THE FALL OF THE FIRST BRITISH EMPIRE

THE FALL OF THE
FIRST BRITISH EMPIRE

Origins of the War of American Independence

ROBERT W. TUCKER AND DAVID C. HENDRICKSON

THE JOHNS HOPKINS UNIVERSITY PRESS
Baltimore and London

This book was presented in part as
the 1981 Jefferson Memorial Lectures at the
University of California, Berkeley, May 19–21, 1981.

This book has been brought to publication
with the generous assistance of the Lehrman Institute.

The Johns Hopkins University Press, Baltimore, Maryland 21218
The Johns Hopkins Press Ltd., London

Library of Congress Cataloging in Publication Data

Tucker, Robert W.
The fall of the first British Empire.

Bibliography: p. 411.
Includes index.
1. United States—History—Revolution, 1775–1783
—Causes. 2. Great Britain—Politics and
government—1760–1789. I. Hendrickson, David C.
II. Title.
E210.T83   1982   973.3'11   82–47977
ISBN 0–8018–2780–9   AACR2

CONTENTS

Preface and Acknowledgments   vii

1. Introduction   1

Part I. The Peace of 1763

2. The Causes of Peace   9
3. The Consequences of Peace   43

Part II. The Status Quo

4. The Historiographical Problem   65
5. Imperial Defense   75
6. The Acts of Trade and Navigation   106
7. Internal Autonomy   146
8. The Issue of Motivation   187

Part III. The Diplomacy of Appeasement

9. The Rockingham Ministry: The Stamp Act Crisis, 1765–66   213
10. The Chatham Ministry: The Townshend Acts, 1767   233
11. The Grafton Ministry: Paper War, 1768–69   250
12. The North Ministry: The Collapse of Imperial Authority, 1770–73   276

Part IV. The Final Reckoning

13. The Coercive Acts, 1774   319
14. The Decision for War, 1775   355
15. The Debate over America   379

Selected Bibliography   411

Index   429

This study began as a collaborative work with my colleague Piero Gleijeses. Undertaken initially in the innocence that attends so many overly ambitious efforts, the project was designed to be a history of America's rise to world power. At the time, this plan to deal with a period extending from the eighteenth to the twentieth century did not appear particularly forbidding. In retrospect, our expectations of the time and effort that would be required to complete a critical history covering almost a century and a half must evoke a mixture of amusement and sadness. What was once intended as an introductory chapter to a work that would end in the years immediately preceding World War I has instead become the first of a two-volume work on the period leading to American independence. The putative second chapter, dealing with the war years, will form a second volume, authored by Professor Gleijeses.

The architecture and basic themes of the present work were set out in a lengthy essay I wrote while under the spell that grips all students of this fascinating period. In the course of proceeding beyond the original essay, David Hendrickson came to play an increasingly important part. From the familiar role of graduate assistant, he progressed—seemingly inexorably—to a position where he was writing very substantial portions of the manuscript. In the end, there was no other equitable solution than to accord him the status of coauthor. The reluctance with which I finally bowed to the inevitable is indicative only of my obtuseness. Dr. Hendrickson's contribution to the study was critical. Without his efforts and irrepressible enthusiasm, I well might have given up. In the end, he took on the indispensable task of editing the final manuscript, reducing it by some 25 percent and thereby improving it enormously.

Throughout the years of writing the book the two of us worked as closely together as coauthors can do. Even so, the chapters that

comprise this work were initially drafted by one person. The breakdown of our efforts should be recorded. I drafted chapters 4, 7, 8,
9, 12, 13, 14, and 15. Chapters 1, 2, 3, 5, 6, 10, and 11 were
undertaken by Dr. Hendrickson. Each chapter, once drafted, went
through several revisions at the hands of both of us.

Many individuals gave us encouragement and help apart, of course,
from Professor Gleijeses. We are grateful to Ed Steiner, Walter
Nelson, David Mapel, and Clelia de Moraes for the valuable contributions each of them made to the work. Also deserving of our
thanks is the staff of the Milton S. Eisenhower Library at The Johns
Hopkins University, and particularly Marilynn Petroff. A number
of historians with a special interest in the colonial period attended
the seminars at The Lehrman Institute, where several chapters of
the manuscript were presented. Two individuals deserve special
acknowledgment: Jack P. Greene and Nicholas X. Rizopoulos. Professor Greene, a colleague at Johns Hopkins and a widely acknowledged master of colonial history, encouraged me from the outset,
and this despite his many reservations and, indeed, disagreements
over the general viewpoint and positions taken in the manuscript.
Both Dr. Hendrickson and I benefited greatly from Professor
Greene's criticisms and wish to express our gratitude for his generous help.

Dr. Rizopoulos, my colleague at The Lehrman Institute, took a
deep interest in the work from its earliest stages. Largely as a result
of his efforts, we received support from the Institute. He also
planned the seminar series at the Institute. Finally, he and Linda
Wrigley—also of the Institute's staff—read the manuscript at various stages and helped us greatly with their instructive editorial
criticism. It is a particular pleasure for me to acknowledge the debt
we owe them for these many efforts.

I also wish to note here—though special acknowledgment is
made elsewhere—that portions of the manuscript were presented
as the 1981 Thomas Jefferson Memorial Lectures at the University
of California, Berkeley.

Finally, thanks must go to Catherine Grover, who not only took
care of this manuscript throughout but did so with her usual efficiency and unfailing good humor.

ROBERT W. TUCKER

THE FALL OF THE FIRST BRITISH EMPIRE

ONE

Introduction

I n 1763 the First British Empire reached its zenith. For almost nine years Great Britain had fought its principal rival, France, on land and at sea for maritime and commercial supremacy. The magnitude of the British victory over France—and, in the concluding stages of the conflict, Spain—was striking. In North America, France was forced to relinquish a position that had been acquired over the better part of a century. The cession of Canada together with the abandonment of claims to all territory east of the Mississippi (except New Orleans) signaled the end of the long contest for empire on the mainland of the American continent. With the acquisition of Florida from Spain, Britain's supremacy over eastern North America was complete.

This triumph over the Bourbon powers, consecrated in the Peace of Paris, signed in February 1763, was shared by the American colonies. In some respects, the colonies were indeed the principal beneficiaries of victory. The French menace from the north and west was at long last removed. And whatever arrangements London might initially make for governing the western territories, it could only be a matter of time before these lands would yield to the pressures of colonial expansion. This deliverance from danger together with the prospect of safe—or safer—expansion were not seen by the colonists simply as gifts of the mother country. The Americans had participated in the conflict. Accordingly, they were entitled to share in the fruits of victory. The nature and extent of their participation, it is true, had occasioned some acrimonious disputes with the metropolis. In the first flush of victory, however, it seemed likely to the colonists that these disputes would be forgotten.

Historians have regularly portrayed the prevailing outlook in the colonies on the morrow of victory as one of deep pride and satisfaction in forming a part—by now, the vital part—of the British

1

Empire. Then, as before, the imperial-colonial relationship was not without its difficulties and points of friction. Colonial dissatisfaction over certain constraints imposed by the imperial system had long been manifest. Colonial resentment over the condescending attitude of the British was never far below the surface. These and other sources of contention evidently must qualify any portrayal of the colonial outlook. Even so, the picture remains of a people who perceived the benefits resulting from membership in the empire as far outweighing the liabilities. Moreover, a cement much stronger than material interest and formed by the sentiments of affection and allegiance presumably bound the colonies to the mother country. These ties, it is usually held, remained very strong in the early 1760s.

Yet within scarcely more than a decade following the 1763 Peace of Paris the colonies had taken the path of armed revolt against Great Britain. The empire that only yesterday had been compared favorably with Rome broke apart. What produced so momentous a change in so brief a period? Were the necessary and, for the most part, even the sufficient conditions for rebellion already present by the early 1760s? If they were present, how are we to reconcile this with the conventional portrayal of the colonial outlook? If, on the other hand, this familiar depiction is substantially accurate, how may one account for an imperial policy either so blind to or so deliberately reckless of its interests that within a very few years it drove loyal subjects to armed rebellion?

If one accepts the prevailing historiography of the causes of the American Revolution, then it is clearly the latter question that is critical. In the prevailing version of the Anglo-American conflict, the Americans had been content with their lot until the time Great Britain set out on its new program of imperial reform. This view taken by current historiography reflects the perspective of the colonists. Before 1763, Benjamin Franklin once noted to interlocutors in Parliament, the colonies had "submitted willingly to the government of the Crown, and paid, in all their courts, obedience to acts of parliament. Numerous as the people are in the several old provinces, they cost [the imperial state] nothing in forts, citadels, garrisons or armies, to keep them in subjection. They were governed by this country at the expense only of a little pen, ink, and paper. They were led by a thread."[1] The Grenville program of 1764 and 1765, however, unnecessarily disrupted this relationship and thus destroyed the conditions for obedience. Dissatisfied with the status quo that had defined the imperial-colonial relationship from virtually the outset of colonization, London set out to tighten imperial ties, to infringe upon long-established relationships, and to assert powers it had never before attempted to assert. It did so in setting forth a new plan for imperial defense and particularly in the method by which this plan was to be supported, in the changes made in the laws and administrative practices governing the system of trade and navigation, and in the limitations imposed upon the autonomy heretofore enjoyed by the colonies in their internal governance.

Armed conflict, however, was at this time avoided. Many of the reforms were withdrawn. It is nevertheless the case that all the essential elements that led to the fall of the First British Empire—the conflicts of interest, the rival ambitions, the profoundly disparate estimates of power—were present in the crisis over the Stamp Act. For current historiography, then, what made conflict inevitable was the persistence in Britain of the outlook that had led to the measures in the first place. The British were not content to leave well enough alone. Obsessed with establishing its supremacy, concerned more with formal submission than with the protection of its interests, the government persisted in a policy that forced the colonists to decide "whether they would be men and not English or whether they would be English and not men."[2] The choice the metropolis posed to America led to the inevitable result.

In seeking to account for the expansion and decline of the First British Empire, historians have concentrated on developments within the metropolis. To the question, What impelled the imperial state to adopt the measures that led from great victory to ignominious

---

[1] *The Papers of Benjamin Franklin*, ed. Leonard W. Labaree et al., 21 vols. to date (New Haven, 1959–), 13:135. "That Franklin was correct in this assessment," Jack P. Greene has noted, "was widely seconded by his contemporaries and has been the considered judgment of the most sophisticated students of the problem over the past quarter of a century"; "An Uneasy Connection: An Analysis of the Preconditions of the American Revolution," in *Essays on the American Revolution*, ed. Stephen G. Kurtz and James H. Hutson (Chapel Hill, 1973), p. 33.

[2] Edmund S. Morgan and Helen M. Morgan, *The Stamp Act Crisis: Prologue to Revolution*, rev. ed. (New York, 1963), p. 152.

defeat? the response has been to point to changes within Britain itself, whether they be the hubris with which Britain emerged from the victorious war, the inexperience, ignorance, and ineptitude of those who directed imperial policy in the 1760s and 1770s, the chaotic state of British politics throughout the period, the financial exigencies under which all ministries labored, or the sudden emergence of a new attitude toward empire. It is particularly the last hypothesis that has struck the deepest roots and found the largest number of adherents. In much of past and current historiography, the acquisition of a large territorial empire in North America in 1763 as well as the enactment of the Grenville reforms of 1764 and 1765 responded to a new attitude toward empire in Britain. Persistently acted upon by metropolitan officials in the decade to follow, this powerful new outlook led inexorably to the American Revolution and to the loss of empire. Whatever the theme adopted, however, the emphasis has been placed on developments in Britain itself. The common view has been that those governing the empire now looked upon the dependencies in a new light, or sought to use such dependencies in a novel fashion, even if such use was restricted to the narrow purposes of politics at home.

This tendency to view the transformation of empire as a consequence of a change in outlook in the metropolis is not peculiar to the historiography of the First British Empire. In the analysis of modern imperialism as well, historians find imperial expansion largely a response to a changed attitude toward empire in Europe. This is so despite the profound differences in circumstances—in social and economic and political organization—separating the old empires in the Americas from the modern empires in Asia, Africa, and the Pacific. The expansion of Europe to Asia and Africa that occurred during the nineteenth century is usually seen as a consequence of the "new imperialism" of the 1870s and 1880s, though bitter argument has raged over the nature of this new imperialism.[3] A similar explanation also figures prominently in accounts of the collapse of the Spanish Empire in the Americas.[4]

---

[3] For a representative sample, see the selections in Harrison M. Wright, ed., *The "New Imperialism": Analysis of Late Nineteenth-Century Expansion*, 2d ed. (Lexington, Mass., 1976). See also Wolfgang J. Mommsen, *Theories of Imperialism* (New York, 1980).

[4] On the Spanish-American Revolutions, see the recent survey by John Lynch, *The Spanish American Revolutions, 1808–1826* (New York, 1973). "[I]n the twilight of empire," Lynch notes, "Spain became not less but more imperialist," and it was this new imperialism that

Nor is it surprising that this explanation should have such wide-spread appeal. The expansion of Europe—what the Indian historian K. M. Panikkar once called the "Vasco de Gama epoch"—ended after all with a world made over in Europe's image; and it seems scarcely remarkable that historians should have sought the source of this boundless activity in Europe itself. The technological and organizational superiority that marked European expansion throughout the modern era made imperialism seem the inevitable consequence of

> . . . the good old rule
> . . . the simple plan,
> That they should take, who have the power,
> And they should keep who can.[5]

The task of the historian became the explanation of the character of Europe's desire; historical controversy, the competitive enumeration of which among the Seven Deadly Sins formed the motivating force behind expansion. Some would erect these desires into the inexorable needs of a particular economic organization; others saw reflected in imperialism the atavistic urges of a landed nobility thrust aside by capitalism. The inventiveness and variety of the explanations offered should not be underestimated, yet they all shared a common structure. They all located the necessary and sufficient conditions of imperial expansion in Europe.

In the case of nineteenth-century European imperialism, this Eurocentric focus has met with some criticism. Much recent historical work has attempted to show that the "new imperialism" of the late nineteenth century was not unlike the old imperialism and that the motivation behind late nineteenth-century British expansion reflected far more continuity than change. What accounted for the extraordinary acquisition of imperial territory during these years, it has been argued, was not primarily new internal social

---

lay behind the growing disaffection of Spanish America from the mother country. "Spanish America was subject in the late eighteenth century to a new imperialism; its administration was reformed, its defence reorganized, its commerce revived. The new policy was essentially an application of control, which sought to increase the colonial status of America and to heighten its dependency. Yet imperial reform planted the seeds of its own destruction: its reformism whetted appetites which it could not satisfy, while its imperialism mounted a direct attack on local interests and disturbed the delicate balance of power within colonial society."

[5] William Wordsworth, "Rob Roy's Grave," 1803, st. 9.

and economic changes in Europe but a variety of changes overseas. Some find the formal annexation of territory to have been a result of a "turbulent frontier" that drew many imperial powers into the constant and unending task of pacification; others find strategic considerations to have been paramount. The role of Great Britain in the partition of Africa, it has been suggested, may be explained very largely in terms of the dangers posed to the security of the route to the East through the Suez Canal or around the Cape of Good Hope. Yet another view is that expansion—or, at least, formal annexation—was the consequence of the response of native populations to earlier informal European penetration. These critics have turned the traditional view of imperial expansion on its head. Instead of finding continuity at the periphery and change at the center, they see change at the periphery and continuity at the center. The phenomenon to be explained in both cases remains the same; but the focus of the explanation has shifted from the "core" to the "periphery"; from Europe to Asia and to Africa; from the metropolis to the provinces.[6]

It is not the intention of the present work to compare the expansion and collapse of the First British Empire with the dynamics of empire on other continents and at other times. Nevertheless, those familiar with the whole of the European imperial experience and the historiography that has emerged to account for this experience cannot fail to be struck by the existence of common explanatory categories across the whole field of modern empire, a fact that reflects the existence of common intellecutal problems. This work should thus be seen as part of this larger inquiry into the processes of imperial expansion and decline. Its point of departure is the thesis that the expansion and collapse of the First British Empire was the consequence of a series of profound upheavals and challenges on the periphery and not the emergence of a new attitude toward empire in the metropolis.

[6] See Ronald Robinson and John Gallagher with Alice Denny, *Africa and the Victorians; The Official Mind of Imperialism* (London, 1961), and two other articles by Robinson and Gallagher: "The Imperialism of Free Trade," *Economic History Review*, 2d ser. 6 (1953):1–15, and "The Partition of Africa," in *The New Cambridge Modern History: XI, Material Progress and World Wide Problems, 1870–98*, ed. F. H. Hinsley (Cambridge, 1962). David K. Fieldhouse, *Economics and Empire, 1830–1914* (Ithaca, 1973), is an excellent introduction to the problem of nineteenth-century imperialism, as is William Roger Louis, ed., *Imperialism: The Robinson and Gallagher Controversy* (New York, 1976). See also John S. Galbraith, "The 'Turbulent Frontier' as a Factor in British Expansion," *Comparative Studies in Society and History* 2 (1960).

PART ONE

THE PEACE OF 1763

TWO

The Causes of Peace

[I]

The 1763 Peace of Paris conferred on Great Britain an imperial position matched by no other power in the eighteenth century. After a disastrous beginning to the Seven Years' War, the British routed the French in most of the principal maritime theaters—North America, the Caribbean, Africa, and India. When Spain renewed the *pacte de famille* with France in 1761 and entered the war the following year, it too went down to defeat. The terms of the peace appeared to give Britain a position of security far stronger than it had previously enjoyed—a security made all the more solid by the prestige conferred through Britain's impressive display of military and financial power.

The following years read like one long fall from grace; and it is difficult to suppress the memory of another peace—also signed near Paris—that left Britain with a similarly exalted imperial position but also with immense vulnerabilities, which the brief passage of time would amply reveal. Fifteen years after the 1763 peace, France changed the character of the War of the American Revolution from a colonial rebellion into a European conflict, thereby ensuring the success of the American revolt. Like that of Britain in 1763, however, France's victory, too, proved bittersweet. Britain emerged from the loss of the American war with its power, if not its empire, almost wholly intact—a denouement that took all the principal antagonists by surprise—while France blundered down the road to bankruptcy and revolution.

The peace settlement of 1763 is of critical interest because it raises the question of whether the explanation for the breakup of the First British Empire, in 1775–83, might be located in the experience and outcome of the preceding war. The view that it may be so located has been maintained by several distinguished

9

historians, though this view has characteristically been given a variety of formulations, some of which are contradictory. The above question also gives rise to another problem: Given that the Peace of Paris contained, in some sense, the seeds of a future war, what considerations led the British to make the peace that they did? If the peacemakers were indeed blind, as many historians have contended, what did they fail to see?

[II]

The Seven Years' War was both a European and an imperial conflict.[1] With distinct origins, the two conflicts merged in 1756 and assumed by early 1758 the relationship they would essentially retain until 1762. Both France and Great Britain entered the war reluctantly. The precipitating incident that unleashed the conflict in North America was the clash of Virginia militia, led by George Washington, with a French and Indian force on the headwaters of the Ohio River in 1754. Each side saw the moves of its rival into the Ohio Valley as a threat to its entire position in North America. The points of difference between Britain and France were not limited to North America, and in North America they were not limited to rival claims to the upper Ohio Valley. These difficulties contributed to the willingness of the British government to stake its prestige on the claims of its colonists. Neither France nor Britain desired war at this time, but neither showed a willingness to retreat from the positions that their respective colonists had marked out for them, and both were convinced that a tough stand would lead their adversaries to beat a retreat. By the spring of 1755, war was inevitable, though it was not formally declared until the following year.

---

[1] The standard works on the continental and imperial phases of the Seven Years' War include the relevant volumes of Lawrence Henry Gipson's monumental *The British Empire before the American Revolution*, 15 vols. (New York, 1936–70); and Max Savelle's *The Origins of American Diplomacy: The International History of Anglo-America, 1492–1763* (New York, 1967). Savelle offers a particularly valuable analysis of the peace negotiations. See also David B. Horn, "The Diplomatic Revolution," and Eric Robson, "The Seven Years' War," in *The New Cambridge Modern History, VII: The Old Regime, 1713–63*, ed. J. O. Lindsay (Cambridge, 1957); Gaston Zeller, *Les Temps modernes, II: De Louis XIV à 1789* (Paris, 1955); and Richard Waddington's unfinished *La Guerre de Sept Ans: Histoire diplomatique et militaire*, 5 vols. (Paris, 1896–1914).

The probability of general war between the two great maritime powers in 1755 had extraordinary repercussions in all the European capitals, where memories of the last war remained vivid. What became a contest for the Austrian Succession began as a commercial dispute between Spain and England, and the peace of Aix-la-Chapelle, which concluded hostilities in 1748, bore witness to the inseparable character of the two conflicts. By the presence of a French army in the Austrian Netherlands, the French succeeded in recovering Louisbourg, a fortress on Cape Breton that American colonials from New England had seized in 1745. In exchange for the evacuation of Flanders, the British restored the fortress that commanded the entrance to the St. Lawrence River and held the "key to Canada." The threat of renewed war in America therefore inevitably drew attention to the vulnerability of British interests on the European continent to French military action. If there were to be a war in America between France and Britain, the French would very likely again pursue the logic of Aix-la-Chapelle.

This is indeed what happened, though not before Europe witnessed a spectacular reversal of traditional diplomatic alignments, an outcome to which British diplomacy during 1755 contributed in no small degree. The events leading to the Diplomatic Revolution of 1756 and to the invasion of Saxony by Prussia in November of that year unsettled all the old diplomatic rules and betrayed all the old expectations. When the dust had cleared, both Austria and the United Provinces—the two powers that had joined with Britain in the Grand Alliance to bring low the ambitions of Louis XIV and that had been troublesome allies in the struggle over the Austrian Succession—were no longer friendly powers. While the Hapsburgs overcame their historic enmity with the Bourbons, the Dutch cowered in profitable neutrality. A formidable coalition arose against the Prussia of Frederick the Great, with whom Britain had concluded, in early 1756, the Treaty of Westminster, a treaty the British believed would ensure the neutrality of Germany and thus provide for the safety of Hanover. By driving a wedge between Prussia and France, who had fought together, intermittently, during the Austrian Succession, the Treaty of Westminster instead ensured the very opposite. It ensured that Germany would be a principal theater of action in the impending war.

In the conflict that ensued, the aspirations of the Two Empresses were so extensively defined that the stake of the war rapidly became the survival of Prussia as a German power. Elizabeth of Russia wished to wrest East Prussia from Frederick, while Maria Theresa of Austria sought to recover Silesia, lost to Prussia during the last war. France's motives were more complicated. It divided its forces between southern and northern Germany, hoping with the southern forces to knock Prussia from the field in the first campaign, in return for which France would receive compensation from Austria in the Hapsburg Netherlands. With the northern army it hoped to capture Hanover. Both would be valuable possessions in their own right, posing a threat to British commercial interests on the continent as well as threatening British naval superiority in the North Sea. Britain would be loath to surrender either in a peace settlement, and not merely because the King of Great Britain, George II, was also the Elector of Hanover. As at Aix-la-Chapelle, the most probable use of France's drive along the North Sea littoral would be to mitigate the French defeat or extend the French victory in the maritime conflict with Britain.

Hostilities in 1757 seemed to confirm the wisdom of the French commitment. The main French army of one hundred and five thousand troops advanced into Hanover during the late summer and forced the "Army of Observation"—a motley force of German mercenaries and Hanoverians commanded by the Duke of Cumberland, the son of George II—to capitulate at Kloster-Zeven in early September. Great Britain seemed poised to abandon the continent, and Frederick's position was one of extraordinary desperation. "The king of Prussia," wrote the English minister in Berlin, "has now against him the Russian army and fleet, 20,000 Swedes, an army of the Empire supported by 30,000 French, and the great Austrian army of 100,000 and, as if he had not enemies enough, the convention to save Hanover from winter quarters will let loose 60 to 80 thousand more French."[2]

At this desperate juncture Frederick earned his sobriquet. After suffering a defeat at Kolin in June 1757, his fortunes turned. At Rossbach, in early November, he crushed the combined forces of the army of the Holy Roman Empire and the French army under Soubise. A month later, in a stunning demonstration of the superior mobility of his army, he defeated the Austrians at Leuthen. His

---

[2] Mitchell to Holderness, August 28, 1757, quoted in Richard Lodge, *Great Britain and Prussia in the Eighteenth Century* (Oxford, 1923), p. 100.

victory at Rossbach broke the indecision of the English: they repudiated, on a specious pretext, the convention of Kloster-Zeven in late November. In less than a month, Frederick's military victories and a change in British policy had combined to alter dramatically the balance of forces. The British increased (from 164,000 to 1,200,000 pounds) their subsidy to the Army of Observation and placed it under the command of a capable general, Prince Ferdinand of Brunswick. In April of the following year the British concluded with Frederick a subsidy treaty that granted him 670,000 pounds a year, a treaty that forbade a separate peace by either side and that was annually renewed until it lapsed with the Anglo-Prussian quarrel in 1762. It was in this manner that the European war came to be joined. The policy of France was that of conquest in Germany in order to pursue its maritime and imperial conflict with Britain; the policy of Britain in Germany was that of denial.

[III]

During the course of the conflict, the problem of British war aims passed through a number of discernible phases, each of which had a direct bearing on the final shape of the peace settlement. Two factors were of the first importance in determining the nature of the peace. One was the surprising progress of British arms, which after a disastrous beginning humiliated the combined power of the House of Bourbon and which, despite numerical inferiority, were used to effect on the European continent. The second was the new political constellation created by the accession of George III to the monarchy in late 1760. The new King, along with his "favorite," John Stuart, third earl of Bute, held views on the war which clashed with those of William Pitt and Thomas Pelham-Holles, the duke of Newcastle. A ministry from which both Pitt and Newcastle had resigned negotiated the final treaty of peace with the French in late 1762. The treaty surpassed all expectations that had been entertained at the outset of the war, but it was nonetheless subjected to harsh criticism, especially by Pitt, whose views of the peace continue to find favor among historians.

For the British, the beginning of the war had been marked by successive military defeats and ministerial crises. Admiral Boscawen failed to intercept the main French fleet from Brest that was sent to Canada in 1755, but his capture of a few ships made Britain appear as the aggressor in the eyes of Europe—the conclusion drawn, or pretext used, by the Dutch to justify their neutrality when called upon by Britain for assistance. Braddock's expedition was cut to pieces in a bloody engagement with the French and Indians on the Monongahela River in 1755, while in the next year the French captured Oswego on Lake Ontario, a British setback with profound implications for the security of New York and the loyalty of the Iroquois Confederation. The loss of Minorca, a British base that played an important role in protecting Britain's Mediterranean commerce and in preventing the French fleet at Toulon from reaching the open seas, came also in 1756.

It was in these circumstances of profound national trauma that George II admitted his theretofore irreconcilable enemy, William Pitt, to the cabinet. Pitt's first efforts were marked by failure. His fragile coalition lacked the support of the King and, with the resignation of Newcastle, it could no longer command the full resources of Parliament. It was only in late 1757, when Pitt formed with Newcastle an administration that included or appeased most of those who might, in opposition, make trouble for it, that the war effort began to turn around. Pitt gave direction and unity to the war effort. He accorded supreme importance to the maritime and colonial struggle with France, but he combined this with assaults on the coast of France that were intended to draw off French military strength from its German campaigns. To Prince Ferdinand and King Frederick he gave support that was sufficient to frustrate French hopes of quick victory on the continent and that led France to dissipate its resources in pursuit of European objectives that remained elusive. By 1758 the strategy began to bear fruit. Louisbourg fell to a British expedition in 1758 and paved the way for an assault up the St. Lawrence on French Canada. Senegal and Goree, major entrepôts of the French slave trade, were taken in the same year. In 1759 Pitt continued his operations in Canada, and General Wolfe succeeded in capturing Quebec, though at the price of his own life. Pitt also began a West Indian campaign that aimed at territorial conquest, and in that year a British expedition, aimed at the outset at Martinique, succeeded in taking Guadeloupe from the French. The victories in India were no less impressive. By 1760 all Canada lay under British military control.

By 1760 the surprising progress of British arms had transformed the debate over war aims. Given Britain's sweeping military victories, it now appeared possible to entertain objectives that had formed no part of the original aims of the war. At this juncture a number of pamphlets appeared, the authors of which proceeded to do battle over the question of what constituted a desirable peace. One side favored the acquisition of Guadeloupe; the other the retention of Canada. With few exceptions—Pitt not among them—neither side believed it possible to insist upon both objectives. By the summer of 1761 the question between the two, insofar as it had disturbed the ministry, was resolved in favor of the acquisition of Canada.

Since the spring, the French and the British had been negotiating in earnest the terms of a peace settlement. There existed a genuine possibility of peace in the summer of 1761. The issue over which the British had been drawn into the war—the security of their North American settlements—was no longer in doubt. By 1761, the colonies could be made secure not merely through the vindication of their claims to the Ohio Valley, or the demolition of all French forts on the Great Lakes, or the permanent withdrawal of French settlers from all of Acadia. The disease itself could be cured through the removal of the French from Canada. Nevertheless, the peace negotiations were placed in jeopardy by the attitude of William Pitt, who desired to placate the French in no quarter and demanded a settlement that would fully recognize the extent of British military successes. For Pitt the aims of the war had become expansive. The security of the American continental colonies receded as the primary object of his policy. Something much greater and more enduring—the permanent humiliation and enfeeblement of France—caught hold of his imagination. To the duc de Choiseul-Stainville, the architect of French policy, as well as to many of Pitt's colleagues in the cabinet, the war aims of the Great Commoner began to seem unlimited. On the fisheries, in particular, Pitt was unrelenting: he demanded the exclusion of the French from both the Newfoundland and the St. Lawrence fisheries. He wished to drive the French from Africa, or at least to restore neither of the conquests that the British had made there. Pitt's fundamental attitude in the summer of 1761 sprang not only from the desire to deprive the French of the sources of their power—the fisheries question, he believed, was intimately related to their maritime strength—but from the conviction that the success of British arms entitled him to *impose* conditions on the French. He would not negotiate with the vanquished power as an equal. It was on this point, more than any other, that the negotiations broke down during the fall of 1761. Choiseul had all along been negotiating with the Spanish to bring them into the war in case the negotiations collapsed. Pitt, however, was absolutely unwilling to moderate his terms in response to the threat of Spanish intervention. The belief of the French that they possessed a counter that entitled them to greater consideration than their conquests warranted, and Pitt's refusal to recognize this latent threat, combined to frustrate the 1761 negotiations. By early fall, Pitt had become convinced that a renewed combination of the Bourbons was inevitable. He urged an immediate declaration of war against Spain. His colleagues in the cabinet were reluctant to enlarge the war, however, except on more reliable indications that Spain had in fact entered into a secret combination with France: if there were no renewed Bourbon alliance, they reasoned, a British declaration of war could only serve French interests. Unwilling to take responsibility for that which he could not direct, Pitt resigned from the cabinet on October 5, 1761.

The resignation of Pitt marked a clear break from the past. Lord Bute, who had become secretary of state for the Northern Department in March 1761, began to assume a clearer role in the direction of policy. He was hostile to the "bloody and expensive" war in Europe. Along with the new King, his first wish was to put an end to the war before all the participants collapsed in exhaustion. Yet the situation he faced was uncertain. The possibility of war with Spain still remained high, and Frederick's 1761 campaign had been full of reverses. One war seemed thus to be on the verge of being lost, another on the verge of beginning. These two prospects, and not simply Bute's stance in favor of a maritime, colonial, and insular Great Britain, reopened the debate over "continental connections."

One of Bute's first steps was to suggest to Frederick that the Anglo-Prussian subsidy treaty of 1758, due to expire in early December 1761, eliminate the provision forbidding either party to negotiate "but in concert and by mutual consent." Before the altered treaty was ready for formal renewal, however, the British ministry hesitated. The occupation of Silesia during the winter of 1761/62 by Austrian troops and the fall of Kolberg to the Russians at the beginning of 1762 seemed to doom the chances of a peace that would leave Prussia territorially intact. With the widening of the war to include Spain, moreover, British land forces would be required to defend Portugal against the inevitable Spanish attack. It seemed unclear whether Britain could any longer support fully its German allies and its enlarged maritime war. Confronted with this serious situation, Whitehall undertook two closely related initiatives.

Through Joseph Yorke, the English ambassador at the Hague, Bute indirectly inquired of Maria Theresa whether she might be interested in abandoning the conquest of Silesia in exchange for British support of Hapsburg pretensions against Spain in Italy. At the same time, Newcastle offered more. In a private letter to Yorke, the duke proposed that intermediaries suggest to Austria that Vienna might receive Silesia in addition to expanded dominions in Italy if Maria Theresa would join England in the war against Spain. Newcastle's private letters to Yorke, not Bute's official dispatch, had contained the suggestion that Austrian participation in the Spanish war would be secured by offering to return to Vienna the province that Frederick had seized during the Austrian Succession, yet it is virtually certain that Bute contemplated a similar exchange. On January 8, 1762, he wrote to Andrew Mitchell, the English ambassador to Prussia, informing him that the subsidy treaty would not be renewed although the money would be granted. The condition of this grant, however, was that Frederick inform Britain of his military resources and plans. Bute urged Frederick to make peace with Austria, and the concessions he had in mind are indicated by his advice that Frederick should suit his terms to the demands he could enforce by the sword. With the Austrians in occupation of Silesia, Bute's advice could be subject to only one interpretation.

Frederick would not learn of the Hague overtures until late in March. When he did, he became enraged. Before then, however, two other events had occurred that had further complicated Anglo-Prussian relations, the most important of which was the death in early January of Czarina Elizabeth, a bitter antagonist of Frederick. She was succeeded by Peter III, a fawning admirer of the King of Prussia. The new Czar showed an immediate desire to take Russia out of its conflict with Prussia, and even to concert with Prussia against Denmark and possibly Austria. Under these novel circumstances—increasing financial demands upon the British and the elimination of Prussia's rival on its eastern flank—Anglo-Prussian relations steadily deteriorated during the spring. Frederick soon received reports, forwarded by the Russian ambassador in England, Count Galitzin, that Bute had urged the Russians not to evacuate their troops from East Prussia so that Frederick could be more easily pressured into concluding a disadvantageous peace. Bute later denied these charges when confronted with Frederick's evidence, and there exists contemporary evidence suggesting that Galitzin was lying. By this time, in any case, the lapse of the subsidy was a foregone conclusion. Bute demanded that Frederick inform London of the King of Prussia's secret and disloyal negotiations with Russia over Denmark. When Frederick refused to accept the conditions under which Bute still seemed, even as late as April, to hold out the payment of the subsidy, the British cut it off.

Newcastle soon resigned from the cabinet, taking his old friend and confidant Lord Hardwicke with him. The occasion for Newcastle's resignation was the April 1762 decision of the ministry, led by Bute and Grenville and supported by an old assistant of Newcastle's at the Treasury, to ask for only another million pounds to carry on the war. Newcastle believed two million was necessary if Britain were to continue meeting its obligations to Prince Ferdinand. As first lord of the Treasury, he deeply resented that his opinion had been overruled on a question belonging to his own department. Shortly thereafter, Newcastle tendered his resignation. Even so, the Bute ministry did not proceed to withdraw British support from the army of Prince Ferdinand. In fact, sufficient supplies flowed to Ferdinand that enabled him to frustrate a planned summer French offensive. The departure of Newcastle, however, did signal a fundamental change in attitude, if not in policy. Through his Prussian diplomacy and through his hints that British support to Ferdinand might soon be coming to an end, Bute was placing Britain on the path to a separate and isolationist peace, one that, his enemies charged, caused Britain to be left without an ally on the continent of Europe.

During the spring, at the time when the negotiations over the Prussian subsidy treaty were coming to a head, the British and the French reopened formal negotiations on the basis of their conversations of the preceding summer and fall. Bute succeeded Newcastle at the Treasury and showed a willingness to concede many

of the issues that had led to the earlier breakdown of the negotiations. In their first proposal, communicated to the French through
intermediaries at the beginning of May 1762, the British had accepted the Canadian boundary proposed by Choiseul the preceding
August. The necessity of receiving an equivalent for the restoration
of Martinique led the British to propose the cession of French
Louisiana east of the Mississippi River. The French were willing
to conclude on these terms, but differences remained over the
precise boundary line in southern Louisiana, and whether Britain
would receive the free navigation of the Mississippi River. The
British were willing to allow the French both Miquelon and St.
Pierre, as well as limited rights of fishing in the Gulf of the St.
Lawrence and off the banks of Newfoundland. Although Choiseul
made noises again about the restoration of Cape Breton, on condition that it would remain unfortified, he assented to the British
terms. In Africa, the British offered to restore the island of Goree,
thus retreating from Pitt's stand of the previous year, and disposing
of the African question as an obstacle to the peace. Bellisle, an
island on the western coast of France that Pitt had seized during
the negotiations during 1761, was to be returned to France in
exchange for Minorca. The British, in conformity to their final offer
during 1761, insisted upon the destruction of the fortifications at
Dunkirk, and to this Choiseul agreed. Finally, the French agreed
to evacuate their troops from Prussia and the rest of Germany, as
well as from Ostend and Nieport, two ports in the Austrian Netherlands that French troops had garrisoned during the war.[3]

Only two issues remained that threatened to break the momentum toward peace: the division of the "neutral islands" of St. Lucia,
Tobago, Dominica, and Grenada; and the question of the Mississippi boundary. Earlier in the spring the British had seemed ame-
nable to the division of the islands proposed by Choiseul, the most
significant feature of which was the French retention of St. Lucia,
an island with an excellent harbor that was indispensable to the
defense of Martinique. Bute and Bedford, the English plenipoten-
tiary of Paris, were both willing to part with St. Lucia, but the
capture of the neutral islands by the British after the fall of Mar-

---

[3] A dispute arose over the precise terms of the evacuation of Prussian territory by the French
in late 1762. Bute believed that he had fulfilled the British obligation to Prussia; Frederick
did not. By this time, however, the Anglo-Prussian relationship had already been irretriev-
ably shattered; see ibid., pp. 129–38.

tinique hardened the terms of the rest of the cabinet, especially those of George Grenville. Unwilling to jeopardize the chances of peace on this point, Bute indicated to the French the willingness of the cabinet to concede St. Lucia "if all other articles are agreed to."[4] He did so without the knowledge of the rest of the cabinet.

Bute also acted without the knowledge of his colleagues in agreeing to a Mississippi boundary that left France in possession of New Orleans and that would have denied British subjects the navigation of the Mississippi had not Grenville raised objections. As it was, the final articles of peace guaranteed to British subjects the free navigation of the river. Only Spain now held up the conclusion of the peace, and that nation's high tone collapsed with the news of the capture of Havana. The English demanded either Puerto Rico or Florida in return for Cuba. The Spanish reluctantly agreed to the cession of Florida, in return for which they received New Orleans and the rest of Louisiana from France.

It is against this general background that the peace treaty ending the drawn-out conflict may be considered. In vivid contrast to the Austro-Prussian Peace of Hubertusburg, which restored the status quo ante on the continent, the Peace of Paris profoundly altered the terms of the ancient rivalry between Britain and France. With the exception of New Orleans and the "barren" lands to the west of the Mississippi, Britain was in complete possession of the North American continent. The French position in both Africa and India had been undermined, and the French would now be forced to carry on the fishery on terms far less advantageous than theretofore. There existed, it is true, an apparent disparity between the sweeping extent of Britain's military victories and the final shape of the peace settlement, but the British had demonstrated their superiority to the combined forces of the Bourbons. Britain had, it would later appear, "conquered in the islands in order to annex on the continent," and the negotiations yielded a settlement that, to a reader of maps, appeared very favorable to the British.[5] Yet it was a peace that was to prove unstable and ultimately fatal to the First British Empire.

In the closing years of the war, the problem of British war aims

[4] George III to Bute, June 21, 1762, *Letters from George III to Lord Bute, 1756–1766*, ed. Romney Sedgwick (London, 1939), pp. 118–19 (hereafter Bute Letters).
[5] Richard Pares, *War and Trade in the West Indies, 1739–1763* (Oxford, 1936), p. 225.

had passed through several discernible phases. A succession of ministries, constantly changing their outward complexion with the fall of Pitt and Newcastle, fearing the retaliation of the mob if they did not conclude a peace that lived up to popular expectations, had made three critical decisions. The first, to restore Guadeloupe to the French while keeping Canada, was taken by a ministry that included Pitt, Newcastle, and Bute. The second lay in the series of diplomatic moves that brought on the rupture with Prussia. The third consisted of the decision to conclude a peace with France and Spain that did not forever break their power. Whereas the decision to take Canada may be identified with a consensus of opinion shared not only by the ministers but also by the "political nation," the second and third rest mainly on the shoulders of the earl of Bute, the duke of Bedford, and George III. In a ministry shorn of Pitt and Newcastle it was Bute and Bedford, adamantly supported by the King, who presided over the break with Frederick and who were largely responsible for the final terms of peace.

[IV]

What considerations led British statesmen to conclude the Peace of Paris on the terms that they did? Many historians have seen in the settlement the emergence of a new concept of empire. To some, it indicated a dramatic shift in the economic utility of the empire, from the view (associated with those who argued for the retention of Guadeloupe) that the primary role of colonies in a self-sufficient empire was to supply the mother country with such commodities and raw materials that it could not supply for itself, to a newer view (associated with those who argued for the retention of Canada) that the primary role of colonies was to receive the manufactures of the mother country.[6] To others, the settlement reflected a turn from "mercantilism" to "imperialism," that is, to a growing belief "that extent of territory and the exercise of authority were more worthy of consideration by a state of real grandeur, such as Great

[6] George L. Beer, *British Colonial Policy, 1754–1765* (New York, 1907), pp. 132–59. See also Vincent T. Harlow, *The Founding of the Second British Empire: Discovery and Revolution*, 2 vols. (London, 1952–64), 1:162–72.

Britain had now become, than were the mere advantages of traffic."[7]
To still others, the statesmen most responsible for the terms of
peace were simply incapable of thinking in grand terms. The ruling
passion of these third-rate politicians, epitomized by Bute, was the
momentary advantage of political factionalism. Bute could be rid
of Pitt only if he had first gotten rid of the war: hence his desire
for an early peace.[8] "Pitt," Richard Pares maintained in a classic
judgment, "was the only man in the first rank of politics who dealt
in terms of economic or strategic value, and considered colonial
acquisitions as something more than so many debating-points for
or against the Ministry." Yet even Pitt, Pares thought, was frequently insincere and demagogic; Pitt too exaggerated and lied
when it suited him.[9] The view that the peace reflected domestic
political considerations is significant, many have held, because it
explains why the Bute ministry made what are largely taken to be
two critical mistakes during 1762: the failure to renew the Prussian
subsidy treaty, and the failure to crush French power in the West
Indies and off Newfoundland. Finally, there are those who discount
the importance of factional considerations but who nonetheless see
the failure to press for more advantageous terms from the French
as deriving from the innocent, though fundamentally wrong-headed,
desire to establish a permanent peace with France;[10] and who see
the rupture with Prussia as proceeding more from unforgiveable
strategic naiveté than from domestic political intrigue.

[7] Charles M. Andrews, *The Colonial Background of the American Revolution* (New Haven,
1924), pp. 126–27. See also David K. Fieldhouse, "British Imperialism in the Late Eighteenth Century," in *Essays in Imperial Government*, ed. K. Robinson and F. Madden
(Oxford, 1963), pp. 24–25.
[8] Scholars who have emphasized the importance of domestic politics in determining the
final shape of the peace include Walter L. Dorn, *Competition for Empire, 1740–1763* (New
York, 1940), p. 379; Jack M. Sosin, *Whitehall and the Wilderness: The Middle West in
British Colonial Policy, 1760–1775* (Lincoln, Neb., 1961), pp. 12, 19; Zenab Esmat Rashed,
The Peace of Paris, 1763 (Liverpool, 1951), p. 206; and Beer, *British Colonial Policy*, p.
132. Cf. Richard Pares, *King George III and the Politicians* (Oxford, 1953), p. 102, n. 4.
[9] *War and Trade*, pp. 609–10. As Edmund S. Morgan has noted, there is a fundamental
incompatibility between "imperial" and "Namierite" interpretations of British politics in
the age of the American Revolution; *The Challenge of the American Revolution* (New York,
1976), pp. 50–51. His generalization applies as well to explanations of the peace. The imperial
historians did attempt to explain British actions in terms of a "theory of empire," though
there remains a great deal of disagreement over what the theory of empire actually was and
whether it underwent a tranformation at mid-century. Lewis Namier and Pares, however,
refused for the most part to see motivation in terms of these larger ideas.
[10] Ronald Hyam, "Imperial Interests and the Peace of Paris (1763)," in *Reappraisals in
British Imperial History*, ed. Ronald Hyam and G. Martin (London, 1975), pp. 33–35; Kate
Hotblack, "The Peace of Paris, 1763," in *Transactions of the Royal Historical Society*, 3d

None of these interpretations is satisfactory. Bute's peace was far more defensible, on premises accepted by most of his opponents, than later historians have been willing to credit. The "Scotch favorite" was at least as consistent in his views as many of his critics. New mercantilist beliefs or new imperialist sentiments, however, were not the basis of this consistency. Nor indeed was petty-minded factional intrigue.

The decisions made in 1761 and 1762 appeared misguided, if not indeed strange, because historians know in retrospect that the premise on which the peacemakers relied—the continued dependence of the American continental colonies—should not have been taken for granted. Yet in fact it was a premise that only a few cared to dispute. A few among the principal peacemakers—Grenville, for example—understood that there was some question about the truth of the premise. But they did not dispute it. This premise was in some fashion connected with the decisions reached at all three stages of the controversy over British war aims. It made sense of the ministry's desire to rid North America of the French, for the latter's removal would provide not only for the security of the continental colonies but also for the effective hegemony of Britain's entire Atlantic empire. The security of their Atlantic empire now virtually assured by their conquests in North America, the British could reexamine the importance of their "continental connection" with Prussia. Finally, the Bute ministry could effectively argue that terms harsher than those accorded to France in the final settlement were unnecessary if the price would be continued war, and that the opponents of the peace were insisting on additional increments of security for an empire already in large measure secure.

[V]

Of the three questions confronting the peacemakers, the first—whether to press for Canada or Guadeloupe—was undoubtedly the

---

ser. 2 (1908):254–55; and J. H. Parry and P. M. Sherlock, *A Short History of the West Indies* (New York, 1966), p. 126. The reorientation of Britain's relations with the continent may also be seen as a consequence of the importance that Great Britain now placed on its North American colonies, and hence as a reflection of the power now exerted over men's minds by the "new imperialism."

most critical. Not only would the decision ultimately reached have a profound effect on the distribution of power in North America, but it conditioned the later debates over the Prussian subsidy treaty and the final terms of the peace settlement. Pitt wondered in early 1760 which possession he would be hanged for not keeping. Happily, by the time the preliminaries were presented to the Commons, he could attempt to hang Lord Bute for not keeping both.[11]

The influence of the pamphlet controversy that was sparked by the "year of victories" in 1759 remains unclear. There is little evidence that any ministers in a position of responsibility contemplated the acquisition of islands in the West Indies at the sacrifice of the retention of Canada. There were too many obstacles to annexing in the islands by conquering on the continent, the greatest of which was that it would leave in jeopardy the objective on behalf of which the war had begun in the first place: the security of the American continental colonies. The ideas presented by the pamphleteers are worthy of some examination if only because they very clearly brought this danger out.

Of all the arguments the pro-Guadeloupe pamphleteers made, the economic argument for retaining the sugar island was the simplest and undoubtedly the most persuasive. The monopoly held by British sugar planters over the home market had driven up the price of sugar to an all-time high. The expansion of supply that would follow from the acquisition of Guadeloupe would lower immediately the price of sugar in the home market as well as extend British control over the European market. Indeed, the price of sugar did begin to decline when sugars from conquered Guadeloupe came upon the British market in 1760. The West Indian possessions of France, many argued, were the foundation of French commercial and maritime power. If the British insisted on conquests in the West Indies, the gain to British wealth and power would stand in direct proportion to a French loss of the same; whereas the acquisition of Canada would be of slight commercial value to Britain, and would detract little from the commercial power of the French. Some of the pamphleteers argued that if Guadeloupe were returned to France, the British continental colonies would have no outlet for their surplus produce. Their spare

[11] Horace Walpole, *Memoirs of the Reign of George III*, ed. Denis le Marchant, 4 vols. (London, 1851), 1:34.

hands would turn to manufactures competitive with those produced at home, and thereby invite the ruin of British wealth and power. Others argued that the American trade to the foreign islands of the West Indies would go on as before, but in that case "a great part of the benefit of the northern colony trade must redound, as it has hitherto done, to those who were lately our enemies, and will always be our rivals."[12] For all these reasons Guadeloupe would be a valuable acquisition; but some went further and added that Canada would prove to be a liability. Not only did it lack immediate commercial value, but the removal of French forces from Canada would free the British colonies from their dependence on the mother country: they would soon, some pamphleteers ominously warned, contend for independence. Even those who urged the retention of Guadeloupe, however, were agreeable to the establishment of secure and stable boundaries in North America, and insofar as this motive had led the British to war in 1754 and 1755, the pamphleteers did not depart from it. Still, the French would remain behind, and "a Neighbor that keeps us in some Awe, is not always the worst of Neighbors."[13]

The most effective reply to these arguments was penned by Benjamin Franklin. In the *Interest of Great Britain Considered* (1760), Franklin argued for the retention of Canada primarily on grounds of security. If the French were to retain their possessions in North America, the borders would have to be secured by forts, which would require large peacetime expenditures; but forts, he insisted, were in any case useless against Indian tribes armed and abetted by the French. The Indians' knowledge of the land and their life of hunting would easily lead them to bypass the principal English fortifications and keep up a continual alarm on the frontier. The disputes between the French and the British would continue to flare up, and Great Britain again would be forced to undertake a war at an immense cost for objectives now within certain reach. He denied that the Americans would turn to manufacturing. The cheapness of land in America, made even cheaper by the annexation

[12] *Annual Register* (1762), p. 59.
[13] William Burke, *Remarks on the Letter Addressed to Two Great Men* (London, 1760), p. 51. Burke insisted on a boundary that would include "all those important Posts and Communications by which alone Canada became in any Degree dangerous to us." He left unexplained precisely in what manner French Canada could secure the dependence of the colonies if it no longer posed a threat to them; (p. 28).

of the new territories, would prevent such a possibility "for some centuries," and the Americans would remain the best—and a growing—market for British manufactures. Franklin further insisted that the internecine quarrels among the colonists would prevent a combination among them opposing the mother country. Their disunion would secure their allegiance—and this, too, presumably "for some centuries."[14]

It has frequently been assumed that the extraordinary economic prospect held out by American expansion into the Mississippi Valley was the decisive consideration for those who urged the annexation of Canada and the Middle West. Yet this assumption is very doubtful. For all those who, like Franklin, saw bright commercial prospects in the expansion of the American settlements beyond the Appalachian Mountains, there were many others who all but dismissed these prospects. Many of these observers held positions of high responsibility. In the spring of 1761 Bute called Canada "a barren country" and inquired of the duke of Bedford if Great Britain should not, "out of all our rich conquests, reserve to posterity something that will bring in a clear and certain additional revenue, to enable them to pay the interest on the enormous debt we have by this most expensive war laid upon them?" He thought little, it would appear, of the prospect of a growing American market for English manufactures which expansion into the West would bring.[15] Pitt, too, contended for the fisheries and Canada in 1761. If he had earlier seen a great market for British manufactures on Voltaire's "few acres of snow," he changed his mind the next year. In opposition to the final treaty, Pitt declared that "the state of the existing trade in the conquests in North America, is extremely low; the speculations of their future are precarious, and the prospect, at the very best, very remote."[16] Neither Newcastle nor Hardwicke thought that the commercial development of North America would flow from Britain's conquests; on the contrary, Hardwicke noted that Canada was "a cold northern climate, unfruitful; furnishes no trade to Europe that I know of, but the fur trade, the most incon-

---

[14] *The Papers of Benjamin Franklin*, 9:66–71, 78, 90–95.
[15] Bute to Bedford, July 12, 1761, *Correspondence of John, Fourth Duke of Bedford*, ed. Lord John Russell, 3 vols. (London, 1842–46), 3:32–33. This "something" out of Britain's "rich conquests" referred to the Newfoundland and Canadian fisheries and not to the West Indies.
[16] *The Parliamentary History of England From the Earliest Period to 1803*, ed. William Cobbett and T. C. Hansard, 36 vols. (London, 1806–20) (hereafter *PH*)15:1265.

siderable of all trades." The sugar islands, however, "must take all the necessaries of life from the Mother Country, as your own islands now do. The sugar trade is a most profitable one, and you may engross almost the whole of it, and serve all the European markets."[17] In contemplating the preliminaries, however, Newcastle adhered to his "opinion that the [French] evacuation of all Canada, possibly in the manner now done, was the first object, we ought to have in view, as that carries security with it for the future."[18]

Among the leading statesmen of Great Britain, then, few, if any, held great hopes for the future commercial development of those territories in North America ceded in the peace. Had considerations of commerical utility been directly determinative, there can be little doubt that nearly all would have opted for the retention of Great Britain's West Indian conquests. The grand prospect of the interior settlement of North America of which Franklin prophesied in his Canada pamphlet was discounted. The confirmation of Britain's title to the upper Ohio Valley as well as the acquisition of Canada were significant because both would lead to the departure of French soldiers, not because either made possible the entry of British settlers. Basically the same estimate was made in 1762 of Louisiana and Florida.[19]

This conclusion is reinforced by British behavior after the war. At the close of hostilities the British limited western settlement on a line approximating that of the watershed of the Appalachians. The sources of this decision were many, but, on balance, the de-

[17] Hardwicke to Newcastle, April 2, 1762, *Anglo-French Boundary Disputes in the West, 1749–1763*, ed., with intro., Theodore C. Pease, Illinois State Historical Library, *Collections* (Springfield, Ill., 1936) (hereafter *IHC*) 27:412–13. See also Egremont's memoir of June 26, 1762, pp. 435–37.
[18] Newcastle to Hardwicke, November 29, 1762, *The Life and Correspondence of Philip Yorke, Earl of Hardwicke*, ed. Philip C. Yorke, 3 vols. (Cambridge, 1913), 3:437–38.
[19] For a similar conclusion, see Lewis Namier, *England in the Age of the American Revolution*, 2d ed. (New York, 1961), p. 276; Fred J. Ericson, "British Motives for Expansion in 1763: Territory, Commerce, or Security?" in *Papers of the Michigan Academy of Sciences, Arts and Letters*, ed. E. McCartney and W. Steere (Ann Arbor, 1942), 27:581–94; Sosin, *Whitehall*, p. 23; and Hyam, "Peace of Paris," p. 32. Earlier works on the Canada-Guadeloupe controversy include William L. Grant, "Canada versus Guadeloupe: An Episode of the Seven Years' War," *American Historical Review* 17 (1912):735–43, and C. E. Fryer, "Further Pamphlets for the Canada-Guadeloupe Controversy," *Mississippi Valley Historical Review* 5 (1917):227–30. Clarence W. Alvord, *The Mississippi Valley in British Politics: A Study of the Trade, Land Speculation, and Experiments in Imperialism Culminating in the American Revolution*, 2 vols. (Cleveland, 1917), included in his work a bibliography of the pamphlets (2:253–64). Alvord attempted to link the attitudes of the pamphleteers with the positions taken by the various parliamentary factions; both Sosin and Namier have noted the difficulties this interpretation presents.

cision reflected the same consideration that had led to the annexation of the territories in the first place: the peace and security of
the frontier. Insofar as the question of commercial exploitation was
raised, the British faced a clear choice between favoring the fur
trade and encouraging white settlement, for the former was based
fundamentally on maintaining cordial relations with the Indians
and protecting their hunting grounds from settlement. Imperial
administrators discouraged interior settlement, security considerations apart, because they believed that colonial settlement beyond
the Alleghenies would place the settlements beyond the reach of
markets in Europe and America, where the settlers might earn the
specie to purchase British manufactures. It is implausible to assume
that British statesmen insisted upon the annexation of Canada and
the Middle West on grounds of prospective commercial utility—
as measured by the expansion of colonial settlement and not the
exploitation of the fur trade—and then reversed these policies upon
the coming of peace.[20]

It was not a new theory of colonization that led the British to
lay so much stress upon the retention of Canada, the return of
which to the French would "lay the Foundation of another War."[21]
Before and after 1745, the approximate year in which Beer detected
a shift taking place in the theory of colonization, "colonies were
highly appreciated as outlets for British manufactures."[22] Before
and after 1745 (or 1763), colonies were valued as suppliers of commodities in the self-sufficient empire.

Beer nevertheless pointed to an important truth. The settlements in North America had become by 1763 the centerpiece of
the old empire. They had eclipsed, in the estimate that was made

---

[20] See chapter 5, section V; Sosin, *Whitehall*, p. 46; and [William Knox], "A Project for
Imperial Reform: 'Hints Respecting the Settlement for our American Provinces,' 1763," ed.
Thomas C. Barrow, *William and Mary Quarterly*, 3d ser. 24 (1967):114–16. The Board of
Trade report of 1768 that clearly rejected the idea of interior colonies on the same reasoning
as Knox noted that "the proposition of forming inland Colonies in America" was "entirely
new"; *Trade and Politics, 1767–1769*, ed. Clarence W. Alvord and C. E. Carter, *IHC*
(Springfield, Ill., 1921), 16:197. Cf. "Barrington's Plan for the West, May 10, 1766," in *The
New Regime, 1765–1767*, ed. Clarence W. Alvord and C. E. Carter, *IHC* (Springfield, Ill.,
1916), 11:235. Harlow, *Founding of the Second British Empire*, 1:172, was forced to see a
reversal of policy in 1763 because he assumed that "the acquisition of Canada and the
'Middle West' as a great potential market for British products was deliberately chosen" by
the peacemakers. This motive hardly squared with the post-1763 attempt to restrict interior
settlement. Yet it is much more plausible to find fault with Harlow's characterization of the
motivation behind the Treaty of Paris than to see an abrupt reversal of British colonial policy
in 1763.
[21] [John Douglas], *A Letter Addressed to Two Great Men* (London, 1760), p. 30.
[22] Klaus E. Knorr, *British Colonial Theories, 1570–1850* (Toronto, 1944), p. 105 n.

of their importance, the sugar islands of the Caribbean. Yet what changed was not the theory of colonization, but the importance of the continental colonies within the terms established by the traditional theory. If anything, it was because the old theory of colonization was now taken with greater seriousness that the British were led to invest so many resources to ensure the security of the seacoast colonies. The southern British colonies on the continent (including Virginia, on whose behalf the war had been undertaken in the first place) fulfilled the primary functions of both "tropical" and "continental" colonization. The continental colonies were also seen to hold the key to the West Indies. They did so, it was believed, by virtue of their strategic proximity and their power of supply. Testifying to their importance as nothing else could was the startling increase in their consumption of British manufactures and in their production of staples—developments that could be charted either in the customs statistics or in a glance at the transformed face of Britain, whose outports on the shores washed by the Atlantic grew steadily during the eighteenth century. It was thus not only that the American continental colonies splendidly performed one function in the self-sufficient empire. Imperial statesmen suddenly appreciated that the continental colonies had become critical to the performance of all the functions. The North American colonies had become the indispensable link in a great chain of empire. With the conquest of Canada they were finally to be secure.[23]

[VI]

The initial British decision to press for Canada in 1761 was in keeping with the widespread public sentiment that the war had been undertaken for the security of the North American colonists.

[23] It may be argued that the decision to annex Canada reflected a preoccupation with continental American security that was new and that indeed would have far-reaching implications at the close of the war. On this view, the significance of the Canada annexation would lie not in its underlying re-evaluation of traditional mercantilist principles but in its "deviationist tendencies from orthodox 'mercantilism' "; Fieldhouse, "British Imperialism," p. 25. In reflecting a turn from "mercantilism" to "imperialism," many have argued, the peace settlement heralded the new sentiments that would promote far-reaching changes in the imperial-colonial status quo at the close of the war—changes that provoked resistance and, finally, revolution. This argument is considered extensively in Part Two of this work. Here it is sufficient to observe that the concern with security may be seen just as plausibly as deriving from external challenge as from internal transformation.

The subsequent behavior of the Bute ministry, both in its conduct toward Prussia and in its disposition to concede many of the issues that had led to the breakdown of the 1761 peace negotiations, must be seen against the background of the decision to annex Canada. The willingness of the French to withdraw from this province signaled that the aim with which the British had begun the war had been achieved. The further prosecution of the conflict would now have to be justified on grounds far different from those that had led the British to take up arms in the first place.

The prospect of a secure imperial peace was increasingly real at precisely the moment when Frederick's prospects on the continent were worsening. All the expedients and talents of that remarkable man appeared incapable of withstanding the sheer weight of the forces gathered against him. By the winter of 1761/62 his army numbered no more than sixty thousand—his defeat seemed all but inevitable. What sacrifices the British were prepared to make in order to stave off this defeat had reopened the debate between the advocates of "continental measures" and the advocates of maritime and colonial warfare. This traditional debate, renewed in the early 1760s, merits investigation not only because of its relationship to the final stages of peacemaking but also because of the light it sheds on the enduring problems of modern British foreign policy and strategy.[24]

From the great wars of the turn of the century against Louis XIV down to the Seven Years' War, the nature of Britain's interests in Europe was the great problem of British diplomacy. Pitt had risen to popularity because of his stridently anti-Hanoverian rhetoric during the War of the Austrian Succession, and in the aftermath of war he continued to champion anticontinental measures. The old debate reached a kind of climax before the outbreak of the Seven Years' War, when Newcastle's subsidy treaties with Russia and Hesse Cassel—engineered largely for securing the neutrality of Germany and, failing that, for the defense of Hanover from the

---

[24] Richard Pares's examination of this debate, "American versus Continental Warfare, 1739–63," *English Historical Review* 51 (1936):429–65, is superb. Two other valuable and more recent works that bear on this controversy are Paul Langford, *Modern British Foreign Policy: The Eighteenth Century, 1688–1815* (New York, 1976),and David B. Horn, *Great Britain and Europe in the Eighteenth Century* (London, 1967). See also, in this connection, Michael Howard's two essays, *The Continental Commitment* (London, 1973) and *The British Way of Warfare: A Reappraisal* (London, 1975).

anticipated attack of Prussia and France—had been subjected to a barrage of criticism by those who dreaded the blood and expense of a war on the continent. The debate took place before the "old system" that bound together the Austrians, the Dutch, and the British was shattered by the *renversement des alliances* of 1756. The impending diplomatic revolution was discernible to neither the supporters nor the opponents of the government's policy, and the position of both sides reflected a combination of unalterable principles and uneasy factual premises.

The disagreement between the two sides centered on the question of Hanover. The heart of the opposition's claim was that the government's policy was designed exclusively for the defense of that "despicable Electorate," an accusation that, if true, rendered the subsidy treaties "expressly contrary to the Act of Settlement," which had placed the Hanoverians on the throne.[25] Supporters of the ministry dismissed this charge. Hardwicke, upset that Hanover had been "so much talked of in this debate," noted that it was a topic "that the disaffected will always make use of, for raising jealousies and distrust in the populace against the illustrious family now upon our throne." For every charge that English policy was made in the interests of Hanover, administration spokesmen were content to hurl back the accusation of Jacobitism—an appropriate quid pro quo, they thought, in the currency of contemporary political abuse. But the heart of the ministry's claim was that "if neither we nor our sovereign had anything to do with the electorate of Hanover, it would nevertheless be necessary for us to have such treaties as these now under our consideration, in order to prevent its being in the power of the French to threaten and compel either the House of Austria, or the Dutch, to join with them in the war against us."[26] It was customary, when speaking of the threat from France, to portray the conflict as a contest with "universal monarchy" and to see French pretensions as a threat to the "balance of power"; but, as Hardwicke noted, the primary threat lay in northern Europe. The principal danger was not that France would unite the resources of Europe under its hostile control, but that it might control the North Sea littoral, with potentially devastating

[25] *PH*, 15:624 (Temple).
[26] Ibid., p. 649 (Hardwicke).

consequences for the prosperity and security of Great Britain.[27]
And to suppose, Chesterfield noted, that a French conquest of
northern Germany "would unite the whole Germanic body against"
France was "to suppose an impossibility." In the German empire,
he noted, they have "what they call a constitution; but if there was
a *vis inertiae* in any body whatsoever, it may justly be said to be
by their constitution in the Germanic body, which renders it impossible for that body to defend itself, or any of its members."[28]

The response of the anticontinentalists to this danger revealed
the ambivalence of their position. Only a few failed to acknowledge
that the balance of power in Europe and the independence of the
Low Countries were objects of British concern. Some denied that
France at any particular moment posed a threat to either the balance of power or the Low Counties; others insisted that the threat,
though real, would be met before it became dangerous to Britain
by the princes of the German empire, whose "jealousy of the French
will always prevent" the possibility that France might "nestle in
the north of Germany"; still others claimed that it was neither
within British power nor consistent with British safety "to defend
Hanover from such an invasion." To become the paymaster of anti-
French forces in Europe would require Britain to neglect "entirely
the prosecution of the war by sea and in America," with consequences that could not fail to be extremely serious. Britain's wealth
and power, Halifax argued, was wholly dependent on its colony
trade and its American plantations: should these "be exposed to
the ravages of the French, a national bankruptcy would probably
in a very few years ensue, which would render us unable to continue the war in Europe for the defense of Hanover, or to prosecute
the war by sea and in America, or even to defend ourselves here
at home." Still, the ambivalence remained. When the government
insisted that an unopposed conquest of Hanover would be followed

---

[27] Cf. the words of the great English naval historian, Julian S. Corbett, *England in the Seven
Years' War: A Study in Combined Strategy*, 2 vols. (London, 1907), 1:18: "It may almost
be said that the dominant note of English foreign policy from time immemorial has been
to prevent either France or Spain securing naval stations beyond the Straits of Dover. It
is upon what may be called the virginity of the Dover defile that the strength of England's
maritime position depends, and no other conceivable naval position could be too valuable
to sacrifice so that this one might be preserved intact." In control of the North Sea coast,
France would also be in a position to inflict a serious blow on English commercial prosperity,
as Napoleon was later to do with his continental system and which was contemplated at the
time by French statesmen.
[28] *PH*, 15:628.

by an attack on the Dutch, Halifax answered that "every independent nation in Europe would resent, and would join in assisting the Dutch to repel such an insolent menace."[29]

On the eve of the Seven Years' War, then, the fundamental contention of those opposed to Britain's involvement on the continent was that Britain's European interests required no such involvement, not that Britain was bereft of European interests. The opposition did not deny that *if* France were to establish itself in the Low Countries and the north of Germany, *then* the consequences for British wealth and power would be exceedingly grave; they did deny that the conditional expressed a meaningful possibility, or that British participation was required to avert it. In so insisting, the opposition was merely echoing positions taken earlier by past opponents of "continental connections."

In the pamphlet controversy over continental connections that occurred during the Seven Years' War, Hanover remained the principal object of declamation. Denunciations of Prussia, however, succeeded the older cries that had once surrounded the Austrians and the Dutch. Israel Mauduit's *Considerations on the Present German War*, published in November 1760, was the most successful of the pamphlets opposing the continental war. It was a remarkable pamphlet not only because of the favor it attracted at the court of George III but also because it reflected the traditional ambivalence felt toward the continent by the representatives of a maritime and insular Great Britain. Like others before him, Mauduit did not deny that the European balance of power was a legitimate object of British concern. His contention was that such an objective had been "made a pretence for so many meaner purposes." He strongly attacked the support that Britain gave to Prussia during the war and compared it to the support Britain had given Austria during the War of the Austrian Succession. In that previous war, instead of making the maritime conquests that would have made the great expense of the conflict worthwhile, "we at last forgot both the Spanish war and the French, and spent our money in Germany against the king of Prussia; for fear he should get, what we are now spending still more millions to prevent his losing."[30] Mauduit insisted that British policy was not only useless but also

---

[29] Ibid., pp. 637–42.
[30] *Considerations on the Present German War*, 1st ed. (London, 1760), pp. 7, 47.

counterproductive. Because France ruled Germany through division, Britain's support of the weaker German states (Austria in the war of 1740–48, Prussia in the war of 1756–63) prevented the emergence of a preeminent German state that would in turn form a natural counterweight to French influence in Germany and hence preserve the balance of power. If his outlook was insular, however, he was not devoid of an enlarged conception of British security. Like other opponents of continental involvement before and since, Mauduit looked for that security across the seas and found it in the empire.

The attitudes that informed the pamphlet were those brought to the monarchy by George III on his accession in 1760. The King was a self-conscious representative of a maritime, insular, and colonial Great Britain. When in his first address he announced to the people of Great Britain that he "gloried in the name of Britain," he was communicating his loathing of continental measures, as he had been taught to do by Lord Bute. The King believed that the true interests of Great Britain had not been maintained by his predecessors in office, that sufficient care had not been "taken to keep the advantages of our insular situation, nor effectual bars put to continental influence."[31] It fell to Lord Bute, who enjoyed the personal confidence of the King, to translate these attitudes into policy. The final year of peacemaking, when Bute's influence was greatest, thus represented a test of the principles of the anticontinentalists.

This test revealed the ambivalence of anticontinental principles. For all of Bute's talk of disengaging from the German war, the responsibilities of power considerably cooled his ardor for a foreign policy free from continental involvement. Like the apostate Pitt at the outset of the Seven Years' War, Bute was an anticontinentalist suddenly in charge of a continental war. Despite all the threats that the nation could not afford the German war and that it might be necessary to withdraw not only the Prussian subsidy but the financial and military support given to Ferdinand, Bute did not so withdraw. Support continued to flow to Ferdinand in 1762. The Army of the Rhine continued to deny to the French the occupation of Hanover.

The great dilemma that Bute faced stemmed from his conviction

[31] Cited in John Brooke, *King George III* (New York, 1972), p. 58.

that Britain could no longer afford the war and his sudden realization that a precipitate withdrawal from the continent risked jeopardizing the overall aims of the settlement. Believing that the whole
system of war credit rested on an extremely precarious foundation,
he greatly feared a national bankruptcy. Yet he began to pay attention to Newcastle's warning that the collapse of the British position in northern Europe would enable France to continue the hostilities indefinitely. Peace was the only answer to the dilemma thus
posed. This would allow for Britain's withdrawal from the continent, but the withdrawal would take place in the context of a
general pacification and not as a result of defeat on the field. The
latter possibility, Bute came to appreciate, might very well prolong
the war, for no one could be sure what price France would demand
in compensation for Hanover. No one could know what arrangement might be made with Austria over the Netherlands. No one
could be certain of the relationship that might emerge between
France and the United Provinces. There was at least the possibility
that the collapse of the British position in Europe would jeopardize
the objectives for which Britain had fought overseas, that the security of the continental colonies might become hostage to the
rapacity of France in Europe. In the past, one of the dominant
themes of the anticontinentalists had been that it was necessary to
choose between the continental and maritime wars. In the actions
that he took after the resignation of Pitt, Bute revealed that he
lived in positive dread of making that choice.[32]

There were times, it is true, when it seemed that such a choice
might be necessary. In January 1762, when the British declaration

---

[32] The implications for the Low Countries of any precipitate withdrawal from the continent
were stressed in one of many answers to Mauduit; see Owen Ruffhead, *The Conduct of the
Ministry Impartially Examined* . . . (London, 1760), pp. 6, 24. Both Pitt and Newcastle
forecasted similar dangers in the event of a sudden withdrawal from the continental war;
PH, 15:1224; Newcastle to Yorke, January 26, 1762, *Hardwicke*, 3:341–42. Bute clearly
stated his attitude in his speech to the Lords on Bedford's motion to withdraw all British
troops from the continent immediately. Although treating with contempt the contention
that America had been conquered in Germany—"that our conquests in Asia, Africa, and
America were gained by Hessians and Hanoverians in the plains of Westphalia"—Bute
noted that the "alteration in the general system" entailed by Bedford's motion would "un-
avoidably retard a peace, by embroiling affairs in a new confusion, by giving cause to our
enemies to exult, and rendering our allies regardless of our interest"; "Sir James Caldwell's
Account of the Speeches in Both Houses of Parliament . . ." in *Sir Henry Cavendish's
Debates of the House of Commons during the Thirteenth Parliament of Great Britain*, ed.
John Wright, 2 vols. (London, 1841), 1:571. Even the duke of Bedford had acknowledged,
in 1761, that England must compensate for Hanover in the event of its conquest by France;
see Bedford to Bute, July 9, 1761, *Bedford*, 3:23–24.

of war against Spain raised the possibility of a Spanish conquest of
Portugal, Bute wondered aloud before the cabinet whether the
withdrawal of British troops from Germany might now be necessary. Prussia was the immediate victim of these anxieties.[33] The
fate of this state, in and of itself, was a matter of indifference to
Bute. He was at least receptive to the idea, if indeed he did not
fully share it, that the Hapsburgs were the natural counterpoint to
the Bourbons in Germany and that the Anglo-Prussian subsidy
treaty was for Britain an alliance with a power that in the German
scale of things stood well below Austria and not much above Hanover. Had Silesia stood in the way of a peace settlement, there can
be little question that Bute would have let it pass to Austria.

Even so, the difference between the continentalists and the insular party can be greatly exaggerated on this point. Even the
continentalists were capable of pursuing a policy of "the most bar-
barous insularity":[34] Newcastle's obsession with the Grand Alliance
reflected this quite as much as Mauduit's pamphlet, for the former
project was informed by little recognition that the aspirations of
Britain's continental allies were centered on provinces far removed
from the wilds of America and the fisheries of Newfoundland. Pitt,
too, prior to his departure from office, had inquired of Frederick
what sacrifices Prussia was prepared to make on behalf of peace.
Newcastle acquiesced in every step away from Frederick that was
taken early in 1762 and changed his mind only when, in April, the
Anglo-Prussian breach was irremediable.[35] The duke's suggestion
in January 1762 that Austria could be detached from the anti-
Prussian coalition through the offer of Silesia was remarkably similar to the pressure that in 1742 Carteret had placed on Maria
Theresa to make peace with Frederick by ceding Silesia to him—
the memory of which undoubtedly lay behind Prince Kaunitz's
determination to separate the fortunes of Austria from those of
England after the War of the Austrian Succession. It perhaps would

[33] On the Anglo-Prussian quarrel—which is usually, though mistakenly, seen as inseparable
from the question of Britain's further participation in the continental war with France on
the Rhine—see Walter L. Dorn, "Frederick the Great and Lord Bute," *Journal of Modern
History* 1 (1929):529–60; Lodge, *Great Britain and Prussia*, pp. 107–38; Frank Spencer,
"The Anglo-Prussian Breach of 1762: An Historical Revision," *History* 41 (1956):100–12;
Herbert Butterfield, "Review Article; British Foreign Policy, 1762–5," *The Historical Journal* 6 (1963):131–40; and Karl W. Schweizer, "Lord Bute, Newcastle, Prussia, and the Hague
Overtures: A Re-examination," *Albion* 9 (1977): 72–97.
[34] Pares, "American versus Continental," p. 433.
[35] See Newcastle to Hardwicke, February 22, 1762, *Hardwicke*, 3:342–43.

have been more difficult for the continentalists than for the isolationists to abandon Prussia to its fate, but even the continentalists were unwilling to go much beyond the payment of the subsidy, and had Frederick not been given his unexpected reprieve in the east, the subsidy would not have saved him.

Once the death of Elizabeth had removed Russia from the anti-Prussian coalition, nothing could stop Frederick from pursuing every avenue he could to solidify his understanding with Peter III, even if this led him, as it did, into undertakings contrary to his understanding with England. The Prussian alliance, considered as something worthy of English cultivation, lapsed the moment Elizabeth died. For with her death Frederick no longer had any real need of the English, and his views on the necessity of living up to one's engagements had the same basic dualism as his private and public thoughts on the Protestant cause. A revolution in the east, and the achievement of British aims in North America, left the two allies without a common enemy. This condition of a successful alliance had barely been satisfied during the war; by 1762 it was utterly lacking. With it went their common action.

[VII]

The lapse of the Anglo-Prussian alliance was coincident with the reopening of peace negotiations with the French. A debate quickly arose within the cabinet and the nation on the terms to insist upon in the final settlement. The 1762 debate was similar to the conflict between Pitt and his colleagues during the 1761 French negotiations, but two new factors had entered the political equation: one was the entry of Spain into the war, the other the additional conquests made by the British during the year. Neither Rodney's conquest of Martinique nor Pocock's capture of Havana was received with enthusiasm by Bute or Bedford, who became worried that an aroused public opinion would demand such stringent terms of the French that the chances of concluding an early peace might be jeopardized. The concessions that Bute made to the French in 1762 led to a revolt within the cabinet, led by George Grenville. Nonetheless, the Bute ministry was determined to avoid another year of war. It pressed on with its aim of concluding an early peace.

This determination sprang from three sources. First, the terms that the British presented to the French in the spring of 1762 amply satisfied the principal aim of the war—the security of the American continental colonies. These terms left the western boundary of the coastal settlements from Carolina northward free from a direct foreign presence capable of further estranging the Indians from the British colonists. As an organized entity capable of severly disrupting the security of the coastal settlements, New France was a thing of the past. Henceforth, whatever problems the French natives remaining in Canada posed to the British would be of a far more limited character. Nor could these problems—essentially those arising from military occupation—be addressed by additional conquests.

Britain's supremacy in North America also appeared to give it a commanding superiority in the North Atlantic, and especially in the theater—the West Indies—that seemed mostly likely to contain the seeds of a future war between France and Britain. The French islands remained dependent on the British continental colonies for some foodstuffs and lumber. In addition, the proximity of the American continent and its resources to the West Indian theater appeared to give Britain a genuine advantage over the French in any future war between them. The fund of talent and resources available in North America, it was thought, would enable Britain to strike at France more easily than France could strike at Britain. During the Seven Years' War, this strategic proximity had greatly aided the British conquest of Canada. The French West Indies were thus seen as potential hostages to a cessation of supply and to a quick descent from the mainland. As a supporter of the peace would write later in the decade, "[w]hoever are masters of the North American continent, and command the intermediate seas, can easily possess themselves of [the French islands]. By stipulating, therefore, for the entire possession of the continent, the restored American islands are become in some measure, dependent on the British empire, and the good faith of France in observing the treaty, is guaranteed by the value at which she estimates their possession."[36]

The conviction that even a relatively lenient peace would leave Britain in a superior position acquired added and decisive impor-

---

[36] William Knox, *The Present State of the Nation, Particularly with Respect of its Trade, Finances* . . . (London, 1768), p. 25. Cf. *Annual Register* (1762), p. 60.

tance, however, because of a third consideration. Another year of war would bring imposing costs and an additional debt on behalf of a war that had cost Britain dearly. The horror with which Bute and Bedford contemplated a further spiraling of the national debt was informed by the belief that such an occurrence would very likely entail disastrous consequences for the wealth and power of Great Britain. These fears did not reflect simply the aversion of the landed interest to a wartime land tax of four shillings in the pound but the conviction that an increase in debt would lead to a diminution of trade and a relaxation of national strength.[37]

The central question before the peacemakers in 1762 was whether these considerations—each of which pointed to the desirability of an early peace—were outweighed by the potential benefits that might be conferred by additional demands upon the French. Would the possible exclusion of France from the northern fisheries or the West Indies provide benefits commensurate with the risks of further war? The Bute ministry, believing that the dangers of another year of war were great, concluded that the additional debt required by a continued prosecution of the conflict would sap the foundations of British power far more reliably than additions to British dominions would add to it. This the opposition, led by Pitt, denied. Pitt remained far more willing to accept a further risk of war in order to achieve a peace that he believed would deny France the means of ever recovering its prodigious losses.

The merit of the opposition's case will be considered shortly. Here it is sufficient to observe that the case the ministry made on behalf of its own conduct during 1762 was by no means an unreasonable one. The factional considerations that some historians have seized upon to explain what would appear to be an inadequate settlement are, on this view, of no fundamental importance. It is true that the opposition to the war maintained by George III and Bute merged with a distrust—for the King, a hatred—of Pitt and

[37] In this opinion the most sophisticated economic thought of the age coincided with the staple contentions of opposition country ideology. See, for example, Adam Smith, *An Inquiry into the Nature and Causes of the Wealth of Nations* (1776; reprint ed. New York, 1937), p. 863; David Hume, "Of Public Credit," in his *Essays and Treatises on Several Subjects,* 2 vols. (London, 1788), 1:314–29; and Henry St. John, Viscount, Lord Bolingbroke, *Some Reflections on The Present State of the Nation, Principally with Regard to her Taxes and her Debts . . .,* in *The Works of the Late Right Honorable Henry St. John, Lord Viscount Bolingbroke,* 3 vols. (London, 1754), 3:159–61. For a remarkable exploration of these themes, see J. G. A. Pocock, *The Machiavellian Moment: Florentine Political Thought and the Atlantic Republican Tradition* (Princeton, 1975), esp. pp. 478–79, 496–97.

Newcastle. It does not follow, however, that these personal antag-
onisms were the cause of Bute and George's desire for an early
peace. Perhaps they were; perhaps, too, private ambition alone
accounts for the opposition to the treaty. What does seem clear is
that ordinary historical methods cannot establish these points one
way or the other, unless one is to reconstruct the motives of political
figures from the recriminations of their enemies.

It is an entirely different matter to believe that the final stages
of the negotiations were heavily influenced both by Bute's determination to conclude an early peace and by his fear that excessive
concessions to the French might undercut the negotiations. These
two considerations, though ultimately complementary, worked at
cross purposes with one another. The former made him anxious to
cede points he believed were "fundamentally inessential" in order
to close with the French, while the latter limited his ability to
retreat very far from the demands Pitt had formulated during 1761.
Once he made the concessions over St. Lucia and the Mississippi
boundary, he was forced to resist pressures from both sides. He
refused to accept the demands of France and Spain for concessions
greater than those he had previously offered, warning the Bourbon
powers that their obduracy might entail the restoration of Pitt to
power—a threat that rapidly softened Choiseul's intermittently av-
aricious disposition. Similarly, he refused to accede to the domestic
clamor for harsher terms, warning the hawks of the dangers of
renewed war. These two sets of calculations were probably most
instrumental in determining the final resolution of the issues dividing the British from the French and Spanish. Considerations of
the respective commercial and strategic utility of Puerto Rico versus Florida were, for the King's favorite, of marginal importance.
This does not mean, however, that Bute was oblivious to the larger
strategic and commercial advantages embedded in the treaty. It
merely shows that, once these larger objectives were secured, he
was no longer willing to justify the continuance of the war on behalf
of what he believed were marginal objectives.[38]

[38] Ronald Hyam has recently suggested that the shape of the peace settlement may be
attributed, at least in part, to Bute's "sincere if misconceived determination to produce a
permanent peace." Hyam discounts the importance of "personal reputation and popularity"
in Bute's designs; "Peace of Paris," pp. 33–34. Yet the two episodes that Hyam cites by
way of evidence do not support his contention. The first was a British demand that the
French accede to the Mississippi boundary; Egremont to Choiseul, July 10, 1762, *Anglo-
French Boundary Disputes*, 27:450. The second was Bute's insistence that the Spanish

[VIII]

The peace settlement of 1763 is significant if only because it demonstrates the enormous importance that was vested in the American continental colonies on the eve of the great postwar crisis in imperial-colonial relations. The settlement represented the strategic equivalent of the economic overinvestment in the colonies which Adam Smith condemned as one of the hurtful effects of the colonial monopoly. "The industry of Great Britain," he said, "instead of being accommodated to a great number of small markets, has been principally suited to one great market. Her commerce, instead of running in a great number of small channels, has been taught to run principally in one great channel."[39] And what was true of British industry and commerce was equally true of British security. By driving the French from North America and returning the sugar islands to their former owners, Britain's security, it seemed, became ever more dependent on its North American colonies. The latter, it seemed to the British, the French, and the Americans, now firmly held the balance of power for the entire North Atlantic. From its secure position on the continent of North America, Great Britain could easily overpower a renewed Bourbon combination against its islands in the West Indies. Everything, it would appear, could easily be seen as dependent on the continued loyalty of the

---

commercial treaties in force before the war be permanently, not temporarily, renewed; Bute to Bedford, September 28, 1762, Bute Letters, pp. 139–40. Both were ultimata presented to the adversary, and though they spoke the language of "permanent peace," they also threatened the continuation of the war. This surely must be judged a remarkable method of encouraging a conciliatory disposition in one's mortal enemies. Hyam's reading of these two episodes confuses a peace designed to remove a hostile disposition in the opponent with one whose unambiguous character prevents either party from escaping or intentionally misinterpreting its terms. It was the latter objective that the British government sought in 1762. Given the relationship between Britain's commercial rights in the Spanish Empire and the outbreak of war between Britain and Spain in 1739, and given the relationship between the unsettled and conflicting boundary claims in North America and the outbreak of conflict between Britain and France in 1754, Britain's insistence on these two points scarcely requires special explanation. Bute's concessions to the French in 1762—his readiness to return St. Lucia, for example—may have been unwise and unnecessary, but they were made because he feared the French would break off negotiations and continue the war, not because he hoped for a change in the hostile disposition of England's great and permanent rival; cf. William Knox, *Extra Official State Papers Addressed to the Right Hon. Lord Rawden . . .*, 2 vols. (London, 1789), 2:37.
[39] *Wealth of Nations*, pp. 570–71.

North American colonists. It was therefore no wonder, as Smith also observed, that "the expectations of a rupture with the colonies . . . struck the people of Great Britain with more terror than they ever felt for a Spanish armada, or a French invasion."[40]

[40] Ibid., p. 571.

THREE

The Consequences of Peace

[I]

Historians of the Peace of Paris of 1763 have never doubted that the consequences of the settlement were far-reaching. The nature of these consequences, however, continues to excite controversy. Many have understood the effects of the peace in terms first popularized by Pitt. He condemned the peace in the Commons because "he saw in them the seeds of a future war. The peace was insecure, because it restored the enemy to her former greatness. The peace was inadequate, because the places gained were no equivalent for the places surrendered."[1] Pitt's view continues to find favor. A distinguished English historian, Richard Pares, has argued that "Pitt was right. France was neither appeased nor crushed."[2] The peacemakers, Pitt contended, "seem to have lost sight of the great fundamental principle, that France is chiefly, if not solely, to be dreaded by us in the light of a maritime and commercial power. And therefore, by restoring to her all the valuable West-India islands, and by our concessions in the Newfoundland fishery, we had given to her the means of recovering her prodigious losses, and of becoming once more formidable to us at sea."[3]

The effect of the European articles of the peace, and, more generally, Bute's diplomacy toward Frederick in 1762, have been condemned with equal severity. "It was no use to conclude a war of intervention by an isolationist peace as Lord Bute did in 1762."[4] This unfavorable view of Bute's continental diplomacy, Ronald Hyam has written,

---

[1] *PH*, 15:1270.
[2] *War and Trade in the West Indies, 1739–1763*, pp. 611–12. See also Julian S. Corbett, *England in the Seven Years' War*, 2:376.
[3] *PH*, 15:1265.
[4] Richard Pares, "American versus Continental Warfare, 1739–63," p. 465.

is essentially uncontroversial, perhaps even incontrovertible. Whatever legitimate disagreement there may be about the peace as an imperial settlement, it is not open to dispute that the European settlement constituted a political error. Though Bute can be defended from charges of moral default towards Britain's Prussian ally, it was unquestionably bad diplomacy to threaten Britain's future international position by cancelling the subsidy to Frederick the Great and forcing an importunate peace upon him, and it was unprecedented to sacrifice continental interests to securing colonial territory and, for domestic reasons, a quick peace.[5]

The argument echoes the position critics took at the time. The "desertion of the King of Prussia," Hardwicke charged in the debate over the preliminaries, had left the British "without any system or connection at all upon the continent."[6] And yet Britain had failed to break the Bourbon alliance. It had abandoned Prussia; it had not forced Spain to abandon France.

The effect of these political errors, it is frequently held, must go a long way toward explaining the disastrous reversal of fortune that the British were to suffer in the War of American Independence. Without an ally on the continent of Europe, and facing a hostile coalition, not only of the Bourbons, but of the League of Armed Neutrals, Britain's divided fleet could not insure the command of the seas that was indispensable to military victory in America. The British defeat at Yorktown in 1781 "demonstrated beyond all doubt that British 'command of the sea' was a precarious monopoly and a deceptive concept unless buttressed by effective alliances on the Continent. Neither administrative weakness, nor military and naval ineptitude, was responsible for the humiliating disaster. The dominating factor was political isolation."[7]

It is, of course, the general effect of the Peace of Paris on the relations between Great Britain and its dependencies in North America that has usually drawn the most attention. Many contemporaries insisted that the removal of the French had had profound effects on the assertiveness of the American colonies. Thomas Hutchinson, the governor and historian of Massachusetts Bay, was convinced by 1773, when his dispute with the Massachusetts as-

---

[5] "Imperial Interests and the Peace of Paris, 1763," pp. 23–24.
[6] *PH*, 15:1255.
[7] Gerald S. Graham, *The Politics of Naval Supremacy* (London, 1965), p. 26, and idem, "Considerations on the War of American Independence," *Bulletin of the Institute of Historical Research* 22 (1949):34. See also Herbert Richmond, *Statesmen and Sea Power* (Oxford, 1943), p. 151.

semby laid bare the irreconcilable positions of the metropolis and the colonies, that had Canada remained in the hands of France, "none of the spirit of opposition to the Mother Country would have yet appeared and I think the effects of [the Canada cession] worse than all we had to fear from the French or Indians."[8] Since it was mostly those who supported the imperial cause who adopted this view, it is indeed surprising that "the Canada cession has emerged as a major cause of the Revolution across the entire interpretive spectrum"[9]—surprising because the dominant interpretation of the Revolution has placed the greatest degree of responsibility on the British for having initiated, with the Grenville reforms of 1764 and 1765, the calamitous chain of events that ended in the Revolution. Recently, however, a view of the Canada cession has emerged that is more consistent with the conventional interpretation of the Revolution, one that pays more attention to what the colonial leaders, and not their imperial adversaries, said of the effects of the French removal. The leaders of the colonial revolt denied with virtually one voice that the removal of the French from Canada had in the slightest degree affected their loyalty to the empire, and insisted that the responsibility for the breach had to be placed squarely on the shoulders of a succession of British governments.

[II]

The failure to destroy the sources of French power, in light of the revenge that France took on Britain during the American war, may seem to be a virtually incontestable criticism of the statesmen who fashioned the Peace of Paris. Britain, it might be thought, gained nothing from its moderation, since France struck back at the first opportunity, and indeed began preparations to that end immediately at the close of hostilities. Great Britain would have had much to gain, on the other hand, had it given no quarter to the French,

---

[8] Cited in Lawrence Henry Gipson's classic essay, "The American Revolution as an Aftermath of the Great War for the Empire, 1754–1763," *Political Science Quarterly* 65 (1950):104. For another formulation of the argument, see George L. Beer, *British Colonial Policy, 1754–1765*, pp. 172–73.

[9] John M. Murrin, "The French and Indian War, the American Revolution, and the Counterfactual Hypothesis: Reflections on Lawrence Henry Gipson and John Shy," *Reviews in American History* 1(1973):307–18.

since French power rested on elements that lay virtually in British hands in 1762. Yet the opportunity had been squandered.

The criticism would appear to have some merit, for it is undeniable that a conciliatory policy was incapable of truly satisfying the French. It was "not the loss of territory, but the loss of the war itself" that created "the desire for revenge."[10] Immediately after the close of the war, the French began preparations for the next one. Choiseul, who remained at the head of French policy until 1770, quickly engaged in the work of rebuilding the shattered French fleet, and he took every care to solidify the alliance with Spain. As noted earlier, however, the fundamental argument between the Bute ministry and Pitt during 1762 did not revolve around the question of whether a lenient peace would remove the hostile disposition of the French. The real argument centered around other considerations: Was it possible for the British to destroy the sources of French power in 1762? And were the potential benefits of this undertaking commensurate with risks of renewed war and a spiraling of the national debt? Or was Pitt aiming impossibly high in demanding the utter prostration of the French menace?

Pitt's criticisms of the peace, it should be noted, were not entirely coherent. In addition to claiming that the peace was insecure "because it restored the enemy to her former greatness"—a charge that could have been directed against the terms he offered the French in 1761—he also berated the failure of the negotiators to obtain a full equivalent in "places gained" for those surrendered.[11] Of the two criticisms, however, only the first deserves serious attention. If the peace were "secure," the failure of the negotiators to insist on greater concessions would have been of little significance. If the peace were insecure, however, it would have mattered little in the end whether the British received their full equivalent in places gained for those surrendered. The first involved a genuine question of national interest, the second merely a point of pride.

Pitt's criticisms of the peace terms are most vulnerable on the first and critical point, for it is difficult to imagine any peace, even one that reflected the additional conquests of a prolonged war, that was capable of destroying the sources of French power. The wealth of France was based predominantly on its internal resources. Even

[10] Pares, *War and Trade*, p. 611.
[11] *PH*, 15:1270.

during the Seven Years' War, British naval superiority was far less significant in the collapse of French finances than the great expense of France's continental strategy. Even if one assumes that an additional year of war would have swept France completely from the West Indies and forced it to relinquish Saint Domingue as well as Guadeloupe and Martinique, the effect would not have been to destroy French economic power, and would have been no more than temporary. It would have entailed a redirection of much French foreign trade; it would not have meant the permanent destruction of its foreign trade, nor of its national wealth.

The effects of France's removal from the Newfoundland fisheries are more problematic. Shortages of trained seamen were endemic in mid-eighteenth-century French naval efforts, and the loss of fishing rights off Newfoundland would have exacerbated this problem. Yet even France's seamen were drawn mainly from a marine that plied the French coastal trade. France would still, even after the loss of its fishing rights, have retained the resources necessary to restore its naval power. The reconstruction of French power that began in the closing stages of the Seven Years' War, and the consequent resurrection of France's ability to strike at Britain, depended ultimately on political will. To deprive France of the internal resources with which it might and did begin the task of recovery was impossible.

None of this means that Britain's retention of the West Indian islands and the complete removal of the French from the fisheries would not have weakened France relative to Great Britain. It is the magnitude and duration of the injury that are in question, and on these points historians have tended to accept uncritically the inflated importance given to the colony trade in the eighteenth century. Moreover, they have assumed that such a weakening of French power relative to Britain would have significantly improved Britain's overall strategic position in the War of American Independence. Yet Britain's critical vulnerability during the American war was the rebellion of the continental colonies, whose defensive power was considerable. Pitt was indifferent to and did not foresee the weakening of British power relative to the continental colonies entailed by the huge expenditures of the Seven Years' War. He saw merely that if Britain grew absolutely weaker because of its massive expenditures on the war, then France would be forced to do the same. Yet this objective made sense only on the assumption that France was not merely the eternal but, united with Spain, the only enemy of Great Britain. This assumption, as the events of the next decade were to make abundantly clear, was false. The significant weakening of French power relative to Britain, even had it been within Britain's reach in 1762, was a result perfectly compatible with a weakening of British power relative to America. Had the war continued another year, this result would have been difficult to avoid.[12]

[III]

The British were politically isolated in Europe from the close of the Seven Years' War until 1787, when a renewed French threat to the United Provinces led the younger Pitt to conclude an alliance with Prussia. Not until French revolutionary armies began their sweep across Europe would Britain again stand at the head of a European coalition. By then, the old issues had been radically transformed by the French discovery of a new source of national power, and the men who had played a great role in earlier years, with the exception of the King, were dead or dying.[13]

 ___ The experience of the Seven Years' War and the peace that closed it exerted a profound influence on the European diplomatic constellation, and it is indeed possible to find the sources of Britain's isolation in that settlement. But the reason that is frequently offered to explain this isolation—the precipitate desertion of Frederick— was of no importance. Of decisive significance was the willingness of France to subordinate its old claim to influence in Europe to the exigencies of redressing English maritime and commercial supremacy. The experience of the Seven Years' War—particularly the disastrous and financially ruinous connection with Austria—

[12] Given the consequences to which the bankruptcy of the *ancien régime* led later in the century, the assertion that the utter destruction of French power would have led to an improved strategic position for Britain during the War of American Independence is not easy to defend. Pitt's view of international order was precisely that against which the Concert of Europe so wisely revolted in the nineteenth century and from whose excesses Britain was to suffer dearly during the Wars of the French Revolution and Napoleon. See F. H. Hinsley, *Power and the Pursuit of Peace* (Cambridge, 1967).

[13] A number of excellent studies have recently been published on British diplomacy during the 1760s and 1770s. See, in particular, Frank Spencer's wide-ranging introduction to *The Fourth Earl of Sandwich; Diplomatic Correspondence, 1763–65* (Manchester, 1961); and Michael Roberts, *Splendid Isolation, 1763–1780* (Reading, Eng., 1970).

upset the traditional opinion that French superiority on land could balance without much difficulty the expected English supremacy at sea; and, in this respect, the French debate over "continental connections," though waged in the Royal Council instead of in the bookstalls, had a more far-reaching effect than the contemporary English debate.

Both in the Austrian Succession and in the Seven Years' War, Britain's position on the continent depended on the role that the French played. Britain's alliances were defensive in both name and intent. Its traditional position was one of great weakness, and though men disputed whether its interests in Hanover, the Netherlands, and Portugal were sufficiently vital to require an active defense in an European land war, they did so against the common assumption that these interests were great liabilities. Pitt's strategy of diversion was instrumental in revising both French and British views over the relative balance of forces between them in Europe. It should be remembered, however, that his strategy depended on denying to French armies the occupation of Hanover: Ferdinand's army was throughout on the strategic, if not always on the tactical, defensive.

In the decade following the Seven Years' War, the attitude of the French remained the crucial pivot on which British involvement on the continent rested. Yet Choiseul clearly subordinated the pursuit of traditional French objectives in Europe to the objective of reducing England's crushing commercial and maritime supremacy. In this he had very little choice. The diplomatic history of the decade after 1763 is largely the story of French isolation, of France's inability to defend its position in Eastern Europe, of the helplessness with which it watched Poland and the Ottoman Empire—two traditional French spheres of influence—being carved up under the malignant direction of Catherine II and Frederick the Great. The participation of Austria in the first partition of Poland completed the isolation of France, a condition that was not materially alleviated by minor French successes in Corsica and Sweden. So long as the understanding between Russia and Prussia remained intact, there were few French opportunities on the continent; and so long as a powerful Britain remained to the north, what opportunities there were could be exploited only by risking a dangerous encirclement. A continental struggle could not be undertaken without some understanding with Britain, and this, despite D'Augillion's overtures in 1772, remained outside the realm of both practical politics and prudence. The structure of French alliances, on the other hand, was well suited to a war of revenge against England, since Austria could protect the continental flank and Spain could proffer some services in the maritime conflict. Choiseul flirted with the possibility of a renewed French attack on Hanover and laid still greater stress on a Spanish attack on Portugal, but the comte de Vergennes remained skeptical of the results and opposed both courses of action.[14] Even Pitt paid mute tribute to the effects of the revision of French policy—a revision that for the most part was not grasped by British statesmen, who continued to fret over Hanover and Portugal—when he said, in 1770, that "they who talk of confining a great war to naval operations only, speak without knowledge or experience. We can no more command the disposition than the events of a war. Wherever we are attacked, there we must defend."[15] It followed that where the French chose not to attack, the British could not defend; and since a defensive policy had been the basis of Britain's traditional commitment on the continent, it was the French decision that insured its "isolation."

[IV]

Historians have traditionally focused not only on the causes of Britain's isolation in the 1760s and 1770s but also on the disastrous consequences to which it presumably gave rise. British diplomacy has usually been seen as singularly ineffective in the period comprehending the fall of the First British Empire, on the reasoning that diplomats cannot escape responsibility for the catastrophes over which they preside. This judgment, however, requires some revision. The fundamental reason for Britain's isolation after the Peace of Paris lay in the absence of a genuine French threat to the

---

[14] On French foreign policy in the 1760s, see J. F. Ramsay, *Anglo-French Relations; A Study of Choiseul's Foreign Policy* (Berkeley, 1939); Ramon E. Abarca, "Classical Diplomacy and Bourbon 'Revanche' Strategy, 1763–1770," *Review of Politics*, 32(1970):313–37; and H. M. Scott, "The Importance of Bourbon Naval Reconstruction to the Strategy of Choiseul after the Seven Years' War," *International History Review* 1 (1979):17–35. Still valuable is Albert Sorel, *The Eastern Question in the Eighteenth Century: The Partition of Poland and the Treaty of Kainardji*, trans. F. C. Bramwell (London, 1898).
[15] *PH*, 16:1104.

"public liberties" of Europe. In this all-important sense, the traditional objectives of Britain's *European* diplomacy were secured at a price far less exacting than that which Britain had traditionally paid. In the 1760s and 1770s a France weakened by the two preceding wars no longer posed the threat that had theretofore been the condition of Britain's involvement on the Continent.

This conclusion does not mean that the European diplomatic alignment was ideal. From the British standpoint, the ideal arrangement would have been one in which its principal maritime rival became embroiled with another powerful continental state in a conflict that affected no vital British interest on the Continent and from which Britain could stand aside. So long as a conflict of this character ended in stalemate and did not threaten to end with the resources of Europe united under a single power or coalition of powers, it would have weakened France relative to Britain, restricted the resources that France could have devoted to its navy, and left Britain dominant in the maritime and colonial sphere. By the same token, however, it is not difficult to imagine a European alignment far worse than the one that Britain confronted from 1763 until the end of the American war, one that involved, simultaneously, the threat of American rebellion and the danger to Britain's vital interests in Europe. If, in imagining the "best-case" European alignment, historians have found the causes of the loss of America in Britain's isolation, they might with equal plausibility imagine the worst case and conclude that the absence of a threat to Britain's vital interests in Europe permitted it to command the resources necessary (though not sufficient) to subdue the American revolt. If the standard of comparison is to be the Anglo-French wars of mid-century, the worst-case analysis is far more plausible than the best-case.

It was a frequent aspiration of British foreign policy during the eighteenth century that Britain's continental allies would bear the brunt of the struggle against France, but this desire was seldom gratified. Britain's alliances with Austria and Prussia during, respectively, the War of the Austrian Succession and the Seven Years' War were with states that stood perilously close to disintegration. As a result—though not without continual recrimination between the allies—Britain shouldered in both conflicts the main burden of the war effort in Flanders and Westphalia, and it was forced to pay expensive subsidies to maintain its continental allies. In neither war would Britain have been able to meet both its continental obligations and the burdens imposed by the American rebellion—burdens far more onerous and costly than those that it had to sustain in the colonial theater during those two conflicts. The same search for a "continental sword" dominated British foreign policy during the 1760s and 1770s, and the argument over continental connections during this period centered on the question of which continental state seemed the most likely to fulfill this role. Russia was the prime candidate for the task, but its asking price remained too high. Despite the instability of cabinet government in the 1760s, successive administrations were remarkably united in wisely refusing to pay that price simply for the sake of "having an ally." Pitt continued to dream longingly of a renewed Prussian alliance; others, like the King, believed that Austria, as the most powerful German state and consequently the "natural enemy" of France, was also the natural ally of Great Britain. Yet neither of the two powerful German states was interested in an alliance with Great Britain, though not because of English perfidy. The "continental sword" remained out of reach because none of the partitioning powers was interested in fighting Britain's battles, especially when such tempting opportunities were available in Eastern Europe. This attitude lay beyond the power of any British policy, however wise and resolute, to change.

The failure to break the Bourbon alliance is another error ascribed to the peacemakers, and, in a sense, the criticism represents the obverse of that directed against Bute's German diplomacy. Victorious Britain emerged isolated from the war, while defeated France emerged with the Bourbon alliance unshaken. "A security against [the Bourbon] league," Edmund Burke wrote, "ought to have been the fundamental point of a pacification with the powers whose compose it. We had materials in our hands to have constructed that security in such a manner as never to be shaken."[16] It is difficult to know what to make of this view. Perhaps it was an error to allow France to seal the Bourbon alliance through the cession of Louisiana to Spain, though it is difficult to see the great consequences that flowed from this decision. Spain's ready adhesion to the *pacte de famille* was based on its jealousy of England,

---

[16] *Observations on a Late Pamphlet*, in *The Works of the Right Honourable Edmund Burke*, 16 vols. (London, 1826), 2:44. His judgment has been endorsed by Hyam, "Peace of Paris," p. 29.

not on its love of France. To have eased this jealousy would have required a conciliatory policy that granted to Spain the terms it desired. The opposition as well as the ministry showed no disposition to make these concessions at the time. Burke himself harshly criticized the leniency of the Spanish articles of the peace. The failure of British policy to break the Bourbon alliance reflected the pervasive consensus that precluded a conciliatory policy toward Spain. But this in turn was not so much a "failure" as a wise refusal to settle the many outstanding differences between the two countries in exchange for the promise of Spanish friendship. A conciliatory policy in 1762, assuming that it did not give way before virtually all Spanish grievances against Britain, would have deprived Britain of the inducements that could have been offered to Spain to ensure Spanish neutrality in the War of American Independence, without at the same time providing an effectual security that Spain would remain true to its obligations.

[V]

The American articles of the peace were those with the greatest consequences. By removing the French from North America, the peace settlement wholly altered the distribution of power on the American continent. As a result of the new territorial dispensation, North America witnessed a diplomatic realignment as far-reaching in its consequences as that which the European state system had undergone in 1756. An old weight was taken from one side of the scale, and added to the other, with profound implications for the control of the North American continent.

The new attitude with which the French viewed North America was of critical importance in altering the distribution of power. From a state whose principal aim was the restriction of the British colonies to a small area along the coast, France became one whose chief desire was to deprive the British of the great benefit that it believed Britain's colonies in North America provided the metropolis. France no longer opposed the interests of the colonies as such, which before the war had been viewed as inseparable from larger British interests. It saw what it had theretofore not seen and what had formed no part of its policy before the Seven Years' War, that it could now strike at Britain by supporting, rather than opposing, the pretensions of the American colonies. It had been decisively beaten at one game; it would now play another.[17]

Metropolitan officials were slow to grasp the full implications of this alteration in French policy. Well after the Peace of Paris, British western policy continued to be informed by the fear that Indian uprisings on the frontier and in the interior, which Whitehall attempted to prevent by the restriction of western settlement and by the regulation of the fur trade, would allow the French to regain their hold on Indian sympathies and upset the stability ostensibly procured by the peace. Similarly, the conciliatory stance that the British adopted toward the old settlers of Quebec reflected, at least in part, a fear that the French might regain their hold on the Canadians and thereby threaten the English colonies in the same manner they had done in the past. A policy dominated by fear of renewed French intrigues on the frontier and in Canada gradually changed into one that recognized the importance of the French Canadians and the Indians as allies to be used against the Americans. It took a long time for this point to sink in, however, and even the Quebec Act of 1774 did not fully reflect the new justification, as against the old, for a conciliatory policy. Once made, the new justification did not require a real departure from past policies, for the requirement of both was a policy of conciliation toward the *habitants* and the Indians. The point remains that at the close of the war, and well beyond, imperial policy toward the conquered territories continued to reflect the fear that the French would resume their old position on the continent by seducing the Indians and the Canadians from the King's interest. There was in this policy little appreciation that a renewed French threat to Britain's seacoast colonies would come from an entirely different quarter, and that the essential interests of the French government would become in great degree hostile to those who had only lately been their dependents.[18]

---

[17] Cf. the "Memoir of La Galissoniere" (1751),in *Anglo-French Boundary Disputes in the West, 1749–1763*, 27:5–22, with Choiseul's "Mémoire justificatif" (1765), in *Mémoires du duc de Choiseul, 1719–1785*, ed. P. Calmettes (Paris, 1904), p. 393.

[18] Cf., e.g., two letters from Guy Carleton, governor of Quebec—the first, dated November 25, 1767, to Shelburne, secretary of state for the Southern Department; the second, dated November 20, 1768, to Hillsborough, secretary of the newly created American Department—for changing assumptions about the relationship between the French, the Canadians, and the Americans; *Documents Relating to the Constitutional History of Canada, 1759–*

The Stamp Act crisis, however, contributed to a growing perception in Great Britain that, in the event of an Anglo-American rupture, France might play a role entirely different from its customary one in North America. For the next ten years, the fear that France, possibly in conjunction with Spain, would enter a war between Britain and the North American colonies operated to weaken Britain's resolution against the colonies. Those in favor of a conciliatory policy made the most of the danger of Bourbon intervention, but such fears were very widely held in governing circles and were by no means the monopoly of the opposition.[19]

1791, ed. A. Shortt and A. G. Doughty, pp. 197–99, 228. On the relationship between the French and the Indians, see *The Correspondence of General Thomas Gage with the Secretaries of State and with the War Office and the Treasury, 1763–1775,* ed. Clarence E. Carter, 2 vols. (New Haven, 1931–33), 1:63; and *Trade and Politics, 1767–1769,* 16:190–91, 193–96.

[19] See Charles Garth to Ringold et al., *Prologue to Revolution: Sources and Documents on the Stamp Act Crisis,* ed. Edmund S. Morgan (Chapel Hill, 1959), p. 153; "The Parliamentary Diaries of Nathaniel Ryder, 1764–7," ed. P. D. G. Thomas, *Camden Miscellany 23 Camden Fourth Series,* vol. 7 (London, 1969), p. 304 (Conway, February 21, 1766); Shelburne to Chatham, February 16, 1767, *Correspondence of William Pitt, Earl of Chatham,* ed. W. S. Taylor and J. H. Pringle, 4 vols. (London, 1838–40) 3:209; and *PH,* 18:1283 (Mansfield). Jack P. Greene has suggested that "perhaps the most important structural change produced by the war was . . . the elimination of France and Spain from eastern North America"; "The Seven Years' War and the American Revolution: The Causal Relationship Reconsidered," in *The British Atlantic Empire before the American Revolution,* ed. Peter Marshall and Glyn Williams (London, 1980). Greene notes the importance that historians have placed on the development "as a precondition for colonial resistance after 1763. Of far greater importance, in all probability, was its effect upon the mentality of those in power in the metropolis. For the destruction of French power not only made the colonists less dependent upon Britain for protection; it also left Britain with a much freer hand to proceed with its program of colonial reform by removing the necessity that had operated so strongly during the first half of the war for conciliatory behavior toward the colonies to encourage them to cooperate against a common enemy" (p. 94). Greene's point seems to be buttressed by the fact that, during war with France, the exigencies of military victory usually prevailed over the need to preserve the constitutional position of the metropolis, and that consequently some of Britain's greatest concessions to the colonists occurred during wartime. Yet it was not the removal of the French from Canada but the end of the war itself that freed the metropolis to proceed with its program of colonial reform. Had a different settlement been made, had Canada been restored to the French, the problem of imperial defense would have been even more pressing than it was in 1763. And since the Grenville administration failed to foresee the resistance which its measures would meet with in the colonies, there are good reasons for believing that some program of imperial defense would have been proposed to—and attempted, at least, to have been imposed on—the colonies. Once the Stamp Act crisis blew up in the face of imperial statesmen—once the *real* effect of the peace on the structure of power became clear—the threat of French intervention in any Anglo-American quarrel operated to weaken, not strengthen, the resolve of the metropolis.

Whether in the absence of such fears Britain would have pursued a different colonial policy from 1766 to 1775 is a difficult question to answer. No government relished the prospect of war with America, and this quite apart from the risks posed by French inter-

Colonial spokesmen also began to grasp the meaning of the new structure of power created by the Peace of Paris; they saw clearly the power that this new relationship conferred upon them. All of a sudden they had a new potential ally, one that would be sure to look benignly on the colonial cause in the event of a civil war within the empire. "Do you think," asked George Mason in 1766, "that all your rival powers in Europe would sit still and see you crush your once flourishing and thriving colonies, unconcerned spectators of such a quarrel?"[20] John Dickinson, in his *Letters from a Farmer*, veiled his threat of French intervention in the words of "some future historian" recording a servile colonial response to the Townshend Duties:

The eighth year of this region was distinguished by *a very memorable event*, the *American* colonies then submitting, for the *FIRST* time, to be *taxed* by the *British* parliament. An attempt of this kind had been made about two years before, but was defeated by the vigorous exertions of the several provinces, in defense of their liberty. Their behavior on that occasion rendered their name celebrated *for a short time* all over *Europe*; all states being extremely attentive to a dispute between *Great-Britain*, and so considerable a part of her dominions. For as she was thought to be grown too powerful, by the successful conclusion of the late war she had been engaged in, it was hoped by many, that as had happened before to other kingdoms, civil discords would afford opportunities of revenging all the injuries supposed to be received from her. However, the cause of dissention was removed, by a repeal of the statute that had given offense. This affair rendered the SUBMISSIVE CONDUCT of the colonies so soon after, the more extraordinary.[21]

---

vention. The prospect of French intervention represented an added danger, but one that is probably neither necessary nor sufficient to explain British conduct from the Stamp Act crisis to the decision for war in 1775. Britain resolved to avoid war with the colonies if it were possible to do so without sacrificing the sovereignty of Parliament and clearly had reasons for avoiding war which went beyond the danger of Bourbon intervention. At the same time, once the government persuaded itself that a war with the colonies was necessary to ensure metropolitan control, it was not stayed by the clear and present danger of Bourbon intervention. Britain did, however, become far more compliant to France.

[20] "Recollect what happened in the Low-Countries a Century or two ago," Mason continued. "Call to Mind the Cause of the Revolt. Call to Mind too the Part that England herself then acted"; George Mason to the Committee of Merchants in London, June 6, 1766, *The Papers of George Mason*, ed. Robert A. Rutland, 3 vols. (Chapel Hill, 1970), 1:70. Franklin would later call to mind the results for Spain: "a broken strength that has never since been recovered"; *The Papers of Benjamin Franklin*, 15:191.

[21] *Letters from a Farmer in Pennsylvania to the Inhabitants of the British Colonies*, in *The Writings of John Dickinson*, ed. Paul L. Ford, vol. 1: *Political Writings, 1764–1774* (Philadelphia, 1895), pp. 384–85, Letter 10.

The radical argument from the Stamp Act crisis to the Declaration of Independence was that conflict between the metropolis and the colonies would bring the French into the war on the side of the Americans. This was a wholly novel line of argument. No colonial spokesman had, within living memory, put forth such an improbable, if not indeed absurd, suggestion. Yet all attempts to conjure up the French menace after the 1763 Peace of Paris, especially when such attempts occurred in the context of moderate or Tory arguments for colonial restraint, were dismissed by the radicals. The famous exchange between Daniel Leonard and John Adams on the eve of independence, in which Leonard sought to renew colonial appreciation of the utility of the imperial tie and America's still great and urgent need for protection from the French, brought harsh ridicule from Adams: "The Canadians and Savages," he noted, "are brought in to thicken the horrors" of the scene imagined by "Massachusettensis," and he agreed that the Quebec Act had "laid a foundation for a fabric, which if not seasonably demolished, may be formidable, if not ruinous to the Colonies, in future times." Still the colonists knew "that these times are yet at a distance; at present we hold the power of the Canadians as nothing. But we know their dispositions are not unfriendly to us. The Savages will be more likely to be our friends than enemies; but if they should not, we know well enough how to defend ourselves against them."[22]

The importance of having removed the French (and Spanish) threat to the colonies can scarcely be appreciated by taking at face value the retrospective judgments that the colonists made of the Great War for the Empire.[23] Indeed, the colonial interpretation of the purposes and effects of the war tends to reinforce its importance, for the Americans had spoken in very different terms before Britain successfully embarked on its supreme effort. From the period of the Stamp Act crisis, colonial revisionists were intent on denying that the coastal colonies faced a serious security crisis before the war. They saw the war as one fought for British, and

[22] *Novanglus and Massachusettensis; or Political Essays, Published in the Years 1774 and 1775, On the Principle Points of Controversy between Great Britain and Her Colonies* . . . (Boston, 1819), p. 33 (Novanglus, Letter 3). Cf. p. 145 (Massachusettensis, Letter 1). Cf. also Murrin, "French and Indian War," p. 311.

[23] Cf. Murrin, "French and Indian War," p. 310; and Bernhard Knollenberg, *Origin of the American Revolution, 1759–1766* (New York, 1965), p. 17.

not colonial, interests. Franklin, in his "Examination" before the House of Commons in February 1766, employed this argument to a very skeptical Commons while arguing for the repeal of the Stamp Act. He knew "the last war is commonly spoke of here, as entered into for the defense, or for the sake, of the people in America. I think it is quite misunderstood." Neither the dispute in Acadia nor the contest on the Ohio, he claimed, engaged the essential interests of the colonies. Before General Braddock's expedition was sent to defend a British, not American, interest in the fur trade, the colonists were "in perfect peace with both French and Indians." The war, he concluded, "as it commenced for the defense of territories of the Crown, the property of no American, and for the defense of a trade purely British, was really a British war—and yet the people of America made no scruple of contributing their utmost towards carrying it on, and bringing it to a happy conclusion."[24]

For Franklin, whose experience with the Albany Plan of Union and whose interest in western colonization pointed to a conclusion directly opposite to the one he drew in 1766, the position that the war was a wholly British war was quite disingenuous, which is not to say that it was out of place. Thomas Paine went even further than Franklin. In the pamphlet that was to make him famous, Paine wrote that "France and Spain never were, nor perhaps ever will be, our enemies as *Americans*, but as our being the *subjects of Great Britain*."[25] This pronouncement could have been made only after the application of British power had driven the French from the continent. It rested on the false assumption that, absent the protection of Great Britain, the defenseless settlements of North America would somehow have had no quarrel with the French or Spanish, that the drive for empire of the Latin powers would somehow have had a different character in North America from that which it assumed elsewhere. Had Paine written these words at the outset of the Great War for the Empire, he would have been looked upon as either a madman or a French agent, features of his character that would not be displayed fully for another generation. His view, however, was widely held in the colonies in the decade after the

[24] "Examination before the Committee of the Whole of the House of Commons," in *Papers of Franklin*, 13:150–51.
[25] *Common Sense* (1776), in *The Writings of Thomas Paine*, ed. M. D. Conway, 4 vols. (New York, 1967) 1:86.

Peace of Paris. This alone demonstrates the enormous transformation wrought by the territorial settlement in North America. The Americans began to interpret their past in terms conformable to their immediate interests and fears—a development that, if neither surprising nor for the most part insincere, must be traced in large measure to the changes resulting from the war.

[VI]

The removal of the French from North America thus made possible a relationship between the French and the Americans that is very difficult to imagine occurring so long as the French retained territorial aspirations in North America and hence represented a threat to the older colonies. To subscribe to this thesis does not diminish the significance of causes intrinsic to the Anglo-American relationship as factors leading to the disruption of the empire. The removal of the French from Canada eliminated a reason for the colonies to stay within the empire, but it did not constitute, in and of itself, a motive for leaving. The motive for leaving must instead be found in the reasons the colonists deemed their situation insufferable.

Was the stability of the imperial-colonial relationship before the Seven Years' War a result of the mild manner in which British rule was exercised over the colonies, or the effect of a French threat that made the continental colonies dependent on the protection of the mother country? Was the instability of the relationship in the aftermath of war a consequence of the novel severity of British rule, or the sudden removal of the French threat? These questions cannot be answered with any finality. The naval protection conferred by the metropolis was far more significant for the colonies than the resources that Parliament devoted during the first half of the eighteenth century to the defense of the colonial frontier.[26] This naval protection continued after the Seven Years' War and yet was not sufficient to reverse the decision for American independence. Nor did metropolitan officials enjoy much success before the war in employing the French and Indian threat as a lever to extract concessions from reluctant colonial assemblies. Indeed, it had been largely over issues related to the defense of the colonial

[26] See chapter 5, note 1.

frontier that the assemblies had risen to the position of power they enjoyed in 1754. On the eve of the Seven Years' War, the assembly of the colony of New York, whose frontier areas were as vulnerable as any other continental colony to French and Indian attack, enjoyed more extensive privileges than any other American assembly under the control of the crown.

This experience, however, hardly signifies that the existence of the common French enemy was not a factor tending to preserve, rather than disrupt, the imperial-colonial relationship.[27] The colonies remained the dependents, the metropolis the protector, even though the promise of protection had seldom been redeemed. The mere threat that it would be so redeemed had conferred an important benefit upon the colonies. The Americans could and did exploit the responsibility vested in the colonial governors for ensuring the defense of the frontiers by refusing money grants save on terms laid down by the assemblies. So long as the French remained, however, the colonists could not threaten to sever their relationship with the metropolis, for this would inevitably have brought a more immediate threat to their own interests than to those of the mother country. In the West Indies, where the British island colonies remained as dependent as ever on British protection against foreign attack and slave revolts, no such severance took place. Where colonies remained truly dependent on British protection, they even submitted to the Stamp Act. Before the removal of the French, there was nothing irreparable about the loss of power suffered by the royal governors to the colonial assemblies. After the Canada cession, there no longer existed the common interest that would have given the two sides an incentive, at least, to reconcile their inevitable differences. Great Britain, having undertaken the war on the assumption that the security of the colonies was virtually identical with the security of the mother country, made a peace that undermined the plausibility of this assumption.

The refusal of the colonial assemblies to yield on their privileges before and during the war underlines the foolhardy nature of the commitment to American security that imperial officials made in 1754.[28] The liberality of the British war effort under Pitt was noth-

[27] Cf. Murrin, "French and Indian War," p. 310.
[28] The title for the conflict chosen by Lawrence Henry Gipson and occasionally employed throughout this work—"The Great War for the Empire"—would be far more appropriate, for all the good reasons Gipson indicates, were it not for its failure to convey the emptiness of the whole enterprise.

ing less than extraordinary, and even here it should be recalled that Pitt only enlarged a policy of commitment to North America that had been undertaken by Newcastle in 1754. A succession of British ministries gradually extended their commitment to North America without first demanding of the colonists a price for this enormous outlay of blood and treasure. The imperial commitment to North America in 1754 was, in the last analysis, unqualified—which is only another way of saying that it was unthinking. During the war, the commitment made it extremely difficult for the British to withdraw their support from the colonies, for this would inevitably have been seen more as a sign of weakness vis-à-vis the French than as a prudent threat against recalcitrant allies. After the war, the results of the commitment—the removal of the French from Canada—deprived the British of the one weapon on which they might have relied to secure the objectives sought in the postwar program of reform. Perhaps this postwar program would have failed in any event; yet in the absence of the Peace of 1763, it is difficult to believe that the consequences of failure would have been as severe as they in fact turned out to be, or that the colonists would have been as intent on forcing the metropolis to yield on matters that the latter considered to be inseparable from the continued integrity of imperial rule. William Pitt, who was most responsible for bringing about this state of affairs, is often thought of as the British statesman who brought the First British Empire to its greatest extent of power and glory. In fact, he was the chief architect of its decline.[29] Pitt asked for very little from America and got even less. The Americans had taken his measure, and it is not remarkable that they came to love the man willing to do so much for them while asking for so little in return.

[VII]

The causal relationship between the outcome of the Seven Years' War and the disruption of the First British Empire is, in some respects, less direct than many have contended. The great sins of omission and commission allegedly committed by British statesmen during the concluding stages of the war—the failure to do the

---

[29] David Hume, who hated the "wicked, madman Pitt," saw this clearly; see J.G.A. Pocock, "Hume and the American Revolution: The Dying Thoughts of a North Briton," in *McGill Hume Studies*, ed. David Norton and Nicholas Capaldi (Austin Hill Press, 1979).

impossible and hence crush French power, the failure to do the
unnecessary and preserve a "continental connection"—in fact had
little bearing on the creation of the vulnerable strategic situation
Britain faced in the 1760s and 1770s. The effect of the experience
and outcome of the war on the imperial-colonial relationship, however, an effect we have only begun to consider, was far more
significant.

The peace settlement gave France a motive to side with the
American colonists; the intractable issues that arose as a consequence of the war as well as the distant danger France now posed
to the Americans, gave it a splendid opportunity. The war heightened Britain's resolve to set its American affairs in order, while
the peace settlement decreased the ability of the metropolis to do
so effectively. The war and the peace settlement confirmed, in the
minds of all participants, the enormous importance of the American
continent as the makeweight of the European balance of power.
For the Americans, this growing sense of self-importance contributed immensely to their desire to establish their relationship with
Britain on the footing of equality; for the British, it underlined the
importance of maintaining the colonists in their traditional status
of dependence. The experience and outcome of the war thus changed
profoundly the imperial-colonial relationship and created expectations in the two sides that were utterly irreconcilable. When the
Grenville reforms and the reaction they elicited in the colonies
produced the first great crisis in imperial-colonial relations, the
arguments introduced by either side were heavily influenced by
the preceding conflict and the changes this conflict had wrought.
To see 1763 as the year in which the positions of the two sides are
to be judged as well as the year establishing the bench mark of
legitimate action is to take a snapshot of a relationship in the process
of upheaval. Begun in 1754, this upheaval bore consequences that
were very far from complete at the formal close of hostilities.

PART TWO

THE STATUS QUO

FOUR

The Historiographical Problem

[I]

In the beginning, there was a status quo. In the historiography of the conflict that resulted in American independence, this premise is so widely shared that it has virtually achieved the status of an a priori judgment. It is the premise that gives an elemental structure to the conflict. It unites those who would otherwise remain divided. Historians may differ over the content and the relative significance of the elements that composed the imperial-colonial status quo. They may argue over its equity and, even more, over the nature of the process that led to its collapse. They rarely differ over the assumption that there was a reasonably well defined status quo in 1763.

The propensity to see a conflict in terms of a set of relationships that presumably defined the positions of the parties at the outset is scarcely distinctive to the history of the Anglo-American conflict. It is apparent in the history of most conflicts. The assumption of a status quo provides historians with a vantage point from which the story they relate can then unfold. What is distinctive about the historiography of the Anglo-American conflict is the emphasis and centrality that has been given to an otherwise familiar device. Here, the status quo does not simply form a useful point of departure. Instead, it is a constant referent, a pervasive standard without which a meaningful account of the conflict hardly seems possible at all. In this respect, as in other respects, the lasting influence of colonial perceptions and arguments is apparent. For it was, of course, the colonists who insisted throughout that the cause—indeed, the only significant cause—of the conflict was the determined attempt by the metropolis to alter the pattern of imperial-colonial relations that had comprised the status quo prior to the close of the Great War for the Empire.

In the colonial version of the controversy that eventuated in war, the Americans had been content with their lot until the time Great Britain set out on its new program of imperial reform. That program sought to effect a far-reaching change in the relationship between metropolis and colonies and to do so irrespective of colonial wishes. Dissatisfied with the status quo that had emerged in the course of many decades, London set out to tighten imperial ties, to infringe upon long-established relationships, and to assert powers it had never before attempted to assert. It did so in setting forth a new plan for imperial defense and particularly in the method by which this plan was to be supported, in the changes made in the laws and administrative practices governing the system of trade and navigation, and in the limitations imposed upon the autonomy heretofore enjoyed by the colonies in their internal governance.

From the initial acts of resistance to these efforts to the final act of armed rebellion against the metropolis, the colonists' position came down to a demand for a return to the status quo. This is the essential meaning of the various resolutions on the Stamp Act passed in 1765 by the provincial assemblies. It is the recurrent theme of the many pamphlets protesting the new policy. In the most famous of these pamphlets, *Letters from a Farmer*, John Dickinson leaves no doubt that all would once again be well if the metropolis would but return to the arrangements that had prevailed prior to 1763.[1] Benjamin Franklin, in his inimitable manner, said the same. Responding in 1769 to the plaintive cry, "Can nobody propose a Plan of Conciliation?" Franklin wrote, "My Answer was, 'Tis easy to propose a Plan; mine may be express'd in a few Words; *Repeal* the Laws, *Renounce* the Right, *Recall* the Troops, *Refund* the Money, and *Return to the old Method of Requisition.*' "[2] In 1774 the First Continental Congress repeatedly returned to this position. Conciliation with the colonies might be effected by a return to the relationship as it presumably stood at the close of the Seven Years' War. "Prior to this era," the Congress reminded the metropolis, "you were content with drawing from us the wealth produced by

---

[1] *Letters from a Farmer in Pennsylvania to the Inhabitants of the British Colonies* (Philadelphia, 1768), in *The Writings of John Dickinson*, 1:312–22, Letter 2.
[2] Franklin to Galloway, January 9, 1769, *The Papers of Benjamin Franklin*, 16:17.

our commerce."[3] Had the mother country only remained content with this benefit the colonies had willingly bestowed upon her all would have been different. There would have been no conflict, now verging on armed rebellion. Even in 1774, though, the Americans insisted the breach was not irreparable. "Place us in the same condition that we were at the close of the last war," the Congress declared, "and our former harmony will be restored."[4]

The prevailing judgment of historians has remained essentially consistent with the position taken by the colonists. In a vast historiography on the conflict that led from empire to independence, the most pervasive theme is that the critical cause of the conflict was the insistent British challenge to the status quo. It appears quite expectedly in the accounts of those who were participants. Yet what is apparent in the first generation of heroic histories is no less apparent in the histories of succeeding generations of nineteenth-century historians. In the work of the great whig historians, among whom George Bancroft must be seen as the leading exemplar, the reader is left in no doubt about the significance of the wholesale attack on the status quo by the metropolis and the role this played in the events that led to war and independence.

Nor have twentieth-century historians abandoned what their predecessors accepted as an article of faith. They, too, take the view that there was a reasonably well defined status quo and that the crisis in imperial-colonial relations was brought on by metropolitan insistence on altering the heretofore accepted dispensation. Whatever the other sins of the progressive historians might have been in the eyes of disapproving colleagues, they did not really controvert this point.[5] The imperial historians, though more difficult to characterize, have not dissented from the fundamental premise respecting the existence of a status quo. On occasion, they have even gone further. In the notable case of Charles Andrews, the collapse of the status quo at the end of the Seven Years' War is directly traced to the change by the metropolis from a policy of mercantilism to one of imperialism.

[3] "Address to the People of Great Britain," in *Journals of the Continental Congress, 1774–1789*, ed. Worthington C. Ford, 34 vols. (Washington, D.C., 1904), 1:84.
[4] *Journals of the Continental Congress*, 1:89. The all-important Statement of Violations of Rights is predicated throughout on the departures from the status quo by the metropolis beginning in 1763.
[5] This is true at least of the newer progressives. See, for instance, Merrill Jensen, *The Founding of a Nation* (New York, 1968), pp. 299, 329–33. But cf. Arthur M. Schlesinger, "The American Revolution Reconsidered," *Political Science Quarterly* 34(1919):76–77.

It is in the prevailing post–World War II history of the Revolution, however, that the colonial version of the crisis leading to independence has attained its fullest expression. The thrust of this writing is indicated by the dicta of Edmund S. Morgan. "All the objectives of the Americans before 1776 could have been attained within the empire and would have cost the mother country little or nothing."[6] The colonies wanted no more than that the status quo not be altered. "If England had been willing, the colonists would have been willing to settle down on this position and search no further."[7] England, however, proved unwilling to settle down on this position—the status quo—and the unwillingness to do so precipitated the crisis that cost the British their empire.

In one sense, at least—however trivial—this view is surely unexceptionable. If the metropolis had refrained from introducing any of the measures the Americans found so threatening to their interests, there would have been no conflict. Even after having introduced these measures, there would have been no war had London simply given way to colonial opposition and abandoned any

---

[6] *The Challenge of the American Revolution*, pp. 56–57. The quotation is taken from the essay "Revisions in Need of Revising," which was originally published in the *William and Mary Quarterly*, 3d ser. 14 (1957): 3–15.

Elsewhere, the principal question this assertion must raise—Why, then, did the metropolis set out on the disastrous course it did?—is given extended consideration. Here, it is useful to ask how Morgan and the many historians who share his view can appear so confident in asserting it. How can they *know* that the objectives sought by the Americans could have been attained without cost to the metropolis? It is another matter to argue that the cost to Great Britain of having pursued the course it did proved greater than the cost entailed by leaving the Americans alone. In fact, the latter cost cannot be known since the British did not leave the Americans alone. Since the ultimate cost of the attempted reforms was a war that resulted in the breakup of the empire, however, it does not seem unreasonable to assume that the cost of the alternative course would have been less, and this quite apart from the eventual consequences to which this course might have led.

Such, however, is not the argument made. Instead, it is that a policy of inaction would have cost the mother country little or nothing. Again, the question arises, How do those making the argument *know* this? The answer, of course, is that they cannot know, that they are dealing with "what might have been," or with what some historians are wont to term "counterfactual history." There is no objection to this device, so long as it is seen for what it is. Indeed, it is difficult to see how an interesting and imaginative inquiry into the causes of the war of independence could be undertaken without resort to what must remain the hypothetical. In doing so, however, such resort should be recognized for what it is and not treated almost as part of the historically known.

[7] Edmund S. Morgan, *The Birth of the Republic, 1763–89* (Chicago, 1956), p. 27. "The net effect of the new studies of the coming of the Revolution," Jack P. Greene wrote in 1968, "has been to reestablish the image of the Revolution as a conservative protest movement against what appeared to the men of the Revolution to have been an unconstitutional and vicious assault upon American liberty and property by a tyrannical and corrupt British government"; *The Reinterpretation of the American Revolution, 1763–1789* (New York, 1968), p. 50.

and all changes to which the colonists took exception. The point was made at the time by a heretical participant in the debate going on in Great Britain and with his customary clarity. Responding to Edmund Burke's plea in 1775 that peace must be preserved, that the colonies must be conciliated, and that time must be permitted to heal the dispute, the dean of Gloucester, Josiah Tucker, wrote: "After all, what is this heaven-born pacific scheme . . .? Why truly: if we will grant the colonies all that they shall require, and stipulate for nothing in return; then they will be at peace with us. I believe it; and on those simple principles of simple peacemaking I will engage to terminate every difference throughout the world."[8]

It is evidently not in this sense that the argument in question must be understood, but in the sense that war might—and, indeed, could—have been avoided without the sacrifice of vital interest by the metropolis.[9] The vital interest of Great Britain was not simply to forestall war with the colonies. Above all, it was to prevent that very independence of the colonies which, though eventually resulting from war, might equally have resulted from a slow yet steady erosion of the British position, an erosion that many observers in London were persuaded was occurring. It will not do, then, to argue that war might have been avoided if the price of such avoidance was to make independence altogether likely, as a practical proposition, through conceding the various issues in dispute with the colonies. At least, it will not do to argue thus unless one assumes the party required to make concessions for peace was persuaded that war could lead only to defeat, in this case to the formal concession of American independence and perhaps even to further sacrifice of other imperial interests. British statesmen may not have been paragons of political wisdom, but this is no reason to accuse them of deliberately pursuing a policy that could lead only to a war they were persuaded Britain could not win.

The concentration of contemporary historians on the immediate origins of the conflict thus provides the most suitable setting for raising the issue of responsibility. The explanation stressing immediate causes suggests a situation in which men were free to

[8] *A Letter to Edmund Burke* (Gloucester, 1775), pp. 44–45.
[9] We say "by the metropolis" rather than "by either side" since those who have urged this view—from the colonists to contemporary historians—simply assume that armed rebellion could have been avoided by the colonists only at the sacrifice of vital interests. By contrast, no such sacrifice is found to have threatened Great Britain.

follow any one of a number of courses. It also raises the question, Who chose to upset the status quo? If the colonists were as content with their lot as Morgan and others find them to have been, and if such objectives as the Americans entertained were compatible with the status quo and would have cost the metropolis little or nothing, there would seem little need to inquire into the more distant origins, the deeper roots, of the conflict. To the question, What impelled the imperial state to attempt to change so satisfactory an arrangement? the answer must be sought for the most part in contemporaneous developments. Whatever the reason, or combination of reasons, given for British policy in the 1760s, the logic of the post–World War II consensus has militated in the direction of emphasizing short-term developments in order to explain the conflict. And that logic has indeed evoked the expected response.

At the same time, the significance of long-term developments affecting the imperial-colonial relationship has not been ignored. Even in the earliest heroic histories of the conflict as well as in the accounts of the great whig historians of the past century, the deeper factors affecting the relationship were not disregarded. In the recent literature, these deeper factors at work have been subject to searching examination by several historians. Thus, Bernard Bailyn has probed the structure of colonial politics in the earlier decades of the eighteenth century, has illuminated the instability of that structure, and has shown how explosive and "latently revolutionary" the American political landscape was by mid-century, even without an ideology that would give transcendent—and revolutionary—meaning to the events of the 1760s and 1770s.[10] And Jack P. Greene has examined with care and insight the long-term conditions that made the imperial-colonial relationship a connection that was not only uneasy long before the great crisis appeared but one that was inherently fragile.[11]

What is relevant, and striking, in this context, however, is that whereas these and other inquiries into the deeper forces determining the evolving relationship necessarily qualify the emphasis so often placed on the immediate origins of the conflict, they are

---

[10] *The Origins of American Politics* (New York, 1967). See also his *The Ideological Origins of the American Revolution* (Cambridge, 1967).

[11] "An Uneasy Connection: An Analysis of the Preconditions of the American Revolution," in *Essays on the American Revolution,* ed. Stephen G. Kurtz and James H. Hutson, pp. 32–80.

not seen to displace the significance commonly given to the proximate causes of the American Revolution. It is Bailyn who has insisted that the latent tendencies of American politics need not have been fulfilled and that without the measures taken by the metropolis "the 'dysfunctions' that may have existed could have continued to function 'dysfunctionally' for ages untold."[12] And Greene, after having laid bare the many and deep "dysfunctions" marking the imperial-colonial relationship, concludes that had the British not altered the character of this relationship so profoundly through the Grenville program, had the metropolis not embarked upon an effort that "seemed to the colonists—and *was in fact*—a fundamental attack upon the extant moral order within the empire as they conceived of that order," it was entirely possible that the Americans would have remained content with their position for a considerable period to come.[13]

Thus, all roads of historical inquiry seem to lead to the same destination. There is, moreover, an apparent plausibility, even persuasiveness, about the directions traced by historical scholarship that discourages the search for different routes that might in turn lead to a different destination. For the British did in fact set out on a program of imperial reform in the 1760s, and in doing so they did introduce a number of measures, some of which were quite clearly novel. Those measures had the evident purpose of altering the existing state of affairs, over which the metropolis was unhappy and apprehensive, and of doing so through a general tightening of imperial ties. All this the British virtually conceded, though they insisted they were taking such measures to preserve the status quo. It is also a fact that imperial officials made little effort to seek the consent of the colonists to these changes. Finally, the dismay and outrage of the colonists can scarcely be controverted any more than their conviction that the imperial state had altered, and in critical measure, the terms of the relationship.

These are weighty facts. What they establish is that the British sought to introduce certain measures following the Great War for the Empire, that the colonists resisted these measures and considered them a grave departure from their understanding of the imperial-colonial status quo, and that the result of this action and

[12] "Central Themes of the American Revolution:" in Kurtz and Hutson, *Essays*, p. 24.
[13] Ibid. "An Uneasy Connection," pp. 79–80.

reaction was the emergence of a crisis that would ultimately be resolved only through war. These facts do not establish, however, that there *was* a status quo—that is, a pattern of relations both reasonably clear to and accepted by the parties—that the British set out to alter radically if not simply to destroy. Indeed, if this were the case we would have the curious, and almost anomalous, situation of a dominant power no longer satisfied with the existing dispensation and a rapidly rising and ambitious power (the colonies being here considered collectively) that is quite content with the status quo. In the normal course of affairs, these roles are reversed. It is the dominant power that meets the challenge to its favored position by invoking the status quo, and the rising power that seeks supremacy, or equality, by condemning the status quo. This is the normal course of affairs for the obvious reason that the status quo is taken to reflect the interests of the dominant power.

Why, then, the reversal of normal roles? Why should the colonies, the rising power, have put themselves in the role of defender of the status quo? The answer, not surprisingly, must be found in the colonists' understanding of the status quo. In this understanding, the colonists were to be allowed to act largely as they pleased, particularly in matters of internal governance, subject to the constraints imposed by the metropolis in the regulation of their trade. Even the power to supervise and regulate trade was, from the American perspective, one attended by conditions and, as matters turned out, very inhibiting conditions. For the imperial state was not to undertake measures for enforcing trade regulations more effectively if such measures were judged by the colonists to threaten their internal autonomy, or, what often came to the same thing, their inalienable rights as Englishmen.

This was, in essence, the colonists' understanding of the status quo. That understanding did not preclude change. Quite the contrary, a certain kind of change was altogether compatible with this conception of the status quo. One may go further and say that this particular status quo amounted to nothing so much as a mechanism for effecting change. The change, however, had to be of a kind favorable to colonial interests and freedom of action. The status quo "moved," as it were, though only in one direction, and the course and meaning of that direction were understood well by the colonists. Change that took a different course and that had a different meaning—unfavorable change that sought to turn back the imperial clock—was a breach of the imperial-colonial understanding. It was, quite simply, illegitimate.

Given this conception of the status quo, it is not surprising that the colonists should have taken a position rising powers have but rarely taken and that they should have resisted the British measures of imperial reform in the name of the status quo. The colonial view impelled them to resist any measures that would have the effect of controlling their freedom of action or of slowing down the change that their understanding of the imperial-colonial relationship permitted. Even small measures taken by the metropolis might have had this result and therefore had to be zealously guarded against, for the cumulative effect of such small measures might have proven considerable. The effect might well have been to stop, if not even to reverse, the movement that was the inevitable result of this status quo. The colonists thus combined a very broad, and certainly unusual, view of the status quo with a very narrow and rigid view resistant to almost any imperial reform, however limited and discrete its character.

Metropolitan officials entertained a very different understanding. To the imperial state, the status quo was identified not only with an overall relationship in which the colonies remained in a clearly subordinate status but also with a relationship that enabled the mother country to take such measures as would insure the continuance of this status. This understanding did not preclude change, a point that is borne out by the entire history of the imperial-colonial relationship; but there were limits to the change it would, and could, permit if the colonies were to remain in a subordinate position. Moreover, in the metropolitan understanding of the status quo, there were no formally acknowledged limitations to the authority it claimed to exercise as of right over the colonies. As a practical matter, this meant that if in the exercise of its powers to regulate the trade of the empire or to provide for imperial defense certain measures were considered necessary, the colonies could not block such measures by contending they were an illegitimate encroachment on their rights. The basic integrity of the imperial system could not be jeopardized by the resistance to specific measures, though those measures imposed constraints that were novel. Discrete and limited aspects of the status quo might be altered in order to preserve the broader status quo, identified with the overall integrity of the system. The metropolis might thus turn back the imperial clock, in the sense of asserting powers since abandoned or even never before asserted, if it considered such action necessary for the general purposes of imperial governance.

These were evidently two very different understandings of the status quo. So long as events did not conspire to bring them into direct conflict, there was no need to attempt their reconciliation. But the events of the 1750s and early 1760s—events principally related to and growing out of the Great War for the Empire—did work to bring about the open confrontation so long avoided. When this occurred, the difficulties inherent in any attempt to reconcile such disparate versions of the status quo were at last laid bare.

These general considerations will be illustrated in some detail in succeeding pages. Here it is sufficient to observe that despite the broad consensus sanctioned by a long-established tradition of historical scholarship, there was no status quo to which common appeal could be made by the parties. The insistence upon identifying the colonial version of the status quo with *the* status quo, hence with the standard of legitimacy by which the claims of the parties might then be judged, has no more justification than the attempt—but rarely made—to identify the status quo with the position taken by the metropolis.

FIVE

Imperial Defense

[I]

At the close of the Seven Years' War, the British stationed an army in North America of unprecedented size and responsibilities. The metropolis limited western settlement on a line approximating that of the watershed of the Appalachian Mountains, and assumed a control over the disposition of Indian territory and the Indian trade which it had never exercised in the past and which theretofore had been left to the provincial governments. In order to finance the costs of this army, the Grenville ministry imposed taxes on the American colonies. Seen against the perspective of a century and a half of colonial development, the Grenville program appeared to the colonists, as it appears to most historians today, to represent a striking usurpation of powers traditionally reserved to the provincial governments. Never before had Parliament attempted to raise a revenue in America, if one excludes a few isolated and, for the most part, insignificant precedents. Never before had the British stationed an army in North America approaching in size the one that they placed there at the close of the Seven Years' War. Never before had the imperial state assumed direct control of Indian relations. In each of these three decisions, historians have found a striking departure from the status quo, a radical subversion of an imperial-colonial relationship that, though never codified in law, was nevertheless well-established in practice.

Yet it is by no means an easy matter to determine the nature of the status quo from which the British presumably departed. Is the legitimate standard of imperial action to be the customary behavior of the metropolis under the security system that prevailed for most of the eighteenth century, or its behavior during the Seven Years' War, a war that in significant measure transformed this older security system? Did the actions that the colonists identified as fundamental challenges to the imperial-colonial status quo spring from a change in British policy, or a change in the circumstances Whitehall suddenly had to confront at mid-century? These questions are worth raising because they indicate the difficulty, particularly in the early 1760s, of defining the imperial-colonial relationship. Even more, they indicate that the status quo contained elements that could no longer be easily reconciled, if indeed they could be reconciled at all.

[II]

There was no novelty as such in Parliament's intervention in colonial affairs. It had claimed the right to legislate for possessions beyond the realm as early as the sixteenth century. During the period of the Commonwealth, in the mid-seventeenth century, that claim was again expressly asserted and acted upon. From the Restoration to the Great War for the Empire, the authority of Parliament to legislate for the colonies, an authority that evidently implied the supremacy of Parliament over the colonies, went unquestioned. That supremacy was carried into practice in a number of spheres, though most notably in the control of commerce. With the exception of a few precedents, none of which produced a significant amount of revenue, Parliament's general legislative supremacy over the colonies had not entailed the practice of taxation.

Parliament's responsibility on behalf of the colonies was as extensive in theory and as limited in practice as its right to tax. The colonists were expected, for the most part, to provide for their own local defense. Parliament's contribution to imperial defense came primarily in the form of the support it gave to the maintenance of British naval power. This protection conferred valuable benefits on the inhabitants of the continental colonies. Without Britain's naval presence in the Mediterranean to protect American commerce—a protection made possible by Parliament's support to the navy and to the army garrisons at Minorca and Gibraltar, the upkeep of which cost £162,956 in 1737—the explosive growth of the colonists' trade to southern Europe would scarcely have been possible. British naval power, moreover, contributed to the growth of colonial commerce in the West Indies. Yet Parliament contributed almost nothing to the support of troops in the continental colonies. In 1737, before the outbreak of the War of Jenkins's Ear, only £10,000 was expended for the maintenance of forces in Georgia and New York; and regular troops were stationed in no other British colony within the area that would, in 1776, secede from the empire.[1]

There were exceptions to the rule that the colonies should provide for their own defense—but these exceptions carried no greater weight than those precedents establishing Parliament's right of taxation. In both cases, the exceptions showed only that, by practice and tradition, Parliament usually did not expend many resources in defense of British subjects outside the realm, and that it usually did not tax where the subjects of taxation were not represented.

There was consequently a kind of reciprocity in the imperial-colonial tie, one that neither the British nor the American found it in their interest to disturb. In the domain of practical policy and settled behavior, though not of right, Parliament's duty of protecting colonial commerce was balanced by its right of regulating the character and growth of this commerce. Its reluctance to impose taxes on its American settlements sprang from Parliament's lack of responsibility in the field of policy that placed—in the eighteenth as in other centuries—the heaviest demands on the public treasury.

This division of responsibility and power was ambiguous in one significant and, as it turned out, all-important respect. It did not make clear the responsibilities that Parliament bore to the colonies, and the corresponding duties that the colonies owed to Parliament, in the event of a threat posed to the American settlements by a foreign power. This problem—one entirely different from the reciprocal rights and duties of the King and his subjects—had seldom been faced.[2] Neither Robert Walpole nor Cardinal Fleury, who respectively dominated British and French political life in the years following the Peace of Utrecht in 1713, was anxious to renew hos-

---

[1] Concerning the upkeep of the army garrisons at Minorca and Gibraltar in 1737, see George L. Beer, *British Colonial Policy, 1754–1765*, p. 12. The expenditures on the navy during 1735 amounted to £1,376,472, and during 1736, to £1,273,687; *Journals of the House of Commons*, 22:527–32, 732–37. For 1765, the cost of the navy alone was approximately £1.44 million; Thomas Whately, *Considerations on the Trade and Finances of This Kingdom, Addressed to the Two Houses of Parliament* (London, 1769), p. 25.

[2] The King and his representatives—the colonial governors—did have the responsibility of defending the colonies against foreign attack, but this function could be carried out only with the cooperation of the colonial assemblies, who raised the troops and supplies.

tilities in the wilderness. The ambiguity of the relationship thus reflected the absence of any great tests to its basic character. This would soon change.

[III]

Problems began to arise in the 1740s with the security system that the traditional division of rights and duties entailed. In form, the complaints were longstanding; they now acquired a scope and an urgency they had never possessed in the past. The reasons for this change are to be found not in the sudden emergence of a new view of empire in the metropolis, but in a profound security challenge arising on the periphery of the American settlements. Only on the Spanish borderland did the disputes that had flared up as a consequence of the War of Jenkins's Ear begin to dissipate, as Britain reached temporary agreement with Spain, with the 1750 Treaty of Madrid, on the many issues that divided them. Elsewhere—in Acadia, whose location made it of critical importance to the New England colonies; in the western and northern approaches to the strategically critical colony of New York; in the Ohio Valley, of greatest importance to Virginia and Pennsylvania, but significant for all the colonies because of its place in a quickened drive to link the French settlements in New France and Louisiana—signs began to multiply that a conflict between the French and British settlements was inevitable. The prospect seemed increasingly real that the French might succeed in restricting the English settlement colonies to a narrow area along the coast and leave the seacoast colonies vulnerable to the permanent menace of French attack. The "contest in America," John Mitchell noted, was not a matter of a "port or two in Nova Scotia, or an Indian fort on the river *Ohio*." It was a struggle "to gain a power and dominion, that must sooner or later command all that continent, with the whole trade of it, if not many other branches of trade; which must all fall into the hands of France, sooner or later if we suffer her to secure her present encroachments on the British dominions in North America."[3]

---

[3] *The Contest in America between Britain and France, with Its Consequences and Importance* . . . (London, 1757), pp. ix–x.

British governments, however, were slow to commit the resources of Parliament in response to these new threats. This reluctance was especially apparent after war broke out between France and Britain in 1744. A detachment of French and Indians from Crown Point descended on Saratoga in 1745 and left it in ruins, killing or capturing more than a hundred colonists. The entire upper Hudson Valley was itself gravely threatened, and many colonists abandoned Albany for the safety of Manhattan. Nor was New York the only colony in peril. The small outposts that settlers from Massachusetts had placed on the Kennebec River were also wiped out with a fury that horrified the more established and secure regions. Yet virtually the only assistance that the British proffered to the colonists—save the usual requests to concert colonial action—was a naval detachment that, in combination with a force of New Englanders commanded by Governor Shirley, successfully overwhelmed Louisbourg in the fall of 1745. Overall, however, the commitment to North America was distinctly limited.

The persistence of the French threat at the close of hostilities in 1748 convinced the home government as well as a number of leading colonists, however, that the ways of the past were no longer adequate. Recognition of the danger facing the older colonies—and a portent of things to come—was the support the government lent to the construction and fortification of the new town of Halifax in Nova Scotia, the parliamentary grants for which totaled five hundred thousand pounds from 1750 to 1757. Yet no one could be certain that the home government would come to the aid of the older colonies before the alarming growth of French power on the periphery. What did seem clear was that traditional arrangements would no longer be sufficient. Franklin summarized the difficulty in the following manner, and his analysis of the problem would have met with no dissent in ministerial circles at home. He reflected on

the difficulties that have always attended the most necessary general measures for the common defence, or for the annoyance of the enemy, when they were to be carried through the several particular assemblies of all the colonies; some assemblies being before at variance with their governors or councils, and the several branches of government not on terms of doing business with each other; others taking the opportunity, when their concurrence is wanted, to push for favourite laws, powers, or points that they think could not at other times be obtained, and so *creating* disputes and quarrels; one assembly waiting to see what another will do, being afraid of doing more than its share, or desirous of doing less; or refusing to do anything, because its country is not at present so much exposed as others, or because another will reap more immediate advantage; from one or other of which causes, the assemblies of six (out of seven) colonies applied to, had granted no assistance to Virginia, when lately invaded by the French, though purposely convened, and the importance of the occasion urged upon them.[4]

Franklin's diagnosis of the difficulty of concerting colonial action pointed to the apparent breakdown of the traditional security system. It represented a confession of the inadequacy of past arrangements. It testified to the danger of retaining the older division of functions which had left each colonial assembly with the responsibility and the power of providing for the security of the seaboard settlements. This division had broken down. It had left the colonists—or at least some of them—vulnerable. It seemed incapable of responding to the new dangers posed by the growth of French power in the interior. Where it would end could not be determined with any precision, but one estimate—of Robert Dinwiddie, the lieutenant-governor of Virginia—was graphic in its depiction of the ruinous consequence that would follow in the absence of corrective action. Virginia alone, he wrote, "is not able to support the whole Burthen; and if some Method is not found to take away these destructive Denials of Assistance from the other Colonies, when it is judged proper to be demanded by his Majesty for the common Good, as now; The Consequence must be, the present Loss of one of the finest and most fertile Countries in America; and the future destruction of all the British Dominions on this Continent."[5]

[IV]

What arrangement would fill the vacuum left by this apparent breakdown of the traditional security system? There were, in essence, three alternatives contemplated at the time. Each would have led to the centralization of power in the colonies. The first would have substituted for the power of the separate provincial

---

[4] "Reasons and Motives for the Albany Plan of Union," in *The Papers of Benjamin Franklin*, 5:399.
[5] Dinwiddie to Thomas Robinson, secretary of state for the Southern Department, June 18, 1754, quoted in Beer, *British Colonial Policy*, p. 43.

assemblies that of a general union; the second would have relied essentially on a strengthened prerogative; and the third would have enhanced the power of Parliament. All would have encroached on the jealously guarded powers of the provincial assemblies.

The colonial conference at Albany, New York, in June 1754, had been suggested by the Board of Trade primarily in order to stem the anticipated defection of the Iroquois to the French. The deliberations quickly moved beyond this limited aim, however, and ultimately produced a plan for a unified government with the responsibility of managing the defense of the colonies. Under the Albany Plan of Union, a president general was to be nominated by the King, but the real locus of control lay in the contemplated Grand Council. The council was to be composed of delegates nominated by the lower houses of the provincial assemblies, with the largest colonies, Virginia and Massachusetts, having no more than seven delegates, the smaller colonies no less than two. The responsibilities of this government were vast, and its powers included that without which there could be little hope of effectiveness: the power of taxation.

The Albany Plan of Union was acceptable neither to the provincial assemblies, which unanimously rejected it, nor to the home government. Their reasons were substantially the same. Both saw in the plan the creation of a body that might prove injurious to their respective interests. The home government objected to the substantial powers that were conferred on the Grand Council and saw in them an ultimate danger to British rule in the colonies. Although Parliament would have to sanction the establishment of the union, the function of Westminster would be that of a joint constituent body with no formal powers over the daily management of affairs, and the British could have no real assurance where such a state of affairs might lead. The maxim that was repeated so often in the following decade—mostly by the British in assuring themselves that conditions in the colonies were not as bad as the evidence made it appear—that colonial disunion would prevent independence, was invoked on this occasion as a justification for the disapproval of the plan.[6]

The British reaction to the Albany Plan of Union illustrated the

[6] Alison Gilbert Olson, "The British Government and Colonial Union, 1754," *William and Mary Quarterly*, 3d ser. 17(1960):22–34.

dilemma confronting the imperial state. Although the metropolis wanted the colonies to provide the means for their own defense on land, thus sparing London the burden, it rejected any mechanism that held out the prospect of posing a yet more effective challenge to imperial authority. The seemingly congenital inability of the colonies to subordinate their separate and often conflicting interests to any common interest was a major reason—perhaps *the* reason—for their inability to defend effectively their frontiers. Colonial disunity, particularly in matters of defense, also limited the pressures that might otherwise have been brought to bear against the mother country. The same disunity, however, implied an unwelcome liability for the metropolis. How to avoid, or at least to limit, this liability without at the same time incurring a still greater liability, in the form of American union, was the essence of the dilemma confronting the imperial state. As matters turned out, the metropolis did manage to resolve the dilemma—or, at any rate, to alter its terms quite radically—though in a manner entirely adverse to the interests of London. The outcome of the Seven Years' War substantially removed one great security threat to the colonies. At the same time, the results of the war did not rid the British of any and all responsibility for colonial defense but instead insured that in attempting to carry out this responsibility the metropolis would have to deal with colonies that, because of their improved security position, no longer felt constrained by the need for protection by the mother country.

These remarks are not intended to imply that at the outset of the Great War for the Empire, Great Britain had a real choice between accepting the Albany Plan of Union for the colonies or accepting the principal burden of colonial defense. There was no such choice, given the reception of the plan by the colonies. Even had there been such choice, though, there is no reason to assume that the metropolis would have acted other than the way it did. In colonial union, London saw the realization of its fears. There was nothing sinister in these fears, just as there was nothing unreasonable in the rejection that the plan met with in the colonies. Still, the question remained, What arrangements would take the place of the old?

Early in 1754, the Board of Trade, under the presidency of the earl of Halifax, had proposed that Parliament lay a tax on the American colonies in order to provide a fund for the common defense. Yet the Newcastle administration, unwilling to risk a battle in Parliament over the plan, and fearing the opposition of Pitt and Fox, was not receptive to the idea. The Board of Trade was consequently asked to prepare a report that, as Halifax put it, was adapted as much as possible "to the Constitution of the Colonies."[7] The object of the plan was to provide for a fund to maintain or further augment forts on the frontiers of the threatened provinces, and also to unify the actions of the colonies in regard to Indian affairs. The fund was to be settled upon by commissioners nominated by the assembly and council in each of the colonies, subject to the approbation of the governor. The apportionment of charges among the colonies was to be guided by "regard for the number of inhabitants, trade, wealth and revenue of each Colony," but each colony was to have only one vote in the proceedings. A commander in chief with final authority over military and Indian affairs in the colonies was also to be appointed by the King. The occupant of this new office would be empowered to draw upon the treasury of each of the colonies in which the funds were raised "such sums as shall be necessary," and he would also be given the task of settling the accounts between the colonies.[8]

It is doubtful that Halifax was convinced of the workability of the plan. The commander-in-chief would represent a new source of power in the colonies, but such powers as he enjoyed would be transferred from the colonial governors, and not from the assemblies. This was true as well of the creation of the Indian superintendents, whose powers were transferred from the colonial governors, not from the assemblies. The plan altered in no significant respect the distribution of political power within each of the provinces. Its only real departure was that the difficulties and obstructions that each of the governors had encountered in securing men and supplies would now be concentrated in one head. Halifax was certainly aware of these considerations, and in the representation that accompanied the plan he warned that if "it should be found upon trial that this measure should be defeated by any of the Colonies" through neglect or refusal, he saw "no other method

[7] Quoted in James A. Henretta, *"Salutary Neglect": Colonial Administration under the Duke of Newcastle* (Princeton, 1972), p. 338.
[8] "Plan for a General Cooperation of the North American Colonies" (August 9, 1754), in *Documents Relative to the Colonial History of the State of New York*, ed. E. B. O'Callaghan, 15 vols. (Albany, 1853–87), 6:903–6 (hereafter *DRCHSNY*).

that can be taken, but that of an application for an interposition of the Authority of Parliament."[9]

Charles Townshend immediately diagnosed the frailty of the proposed union: "It is impossible to imagine that so many different representatives of so many different provinces, divided in interest and alienated by jealousy and inveterate prejudice, should ever be able to resolve upon a plan of mutual security and reciprocal expense." He noted that some of the least peopled and considerable colonies are most connected with large tribes of Indians and most exposed to an invasion, while the most peopled and more flourishing are most remote from the danger." It would be difficult, he concluded, "to persuade the more wealthy colonies not immediately interested to take upon them the charge of defending their neighbours upon their own allegation of their own inability.[10]

The warnings of Halifax and Townshend were prophetic. When General Braddock met with the colonial governors in April 1755, in conformity with the plan the Board of Trade had proposed the preceding August, the governors gave "as their unanimous opinion that such a Fund can never be established in the Colonies without the aid of Parliament."[11] The response of the government was neither to threaten to withdraw its support from the colonies, nor to impose a parliamentary tax upon them, but to assume the cost itself. The pattern of politics during the Seven Years' War was thus established at the very beginning. The secret instructions that were prepared for Braddock ordered him to secure as much support as he could from the colonial assemblies, but in the event of failure he was notified that the crown was prepared to bear the expenses of his expedition. "The first point" that was laid down by the Newcastle ministry when informed of the French encroachments in North America—"that the colonies must not be abandoned"[12]— was also, as it turned out, the last. Convinced of the importance of its plantations in North America and the consequent necessity of driving the French from their threatening positions on the periphery of the American settlements, the government gradually

[9] "Representation to the King with plan of General Concert," in *DRCHSNY*, 6:902.
[10] Quoted in Lewis Namier and John Brooke, *Charles Townshend* (London, 1964), p. 39.
[11] Quoted in Alan Rogers, *Empire and Liberty: American Resistance to British Authority, 1755–1763* (Berkeley, 1974), p. 106.
[12] Quoted in Olson, "Colonial Union," p. 27.

became insensibly preoccupied with military victory on the periphery and ultimately abandoned all other considerations to that end.

The relationship that Braddock and his three successors—Governor William Shirley, Lord Loudon, and Jeffery Amherst—enjoyed with the colonial assemblies was never a happy one. Jealous of their rights, the colonial assemblies insisted upon contributing aid in their own way and with the understanding that their respective contributions had to be regarded as free gifts to the metropolis. The latter condition meant that the call for requisitions might or might not be honored; in any event, it could not be attended by coercion. The former condition left each colony that did contribute free to attach such conditions as it saw fit. These conditions might, and regularly did, severely restrict the place where the troops of a particular colony could be employed as well as the period of employment. Loudon became so frustrated that he wrote to Pitt that "every Man in this Country, would if possible, throw the whole Expense on the Publick, and save the Province from being at one Shilling Expence for the Common Cause."[13]

Under Amherst, who replaced Loudon in the spring of 1758, relations with the colonial assemblies improved. At the moment when it appeared that Loudon and representatives of the northern assemblies were heading toward a confrontation over the question of providing troops, a letter arrived from Pitt announcing Loudon's recall and promising the colonial assemblies that Britain would amply reimburse their efforts to raise troops for the coming campaign. The new policy gave the colonists, in effect, all that they had been asking for, and many of the assemblies responded with enthusiasm.[14] Despite the large number of provincial troops that were raised, however, victory in North America was due primarily to the exertions of the regular British army. Regular forces bore the brunt of the fighting. They were largely responsible for the great British victories of the war: the successful assault on Louisbourg in 1758, on Quebec in 1759, and on Montreal in 1760. Some colonial forces distinguished themselves in action; for the most part,

[13] *Correspondence of William Pitt, Earl of Chatham,* 1:56.
[14] Rogers, *Empire and Liberty,* p. 114.

however, the role of the colonial forces was confined to supporting the movements of the main British armies.[15]

The conflicts that arose between the British commanders and the colonial assemblies in the beginning stages of the war, and the subsequent resolution of these conflicts in favor of the latter, were indicative of the uncertain political relationship between the North American assemblies and the metropolis at the end of the war. Britain had assumed primary responsibility for the security of the North American colonies, largely at their behest. The half-hearted British attempts to assume powers commensurate with these responsibilities, however, had ended in failure. In matters relating to imperial defense, the significance of the Great War for the Empire lay in its implicit abandonment of a fundamental feature of the traditional relationship between Britain and its colonies. What emerged in its stead during the war, however, was an unstable arrangement that could not long endure, the central feature of which was a marked disparity between the responsibilities that the metropolis had undertaken on behalf of America and the powers it could exercise over America. The war had both greatly expanded its responsibilities and revealed the debility of the instrument—prerogative—by which it had theretofore attempted to meet them.

This assumption of responsibility—the scope of which can be measured roughly by the cost of the war to Great Britain and the concomitant rise of the national debt—represented a fundamental change in the imperial-colonial relationship. On behalf of its colonies as a whole—but particularly on behalf of the continental colonies—Parliament's expenses in the past were miniscule in comparison with what they would become during the Seven Years'

---

[15] Stanley M. Pargellis, *Lord Loudon in North America* (New Haven, 1933), pp. 354–55; and John Shy, *Toward Lexington: The Role of the British Army in the Coming of the American Revolution* (Princeton, 1965), p. 19. In 1756, Parliament granted one hundred fifteen thousand pounds to the northern colonies for part of their expenses during the preceding campaign and later in the year granted another fifty thousand pounds to the southern colonies for their prior expenditures. The commitment to reimburse, however, was never fully elaborated to the colonial governors until late 1757, when Pitt requested that the governors attempt to raise from their respective assemblies as large a force as was practicable and promised that the King would recommend that Parliament reimburse the colonies in part for these efforts. In fulfillment of the promise, Parliament voted two hundred thousand pounds for the colonies for their assistance in the 1758 campaign. It voted the same amount for the 1759 and 1760 campaigns. Thereafter, with the need for colonial troops less pressing, it reduced the reimbursement to £133,333 for 1761 and 1762. The distribution of the funds among the various colonies was decided upon by informal agreement between the Treasury and the colonial agents.

War. From annual expenses of £10,000, Britain was suddenly bur-
dened with a war whose total cost was £100,000,000. By the end
of the war the national debt had risen from £72,500,000 to
£137,000,000. The interest on this debt constituted an extraordinary £4,700,000 out of an annual budget of £8,000,000.

The political history of the next few years after 1763, insofar as
it concerned the problem of imperial defense, consisted in the
attempts of the British to lessen this disparity between power and
responsibility. The continuation of existing arrangements—in which
American security was provided for out of Britain's own resources—
was politically out of the question. In this sense, the instability of
the disjunction between power and responsibility resided essentially in the inequitable burdens that the British believed it imposed
upon them. This being so, the British faced only two alternatives:
one was to lessen their responsibility for the security of their North
American colonies; the other, to gain the assistance of the Americans in paying for the cost of the army. The first alternative promised to undo the efforts of nearly a decade, but the second raised
the difficult question of how the contributions would be raised.

[V]

None of the measures that the British took at the close of hostilities
is intelligible without keeping in mind the fundamental desidera-
tum that lay behind the war effort: to secure the North American
colonies from the encirclement and attack of New France. Once
the war had broken out and the British embarked on their succession of victories, only the expulsion of France from the North
American continent seemed to hold out the prospect of security.
But military victory, though transforming the security problem,
did not end it. It scarcely constituted a permanent solution to the
security problem of the North American colonies and could have
done so only by the expulsion or extermination of those the Anglo-
Americans had just defeated.

What was to be done with the now greatly expanded empire in
North America? In large measure, the British response was determined by the course and consequences of the war. Having conquered vast new lands in the north, south, and west, a substantial
military force was needed to occupy and to secure them. In the

St. Lawrence valley, between eighty and ninety thousand French settlers had to be kept in subjection, and previous experience with a much smaller population in Acadia had shown that the obedience of the *Canadiens* could not simply be taken for granted. In the Floridas, the harbors of St. Augustine, Pensacola, and Mobile had to be garrisoned. Finally, in the area bounded by the Appalachians and the Mississippi to the east and west, and by the Floridas and the Great Lakes to the south and north, a military force was required for the effective occupation of territories on which claims to sovereign possession rested.

These requirements followed from the nature of the peace settlement. They could be avoided only by jeopardizing the settlement and thereby jeopardizing as well the goals for which the war had been fought. Although the defense of North America would rest primarily on British naval supremacy, and although Britain emerged from the war clearly the predominant naval power, the security of the newly won possessions—and thus the security of the established American colonies—could not be left to naval power alone. At the time, few observers contended otherwise, whether in London or in the colonies. Nor was it seriously argued that the defense requirements entailed by the peace could be met by the colonists. Regular troops were needed. The decision to maintain a British army in postwar America was not, as such, a matter of controversy. The size and deployment of the force were largely determined by the essential functions it would be called upon to perform.[16]

The metropolis was also intent upon managing relations between the Indians and the colonists in such manner as to insure the peace and stability of the frontier and interior and for these objects as well regular troops were needed. Why it was so intent may be understood by recalling the origins and course of the war, for it was particularly the experience of the war that prompted the de-

---

[16] The most detailed and lucid analysis of the 1763 decision to station a peacetime army in America is to be found in Shy, *Toward Lexington*, pp. 52–83. Shy argues "that the great extension of territorial control . . . made the traditional system of local self-defense inapplicable" and "that the structure of the peace settlement largely determined not only the existence of a British army in postwar America, but its approximate size and deployment as well"; p. 56. Of the fifteen regiments to be stationed on the North American continent, three were to be deployed in Nova Scotia, four in Canada, four in Florida, and the remaining four divided between the Atlantic seaboard, the frontier, and the interior. The inapplicability of the traditional system of local self-defense was earlier emphasized by Beer, *British Colonial Policy*, pp. 252–73, and more recently by Jack M. Sosin, *Whitehall and the Wilderness*, pp. 27–51.

termination of the imperial government to control Indian affairs. Traditionally, Great Britain had left the management of Indian relations to the separate colonies. The history of these relations had never been very satisfactory, however, and in the years preceding the war the dissatisfaction of British officials with colonial handling of the natives had grown. In part, the difficulty stemmed from the trading practices of the Americans, practices that were aggravated by the competition of the colonies for the Indian trade. The poor state of Indian relations was also the result of the colonists' relentless drive to occupy the lands the Indians claimed as their own. By contrast with the Americans, the French, who showed greater moderation (and greater generosity) in their trading practices and who had no interest in dispossessing the Indians of their land, enjoyed far better relations. In time, they succeeded in further alienating the Indians from the colonists and, during the war, many of the native tribes on the frontier and in the interior became their allies.

With the active intervention of the metropolis in the growing conflict, responsibility for the frontier was assumed by Great Britain and, to an increasing degree, so was the active management of Indian affairs. Anxious to obtain the support—or, at least, the neutrality—of the Indians, and aware that this would prove very difficult as long as past practices were retained, the imperial government took measures to exert greater control over trade (though no comprehensive system of regulation was introduced during the war). At the same time, efforts were made to assure the Indians that they would not be dispossessed of their lands against their will. Such assurances were even subscribed to on occasion by colonial representatives. At the Albany Congress, the colonial commissioners, bidding for the friendship of the western tribes, had recommended that colonial claims to territory be limited to the Appalachian Mountains. It was the government in London, however, that in unmistakable terms committed the empire to respect the Indian claims. During the war, the British, on at least three major occasions—at Easton in 1758, at Lancaster in 1760, and at Detroit in 1761—undertook solemn treaty commitments that reaffirmed roughly the Appalachian boundary line. These commitments, though made under pressure of wartime necessity, were considered by the imperial government as quite binding at the end of the war and in its interest to honor if further hostilities with the

Indians were to be avoided. Finally, as the war progressed in the interior and the British army took numerous forts and outposts formerly held by the French, a regime of military occupation was established on the lands that were to be held in reserve for the native tribes.

The royal proclamation of October 7, 1763, formalized the elements of an Indian policy that had already taken shape during the years of conflict. Apart from naming the three new North American provinces of East Florida, West Florida, and Quebec, defining their boundaries, and providing them with a form of government patterned after the older established provinces, the proclamation stipulated that the lands west of the Appalachians from Georgia to Quebec were to be reserved for the Indians. In consequence, these lands could not be purchased or settled on without special permission of imperial authority. This vast Indian reserve might be entered by those in pursuit of trade with the native tribes. The trade was to be free and open to all English subjects who were properly licensed and who gave security to observe those regulations laid down by imperial authority. The proclamation made no express provision for the government of the Indian territory. In practice, governing power rested immediately in the hands of the commander-in-chief of the British army, an office soon filled by General Thomas Gage. He, in turn, was assisted by two Indian superintendents, William Johnson for the Northern Department and John Stuart for the Southern Department, whose offices had been created in 1755 to manage political relations with the Indians.[17]

In the provisions dealing with the Indian problem, the proclamation responded to what its authors regarded as the lessons of the war. One lesson was that peace and stability on the frontier required a consistent and comprehensive Indian policy. Another was that the colonies could not be expected to provide such policy, whether in regulating trade, or in controlling expansion into lands the Indians claimed, or, finally, in providing an effective defense against the inevitable uprisings. Still another lesson was that the measures taken by the imperial government during the war, meas-

[17] Johnson served from 1755 until his death in 1774; Stuart, from 1763 until 1779. Edmund Atkin, who preceded Stuart in the southern department, served in the post from 1756 to 1761; see John R. Alden, *John Stuart and the Southern Colonial Frontier* (Ann Arbor, 1944), p. 139.

ures that found expression in the proclamation, represented commitments to the Indians which London could now ignore only by breaking faith with the native tribes, an act that was seen to imply the virtual certainty of renewed violence. The proclamation did not draw out these lessons in detailed and irrevocable terms. The provision respecting trade regulation was left quite general. The restrictions on private land purchases and settlement were intended not as a standing barrier to further westward expansion by the colonists but as means enabling expansion to occur without violence and with the consent of the natives. Once the imperial government acquired Indian property by fair purchase, the frontier could be extended westward.[18]

Not only was the experience of the war found to justify the proclamation, but the great Indian uprising that began in the late spring of 1763 was taken as further evidence of the need for imperial control of the frontier and the interior. The origins of Pontiac's rebellion remain a matter of uncertainty and controversy. In the view of imperial officials on the scene, the French had instigated the uprising. If the French did play a significant role in inciting the Indian tribes to violence, however, it was largely because the ground was already well-prepared. Despite British efforts during the war to regulate trade and to assuage Indian apprehensions over the security of their lands, these efforts enjoyed no more than modest success. When the war came to an end, the perennial sources of Indian discontent remained apparently as strong as ever. Moreover, the removal of the French added fuel to an already smoldering fire, if for no other reason than that the Indians resented

[18] Historians have found other motives in the creation of an Indian reservation beyond the mountains, where settlement was forbidden for the time. Bernhard Knollenberg, while not denying the importance of protecting and pacifying the Indians, argues that another important motive for the 1763 Indian boundary line was the desire "to discourage settlement in the West as a means of conserving the colonial market for British exports"; *Origin of the American Revolution, 1759–1766*, pp. 101–2. On this view, imperial officials feared that new colonies beyond the mountains would escape the control of the metropolis. The interior colonies would soon develop not only economic self-sufficiency but this would be attended by parallel political development. To ward off this prospect, at the close of the war imperial officials sought to encourage settlement in the North and South while discouraging it in the West. It is very doubtful, however, that these considerations would have been sufficient to prompt British acceptance of the frontier as an imperial responsibility in the absence of the Indian problem. The prospects held out by expansion to the West, if the problem of the Indians was set aside, lay in the future and were, in any event, much controverted. But the problem of the Indians was immediate and the need to deal with this problem very real. The setting of the 1763 boundary line responded, first and foremost, to the strong desire to pacify the Indians and to avoid further conflict.

British claims to sovereignty over territory the native tribes had never ceded to European powers. In the eyes of the Indians, the French (and Spanish) had no right to cede the lands of the great interior to the British since these lands had never been theirs to cede. Nor did the Indians appreciate the distinction drawn by Britain between sovereign right over territory and ownership of land. Instead, they feared, and not without reason, that the control claimed by Great Britain would, despite solemn promises to the contrary, eventually lead to their being dispossessed of the lands. Their apprehensions were sharpened when the British occupied the forts in the interior abandoned by the French and, in several instances, strengthened these forts while building settlements around them. The successors to the French appeared to be entering in force. At the same time, they displayed no affection for the Indians. Arrogant and aloof as compared with the French, the British were also far less liberal in their dealings with the Indians on such matters as providing ammunition for hunting, giving presents, and supplying rum.[19]

Whatever the degree of responsibility the imperial government itself bore for the 1763 uprising, British officials found in the colonial response to the rebellion confirmation of the view that there could be no return to the previous arrangements. Although some of the colonies responded to the call for troops to support a depleted British army, a considerable part of which was tied to garrison duty, even those that did failed to raise the forces requested. To British commanders, the experience of the early years of the Seven Years' War was being replayed. The inadequacies of the requisition system seemed no less apparent in 1763 than they had in 1754. The difference was that in 1763 these inadequacies proved much less serious, owing to shortages of ammunition suffered by the Indians and their inability to achieve the degree of unity necessary to make a sustained effort. Although by the fall of 1764 the rebellion

---

[19] The origins of Pontiac's Rebellion are examined at length by Howard H. Peckham, *Pontiac and the Indian Uprising* (Princeton, 1947), pp. 70–111. Peckham places a large measure of responsibility for the uprising on British policy, as does Shy, *Toward Lexington*, pp. 104ff, who emphasizes the role of Amherst in the affair. In this respect, Knollenberg, *Origin*, pp. 103–11, is the most extreme in placing responsibility for the uprising on the British commander-in-chief. In the context of the issues discussed in these pages, the issue of British responsibility appears irrelevant. The choice was not between an all-wise British policy and the one that was in fact followed, but between the policy followed by the metropolis and the behavior that might have been expected from the colonies had they been left to do as they pleased. Surely this behavior cannot be expected to have led to a more favorable Indian response.

had collapsed, it left a deep impression on imperial officials. The frontier, they concluded, would have to be garrisoned. In addition, the forts in the interior that had fallen before the Indian attack would have to be reoccupied, and this despite their ineffectiveness in stopping the Indians. Finally, the program for managing Indian relations set forth in the 1763 proclamation would have to be given more detailed form and put into operation. In the summer of 1764 the plan to regulate Indian affairs was completed. Encompassing both commercial and political relations, the new program would virtually eliminate the influence of the colonies. Trade with the Indians could be undertaken only at specially designated locations. Although open to all, it was to be closely regulated, traders being required to have licenses and to post bond. Before the plan could be put fully into operation, however, a new source of revenue would have to be found. Until such time, the system that had evolved from the war and that was itself a modest version of the 1764 plan would prevail.

It is not difficult to make an impressive case against the measures affecting their new conquests that the British adopted at the close of the Seven Years' War. For the ostensible purpose of this army was to bring order to the new conquests and security to the older colonies. The undeniable result was to bring disorder to the older colonies and insecurity to the empire as a whole. The sizable costs of this standing force led the Grenville administration to impose sugar duties and stamp taxes on the American colonies, which in turn sparked a revolt that brought civil government in many of the seaboard colonies to a standstill. The Americans argued at the time, and many historians have since followed them in arguing, that the Indian program was not necessary, that the colonists had defended themselves in the past against the Indians and that they could continue to do so in the future—particularly if the Indians were no longer supported by the French.[20] Yet this criticism need not be accepted in order to find fault with the government's Indian program. Even if it were true that the colonists were incapable of defending themselves, it may be argued that they should nevertheless have been allowed to suffer the consequences of their own negligence, and that the responsibility for the security of the continental colonies against Indian attack was a burden of which the

---

[20] See, for example, John R. Alden: *The South in the Revolution 1763–1789* (Baton Rouge, 1957), pp. 45–55.

metropolis ought to have relieved itself. Whatever risks a policy of indifference entailed, they were surely far less imposing than the risks run by the course of action that was followed.

Yet, as has been noted, the principal functions of the army were not seen in terms of the Indian problem but in the context of the indispensable tasks it would have to perform in the North, South, and West. A policy of minimal Indian regulation—in which the metropolis returned the care of Indian affairs to the individual colonies—was at least a possibility in the aftermath of war; but to whom would the British have turned over the problems of Canada or Florida? There was no existing colonial authority prepared to take responsibility for territories so distant from the older settlements, and no colonists suggested that the administration of these areas be somehow removed from the control of Whitehall and Westminster. In the absence of the 1763–64 policy for managing Indian relations, an army in North America would still have been required. In the absence of this Indian policy, the cost of maintaining an army in America would still have been seen to require an American revenue. For the territories in which the army was stationed were significant only because their possession by a foreign power would pose a threat to the seacoast colonies, not for any intrinsic worth they may have had as objects of English commerce or colonization. The point is important, since the British attempt to obtain a revenue from America, an attempt that would have such fateful consequences, is often seen as following from the particular postwar policy adopted by the metropolis for managing Indian relations. Since that policy is just as often attacked by historians as having been misguided and unnecessary, it seems to follow that the search for a revenue in this country was also misguided and unnecessary. But if the Indian policy adopted by the imperial government in 1763–64 made the insistence upon obtaining an American revenue greater than it otherwise would have been, which was undoubtedly the case, it did not create that insistence. Rather, the new territorial status quo did so, since it required an army that London was determined from the outset the Americans should help to support.[21]

---

[21] The yearly cost of the British army in North America has been variously estimated between two hundred fifty thousand and four hundred thousand pounds. This cost was largely independent of the added outlays resulting from the Indian program, which went as high as three hundred thousand pounds. The Indian program was expensive primarily because the supply of distant forts was extremely difficult.

Was, then, the Indian policy of the Grenville ministry necessary? In a narrow sense, it is difficult to think that it was. Great Britain might have adopted a different policy, as indeed it eventually did in 1768, when the many obstacles in the way of implementing the plan of 1763–64 had become apparent, when the prospects of obtaining colonial support for the costly plan by means of a colonial revenue had all but disappeared, and when the mounting unrest of the colonies appeared to require the presence of troops on the seaboard. Yet, once the prospect of a standing force was accepted as necessary—and this occurred to imperial officials immediately after the general shape of the peace settlement became clear—it was a small step to contemplating the use of this force as an aid in settling some Indian problems of long standing. The particular expedient adopted failed, and in retrospect it is difficult to avoid the conclusion that it was too ambitious. In adopting it, however, the Grenville ministry yielded to the advice of its officials on the spot—particularly that of William Johnson, whose knowledge of Indian affairs was intimate and of long standing. The government could not be sure that French power on the continent was broken beyond repair—indeed, Pontiac's Rebellion was attributed very widely by imperial officials to French incitement. If the Indians were to remain hostile, the French might once again be afforded the opportunity of extending their influence. However misguided in some respects it may have been, London's concern with pacifying the Indians was altogether understandable. Equally understandable was the conviction that, in dealing with the Indians, a return to the old ways would no longer suffice. For these ways were seen as bound to provoke the native tribes to continued violence. The old ways were also seen to hold out the prospect that the imperial government would once again and at great cost have to intervene on behalf of the colonies. Although Great Britain would remain responsible for the consequences that might follow, it would surrender at the outset the prospect of controlling those consequences.

[VI]

The decision to station an army in North America in 1763 aroused little critical comment at the time. Rather, it was the manner in which the Grenville ministry went about paying the costs of this army that stimulated opposition in the American provinces. This decision to impose taxes on the American settlements has been attacked and condemned on a variety of grounds; some have viewed it as unjust, others have conceded its equity but have questioned its constitutionality. Perhaps the most damning criticism, however, is the view that the whole program of taxation was unnecessary; that the objects that the Grenville administration would otherwise seek in vain could have been achieved had other considerations not been uppermost in the minds of those who ruled the empire.

This view has been given a variety of expressions. The most recent is John Murrin's suggestion that Britain possessed "two sets of imperial precedents after 1763. To govern her colonies she could extend the lessons of victory by continuing to do what had won the war. Or she could revert to earlier, more strident suggestions about how she *ought* to have won the war." In reverting after the peace to the "attitudes of 1754–57"—years during which "the traditional requisition system had revealed its inability to provide badly needed revenues"—London neglected the "lessons of victory." Pitt's subsidy policy—"in which Parliament used specie grants to reimburse particular colonies in direct ratio to their military efforts"—succeeded admirably in reconciling *imperium et libertas*: "With reasonable efficiency it provided provincial troops in large numbers, probably stimulated a dramatic rise in colonial importations of British goods, helped to stabilize paper currencies, and encouraged hearty cooperation with the mother country—all of this while respecting traditional colonial liberties." Yet despite the conspicuous success of this policy, Britain abandoned it after the war: "Direct taxation of the colonies promised to raise only about a fourth of the annual £400,000 needed to maintain ten thousand redcoats in America after 1763. Well placed subsidies might have fielded as many provincials at less cost to Britain by stimulating a larger voluntary response from the colonies."[22]

It is revealing that Murrin makes no attempt to describe how such a system would have functioned under peacetime conditions. To have done so would have brought out the many difficulties to be overcome were this expedient to have been adopted. Only if forces under colonial control had been capable of discharging the responsibilities that were entrusted to the British regular army

[22] "The French and Indian War, the American Revolution, and the Counterfactual Hypothesis," pp. 314–15.

after the war would the expedient recommended by Murrin have made much sense. Yet every attempt to utilize colonials for regular garrison duty during the Seven Years' War, as Lawrence Henry Gipson has noted, "had led to the deepest sort of unrest and only too frequently to widespread desertion."[23] This being so, there was no alternative to the employment of regular troops.

The system by which the British government had secured the support of the American assemblies for the war effort was designed for war and could not be transferred to the problems of peace. The device that had made the requisition system workable in time of war—reimbursements—was irrelevant to the conditions of peace. The problem facing the Grenville administration at the close of the war was how to find money to support an army that was already in being, rather than to raise additional forces the expense of which might partially have been reimbursed by Parliament.[24]

---

[23] The British Empire before the American Revolution, 9;42.

[24] It is generally agreed that the prospect of using the army against the seacoast colonies was not the primary motive in leading the ministry to station regular troops in North America. Jack P. Greene's judgment is characteristic: "The decision to keep a large contingent of troops in America following the war was almost certainly not the result of the sort of calculated deception suggested by Captain Walter Rutherford, . . . who proposed in 1759 that troops he retained in the colonies 'apparently for their defence, but also to keep them in proper subjection to the Mother Country.' But neither, as some later historians have contended, were security of the new conquests against their former possessors nor the desirability of distributing troops 'amongst the several Members' of the 'Empire, in proportion to their ability to support them' the only considerations behind this decision"; "The Seven Years' War and the American Revolution," pp. 93–94. Greene cites the now-famous memorandum of William Knox, who noted that "one great purpose of stationing a large Body of Troops in America" was "to secure the Dependence of the Colonys on Great Britain"; see [William Knox], "A Project for Imperial Reform." "With such a large—7,500 troops in all—military force in the colonies," Greene writes, "metropolitan officials at the end of the Seven Years' War could now proceed with the business of imperial reconstruction with reasonable confidence that they had the resources near at hand to suppress any potential colonial opposition." (For similar judgments, see Shy, Toward Lexington, pp. 62–68; and Knollenberg, Origin, p. 94.)

This prospect, moreover, was powerfully reinforced by the experience of the war. The British had concluded, Greene notes, that the colonists would react against a concerted effort by the metropolis to reorder the Anglo-American relationship in the same manner in which they had reacted against the French. All the reasons that made the colonists incapable of fighting the French enemy—their disunity, their inability to produce good and courageous soldiers—would render them incapable of resisting the reforms imposed by the metropolis.

Greene's thesis is certainly plausible. Since the problem of military coercion against the seacoast colonies would suddenly emerge as a possible option of British policy in the aftermath of the disturbances over the Stamp Act, it seems difficult to imagine that this prospect was not seriously considered by imperial officials before the crisis broke upon them. Nevertheless, there are many indications that this was the case, that the Grenville administration did not give the problem of coercion the serious consideration it obviously deserved. Instead of proceeding "with reasonable confidence that they had the resources near at hand to suppress any potential colonial opposition," the architects of the Grenville

[VII]

A far more direct challenge to the necessity of the Grenville program was made later by Edmund Burke, whose judgment on this
issue, as on so many others, has been shared by most historians.
Burke saw the employment of the requisition system as the means
by which the claims of sovereignty and freedom could have been
reconciled, the means by which the substantial interests of either
side could have been preserved without raising the issue—the
sovereignty of Parliament "in all cases whatsoever"—that would
ultimately disrupt the empire. A willingness to rely on requisitions
to finance the costs of the army in North America represents the
road not taken. In 1774, Burke was "morally certain" that the
British, by refusing to consider this course, "had lost at least a
million of free grants since the peace. I think we have lost a great
deal more, and that those who look for a revenue from the provinces
never could have pursued . . . a course more directly repugnant
to their purposes."[25] Why was it abandoned?

---

program simply failed to foresee that America would object violently to their handiwork,
and it was the prospect of widespread American civil disobedience which alone could have
made the problem of coercion meaningful and which would have allowed the British to
resolve it in the manner Greene indicates. In retrospect, historians may judge it a peculiar
kind of hubris that Grenville, convinced of the equity of his program and its benefits to
Britain and America alike, did not foresee the storm of opposition it would provoke, but
his lack of foresight was shared by many others, including Benjamin Franklin. Moreover,
once it was clear that the colonies were utterly out of sympathy with the postwar program
of reform, imperial officials acted in a very strange fashion for men who thought of the army
as a means of enforcing their will over America. British troops, as Gage noted to his superiors
after the Stamp Act riots, were "scattered and divided over this vast Continent. . . . [V]ery
few could be collected in Case of sudden Emergencys, in any part, except in Canada";
Gage to Conway, September 23, 1765, *The Correspondence of General Thomas Gage with
the Secretaries of State and with the War Office and the Treasury, 1763–1775*, 1:68. Before
these riots occurred—at a time when the ministry received full and ample warning of the
opposition of the American assemblies to the Stamp Act—Gage's superiors made no suggestion, even obliquely, that the army might be needed to fulfill such a function. Finally,
the contempt for the colonial soldier that so often appears in the correspondence of members
of the British military establishes very little. Although such contempt was shared in many
instances by civilian statesmen, the latter did not display any confidence at all in a military
solution to the American problem during and after the Stamp Act crisis, and they seem, as
noted earlier, to have given it very little thought beforehand.

[25] *PH*, 17:1268. "It is not impossible," Edmund S. Morgan and Helen M. Morgan have
written of the successors to the Grenville ministry—but in words that apply to them all—
"that a ministry disposed to moderation might have obtained money from America without
reviving the conflict between colonies and Parliament: in return for the voluntary contributions which the Americans offered to make if called upon in a constitutional manner,
Parliament might have been persuaded to leave its avowed authority unexercised. But the
men in control after the fall of Rockingham were not interested in voluntary contributions
and would not leave the question of right alone"; *The Stamp Act Crisis*, p. 362.

One problem with the system lay in finding a formula of apportioning the burden among twenty-six colonies whose circumstances were vastly different.[26] The list of potential formulas was virtually endless; that which the Board of Trade devised in 1754, when it called for the creation of a common treasury into which colonial contributions for the war effort might be made, was really only an agenda of items to be discussed. The colonies were to be guided, the board said, "by regard for the number of inhabitants, trade, wealth, and revenue of each Colony."[27] Each of the four items, however, would have favored some colonies at the expense of others. None of the items was unambiguous. If population were the formula, it would matter immensely whether both slaves and freemen were included, and the northern and southern colonies would predictably differ on this question. The difficulties of measuring either "trade" or "wealth" as a guide to "ability to pay" were nearly insurmountable. What trade would be measured? If external commerce were taken as the basis of the formula, this would adversely affect the interests of those colonies who handled much of their neighbor's commerce. This would have left New Jersey, much of whose commerce passed through New York and Philadelphia, almost exempt from requisitions. The same was true of New Hampshire and North Carolina, much of whose commerce also passed through the ports of neighboring colonies. Nor did there exist any common definition of the nature of wealth. Did it consist in the ownership of land? Was all land to be equally valued? Or did improvements on property better signify the amount of wealth that could be spared for purposes of taxation? How was one to measure improvements? None of these questions was a "technical" matter that could be referred to some body of experts. Each involved political considerations that might bear mightily on the level of taxation imposed within a colony and on its prospects for the future.[28]

All the formulas suggested above shared the assumption that

[26] The West Indian islands could not be fairly excluded from the burden, for the war, by improving Britain's overall position in the North Atlantic, had apparently brought important benefits to the sugar islands.

[27] "Plan for General Cooperation," in *DRCHSNY*, 6:904.

[28] Each of these questions, and several others, was raised during the American Confederation. The attempt to find a basis for the settlement of the accounts of the union, and the attempt to implement the formulas that were from time to time agreed upon, preoccupied the Continental Congress during and after the war. On these conflicts see particularly E. James Ferguson, *The Power of the Purse: A History of American Public Finance, 1776–1790* (Chapel Hill, 1961).

"ability to pay" was the proper measure for apportioning the burden among the American colonies. There is, however, little reason to suppose that an agreement on this principle existed in the American colonies. "Need" was a criterion that perhaps was just as appropriate to the circumstances—at least, those who were least in need of assistance could so argue. The grounds for asking Maryland to help finance the costs of the subjugation of Canada were that the American colonies shared a degree of interest with one another that should have been sufficient to overcome all other obstacles. But a war had been fought and a commitment had been made that flew in the face of this assumption. The acceptance of "ability to pay" as the criterion for apportioning the burdens of imperial defense presumed a sense of common interest among the colonies which was altogether lacking. It implied that, for certain purposes, the colonies were to be treated and thought of as one political unit with one political interest, when such a development would come about only after two decades, at a time when American statesmen were forced to admit the inadequacy of ideas and measures that had brought them very nearly to disaster. On the eve of the Stamp Act crisis, there was only one point on which the American assemblies recognized an overwhelming common interest. It consisted in their right to determine the occasions on which and the mode by which they would each respectively contribute to the common treasury. These sentiments, however, were capable only of frustrating a program of common action. The colonies were incapable of formulating a program of common action on anything save a right to maintain their separate and discordant action. This made parliamentary taxation necessary; but it also increased the likelihood that any such program would be resisted.

This prospect is underlined by the responses of the colonial assemblies to the Stamp Act. The frequent charge that the Stamp Act would drain the colonial economies of specie meant that the colonists were incapable of making contributions on the scale desired by the British, quite apart from the manner in which the British sought to raise the funds. Many colonists also questioned the assertion that the colonists were bound, in equity, to support the army stationed on the periphery. Some did so by challenging the opinion, widely held in Britain, that the "Great War for the Empire" had been fought on behalf of the American settlements;

others, by maintaining that the British monopoly of colonial trade represented an already existing and onerous form of taxation.[29] Still other colonists questioned the need for stationing troops on the periphery. Some wondered whether the troops under Amherst were primarily responsible for the Indian rebellion that had broken out at the close of the war. The implication was that the royal army had, in fact, contributed to and aggravated the very problem it had been designed to solve. Policy would presumably require the removal of these troops.[30] Each of the three objections—that the army was unnecessary, that it was inequitable to ask the colonists to pay for it, and that in any case they were incapable of doing so—would have applied as much to a request for requisitions as to the Stamp Act. The character of the objection indicates that Grenville was not mistaken in thinking a requisition system unworkable in the circumstances after the war.

The difficulty of establishing a proper criterion to guide the apportionment of the burden, the obstacles in the way of applying whatever criterion was agreed upon to the circumstances of American life, and the substantive objections that the Americans made to supporting the army were large obstacles to a plan of requisitions. Even these, however, did not reach the heart of the problem, which lay in the tendency of the requisition system to depress the contributions of the participants to the lowest common denominator. It made the action of the least zealous the effective standard

[29] See, e.g., "A Letter to Dennis De Berdt," in *A Collection of Interesting, Authentic Papers Relative to the Dispute Between Great Britain and America, 1764–1775*, ed. John Almon (London, 1777), pp. 170, 174; *Papers of Franklin*, 13:150–51; "Letters of William Samuel Johnson to the Governors of Connecticut," [1766–1771], Massachusetts Historical Society, *Collections*, Trumbull Papers, 5th ser., vol. 9 (Boston, 1855) pp. 337–38 (hereafter Trumbull Papers); John Dickinson, *Letters from a Farmer in Pennsylvania to the Inhabitants of the British Colonies*, in *The Writings of John Dickinson*, pp. 358–64, Letter 8.

[30] See the discussion and sources in Shy, *Toward Lexington*, pp. 140–43. Stationing the army in North America, Dennys De Berdt wrote, "is as absurd as it is needless." The treasurer of New Jersey wondered, "What occasion is there for garrisons and forts hundreds of miles in the Indian country. These are so far from protecting that they are the very cause of our Indian wars, and the monstrous expenses attending them." Shy cites a number of other colonial complaints against the army but notes "the one point all of them have in common: none is an objection to the army as such. Almost all date many months *after* the decision to keep a garrison in America was made known; and they all appear in a context that makes it clear that the basic complaint is against taxation, with the army simply recognized as the source of this difficulty"; pp. 142–43. The basic complaint, however, would appear to be not simply taxation but the request for American support of the army, whatever the mode adopted.

for the action of all.[31] Because differential tax rates raised the prospect of depopulation, each colony had good reasons for keeping tax levels, and hence contributions, on a par with those of neighboring colonies—reasons that would have hampered the operation of the requisition system even assuming a willingness to provide an "equitable" share of the burden and a general agreement with the overall aims of British policy. And these commitments, in the event, were not present.

This tendency was not really given full play during the Seven Years' War, since Parliament reimbursed the colonies for many of their expenses. It was the promise of reimbursement that gave the system whatever success it enjoyed.[32] The effective referent for each of the colonial assemblies during the Seven Years' War was not what their fellow colonials had contributed; the contributions of neighboring colonies could effectively be disregarded. Instead, reimbursements came directly from the mother country and had little to do with what contributions came from a neighboring quarter. The negligence of some was not allowed to impair the cooperative spirit of others.

At the close of the war, however, this situation no longer prevailed. More instructive, therefore, is the response of the assemblies to the calls of Amherst for reinforcements during Pontiac's Rebellion, at a time when the assemblies were informed that Britain would not reimburse them on behalf of what was regarded as an indigenous problem. Each colony kept a close watch on the contributions its neighbors would make. Each was reluctant to act until it had received information on the actual provisions its neighbors had contributed. The referent for equitable contribution became what those least disposed to aid, or those furthest from the danger, judged equitable for themselves.[33] It is implausible to assume that those colonies who faithfully fulfilled their requisitions during the war would have continued to do so had their neighbors

---

[31] Beer, *British Colonial Policy*, p. 70. Cf. Madison to Jefferson, October 3, 1785, *The Papers of James Madison*, ed. William T. Hutchinson et al., vols. 1–10 (Chicago, 1962–77), vols. 11–13 (Charlottesville, 1977–), 8:374; and "Circular to the Governors of the States," *The Papers of Robert Morris, 1781–1784*, ed. E. James Ferguson, 5 vols. to date (Pittsburgh, 1973–), 1:380.

[32] Cf. Pargellis, *Lord Loudon*, pp. 352–53.

[33] See Beer, *British Colonial Policy*, pp. 263–64. In his letters to the earl of Halifax, which bear out Beer's account, Gage elaborated on his difficulties in obtaining colonial contributions; see *Gage*, 1:3, 7, 12, 13, 17–18, 22, 27.

been negligent in the fulfillment of their duties. Massachusetts gave no evidence of such a commitment when called upon for reinforcements during Pontiac's Rebellion, when the prospects for reimbursements were no longer present.

This was precisely the difficulty that doomed the finances of the Confederation in the late 1770s. For when it became clear that the Congress might very well lack the capability of settling the accounts of the Union, contributions virtually ceased coming into the public treasury. The train of thought that led Grenville to his conclusion that a general tax was required followed the same steps that would be taken by American statesmen who would witness the collapse of the finances of the Confederation in the late seventies. If the public virtue of the revolutionary generation was not sufficient to make a system depending on the free grants of sovereign assemblies a workable one during the revolutionary war itself—when the dangers posed by failure were infinitely greater than they had been before the outbreak of war—the "affection" of the colonists for the mother country was scarcely likely to issue in a different response. All the evidence indicates that this response would have been far worse.

The American demand for a return to requisitions, then, did not signify an acknowledgment of either the duty or the willingness of the colonists to share the expenses of the army stationed in North America. Even had it done so, there are good reasons for questioning the efficacy of the system. The determination that the Americans ought to share part of the burden of the army thus made a conflict over the sovereignty of Parliament inevitable, for the failure of the requisition system would then have required the interposition of parliamentary power, a point that Grenville clearly recognized.[34] Yet the colonists' position on such a possibility was unmistakable. Either free grants were free grants or they were not. If, in case of colonial refusal, the supreme authority of Parliament could be interposed, they were not free.

The British could not have avoided coming to terms with this claim and its explosive implications even had they clearly wanted to do so. To this extent, it was not a matter of British capability of shouldering the entire burden of imperial defense in North Amer-

---

[34] Charles Garth to the Committee of Correspondence of the South Carolina Assembly, June 5, 1764, *Prologue to Revolution*, p. 28.

ica. The imperial state could have done so—indeed, for all intents and purposes, it did do so—though the inequity of the arrangement would have been apparent and galling. Even so, the issue of parliamentary sovereignty would not have been avoided. It would simply have been resolved in favor of the colonial assemblies. It would have established once and for all that free grants were the only arrangement possible with assemblies that enjoyed powers equivalent to those of the House of Commons.

[VIII]

"It was the fate of the times," Horace Walpole wrote of the administrations of Bute and Grenville, "to stir questions which, for the happiness of the whole, had better slept in oblivion."[35] His judgment has been widely echoed by historians. The inarticulate premise of this conclusion, however, is that some path lay open to the British which would have succeeded in evading the question of sovereignty; that some approach existed which would have left Parliament in a position to exercise its general superintending power over the empire, while not threatening the internal autonomy of the provincial governments; that there was some way of preserving the ambiguity of the imperial-colonial relationship and shielding its character from scrutiny. For Walpole, as for others, such a path did exist. It consisted of an adherence by the metropolis to the status quo.

We return, then, to the question posed at the outset: What was the status quo and who sought to challenge it? Was it the metropolis, in deciding to maintain a peacetime army in America, in assuming responsibility for the peace and stability of the frontier, and in insisting that the colonies share in the costs of the imperial establishment? Or was it the colonies, in challenging the imperial program for the wilderness and in refusing to share in the costs of the imperial establishment save by a method—requisitions—that experience had shown to be less than reliable? There is no simple answer to these questions. Clearly, it will not do to attempt to answer them by going back to the period before the war and identifying the arrangements that had then obtained with *the* status

[35] *Memoirs of the Reign of King George the Third,* 2:71–72.

quo. For the war profoundly disturbed the old relationship. It deranged the "extant moral order within the empire." This order had rested on a practical division of rights and duties that seemed incapable—so articulate opinion in the colonies and Britain held in 1754—of meeting the new challenges posed by the French. Parliament thus assumed wide responsibility for the security and defense of the American settlements. For the first time, it expended enormous sums on behalf of America. Yet the question of what this assumption of responsibility implied for the division of power was left unresolved till the end of the war, largely because Pitt felt that nothing was so important as military victory and obsessively sacrificed all considerations to that end.

By the close of the war, this question could no longer be avoided. The disjunction between power and responsibility introduced by the war could not persist. It is scarcely remarkable that the Grenville administration, in attempting to overcome this disjunction, imposed taxes on the American settlements rather than abdicate Parliament's new-found responsibility for American security. Grenville could not turn responsibility for the new conquests over to another authority. No such authority existed. He could not simply return to the arrangements of the past. The *status quo ante bellum* had ceased to exist. Yet the *status quo inter bellum* was no longer relevant. The British could see no other way to discharge the responsibility for American security they had clearly assumed in 1754 than through the use of regular troops. They concluded that no other method could ensure the fair distribution of the burden of supporting these troops than parliamentary taxation. The larger issue, then, was simply this: If London challenged one feature of the status quo, it was because other features of the status quo had changed and these changes could no longer be dealt with satisfactorily by the methods of the past. The problems inherited from the war and from the peace settlement that followed demonstrated the ambiguity of the imperial-colonial relationship in the early 1760s. Even more, they revealed that both sides now entertained conceptions of their rights and duties within the empire which would be increasingly difficult, if not indeed impossible, to reconcile.

SIX

The Acts of Trade and Navigation

[I]

Following the Seven Years' War the British made a number of changes in the regulations affecting the trade of the empire and in the administration of those laws. The conventional view of the reforms emphasizes that they reflected a fundamental change of policy, from one concerned almost exclusively with the regulation of trade to one reflecting the pressing revenue requirements of Great Britain after the war. The so-called changes in the "laws of trade" during 1764 reflected the turn from mercantilism to imperialism quite as much as did the Stamp Act and imperial policy on the periphery; indeed, according to this view, all of the old objectives were sacrificed after 1763 on the altar of the new imperialism. It was to this new turn of policy—but to this alone—that the American continental colonies objected. The colonists, according to this view, were basically content with their status of commercial subordination. If they wanted no more than what they had, however, they also would not settle for any less, and they were willing to fight for it. Yet the British were not content with their old and settled position; they had all the immoderation of those who, like Thucydides' Cleon, "wanted more."[1]

[1] Though it has been challenged in recent years, this understanding of the transformation of British policy in the aftermath of the war and the response it evoked in the colonies continues to find broad support. The real bitterness of the colonists, Esmond Wright has written, was felt "not for the old mercantilism, but for the new imperialism"; *Fabric of Freedom, 1763–1800*, rev. ed. (New York, 1978), p. 36. Oliver M. Dickerson, *The Navigation Acts and the American Revolution* (Philadelphia, 1951), remains the basic text for those who find this view persuasive. Recent works that recognize the importance of the traditional aims of the "mercantile system" in the reforms that the British adopted in 1764 include Lawrence Henry Gipson, *The British Empire before the American Revolution, vol. 10, Thunderclouds Gather in the West, 1763–1766;* Ian R. Christie and Benjamin Woods Labaree, *Empire or Independence, 1760–1776* (New York, 1976); and Thomas Barrow, "Background to the Grenville Program, 1757–1763," *William and Mary Quarterly,* 3d ser. 22 (1965):93–104, and *Trade and Empire, The British Customs Service in Colonial America, 1660–1775* (Cambridge, Mass., 1967).

Yet it is by no means an easy matter to determine the nature of the status quo from which the British are supposed to have departed and to which the colonists wished to return. The British presumably had the right to regulate the trade of the empire. Was this right unlimited? Could it legitimately be exercised in areas where it had fallen into disuse or been ignored during the preceding regime of "salutary neglect"? Did Britain's right to regulate trade mean that it could take any measures it deemed necessary in order to see to the enforcement of the laws directing trade? Could it change the reasons—or mixture of reasons—for regulating trade, or were only certain purposes admissible and others forbidden? Merely to ask these questions points to the uncertainty marking the imperial-colonial relationship on the eve of the Grenville reforms, an uncertainty illuminated by the conflicts that arose over the enforcement of the trade laws during the Seven Years' War. Here, too, as with imperial defense, the questions indicate that each side entertained understandings of the status quo which, once illuminated, would be exceedingly difficult to reconcile, if indeed they could be reconciled at all.

[II]

In 1763 Great Britain superintended the resources of a far flung and complex commercial empire. The most valuable part of Britain's dependencies lay across the North Atlantic on a long and ragged arc beginning in the West Indies and stretching northward to Nova Scotia and Newfoundland. The commerce of these plantations conformed to two broad patterns. All the colonies were important as markets for British manufactures, but they earned their remittances for this important trade in two broadly distinct ways. The "bread colonies" of the middle Atlantic, whose commerce centered in the ports of New York and Philadelphia, and the fisheries of New England, whose principal port was Boston, found their best markets in the foreign West Indies and southern Europe. The specie and bills of exchange they derived from the sale of their exports and from their carrying trade constituted the chief source of their remittances to the mother country, in return for which they took off British manufactures in ever increasing volume. The southern American colonies and the British West

Indian islands traded, for the most part, directly with Great Britain. Direct remittances, and the extension of credit by British merchant houses, were their principal means of payment for British manufactures.

There were exceptions to these two principal trading patterns. The colonial shipbuilders, who were centered in New England and who supported a wide range of occupations, frequently sold their products directly in Great Britain. The white pines of New Hampshire, marked by a broad arrow for their suitability as masts in the Royal Navy, were also exported straight to the metropolis. The flax produced in the middle colonies formed the principal raw material in the manufacture of linens and was exported directly to Great Britain and Ireland. Iron in its unfinished state was sent to Great Britain, to return in the form of a wide range of implements indispensable to a largely agricultural nation. The southern colonies, on the other hand, traded with the British and foreign West Indies as well as with southern Europe. South Carolina sent a large portion of its rice to the Mediterranean and, during the Seven Years' War, also found a significant market for its principal export in the West Indies. There had also developed by mid-century an extensive intercolonial commerce. In the broadest terms, however, the commerce of the American colonies conformed to the two broad patterns noted above. 99.6 percent of American tobacco was exported directly to Great Britain, of which 91 percent was reexported to markets in northern Europe. 52 percent of American rice was sent to the British entrepot, of which 79 percent was re-exported to northern European markets. Only on the most infrequent occasions, when crops in Britain suffered from drought, was American wheat and flour exported directly to markets in the metropolis, and the northern European reexport trade in foodstuffs was as yet of minor significance. The same basic pattern held for the fisheries of New England.[2]

Superimposed on this system of trade and navigation were a number of regulations by which the British attempted to direct the

[2] See *The Statistical History of the United States from Colonial Times to the Present*, ed. Ben Wattenberg (New York, 1976), ser. Z, pp. 449, 454, 460, 486–92. The most recent work on the trading patterns of the American colonies before the Revolution is James F. Shepherd and Gary M. Walton, *Shipping, Maritime Trade, and the Economic Development of Colonial North America* (London, 1972). See also Marc Egnal, "The Economic Development of the Thirteen Continental Colonies, 1720–1775," *William and Mary Quarterly*, 3d ser. 32 (1975):191–222.

trade into what they considered to be its proper channels. The basic features of the Acts of Trade and Navigation were well established at the close of the seventeenth century, and they remained so until the Revolution disrupted the economy of the First British Empire.[3] Various features of this system underwent periodic revision and were the subject of continual debate in Great Britain, but the basic assumption that the mercantile system was responsible for the great wealth and power of eighteenth-century Britain went, for the most part, unchallenged. In the decade before the Revolution a number of the pamphlets of older mercantilist writers were reprinted by those who insisted upon their relevance to contemporary issues, and fresh reformulations of the basic design of the mercantile system continually appeared. Only in 1776, a year after the outbreak of armed hostilities, did Adam Smith comprehensively challenge the body of assumptions on which it was based. Smith, however, stood virtually alone: the British "political nation" held firmly to the older ideas.

The mercantile system was designed to augment both the wealth and power of the empire in an age in which both objectives were closely associated. "Power," as William Wood wrote, "is not to be compassed or secured but by riches, and a country cannot become rich but by the help of a well managed and extended traffic."[4] Wealth made its contribution to political power in two distinct ways. The rise of the public debts during the eighteenth century seemed to demonstrate the truth of the maxim that "money is the sinews of war." And while many were convinced that Britain's indebtedness would ultimately be the cause of the nation's ruin, it was also understood that the indebtedness was a sign of immense strength. The British experience in war during the eighteenth century testified to the intimate relationship between economic wealth and political power, linked by the capacity of the state to borrow immense funds in time of war. By the middle of the century, it had become a commonplace that British power was based fundamentally on British wealth, and the latter on the trade of its col-

---

[3] See Lawrence H. Harper, "The Effect of the Navigation Acts on the Thirteen Colonies," in *The Era of the American Revolution*, ed. Richard B. Morris (New York, 1939), for the most succinct description of the regulatory system governing the commerce of the North American colonies.

[4] Quoted in William S. Sachs and Ari Hoogenboom, *The Enterprising Colonials: Society on the Eve of the Revolution*, p. 139. See also Klaus Knorr, *British Colonial Theories, 1570–1850*.

onies. The notion was seemingly confirmed beyond all doubt by the experience of the Seven Years' War, when the army commanded by Prince Ferdinand, placed in the field by British subsidies, and the army of Frederick II of Prussia, maintained there by British subsidies, had been able to repulse effectively the overpowering coalition directed against them. The immense financial strength of the English was to the wars of the mid-eighteenth century what the *levée en masse* was to be for the wars of the French Revolution and Napoleon: an addition of strength to one side that overthrew all previous calculations of power.

External commerce also made a direct contribution to British naval power. The Acts of Navigation, first applied to America by the Commonwealth in 1651 and successively modified until the end of the seventeenth century, forbade trade in any commodity in American ports save in English—later British—owned ships whose master and three-fourths of the crew were also British subjects. The requirement that colonial staples, with certain exceptions, pass through the British entrepot before reaching their European markets ensured, in turn, that these seamen were readily available, through impressment if necessary, for service in the Royal Navy at the first outbreak of war.[5] Bounties were given on a wide range of naval stores in order to lessen the dependence of Great Britain on the Baltic powers for supplies in times of public emergency. The same policy was followed for certain raw materials that were necessary in the production of British manufactures and of which hostile nations might deprive the British in time of war.

The colony trade to the Americas absorbed nearly all of the remarkable growth of total British exports during the eighteenth century. The total proportion of English exports that went to Asia, Africa, and America rose from 10.3 percent in 1700 to nearly 31.1 percent in 1772. Perhaps it was because all visible changes in the trade of Great Britain seemed to be due to the colonies that con-

---

[5] The importance of the principle of "making all goods as much as possible center in England" is underscored by the reluctance of the British to resort to impressment in American ports, the effect of which was to confer an immunity on "service" in the Royal Navy for those seamen who plied the American trade to and from the West Indies and southern Europe. On impressment during the revolutionary decade, see Neil R. Stout, "Manning the Royal Navy in North America, 1763–1775," *American Neptune* 23 (1963):174–85. For a more general survey, see Dora Mae Clark, "The Impressment of Seamen in the American Colonies," in *Essays in Colonial History Presented to Charles McLean Andrews by His Students* (London and New Haven, 1931), pp. 198–224.

temporaries invested an importance in them which has frequently baffled more recent and detached observers.[6] Whereas European markets were stagnating, those in America seemed capable of unlimited growth. Nor was it unreasonable to believe, though in retrospect the belief would appear to be mistaken, that the laws of Great Britain which confined the commerce of the colonies to the mother country were in large measure responsible for this sudden and remarkable prosperity, that wise policy, and not simply the superior qualities of British merchandise and credit, had secured the British such great advantages over their European rivals. It was not so much the maxims of the mercantile system that, by their persuasiveness, had secured the allegiance of the minds of Englishmen, as the indisputable statistics of the customs service—with these, it seemed, no men could quarrel. Edmund Burke's first speech on conciliation with America consisted in no small part of a great statistical exercise on the value of the colony trade.[7] It was a speech that, in the time it devoted to the sheer amount of the trade, with only passing references to the maxims of the mercantile system, confirmed Adam Smith's observation that one of the principal effects of the discovery and settlement of the Americas had "been to raise the mercantile system to a degree of splendour and glory which it could never otherwise have attained to."[8]

The "splendour and glory" of the mercantile system had consequences of abiding importance for the American Revolution. From the wealth and power that it appeared to confer upon Great Britain, conclusions would be drawn, by all parties to the quarrel, that colored virtually every aspect of the controversy. It gave the colonists themselves a sense of self-importance and power that can scarcely be overestimated. From the beginning of the conflict they had become fully convinced that they were capable, if united, of inflicting a terrible wound on Great Britain from which it would never recover. Nor were such beliefs confined to the colonies. Writing only shortly after events had belied the worst prophecies

[6] On the importance of the colony trade, see Ralph Davis, "English Foreign Trade, 1700–1774," *Economic History Review*, 2d ser. 15 (1962–3):285–303. Richard Pares, "American versus Continental Warfare, 1739–1763," pp. 441–42, has noted the extraordinary over-valuation of the colony trade and has expressed amazement that the opinion was held not only by the advocates of maritime war but also by those, such as Hardwicke, "who had no motive for exaggerating in this respect."

[7] *PH*, 18:484–90 (March 22, 1775).

[8] Adam Smith, *An Inquiry into the Nature and Causes of the Wealth of Nations*, p. 591.

of commercial doom, Adam Smith recalled that "in the total exclusion from the colony market, was it to last only a few years, the
greater part of our merchants used to fancy that they foresaw an
entire stop to their trade; the greater part of our master manufactures, the entire ruin of their business; and the greater part of our
workmen, an end of their employment."[9]

When, in 1779, George III outlined to his first minister, Lord
North, the reasons why he considered the war with America "as
the most serious in which any country was ever engaged," he
articulated a view that, in its estimate of the consequences American independence would presumably entail, had formed the common ground of political debate for more than a decade.[10] American
independence would not only deprive England of its monopoly of
American trade and, for this reason alone, markedly weaken its
power relative to that of France. Equally important, American
independence would disrupt the entire system of trade relations
within the empire. In this complex and interdependent system,
the continental colonies played a key role. If they were to break
away, the adjustments that would be required to compensate for
their loss might well prove too difficult for the metropolis to manage. The critically important trade ties between the northern American colonies and the British West Indies would be broken with
no apparently satisfactory alternatives to replace them. So, too, the
defense of Britain's West Indian possessions might well prove impossible without the bases provided by the continental colonies.
To these considerations was added the significance of Anglo-American trade for the maintenance of Britain's naval power. If the
control of this trade were once successfully challenged and broken,
as would presumably be the result of American independence, both
the economic and the military bases of Britain's power would be
destroyed.[11]

Such were, in brief, the considerations that led British statesmen
to equate the future of the metropolis with the retention of the
American colonies. The same considerations later led George III

---

[9] Ibid., p. 571.
[10] George to Lord North, June 11, 1779, *The Correspondence of King George the Third
from 1760 to December 1783*, ed. John Fortescue, 6 vols. (London, 1927–28), 4:351.
[11] An excellent summary of the case for British dependence on America has been given by
Jonathan Dull, *The French Navy and American Independence* (Princeton, 1975), pp. 36–
44.

to conclude that "should America succeed in that [independence], the West Indies must follow them, not independence, but must for its own interest be dependent on North America; Ireland would soon follow the same plan and be a separate State, then this Island would be reduced to itself, and soon would be a poor Island indeed, for reduced in Her Trade Merchants would retire with their Wealth to Climates more to their Advantage, and Shoals of Manufacturers would leave this country for the New Empire."[12] These sentiments differed in no essential respect from the views that the Americans themselves entertained—views that lay at the heart of their policy of commercial intimidation and that also contributed to their insistence that the old colonial system imposed severe burdens on the American settlements.

The irony of this state of affairs should not go unnoticed. The principal justification for defending and securing the colonies rested on the contribution they made to British wealth and power. It was not only, however, that the American colonies were a great market for British manufactures: they had also the advantage of being a secure market. It was not only that they produced commodities indispensable to British naval strength and to the production of British manufactures: these products would also be available in time of war. In order to relieve their dependence on potentially hostile nations for markets and supplies, the British had created one great market and one great supplier. As the crisis with the colonies loomed, the British realized that they had come full circle. They had not, in fact, relieved their dependence on others. They had exchanged and concentrated their dependency.

The British thus emerged from the Seven Years' War convinced that their empire in North America was the principal source of their wealth and power. This belief had underlain the conduct of the Seven Years' War and the negotiations ending it. This belief also underlay the two fears that informed so much of subsequent British conduct: that the Americans were undermining various features of the mercantile system and that the colonists might exclude the British, by economic boycott, from the American market. The first presented a prospect of gradual erosion; the second, the prospect of immediate distress. The first was by far the more important in explaining the reforms that the Grenville ministry undertook in

---

[12] *George III*, 4:351.

1764; the second, the retreat of subsequent ministries. In the end, however, the prospect that each fear held out was the same, and the British were left wondering whether they should witness their eventual loss of power in one act or five.[13]

[III]

There were two difficulties in the relationship between the metropolis and the colonies which the war had magnified and which, in the view of imperial officials, now required immediate attention. The first centered around the import trade of the colonies, and it led to a whole series of legislative and administrative reforms, the centerpiece of which was the Sugar Act of 1764. The second problem revolved around the security of private debts owed to British merchants by the colonists. It too was magnified by the war. In order to finance the colonial war effort, provincial legislatures had issued paper money in large amounts. Since debts to British merchants were at times payable in both local and sterling currency, the rise of colonial exchange rates, brought on at least partly by excessive issues, adversely affected the interests of the British creditors. The problem was gravely accentuated by the economic depression that struck Britain at the close of the Seven Years' War, and the currency of Virginia, where the problem was most acute, steadily lost its value in relation to pounds sterling. To this problem the British responded with the Currency Act of 1764.

The Currency Act deprived colonial currency emissions south of New England of their legal tender status. In certain respects it represented an extension to the other colonies of the principles that had been applied to New England in the Currency Act of 1751. It prohibited the issue of any further paper currencies "to be legal Tender in Payment of any Bargains, Contracts, Dues or Demands whatsoever" after September 1, 1764. The statute did not deprive existing emissions of their legal tender, but provided that the "con-

---

[13] Cf. Knox to Grenville, September 19, 1769, *The Grenville Papers: Being the Correspondence of Richard Grenville, Earl Temple, K. G., and the Right Hon. George Grenville . . .*, ed. W. J. Smith, 4 vols. (London, 1852–53), 4:456; and Samuel Johnson, *Taxation No Tyranny: An Answer to the Resolutions and Addresses of the American Congress* (London, 1775), pp. 8–9: "Concessions may promote [our commerce with America] for a moment, but superiority only can ensure its continuance."

ditions and terms, upon which such Bills have been emitted, should not be varied or prolonged, so as to continue the legal Tender thereof beyond the Terms respectively fixed by such Acts for calling in and discharging such Bills."[14]

The Currency Act was a response to profound changes in the structure of the Atlantic economy. After the conclusion of the Treaty of Aix la Chapelle in 1748, the colonial economy entered a period of rapid growth. Consumption of British manufactures rose spectacularly and far outpaced the concomitant increase in the value and volume of colonial produce. Such activity resulted in a large accumulation of debts and a serious erosion in the international financial position of the American colonies. The situation was most acute in the tobacco colonies of the Chesapeake. The growing indebtedness of the planters had made them acutely dependent on economic fluctuations in the mother country; whenever British firms were called upon to honor their debts, which occurred in the financial bust following the Seven Years' War, the consequences were felt immediately in the Chesapeake, where credit lines tightened and outstanding debts were called in.

The effects of financial crises in Great Britain were thus transmitted directly to the Chesapeake economy; the most visible manifestation was the rising price of local Virginian currency in relation to pounds sterling. Exchange rates moved above par (125) in 1756 and hovered around 140 until early 1762, when they shot up to 160. It was this dramatic exchange movement that prompted English merchants to lobby for enactment of the Currency Act.[15]

To a certain extent the Currency Act of 1764, especially as it would later be interpreted, represented a hardship to colonial interests beyond the degree required to secure British investments in the colonies. For this reason English merchants, whose complaints were largely responsible for the measure in the first place, lobbied for its repeal after 1765. Benjamin Franklin convinced the English merchants that colonial legal tender currency would not harm their interests so long as sterling debts were computed ac-

---

[14] *Statutes at Large,* 4 Geo. 3, c. 34. Both provisions were subjected to differing interpretations by imperial and colonial leaders in the years ahead. On these conflicts, see Joseph A. Ernst, *Money and Politics in America, 1755–1775* (Chapel Hill, 1973). The following section is based largely on Ernst's illuminating work.

[15] On the differing reactions and interests of English and Scottish firms, see Ernst, *Money and Politics,* pp. 43–88.

cording to the market rate of exchange. Even so, Parliament did not grant relief from the Currency Act until 1770, when it passed a measure, restricted to a proposed New York emission, that allowed the New York legislature to establish a loan office whose notes would be a legal tender for all public obligations. In 1773, the privilege was extended to the rest of the colonies covered by the Currency Act of 1764.

Did the act of 1773 represent the basis on which the interests of the colonists and the metropolis could have been reconciled? The answer is unclear.[16] By 1774 the right of Parliament to regulate colonial currency was explicitly denied by the Continental Congress; the Currency Act of 1764 was included in the statement of colonial rights and grievances (though not in the association) of the Congress. Many colonists continued to believe that their paper emissions required the support of a legal tender provision for the payment of private as well as public debts, in order to secure the value of the paper, and the 1773 act did not respond to this objective.

In retrospect the wisdom of the 1764 Currency Act seems open to question, especially the provision that forbade the use of paper money in the payment of taxes. This injudiciousness was indeed recognized by Parliament, which consented to a repeal of the objectionable measure. Yet it is scarcely possible to conclude that the Currency Act represented a challenge to the status quo, in the sense that it was an illegitimate exertion of parliamentary power. No colonists, at least at the beginning of the decade, questioned the right of Parliament to regulate the currency of the colonies. Nor was Parliament's interference in currency regulation an instance of the application of power that, while admittedly legitimate, ruffled previously undisturbed waters, for Parliament's interest in currency regulation was of long standing.

The broader significance of the Currency Act lay in the fact that it was a response to changes in the economic relationship between colonies and metropolis—a relationship with which the former were increasingly uneasy. The anxiety that the acute dependence on British credit bred in the tobacco planters was reflected in the growing belief that the "mercantile system" fostered an inherently

[16] Cf. Jack P. Greene and Richard M. Jellison, "The Currency Act of 1764 in Imperial-Colonial Relations, 1764–1776," *William and Mary Quarterly*, 3d ser. 18 (1961):485–86, 518.

exploitative relationship between merchant and planter, a belief that underlay the overall colonial response to the reforms of the Grenville administration and that significantly affected colonial aims as the colonists drew apart from the metropolis during the final crisis.

[IV]

The 1764 Sugar Act and the administrative measures that accompanied it proved to be of more far-reaching importance than the Currency Act. Not only did the former represent, at least in part, an attempt to raise a revenue in the colonies, but it did so by means that curtailed the internal autonomy of the provincial governments. Like those of the Currency Act, some of the provisions of the Sugar Act were altered or repealed after its initial passage. Yet those that remained accounted for much of the bitterness that prevailed in Anglo-American relations between 1764 and the onset of war, especially in the province—Massachusetts Bay—that became the center of the rebellion.

The Sugar Act centered around the import trade of the colonies. Unlike the southern tobacco- and rice-producing colonies, the northern provinces were beset with few restrictions on their export trade. With the exception of the shipping industry, the largest markets of the northern colonies lay outside the empire. Since a principal feature of the mercantile system was the desire to establish a favorable balance of trade, the metropolis placed few restrictions on the trade of the northern colonies to foreign ports. The British, however, did seek to regulate the import trade of the colonies with foreign regions. The most famous restriction was the six-pence tax on molasses imported from the foreign islands of the West Indies, but the system of regulation also forbade the direct importation of European manufactures, of wines from southern Europe, and of tea handled by rival European tea companies and smuggled into America from northern Europe and the West Indies. The British were worried about the evasion of the regulations governing all these trades, and the upshot of their anxiety was the Sugar Act.

"The great object," Grenville said in introducing the Sugar Act before Parliament, is "to reconcile the regulation of commerce with an increase of revenue."[17] The large increase in the national debt formed an important background for both purposes. Anxiety over its immense size not only increased the pressure on the ministry to find new sources of revenue, but also contributed to fears that the colonists were directly importing increasing amounts of manufactures from Europe in violation of perhaps the most basic provision of the Acts of Trade and Navigation. Grenville estimated the illegal imports from northern European ports at over five-hundred thousand pounds. Such wholesale smuggling represented "a loss of that Sum to Great Britain, her Trade and Manufactures & an Encouragement & Advantage in the same Proportion to the Commerce of our Rivals."[18]

Thomas Whately, Grenville's assistant at the Treasury, estimated the value of goods smuggled into the American colonies at seven hundred thousand pounds and indicated, in reasoning employed throughout the decade, why it might be expected to climb even higher.[19] The "number and the Weight of the new Taxes" required by the service of the national debt had the consequence that "rival Nations who were not before, may now be able in many articles to undersell us at Foreign Markets, and even become Competitors at our own."[20] The direct trade with Europe struck at the very heart of the mercantile system. "The extent of that trade was enormous, and it was all stolen from the Commerce, and Part of it from the Manufactures of Great Britain, contrary to the fundamental Principle of Colonization, to every Maxim of Policy, and to the express Provision of the Law."[21]

Moreover, the specter of foreign competition over colonial markets was one that, once loosed, could not easily be contained. The decline in the consumption of British manufactures would have further consequences for the revenue, and to meet this shortfall additional taxes might have to be levied, further imperiling the consumption and the revenue. Around and around, it seemed, the vicious circle went. To break it was the task of the Sugar Act, and

---

[17] Ryder Diaries, p. 234.
[18] Quoted in Gipson, *British Empire*, 10:203. See also Ryder Diaries, p. 234.
[19] *The Regulations Lately Made with Respect to the Colonies Considered* (London, 1765), p. 60.
[20] *Considerations on the Trade and Finances of This Kingdom, Addressed to the Two Houses of Parliament*, p. 3. Cf. Josiah Tucker, *The Case of Going to War for the Sake of Trade* . . . (1763), in *Four Tracts* . . . (Gloucester, 1774), pp. 86–87.
[21] Whately, *Considerations*, p. 65.

Whately introduced the subject of the import trade in European manufactures in his pamphlet justifying the act in terms that indicated the importance of the direct European trade: the American revenue, he held, "came under the Deliberation of Parliament the last Winter, and by their Wisdom an Act was passed to be the Foundation of an American Revenue, which is formed upon such Principles, that the Increase in the Revenue, which may be expected from it, tho' very considerable, seems the least important Object; so very judicious, so very interesting are the several Provisions of this Act, for the Purposes of Commerce and Colonization."[22]

Compared with this important purpose the adjustment of duties in the Sugar Act affecting the direct trade to Europe was of minor importance. Half of the "old subsidy," an ad valorem tax on European goods entering England, had traditionally been drawn back on re-export to America. The Sugar Act eliminated the drawback and placed the effective duty at 5, instead of 2.5, percent. The adjustment reflected no fundamental change of policy. It would represent a slight addition to the revenue while in some cases securing added protection to British manufactures. "The imposition," wrote Whately, "is not indeed very heavy; but so far as it extends, it is in favour of the British Manufactures."[23] The British also placed a large duty on French lawns and cambrics, rendering their re-export to America prohibitively expensive. The measure was similar to prior regulations governing the re-export to America of unwrought iron or steel, cordage, sailcloth, paper, oysters, and unwrought hemp.[24] Like these earlier measures, the intent of this provision of the Sugar Act was prohibitive: to discourage the con-

[22] *Regulations*, p. 58. The passage was not merely a rhetorical flourish. Later in the pamphlet, which in view of Whately's close ties to Grenville should be seen as the official statement of the Grenville administration's views, Whately wrote that the duties "appear to have been judiciously chosen, not only with a View to the Revenue, which they will produce: but for other, and in my Opinion, greater political Purposes, which each of them will respectively answer; and besides those already mentioned, there is one general Effect that will result from the whole, which will be of the utmost Importance to the Trade of Great Britain and to the Connection between her and her Colonies; tho' the Duties are very low, the Articles on which they are laid are numerous, and comprehend all that have been the Subjects of a contraband Trade, with those Parts of Europe which the Colonies are not allowed to trade to"; p. 87.
[23] *Considerations*, p. 65. Harper estimated that the duties on foreign goods re-exported to the colonies amounted to approximately twenty thousand pounds in 1773; Harper, "Effect of Navigation Acts," p. 28.
[24] Harper, "Effect of Navigation Acts," p. 11.

sumption of foreign manufactures and to assist those of Great Britain. Yet overall the adjustments that the act made in the duties were minor. Of far greater importance was the determination to enforce existing regulations forbidding the direct traffic.[25]

More far-reaching alterations were made in the laws governing the West Indian trade of the continental colonies. In the early eighteenth century sweeping changes began to occur in the economic relationship between the West Indies and the American continental colonies. The French and Dutch islands entered a period of prosperity and gradually began to displace the sugars of the British islands in the European market. They also made inroads on the trade with the American continent. By the early 1700s the intimate commercial ties between the British North American colonies and the foreign islands of the West Indies had been well established, never again to be broken. The home governments in Britain and France, however, were not entirely happy with this arrangement. Each reasoned that any drain of specie caused by an unfavorable balance of trade in any part of their respective empires would decrease by a proportionate amount the wealth of the whole. This reasoning, along with the pressure exerted by the groups directly interested in a prohibitive policy, led both powers to confine importations to sources from within their respective empires and to encourage exports to the lands of their rivals. French domestic producers, however, were incapable of supplying some essential commodities to their West Indian planters, and those commodities they could supply often came at a higher price. The French government, at home and in the islands, therefore frequently found it necessary to open the islands to a limited range of products from the American continental colonies and Ireland. The French soon discovered, however, that to open the islands to some traffic had the effect of opening it to all; and that if British ships brought lumber, which was allowed, they could easily smuggle flour, which was forbidden. On occasion, domestic monopolists exerted suffi-

[25] "The question of the content and the volume of" the illegal trade in European goods remains a subject of great dispute, but Barrow hazards "a generalization on the content of illegal trade" before the Seven Years' War: "the goods involved were those which at a given moment England could not, or would not through its tax policies, supply as plentifully or as cheaply as other areas. Other than molasses, most of these items were procured through Holland or the Dutch islands in the West Indies"; Barrow, *Trade and Empire*, p. 149; see pp. 143–59 for an excellent disscussion of this question. For a different view, see Dickerson, *The Navigation Acts*, pp. 69–79.

cient pressure to close the islands entirely to foreign imports, but this so outraged the planters that such regulations were soon relaxed.[26]

The British faced similar problems. Since the northern colonists relied on markets in the foreign islands to purchase the specie and bills of exchange that were used in the purchase of British manufactures, the attempt by the British sugar planters to entirely close this trade was doomed to failure. With the Molasses Act of 1733, the sugar planters had to settle for a prohibitive tax on foreign sugars imported into the mainland colonies, but the implausibility of relaxing one part, and forbidding another, of an exceedingly profitable exchange of products made the law virtually a dead letter. In passing the Molasses Act, Parliament had also given thought to the loss of revenue occasioned by the importation of foreign sugars; for theretofore the foreign sugars had been immune from taxation, unlike the "dead produce" of Barbados and the Leeward Islands, which was taxed at a rate of 4.5 percent. A fiscal motive was thus present in the 1733 legislation, but not in the sugar duties themselves, which were prohibitive.[27] The law, however, lay unenforced from the very beginning. Customs officials soon learned that attempts to enforce the law only courted the considerable retaliatory powers of the North Americans, and the officials quickly surrendered their short-lived attempts to do so.

The exigencies of war required the reversal of the policies that the European powers had announced, but had experienced such difficulty in enforcing, during peacetime. The interest of the British in maintaining a "favorable balance of trade" between the continental colonies and the French islands became plainly subordinate to the strategic objective of depriving the French islands and French military forces of their sources of supply. For the French, the commercial objectives of self-sufficiency and home monopoly became subordinate to the necessity of obtaining supplies wherever they could find them. Thus in peace and war did the respective policies of the British and the French remain faithfully antagonistic.

It has already been noted how the failure of the customs officials to enforce the forbidden wartime trade from the American mainland to the foreign West Indies drew attention to the overall in-

[26] Dorothy Burne Goebel, " 'The New England Trade' and the French West Indies, 1763–1774: A Study in Trade Policies," *William and Mary Quarterly*, 3d ser. 20 (1963):331–72.
[27] Barrow, *Trade and Empire*, pp. 134–36.

tegrity of the mercantile system itself. Interestingly enough, the British treated the six-pence tax on foreign molasses as a revenue measure, and not as a prohibitive regulation, when they called for its enforcement during the war, and the duties remained at six pence when the enforcement program was pursued with renewed vigor at the close of the war. There was considerable recognition in Britain, however, that the trade could not bear so large a tax, and that to place it at so high a level would only offer irresistable temptations to smugglers. The Commissioners of the Customs recommended, therefore, that it be reduced. There can be little doubt that Grenville's primary consideration in determining the proper size of the duty was the level that would secure to the Treasury the most revenue, and there are indications that he would have settled for a duty of two pence had not the West Indian interest demanded a greater measure of protection against competition from the French islands. At the basis of the lowered duty lay the recognition that a prohibition of this trade now lacked even the appearance of feasibility, let alone of expediency, so that the effective choice of the British was between regulation that allowed the trade to proceed and that would bear a revenue or no regulation at all.[28]

The chief precedent for the reduction of the molasses duty was the arrangement governing the export trade in rice. Enumerated commodities, of which rice was one, could reach Europe only through the English entrepot. In England rice was subjected to high import duties, of which all save seven pence per hundredweight were withdrawn on re-export to Europe. In the 1720s, Carolinian merchants complained that the additional freight charges and delays occasioned by the policy of enumeration were severely hampering the market for rice in southern Europe. Accordingly, in 1730, Parliament allowed direct shipment of Carolina rice to

[28] On the motives of the Grenville ministry in reducing the tax on molasses, see Barrow, *Trade and Empire;* idem, "Background to Grenville Program," pp. 93–104; Jack M. Sosin, *Agents and Merchants: British Colonial Policy and the Origins of the American Revolution, 1763–1775* (Lincoln, Neb., 1965), pp. 36–49; and Allen S. Johnson, "The Passage of the Sugar Act," *William and Mary Quarterly,* 3d ser. 16 (1959):507–14. Britain claimed a right to control and to benefit from colonial trade. It is likely that at some point this right would have been reasserted with respect to the West Indian trade, even in the absence of the exiguous financial condition in which Britain found itself after the war, and perhaps in the absence of the commitment of a standing army on the order of the one established in North America after the war. It is thus somewhat misleading to see the changes governing the West Indian trade as stemming from the same calculus—an American army requires an American revenue—that brought on the Stamp Act.

southern Europe but continued to require the seven-pence duty. A similar arrangement was made in 1764 for rice shipped to the foreign West Indies, where rice had secured a sizable market when the British occupied the French islands during the Seven Years' War. There was no more fundamental change of policy in the Sugar Act than in the earlier acts granting relief to the producers of rice. Each involved the partial abandonment of prohibitive regulations, on a showing of inexpediency, and the substitution in their place of less onerous fiscal duties.[29]

The same combination of commercial and fiscal objectives that appeared in the regulations of the Sugar Act governing the importation of European manufactures and foreign sugars, was also present in the regulations governing the colonial import trade in tea and wine. The East Indian trade was directly considered in the Sugar Act only in the prohibitive regulations affecting the colonial importation of Indian textiles, but the prohibition of tea smuggling, though not mentioned, formed an important objective of the act itself.[30] The British East India Company monopolized the British trade with Asia. The company's imports of tea into the great London merchant firms were a staple of home taxation, and only a portion of the taxes were withdrawn on re-export to America, the tax on American tea amounting to approximately one shilling per pound. The difference in price between tea purchased in Holland and in England was often quite substantial—the latter being at times over 200 percent more expensive—because Dutch East Indian tea was immune from taxation by the United Provinces. The price differential created an incentive to smuggle from other European nations or from entrepôts in the West Indies, which American merchants, it is generally conceded, could not resist. The most recent authority estimates that 1.2 million pounds of tea a year were consumed in the colonies during the early sixties, "three quarters of which were smuggled."[31]

Restricting the tea trade to the East India Company was a primary objective of policy, one that American imports from Europe—

[29] For a summary of the relevant statutes, see Charles Andrews, *The Colonial Period of American History*, vol. 4: *England's Commercial and Colonial Policy* (New Haven, 1938), pp. 95–98.
[30] See Whately, *Regulations*, p. 93; and *Journals of the House of Commons*, 29:933.
[31] Benjamin Woods Labaree, *The Boston Tea Party* (New York, 1964), p. 7. See chap. 1, for an enlightening discussion.

in effect, from rival Europeans tea traders—directly undermined. The prohibition of smuggling was consequential, moreover, not only in terms of the revenue—and, as developments later in the decade would show, in terms of the overall financial stability of the East India Company. The East India trade, in addition, was believed to be a far better apprenticeship to service in the Royal Navy than the coastal trade in coal. "It is certainly of consequence to the British Navigation," Whately wrote, "to have the Carriage of all that is consumed by British subjects; but of so much as is run in here, or in the Colonies, other Nations have the Carriage from India to Europe, and perhaps, from Europe to America: and to recover the Navigation of such long Voyages, and the direct Importation of the vast Quantities of Goods now brought for our Use by Foreigners, are important national Objects."[32]

The reduction of the duties on tea brought about by the Chatham administration in 1767 was intended to bring these partially incompatible fiscal, commercial, and strategic requirements more into line. The approximate one-shilling tax, collected in England, had led to widespread smuggling. The government drew back all taxes on tea re-exported to America and imposed a three-pence duty to be collected in American ports. Townshend, estimating American consumption at 1.6 million pounds of tea a year, hoped to raise a revenue of twenty thousand pounds from the three-pence duty, but there were collateral advantages that would be realized even if the American consumption was not as high as he had reckoned. Confining importations to British East India tea would help stabilize the finances of the East India Company; the carrying trade would be conducted in British ships, and American smugglers would have less incentive to touch at Holland or the Dutch West Indies and there procure other foreign goods to complement their cargoes of illicit tea. Neither the determination of the Grenville administration to enforce existing regulations, nor the alteration of these regulations by Townshend, reflected an abandonment of the traditional ends sought by the regulation of the tea trade. The primary innovation of the latter lay in Townshend's belief that a reduction of the tea duty would more effectively reconcile the regulation of trade with an increase of revenue.

The Grenville administration also adjusted the duties governing

[32] *Considerations*, p. 67.

the colonial import trade in wines from southern Europe and the wine islands of the middle Atlantic. The export trade to southern Europe was of immense importance to the colonists. The best markets for both the fish of New England and the wheat and flour of the middle colonies frequently lay in this region. In the return voyage were included a variety of articles. Parliament allowed colonial shippers to import salt directly to New England for use in the fisheries, and assorted cargoes of wine, fruit, and oil were also imported directly to America.[33] If of European origin, such importation was forbidden by the Acts of Navigation. But the wine islands of the middle Atlantic, with one ambiguous exception (the Canaries), were considered to be part of Africa, and as such the direct importation of wines and other tropical products from thence was left unregulated until 1764.[34] The adjustment in duties undertaken by the Grenville ministry reflected the policy that the colonists should import more wines of European origin, which in turn would be required to pass through Great Britain. Even though Madeira was more expensive than port, the absence of a tax on the former, coupled with a tax of 11.1 pence per gallon and greater freight charges on the latter, had given a preference to Madeira.

In the Sugar Act, the Grenville ministry decreased the tax on European wines imported by way of Great Britain (from 11.1 to 3.8 pence per gallon) and subjected the wines that could be imported directly to America to a tax of 6.6 pence per gallon. Such wines "as are carried from hence," wrote Whately, "will certainly be cheaper . . . than they used to be; they will for the most Part too be cheaper than those of the Madeiras, their original Price, and the Duty upon them being so much less, as to overballance the Difference of Freight." The intent was partly prohibitive and partly fiscal: "this Tax upon a Luxury of foreign Growth, co-operating with the Encouragement given to Exportation from hence, will have the still further beneficial Effects of improving at the same time Navigation and Revenue."[35]

The extent to which the new schedule of duties was formulated with the traditional objectives of the Acts of Navigation in view is

---

[33] See James G. Lydon, "Fish and Flour for Gold: Southern Europe and the Colonial American Balance of Payments," *Business History Review* 39 (1965):171–83.

[34] On the Canaries, see Andrews, *Commercial and Colonial Policy*, pp. 110–13.

[35] *Regulations*, p. 75. The duties were calculated in terms of tuns (one tun equals 252 gallons), which we have reduced to pence per gallon.

borne out by a later dispute in Britain over the proposed revision of the regulations governing this trade. Both the Rockingham administration and Townshend toyed with the idea of allowing the direct importation of European wines, subject to the same rate of taxation the Grenville ministry applied to Madeira (6.6 pence per gallon, or 7 pounds a tun.) The proposal was attacked by Grenville as a violation of the principles of the Acts of Navigation, and Townshend abandoned the scheme—partly, it would appear, at the request of the London wine merchants.[36] The controversy illustrates that attempts to frame legislation that took account of American commercial interests frequently involved eliminating the traditional forms of subordination required by the Acts of Navigation—which had not been onerous only because they had been disobeyed—and substituting in their place measures of light taxation, whose only drawback was that they were unconstitutional precisely because they were less onerous.

The features of the Sugar Act governing the import trade of the colonies thus seemed well designed "to reconcile the regulation of commerce with an increase in revenue."[37] Such an aspiration scarcely reflected a grand departure in policy. With respect to the trades in tea, wine, and foreign manufactures, the British continued to place primary emphasis on retaining their role as sole supplier to the colonies, reaffirming the traditional policy of making "all goods center as much as possible in England."[38] Revenue considerations played a role in the readjustment of the duties, particularly in the case of the adjustment of the old subsidy, but this scarcely represented a novel approach to trade regulation. Considerations of revenue had played a role in the regulations that underwent revision in 1764. In the case of the West Indian trade in molasses, considerations of revenue were now clearly paramount, though the three-pence duty did secure a degree of protection to the West Indian interest. Yet even here fiscal motives had not been wholly absent in the past. More importantly, the prohibition of imports of foreign molasses into the continental colonies was now clearly found to be unfeasible. Recognition of this fact in imperial circles

[36] See *The Papers of Benjamin Franklin*, 14:184; Lewis Namier and John Brooke, *Charles Townshend*, p. 187; and P. D. G. Thomas, *British Politics and the Stamp Act Crisis* (Oxford, 1975), p. 352.

[37] George Grenville, quoted in Ryder Diaries, p. 234.

[38] William Baker, quoted in Ryder Diaries, p. 236.

scarcely qualifies as the sea change in assumptions about empire that historians have diagnosed as the transformation of mercantilism to imperialism.

[V]

The real novelty of the Grenville program did not lie in the changed purposes of the laws regulating the external commerce of the empire but in the determination to enforce these trade laws, whatever their purpose. The paper restrictions the government introduced in the Sugar Act would all have been for naught had the ministry not moved on a broad front to reform the administration of the trade laws in America.

It has been noted how the British emerged from the Seven Years' War acutely conscious of the inadequacies of the "requisition system" and convinced of the equity of requiring the Americans to share the expense of the British army that was now stationed in North America. If the failure of the requisition system formed the immediate background for the Grenville program of taxation, it is equally true that the evasion of the trade laws during the Seven Years' War brought to light, in compelling fashion, the inadequacy of the older and lax policy of trade enforcement. The war demonstrated the almost total weakness of British customs officials in enforcing the laws of trade. It did so at a time when the avowed purpose of the regulations was neither fiscal nor commercial, but strategic: preventing the French from provisioning their troops and fleets with foodstuffs from the American continental colonies and Ireland. The inability of the customs officials to enforce the laws of trade, even in times of public emergency when failure to do so might lead to the failure of military operations and hence to the deaths of British soldiers and seamen, inevitably drew attention to the integrity of the mercantile system itself. If the enforcement mechanism was ineffective in time of war, the British thought, there was little reason to assume its effectiveness in the coming period of peace. Long and repeated warnings of the inefficiency and venality of the customs service, for the most part ignored in the past, seemed finally to be vindicated.

The devices by which colonial traders evaded the restrictions were manifold. It was not simply a matter, however, of wily traders frustrating the efforts of customs officials. The customs officials themselves frequently partook of the fruits of this illegal trade. Nor was the problem only that the judges of the vice-Admiralty courts were frustrated by writs of prohibition issued by colonial courts that enjoined further proceedings in smuggling cases. The judges themselves, who were frequently native-born colonists with the interests of their own communities at heart, aided and abetted the illicit traffic. Nor were the governors blameless. The most famous abuse during the Seven Years' War was the assistance some governors gave to illicit traders by selling to the highest bidder "flags of truce" that allowed the merchants to trade with the French islands on the pretense that the basic purpose of the traffic was the exchange of French prisoners. There were other sins of omission as well as commission, however, and most of the governors seemed intent merely on placing the blame on others rather than on uprooting the evil.[39] The evil, indeed, was systemic. The reform, the British concluded, would have to be comprehensive.

The decision to station a squadron of twenty-one ships in Halifax to patrol North American waters was made immediately after the conclusion of hostilities. That a large peacetime naval establishment of sufficient size was required to respond to imperial needs at the first outbreak of war was an obvious conclusion for those who had suffered through the string of British disasters at the outset of the Seven Years' War. "We have learned by fatal Experience," wrote Whately, "that 10,000 Seamen were not a sufficient Preparative for War in Times of perfect Tranquillity; for the Losses sustained at the breaking out of the last were chiefly owing to the Want of Hands, which could not be procured so soon as the Occasion required, by the most vigorous Press, and the most liberal Bounties."[40] The decision to use the peacetime naval establishment of sixteen thousand sailors in the prevention of clandestine trade, in both Great Britain and America, followed naturally from the increased security requirements that the British found placed upon

[39] On the problem of the illegal trade between the American continental colonies and the French and later Spanish West Indies, and the efforts by the British to prohibit it, see Neil R. Stout, *The Royal Navy in America, 1760–1775: A Study of Enforcement of British Colonial Policy in the Era of the American Revolution* (Annapolis, Md., 1973); George L. Beer, *British Colonial Policy, 1754–1765;* and Richard Pares, *War and Trade in the West Indies, 1739–1763*. For a different view of illegal American trade during the war, see Alan Rogers, *Empire and Liberty*, pp. 90–104.
[40] *Considerations*, p. 25.

themselves after the war. That a dual purpose could be served was doubtless a welcome relief for those in Britain alarmed at the fiscal crisis of the state and the possibility of a war of revenge launched by the French. "The making them serve on board the Smuggling Cutters, at the same Time preserves the Vigour of our Naval Force, and improves the Means of supporting it."[41]

The British, moreover, had employed the navy extensively during the Seven Years' War in an attempt to stop the provision trade between the continental colonies and the French West Indies, and colonial governors had given very favorable reports of the navy's performance.[42] The British decision to employ the fleet after the war thus continued a practice that had apparently demonstrated its efficacy in cramping the illicit traffic. That a much larger squadron was deputized for similar purposes in English waters demonstrates that the action was designed neither as punishment of the colonists nor as the opening salvo in a "war against colonial commerce."[43] The British were attempting to put a stop to illicit traffic, and in doing so they grasped those tools that had apparently been effective in the past and that at present lay closest to hand.

The Grenville ministry also moved on a broad front to reform the many deficiencies in the customs establishment. Absentees were ordered back to their posts in the spring of 1763. Those officials who had collaborated with local merchants in evading the trade laws were threatened with removal.[44] The size of the customs establishment in the colonies was increased: twenty-five additional comptrollers, who served to check the activities of the regular customs officials, were added to the staff between 1764 and 1766. Additional surveyors general, who supervised the work of the customs establishment in the colonies, were appointed and the districts that the posts covered were divided in order to ensure more effective supervision.[45]

The absence of effective means of supervising the work of the colonial customs establishment finally led, in 1767, to the creation of the American Board of Customs Commissioners. No new powers were conferred on the board. The traditional powers possessed by

[41] Ibid., p. 26.
[42] Stout, *The Royal Navy*, pp. 19–22.
[43] This was Dickerson's charge in *The Navigation Acts*, pp. 169–70.
[44] See Barrow, *Trade and Empire*, p. 181.
[45] Ibid., p. 189.

the English Board of Customs were simply transferred to the new establishment in the colonies, with the understanding that closer supervision would lead to greater efficiency and would leave less room for the confusion attendant on conflicting reports which disputes involving the customs had inevitably entailed in the past in America.

Without other changes, however, these reforms likely would have been for naught. The customs service in the colonies had decayed not simply through venality or indifference. Provincial interests possessed a considerable array of legal weapons that could be employed against the overly diligent customs official. The most important was the vulnerability of the customs officials to a civil suit in a provincial common-law court brought by the owner of the seized vessel. The Sugar Act limited this vulnerability; so long as the judge proclaimed that there existed a probable cause of seizure, the customs official and deputized naval officer who brought the case would be liable for neither the costs of suit nor a damage suit brought in another court.[46]

The Grenville administration also made a start toward reinvigorating the powers of the courts of vice-Admiralty. Provincial common-law courts and provincial vice-Admiralty courts existed side by side in America during the eighteenth century. The practical, if not the formal, jurisdiction of the latter was confined mostly to cases of seizure during wartime and to contractual disagreements between merchants and seamen. The authority of the vice-Admiralty courts to hear cases involving violations of the laws of trade, ostensibly granted by Parliament in 1696, had been undermined by a variety of factors, one of which was the power of a provincial court of common law to issue a writ of prohibition banning further proceedings in the admiralty court on the grounds that it had exceeded its jurisdiction.[47] The real deficiency of the vice-Admiralty courts, however, lay not so much in their uncertain jurisdiction as in the fact that they were largely staffed by provincials— men who, like the governors and the customs officials, had "de-

---

[46] *Statutes at Large*, 4 George 3, c. 15, no. 46, For an example of the vulnerability of the customs officials to damage suits from aggrieved merchants, see Gipson, *British Empire*, 10:228–29.

[47] M. H. Smith, *The Writs of Assistance Case* (Berkeley, 1978), pp. 54–57; and Andrews, *Commercial and Colonial Policy*, pp. 261–68.

generate[d] into Creoles."[48] The judges received no salary, and the small fees granted to them were regulated by the colonial assemblies. For all, their service on the bench was more honorific than remunerative; many were lawyers whose principal business was with the merchants of the community, and as a result they usually had no desire to swim against the tide of local mercantile or political sentiment.[49]

In retrospect, what appears surprising is not the changes that were made in 1764 but the very limited scope of the innovations. In the Sugar Act, Parliament authorized the establishment of a court of vice-Admiralty with original, but not appellate, jurisdiction over violations of the trade laws in "all America." The new court was placed at Halifax. Customs officials (as well as the navy) had the right to bring suit in any court with jurisdiction over violations of the trade and revenue laws, but the new court heard very few cases.[50] Insofar as the intention was to utilize the new court in only those provinces, especially New England, whose reputation for smuggling exceeded all others, it was left unrealized. Both the distance from the original seizure and the great local hostility against the new court compromised the efforts of customs officials to employ it against colonial smugglers.

Only in 1768 did the British respond to the difficulties that the customs officials and the navy had encountered in utilizing the new court in Halifax. They did so by abolishing the court and replacing it with four new courts—to be established in Halifax, Boston, Philadelphia, and Charleston—with both original and appellate jurisdiction over violations of the laws of trade. The British intended the new courts to displace the older provincial vice-admiralty courts in cases concerning violations of the trade and revenue laws, but the displacement was usually limited to the provinces where the new courts were established. The fundamental purpose of the new courts was to lessen the dependence of the judges on the local merchant community. Each judge was to receive a salary of six hundred pounds a year, and though it would be paid from proceeds

---

[48] "We are here removed at a great distance from our superiors," one customs official wrote, "and continuing long in the same Place degenerate into Creoles, and at length forget Mother Country and her interests." Quoted in Smith, Writs of Assistance, pp. 64–65.
[49] See Carl Ubbelohde, The Vice-Admiralty Courts and the American Revolution (Chapel Hill, 1960), pp. 5–12, and Smith, Writs of Assistance, pp. 57–58.
[50] Ubberlohde, Vice-Admiralty Courts, pp. 23–54, 81–82.

of condemnations in his court, the salary itself was not dependent on the size of the condemnations. If the revenue from condemnations were insufficient, the judge would receive his salary from other sources. The new salary structure represented an attempt by the British to placate colonial fears that the judge would be given an interest in the number of condemnations while yet removing him from local pressures. Finally, the men chosen were those who had demonstrated their loyalty to the metropolis at various times during the previous decade and who could be expected to buck the tide of popular sentiment again.[51]

There is no reason to consider these changes in the machinery of enforcement as being linked primarily to the desire of raising a revenue in the colonies, a view maintained even by those historians who recognize that the adjustment of duties in the Sugar Act reflected many of the traditional aims of the regulatory system.[52] The changes in the machinery concerned the customs, it is true; but, as Whately noted, "in other Countries Custom house Duties are for the most Part, little more than a Branch of the Revenue: In the colonies they are a political Regulation, and enforce the Observance of those wise Laws to which the great Increase of our Trade and naval Power are principally owing."[53]

Did the measures taken by Grenville and succeeding administrations to enforce the laws of trade and revenue constitute a challenge to the status quo? The colonists evidently thought so. Their view is shared by most historians. Certainly, there is no question that changes were made. There is also little question, however, that the most significant of these changes lay in the overhaul of the machinery of enforcement and not in the larger purposes on behalf of which this machinery existed. If such was indeed the case, was it unreasonable or in some way peculiar—did it reveal a sudden and profound inflexibility—for the British to insist on the integrity of this machinery?[54] Certainly, no novel principle was introduced by doing so. The guiding principle that had led to the establishment of the customs service in the colonies and to the creation of the

---

[51] Ibid., pp. 128–71.
[52] Gipson, *British Empire*, 10:231.
[53] *Regulations*, p. 88.
[54] Cf. Alison Gilbert Olson, "Parliament, Empire, and Parliamentary Law, 1776," in *Three British Revolutions: 1641, 1688, 1776*, ed. J.G.A. Pocock (Princeton, 1980).

colonial vice-Admiralty courts in the late seventeenth century was that the American colonists should not be judges in their own cause when this cause concerned the Acts of Trade and Navigation. The principle had been neglected by imperial officials and undercut by resourceful colonists in the succeeding half-century. It had never been forgotten. When the alarming extent to which the principle had in practice been compromised became apparent during the Seven Years' War, it was reaffirmed in the reforms of the mid-sixties, for the British did not consider violations of the law as precedents to be respected. They did not deny that they were making significant changes; they did contend that such changes were necessary in order to maintain the integrity of the mercantile system.

[VI]

The attempt to change certain discrete features of the status quo in order to preserve the larger status quo—what the British saw as the larger purposes of imperial rule—was never accepted as legitimate by the colonists. It has seldom been adequately understood by historians, who have viewed it in terms first established by the colonists and little altered since. The American response has also been frequently misunderstood. The traditional, or whig, view emphasizes the essentially defensive character of this response: the Americans asked for no more, and no less, than to be placed again in the position they enjoyed before the Grenville administration embarked on its campaign to extinguish the traditional rights of the British American colonies.[55] The Americans, according to this view, drew a line only at the constitutional innovations of Parliament. These innovations, the colonists said, had two paramount features: the attempt to raise a revenue in the colonies, and the extension of the complicated machinery of enforcement which the colonies insisted was inseparably connected with revenue collection. Yet the colonists made no challenge to Parliament's right to regulate the trade of the empire; even when they did challenge this right, as in 1774, they nevertheless offered

[55] Edmund S. Morgan, *The Birth of the Republic, 1763–89*, p. 27.

to consent to regulations of trade that were not revenue measures in disguise.

Most historians have viewed this offer as unproblematic. Perhaps more than anything else, the refusal of the British to accept it makes imperial action in the sixties and seventies appear almost wilfully contrary to British self-interest. It is thus not surprising that historical inquiry has focused on the sources of this perverse obstinacy rather than on the purposes to which imperial officialdom avowedly addressed its efforts. The result has been a line of inquiry that has obscured the nature of the colonial offer to allow Parliament the right to regulate the trade of the empire. This offer was in fact anything but unproblematic.

The investigation of the American position has mostly taken the form of an analysis of American constitutional doctrine in the 1760s. Two views of this doctrine have emerged. The first, and older, view was that, in response to the Sugar and Stamp Acts, "the colonies admitted the right of Parliament to levy customs duties (external taxes), but denied the right of Parliament to levy excise taxes (internal taxes) upon them." The Sugar Act was constitutional, according to this understanding of the colonial position; the Stamp Act was not. In the aftermath of the 1767 Townshend Revenue Act, which was clearly fiscal in intent, the colonies advanced to a second stage. Then, they "conceded the right of Parliament to regulate the trade of the Empire, and hence exercise a legislative authority over the unrepresented colonies, but denied the right of Parliament to levy taxes of any kind whatever, internal or external."[56]

Edmund S. Morgan has sharply criticized this older view of the progress of American constitutional doctrine. It is a "Tory libel," he has written, for it indicts the colonists for "skipping from one constitutional theory to another, like so many grasshoppers." Morgan's view is that there was no difference between the constitutional position of the colonists in 1764–65 and 1767–68. On the earlier occasion, no less than on the latter, the Americans condemned as unconstitutional all revenue taxes. According to Morgan, the Americans viewed both the Sugar and Stamp acts as unconstitutional, the Sugar Act because "Parliament made use of trade regulations

---

[56] Randolph G. Adams, *Political Ideas of the American Revolution*, 3d ed. (New York, 1958), p. 91.

to raise money." The American position was remarkably consistent: when the colonists "objected to the Townshend duties in 1767, they had in no way changed the conception of Parliamentary power which they avowed at the time of the Stamp Act; they still admitted the authority of Parliament to regulate trade and to legislate in other ways for the whole empire; they still denied that Parliament had a right to tax them."[57]

Neither view is wholly persuasive. Morgan correctly notes that most colonial assemblies condemned as unconstitutional parliamentary taxation as such, and that most assemblies did not bother with the distinction between internal and external taxation. He makes out a persuasive case showing that the colonists, in 1764–65, usually did not *admit* that Parliament had the constitutional right to lay revenue taxes on the external commerce of the colonies. Nevertheless, he fails to note that the Sugar Act, save on the rarest of occasions, was not explicitly *condemned* as unconstitutional by the colonists. Morgan notes that some of the assemblies and pamphleteers of the New England colonies, where the primary burden of the Sugar Act fell, did not challenge the constitutionality of the Sugar Act but objected instead to its inexpediency and inequity; yet he implies that this ambiguous position was restricted to the New England colonies. Such was not the case. Nearly all statements of the colonial posture in the wheat, tobacco, and rice colonies reflected a similarly ambiguous position. A few wrote or said that

---

[57] "Colonial Ideas of Parliamentary Power, 1764–1766," *William and Mary Quarterly*, 3d ser. 5 (July 1948):311–42; reprinted in Morgan, *The Challenge of the American Revolution* pp. 42, 8, 41–42. Morgan, who quotes the statement of Randolph Adams noted above, also cites other representatives of this school of thought; see p. 7.

William Knox, in response to John Dickinson, characterized the distinction in the following manner: "The right of Parliament to charge foreign molasses with a duty of six-pence a gallon was unquestionable; but, for parliament to *reduce* the six-pence to three-pence, is a violent usurpation of unconstitutional authority, and an infringement of the rights and privileges of the people in the Colonies. The reduction of the duties on black teas too was another intolerable grievance: whilst they carried out with them a duty of one shilling a pound, paid at the East-India Company's sales, which, by the ordinary increase of charges, amounted to near eighteen pence when the teas arrived in America, things went on very well; but when parliament took off that shilling, and instead thereof laid on a duty of three pence, to be paid on importation of tea into the Colonies, which precluded all increase of charges, then were the Colonies undone. . . . I believe it is the first time that the Colonies of any state have complained of the injustice of the mother-country in laying taxes upon them which were not *sufficiently heavy*; nor was it ever before discovered, that the proper means to redress the grievances of any people, were to increase their taxes"; *The Controversy between Great Britain and Her Colonies Reviewed* . . . (London, 1769), pp. 36–37.

the Sugar Act was unconstitutional because it sought to raise a revenue in the colonies; a few others just as clearly admitted the constitutionality of revenue taxes on external commerce and acknowledged that the 1764 Sugar Act fit this description. Generally, however, the colonial position in 1764 and 1765 consisted of a blanket condemnation of revenue taxes that *would* have applied just as much to external (revenue) taxes as to internal ones but which was usually not applied to the Sugar Act.

There is a more serious difficulty with the way in which the American position in 1764–65 has been characterized. Most historians appear to assume that the constitutional position of the colonists was equivalent to their practical position, and that if the colonists acknowledged the *right* of Parliament to regulate their trade, they also by this very acknowledgment gave notice that they would submit to whatever measures Parliament thought it expedient to take. No such conclusion is warranted. In the course of a decade, the principles underlying the regulation of trade from the foreign West Indies to the American continental colonies had undergone a series of changes. From a policy of import prohibition, designed for the sustenance of the British West Indian colonies, British policy had passed to one of both export and import prohibition, dictated by the strategic requirements of the Seven Years' War, and finally to one in which revenue requirements were paramount. New England traders had opposed each successive phase, and they had done so successfully. There is every reason to think that they would have acted in the same way in the future. No regulation of the molasses trade that had prohibitory aims would have been considered as legitimate by politically effective opinion or had its terms respected by the traders in this commodity. It is true that the merchants, though not others in the port towns of New England, finally came around to grudgingly accepting the one-pence tax on both foreign and British molasses imposed by the Rockingham administration. This tax imposed by the friends of America was wholly a revenue measure, however, and hence was unconstitutional. If political considerations dictated that it not be actively opposed, constitutional considerations ensured, especially in the aftermath of the controversy produced by the Townshend Acts, that it would never be considered as legitimate.

A similar conclusion appears inescapable with respect to the tea and wine trades. The duties affecting tea had always been framed at least partly with fiscal purposes in mind, and the 1767 readjustment of the tea duties was not fundamentally different in this respect. The effective opposition to all such regulation, before and after 1767, indicates that Great Britain could have secured the acquiescence of the colonists in the regulations affecting tea only by making British teas competitive in price to the teas of rival European traders. By the early 1770s, even this had become insufficient. By then, it had become necessary to withdraw all taxes. The return to the status quo meant a return to the days of easy smuggling and the withdrawal of any restrictive regulation on the colonial tea trade. The same pattern of opposition is evident with respect to the colonial import trade from southern Europe and the wine islands. There existed no sympathy in America with the attempt by the Grenville administration to make Portuguese wines—required by the Act of Navigation to pass through British entrepots—cheaper in price than those of Madeira. Whether the new taxes on Madeira were one part of a larger and traditional regulatory policy or whether they were wholly revenue measures was a distinction of relevance to American constitutional doctrine. It was irrelevant to the practical position of the colonists, who were determined to oppose those restrictions quite apart from the intricate reasoning that led Parliament to enact them.

The colonial offer to allow Parliament to regulate the trade of the empire was not, then, as open-ended as it may seem. Indeed, the offer, so far as it extended to the regulation of the trades in molasses, tea, and wine, was so qualified as to be scarcely an offer at all. There were, in general, two strategies of opposition to parliamentary measures that concerned the external commerce of the empire. One was to question the legitimacy of the end; the other, to challenge the legitimacy of the means.

The attack on the legitimacy of the means was widespread and insistent. Throughout the decade of crisis the colonists regarded these measures as intolerable infringements on their individual and collective rights. There were variations on the theme of the parliamentary regulation of the external commerce of the colonies, but the note that the colonists struck on the enforcement of these regulations was unvarying and undisturbed by discordant responses. Throughout the decade the offer to allow Parliament the right to regulate the trade of the colonies was coupled with the assertion that the means of enforcement had to be left in the hands of the colonists themselves, and that these means of enforcement had scrupulously to respect the common-law rights of Englishmen. British pleas of necessity failed to override the constitutional rights of British subjects. There is no reason to question the sincerity of the American belief that these measures were intolerable infringements upon their individual and collective liberty; at the same time, American complaints could be satisfied only by leaving the enforcement mechanism of the Acts of Trade and Navigation in colonial hands. The practical result would have been to allow the colonists to obey only those laws they wished to obey.

The colonists also frequently challenged the legitimacy of the end, even when this end concerned the "regulation of trade" and not the collection of revenue. The colonists, it is true, did not directly challenge the right of Parliament to regulate the trade of the empire; they did, however, qualify the right by a "rule of reason." Differing formulations were given of it throughout the decade, but fundamentally the rule was that the British right of regulating the external commerce of the empire carried with it a duty to legislate for the "general good" of the empire. There was scarcely anything objectionable in the formulation, for the British claimed to be doing just that. The Americans, however, understood the "general good" of the empire as one in which their own interests were not sacrificed—whether it be to West Indian nabobs, London wine merchants, or the East India Company. They had come to embrace, as Arthur M. Schlesinger once said, "a Ptolemaic conception of the empire, with England as the sun and America the earth about which the sun revolved; while the statesmen at home justified their course in the terms of the Copernican theory."[58]

The response of the New York assembly to the Sugar Act contained the most explicit statement of the principle that Parliament's right to regulate trade had to be tempered by the equity of the results, yet the thrust of its comments was not very different from that of other assemblies. Parliament had the right to "model the Trade of the whole Empire, so as to subserve the interest of her own, . . . But a Freedom to drive all Kinds of Traffic in a Subordination to, and not inconsistent with, the British trade; and an Exemption from all Duties in such a Course of Commerce, is

[58] *The Colonial Merchants and the American Revolution, 1763–1776* (New York, 1918), p. 51.

humbly claimed by the Colonies as the most essential of all the Rights to which they are intitled." They asked that Parliament "charge our Commerce with no other Duties, than a necessary Regard to the particular Trade of Great Britain, evidently demands." It is not unreasonable to understand this as an exemption from restrictions on the molasses, tea, and wine trades, for none of these commodities was produced in Britain itself—none was competitive, or so it could be claimed, with the "particular trade of Great Britain." If the principle were accepted, regulations of trade would have to be submitted to the colonists' scrutiny and consent before they could be accepted as legitimate. It was a grant of power qualified by a test of reasonableness, and the petition of the New York assembly could leave little doubt that the reasonableness of the legislation was a determination which each colonial assembly, and not Parliament, was best equipped to make.[59] The constitutional niceties of their position apart, the colonists never surrendered the right "that all free states have, of judging when their privileges are invaded, and of using all prudent measures for preserving them."[60]

The distinction between internal and external taxation, or taxation on behalf of the regulation of trade and that on behalf of revenue, was thus irrelevant to the colonial position regarding their trade in tea, wine, and molasses. They wished these trades to be placed under no regulation; if regulated, they sought to frustrate the effectiveness of those charged with enforcing the laws. When the Americans asked for a return to the status quo, they meant the one summed up by the phrase "salutary neglect," not the one comprehended by the distinction between revenue taxes and regulations of trade. The colonists' incessant attack on parliamentary taxation throughout the 1760s ought not to lead us to conclude that the colonists would have gladly suffered the prohibition of their

---

[59] Edmund S. Morgan and Helen M. Morgan, who cite the New York petition in *The Stamp Act Crisis*, comment that "the molasses duty might be beneficial to the West Indies planters but certainly not to the commerce or manufacturers of the mother country. It was therefore an abuse of the Parliamentary power to regulate trade"; pp. 56–57. The proper conclusion, however, is not, as the Morgans earlier assert, that the colonists were demanding that "regulations of trade be regulations of trade," but that regulations of trade be framed in light of the increasing stature of the American colonies within the empire; that the regulations be framed with a degree of reasonableness and equity of which only the Americans themselves could be the final judge.

[60] John Dickinson, *Letters from a Farmer in Pennsylvania to the Inhabitants of the British Colonies*, in *The Writings of John Dickinson*, p. 349, Letter 6.

trade in molasses, wine, and tea because the enacting legislation contained a suitable preamble that made no mention of the revenue, John Dickinson to the contrary notwithstanding. The colonial position regarding the restrictions on these trades boiled down to a few mutually reinforcing propositions: prohibitory tariffs, although superficially legitimate, violated the injunction that Parliament must legislate for the general good of the empire, and revenue tariffs were unconstitutional exercises of parliamentary power. Burdensome regulations were unreasonable and inexpediential, hence offering occasions for legitimate evasion. Less burdensome regulations were unconstitutional, offering occasions for declamations against the violations of rights. Both kinds of regulation could not be enforced by means that infringed the constitutional rights of the colonists. Both offered occasions for resistance, armed and otherwise.

[VII]

The only restrictions seemingly immune from the charge that they violated the duty to respect the general good of the empire were those governing the northern European trade in foreign manufactures. The concession to Parliament of a right to regulate the external commerce of the empire meant, for most colonists, the concession of the right to regulate this particular trade. Many colonists explicitly offered to preserve the policy that confined the American trade to Europe to the British entrepot. Many did so in 1774 and 1775 as well as in 1765, though in the final years of crisis those colonists who offered the concession treated the restriction as one that Parliament had no inherent right to make apart from the consent of the colonies.

The colonial position regarding the northern European trade, however, was delicate, and not as straightforward as many have assumed. It began with a premise—that the commercial dependence of the American colonies on Great Britain was the source of British wealth and power—that few in Britain were inclined to dispute. "The subordination of the Colonies," Daniel Dulany wrote, "and the authority of the Parliament to preserve it, have been fully acknowledged. Not only the Welfare, but perhaps the Existence of the Mother Country as an independent Kingdom, may rest upon her Trade and Navigation, and these so far upon her intercourse with the Colonies, that, if this should be neglected, there would soon be an End to that Commerce, whence her greatest Wealth is derived, and upon which her Maritime Power is principally founded."[61]

What conclusions followed from this premise? For Dulany, as for others who employed this argument, the necessary conclusion was that Parliament had a right to regulate the trade of the empire. But colonial speculations did not end there. Indeed, the very arguments that the colonists introduced in the course of conceding to Parliament the right to direct the trade of the empire led inescapably to a host of other conclusions. It followed that Great Britain was absolutely dependent on the colonies, which were the principal sources of its greatness. It also followed that a policy of nonimportation of British manufactures, to be employed as an instrument of coercion, would leave the British with no choice but to capitulate. It further followed that the Acts of Trade and Navigation secured for the British a share of the colonial trade which they would not otherwise have possessed; that the British monopoly of the colonial market was itself a form of taxation. Once having emphasized all these considerations, once having articulated premises that led inescapably to the conclusion that the Americans were victims of the mercantile system, the colonists drew back. With John Dickinson, whose *Letters from a Farmer* of 1767 constitute a shrill indictment of virtually every aspect of parliamentary regulation, they said: "We do not complain of these measures. These burdens we bear heavily but gladly, as a token of our affection."[62]

Stripped of the quarrelsome language in which the colonists cast it, this evaluation of the burden imposed by the confinement of the colonial market to British manufactures was shared by nearly all parties to the dispute. The consensus in Great Britain was that the imperial-colonial relationship—considered in all its aspects—was advantageous, and hence equitable, to both sides, but no one doubted that the restraints imposed by confinement of the colonial market to British manufacturers were onerous for the colonies. Even Adam Smith believed that this restriction entailed severe

---

[61] *Considerations on the Propriety of Imposing Taxes in the British Colonies for the Purpose of Raising a Revenue* . . . (Annapolis, 1765), in *Pamphlets of the American Revolution, 1750–1776*, ed. Bernard Bailyn, 1 vol. to date (Cambridge, Mass., 1965), 1:638. Cf. p. 622.
[62] *Letters*, p. 14.

disadvantages for the colonists. The novelty of his thesis lay in his belief that the disadvantages for the colonists did not bring comparable advantages to the British nation, though he noted that the monopoly might bring partial benefits to British merchants and manufacturers.

The shared perception of the burdens imposed by the colonial monopoly gave a fundamental saliency to the issue of the integrity of the mechanism for enforcing the Acts of Trade and Navigation. For if the essential tie that bound the trade of the colonies to Great Britain lay not in the interest of each who bought and sold—if the trade laws were not self-enforcing—then law would be necessary to ensure that the commercial connection persisted. From 1764 and 1765, the colonists insisted that the mechanism to enforce the law remain in their hands. The Acts of Trade and Navigation were to be enforced not by commercial preference, nor by a mechanism controlled by imperial officials, but by the colonists themselves. The security that the colonists offered for the continued integrity of the laws on which the preservation of the empire depended was their good faith and affection.

This being so, it should scarcely occasion much surprise that the British were unwilling to accept the proposal. By refusing to offer any security that their concession would be adhered to, the Americans offered a ground of reconciliation to which the British could not subscribe. The colonial "concession" offered to Parliament the right to make regulations while reserving to the local mercantile communities themselves the right to determine the occasions on which that right would be anything other than an empty claim. Had the colonial record been other than it was and had the British not just lived through a war that amply demonstrated the inadequacy of the old system of enforcement, there perhaps would have been solid grounds for accepting the offer. Under the circumstances, however, acceptance would have meant abandoning the assumptions that informed the debate on both sides, the most important of which was that law, and not commercial preference, secured the trade of the American colonies to Great Britain. So long as the right to regulate the external commerce of the empire was coupled with a denial of the right to see to the enforcement of the regulations, the British viewed the concession as an empty one. The rights of Englishmen became, in England, a buzzword for wholesale violations of the laws of trade; and the measures that the Grenville ministry had undertaken to ensure the observance of these laws—measures that not even the most conciliatory ministry was prepared to abandon—came to be viewed as inseparable from the basic integrity of the mercantile system itself.

[VIII]

What was the relationship of the Acts of Trade and Navigation to the conflict that would lead to the disruption of the First British Empire? The traditional view is that the laws of trade had very little relation to the conflict, that the metropolis embarked on a new policy at the close of the Seven Years' War in pursuit of objectives wholly different from those sought by the laws of trade; that, in pursuit of a revenue, it introduced changes in the administration of the trade and revenue laws, severely clogging the legitimate commerce of the colonies and representing an unnecessary violation of the colonists' constitutional rights; that the colonists, in objecting to these new measures and to the change in British policy they reflected, made no challenge to other features of the English commercial system; that the colonists would have been content had Great Britain only pursued its older objectives and allowed the colonists to return to the constitutional position they had enjoyed in 1763.

The peculiar feature of this position is that, despite the concession of extensive theoretical powers of action to the imperial state, it nevertheless placed virtually no restraints on the practical area of freedom enjoyed by the colonists. Although the Americans did not challenge the legitimacy of the theoretical right of Parliament to regulate the trade of the empire, they did insist that this right not be employed to violate the relationship as it stood at the close of the Great War for the Empire. Imperial authorities were expected to refrain from imposing any trade restraints that did not form a part of the system in practice as it stood before the Grenville reforms. If accepted by Great Britain, this position would have legitimized the departure of the colonists from the restraints provided for in the laws of trade so long as these restraints had not been enforced by the mother country.

In the manner in which the colonists formulated their claims, the right of Parliament to regulate the trade of the empire was thus

not placed directly in contention until the final crisis of 1774. Indirectly, however, the right was all but obliterated, primarily through
the colonists' denial to Great Britain of the means to enforce effectively the restrictions that once had merely gathered dust in the
law books. This claim to effective control became the fundamental
issue in the imperial-colonial conflict. It was an issue on which
neither side showed the slightest disposition to compromise.

The British could not accept the American understanding of the
status quo as the unquestionable mark of legitimate imperial action.
They refused to acknowledge that previous violations of the law
had established a precedent limiting the powers of the Parliament
of Great Britain. Nor could they acquiesce in an understanding of
the status quo that forbade change detrimental to colonial interests,
especially when such change was necessary—as the British believed it was—in order to maintain the larger integrity of the mercantile system. The evasions of the mercantile system which the
colonists considered to be *the* status quo were considered by the
British to be "contrary to the fundamental Principle of Colonization, to every Maxim of Policy, and to the express provision of the
law."[63] Acceptance of the colonial position would have meant not
the reform, but the end, of empire.

To those who worried that the great increase of wealth, population and territory in the colonies might lead them to "break off
their Connections with Great Britain," Whately insisted that the
"Connection is actually broken already, wherever the Acts of Navigation are disregarded; and for so much of their Trade as is thereby
diverted from its proper Channel, they are no longer British colonies, but Colonies of the Countries they trade to."[64] From this
vantage point, the complaints of the colonists were profoundly
unsettling. The British could have responded to them only by
conceding in effect the claim to control that formed the basis of
the mercantile system. The abandonment of the measures designed
to insure more effective observance of the laws of trade would have
been tantamount to an admission that these laws could not be
enforced at all and that their observance depended entirely upon
the willingness of the colonies to comply with them. The objectives

---

[63] Whately, *Considerations*, p. 65.
[64] *Regulations*, p. 92. Cf. Charles Jenkinson to R. Walters, January 18, 1765, *The Jenkinson
Papers, 1760–1766*, ed. Ninetta S. Jucker (London, 1949), pp. 347–48.

partially sought through the 1764 Sugar Act could have been given up only by acknowledging that the metropolis was no longer able to direct the trade of the colonies when such direction did not correspond with colonial interests.

SEVEN

Internal Autonomy

[I]

I n dealing with the problems of imperial defense and trade, the British laid bare the issue that almost at once became the heart of the American crisis: the internal autonomy of the colonies. The folly of having done so has been noted by historians from that day to the present. "Happy would it have been had the question never been agitated," David Ramsey wrote in the years immediately following the war of independence. "An original genius, unfettered with precedents, and exalted with just ideas of the rights of human nature, and the obligations of universal benevolence, might have struck out a middle line which would have secured as much liberty to the Colonies, and as great a degree of supremacy to the Parent state, as their common good required. But the helm of Great Britain was not in such hands."[1] The metropolis was not content to leave Pandora's box unopened. "Not for the first time," a recent account reads, "the British could not leave well alone."[2] With the advent of the Bute ministry, another historian declares, Britain was now led by men whose "ignorance and inexperience led them to adopt measures which Newcastle [and Pitt] presumably would have avoided."[3] Determined to rationalize and make explicit a relationship that could be maintained only by shielding it from too close a scrutiny, the Bute and Grenville governments instead pursued a course that revealed the widely different—indeed, irreconcilable—views the parties entertained of the relationship.

This criticism betrays a retrospective wisdom that has the modest advantage of knowing what resulted from having illuminated too brightly the issue of internal autonomy. Even so, it is partially

---

[1] *The History of the American Revolution*, 2 vols. (London, 1793), 1:54–55.
[2] Eric Robson, *The American Revolution in its Political and Military Aspects, 1763–1783* (New York, 1966), p. 14.
[3] Bernhard Knollenberg, *Origin of the American Revolution, 1759–1766*, p. 31.

misleading in its suggestion that the British were determined to clarify what prudence enjoined to obscure. What imperial authorities were clearly determined upon was to shore up a system of defense and trade that seemed to them seriously defective. The purpose of raising a colonial revenue to help defray the costs of imperial defense, and of adjusting the laws of trade, were not informed by the desire to assert Parliament's supremacy. Certainly, this was not their primary intent. Instead, it was mainly in order to secure these purposes that the British were driven to insist upon colonial acknowledgment of Parliament's supremacy. This insistence did not precede, but followed, the American challenge to parliamentary authority.

The view that the metropolis should have avoided any course of action that touched upon the vital nerve of the imperial relationship is itself indicative of the uncertainty marking the relationship. Whether it was open to British ministries to have left well alone is a critical question. But even if we assume that Whitehall might have done so, the imprudence of pursuing the course it did follow was not in tampering with a constitutional status quo that was clear and acceptable to the parties involved. On the contrary, the persuasiveness of this view rests on the assumption that the status quo was unclear, that the parties had come to entertain very different notions of it, and that, in these circumstances, wisdom dictated a policy of avoiding any measures that would awaken the parties to their as yet not openly articulated, though profound, differences.[4]

These differences were far from novel. By the early 1760s they

---

[4] At the time, many on both sides did not appreciate the course of action wisdom dictated, though they clearly appreciated the unsettled character of the relationship. Two expressions of this appreciation are worth recalling. In his *Administration of the Colonies*, 2d ed. (London, 1765), p. 42, Thomas Pownall urged that the determination be made "whether in fact or deed, the people of the colonies, having every right to the full power of government and to *a whole legislative power*, are under this claim entitled, in the powers of legislature and the administration of government, to use and exercise in conformity to the laws of Great Britain, the same full, free, independent, unrestrained power and legislative will . . . as the government and legislature of Great Britain holds by its constitution and under the great charter." Pownall had been governor of Massachusetts and his knowledge of the colonial problem was considerable. Yet he expressed genuine uncertainty over the vital issue dealt with in these pages. In the same year that the first edition of *The Administration of the Colonies* appeared (1764) the Virginia Committee of Correspondence wrote the following to its London agent: "It may, perhaps, be thought presumptuous in us to attempt or even to desire any Thing which may look like a restraint upon the controlling Power of Parliament; we only wish that our just Liberties and Privileges as free born British Subjects were once properly defined"; quoted in George L. Beer, *British Colonial Policy, 1754–1765*, p. 308. Within a year the Burgesses were in much less doubt about the definition of their liberties and privileges in relation to Parliament; but this new-found certainty came only with the outbreak of the Stamp Act crisis.

had characterized the imperial-colonial relationship for nearly a century. Ranging across the broad spectrum of this relationship, their center of gravity was to be found in the disparity of views over the origin and nature of the provincial assembly. In his study of the British colonial system before 1783, Leonard W. Labaree summarized the difference in this manner:

The colonists felt that, as Englishmen, they had a right to share in making laws and laying taxes through agents of their own election. They believed that the summoning of an assembly by a royal governor in accordance with his commission and instructions was nothing but the recognition of this right and that this right could not be denied them. Therefore, the assembly, though called into being by a royal act, was just as fundamental and essential a part of the provincial constitution as the King's own representatives. Its position, they thought, should be equally independent and assured. But the ministers and agents of the crown saw the matter in a different light. They generally admitted the right of all Englishmen to a share, actual or theoretical, in legislation and taxation. But they would not concede that the only means to accomplish that end was a local assembly exercising powers equivalent to those of parliament. In their opinion, parliament itself might pass laws for or impose taxes upon the colonies, as it actually did after 1763. Or a local elective body similar to an English municipal council might serve the purpose. In any case, the actual creation of an assembly was an act of royal grace and favor. The legislature so established could have no power greater than was provided in the commission and instructions upon which it was founded. Therefore the British officials vigorously opposed the tendency of the assemblies to exercise freedom of action equal to that of parliament. These views were never reconciled in the period before the American Revolution.[5]

The colonial position was supported by the uniform practice of eighteenth-century British governments of denying royal governors the sole authority to legislate for a province that was settled by a substantial number of English subjects. In all such provinces, an elective assembly formed an integral part of the legislative process. This practice supported the colonial claim that provincial assemblies existed as a matter of right, independent of "royal grace and favor." Crown officials countered the colonial position by contending that the assembly was the creation of prerogative, that its functioning depended entirely upon the King or his governor, and that such legislative power as had been given by virtue of "royal grace

[5] *Royal Government in America: A Study of the British Colonial System Before 1783* (New Haven, 1930), pp. 174–75.

and favor" could be limited or, for that matter, taken away by the giver.

Thus, the very basis of the provincial assembly remained a matter attended by controversy and uncertainty. The colonial position, carried to its logical conclusion, implied that the scope of legislative action to which the assemblies might lay legitimate claim could be limited only by those powers expressly reserved to the King or his governor. Laws passed by colonial legislatures could be vetoed by the governor or, even though approved by him, subsequently disallowed by the Privy Council. Disallowance, moreover, need not be exercised upon reception of the legislation in England. A delay of several years in disallowing acts might be resorted to. Pending disallowance, the imperial government might require that certain types of bills contain a suspending clause, which had the effect of postponing their operation until royal consent was given in council. But these powers of veto, disallowance, and suspension—powers that found no parallel in the case of the Parliament at Westminster—did not prevent the colonists from considering their elected assemblies as founded on essentially the same basis as the imperial Parliament and as possessing similar powers in matters of internal governance.[6]

Given the broad and persisting disparity of view over the nature and powers of the provincial assembly, struggle between royal officials and colonial lower houses was inevitable. It proved to be very much a one-sided conflict. In imperial design, the governor was intended to be the undisputed master of his colonial house, with the assembly relegated to a distinctly subordinate and passive role. In practice, it was the assembly that almost everywhere emerged in the eighteenth century as master of the province, and the governor who was increasingly forced to accept a subordinate and passive role. The period from the end of the seventeenth century to the years immediately following the Seven Years' War is marked

---

[6] The standard works on the governance of the British colonies are Labaree's monograph (ibid.); *Royal Instructions to British Colonial Governors, 1670–1776*, ed. Leonard W. Labaree (New York, 1935); and A. Berriedale Keith, *Constitutional History of the First British Empire* (Oxford, 1930). The rise of the colonial assemblies is dealt with by Jack P. Greene in *The Quest For Power: The Lower Houses of Assembly in the Southern Royal Colonies, 1689–1776* (New York, 1963); colonial administration in the age of Newcastle is examined by James Henretta in *"Salutary Neglect."* Finally, Bernard Bailyn has set the problems of royal government in America within the broad framework of colonial politics in his remarkable essay, *The Origins of American Politics*.

throughout by the rise in significance of the lower houses of assembly and a corresponding decline in the position of the governors (and councils). By the 1760s the provincial assemblies had become the effective centers of political life in the colonies. In contrast, the position of the governors had increasingly taken on the appearance of a shadow devoid of any real substance.

[II]

This development, one momentous in its significance for the course of the conflict that eventuated in war between the metropolis and its American colonies, must in part be traced to forces that were largely beyond the control of any imperial policy, however wise and resolute. The astonishingly rapid growth in population and wealth of the continental colonies insured that the power of the Americans would steadily improve relative to Great Britain and that, in all likelihood, with this ever more favorable power position would go an ever greater assertiveness. Even had the metropolis desired to place limits on colonial growth out of apprehension over the consequences to which it might one day lead, there was no apparent way by which this could be done. If the drive for an ever greater autonomy, one which expectedly found its principal expression in the provincial assemblies, were to be contained, it would have to be sought by other means; but these other means were either rejected or pursued half-heartedly and too late.

The emergence of colonial elites went hand in hand with the almost meteoric development in population and wealth. What was the metropolis to do with these emergent elites? How was it to channel their natural aspirations to an authority and status commensurate to their growing economic and social power? Might the metropolis have turned aside the energies of the colonial elites to its own purposes, had it made the attempt at an early date? Imperial officialdom seems never to have seriously asked itself these questions, let alone to have sought to work out a strategy that might have responded effectively to the problem. Admittedly, the prospects of success for such a strategy were never more than marginal. Only two paths lay open to the British. They could have attempted to draw the colonial elites into the political center of the empire, a step that presupposed, at the very least, colonial representation in Parliament. The second alternative required that an attempt be made to satisfy the energy and ambition of emergent elites through such prizes as the governor had at his disposal.

Neither strategy promised much success. In urging that the colonies be represented in Parliament, Adam Smith argued that in taking this step "a new method of acquiring importance, a new and more dazzling object of ambition would be presented to the leading men of each colony. Instead of piddling for the little prizes which are to be found in . . . the paltry raffle of colony faction . . . they might then hope, from the presumption which men naturally have in their own ability and good fortune, to draw some of the great prizes which sometimes come from the wheel of the great state lottery of British politicks." When Smith made his argument (1776) events had already transformed the little prizes to be won in the paltry raffle of colony faction into something considerably greater, as he was ruefully to acknowledge. "From shopkeepers, tradesmen, and attornies," he noted, "they are become statesmen and legislators, and are employed in contriving a new form of government for an extensive empire, which, they flatter themselves, will become, and which, indeed, seems very likely to become, one of the greatest and most formidable that ever was in the world."[7]

At no time was either side prepared seriously to consider, let alone to accept, colonial representation in Parliament. Particularly on the American side, it appeared unattractive from almost every vantage point. Quite apart from the impediments posed by distance and time, representation in Parliament would have run counter to a growing sense of American separateness, the harbinger of a sense of national identity. At best, the Americans could expect to form no more than a small minority in Parliament, a position the disadvantages of which were not compensated for by the prospect that, in time, they might become a majority. Indeed, it was this very prospect that led even the great friends of America in Parliament to oppose the idea of colonial representation. Burke was content simply to dismiss the idea as "against nature." But Isaac Barré, in the course of debate over the repeal of the Stamp Act, rejected it as "dangerous, absurd, and impracticable. They will grow more numerous than we are, and then how inconvenient and dangerous would it be to have representatives of 7 millions there

[7] *An Inquiry into the Nature and Causes of the Wealth of Nations*, pp. 587–88.

meet the representatives of 7 millions here."[8] Nor would colonial representation have resolved the issues increasingly disputed between Great Britain and America. Participation in Parliament's proceedings would scarcely have removed colonial opposition to legislation considered injurious to American interests in matters of trade and commerce. The colonists would still have insisted upon controlling their internal affairs, leaving to Parliament the right to deal with external matters of general imperial concern. In this case, however, the same difficulties would have persisted.[9]

The other alternative presupposed that if British governments were prepared to leave patronage entirely in the hands of the governors, they might have used it successfully to secure the support and allegiance of colonial elites—or, at any rate, a substantial portion of these elites—and thereby establish, both within and without the provincial assemblies, a favorable balance of power. Quite apart from the persistent indisposition of the metropolis to pursue a strategy of co-option, however, it is very doubtful that the requisite conditions obtained in the colonies for its success. Possessed of a developed sense of separateness from the mother country, markedly parochial in outlook, and increasingly sensitive of their importance to the metropolis, these elites were scarcely the likely subjects of a strategy of co-option that would, after all, still have left them in a subordinate status.[10]

[III]

The rise to preeminence of the provincial assembly, then, and the portentous consequences that would attend this rise, may have been impossible to prevent even by an imperial officialdom acutely conscious of its interest in holding the colonies to a subordinate status for as long a period as possible. At the same time, until the Grenville reforms during the early 1760s, successive governments in London made no small contribution to developments that would in the end lead to the demise of the First British Empire. In almost

[8] Ryder Diaries, p. 274.
[9] These and other points were made by Josiah Tucker in his critique of proposals for American representation, *The True Interest of Great Britain Set Forth in Regard to the Colonies* (Gloucester, 1774), Tract 4, pp. 164–88.
[10] See Bailyn, *Origins of American Politics*, pp. 72–105.

every possible way, imperial policy contributed to the increasing debility of royal government in America. When the crisis attending the attempt to tax the colonists broke upon a stunned metropolis, the extent to which imperial power had eroded in America was laid bare with sudden brutality. For those who wanted to see, it was apparent that a policy of "salutary neglect," in Burke's phrase, had promoted the requisite conditions, not merely for an extraordinary degree of local self-government, but for an autonomy almost akin to independence.

Such a result did not come through formal concessions on the part of the metropolis. With rare exception, British governments had not made formal concessions of power to the colonies. Quite the contrary, from the Navigation Act of 1696 to the Declaratory Act of 1766, the assertion of imperial supremacy had been reaffirmed on a number of occasions and had gone uncontested by the colonies. Still, powers that in form were always very considerable, and in substance were not negligible even at a relatively late date, underwent progressive debilitation throughout the eighteenth century. It remains an open question whether they did so for the most part because the metropolis insistently pursued a system of "government by instruction," which in its rigidity was incapable of adjusting to a rapidly changing colonial reality,[11] or rather because from the outset the system was too permissive in practice, however strict it may have appeared in theory. The weight of historical opinion favors the first explanation, which has been regularly supplemented by an emphasis on the inventiveness, persistence, and determination that characterized the efforts of provincial assemblies in wresting power from governors and crown officials.

There is an apparent plausibility to the prevailing view. In the century preceding the American Revolution, the system of imperial governance underwent very little formal alteration. In the governors' commissions and instuctions for the royal provinces such changes as were made dealt with matters of no more than peripheral significance. Not only did the system of "government by instruction" fail to respond to the great changes occurring in the colonies during this period; in the uniformity of the instructions given to governors there was also a persistent failure to appreciate the widely varying conditions in which royal government in the colonies had to be

[11] As Labaree, *Royal Government*, pp. 420–48, strongly insists.

conducted. "The officials in Whitehall who drafted these documents," Labaree has written, "were as unmoved by the changes in America as they would have been if these changes had taken place on another planet. Inevitably, therefore, the system of government by instruction proved more and more unworkable the longer it was in force."[12] Until it was too late, this argument runs, authorities in London could find no reason to change a system that events had long overtaken. Nor would they permit a governor the kind of discretion in applying his instructions that circumstances might require. Obligated to keep his instructions confidential, the governor was inhibited from making such effort as might have resulted in the sharing of responsibility for observing the instructions with the provincial assembly and council. Not surprisingly, the insistence upon the sole responsibility of the governor contributed in significant measure to the colonial view that the instructions bound the governor but could not be considered as binding upon the assembly. Even had the instructions not betrayed an evident partiality to British over colonial interests, their secretive and inflexible character insured that what the imperial government considered to be the foundation of its authority in the colonies and the basic framework of the colonial constitution would fail to secure the loyalty of those whose behavior they were designed to regulate. It is primarily for these reasons that the standard work on royal government in America concluded, "Responsibility for the catastrophe that followed must rest primarily upon the shoulders of those who prepared the commissions and instructions and who failed to see that the system of 'government by instruction' was no longer suitable as the foundation of the colonial constitution. For they thought only in terms of the past and of government 'by royal grace and favor,' ignoring the new principle of government 'by the consent of the governed.' "[13]

The difficulty with this view lies not in what it has to say about the formal system of "government by instruction" but in the judgment it draws about the significance of this system in accounting for the steady decline of imperial authority. There is no persuasive reason to assume that a more flexible and liberal system of royal government would have prevented the same erosion of British

[12] Ibid., p. 447.
[13] Ibid., p. 448.

power in the colonies. Even to put the matter in this way is misleading, since it appears to accept the notion that British rule in America was both in theory and in practice inflexible and illiberal. Such was not the case, however, as almost all accounts of this rule—including the aforementioned account—attest. The inflexibility and illiberality of the British colonial system was very largely a matter of form, not of substance, else it would be impossible to account for the extraordinary degree of autonomy the colonies enjoyed in the conduct of their internal affairs. What is striking about royal government in America from the beginning to the end is not its inflexibility but its permissiveness. The phrase—now almost hackneyed—that the freest of peoples were the first to rebel remains acutely expressive of the American colonial experience.

The growth of self-government in the continental colonies was not marked by a series of sanguinary struggles with the metropolis. Until the final crisis of 1774–75, the American experience consisted of a succession of bloodless victories won against an imperial power that regularly submitted in the end to colonial demands for an ever greater autonomy. It is true that such submission normally remained informal, the metropolis conceding in fact what it refused to concede as a matter of right. Even when concessions by the metropolis were made, or appeared to have been made, as a matter of right, they were often attended by persisting disagreement between crown officials and colonists over the consequences that presumably followed from them. The development of colonial autonomy was therefore marked throughout by controversy and uncertainty.

These characteristics are everywhere apparent in the crucial relationship between the governor and the provincial assembly. According to imperial design, it was the governors who were to exercise the initiative in making laws for the colonies, an initiative expressly conferred upon them by their commission from the King. The assembly, having no inherent right to legislate, was relegated to the role of advice and consent. In practice, and virtually from the outset, the initiative in legislation gravitated to the assembly, with the governor's role limited to that of consenting to bills. The metropolis had sought to change this practice in the latter part of the seventeenth century and to insure that the legislative initiative would rest with the governor. The attempt failed, however, and from the 1680s the assembly's power and, indeed, right to initiate legislation went unchallenged, while the governor's role became limited to that of assenting to bills. He might still refuse to give his assent. He might threaten to prorogue or dissolve the assembly if it persisted in a course of action he opposed. The price of exercising these powers, however, could prove to be quite high. Even if and when exercised, the governor's powers could not substantially alter the considerable advantages accruing to the assembly from its power to initiate bills, advantages for which the governor could never find adequate compensation.

Nowhere was this initiative of the assembly exercised with more significant effect than in matters of finance. By the eighteenth century, the accepted view of the crown's law officers had become that in the absence of taxation by Parliament a colony of English subjects could be taxed only by an assembly of local representatives. Until the 1760s, insignificant exceptions apart, Parliament refrained from attempting to tax the colonies. In consequence, the power of taxation, as well as of appropriation, was left almost entirely to the provincial assemblies.

Why royal authorities permitted this development, which rendered imperial government crucially dependent in each province upon the local legislature, must remain one of the many mysteries attending the governance of the First British Empire. It was not as though metropolitan officials were blind to the effects of leaving so potent an instrument in the control of provincial assemblies. Sensitive to the threat held out to prerogative by colonial control of finance, they sought to counter it by some arrangement that would provide support for royal government while escaping control by the assembly. The efforts resembled the proverbial attempt to square the circle and were no more successful. This was particularly true of the scheme to obtain from the assemblies a permanent revenue to meet the needs of local government and to be left to the sole disposition of the King. The assemblies, predictably, had no intention of neutralizing their most potent instrument of power by granting a permanent revenue to the crown.

The provincial lower houses thus sought to make the most of their control over finance. They did so with devastating effect on the power and independence of the governor. Every device possible was employed to cut down the scope of prerogative and establish the supremacy of the assembly. Whereas royal authorities had pressed for permanent grants of revenue, the assemblies insisted upon passing revenue bills for brief periods. Even then, the appropriations were made so specific as to leave little, if any, discretion in their expenditure. Where these controls proved insufficient, they were complemented by assembly control of the appointment of the treasurer and by the power to withhold the payment of monies not directly authorized by the assembly. Finally, in a number of colonies the salaries of the governor and other royal officials were dependent upon annual appropriations of the lower house.

In certain respects, the metropolis appeared almost to cooperate in creating nemesis. It did so, for example, in insisting that the assemblies model themselves after, as well as pattern their procedures on, the House of Commons. Having done so, there remained for the provincial legislatures to take what appeared to them as the next logical step: to interpret their powers in internal affairs as substantially comparable to those of the House of Commons. The implications of this view could scarcely be reconciled with the British position that the assembly was the creation of prerogative and that it remained dependent on royal grace and favor. In their contest with royal authority, the assemblies saw themselves as fighting the same battle against prerogative that the House of Commons had fought and for the same purpose: to secure for the conduct of their internal affairs those "ancient rights and privileges" enjoyed by Westminster. But the achievement of these rights and privileges, which the colonists considered themselves entitled to as Englishmen, could have no other result than to pose a continual challenge to British authority, since until the 1760s this authority had been exercised almost entirely through the King's prerogative. Until that time, the assemblies had never overtly challenged the authority of Parliament, by denying that body's legislative competence over the colonies, since there had been no real need to do so. Only when it became apparent that government by instruction was insufficient to contain the claims to autonomy of the assemblies, and that such claims threatened the larger purposes of imperial rule, did British governments call upon Parliament to interfere directly in colonial affairs. By this time, however, it was very late.

British policy not only encouraged the provincial assemblies to assume that in respect of their internal affairs they were entitled to the rights and privileges of the House of Commons; more important, it insured that the balance of power between assembly and governor would increasingly favor the former by denying the latter such instruments as might better have sustained his position. Of these instruments, patronage was by far the most critical. Even with an abundance of patronage, it is very doubtful that a governor could have maintained an independent, let alone a favorable, position in relation to the assembly since the other conditions that made possible the success of the mixed and balanced constitution in Great Britain were largely absent in the colonies. Without substantial patronage, however, it was virtually certain that a governor could not hope to forge an effective administration and compete on anything near equal terms with the assembly. The provincial assemblies were not slow in recognizing this and as their power grew, particularly over finance, so did their measures to restrict and to cut away the governor's patronage. Imposing residence requirements, restricting the periods of tenure, withholding salaries or granting them on an annual basis, and converting many appointive into elective offices were among the more effective devices. For these measures, the metropolis, with its ever permissive policy, could be held only indirectly responsible. The same cannot be said of the approval by crown officials in London of the assembly's right to select the provincial treasurer, a post that controlled public expenditures and, for that reason alone, carried with it immense political influence. Nor, for that matter, did British governments refrain from depriving governors of such patronage as the lower houses of assembly were unable to get. From a very early date, ministries in London made use of a substantial number of colonial posts to strengthen their political base at home, though in doing so they weakened that of the governor. This practice continued through the eighteenth century, reaching its high point, ironically, under the earl of Halifax, the president of the Board of Trade from 1748 to 1761 and the colonial official most intent during these critical years on reasserting a more centralized and effective control over the colonies.

These and yet other characteristics of royal government in America do not so much bear out the view of an imperial system that foundered because of its excessive rigidity as they do of a system that paved the way for its demise through an extraordinary permissiveness. In clinging to formal powers that remained very considerable, the metropolis did little to assuage the ingrained fears and suspicions of the colonists that one day these powers might be employed to arbitrary ends. Yet in the surrender of substantive controls to the lower houses of assembly, crown officials fed an appetite that was quite insatiable. Resistant to change in matters of form, imperial authorities were remarkably pliant in matters of substance. The combination resulted in the worst of all possible worlds for the metropolis.[14]

[IV]

The dilemma increasingly confronting imperial authorities committed to rule with the consent of the governed, but nevertheless committed to rule, did not go unnoticed until the years of crisis. The record from the early 1700s is replete with warnings from crown officials in the colonies of the consequences to which the above developments might one day lead if they were not checked. Until the 1740s the warnings met with little response at higher levels. Instead, a remarkable passivity reigned, a passivity that reflected the casual way in which colonial affairs had long been dealt with by London. It was only in the years preceding the outbreak of the Great War for the Empire that metropolitan officials began to register serious concern over trends in the colonies. Although slow in coming, by the late 1740s and early 1750s growing dissatisfaction had become apparent in Whitehall.

This dissatisfaction did not have preordained results. It might have taken any number of expressions and, given the British penchant for drift in colonial affairs, might well have resulted in no

---

[14] Thomas Barrow, *Trade and Empire*, pp. 106–33, gives an illuminating picture of the "inefficiency in departmental organization, indifference to reform, and the misuse of the power of patronage" that characterized the administration of the old colonial system in the four decades preceding the outbreak of the crisis in the 1760s. " 'Salutary neglect,' " he writes, "was not an accident but a precise policy." Aimed at keeping the colonies content, the policy of Walpole and his successors required a policy of appeasement, the guiding principle of which was to let well enough alone. The result of this policy, as Barrow persuasively shows, was the steady erosion of royal authority in the colonies. "It should have been no surprise to anyone that eventually it would be not just the local royal representatives but the home authorities themselves whom the colonists would 'look upon . . . with Disdain and bid . . . Defiance' "; p. 133. The colonial policy of Walpole and his successors, so often praised by historians for its restraint and prudence, set the stage for the disaster that followed.

serious attempts to alter imperial policy at all. [15] The war, however, proved to be a forcing ground. On more than one occasion in the past, the provincial assemblies had taken advantage of the pressures exerted by war on the metropolis to exact concessions from royal authority. In the course of the Seven Years' War they did so again and with marked success. The imperial government, engaged in a global conflict with its great rival, considered itself in no position to contest colonial claims, let alone to force the colonies on a course they were evidently unwilling to follow. Accordingly, it bent every effort, particularly under Pitt, to placate the colonies while seeking their cooperation through measures that would avoid, so far as possible, charges of dictation and infringement upon cherished colonial "rights." Colonial governments—in effect, the assem-

---

[15] The position taken in the text is at variance with that taken by Jack P. Greene in his valuable essay, " 'A Posture of Hostility.' " Greene argues that during the years 1748–56 there occurred an important redirection of British colonial policy, from one characterized by permissiveness to one intended to secure close control over the colonies; that the war momentarily interrupted this policy spearheaded by the energetic president of the Board of Trade, the earl of Halifax; and that, with the termination of the war, metropolitan officials, in effect, took up with even greater determination the policy of the prewar period. Greene acknowledges that the efforts of the years 1748–56 had no considerable results, though why this was so if imperial officialdom was determined to impose a much tighter regime on the colonies is not quite clear. Of course, the colonists opposed the board's efforts whenever and wherever possible. But this scarcely covers the ground. Of equal, if not greater, importance was—as Greene notes (p. 49)—the lack of ministerial support for the reforms pushed by the Board of Trade and the unwillingness of governments to call for significant parliamentary intervention in colonial affairs (p. 62). In view of this, however, one must treat with caution the assertion that "the efforts of Halifax and his colleagues between 1748 and 1756 clearly constituted a major transformation in metropolitan behavior towards the colonies" (pp. 65–66), for on Greene's own account not only was that policy "transformation" largely abortive but was so because it failed to secure real ministerial support. The transformation, then, did not really occur. Halifax's vision of a reformed and centralized empire remained just that—a vision—and this quite apart from the persisting doubt over just how sweeping that vision was.

What is of critical significance is Greene's assessment of the significance of this earlier failure to reform the empire. That significance must be found, he argues, not so much in its effects on the colonies but, instead, on the metropolis. "For this failure served both to intensify metropolitan fears that the colonies would sooner or later get completely out of hand and to increase—almost to the point of obsession—metropolitan determination to secure tighter control over the colonies" (p. 66). Thus, what is very nearly a straight line is drawn between the efforts of 1748–56 and the ostensibly "new" policy of the 1760s. It turns out that the new policy was not new at all but simply a renewal of earlier policy, though now pursued with far greater determination because of the initial failure and (a point we deal with elsewhere) because of the heightened confidence of the metropolis, in the wake of the war, that it was in a much better position to impose its will on the colonies.

In contrast, then, to the view taken in these pages, the "compulsion" behind the new policy of the 1760s does not stem primarily from the experience of the war and from the problems created by the conflict, problems British statesmen had somehow to resolve. It was rather the "posture of hostility" already well formed in the years preceding the war that led to the great confrontation.

blies—were left at liberty to decide the manner and extent of their participation in the war, and this quite apart from the interests that a particular colony might have at stake in the conflict.

Although the years of war were marked by further erosion of imperial authority in America, the significance of the conflict for the constitutional relationship between metropolis and colonies is not to be found in the opening up of new issues. The provincial assemblies did not lay claim to powers that they had not previously claimed. They did press, however, for the consolidation of positions that the imperial state had been reluctant to concede in the past and, aware of the exigent condition of the metropolis, they did so with considerable success. In this respect, the significance of the war must be found, on the one hand, in the momentum it gave to pre-existent colonial claims to autonomy and, on the other hand, in awakening the British as never before to the broad scope of these claims. In the course of the war, the colonists—principally through the provincial assemblies—elaborated their views on constitutional questions and did so in a remarkably thorough manner. Indeed, in the crisis brought on by the British measures of 1764–65, there was scarcely an issue touched upon that had not been raised during the war and scarcely a position taken by the colonists that had not been set out in the preceding decade.

[V]

Considerations of equity and expediency figured prominently in the colonial armory of arguments against the Stamp and Sugar acts. Nonetheless, the principal basis of the attack rested on constitutional grounds—whether these grounds were defined in terms of charter rights (applicable only to the few colonies possessing charters); or in terms of those rights and privileges to which Englishmen everywhere were entitled; or in terms of a higher law that the English constitution was found to incorporate; or, finally, in terms of what the colonists had come to see as their own constitutional orders, made up of local tradition, precedent, and statute and sanctioned by time and imperial passivity (such passivity being more often than not equated with imperial acceptance). In turn, the constitutional grounds might have reference either to the rights of individuals or to the rights (or powers) of political collectives.

For all practical purposes, the collective was virtually synonymous with the provincial assembly, since it was the assembly that represented the collective not only in the literal sense but also in the sense of forming the principal institutionalized manifestation of opposition to the metropolis.

It was in the assembly that opposition to imperial measures initially found effective expression and, for this reason alone, it was the assembly that took on the attributes of an embryonic government. This development perhaps explains the no little difficulty encountered in separating individual and collective rights in the colonial position. The assemblies were seen during this period, as they were seen in an earlier period, to be the protector of both individual liberties and collective autonomy. Indeed, the implicit, and even explicit, argument was that there could be no effective guarantee of individual rights without the effective guarantee of collective rights (or powers), that is, the rights of the provincial assemblies. The issue of taxation afforded the clearest, and most important, illustration of the argument. The right of individuals not to be deprived of their property without their consent could be adequately safeguarded only by the right (power) of the assembly alone to levy taxes. The dependence of individual rights on collective status meant that the central issue raised by the measures of the Grenville ministry concerned the role and power of the provincial assembly. This had always been the central issue in the imperial-colonial relationship. Before, the issue had been between assembly and governor; now it was between assembly and Parliament.

What then, was the constitutional position taken by the colonists in responding to the various parliamentary measures of 1764 and 1765? In essence, this response was that Parliament could not do what a governor could not do and for substantially the same reasons. The supremacy of Parliament both within the realm and over the colonies was not challenged. But that supremacy was not without limits and these limits, themselves an integral part of the British constitution, could not be transgressed. They were as valid for the King's subjects in the colonies as they were for his subjects at home. They defined the fundamental rights of Englishmen, rights that were inalienable and, as such, could not be abridged or destroyed by any means. This position was made apparent in the resistance of the colonists to the acts of Parliament extending Admiralty jurisdiction. The colonists had long contended that such jurisdiction had the effect of subverting their rights and liberties as Englishmen—above all, by depriving them of their right to trial by jury. That this extended jurisdiction was sanctioned by acts of Parliament did not in the least alter colonial opposition.

It was, of course, the Stamp Act that brought on the great crisis in the relationship between metropolis and colonies and, in so doing, laid bare as never before the American challenge to imperial supremacy. Here again, the first line of colonial defense centered on the rights of Englishmen, in this instance the right not to be taxed save by their own consent, whether given directly or through their chosen representatives. Unrepresented in Parliament and incapable of being represented because of their situation, they could not be taxed by Parliament but only by their local legislatures. The "freedom of a people, and the undoubted Right of Englishmen," the Declaration of the Stamp Act Congress read, made it essential "that no taxes be imposed on them, but with their own Consent, given personally, or by their Representatives."

Was the position taken with respect to the Stamp Act rooted simply in the special character of taxation, which presumably distinguished it from other forms of legislation? If taxes were, as the colonists contended, a "free gift of the people," and for this reason could be levied only by the people themselves or by those who directly represented the people, did this mean that the requirement of representation was less stringent, and perhaps even nonexistent, when applied to other forms of legislation affecting the internal governance of the colonies? Or did the rights of Englishmen also include a right to representation in matters that went considerably beyond taxation? The general issue implicit in these questions was by no means unfamiliar. It had been raised almost from the beginnings of colonial government. In an earlier period, it had been reflected in the running dispute over whether representative institutions, and the amplitude of legislative competence that was claimed to inhere in these institutions, existed by virtue of a right independent of, and free from infringement by, the prerogative. What the colonists had once claimed against prerogative they would now claim against Parliament, and this despite their acknowledgment of parliamentary supremacy. A right of representation did not exist by virtue of Parliament.

If this were so, if a right of representation existed independently of any outside authority, what followed from the right (the issue of taxation apart)? Was it not meaningless to assert the right unless it implied the general and exclusive competence to make such laws as were necessary for the internal governance of the colonies? Such was the conclusion drawn by the Virginia House of Burgesses in its 1764 petition to the King protesting the proposed stamp duties. Virginians, the petition read, had an "ancient and inestimable Right of being governed by such Laws respecting their internal Polity and Taxation as are derived from their own Consent."[16] The petition stopped short of expressly claiming an exclusive jurisdiction in matters of internal governance. It did not assert a right of being governed *only* by such laws respecting their internal polity as were derived from their own consent. There was no need, however, for the kind of explicitness the governor of Rhode Island voiced by the rhetorical question: "What have the King and Parliament to do with making a law or laws to govern us by, any more than the Mohawks have?"[17]

Apart from the fact—and, admittedly, it was all important—that parliamentary supremacy had now been squarely called into question, the American response to the measures of imperial reform taken in 1764 and 1765 represented continuity rather than change. The colonists had long asserted that the rights they exercised through their provincial assemblies did not depend upon the sufferance of others. Heretofore directed against prerogative, the claim was now directed against Parliament. Only the scope of the claim was left vague in the colonial response. In theory the colonists recognized that some questions were indeed of a general character and thus lay within the jurisdiction of Parliament. In practice the colonial legislatures never surrendered the right to determine which were the general—or external—questions and which the local—or internal—ones. This was the core of the colonial position. It could be accepted by the metropolis only by the concession—which must now be definitive, because made by Parliament—of imperial supremacy.

---

[16] William J. Von Schreeven and Robert L. Scribner, eds., *Revolutionary Virginia: The Road to Independence*, 6 vols. to date (Charlottesville, 1973–), 1:11.
[17] Quoted in Beer, *British Colonial Policy*, p. 310.

[VI]

Although the crisis that ensued upon imposition of the Stamp Act raised the most fundamental of constitutional issues, it was not these issues that were to claim the preponderant attention of Westminster and Whitehall. In the debate that attended passage of the Declaratory Act and repeal of the Stamp Act, considerations of policy—that is, of expedience, prudence, and equity—played much the more prominent role. This emphasis is not surprising. From the outset of the crisis to its apparent termination there was a virtual consensus in the British political establishment on the issue of right. The authority of Parliament to legislate on any and all matters affecting the colonies was thus taken for granted. In introducing the revenue measures of 1764 and 1765, Grenville had asserted that if any member of the Commons doubted the right of Parliament to tax North America he was ready to take the opinion of the House.[18] But Grenville's assertion had gone unchallenged.

It was only at a later date, in February 1766, after news of the bitter opposition of the colonists had reached the metropolis, that the constitutional issue was taken up and given serious consideration. Even then, the opponents of Parliament's right to tax the colonists—whether in the form of an external or an internal tax—comprised no more than a small minority. The government then in power, led by Lord Rockingham, did not take a position on constitutional principle that broke from the preceding government. Although intent on repealing the Stamp Act, the Rockingham ministry reaffirmed, through the Declaratory Act, the supremacy of Parliament, a supremacy that encompassed the right to lay an internal tax on the colonies. The ministry's attitude was succinctly summarized at the time by General Conway, the secretary of state for the Southern Department, who declared that he "never was nor ever shall be a friend to internal taxation in America." He did not deny the legal right, but he thought "in point of policy and justice this ought not to have been attempted."[19]

The very few who denied Parliament's right to tax the colonies did not deny the supremacy of Westminster in every other respect.

[18] Ryder Diaries (March 9, 1764), p. 235.
[19] Ryder Diaries (February 3, 1766), p. 261. Conway, though a member of the Rockingham ministry, was an admirer of Pitt.

Taxation apart, there was no one more emphatic than Pitt on Parliament's right to legislate on all other matters for the colonies. If the Americans were not content with repeal of the Stamp Act, if they otherwise challenged the supremacy of Parliament, Pitt pledged to teach them to submit and promised to "second any vigorous resolution and give his vote for employing the last ship and the last man in this country to force them to perfect obedience."[20] Events would prove that these were but empty words and that neither for Pitt nor for those—like the Rockinghamites—who opposed exercise of the right of taxation on grounds of policy would

[20] Ryder Diaries (February 21, 1766), p. 308. Pitt prefaced these words with this advice: "Throw the rod away and shame them to submission; if that will not be effectual, you must use the power of this country to force them to obedience. Give them satisfaction in one point in order to make your stand on better ground." Pitt's position on Parliament's right of taxation, as distinguished from the justice or expediency of taxing the colonies, remains a matter of some uncertainty and controversy. The principal difference is over whether his position disavowed the right of Parliament to raise a revenue in America by "internal" duties alone, or whether it also forbade fiscal purposes in parliamentary legislation affecting American external commerce. Edmund S. Morgan and Helen M. Morgan, *The Stamp Act Crisis*, pp. 273–75, take the view that Pitt denied Parliament's right in both instances. The Morgans rely primarily on Pitt's speech before the House on January 14, 1766, in which he replied to Grenville's complaint of not understanding the distinction Pitt had earlier drawn between taxation and legislation. (Pitt had declared that "taxation is no part of the governing or legislative power. The taxes are a voluntary gift and grant of the Commons alone.") In answer to Grenville's complaint of not understanding the difference between internal and external taxes, Pitt stated, "There is a plain distinction between taxes levied for the purposes of raising a revenue and duties imposed for the regulation of trade, for the accommodation of the subject; although, in the consequences, some revenue might incidentally arise from the latter." These statements are taken from the printed version of the debate in *PH*, 16:99–104.

   This account of the debate has been seriously questioned in recent years. P. D. G. Thomas, *British Politics and the Stamp Act Crisis*, pp. 171–73, assumes that Pitt understood the distinction between internal and external taxation, not, as the Morgans do, in terms of legislative intention, but in terms of the objects of taxation. Pitt, according to this view, did not challenge the constitutionality of revenue taxes on external commerce. The issue is also examined, and in considerable detail, by Ian R. Christie, "William Pitt and American Taxation, 1766: A Problem of Parliamentary Reporting," *Studies in Burke and his Time* 17 (1976):167–79, who reaches substantially the same conclusions as Thomas, while placing emphasis on Pitt's political motives at the time: "Playing the great game for office and power [which were to fall into his hands within the next few months], intent on downing all rivals, anxious on the one hand to rub Grenville's nose in the mud and on the other to demonstrate the weakness of the Rockingham ministry, he had been swept into indiscretions by the flights of his own rhetoric and the heat of impromptu argument" (p. 179). Both Thomas and Christie rely partly on the summary made of the January 14 debate by James West, former Treasury secretary to Newcastle; and both also note the support given this depiction of Pitt's position by others attending the debate (including Edmund Burke, Benjamin Franklin, Charles Garth, and Horace Walpole). This evidence, unfortunately, is less conclusive than it may appear, since these sources show only that Pitt condemned internal taxation as unconstitutional but do not show the precise manner in which the Great Commoner distinguished between internal and external taxation. Nor do they show that Pitt positively supported the constitutionality of revenue taxes on external commerce in debate. Far more persuasive evidence of the view that Pitt did not challenge the constitutionality of revenue

the appropriate time ever come when they were prepared to support parliamentary supremacy through force of arms. Still, these considerations do not detract from the very general affirmation of imperial supremacy at the time of the Stamp Act crisis by opponents of Parliament's right to tax America. The most impassioned among them, Lord Camden, left no doubt on this point. Though he promised to maintain to his "last hour" that "taxation and representation are inseparable," that "this position is founded on the laws of nature," and that whoever attempts to take what is a man's own without his consent "attempts an injury" and, if successful, "commits a robbery," Camden did not believe he was betraying the principle of parliamentary supremacy.[21] Quite the contrary, it was those who would assert a power that Parliament did not have who were subverting the rights of Parliament and the tenets of the British constitution. In opposing the Declaratory Act, which opened the way for repeal of the Stamp Act by asserting Parliament's authority over the colonies "in all cases whatsoever," Camden and Pitt were simply expressing their opposition to the implicit claim of a right to tax America and not to the pretention in all other respects of supremacy over the colonies.[22]

The doctrine on which nearly all in the metropolis agreed did not go unexamined in the crisis brought on by the Stamp Act. The most lucid statement of Parliament's right to tax the colonies—and, beyond this, of Parliament's supremacy generally—was given by Lord Chief Justice Mansfield. It rested on two principles:

---

taxes on external commerce is provided by the record of the Chatham ministry. This ministry not only passed the Townshend Revenue Act, but in parliamentary debate both Townshend and Grenville made assertions as to the distinction between internal and external taxation and the character of Pitt's position on this question which, as Christie notes, "would have been meaningless had not all or virtually all members of the Commons understood" that Chatham approved of revenue taxes on external commerce but thought unconstitutional revenue taxes on "internal" objects, like stamps. There nevertheless remains the strong possibility that Pitt did not fully know his own mind on this difficult question and that in the heat of debate he made assertions, particularly with respect to the relationship between representation and taxation, that were inconsistent with his conception of the extent of parliamentary power.

[21] *PH*, 16:178.

[22] The text of the Declaratory Act read: "That the King's Majesty, by and with the advice and consent of the Lords spiritual and temporal and Commons of Great Britain in parliament assembled, had, hath, and of right ought to have, full power and authority to make laws and statutes, of sufficient force and validity to bind the colonies and people of America, subjects of the crown of Great Britain, in all cases whatsoever."

1st, That the British legislature, as to the power of making laws, represents the whole British empire, and has authority to bind every part and every subject without the least distinction, whether such subjects have a right to vote or not, or whether the law binds places within the realm or without.

2nd, That the colonists, by the condition on which they migrated, settled, and now exist, are more emphatically subjects of Great Britain than those within the realm; and that the British legislature have in every instance exercised their right of legislation over them without any dispute or question till the 14th of January last.[23]

Mansfield's argument begins with the assertion—taken as a self-evident truth—"that in every government the legislative power must be lodged somewhere, and the executive must likewise be lodged somewhere. In Great Britain the legislative is in parliament, the executive in the crown." Were there any inherent limits to Parliament's legislative authority? Mansfield did not take up the question. Instead, he addressed the issue of whether Parliament may take a man's property without compensation and without his consent, given directly or through chosen representatives. The colonists had responded with an emphatic negative to both and their case had been put with considerable force in the House of Lords by Camden. Mansfield rejected the case *in toto*. Against Camden's assertion that Parliament cannot "take away any man's private property without making him a compensation," Mansfield replied that "it frequently takes private property without making what the owner thinks a compensation." In response to Camden's claim that private property can be taken only through consent, whether given directly or by chosen representatives, Mansfield argued that consent was a term with no precise meaning; acts of the legislature had been resisted in the past, yet by their enforcement they had eventually been accepted.[24]

Mansfield did not simply dismiss the issue of representation, but he did come very close to equating representation with effective authority. The British legislature represents the whole British empire, he contended, because it has the authority to bind every part and every subject, without the least distinction. Does it follow that authority, where effectively exercised, is of necessity also representative? Mansfield would not say so. He was content with as-

[23] *PH*, 16:173.
[24] Ibid., pp. 173–74.

serting that representation first arose by favor of the crown, that it had never been completed, and that the notion "that every subject must be represented by deputy, if he does not vote in parliament himself, is merely ideal." The established rule of construction, heretofore not disputed by the colonists, that no parts without the realm were bound by an act of Parliament unless so stipulated in the act, was meaningless if not based on a right of Parliament to bind all parts of the empire by its laws. This right, or authority, was further confirmed by past practice, and Mansfield invoked a number of instances—almost all of which were disputed by Camden—to show that territories had been subject to Parliament's laws, taxation included, without being either united or, even though part of the realm, represented.[25]

In the case of the colonists, Mansfield argued, "they migrated with leave as colonies, and therefore from the very meaning of the word were, are, and must be subjects, and owe allegiance and subjection to the mother country. This allegiance was not affected by the type of colony, that is, whether it was royal, proprietary, or chartered." With respect to charter governments, however, their dependence was particularly clear, for they had no standing materially different from the great corporations. The charter of Massachusetts, Mansfield noted, had been revoked in 1684. Yet it was now contended that a colonial legislature "can exist with a sole power of laying taxes, which legislature may be destroyed here by a process in the courts of Chancery or Kingsbench." Finally, Mansfield found nothing in the history of colonial response to parliamentary acts that disputed the unqualified authority of Parliament to legislate for the colonies until the passage of the Stamp Act. The subjection of the colonies to England did not exclude taxation. Thus, "there are many statutes laying taxes in America; I know no difference between laying internal and external taxes; but if such difference should be taken, are not the acts giving duties, customs, and erecting a post office, to be considered as laying an internal Tax."[26]

---

[25] Ibid.

[26] Ibid., pp. 175–76. Mansfield need not have offered these examples in support of his case. On strict constitutional grounds they added little to his argument that Parliament possessed the power to impose taxation on the colonies, and from a broader perspective they served only to point out that by practice and tradition Parliament usually did not tax where the subjects of taxation were not represented.

Mansfield's position was singularly austere. Although even he had made a bow to the principle of representation, it had been a very curt gesture. Not so with the other champions of Parliament's unqualified supremacy. Almost all affirmed that the right of Parliament to tax the colonies depended upon the representative character of that body. Grenville was as clear and emphatic on this as any. In rejecting the need for actual representation, he did not deny the principle of representation itself as applied to the colonies. Later in the decade, he even considered a plan to give the colonies actual representation at Westminster. Nor did he restrict the need of representation to taxation. "The objection of the colonies," he declared during the debate over repeal of the Stamp Act," is from the general right of mankind not to be taxed but by their representatives. This goes to all laws in general. The Parliament of Great Britain virtually represents the whole Kingdom. . . . Not a twentieth part of the people are actually represented."[27] What is significant in this statement, as in the many similar statements made in Parliament at the time, is not so much the form of representation the colonists were alleged to possess, which was considered by Grenville and others as satisfactory, if not ideal, but the admission that the authority of Parliament derived from its representative character. However defective and inadequate the doctrine of virtual representation may have been considered, the point remains that it clearly acknowledged the legitimacy of the requirement for some kind of representation to give the law its authority.[28] If so, there was no apparent reason for applying this requirement only to taxation, to the property of the subject, and not to his life and liberty.[29]

The colonists, of course, vehemently rejected the form of representation put forward by Grenville. At the same time, they rejected just as vehemently proposals for actual representation in Parliament. Whereas actual representation was considered alto-

---

[27] Ryder Diaries, p. 254.
[28] Cf. J. R. Pole, *Political Representation in England and the Origins of the American Republic* (New York, 1966), p. 339.
[29] The point was made on several occasions in parliamentary debate, even by those who otherwise opposed exercise of the right. Thus, Richard Hussey declared that he could "find no distinction between taxation and any other law. Consent seems as necessary to cases where the life and liberty of the subject is concerned as where the property is concerned. . . . If the Stamp Act is illegal, the law of navigation is not legal, and the rights of taxation and of laying charges upon goods and merchandise"; Ryder Diaries, p. 270.

gether unworkable, virtual representation was judged utterly meaningless. This judgment of virtual representation has prevailed, so much so that later scholars have scarcely deemed the doctrine worthy of serious consideration. "The whole theory of virtual representation," Charles McIlwain wrote many years ago, "was as empty in law as it was unjust in policy. Of all the arguments urged in England against the American claims it was the least weighty," and if for no other reason than its "fatal confusion of under-representation and non-representation."[30] Many of the great centers of population in England were terribly underrepresented. Still, there was actual representation in England, however inadequate. In America, though, the euphemism that passed for virtual representation meant that there would be no representation at all.

The case for virtual representation was not quite so threadbare. It did not simply depend, as its supporters too often seemed to imply, on the fact that more than nine-tenths of the people of Great Britain were not electors and that, in consequence, Americans were no more underprivileged than the vast majority of Englishmen at home. Among others, this had been an argument of Thomas Whately, who concluded that the colonists were in the same position as the people of Great Britain: "All *British* subects are really in the same; none are actually, all are virtually represented in Parliament; for every Member of Parliament sits in the House, not as Representative of his own Constituents, but as one of that august Assembly by which all the Commons of *Great Britain* are represented."[31] Whately's argument cannot be taken literally, for it is evidently untrue. The defense of virtual representation, however, did not rest in the main on the proposition that all British subjects were literally in the same situation. Instead, it rested on the proposition, as Whately also argued, that the interests of all British subjects were given due consideration by Parliament and not sacrificed to partial advantage. Applied to the colonies, the doctrine of virtual representation was effectively a claim that, overall, the imperial-colonial relationship was an equitable one and that it was so because Parliament, despite its admitted shortcomings, did normally manage to balance the interests of the various parts of the empire for the greater good of the whole. Virtual representation secured for

---

[30] *The American Revolution: A Constitutional Interpretation* (New York, 1923), pp. 169–70.

[31] *The Regulations Lately Made with Respect to the Colonies Considered*, p. 109.

the colonists roughly what they would have otherwise secured through actual representation.

The point remains that virtual representation was not actual representation. Pitt pronounced the idea of virtual representation "the most contemptible idea that ever entered into the head of a man; it does not deserve a serious refutation."[32] It was contemptible because it took money out of the Americans' pockets without their consent. Pitt, however, entertained no doubts about the right of Parliament to govern the Americans in every other respect without their consent. He did not so much as even trouble himself with attempting to justify "the supreme legislative and governing power" of Parliament. It was enough that Parliament had "always bound the colonies by her laws." The consent of Americans was necessary only for the "giving and granting their own money. They would have been slaves had they not enjoyed it."[33] The Americans agreed, though as events were to show, where Pitt stopped with the requirement of consent the Americans only began.

[VII]

In a classic essay written more than half a century ago, the constitutional historian Andrew C. McLaughlin contended that the constitutional structure of the First British Empire was a "federal" one. In examining the "old empire as it was, let us say in 1760," McLaughlin found "that it was a composite empire, not simple and centralized," though he emphasized that he was speaking not "of any theory of the law of the empire but of its actual institutions and their practical operation." The division of powers between the parts and the center under the old imperial constitution, McLaughlin argued, was to a very marked degree "the distribution of powers characteristic of American federalism. In fact, if we add to the powers of the central authority in the old empire the single

---

[32] *PH*, 16:100.
[33] Ibid. Taxation apart, it is difficult to distinguish Pitt from Grenville on the issue of parliamentary supremacy. Indeed, as between the two, Grenville was more at pains to justify this supremacy than was Pitt, for whom it needed no justification. Pitt's commitment to parliamentary supremacy was later to evoke the bitter comment of John Adams: "He died a martyr to his idol. He fell in the House of Lords with the sovereignty of Parliament in his mouth"; *The Works of John Adams*, ed. Charles F. Adams, 10 vols. (Boston, 1856), 10:193.

power to obtain money by direct or indirect taxation immediately from the colonists for imperial purposes, we have almost exactly the scheme of distribution of our own constitutional system."[34]

McLaughlin's depiction of the old empire as a federal one is still widely accepted today; so, too, is his assumption that, in the aftermath of the Seven Years' War, the British asserted a "theory of centralized legislative omnipotence" that challenged profoundly the existing "principle of differentiation." Because Parliament "insisted on the existence of unlimited power—asserted, one might not unjustly say, that Parliament was above the law," the Americans were driven to stake out an equally extreme position. The American utterances that sought to "divide sovereignty" and that thus anticipated the theory and practice of American federalism broke down before the "inflexible" and "rigid" character of the opposing parliamentary claim. In the face of such inflexibility, there was little point, Bernard Bailyn has written, "in continuing to press for a formal classification and division of Parliament's powers. Defenders of American claims were forced to move onto the politically more extreme position that the Massachusetts House" would maintain in 1773—a position that denied altogether the authority of Parliament over the colonies.[35]

McLaughlin defined federalism as a system of government "in which powers of government are separated and distinguished and in which these powers are distributed among governments, each government having its quota of authority and each its distinct sphere of activity."[36] The definition, however, is in some ways inadequate. It says nothing about whether the distinct governments must be independent of one another, and it does not indicate by whom or what the distinct quotas of authority are allocated or derived. K. C. Wheare, the distinguished analyst of federal government, proposed a different and more restrictive test: "Does a system of government," Wheare asked, "embody predominantly a division of powers between general and regional authorities, each of which, in its own sphere, is co-ordinate with the others and independent

---

[34] "The Background of American Federalism," *American Political Science Review*, 12 (1918): 215–17.
[35] Ibid., pp. 222, and 232; Bernard Bailyn, *The Ideological Origins of the American Revolution*, pp. 223–24. Cf. Charles H. McIlwain, "The Historical Background of Federal Government," in *Federalism as a Democratic Process*, ed. Roscoe Pound et al. (New Brunswick, N.J., 1942), pp. 34–35.
[36] "Background of Federalism," p. 215.

of them?" Neither the general government nor the regional governments, according to Wheare, can be the source of the division of powers—otherwise the arrangement would cease to be federal in principle, though it might remain so in practice. A system in which the regional governments are dependent on the general government—even though the regional governments may enjoy extensive powers of conducting their own affairs—is a unitary state organized on the principle of devolution, for the powers of the regional governments are exercised subject to the supremacy of the general government and are in principle revokable. A system in which the general government is dependent on the regional governments—the foremost example being the government created by the Articles of Confederation—Wheare calls "confederal."[37]

When considered from this perspective, it is evident that the constitution of the First British Empire was neither federal in principle nor federal in practice. More than anything else, the institution of royal government prevents it from being so considered. Royal government meant that the regional governments, in their very composition, were dependent on the general government for their chief executive officer. Through the powers of disallowance and veto, moreover, the agents of the general government were capable of blocking the will of the provincial assemblies, even on issues of merely local importance. Finally, the privileges

---

[37] *Federal Government*, 4th ed. (London, 1963), pp. 29–33. Wheare did not regard "the federal principle as present to a sufficient degree in the Articles of Confederation of the United States of 1777, in the Austro-Hungarian Compromise of 1867, . . . or in the Covenant of the League of Nations, to give them the name federal. Nor in the practical working of these constitutions," he noted, "was federal government produced. The predominant principle in practice as in theory was the subordination of the federal governments to the regional governments." Since the distinctions introduced by Wheare are followed closely in the text, it may not be amiss to draw attention to his discussion of the devolutionary principle. Neither the government of the Union of South Africa, nor the Constitution of India of 1919, nor the relation between the Parliament of the United Kingdom and that of Northern Ireland, are instances, according to Wheare, of federal government. "It is true that the people of Northern Ireland are subject to two governments, one at Stormont, near Belfast, the other at Westminster, just as two people in an American state are subject to two governments. But the two governments for Northern Ireland are not co-ordinate"—there is no legal presumption that, once it is granted that the local government is acting within its allotted sphere, it is supreme and subordinate to no other. "There is nothing in law to prevent the parliament of the United Kingdom from passing laws for Northern Ireland not merely on the specified reserved subjects, but on any subject whatever. Moreover, the parliament of Northern Ireland received its powers from the parliament of the United Kingdom, and the latter can reduce or increase or abolish these powers. . . . And thus although great consideration is shown to Northern Ireland and no interference in provincial affairs occurs unless absolutely necessary, there is here no example of federal government."

of the colonial assembly were merely privileges, not rights. Throughout the crisis of the 1760s and 1770s, the British insisted that sovereignty was vested in Parliament. The empire, they believed, was organized on the principle of devolution, and had been always. This meant that colonial autonomy was subject to the discretion of Parliament and could, *in extremis*, be curtailed.

All these features of the old imperial constitution were incompatible with a scheme of government predominantly federal. Considered alone, they are the arrangements of a centralized, unitary state. And yet the very institution—royal government—that gave the imperial constitution many of its unitary features also made it predominantly confederal in practice. Unlike the American federal structure, in which the national government and the state governments are, with few exceptions, independent, the effectiveness of royal government in America was critically dependent on provincial authorities. This was nowhere more apparent than in the indefinite discretion vested in the crown to make requisitions for men and money. In practice, these requisitions were mere recommendations that the colonial assemblies observed or disregarded at their option. Save as the imperial Parliament was willing to draw on the resources of its subjects in the British Isles for the defense and protection of its subjects in America, the general government could do very little but with the approval and cooperation of the colonial assemblies. The subordination of the general government to the regional governments was also evident insofar as jurisdiction over the trade laws was held by colonial courts of common law, for this arrangement made the efficacy of the administration of the trade laws dependent on the cooperation of local juries.

The constitution of the First British Empire, then, was in critical respects neither federal in theory nor federal in fact. It was not, however, entirely without federal features. There did exist a "national Parliament" that, in the normal exercise of its legislative powers, confined itself to objects of government beyond the ability of the provincial legislatures to deal with satisfactorily from their separate and limited stations. The distinction between imperial and provincial purposes, between general and local areas of concern, between external and internal objects—the appeal, in other words, to principles recognizably federal—came naturally to men on both sides of the Atlantic when forced, during the crisis brought on by the Stamp Act, to articulate the character of the imperial constitution. This is commonly recognized in the case of the colonists.[38] It is no less true, however, of the position of the metropolis.

On the British side, the most striking appeal to the federal character of the empire and to the division of powers characteristic of federalism was made by Thomas Whately, in his apologia for the Grenville program, *The Regulations Lately Made*. Both the "national Parliament" and the "provincial Legislatures," Whately argued, were representative of the people and were vested with "equal legislative Powers." The difference was that the one was "exercised for local and the other for general Purposes." Far from being incompatible, the two were complementary and would seldom "interfere with one another: The Parliament will not often have occasion to exercise its Power over the Colonies, except for those Purposes, which the Assemblies cannot provide for. A general Tax," Whately insisted, "is of this Kind; the Necessity for it, the Extent, the Application of it, are Matters which Councils limited in their Views and in their Operations cannot properly judge of."[39] Even those writers, like Samuel Johnson and Thomas Hutchinson, usually cited to demonstrate the inflexible character of the British position, paid tribute to the "spirit of liberty" that informed the organization of the empire. "As men are placed at a greater distance from the Supreme Council of the kingdom," Johnson acknowledged, "they must be entrusted with ampler liberty of regulating their conduct by their own wisdom. As they are more secluded from easy recourse to national judicature, they must be more extensively commissioned to pass judgment on each other. For this reason," he noted, "our more important and opulent Colonies see the appearance and feel the effect of a regular Legislature, which in some places has acted so long with unquestioned authority, that it has been forgotten whence that authority was originally derived."[40]

It is not only the existence of a "national Parliament" which

---

[38] See Bailyn's illuminating discussion of the development of colonial thought on this question, in *Ideological Origins*, pp. 209–17.

[39] *Regulations*, pp. 109–113.

[40] "Speech of the Governor to the Two Houses, January 6, 1773," in James K. Hosmer, *The Life of Thomas Hutchison: Royal Governor of the Province of Massachusetts Bay* (Boston, 1896), pp. 364, 367; and Samuel Johnson, *Taxation No Tyranny*, p. 26. Cf. William Blackstone, *Commentaries on the Laws of England*, 4 vols., 3d ed. (London, 1768), 1:107; and Bailyn, *Ideological Origins*, pp. 226–27.

makes the old imperial constitution resemble a federal one. Though
in critical respects nonfederal in both theory and practice, the
empire was nevertheless federal in spirit. It had nonfederal institutions and practices whose purpose, it was agreed by Englishmen
and Americans alike, was to fulfill a federal design. Metropolitan
officials, whether at home or in the colonies, concerned themselves
mostly with general objects. On matters of provincial concern, the
colonists were left to do pretty much as they pleased. "The generalization is probably just," McLaughlin noted, "that instruction
and disallowance were exercised chiefly for essentially nonlocal,
imperial purposes, the maintenance of the character and aim of
the empire."[41] This was undoubtedly the case. It was also the case
that in the practical working of the colonial constitutions, confederal
practices had won out over unitary practices. The negative powers
of the assembly had proved more potent than the negative powers
of the crown, with the result that the assembly had risen to the
commanding position it enjoyed at the end of the Seven Years'
War—and not only on matters of local concern. The purposes and
aspirations of imperial rule, dependent on the efficacy of royal
government, were consequently placed in increasing jeopardy. In
this lay the crisis of the imperial constitution. In practice, the
imperial constitution came to share what Alexander Hamilton would
later call "the great and radical vice in the construction" of the
Articles of Confederation. This consisted of "the principle of LEG-
ISLATION for STATES or GOVERNMENTS, in their CORPO-
RATE or COLLECTIVE CAPACITIES, and as contradistin-
guished from the INDIVIDUALS of whom they consist."[42]

The nature of the constitutional conflict that arose after 1763 may
now be placed in better perspective. Whether one considers the
acts imposing federal taxes on individuals in the colonies, to be
collected by federal officials, and the violations of which were to
be punished in federal courts, or the reforms in the machinery for
enforcing the laws of trade all were intended to make the action
of the general government independent of the cooperation of the
parts. Far from representing a departure from federal practices,
the Grenville reforms represented a partial abandonment of confederal arrangements and the institution—or reaffirmation—of fed-

---

[41] "Background of Federalism," p. 217.
[42] Federalist no. 15, *The Federalist Papers*, ed. Clinton Rossiter (New York, 1961), p. 108.

eral practices. The animating purpose of the Grenville reforms was something akin to that which animated the American constitutional reformers of the 1780s. Nor should this seem surprising. The Grenville reforms cannot be seen apart from the crisis in royal government and the consequent breakdown of government by instruction—a breakdown that had the same symptoms and the same causes as the crisis of the American Confederation in the 1780s.

The colonial understanding of the dangers of central rule would profoundly influence the development of the Articles of Confederation. Royal government was gone; but the effective principle of that government—the subordination of the general government to the regional governments—remained. Under the articles, the power of the Continental Congress derived merely from the sense of common danger that British invasion had hammered into the colonists; its basis lay less in an incipient nationalism than in the conviction that if the colonists did not hang together they would hang separately. It thus came to depend, like the imperial constitution, on the affection of the parts, not the power of the center. The crisis of the Confederation arose because the general responsibilities that the articles had vested in the Continental Congress could not be discharged under a legal and institutional framework that was confederal in both theory and practice. It was thus subjected to all the strains of alliance politics, strains that the Continental Congress, with its inflated responsibilities and deflated power, soon found itself incapable of mastering.

The crisis of the imperial constitution was quite similar. Here, too, a disjunction had arisen between the responsibilities of the general government and its powers. Here, too, the disjunction could be overcome only by enabling the general government to operate without the cooperation, and despite the opposition, of the parts. Whether the British Empire would be, in some sense, a federal one, was indeed a stake of the conflict between metropolis and colonies; federal arrangements, however, underwent their severest challenge from the Americans, not from the British. At stake in the conflict over the Grenville reforms was not whether the regional governments would continue to enjoy power over local affairs, but whether the general government would enjoy powers commensurate with its responsibilities over the whole.

It may, of course, be objected that the location of sovereignty in Parliament was inconsistent with the federal principle, and so it was. But this shows only that, if the empire were to become more like a federal state in practice, it could not be federal in principle. Those whose consent would have been required to reconstitute the empire on the federal principle—the American colonists—did not want an empire predominantly federal in practice. They wanted the operation of the empire to depend on, and hence in critical respects to be subordinate to, provincial institutions— above all, the provincial assemblies. Nor did the Americans want representation in Parliament, which they saw—correctly—as merely a device to legitimate the exercise of parliamentary power. They wanted the power to determine their destiny, and the only institutions that promised to secure this aspiration were to be found on the provincial level. The only scheme of government consistent with such an aim—so long as the Americans formed a part of the British Empire—was one that was predominantly confederal in practice.

Did Parliament, then, as McLaughlin claimed, insist "on the existence of unlimited power" and assert "that Parliament was above the law"? In one critical respect, it did. The essence of the imperial claim was that Parliament's right to determine the limits of its own power was illimitable. It is not difficult to see why the Americans found the claim unacceptable. They did not share the assumption— made regularly by British writers—that Parliament would exercise its power with justice, and that the sovereignty of Parliament was compatible with the preservation by the colonial assemblies of their traditional privileges and hence with a kind of federal scheme. The claim was the only solution available to the British, however, that provided a basis for effective imperial rule over the colonies. The British located sovereignty in Parliament not because they could not imagine locating it anywhere else, but because they were persuaded that the consequences of doing so would lead to the loss of their claim to control over the colonies. The inflexibility of the position stemmed, not from the peculiar manner in which sovereignty was defined, but from the intractable character of the conflict.[43]

---

[43] The charge of inflexibility has been made in a number of ways, not all of which are considered in the text. In one of his most striking formulations, McLaughlin argued that "nothing could more fully discredit legalism when dealing with a practical problem of statesmanship" than the British doctrine of parliamentary supremacy; for this doctrine in effect held "that Parliament could not recognize the illegality of doing what in practice it actually had not done and what the passing years were proving it could in reality not do"— tax the colonies. The British failure, according to McLaughlin, consisted in their inability

[VIII]

It is a commonplace among historians to observe that the British measures of 1764–65 and the colonial reaction to them brought into sharp relief what should have been long apparent: that the colonies had reached a stage of maturity and power where they could no longer be treated as weak dependencies. Not only had they outgrown the institutional forms that had once adequately reflected their infant status, but they had increasingly come to resent the central principle on which the imperial-colonial rela-

---

to recognize the illegality of their action, not simply the impolicy of it. Hence the critical question, to him, was whether Englishmen or Americans were "capable of finding a law of the empire"; "Background of Federalism," pp. 228–29.

McLaughlin's position is not without difficulty. A mere parliamentary act—even if made by an "extraordinary Parliament, in which there were to be American representatives," as Francis Bernard proposed in 1765—would not have changed the constitution of the empire, in law, from a unitary to a federal one (p. 228). So long as the concession was made by Parliament, it could be withdrawn by the same body, for no Parliament can bind its successor—or even itself. Such a concession, even if considered wise from a political standpoint, would not have changed the constitution of the empire from a legal perspective. On this point, see the still valuable discussion of A. V. Dicey, *Introduction to the Study of the Law of the Constitution*, 8th ed. (London, 1927), pp. 64–66.

McLaughlin's position must be distinguished from that of Bernard Bailyn, who criticizes the inflexibility of the position adopted by British writers on the basis of their failure to recognize that "Parliament's sovereignty might be divisible"; *Ideological Origins*, p. 224. This contention, however, is also difficult to sustain. Whether sovereignty is regarded as divisible or not—a question into which it is pointless to enter here—it cannot be maintained that the doctrine of indivisible sovereignty is incompatible with "the federalist tradition," as Bailyn seems to imply (pp. 228–29). In the scheme of American constitutionalism—to which critics of the British doctrine make appeal—it is legislative and other powers that are divided, not sovereignty; cf. Dicey, *Law of the Constitution*, pp. 140–41; Wheare, *Federal Government*, p. 53; and Gordon Wood, *The Creation of the American Republic, 1776–1787* (New York, 1969), p. 530.

It is true that most British writers failed to draw clearly, if at all, the distinction between fundamental and statutory law, or between constituent and legislative power, which comes so easily to us now; cf. particularly Johnson, *Taxation No Tyranny*, p. 26. If British writers may be plausibly charged with intellectual rigidity, the accusation must center on their failure to anticipate what would later become the central doctrine of American constitutionalism—a doctrine that located sovereignty in the people, who in turn delegated governing power through the instrument of a written, supreme constitution. The positions of Bailyn and McLaughlin, if considered sympathetically, may be so read. Yet such an indictment would have to rest on the assumption that a British offer to form a written constitution fixing the rights of the imperial and provincial legislatures would have led to a result satisfactory to both sides. This assumption is very questionable. The direction taken by the conflict would, if anything, seem to indicate the reverse—that the viability of the old imperial constitution lay precisely in its ambiguity. If the failure of any such effort is assumed, it becomes much easier to understand why British thought did not move in the direction taken at the time and subsequently by American thought. The mere offer to locate sovereignty somewhere other than in Parliament would have represented an acknowledg-

tionship had always been based. The principle of inequality underlay the whole of the system regulating colonial trade and commerce, just as it underlay the whole of the system of government by instruction. The measures of the Grenville ministry were premised on the assumption that the colonies could still be treated as they had once been treated, that the clock could be turned back to an earlier time, and that the colonists could somehow be made to accept a reform of the imperial relationship which set distinct limits to the ever-growing claims of provincial assemblies. Yet the crisis that erupted with the passage of the Stamp Act laid bare the dangers of this assumption. At the same time, the crisis pointed up as never before the difficulties of resorting to a policy of coercion. Not the least of these difficulties sprang from the conviction that the British Empire was one based on the premise that the colonists, as Englishmen, carried with them to all parts of the empire essentially the same rights and privileges as enjoyed by Englishmen at home. In the words of Lawrence Henry Gipson, "The British Empire of the eighteenth century was based on the idea of government by consent of the people as free men and as inheritors of the great tradition of English liberty. Only through just laws and

---

ment by the metropolis of the many difficulties of locating sovereign power in Parliament—and hence making Parliament the judge of its own cause. The offer itself would consequently have entailed the prior concession of the central constitutional issue in dispute between Britain and America, for it would have signified that Parliament recognized that its rule depended on the consent of the colonists, and that it—because unrepresentative—was incapable of giving such consent. Once having made this concession, it could not then retreat to its former position if negotiations between the metropolis and the colonies for a written constitution were unsuccessful.

It may be argued, finally, that an act—such as that which Parliament made in 1778, declaring that it would not impose revenue taxes on the colonies—would have satisfied the aspirations of both parties and hence was the course marked out by true statesmanship. The unwillingness of the British political nation to adopt this position, however, sprang from the recognition that the Americans claimed the exemption on the grounds that Parliament was not representative. Thus, the reflection followed immediately that acceptance of the colonial position would have given the Americans a principled basis on which to oppose any and all imperial legislation. This was the primary basis for the position—so often ridiculed—of William Knox, that "either the colonies are a part of the community of Great Britain, or they are in a state of nature with respect to her, and in no case can be subject to the jurisdiction of that legislative power which represents her community, which is the British Parliament"; quoted in McLaughlin, "Background of Federalism," p. 228. If the national Parliament was not representative of the whole, the British believed, the basis for its rule over the parts was destroyed. Nor does the fact that the British made the offer in 1778 show that the offer, if made at an earlier time, would not have had this consequence. It may show simply that the position of the British in 1778 was desperate indeed, and that by this time they were grasping at straws.

a mild type of control could an empire of this type be held together. For basically, only moral force united the various elements of the Empire."[44]

The broad constitutional dilemma that must sooner or later confront an empire such as this is evident. Burke articulated it at the time with his customary felicity of expression, though not uncharacteristically he had neither then nor in later years a viable solution. "An Englishman must be subordinate to England, but he must be governed according to the opinion of a free land. Without subordination, it would not be one Empire. Without freedom, it would not be the British Empire."[45] Was there a solution that would accommodate the claims of subordination and freedom? Certainly, a solution existed that would have satisfied the claim of freedom, though at the sacrifice of the claim of subordination: Britain had only to relinquish its sovereignty over the colonies. The colonists were to propose this solution at the time of the First Continental Congress in 1774. Their "federalistic empire" would have been made up of equal and independent legislatures (that is, independent states), whose principal bond would be their common allegiance to the person of the King. The result, however, would not have been a transformation of empire but its abandonment. And what remained would certainly not have been federal.

In the absence of this radical solution, was there an arrangement that, though perhaps far from ideal, would nonetheless have satisfied the conflicting claims of subordination and freedom? As we have noted, the preponderant view of historians, following the view taken at the time by the colonists, is that there was a viable arrangement, which consisted simply in the adherence of both sides to the status quo, constitutional and otherwise. The metropolis had only to remain content with the imperial-colonial relationship in the form in which it appeared at the close of the Seven Years' War, and the challenge made to its authority in the 1760s would have been avoided. Moreover, it presumably would have been avoided at no substantial sacrifice of British interests. Once again we are reminded of Edmund S. Morgan's dictum: "All the objectives of the Americans before 1776 could have been attained within the empire and would have cost the mother country little or nothing."[46]

[44] *The British Empire before the American Revolution*, 10:294.
[45] Ryder Diaries, p. 273.
[46] *The Challenge of the American Revolution*, pp. 55–56.

In the context of the critically important relationship between the metropolis and the colonial assemblies, Jack P. Greene has elaborated this recurrent theme. A working arrangement, he has argued, had developed in the course of the eighteenth century which, if left unchallenged, might well have persisted for a substantial period of time. Greene acknowledges, and even emphasizes, the widening disparity between the formal powers still laid claim to by the metropolis and the steady expansion of the powers effectively exercised by the lower houses of assembly. Yet he writes that this "growing divergence between imperial theory and colonial practice mattered little so long as each refrained from openly challenging the other." Such, unfortunately, was not the case. For the new policy inaugurated by British governments in the wake of the war "threatened to upset this arrangement by implementing the old ideals long after the conditions that produced them had ceased to exist. Aimed at bringing the colonies more closely under imperial control, this policy inevitably sought to curtail the influence of the lower houses, directly challenging many of the powers they had acquired over the previous century." Inevitably, the challenge, once issued, evoked strong response by the provincial assemblies, with the result that the wide gulf separating imperial theory and colonial practice was laid bare. The exposure made colonial lawmakers much more conscious of, and sensitive to, the significance of the constitutional issue than they had previously been. They were also more determined than ever to hold on to the powers they had acquired during the preceding century, powers now threatened by measures that the metropolis appeared determined to impose on them. The conviction was not slow in developing that these powers could be assured only by the provincial assemblies achieving a status of complete equality with the imperial Parliament. Thus, the new policy not only challenged the status quo but, in doing so, made impossible "a return to the old inarticulated and undefined pattern of accommodation between imperial theory and colonial practice that had existed through most of the period between 1689 and 1763."[47]

In this view, then, the constitutional status quo consisted, as it were, of two worlds—the ideal and the real, or, the theoretical and the practical—and the viability of this status quo depended

[47] *Quest for Power*, pp. 357–79.

upon neither world moving beyond its designated orbit. The British, occupying the ideal world, were to remain satisfied with the forms of power, however empty and fictitious they might become; the colonists, occupying the world of practice, were to enjoy the substance of power though at the price of an occasional bow, when expedient, to imperial theory. They were, in other words, to acknowledge imperial supremacy in theory even while defying it in practice, just as the British were to relinquish imperial supremacy in practice even while continuing to proclaim it in theory.

Clearly, this was not the British understanding of the constitutional status quo, though it was certainly their fear of what the constitutional relationship might soon become if imperial supremacy were not effectively asserted. Aware that a policy of salutary neglect had led to the debility of royal authority in the colonies and that government by instruction was no longer able to control the power of the lower houses of assembly, imperial officials determined to employ the authority of Parliament to undertake reforms they had come to regard as indispensable. The colonists had seldom challenged the authority of Parliament in the manner they came to challenge government by instruction, if for no other reason than that Parliament's intervention in colonial affairs had been infrequent. Until the Great War for the Empire, they had seldom contended that the laws of the provincial assemblies were to be treated as equal to those of Parliament. It was only in the war years that the arguments later used in responding to the Stamp Act were widely advanced.

Did the postwar intervention by Parliament in colonial affairs itself represent a challenge to the status quo? In a significant sense, it clearly did. At the same time, however, the actions of the colonial assemblies which had led to the breakdown of government by instruction also represented a challenge to the status quo. Moreover, colonial rejection of parliamentary authority in internal taxation and in other matters affecting their "internal" governance represented such a challenge as well. It was one thing to defy the authority of the governor and quite another to defy the authority of Parliament. By doing the latter, the colonial assemblies challenged imperial supremacy in a manner they had not done before.

The various measures taken by Parliament addressed problems that, in the eyes of imperial authorities, required immediate remedy, problems experience had shown could not satisfactorily be addressed by the arrangements of the past. Quite the contrary, these arrangements had largely given rise to the problems. Although the intervention of Parliament was not primarily informed by the purpose of reforming the constitutional relationship between metropolis and colonies, there is no gainsaying the point that the measures of 1763–65, if effective, would have had this result. They would have challenged what had by this time become the provincial assemblies' claim of exclusive power to tax. In a number of other respects, they would have set limits to, if not have diminished, the pretensions of the colonial legislatures. Morevoer, the colonists had no way of knowing the measures that Parliament might take in the future if its present intervention were to prove successful. The assurances of the Grenville government, even if sincerely given, might not operate to bind its successors. The metropolis, after all, still claimed very imposing formal powers over the colonies. Given encouragement, might not a future government attempt to activate powers long in disuse and to reduce colonial self-government to a vanishing point? And if this should happen, what would prevent the imposition on the colonies of a tax burden that might crush them, particularly given the intense desire of British governments to lighten the burden of taxation at home?

Thus the new policy of the metropolis not only struck at the pretensions of the colonies, it also activated fears that, however exaggerated and even imaginary, were never far below the surface. It reminded them that what they had come to identify as the status quo had never been accepted by the imperial power, however permissive and casual the latter had regularly been in the past. Given this combination of colonial hubris and fear, the reaction of the Americans is scarcely surprising.

The dilemma confronting the metropolis, however, was no less real and profound. To view its response as a deliberate and quite unnecessary assault upon *the* status quo is to trivialize, if not simply to overlook, the problems it faced. Nor will it do to apply a retrospective wisdom to imperial action and, not surprisingly, to find this action sadly wanting. The problems imperial officials confronted in the early 1760s appeared, not unreasonably, as both serious and pressing. Yet it was impossible to resolve them if the claims to autonomy of the colonies were honored. The American position would require the metropolis either to carry the entire burden of imperial defense or to accept a system that was for the most part quite unreliable (and, to the extent it might be relied upon, would likely be used by the colonists to exact further concessions from Great Britain). The American position would also require the metropolis to trust to colonial self-interest in preserving the integrity of the system of trade and navigation, since measures of effective enforcement invariably were resisted on grounds that they violated the colonists' rights as Englishmen or the legitimate powers of the provincial assemblies.

The American position, in a word, left the British with virtually no authority to enforce and no status quo to defend. If accepted, it would have left them with their "ideals" and an "imperial theory" that even then bore little meaningful relationship to the realities of colonial practice. Even if the colonial version of the constitutional status quo were to be accepted (and this version was itself a matter of intense controversy and uncertainty), its acceptance would threaten to disintegrate an already weakened imperial structure. What the British regarded as the larger status quo, one the legitimacy and necessity of which they did not for a moment doubt, was accordingly jeopardized by the smaller status quo, the legitimacy of which continued to provoke considerable doubt. That doubt could be resolved only by colonial submission or by denial of the sovereignty of Parliament, the foundation on which the empire rested.

The Issue of Motivation

[I]

The classic whig explanation of postwar British imperial policy located its motive force in the aggressiveness of men who, at the moment of victory over Britain's great rival, determined to suffer no further impediments to their will to unlimited power. This was the explanation of the great nineteenth-century American historian George Bancroft. "Allured by a phantom of absolute authority over the colonies," Bancroft wrote, British governments "made war on human freedom."[1] It was this interpretation that understandably found favor with the majority of the colonists. The rebellion against Great Britain was a rebellion against a tyranny in some measure attempted and in greater measure planned. Although given more sophisticated expression, and embedded in a far more complex account of the causes of conflict between metropolis and colonies, this view has by no means disappeared today. The conspiratorial dimension once attributed to ministerial policy is now largely discounted.[2] A deliberate intent to reduce the colonies to a condition of servitude is seldom avowed.[3] Still, the core of the colonial charge against the mother country continues to find favor.[4] What else can be the meaning of the theme—as pervasive today perhaps as it has ever

---

[1] *History of the United States of America, from the Discovery of the Continent*, 6 vols. (New York, 1883–85), 3:482.
[2] Although it continues to find subtle expression in contemporary historiography. A not so subtle expression is given by Oliver M. Dickerson, *The Navigation Acts and the American Revolution*.
[3] Yet how else is one to account for the view entertained by a number of historians that Bernard Bailyn is a "tory" historian, and this because Bailyn presumably suggests that the ideological lens through which the colonists saw the struggle with the metropolis distorted as much as it informed? See, for example, Kenneth Lynn, "Regressive Historians," *American Scholar*, Autumn 1978, pp. 472–80.
[4] It clearly does, for example, in the recent collected essays of Edmund S. Morgan, *The Challenge of the American Revolution*.

been—that the American Revolution was, first and foremost, a struggle for liberty of the individual and not for independence of the collective? It was presumably because successive British governments, joined and supported by Parliament, threatened to destroy fundamental human rights—and not only the right of property, though this right was and is found critical since so many other freedoms depended upon security of property—that the colonists first resisted and finally rebelled. To defend these rights, political independence ultimately appeared indispensable. But independence must be seen, on this view, as a means—however important this means may have been—and not as an end. Independence emerged, as it were, as a byproduct, a happy consequence, of efforts to preserve human rights placed in jeopardy by a design for empire in which these rights would have been subordinated to, if not in the end destroyed in the name of, imperial necessity.

There is no way of proving what successive British governments would have done had they not been resisted. Conceivably, the measures taken in 1763–65, had they gone unopposed, might have whetted an imperial appetite that knew few limits. There is no evidence, however, that the prospect of exercising unlimited and arbitrary power over the colonies, of reducing the colonists to a condition of abject dependence indistinguishable from servitude, held any attraction to the men who governed the empire during these years. Would-be tyrants do not generally betray indecision, inconsistency, and sheer inadvertence in carrying out their designs. Nor is it their habit to shrink from using force when their will is openly flouted. Tyranny does not commonly advance its cause by permitting resistance groups openly to flourish, to organize, to sign pamphlets, and to resort to violence that goes unpunished. Nor does it usually fail to defend effectively those who have the temerity—or bravery—to support the tyrant's measures to undermine the confidence of those who continued to support the metropolis. Yet this was the pattern of British behavior in the first, and critical, contest with the colonies, as it was to be the pattern of British behavior until—and, indeed, even after—the die for war was cast.

A more sophisticated and detached view of the motivation behind Britain's postwar imperial policy attributes this policy to the compulsions exercised by a new concept of empire. There is no uniform expression given this new concept, just as there is no uniform account of the origins of the changed outlook toward empire. To Charles M. Andrews, the discontinuity between the traditional policy of salutary neglect and the policy pursued in the 1760s reflected a shift from a mercantile to an imperial outlook. The change, he argued, was a radical one, for mercantilism and imperialism had nothing in common. Mercantilism was based on the business man's view of "pay as you go." Prosperity here and now was its aim, not glory. Territorial acquisition was to be avoided, save as it would promise a quick and adequate return on the investment.[5]

The outlook of imperialism, by contrast, was not content with mercantilist goals. To imperialism, the mere advantages of traffic were not enough for a state of real grandeur; instead, the extent of territory and the exercise of authority were now considered more worthy of consideration. It was, Andrews concluded, the substitution of these new ideas for the principles and methods of the old colonial policy that lay at the core of the gathering crisis. For it was the new concept of empire that led to the measures against which the colonists first protested, then resisted, and finally rebelled. "The fact that the colonists over and over again declared that they had no intention of objecting to any act of parliament relative to trade and asked only for a return to conditions as they had existed before the Sugar Act of 1764 shows that imperialism and not mercantilism was the first cause of the eventual rupture."[6]

Andrews does not make clear what prompted the fateful conversion to imperialism, with all its baleful effects for policy. He was content to describe the change he found—though the contrast he drew between mercantilism and imperialism is as confusing as it is enlightening—[7] and to insist that it was the prime factor in

---

[5] *The Colonial Background of the American Revolution*, pp. 121ff.
[6] Ibid., p. 129.
[7] Andrews saw the "self-sufficient empire of the mercantilists" as something radically different from the "thing of territory, centralization, maintenance, and authority" that emerged in 1763. In metropolitan thought, however, the self-sufficient commercial empire was inconceivable in the absence of the framework of imperial law that channeled the growth of colonial commerce, a framework that inevitably made the empire, at least partly, a "thing of territory, centralization, maintenance, and authority." It is misleading, moreover, to place the concern for power in opposition to the desire for wealth, for contemporaries saw "power and plenty" as complementary, not contradictory, objectives. This was the case with respect to both the contribution that the carrying trade made to naval power and to the support that the wealth created by the transatlantic commerce lent to the stability of British public credit. Contemporaries sometimes fretted over the instability of the nation's credit, but they did so against the assumption that the colony trade was very largely responsible

prompting the policy that eventually led to war between the metropolis and its American colonies. Once the "new issue . . . of
territorial imperialism emerged to perplex the souls of British
statesmen," the rest of the story seems to follow almost as a matter
of course.[8] It does so because this altered view of empire, though
new, at once became deeply ingrained in departmental habits of
thought and routine. The change, once made, defined the "givens"
of political thought and action and radically foreclosed the range
of historical possibilities. Although Andrews did not explicitly say
so, the reasonable conclusion to be drawn from his argument is
that once the new view of empire had triumphed, for whatever
reasons, war with America was virtually inevitable.

What Andrews left implicit, another distinguished historian, John
Shy, has recently made explicit. In the manner of Andrews, Shy
also finds the underlying motivation of British action in a new view
of empire. Although Shy, again in the manner of Andrews, is not
disposed to inquire into the origins and causes of this change in
outlook, he entertains little doubt over its great significance in
determining the fate of the First British Empire. "The impulse
that swept the British Empire toward civil war was powerful," Shy
declares in his arresting essay on the spectrum of possibilities in
the years 1763–75, "and did not admit of any real choice." For that
impulse, though new, expressed men's deepest convictions "on the
objectives of politics, and on the goals of life itself." It is only by
understanding the hold that these convictions exercised over men's
imagination that one can understand the deep consensus that, despite surface appearances to the contrary, underlay British political
life and, in particular, conditioned men's thoughts and assumptions
about empire. Rejecting the labels "liberal" and "conservative,"
Shy considers the new outlook best described by the term "en-

---

for whatever solidity it possessed. See Jacob Viner, "Power versus Plenty as Objectives of
Foreign Policy in the Seventeenth and Eighteenth Centuries," *World Politics* 1 (1948):1–
29; and Charles Wilson, " 'Mercantilism': Some Vicissitudes of an Idea," *Economic History
Review*, 2d ser. 10 (1957): 181–88. The economic and intellectual historians who have most
recently examined the character of "the mercantile system" have not contested the view
that the power of the collective remained an omnipresent justification for mercantilist
policies. Both Viner and Eli F. Heckscher, in *Mercantilism*, trans. Mendel Shapiro, rev.
ed., E. F. Söderünd, 2 vols. (London, 1955), simply insisted that the range of objectives
was wider than nineteenth-century German and English historians (who attributed an almost
exclusive emphasis on the objective of power) believed.
[8] Andrews, *Colonial Background*, p. 123.

lightened." "It was, or purported to be, factually better informed than previously held opinions about the colonies, and it took a broader view of relationships, a deeper view of value, and a longer view of time. Above all, it sought rationality."[9]

The rationalization of imperial policy presumably meant not only ridding policy of contradiction and of arrangements that defied logical explanation; it also meant that the keys to a policy based on reason were to be found in the ideals of "equity" and "efficiency." And despite the difficulties that might, and would, arise over precisely what these ideals implied in practice, there was no doubt over their core meaning. Equity dictated that the Americans share in the burden of empire, and efficiency required that the colonies acknowledge the sovereignty of Parliament.

The views of Andrews and Shy provide one answer to the question of why postwar British governments acted as they did. Whatever the merits of the answers, their general implications are clear enough. The new view of empire prompted a policy that represented a departure from the imperial-colonial status quo. The crisis that ensued must be traced, then, to this change in the outlook toward empire. The change made conflict inevitable not only because of the hold it enjoyed over the imagination of imperial officialdom, and the British political nation generally, but because its character placed severe restrictions on the range of historical possibilities. It imposed the narrowest of limits upon what was conceivable in setting American policy. This is only to say, however, that the conflict was at root brought on by the metropolis and not by the colonies, that if war was inevitable it was because British statesmen acted under the spell of an impulse that did not admit of any real choice. And although the inevitability of an event is generally understood to relieve the actors of responsibility for its occurrence, the view here considered nevertheless manages to encompass both worlds. That is perhaps one reason why it must prove so attractive. There is no design of tyranny, no conscious intent to reduce the colonists to a position of abject independence, no desire to make war on human freedom. Instead, there is a pattern of behavior that, even though it might have the same objective consequences as the most ominous of conspiracies, is oc-

[9] "Thomas Pownall, Henry Ellis, and the Spectrum of Possibilities, 1763–1775." in his *A People Numerous and Armed* (Oxford, 1976), pp. 68–72. When judged in terms of its consequences, the irony of Shy's description of the new outlook will not escape the reader.

casioned by an outlook, a world view, whose hold on men is such that they can scarcely imagine acting other than in conformity with the apparent dictates of this view. In this manner, the issue of responsibility is moderated, if only by being depersonalized. In place of George Grenville, Charles Townshend, George III, ideas apparently held men in utter thralldom and produced a consensus that virtually precluded the search for alternative courses of action. Still, the issue of responsibility for the crisis that eventuated in war remains, and it continues to rest squarely on British shoulders. For the assumption that forms the basis of this more subtle and sophisticated view is identical with the assumption that forms the basis of whig historiography generally, whether old or new. It is that the metropolis could have preserved the substance of its interests and position had it only remained faithful to the old colonial policy.

If those responsible for the empire did not see matters in this light, however, it is doubtful that they failed to do so due to a new view of empire. A conviction that the ways of the past would no longer suffice, that these ways had led to serious lapses in the system of imperial control, and that the wartime experience had illuminated as never before the need for reform of the system, was surely there. This conviction, however, need not be seen in terms of a new view of empire, and the attempt to do so only confuses matters. There was little, indeed, that was "new" about the ideas entertained by Grenville and his associates; little that had not been urged, and sometimes achieved, by imperial officials in the past; little that represented a departure from earlier thinking about the relationship of the colonies to the mother country. In the history of the imperial-colonial relationship, various methods of satisfying imperial interests were experimented with. Especially at the outset of colonization, some of these involved the contractual relationships that the colonists would ultimately find as an emblem of their equality with the mother country; other methods, particularly after the Restoration, involved the more direct assertion of imperial control. Such assertions of imperial control, it is true, were regularly followed by relaxations in practice of sufficient scope that the colonists were able to formulate a version of the relationship that allowed little room for their own subordination. Yet the colonial claim of freedom never wholly displaced the imperial claim of subordination, even during the reign of Walpole and Newcastle, when the institutions of imperial control were allowed to decay to a remarkable extent. Neither the metropolitan desire to assert control nor the colonial desire to be free arose suddenly in 1763. The predicament that arose from the contradictory character of these desires was "coeval with colonization itself."[10]

There were differences, of course—profound differences even—in the policy of those who governed the British Empire in the aftermath of the Seven Years' War and of those who presided over the preceding policy of "salutary neglect," which spanned roughly the years from Walpole's unwillingness to implement the recommendations presented in Spotswood's 1721 report to the Board of Trade to the appointment of George Dunk, earl of Halifax, to the presidency of the Board of Trade in 1748. The Grenville administration did implement a program that had not been implemented by its predecessors. Yet neither in the sphere of imperial defense nor in the administration of the Acts of Trade and Navigation is it accurate to characterize the difference between the two policies as one involving the fundamental purposes of imperial rule. There was a change of policy, not of basic outlook; a change of means, not ends. At the core of the new policy was the conviction that the preceding policy had led to a basic undermining of the system of imperial control and that new challenges and novel circumstances had made a policy of loose regulation incapable of securing the great objects of empire. By the same token, the most ambitious attempt to articulate the purposes and assumptions that lay behind the policy of "salutary neglect"—that of Edmund Burke, in his great speeches on America in 1774 and 1775—makes it apparent that at the core of this policy was the conviction that the principal aspirations of imperial rule could be secured through loose regu-

---

[10] On this point, see Stephen Saunders Webb, *The Governors-general: The English Army and the Definition of the Empire, 1569–1681* (Chapel Hill, 1979), esp. pp. 461–66. Webb argues that the "new" imperialism of 1763 was not new, that the Knox memorandum, discussed earlier, "proclaimed not the arrival but rather the return to Anglo-American preeminence of coerciveness and power-hunger, of paternalism and militarism." Why Webb finds it necessary to characterize this imperial program in language to which its adherents would have objected—and indeed would have found offensive—is unclear; nevertheless, his emphasis on the resemblance of the Knox memorandum—and by implication the Grenville program—to metropolitan aspirations at other times in the history of the empire remains valid. It is important, however, not to confuse the question of the relationship of the Grenville program to prior imperial aspiration with the question of the causes of the emergence of the Grenville program in the mid-sixties. Webb, too, would presumably locate the causes of the Grenville program in a "revived view of empire" and hence in a change in outlook in the metropolis rather than in a change in circumstances on the periphery.

lation. The pervasive consensus in Great Britain to which Shy and others have drawn attention is testimony, not of the emergence of a new view of empire, but of the profound continuity in the purposes and aspirations of imperial rule. Circumstances, however, were capable of radically undermining the Burkean vision, and in the 1740s and 1750s they increasingly did so. Walpole's advice to let sleeping dogs lie was not applicable, after all, to dogs that were not sleeping.

Across the whole field of colonial administration, the arrangements in which Walpole and Newcastle had acquiesced were not working. In the 1740s many provinces became all but ungovernable as popular parties in several assemblies waged protracted war against their governors. The system of government by instruction was clearly breaking down. The system of imperial defense was deemed incapable of responding to the emergence of a powerful external threat, and not only by the "new imperialists": it was Franklin who pronounced the older system unworkable, it was Newcastle who would not abandon the colonies to their fate in 1754. And all the while evidence accumulated that the system for the administration of the trade laws was being systematically undermined. These problems were apparent to discerning observers, like Halifax, well before the outbreak of the Great War for the Empire, yet at that time they had no decisive consequences for policy. The war brought them all, as it were, to maturation. The experience of the war underlined the weakness of the governors and the inadequacy of the enforcement mechanism of the laws of trade; and the outcome of the war transformed, though it did not eliminate, the security problem of the colonies.

One new element had entered the situation: Parliament's acceptance of responsibility for American security was of a different order from that which Parliament had discharged in the past. It led directly to a novel assumption of parliamentary power. Yet this novel assumption of responsibility arose from the apparent breakdown of the security system of the colonies before the outbreak of the Seven Years' War, a breakdown that testified to the inadequacy of past arrangements and to the necessity of a more activist imperial role. It may be argued that, in the aftermath of war, the British discharged their new responsibility for American security in the way that they did because of a new view of empire. But that argument is persuasive only to the degree it can be shown that other and equally effective methods could have been employed to secure the newly acquired territories and to insure peace on the imperial frontier. In fact, what can be shown is only that there were no other methods which held out the promise of securing these ends.

Did the British insistence that the colonies share in the burden of imperial defense arise from the hold that an ideal of equity suddenly exercised over men's minds? A positive answer requires a curious reading of human motivation. Nothing seems more readily explicable in terms of normal reaction than this insistence. Indeed, what would require special explanation would be a reaction quite different from the one that did occur, that is, a willingness on the part of the metropolis to shoulder the entire burden of imperial defense in North America. Its unwillingness to do so led directly to the taxation of the colonies, thereby provoking a challenge to the sovereignty of Parliament. Was it a new view of empire that led the metropolis to react so strongly to this challenge? Was it, as Shy asserts, an ideal of efficiency that impelled the British to insist upon colonial acknowledgement of parliamentary supremacy? The questions themselves appear curious. They suggest that the issue of sovereignty was, at least in the way that British governments and Parliament dealt with it, not merely pointless, but a case in which the insistence upon form came to prejudice and even to render impossible a resolution of substantive differences. These differences might well have been compromised, it is often implied, but the issue of sovereignty, in the maner in which the British insisted upon defining it, was not susceptible of compromise. This is, presumably, why it should never have been brought to the fore, or, even once it had been raised, why it should have been quietly dropped. But the obsession with sovereignty drove the British to risk their all on this issue and, in the end, it cost them their empire.

Yet there was nothing peculiar either in the importance that the imperial state attached to the claim of parliamentary sovereignty or in the manner in which the claim was defined. That the claim could not be compromised is clear. It was impossible to compromise, however, not because of the manner in which the imperial state defined it, but simply because the nature of the issue is such that it does not permit the kind of compromise that may attend the resolution of other political conflicts. The British did not treat the issue of sovereignty in terms of some intrinsically elusive or

abstract manner, which, for this reason, made the issue refractory
to the ordinary methods of political give and take. They dealt with
it in the only way they could—consistent with the preservation of
their position and their claim to rule. Challenged in its claim by
the colonies—and it was the challenge that raised the issue, not
the prior exercise of power—the metropolis had the alternative
either of insisting upon its claim or, by its silence, of acquiescing
in the colonial position. The issue of sovereignty, once raised,
immediately became the intractable core of the controversy between metropolis and colonies.

Even when these considerations are acknowledged, and the difficulties attending the issue of sovereignty granted, the significance
of the controversy over sovereignty is often missed or obscured.
What, it is often asked, did the British stand to gain by taking so
adamant a position on Parliament's supremacy and by refusing to
yield gracefully on issues that, even if symbolic of this supremacy,
were in themselves quite insignificant? The more revealing question to ask, however, is what the British might not unreasonably
have thought they stood to lose by failing to assert effectively the
authority they believed they had always enjoyed, and continued
to enjoy, over the colonies. It is easy to respond that wiser men
would have seen that they could stand only to lose by such assertion. As matters turned out, this was indeed the case, though the
absence of determination attending the assertion made no small
contribution to the final result. Even so, what does the response
signify other than that the metropolis should have conceded the
issue of sovereignty and, by that concession, acknowledged the de
facto equality of the colonies?

The refusal to consider such course is not to be traced to some
mysterious obsession with sovereignty which gripped the minds of
eighteenth-century Englishmen. Nor is it to be attributed in the
first place to imperial pride, though this consideration surely played
its part. Above all, it must be found in the equation of sovereignty
with the preservation of those interests that were considered indispensable to Britain's status as a great power and without which
not only the nation's leading position among the powers but also
its very security and material well-being would be jeopardized.
Events were to show that the equation was unfounded, that the
interests that were indispensable to Britain's position in the world
did not require retaining sovereign control over the American colonies. At the time, however, the insight that enabled an accurate

reading of Britain's future was the possession of but a select few. These seers apart, the British political nation found in the equation a proposition so self-evident as scarcely to warrant serious discussion.

The key to post–1763 imperial policy, then, must be found above all in what was at the time the conventional wisdom respecting the foundations of national power and greatness, a wisdom shared entirely by Britain's rivals, rather than in a new concept of empire that had suddenly taken hold of men's imagination. In place of the attempt to explain postwar policy in terms of a new concept of empire, it seems far more useful to see this policy as an intensification of quite traditional views and concerns. If in the years immediately following the Seven Years' War the problems of the empire were taken more seriously than before, it was because British statesmen were now more sensitive to the importance of the empire than they once had been. They were more sensitive because they were persuaded the empire had become far more important to Britain than ever before, because its sudden expansion through war presented problems that—though they were not novel—could not be satisfactorily dealt with merely by following the ways of the past, and because the experience of the war persuaded them that the relationship with the American colonies had to be tightened overall, else imperial authority would soon become irrelevant.

The motivation of British postwar policy may now be seen in truer dimension. An element of aggressiveness was surely there, but it was compounded in at least equal measure by fear. If anything, it was largely the result of fear, and this despite the apparent confidence of the metropolis in the aftermath of the Great War for the Empire. If the colonies increasingly held the balance of power between Great Britain and a bitterly revanchist France, it was vital that Whitehall prevent their slipping from the control of the metropolis. The greater the persuasion that the security and well-being of the metropolis depended upon retaining the colonies, the more urgent the need to assure control over them. Yet the more urgent this felt need, the stronger the determination to take measures that might and, of course, did provoke resistance and further imperil the relationship.[11]

Could this apparently vicious circle have been avoided at the

[11] In a recent essay, Ian R. Christie has drawn attention to these basic concerns of British ministers in the years that followed the war; "British Politics and the American Revolution," *Albion* 9 (Fall 1977): 208–13.

outset by a policy of inaction? To the great majority of historians of the period, this question will appear little more than rhetorical. Now, as in the past, the prevailing consensus is that the metropolis need not have provoked the challenge it did to imperial authority and that the vicious circle British governments were to find themselves in was, for this reason, very largely one of their own making. Although the potential for conflict between metropolis and colonies had become considerable by the 1760s, it might nevertheless have been kept under control for a very long time had the metropolis not sought to alter the terms of its relationship with the colonies. Thus, the measure of the folly of those steps taken by the imperial state in the years 1763–65 must be found, not simply in the disastrous results to which they led, or even in the utter inability of the statesmen responsible for them to have foreseen the consequences to which they would lead, but in the failure to have appreciated that these measures were unnecessary in order to retain the interests vital to Great Britain. The argument, by now, is thoroughly familiar: the fears that Great Britain entertained of the colonies could have been avoided only by a policy that faithfully adhered to the imperial-colonial status quo. Given the meaning attached to the status quo, however, this is but a euphemism for a policy of conciliation. In turn, conciliation implied in this early period roughly what it would imply in later years when employed by opponents of a coercive policy. The Americans must be left to do more or less as they pleased. In 1763–65 this would have meant no attempt to reform and to enforce the laws of trade. Above all, it ruled out the Stamp Act or any other measure that imposed an internal tax (or, for that matter, an external tax). These measures would have been unnecessary in any event, since a policy of conciliation was probably incompatible with the retention of a British army in America, an army that, quite apart from the expense it entailed and the immediate purposes it was to serve, awakened colonial fears of the uses to which it might one day be put.

Were these consequences of conciliation—in effect, capitulation—"unthinkable" for any imperial state, particularly one whose rulers believed that in victory over the Bourbon powers they had recreated the glory of Rome? Very likely, they were. A policy of conciliation in the circumstances immediately following the Great War for the Empire required that Great Britain accept instead a relationship of de facto equality with the colonies and, in effect, surrender its pretension of ruling the colonies at all. For the war had raised issues of contention between London and America that could be left in abeyance by the imperial state only by the admission that the continental provinces were no longer subordinate. The metropolis would henceforth have to obtain the consent of the colonies to any measures that significantly affected the latter's interests.

[II]

The colonial reaction to measures taken by the metropolis raises the question posed earlier. If the ties of allegiance and affection binding the colonies to the mother country were as strong as they are commonly portrayed by historians, how is the American reaction to the measures of 1763–65 to be explained? Objection may, of course, be taken to the question itself, or, at any rate, to the evident implication held out. It may be argued that the colonial reaction testifies to the significance of these ties in the sense that without them the response would have been more serious than it was. But this objection seems more clever than substantial. By almost any reasonable standard, the American reaction, particularly to the Stamp Act, was severe. Its severity, moreover, cannot be diminished by pointing to a tradition of civil disturbances that marked the history of a number of colonies. These disturbances did not involve a direct challenge to imperial authority. They did not have the scope and magnitude of the measures taken to resist implementation of the Stamp Act. Nor did they have the approval, whether express or tacit, of a broad segment of colonial political leadership. In these, and yet other, respects the American response to the actions of the metropolis was unprecedented. It not only astonished the British—including many who were well informed on colonial affairs—but surprised not a few Americans.

The colonists' reaction may nevertheless be seen as the expected and, indeed, proportionate response to measures that were themselves startling in their severity.[12] The ties of allegiance and affection were not, after all, unconditional. They could not be expected

---

[12] Pauline Maier so argues in her study, *From Resistance to Revolution: Colonial Radicals and the Development of American Opposition to Great Britain, 1765–1776* (New York, 1972).

to withstand an assault on almost every aspect of the relationship. Strong as these bonds presumably were, the actions of the metropolis tested them beyond the point where they could reasonably be expected to exact obedience. On this view, there is no mystery in the response of otherwise faithful and contented colonies to measures threatening their liberty and well-being.

Such was, in effect, the response of the colonists and it remains today the essential response of historians who endorse the colonial position. Still, it lacks persuasiveness as an explanation of the issue raised here. Obviously, the colonists found the measures of the metropolis severe, else they would not have reacted to them as they did. Without calling for a directed verdict, however, one cannot determine the severity of the British measures simply by invoking the colonial response to them. Instead, one must ask, Whatever the colonists thought of the measures taken by the mother country, were they of such severity and of so threatening a character as to subordinate imperatives one would normally expect to arise from strong bonds of allegiance and affection? Certainly, it was— and is—nonsense to pretend that the revenue acts, even had they become fully effective, would have represented a crushing burden for the colonists. Despite the arguments of Franklin and others, the wealth of the American provinces could easily have supported these measures, which would have left the burden of taxation in the colonies no more than a modest fraction of the tax burden in the metropolis. Of course, where taxes are so nominal that they scarcely deserve the name, an increase in the order represented by the Stamp Act may readily appear severe and threatening. Similarly, where burdensome constraints on trade are disregarded with impunity, measures taken to reform patent abuses and to insure a greater measure of compliance also appear severe and threatening. This establishes very little, however, save that where men are at liberty in their behavior, they will view with considerable disfavor any attempts to constrain them.

If the larger issues attending the measures of the Grenville ministry are put to one side, there is no apparent reason for considering the measures of such severity as to provoke the response they did. The colonial reaction to the program of imperial reform can be understood only by largely abandoning the picture so often drawn of faithful colonies, closely bound to the metropolis by ties of allegiance and affection. It is clear that there were limits—and, as it turned out, rather sharp limits—to these affective sentiments. Taken together, they denote a willingness to make sacrifices for the interests of the greater collective—even more, a self-acknowledged duty to do so. Such willingness had rarely been demonstrated by the colonies, whether toward one another or toward the distant metropolis. In their mutual relations, they appear to have been almost congenitally incapable even of defining common colonial interests, let alone of acting upon and making sacrifices for such interests. Their relations with the metropolis did not deviate from this pattern of provincialism and of reluctance to acknowledge interests transcending the particular concerns of each colony. The old colonial system was not undergirded by bonds of affection and allegiance. Compliance with its laws and regulations was the result of perceived interest and advantage. Where the system worked to colonial disadvantage it was observed in the breach. So, too, in matters of imperial defense there was little record of willingness to sacrifice for interests of the greater whole.

In the light of these considerations, the emphasis that is regularly placed on the affection and allegiance of the colonies is difficult to understand. Of what did this allegiance and affection consist? The frequency of verbal declarations apart, evidence for the affective sentiments of the colonists is chiefly found in their presumed desire to remain a part of the empire. There is no reason to doubt the reality of that desire—at least, until a very late stage of the unfolding crisis. But the wish to remain a part of the empire testified primarily to the fear of the hazards and uncertainties independence would hold out for colonies that had flourished within the protective imperial cover and that, when left to their own devices, had never shown themselves able to unite their efforts. Rather than independence, those colonists who led the growing resistance to imperial authority wanted to enjoy the benefits of independence while avoiding as many of its burdens as possible. This was the essential meaning of the equality, or equivalence, sought by the colonists, a condition in many respects distinctly more advantageous for fractious provinces than was independence.[13] The desire to attain a status of equality was altogether understandable. At the same time, it requires a curious reading of the colonial outlook to see in the

---

[13] Cf. William Knox, *The Interest of the Merchants and Manufacturers of Great Britain in the Present Contest with the Colonies Stated and Considered* (London, 1774), pp. 43–45.

Americans' drive for equality evidence of the strength of affective sentiments.

It would be absurd simply to dismiss the significance of the moral and psychological bonds that tied the colonists to the mother country. Calculations of interest and advantage, however, were also significant in explaining colonial behavior, as were habit and fear. Moreover, the strength of the affective sentiments was largely a function of what can perhaps best be termed the utilitarian basis of the relationship. This is commonly recognized in the case of the metropolis. Thomas Paine's characterization of British motivation in protecting the colonies—"*interest*, not *attachment*"[14]—has been seen by historians as essentially accurate. Yet when similar motivation has been ascribed to the colonies, it has drawn objection. There is no apparent reason though for believing it to be any less true in the case of the colonies. Certainly, the Americans went to greater lengths in professing their attachment; but the frequency of such profession cannot be taken as reliable evidence for the strength of affective sentiments. The colonial record shows how conditional these sentiments were.

The burst of patriotism that attended the end of the Great War for the Empire, and that historians have so often remarked upon, followed years during which colonial conditions for displaying affection—at least verbally—had been amply satisfied by the metropolis. The rapidity with which this attachment was withdrawn once the requisite conditions were not met is impressive. Thus, the well-known statement of the colonial leader, William Smith, on the effects of passage of the Stamp Act: "This single stroke has lost Great Britain the affection of all her colonies." So long as the colonists were left at liberty to pursue their respective interests, so long as imperial authorities refrained from infringing on their internal autonomy, and so long as the mother country continued to provide the necessary framework of security within which they might and did prosper (while not enforcing those constraints of the old colonial system that would adversely affect prosperity and liberty), the Americans would remain faithful children of the empire.

---

[14] *Common Sense* (1776), in *Writings of Paine*, 1:86. The complete quotation is, "We have boasted the protection of Great Britain, without considering that her motive was *interest*, not *attachment*; and that she did not protect us from *our enemies on our account*, but from *her enemies*, on *her own account*."

Their patriotism and affection were thus vitally contingent on the promise of mother's continued benign behavior.[15]

The intensity of the colonial reaction to the postwar measures of the metropolis may in large part be accounted for by the expectations the Americans had formed of the imperial relationship and the blow administered these expectations by the imperial state. The colonists saw in the program of imperial reform a threat to their interests and a denial of their pretensions. It is not surprising that they should have done so. The postwar policy of Great Britain did indeed threaten a number of American interests and deny the colonies' most cherished pretensions. The shock and the subsequent outrage with which the colonists received the new measures must be seen against the background of the imperial policy of preceding decades.

Then, too, colonial expectations had been considerably inflated by the experience of the war. Whatever their later reading of British motivation and interest, the colonists understood the implications of the commitment the metropolis had made to expel the French from North America. The generous estimate Americans had long made of their significance to the empire was now measurably increased. Not only did they consider themselves to form the vital core of the empire; even more, they had come to represent the margin of power that enabled England to maintain supremacy over its Bourbon rivals. Nor was it only the Americans who had given themselves this exalted position. The British had also encouraged them in this respect, thereby aggravating the imperial state's difficulties by confirming the vision the colonies already entertained of themselves. When to these considerations is added the colonial

---

[15] Jack P. Greene, "An Uneasy Connection: An Analysis of the Preconditions of the American Revolution," in *Essays on the American Revolution* ed. Stephen G. Kurtz and James H. Huston, pp. 55ff, has examined what he terms the "basic substructure of expectations" entertained of the mother country by the colonists. These imperial duties of "nurturance and protection" were seen to constitute "a kind of sacred, if not entirely explicit, moral order, the preservation of which was felt to be absolutely essential to the continuation of a just—and, therefore, acceptable—relationship between Britain and the colonies." In general, Greene makes clear, the basic norm of this "sacred moral order" was the obligation of the metropolis to further the individual and group interests of the colonists and to do nothing to hinder those interests. But this is only to confirm that the sentiments of affection and allegiance were contingent on utilitarian considerations. The sacred moral order of the colonists was simply the order of their expectations, an order which in its scope and magnitude was astonishing. Significantly, Greene has almost nothing to say about the duties owed by the colonies to the mother country. Even affection and allegiance are not conceived as duties. They are simply the freely given response to the fulfillment by the metropolis of its duties.

estimate of the role they played in the war—a role seen as nothing less than that of a worthy and equal ally of Great Britian—the claim to de facto equality with the metropolis becomes entirely understandable. That claim, moreover, had been given vivid expression during the war years when an exigent metropolis had time and again backed away from confrontation with colonies whose defiance of imperial authority was overt and frequent.

The war once over, the colonists looked forward to a future relationship with the metropolis even more promising than their relationship of the recent past. Suddenly, their expectations were dashed by a program of imperial reform that appeared to them to revive imperial claims they considered long ago conceded, that illuminated as never before the conflicts of interest between them and the metropolis, and that bore unmistakable evidence that the metropolis had not the slightest intention of considering them in other than a clearly subordinate status. Indeed, the new policy simply dismissed colonial pretensions to equality of status. The limitations placed on colonial freedom still left the colonists with a very considerable area of freedom; the tightening of imperial ties still left the colonies with a degree of internal autonomy that, for colonies, was remarkable by almost any standard. These considerations proved largely irrelevant, however, for colonies that had come to equate their accustomed freedom of action with the moral order, the mother country's toleration—and protection—of this freedom with its solemn duty, and the resistance to metropolitan constraints with their sacred rights.[16]

---

[16] In his now famous essay, "Revisions in Need of Revising," in his *Challenge of the American Revolution*, pp. 50–52, Edmund S. Morgan writes that the Revolution "is one of those brute facts which historians must account for" and that it cannot be accounted for if one assumes that the empire was as "fairly administered" as the imperial historians have done. "If the British government could not run the empire without bringing on evils that appeared insufferable to men like Washington, Jefferson, John Adams, and Franklin," Morgan continues, "then the burden of proof would seem to be on those who maintain that it was fit to run an empire." In one sense, at least, Morgan's argument is unexceptionable. If the "brute fact" that the Revolution occurred is the test of whether or not the empire was "fairly administered," then obviously one can only conclude that it was not. If the great American leaders are the arbiters of whether or not Britain was "fit to run an empire," then obviously one can only conclude that it was not. What does this argument prove, however, save that men rebel when they consider their position, for whatever reasons, insufferable? Nor does the appeal to Washington, Jefferson, etc., add much, unless one assumes that they embodied the standards of insufferability and unfitness on which all reasonable men might agree. Suppose we reverse the argument and say that even if such critics of imperial policy as Chatham and Burke did not think the empire insufferable, then the burden of proof is on those who maintain that Britain was not fit to run an empire. Does this establish that, on balance, Britain was fit to run an empire?

·

These considerations have put aside the larger issues attending the measures of the Grenville government. The colonists argued that it was precisely the larger issues that could not be put aside and, here again, historians have followed them in this argument. Even if the purposes that the metropolis ostensibly sought through its measures were both limited and reasonable—though plenty of doubt and controversy arose here—and even if the measures themselves were not odious—a matter of still greater controversy—the methods these measures employed constituted an attack upon the liberties of the colonists. It was not simply what England was doing that provoked the colonial reaction, though this was bad enough, but what it might—indeed, in all likelihood, would—do if permitted to exercise the powers inherent in the measures taken to reform the system of trade and, above all, to raise a colonial revenue. Thus, the well-known statement of Moses Coit Tyler that the colonies acted "not against tyranny inflicted, but also against tyranny anticipated."[17] Yet the apparent alacrity and determination with which tyranny was anticipated does not easily square with the picture otherwise drawn of colonies closely bound to the mother country by sturdy ties of allegiance and affection. Nor is this curious juxtaposition of a belief in a ministerial conspiracy to destroy colonial liberties—for that is what "tyranny anticipated" must mean— and a devotion to the metropolis accounted for by calling attention to a political culture that nourished such belief and swiftly brought it to the surface of political life with little provocation. This may in part explain the otherwise mystifying coexistence between the dark suspicions entertained almost from the outset of the mother country's designs and the continued professions of allegiance and affection. It does little to establish the significance of these professions.

The fears and suspicions over British intentions entertained by the Americans have always been emphasized by historians when considering the springs of colonial behavior. In responding to the postwar measures of the metropolis, the colonists were not only alarmed over what they saw as a direct challenge to their interests, they were equally—if not more—concerned over the ultimate consequences of conceding the immediate issues in dispute. Once made, where would such concessions lead? Where would imperial

[17] *The Literary History of the American Revolution, 1763–1783*, 2 vols. (New York, 1897) 1:100.

authorities stop in their program of reform? Taken by themselves, the measures of the Grenville government could scarcely be seen as destroying the liberties of the colonists. Although these measures clearly challenged colonial autonomy at a number of critical points, though they denied some of the Americans' most cherished pretensions, they could hardly be considered as tyrannical. The freedom of action left to the colonists was still quite spacious; the degree of internal autonomy that remained was, for colonies, still quite extraordinary. But would the foundations of the colonial position remain secure if the new measures went unresisted? Having succeeded in their initial efforts to tighten imperial ties, would the British then rest content or would they look upon their success as an invitation to assert an ever greater control? The formal basis for claiming a control that would radically constrict the autonomy long enjoyed by the colonies had, after all, never been abandoned. The powers still claimed on behalf of colonial governors, acting through prerogative, were very considerable, and above and beyond these powers there was the sovereign authority of Parliament, an authority whose unlimited sway over the colonies went virtually unchallenged in the metropolis. The measures of the Grenville government awakened memories of past controversy over formal powers the metropolis had persistently clung to, whatever its actual practice; they aggravated fears that these powers would now be increasingly employed; and they served as a forceful reminder to many in the colonies that their situation remained ambiguous, and thus insecure.

These were the larger considerations raised by the measures of the Grenville government, and undoubtedly they played a critical role in determining the reaction of the Americans. There is little reason to doubt the sincerity and conviction with which the colonists held to them. The very ambitions of the Americans served only to strengthen their persuasion that the metropolis was now intent upon a course that, if unresisted, would lead to the loss of an autonomy the colonists had taken a century to acquire and that, once lost, would leave them entirely vulnerable to such measures future British governments might consider desirable to impose. Even if a substantial measure of trust had been entertained in the intentions of the Grenville ministry, there was no way of knowing the intentions of future ministries. The American revenue measures had been taken because of London's financially straitened position after the war. The proceeds from these measures, however, even if they had been fully realized, would not materially have eased the needs of this or succeeding governments. If equity required that the Americans shoulder part of the burden of empire, and that they do so in the manner London now prescribed, it still left open the question of what that part might eventually come to represent. The colonists could not know. At best, they could only trust—and hope—that London would remain content with the quite modest revenue it now obtained from the Americans.

The fears and suspicions with which the colonists received the measures of imperial reform not only were deeply felt; given the essential nature of the growing conflict between metropolis and colonies, they were also reasonable. In fact, the colonists had no reliable assurance with respect to the future behavior of the imperial state if its present demands were once conceded. Of course, they had no reliable assurance in any event. Even so, to concede the demands now being made upon them could scarcely improve their situation. If anything, concessions would simply encourage the metropolis to go still further in the direction it was already seen to be clearly moving.

The colonial reaction thus responded to the logic of the situation that defined the relationship, and the growing conflict, with the metropolis. Given the interests to which the Americans laid claim and the pretensions to which they aspired, the fears and suspicions aroused by the British measures were not only reasonable but compelling. Those fears and suspicions were no doubt reenforced by a political outlook that found in virtually every imperial action evidence of a design by government ministers to destroy the liberties of the colonists and to do so largely through the same corrupt use of influence that was leading to the downfall of free government in England. In the works of one leading colonial historian, however, the vision of politics held by the colonists did not merely reenforce the colonial reaction to the program of imperial reform; more than any other factor, this vision determined the reaction that was to lead first to resistance and then to rebellion. In the end, Bernard Bailyn has written, it is the "bearing of certain eighteenth-century British political ideas on the realities of politics in pre-Revolutionary America . . . that provides the sufficient background for understanding why there was a Revolution."[18] It was "a pattern of ideas, assumptions, attitudes and beliefs given distinctive shape by the opposition elements in English politics" through which the colonists "saw the world and in terms of which they themselves became participants in politics."[19] It was this ideology that, when combined with the fragile and unstable political structure in the colonies, produced the explosive amalgam that needed only the shock provided by the new imperial policy to set off the forces culminating in revolution. For every measure of the new policy was but further confirmation of what the colonists had long believed: that a comprehensive conspiracy against liberty was in train throughout the English-speaking world, a conspiracy nourished in corruption, determined upon aggrandisement, and intent upon realizing its ambitions first in America.[20]

Is it necessary, let alone sufficient, to account for the fears and suspicions of the colonists in these terms? Does the reaction of the colonists remain inexplicable, or very nearly so, in the absence of the outlook which was, as Bailyn insists, determinative of the political understanding of eighteenth-century Americans? It would not seem so. The fears and suspicions the colonists harbored, the design they professed to see in ministerial actions, are surely not distinctive only of the political culture Bailyn has analyzed with such care and imagination. These same fears and suspicions, when stripped of the admittedly distinctive terms of eighteenth-century opposition ideology, form the staple elements of nearly every conflict that, in its structural features, bears a rough comparison with the conflict that arose between England and the colonies. What Bailyn has written of the eighteenth century—that it was "an age of ideology" and that "the beliefs and fears on one side of the

---

[18] *The Origins of American Politics*, p. 13. In the foreword to his *The Ideological Origins of the American Revolution*, Bailyn writes in a similar vein: "In the end I was convinced that the fear of a comprehensive conspiracy against liberty throughout the English-speaking world . . . lay at the heart of the Revolutionary movement." In a later essay that looks back on his two influential books Bailyn declares: "American resistance in the 1760s and 1770s was a response to acts of power deemed arbitrary, degrading, and uncontrollable—a response, in itself objectively reasonable, that was inflamed to the point of explosion by ideological currents generating fears everywhere in America that irresponsible and self-seeking adventurers—what the twentieth century would call political gangsters—had gained the power of the English government and were turning first, for reasons that were variously explained, to that Rhineland of their aggressions, the colonies"; "The Central Themes of the American Revolution: An Interpretation," in Kurtz and Hutson, eds., *Essays*, p. 13.
[19] *Origins of American Politics*, p. 57.
[20] Bailyn, *Ideological Origins*, pp. 94–159.

Revolutionary controversy were as sincere as those expressed on the other"—may be written of most centuries, just as the structure of reciprocal fears he has described may serve as a description of most great conflicts. The imperial-colonial conflict arose from a desire of provincial elites to be free from external control, and from the unwillingness of metropolitan officials to acquiesce in the full development of this condition. Neither the colonial desire to be free, nor the metropolitan desire to assert control, were passions that needed special instruction from the exigencies of eighteenth-century political discourse. Clearly, an understanding of the depth and intensity of the fears entertained by the colonists is considerably enhanced by an examination of the ideology they entertained. To view this ideology as the prime causative agent in determining the colonial response is quite another matter.

In the end, the critical issue raised by the colonists' reaction to the metropolis does not concern the sources of their fears and suspicions but the possible response that Great Britain might have made to them. What could satisfactorily assuage these suspicions and fears short of a revolutionary change in the structure of the empire, a change that, even if it had been constitutionally possible, signified to the English the end of empire? For the security that the colonies were in effect demanding was no longer one that could be satisfied by their pre–1763 status. However insistent they were on returning to their previous situation, it had been precisely the ambiguities characterizing this situation that had left the way open to measures that now threatened their liberties. The response of the colonies to the measures of the imperial state went beyond the measures themselves; its intensity reflected the desire to remove the remaining reasons—or pretexts—for imperial intrusion in colonial affairs. Short of independence, this could be assured only by British acknowledgment that the colonies enjoyed a status of equality within the empire.

PART THREE

THE DIPLOMACY OF APPEASEMENT

The Rockingham Ministry

The Stamp Act Crisis, 1765–66

There is a familiar pattern to conflicts in which the parties believe that vital interests are at stake. In such conflicts perhaps the most characteristic feature is the obsession to find in almost any discrete issue arising between the parties a symbol of the larger issue and to relate virtually any conflict of interest to the underlying conflict of interest. In this manner, the conflict becomes all-pervasive. It suffuses every aspect of the relationship. Any difference, however, trivial, may be invested with great significance, for any confrontation may—and likely will—be seen as a test of the will to resist and, ultimately, to prevail. Long ago, one of the greatest of historians illuminated this pattern. In urging the Athenians to reject Sparta's ultimatum, Thucydides has Pericles say: "Let none of you think that we should be going to war for a trifle if we refuse to revoke the Megarian decree. It is a point they make much of, and say that war need not take place if we revoke this decree; but, if we do go to war, let there be no kind of suspicion in your hearts that the war was over a small matter. For you this trifle is both the assurance and the proof of your determination. If you give in, you will immediately be confronted with some greater demand, since they will think that you only gave way on this point through fear."[1]

It is roughly in these terms that the course of the crisis that led to war between Great Britain and the American colonies may be understood. Both sides believed, or came to believe, that vital interests were at stake. Both sides came to find in almost any issue arising between them a symbol of the larger issue and to relate virtually any conflict of interest to the underlying conflict of interest. To the metropolis, the survival of the empire, and consequently

[1] *History of the Peloponnesian War*, trans. Rex Warner (London, 1954), p. 92.

of Great Britain's security and well-being, depended upon colonial acknowledgment of Parliament's supreme legislative authority. To the colonies, such acknowledgment was seen to threaten the entire foundation of colonial autonomy and to open the way to the exercise of uncontrolled power. Thus, the growing colonial demand for equality of status within the empire was also centrally equated with security, for without equality, the argument ran, there could be no security. Once the issue was squarely joined in the period of the Stamp Act crisis, it came to suffuse every aspect of the relationship. On the imperial side, it explains the subsequent adoption of measures that had little relation to the objectives Britain initially had sought in reforming the empire. On the colonial side, it explains responses that seem out of all proportion to the actions that are found as causes. On either side, though particularly on the side of the colonies, what would in former circumstances have been viewed as matters of secondary importance were ultimately seen as critical tests of will. War was the only outcome that could be expected in this atmosphere, barring the capitulation of one party.

On more than one occasion, however, the British came close to a position of capitulation, only to draw back after virtually all but the one vital concession—parliamentary supremacy—had been made. On this issue, the imperial state was indeed unyielding. This issue apart, however, the record is full of concessions on the part of London. The retreat of the metropolis before American resistance, its willingness to compromise and even to abandon its policy for the colonies, is not, as has frequently been contended, indicative of a rigidity that, in the circumstances, was somehow unusual. It is not rigidity that primarily characterizes Whitehall's policy during the years of crisis, but an inconstancy that transcends mere inadvertence and that, in retrospect, still appears bewildering. For this inconstancy the British would ultimately pay a heavy price.

Until the reaction to the Stamp Act, imperial policy had had an inner coherence. Its great weakness was the lack of awareness of the imposing conditions in which it would have to be implemented. Metropolitan officials did not appreciate the depth and intensity of the desire in the continental provinces for an equality of status that was utterly incompatible with the imperial structure and design. The resistance to the Stamp Act should have left no doubt on this score. In the wake of such resistance, there was no longer the slightest excuse for ignorance over conditions in the colonies.

Yet British governments did not behave accordingly. Although a huge flash of lightning had suddenly illuminated the landscape for them, they appeared to grope about much the same as before—though not quite the same as before, of course, since they had seen something. What is astonishing is the persistent inability to act on the basis of what they had seen. If the British had consciously and deliberately sought to create an effective resistance in the colonies, while at the same time destroying what remaining authority they possessed, they could scarcely have gone about doing it in a more effective manner than they did. Step by step, they prepared the colonies—in almost every way—for armed rebellion. All they did not do was to give those who rebelled the arms with which to wage war. And in a way they did this too in the end.

[I]

If the decade-long crisis that was to lead from resistance to rebellion is considered as a drama, the opposition to the Stamp Act appears as the first act. In the conventional historiography of the period it is so treated. Although the act is deemed to be very important, it is still seen as only one of several. Even if it sets the tone for the acts that are to follow, it does not determine the outcome of the play. The intervening acts have an integrity of their own. Each contributes to the tragic denouement, which, though becoming more likely with each successive act, remains uncertain almost to the end. This perception of the Stamp Act crisis, however, misses its true significance. The Stamp Act crisis was not merely one act in a much larger drama; it was very nearly the drama itself. What follows seems almost to resemble a set piece, a fulfillment of destinies that cannot be altered, a kind of long epilogue.

This is so if only for the reason that the Stamp Act crisis raised to the surface, and did so with explosive suddenness, the issue—parliamentary sovereignty—that would henceforth dominate the transatlantic relationship. It would dominate the relationship because it went to the very heart of the relationship. Moreover, the issue was one that could not readily be compromised, if at all. As a matter of policy, it might be left in abeyance for an indefinite period, though this would have proven very difficult and particularly so once the issue had been brought into the open. This tenuous prospect apart, however, there was no apparent way by which the issue might have been compromised. In this respect, those statesmen—from Grenville on—who argued that Parliament either was or was not sovereign in its authority over the colonies held a position difficult to refute. The colonies, in fact, did not refute it but, if anything, confirmed it. They did so not primarily by insisting that Parliament's authority over the colonies did not comprise the power of taxation, important though this denial undoubtedly was, but by implying from the outset that the "due subordination" owed to Parliament was itself a matter that the colonies had as much right to determine as did the legislative body of the mother country. This claim was inherent in the logic of a position that sought from the beginning to place effective restraint on the controlling power of Parliament, and in the declarations of the Stamp Act Congress that logic is apparent. The levying of taxes was seen as the most important manifestation of this power and accordingly the greatest threat to the colonies. But it was not the only power, just as it was not the only threat.

The authority of empire is endangered by verbal defiance that goes unpunished. It is lost through the failure to respond effectively to active resistance. The Stamp Act crisis dealt a crippling blow to the substance of British authority in the colonies. The effect of the crisis was to begin the process of turning the imperial presence into an object of scorn and contempt. At almost every stage of the crisis it was the imperial state that betrayed weakness, timidity, and indecision, whereas the colonies projected strength, audacity, and a sense of direction. The one example of apparent resolution— whatever its wisdom—shown by the metropolis was the decision to enact the Stamp Bill. Taken in response to the direct challenge thrown down by the colonies during the immediately preceding months, this one example of imperial resolution was only apparent. The colonial response to passage of the Stamp Bill swiftly laid bare for all to see the fragility of imperial authority when challenged and the irresolution of imperial will effectively to confront the challenge. Frustrated at every turn in its efforts to implement the tax, its officials threatened with violence if they supported the measure (and, on occasion, even if they did not, as in the case of Massachusetts Lieutenant Governor Thomas Hutchinson), the power that had supposedly recreated the glory of Rome remained passive. Colonial resistance revealed in striking manner the weakness of

what Whitehall was still wont to consider normal means for asserting imperial authority. These means depended for their effectiveness on crown officials who proved to be impotent once the
crisis broke. When colonial governors called for the support of
militias, the latter failed to respond. Similarly, local magistrates
refused to enforce the tax and to punish those resisting implementation of the law. Crown officials were thus isolated and, in a
number of instances, intimidated. Not surprisingly, few showed
any eagerness to take a firm stand against violators of the Stamp
Act.

[II]

Although forewarned that the tax might provoke some resistance,
the British were stunned by the scope and intensity of the colonial
reaction.[2] A new government was left to deal with the full-blown
crisis. In theory, at any rate, several courses of action were open
to the Rockingham ministry. It might adopt a policy of enforcement.
At the other extreme, it might concede with no qualification. Alternatively, it might concede the immediate issue in dispute, the
Stamp Act, while preserving its position in principle. Yet another
course was to modify the Stamp Act. Finally, the act might be
suspended, whether for a limited period or permanently.

In practice, the choice was much narrower, for the two extreme
options were virtually ruled out from the start. Although the Rockingham administration would not give serious consideration to a
policy of enforcement, it also could not give serious consideration
to a policy of concession with no attending qualification. The latter
course would have been seen on almost all sides to concede the
issue of parliamentary supremacy, certainly in matters of taxation
and possibly beyond, and could not have been carried through
Parliament even had the ministry wanted to do so. Modification
raised the questions of what was to be modified and whether such

---

[2] Years later, in the debate in Commons over repeal of the Townshend duties, Grenville,
in recalling the opposition to the Stamp Act, declared: "that opposition I own I did not
foresee. If I had imagined, that great bodies of people would, in the space of a few months,
have changed their opinions, I would not have proposed it; because I wished too well to
the safety of Great Britain, to have made such a proposition, under such circumstances";
*Sir Henry Cavendish's Debates of the House of Commons during the Thirteenth Parliament
of Great Britain,* 1:494–95.

modifications as might be agreed upon would prove acceptable to the colonies. Even a very watered down act might nevertheless be rejected by the colonists and for substantially the same reasons that they had rejected the original act. Rejection would raise once again—though now perhaps in more pointed form—the dreaded prospect of enforcement. Suspension, if temporary, would only put off the day when a choice would have to be made. If permanent, it would be a barely disguised functional equivalent of concession without qualification.

Thus, the avoidance of enforcement and of concession without qualification left the Rockingham government with a narrow range of choice. Little was left save the course that was finally chosen: repeal of the Stamp Bill attended by the affirmation of Parliament's unqualified supremacy over the colonies. To the extent the Rockingham ministry demonstrated ingenuity and effectiveness in its handling of the crisis, these qualities were not so much apparent in the course finally marked out as in the rationale given for, and the tactics employed in, taking that course.

Was the rejection of a policy of enforcement the result mainly of the contingent event that, in the fall of 1765, a government was in office composed mostly of men inclined to conciliate the colonies?[3] The Grenville ministry had come to an end the preceding summer for reasons quite unconnected with the American crisis. Had Grenville been able to sustain a different personal relationship with the King, his administration would have had to deal with the effects brought on by his creation, the Stamp Act. Would it have followed a policy of enforcement, as Grenville was later to insist upon and to move for in the Commons during debate over repeal of the Stamp Act?[4]

The question at issue also arises for the early period of the Rockingham ministry itself. Until the end of October, 1765, the effective head of the government of "old Whigs" was not Lord Rockingham but the King's uncle, the duke of Cumberland. Without question, Cumberland took a harder attitude toward the first signs of colonial resistance to the Stamp Act than did Rockingham or the two sec-

---

[3] This is the conclusion suggested by Ian R. Christie and Benjamin Woods Labaree, *Empire or Independence, 1760–1776*, p. 64.
[4] On February 7, 1766, Grenville moved before the Committee of the Whole House on America for enforcement of the Stamp Act; Ryder Diaries, pp. 282ff.

retaries of state, Conway and Grafton.[5] Yet at the very time that the full extent and seriousness of the colonial reaction were first becoming apparent to the government, Cumberland suddenly died. His death ended the possibility—such as it was—that the government might pursue a policy of enforcement. Not only did his death remove the one commanding figure from the administration, thereby markedly increasing its dependence on the man—William Pitt— the Rockinghamites from the outset had wanted as their leader, it weakened the position of those disposed to take a firm position on American policy while strengthening the position of those favoring a conciliatory line.

The question persists, Would the preceding government of Grenville or the Rockingham ministry, with Cumberland, have taken the path of enforcement? Serious doubt must persist that either would have done so. This doubt does not rest, in the main, on the practical problems attending enforcement. These problems—the legal obstacles in the way of employing the military in the colonies, the very modest forces available, the highly inconvenient deployment of these forces, and the striking debility betrayed by royal officials in responding to the colonial challenge — were certainly real enough. At the same time, none prevented the metropolis from the serious attempt to enforce the Stamp Act had the determination to do so been there. Nearly a decade later, most of these same problems confronted the North government in the final crisis that would lead to war. By then, however, the illusions that would persist for a decade had finally been dispelled—at least for most—and the North ministry recognized, however reluctantly, that its choice was one between employing force and abandoning even the pretense that the colonies were still subordinate to the King-in-Parliament.

In 1765, the British political nation was still very far from confronting the reality of this choice. Although there were those who warned that the choice would one day have to be made, they were

[5] Indeed, Conway, the secretary of state for the Southern Department, had taken the American position at the time of the passage of the Stamp Act in the spring of 1765. It remains true that Rockingham and most of his followers had not come to office with any articulated view toward the Stamp Act. Insofar as they were intent on reversing the work of the previous ministry, their resolution was confined to Grenville's 1764 legislation, and even here their concern was mostly focused on matters—the Spanish logwood and bullion trades—that were among the least important of American complaints; see Paul Langford, *The First Rockingham Administration, 1765–1766* (Oxford, 1973), pp. 112–17.

as yet a minority and would remain so for years to come. In the meantime, what was real and immediate were the costs and hazards of employing force to obtain colonial obedience. After the death of Cumberland, the Rockingham government clearly entertained no intention of incurring these costs and hazards.

Still, it is altogether likely that a more self-assured and more hardline adminstration would also have sought a solution to the Stamp Act crisis which, in principle, reaffirmed Parliament's supremacy over the colonies while, in practice, compromising— whether through repeal, modification, or suspension—this supremacy in the critical instance of taxation. Much has been made by historians of the political consensus in the metropolis on the issue of parliamentary supremacy over America. But there was another consensus as well. Although less articulate, it drew the line short of a policy of enforcement when treating with the continental colonies. A Grenville administration, no less than a Rockingham administration, would have been hard-pressed in any attempt to break this line. Almost a decade later, with a government that was presumably much more hard line than the Rockingham government, in economic circumstances seen as much more favorable to Great Britain than those of 1765, and with a political crisis that appeared to the large majority of the political nation as much more serious than the Stamp Act crisis had been, it was still very difficult for the North ministry to make a clear choice for a policy of enforcement. Indeed, the choice was not made with the Coercive Acts, but only when the failure of those acts had become glaringly apparent. These considerations, it would seem, must qualify the conclusion drawn by some historians that in late 1765 a civil war was avoided because the British government was led by conciliatory men. This it was, but even less conciliatory men would have hesitated to draw the sword, given the prevailing consensus. It was this consensus that must account for a policy of concession.[6]

---

[6] In the case of the Rockingham administration before the death of Cumberland on October 31, 1765—a period of three months during which Cumberland, though holding no office, was the real force—there is a disparity of opinion among historians. Paul Langford has written that "in fact it is perfectly clear that, at the time, Conway and his colleagues really did intend the use of force in America"; ibid., p. 81. The "time" to which Langford refers is October, the month when Whitehall first became aware of the colonial reaction in the preceding August. The evidence in support of this view is, in the main, the orders sent by the secretary of state for the Southern Department, Conway, to General Gage, the British

[III]

This consensus also accounts for the strategy the Rockingham ministry adopted to resolve the crisis brought on by the Stamp Act. The strategy had to respond to two imperatives. It had to meet the requirement that a solution not be seen to compromise Parliament's supremacy. At the same time, it had to persuade those otherwise opposed to repeal that retention of the Stamp Act would prove injurious not only to colonial but, above all, to metropolitan interests. The first imperative could be met by the reaffirmation

---

army commander in North America, and the instructions, also sent by Conway, to the several colonial governors. The orders to Gage, dated October 24, were very general and very cautionary in tone. Having taken note of the "disturbances" in the colonies, Conway wrote: "These Events will probably create Applications to You, in which the utmost Exertion of your Prudence may be necessary, so as justly to temper your Conduct between that Caution and Coolness, which the Delicacy of such a Situation may demand, on the one hand, and the Vigour necessary to suppress Outrage and Violence, on the other." Gage was told that "positive instructions" are not possible, and that he must act as circumstances require according to his judgment. The operative passage reads: "But, having taken every Step, which the utmost Prudence and Lenity can dictate, in compassion to the Folly and ignorance of some misguided People, You will not . . . where your Assistance may be wanted to strengthen the hand of Government, fail to concur, in every proper Measure, for its Support, by such a timely Exertion of Force, as may be necessary to repell Acts of Violence and Outrage, and to provide for the Maintenance of Peace, and good Order in The Provinces"; *The Correspondence of General Thomas Gage with the Secretaries of State and with the War Office and the Treasury, 1763–1775,* 2:28–29. This was, admittedly, an order to employ force after having exhausted all other means. In context, however, it was so encumbered by qualifications as to leave everything to Gage. Its effect could hardly be other than to remind Gage that he would be held strictly accountable in the event he used his forces unwisely. In Conway's circular letter of October 24 to the governors in North America, much the same language is repeated and the governors are instructed "if a timely exertion of force is necessary" to "make the proper application to general Gage, or lord Colvil, commanders of his Majesty's land and naval forces in America." The circular letter continues: "For however unwillingly his Majesty may consent to the exertion of such powers as may endanger the safety of a single subject; yet can he not permit his own dignity, and the authority of the British legislature, to be trampled on by force and violence, and in avowed contempt of all order, duty and decorum"; *PH,* 16:117. By mid-December, Conway's flight from the course of coercion is clear. In a letter of December 15 to Gage, he wrote: "Your Situation is certainly delicate and difficult; it requires both Prudence and Firmness in the Conduct of all employed for His Majesty's Service there, especially considering what you say of the Difficulty, or rather Impossibility of drawing any considerable Number of Men together, and of the Impracticability of attempting any Thing by Force in the present Disposition of the People, without a respectable Body of Troops"; *Gage,* 2:30. Gage's lack of forces was well known to Conway in October, when the secretary had sent the instructions some have interpreted as intending the use of force. Nothing had changed in the period between late October and mid-December, save the determination of the government to settle the crisis through some form of concession. Yet this determination says nothing one way or the other about the government's intent in October. In later debate (February 3, 1766) in Commons, Conway declared that he could "never consent to . . . enforcing the Stamp Law by a military force." In reply, Grenville, pointing to Conway's instructions of October 24, asked: "Has not Conway ordered force himself? Was it because he knew Gage

of parliamentary authority over the colonies and, by the end of December, the ministry had determined upon the Declaratory Act. The assertion of principle would have to come first, for without it there could be little, if any, prospect of obtaining the abandonment of principle in practice. The second imperative proved more difficult to satisfy. A careful case for repeal had to be built. It had to be seen as responding to important interests. Pressures for repeal had already begun in November by British merchants prominent in American trade. Although colonial nonimportation agreements were concluded only in October, November, and December of 1765, the merchants had anticipated these agreements for several months. In December, the merchants' appeals to the ministry to repeal the Stamp Act were given added strength by those manufacturers with a stake in the American trade.[7]

The campaign for repeal found a receptive target in Rockingham. It did so if for no other reason than the ties Rockingham had always maintained with commercial interests. The merchants had long formed a part of the political base that supported the old Whigs. Not surprisingly, the persuasion of the mercantile elements that a drying up of the American trade would spell catastrophe for many

and Colville could send no force or no ships, that he gave these specious but delusive directions?" Ryder Diaries, pp. 261, 275.

Who, then, was the "real" Conway? P.D.G. Thomas, British Politics and the Stamp Act Crisis, p. 138, is of the opinion that the instructions of October 24 did not embody any decision on colonial policy, that the orders were not intended to be put into force, that any administration faced with the colonial crisis would have had to issue similar instructions (which their recipients knew how to interpret), and that the ministers were in any case aware that circumstances—above all, the inadequate state of the military forces—would prevent any effective action. Thomas concludes: "The instructions were a piece of face-saving, promulgated to avoid any subsequent charge of negligence." The disparity between Langford and Thomas is not over the viability of the ministry's orders. Both are of the view that, in the circumstances, the orders could not have been executed. Disagreement centers, instead, on the intent of those sending the instructions, and on this issue, it would seem, Thomas is closer to the mark. Of course, the further question is what might have happened had the duke of Cumberland lived. Would he have insisted upon pursuing a policy of enforcement and thereby overcome the obstacles that, in October, remained in the way of such policy? Whereas Langford believes this highly likely, Thomas is more reserved. Christie and Labaree, Empire or Independence, p. 64, agree with Langford. "Cumberland's death . . . perhaps alone prevented the cabinet from committing itself a second time, and irrevocably, to an immediate armed conflict in North America." As noted in the text, the difficulty with this view is that it largely neglects the broader consensus prevailing in Britain at the time, a consensus that militated against a resolution of the colonial conflict by armed force. It strains the imagination to believe that Cumberland's presence would have sufficed to break the bounds of this consensus.

[7] On the relationship between the ministry and various economic interests, see Langford, Rockingham Administration, pp. 119–25, 188–90.

of them made an immediate impression on Rockingham. Yet the alacrity with which Rockingham embraced their cause and sought their relief was also due to his immediate perception that he had found a way out of the crisis. Unable to see any acceptable way of implementing the Stamp Act, yet fearful of an admission of impotence that would invite political attack and only serve to strengthen resistance in Parliament to repeal, the ministry could respond to what might plausibly be held up as a compelling interest now endangered by legislation that, for reasons quite apart from principle, ought never to have been enacted.

Still, a timid and never quite united ministry had to be given a final push. It was provided by Pitt. In mid-January 1766, the hero of the Great War for the Empire finally revealed his position on the American crisis. The Stamp Act, Pitt declared in his long-awaited speech to the House of Commons, had to be repealed, and this because it was unconstitutional. The Americans not being represented in Parliament, the Commons had no right to lay an internal tax upon them. Pitt had gone measurably further than the administration had wanted to go. Rockingham and his ministerial allies would not, and could not, disavow Parliament's right to tax the colonies. The tax they were ready to repeal was considered unwise, imprudent, even inequitable, but it was not deemed unconstitutional. On the last claim, the man they had in vain entreated to lead them would have to stand alone.

Pitt's call for repeal of the Stamp Act nevertheless served to crystallize opinion within the government and to push it toward a decision. By late January, the substance of the decision had become clear and had found general support within the government. The ministry would press for repeal of the Stamp Act. The preliminary step to doing so, however, would have to be the solemn affirmation of Parliament's supremacy. Moreover, to appease those—in the ministry, in Parliament, and in the country—who might yet entertain reservations over the determination of the government to preserve imperial authority over the colonies, the government would propose additional resolutions condemning the unlawful activities of the colonists. The resolutions disapproved the measures taken by the colonial assemblies to foment resistance, recommended that the King order the colonial governors to see to the proper punishment of the instigators of the riots, and proposed that the King recommend to the governors that they should recommend to their respective assemblies the affording of compensation to those who, in attempting to uphold the act, had suffered in their persons and property. These resolutions, subscribed to without enthusiasm by Rockingham, were the price required for repeal.[8] In the immediate aftermath of the crisis, the colonists would leave little doubt over their attitude toward these largely symbolic gestures. They would be given short shrift as, indeed, that greater symbol, the Declaratory Act, would be given.

The tactics of the government were no less simple than its strategy for securing repeal of the Stamp Act. Once the passage of the resolutions had paved the way for consideration of the bill for repealing the tax, the government would make every effort to narrow the debate to those issues in which it presumably held the high ground. This meant the avoidance, so far as possible, of constitutional issues and of the challenge the colonists had thrown down to the authority of Parliament. It was not law but economics, not principle but expediency, that the ministry was intent on emphasizing. The Stamp Act had to be repealed, the government's brief ran, because the economic consequences of the act threatened both the metropolis and the colonies. The latter could not, even if they would, pay the tax and continue to buy a similar quantity of British goods. The decline in trade, particularly when the full effects of the nonimportation acts were once felt, would strike at the interests of merchants and manufacturers alike. A decline in

[8] Pitt apart, a principal reason for delay in reaching a policy decision was the persisting division within the ministry. With three important figures opposed to repeal—Northington, Yorke, and Townshend—the fate of any attempt to push repeal through Parliament would be, at best, uncertain. Moreover, the King was reluctant from the outset to agree to repeal. In mid-January he voiced his desire that the government "act firmly until the arduous business of the American colonys is over;" George to Lord Egmont, *The Correspondence of King George the Third from 1760 to December 1783*, 1:220. What did acting firmly mean for him? There is no evidence that it ever meant enforcement. Instead, the King wanted to keep the act, though in modified form, and he expressed this in a memorandum of February 10, following a misunderstanding with Rockingham, which read; "I told him [Rockingham] I had . . . given him permission to say I prefer'd Repealing to Enforcing the Stamp Act; but that Modification I had ever thought both more consistent with the honour of this Country, and all the Americans would with any degree of Justice hope for"; 1:268–69. George III was never quite clear on what modification meant for him, however, and in the end submitted to Rockingham's argument that the only real choice was between enforcement and repeal. Yorke, the attorney general, was clearer on this matter and in pushing for modification proposed that an amended Stamp Act remedy colonial objections respecting the specie shortage, the vice-Admiralty courts, and stamp duties on customs clearances; Langford, *Rockingham Administration*, p. 130. In January, the opposition of those in the ministry who wished to take a firmer position than Rockingham—though who also drew back from force—was largely mollified by the resolutions noted in the text, in the final formulation of which Yorke had been closely involved.

manufactures would mean a rise in unemployment and the prospect of domestic instability. These threatening prospects could be relieved, the government insisted, only by repeal of the Stamp Act. Once the act was repealed, a grateful and again submissive America would bear out the wisdom of the ministry's policy.

This was the burden of the government's case for repeal. To support its position, an impressive array of witnesses testified to the dire consequences that would follow for Britain's commercial interests and domestic tranquillity in the absence of repeal. It was this testimony and evidence that a number of historians have seen as decisive in securing repeal of the Stamp Act. In reply to the government's case, the opposition did not effectively respond in terms of economic interest. By failing to do so, it has been suggested, they virtually conceded the considerations of expediency invoked by the government. Instead, the chosen grounds for the opposition's case against repeal were the dangers of the grave constitutional issues raised by the colonial challenge, the ultimate aspirations entertained by the Americans, and the encouragement repeal would give to those aspirations. The thrust of the opposition's argument, however, was blunted by the Declaratory Act. Having thus largely neutralized the opposition, there remained the impression the government's case had made on the large, and indispensable, independent vote. In the end, the support given the ministry by the independents insured passage of the bill repealing the Stamp Tax.

Was the Rockingham government's case for repeal well-founded and did the ministry believe its own brief? Recent historiography has replied in the negative to the first question. The causal connection drawn between the Stamp Act and the recession in Britain was without foundation. The recession antedated the crisis. Its roots lay in the general depression of trade and industry which followed an immediate postwar boom. The decline had begun in 1764 and had persisted throughout 1765, whereas the effects of Grenville's American legislation—and certainly the effects of the Stamp Act—could not have been registered before early 1766 at the earliest. The government, however, had found these effects even before the nonimportation acts had gone into effect.[9]

Does this response effectively refute the case for repeal made

[9] See Langford, *Rockingham Administration*, pp. 185–89; and Thomas, *Stamp Act Crisis*, pp. 214–16.

by the Rockingham ministry? It would not appear so, for the reason that the refutation does not really meet the case to which it is ostensibly addressed. In examining the link between Britain's economic distress and the Stamp Act, historians have addressed the past, that is, the period prior to early 1766. But the ministry's case was addressed, in the main, to the present and future, that is, to early 1766 and beyond. Clearly, no credence could be attached to the alleged effects of actions that had yet to be taken. The government did not pretend otherwise. It did not argue in late 1765 that the decline of trade with the colonies was the result of a reaction that had not occurred. It did contend that this decline was due in part to the 1764 American legislation of the Grenville ministry, a charge that was not and could not be substantiated.

If the effects attributed to the 1764 legislation were without foundation, the same must be said of the critique the Rockingham government made of the Stamp Act itself. The burden of this critique, with its emphasis on the inability of the colonists to pay the stamp taxes, was not difficult to refute. Neither the alleged poverty of the colonies nor the shortage of specie, which was real enough, was an imposing obstacle to the annual payment of approximately sixty thousand pounds.[10] In the House of Lords protest of March 11, 1766, against committing the bill to repeal the Stamp Act, it was noted that the tax

if divided amongst 1,200,000 people . . . would be only one shilling per head a year; which is but a third of the wages usually paid to every labourer or manufacturer there for one day's labour . . . that of the debts contracted by those colonies in the last war, above £1,755,000 has already been discharged, during the course of three years only . . . that the bounties and advantages given to them by parliament in 1764 and 1765, and the duties thereby lost to Great Britain for their service, and, in order to enable them the more easily to pay this tax, must necessarily amount, in a few years, to a far greater sum than the produce thereof.[11]

If the argument of this unavailing protest was in some respects exaggerated—particularly the estimate given to the benefits conferred on America by the 1764 and 1765 legislation—it was basically

---

[10] The total annual revenue expected from the Stamp Act was approximately one hundred ten thousand pounds, but fifty thousand pounds were to come from the British West Indies. Although the Stamp Act specified that the revenues collected in America were to be spent in North America, this still did not prevent the shift of specie from the major seaboard colonies to sites—Canada and the Floridas—where the British army was concentrated.
[11] PH, 16:183–84.

well-founded. The argument of incapacity was no more persuasive than the argument that payment of the tax would gravely impair the ability of the colonists to sustain the same level of British exports as before. At most, the economic effects of the tax would have acted as a modest depressant upon the general level of trade.

The burden of the government's case for repeal did not, in fact, rest upon these considerations. Nor did the failure of the opposition to mount a persuasive response indicate otherwise. Grenville and his allies could have met the attack upon the alleged economic effects of the 1764 American legislation, just as they could have disposed effectively of the economic critique leveled against the Stamp Act. What they could not easily dispose of were the economic consequences held out by the political weapon of nonimportation. They could, and did, point out that the nonimportation resolutions were themselves a grave challenge to imperial authority over the colonies and that to give way before the threat of these acts would only encourage the colonies to make new demands. This argument, however, did not and could not meet the fears on which the ministry had based its case. The economic threat held out by nonimportation remained. In the absence of an acceptable alternative political solution to that threat, there was no apparent way by which it could be shunted aside. The economic interests at stake were significant; the government's arguments were persuasive because, considered within their own terms, they had a solid foundation.

There is, moreover, no reason to doubt that the Rockingham ministry believed in the essential case it made for repeal. The government was insincere in not admitting that it was yielding to force, or, to put the matter differently, that it was yielding to a threat that could be countered effectively only by force. The resort to nonimportation, once implemented, would leave no real option to the government other than force, should repeal be rejected. In this light, the course on which the government set out was not one merely characterized by expediency. It did not partake of a free choice. At least, the principal actors did not think so and their arguments, when carefully considered, do not yield a contrary impression. If it is still maintained that the ministry was less than candid in presenting its case, it must also be said that, as such matters go, the Rockingham government was not particularly mendacious, given the limits within which it had determined to act.

These limits, moreover, were known to, and largely accepted by, almost all the participants in the debate.[12]

[IV]

There is no simple, yet satisfactory, manner in which the debate over repeal of the Stamp Act may be characterized. Reflecting the disparate and even contradictory motives that already formed the basis of British policy toward America and that were to continue to inform policy in the decade ahead, the debate may perhaps best be seen as a kind of prelude to the policy dilemmas that faced the metropolis in the coming decade. It also provides a partial explanation of what otherwise may appear inexplicable in British policy during these years of deepening crisis.

Although the dilemmas of policy assumed a variety of expressions, in the end they could be reduced to one. Without the effective assertion of sovereign authority over the colonies, there was no apparent way by which the metropolis could be assured of retaining an interest considered vital to its security, status, and material well-being. Yet the reaction to the Stamp Act revealed

---

[12] Evidence of this second consensus against the use of force is provided by the vote on Grenville's February 7 motion for a formal address to the crown, requesting the enforcement of all laws, including the Stamp Act. It was anticipated that the motion would destroy the ministry. Instead, the government defeated it by a stunning 140-vote majority. As Thomas rightly emphasizes, this signaled the end for a policy of enforcement; thereafter the issue was whether modification or repeal was the best manner of conciliation; *Stamp Act Crisis*, p. 212.

The February 7 vote is of relevance to what Langford has called "the central problem in the passing of the repeal of the Stamp Act; what persuaded so many Independents, who had no interest in political or personal profit, 'so grossly,' as one of their opponents put it, to 'Change their late opinion'?" *Rockingham Administration*, p. 175. Langford's answer is that the Independents shifted to the side of the administration because they accepted a causal link between Grenville's American legislation and the commercial and industrial crisis in Britain. This early vote is important if only because it shows an Independent shift occurring before the Rockinghams had a chance to present their battery of witnesses. In explaining why the Independents voted so decisively with the ministry, one cannot rely on the economic case presented by the government. It is true that Langford is seeking to explain why the Independents favored repeal rather than modification, whereas the February 7 vote concerns the question of immediate enforcement of the act. The earlier vote, however, set the conditions under which the question of modification had to be considered. What that vote revealed was a reluctance to deal with the problems that modification would have kept open.

043198$$31   06-11-82 17-18-10

that there was no apparent way of effectively—and not merely formally—asserting sovereign authority without a willingness to enforce that authority. The central dilemma of policy arose from the fact that the insistence upon exercising Parliament's supremacy over the colonies was matched by the insistence upon avoiding the consequences to which this exercise might now be expected to lead. The inconstancy that otherwise seems inexplicable in British policy reflected the tortuous route taken by successive governments in London in their attempts to escape from the horns of this dilemma. In the end, each attempt necessarily failed.

The chief significance, then, of the debate over repeal of the Stamp Act is that, despite the efforts of the Rockingham government, it laid bare the great dilemma of policy. The debate illuminated the twofold consensus that conditioned Britain's American policy until 1775 and that made a viable resolution of the dilemma impossible. For if one part of this consensus pointed to enforcement, the other part drew the line at enforcement. Given the circumstances in which conflict between metropolis and colonies arose, the practical outcome of this antinomy could be only the steady concession of effective authority by the metropolis. This was of course a solution of sorts, but it was scarcely a viable one. Eventually the metropolis would either have to concede even its formal authority or breach the line that fell short of enforcement. The parliamentary opposition—led by Grenville—saw this clearly enough in 1766, even if its determination to breach that line must be questioned.

In 1766, the Rockingham whigs were an accurate barometer of politically effective opinion. The British political nation was no more willing to enforce parliamentary supremacy in 1766 than was the ministry. The debate over repeal is significant not only in demonstrating this unwillingness but in illuminating the reasons for it as well. Clearly, the major reason was fear of the consequences of not repealing the Stamp Act. Had there been other, equally important reasons they would have been apparent before the late fall of 1765; but they had not been apparent. There had been only token opposition to the passage of the Stamp Act in the spring of 1765. Later, during the summer, when the new ministry came to office, it did not bring a commitment to repeal the tax. The move toward repeal was clearly prompted by colonial opposition. Had the Americans submitted to the measure, there is little reason to believe that the Rockingham ministry would have sought to undo Grenville's work, and there is even less reason to believe they could have succeeded.

The fear that formed so pervasive a motivation in British policy is easily misunderstood. Englishmen did not doubt that the metropolis could crush America to atoms, as the great Pitt had assured them. Indeed, they would cherish the conviction of their military invincibility to the very end, just as they would not be shaken from their belief in the military incompetence of America until they were faced with defeat. Still, the danger that the Bourbon powers would enter any war that arose between the metropolis and the colonies could not be discounted, and in this case Britain's military superiority over the colonies might prove irrelevant. Even if this worry could be overcome, as it sometimes was, imperial hubris did not prevent the British from asking what price they might pay for a "successful" conquest. The costs and consequences of war with America were incalculable. For both Britain and America, war might well mean economic ruin, "death to both countries," as Conway put it in debate. For the metropolis, it would leave a debt that, coming on top of the already burdensome debt resulting from the Seven Years' War, was likely to prove totally unmanageable. Those who were otherwise most severe in their attitude toward the colonies—Grenville, Bedford, and Halifax—were of all statesmen the least likely to take measures that would increase a debt they believed was already ruinous. All the reasons that had fueled the traditional country and anticontinentalist opposition toward war came into play to weaken metropolitan resolve. The effects of a successful conquest on the distribution of power at home could not be fully known. In the same speech that Pitt assured the British of their strength, he added, "In such a case, your success would be hazardous. America, if she fell, would fall like a strong man. She would embrace the pillars of the state, and pull down the constitution along with her."[13]

These were the considerations that ultimately conditioned debate over repeal of the Stamp Act. The pattern of policy that resulted—and that would persist for nearly a decade—was one of

[13] *PH*, 16:107.

04319$$$32   06-11-82 17-19-00

appeasement. The Rockingham ministry's emphasis on the commercial interest and the injury done to this interest by the Stamp Act should not be seen to alter this conclusion, for appeasement is nearly always marked by self-deception. To believe that it is undertaken for reasons other than fear and a sense of impotence is part of its pathology. For the appeaser, the will to believe is substituted for the will to act. Thus the illusions generated by appeasement will persist in the face of a reality that by any normal reckoning ought to dispel them. Thus it was for Rockingham. And thus it would be for his successors.

[V]

It is in the effects on the colonies that the true significance of the Stamp Act crisis must ultimately be seen. Although in 1766 the Declaration of Independence remained a decade away, its moral and psychological cornerstone had now been laid. The course and outcome of the crisis gave the colonies a confidence in dealing with the metropolis they had never before possessed and would never lose. The crisis opened their eyes to the benefits that even a modest degree of intercolonial cooperation might bring. More important still was the lesson it conveyed to them of their economic power and importance. In this respect, a keen observer of the change that occurred in the colonies wrote:

Elevated with the advantage they had gained, from that day forward, instead of feeling themselves dependent on Great Britain, they conceived that, in respect to commerce, she was dependent on them. It inspired them with such ideas of the importance of their trade, that they considered the Mother Country to be brought under greater obligations to them, for purchasing her manufactures, than they were to her for protection and the administration of civil government. The freemen of British America . . . conceived it to be within their power, by future combinations, at any time to convulse, if not to bankrupt, the nation from which they sprung.[14]

Thus, what had heretofore been intimations of greatness were suddenly transformed into realities for the colonists.

[14] David Ramsay, *The History of the American Revolution*, 1:74–75.

The rejoicing in the colonies, on hearing the news of the repeal, was spontaneous and unaffected. Many colonists believed that some, at least, of their English friends had acted on the basis of principles similar to those which the colonists had themselves urged. South Carolina erected a statue of Pitt, whose name was honored throughout the colonies. Yet these warm expressions of friendship could not obscure the deeper meaning of British conciliation. The Americans understood that repeal had been secured not primarily because Parliament had come to see the justice of their position, but because vigorous opposition in the colonies had left the metropolis with virtually no alternative but to retreat. The colonists believed—and in this there was no self-deception—that it was their own conduct, not the pressures of the merchants and manufacturers of Great Britain, and not even the sentiments of their English friends, that had brought them relief.[15] The London merchants advised their colonial correspondents that "it has been a constant argument against the repeal that . . . the Parliamentary vote of right will be waste paper, and that the colonies will understand very well that what is pretended to be adopted on mere commercial principles of expedience is really yielded through fear,"[16] and consequently warned the colonists to behave. Yet the plea of the London Merchants could not wipe clean the record of the previous year. The crisis had shown that the authority of the imperial state could directly and successfully be defied. In the end, this was the only lesson that would matter.[17]

---

[15] Cf. John Dickinson, *An Address to the Committee of Correspondence in Barbados* . . . (Philadelphia, 1766), in *The Writings of John Dickinson*, pp. 269–70; *The Papers of John Adams*, 4 vols. to date (Cambridge, Mass., 1977–), 1:189; and *The Papers of George Mason*, 1:65–66, 69.

[16] Reprinted in Edmund S. Morgan, ed., *Prologue to Revolution* (Chapel Hill, 1959), p. 157.

[17] In later years, William Knox recalled that "the morning after the resolution passed in the House of Commons, to repeal the stamp act, and to bring in the declaratory bill, I was sent for to a meeting of the Opposition at Mr. Rigby's in Parliament Street. When I came there, Mr. Grenville and Mr. Rigby came out to me and told me, the Duke of Bedford and several others desired to know my opinion of the effects which those resolutions would produce in America. My answer was in a few words—addresses of thanks and measures of rebellion. Mr. Grenville smiled and shook his head, and Mr. Rigby swore by God he thought so, and both wished me a good morning"; *Cavendish Debates*, 2:34.

TEN

The Chatham Ministry

The Townshend Acts, 1767

[I]

The Rockingham administration had undertaken the repeal of the Stamp Act and the modification of the Sugar Act in the expectation that its action would constitute a general settlement with the American colonies, restoring the former "unsuspecting harmony" rudely shattered by Grenville's disruptive two years at the helm. The following year, however, was to witness a resurgence of American troubles. The Massachusetts assembly refused to grant compensation to the sufferers of the Stamp Act riots unless the rioters were granted a general pardon, a course of action directly contrary to the parliamentary resolutions accompanying the repeal of the Stamp Act. The New York and Boston merchant communities drew up petitions complaining of continuing restrictions on their trade, while the southern assemblies affected by the 1764 Currency Act sought relief from a measure they found burdensome and injudicious. Rhode Island flatly refused a grant of compensation to Martin Howard and Thomas Moffat, victims of the 1765 riots and notorious for their defense of the Stamp Act. Customs officials continued to be victimized; their tormenters remained at large. Only a few assemblies paid deference to Parliament's Quartering Act in responding to General Gage's request for quarters and rations. In all matters touching their commercial interests, the colonists continued to display the assertiveness that would be seen on the other side of the Atlantic as a mark of ingratitude and petulance. In all matters affecting their political rights, they continued to display an aggressiveness that would prove difficult to ignore in a Parliament that had only recently reaffirmed its right over the colonies "in all cases whatsoever."

The metropolis countered these colonial actions with a number of measures of its own. In 1767 the Privy Council disallowed *ab initio* the Act of Indemnity that the Massachusetts assembly had attached to the bill compensating the victims of the Stamp Act riots. Parliament forbade any activity from the New York assembly until it had fully complied with the terms of the Quartering Act. It also established an American Board of Customs Commissioners, which the ministry located in Boston, and approved a new tax bill whose preamble held that "it is expedient that a Revenue should be raised . . . for making a more certain and adequate Provision for defraying the Charge of the Administration of Justice, and the Support of Civil Government, in such Provinces where it shall be found necessary; and towards further defraying the Expences of defending, protecting, and securing" the American colonies. Some of this action, particularly that referring to New York and Massachusetts, represented a response to provocations thrown down by the colonists. The Townshend program of taxation and the establishment of the Board of Customs Commissioners is not so easily characterized.

William Pitt, now elevated to the peerage as Lord Chatham, formed the new administration in July 1766. The opponents of the repeal of the Stamp Act had predicted a resurgence of American troubles, but their sentiments were not shared by the new administration. Chatham and his allies were among the warmest "friends of America." Three of their number—Shelburne, Camden, and Pitt himself—had voted against the Declaratory Act and had apparently subscribed to the American position on internal taxation; others, like Charles Townshend, the new chancellor of the Exchequer, had supported the repeal. As secretary of state for the Southern Department, Lord Shelburne would play an important role in American affairs, and the colonial agents believed that his role, like Townshend's, would prove favorable to American interests. The colonial agents soon began earnest efforts to secure the repeal of the Currency Act and to pave the way for expansion into the West. The new ministers appeared favorable; the colonies appeared calm. Shelburne surveyed the colonial scene and found little cause for alarm. "At New York they have made difficulties about quarters," he wrote to Chatham, "but it appears to me by the letters that it's only the remains of a storm, and wants a little good humour and firmness to finish."[1]

By February of the following year the political mood had drastically altered. In swift succession letters from America revealed that the actions of the previous administration had not succeeded in composing the disputes between Great Britain and America. In late January, a petition from 240 New York merchants arrived complaining that the modifications of the 1764 Sugar Act introduced by the Rockingham administration did not sufficiently relieve the restrictions on American commerce and asking, among other things, for "Liberty to import into the Colonies all West India Productions."[2] Chatham found the petition "highly improper: in point of time, most absurd; in the extent of their pretensions, most excessive; and in the reasoning, most grossly fallacious and offensive."[3] On February 4 the ministry received word that the Massachusetts assembly had relieved the perpetrators as well as the victims of the Stamp Act riots by attaching a general pardon to its Act of Compensation. On the same day came reports of the defiance of the Quartering Act by the New York and New Jersey assemblies. Chatham commented that "New York has drunk the deepest of the baneful cup of infatuation, but none seem to be quite sober and in full possession of reason."[4] His view was shared by many others, as Charles Garth reported to the South Carolina assembly: "Administration much displeased and Opposition appealing thereto for a confirmation of the opinions expressed last year that nothing will give satisfaction to the colonists but an absolute repeal of all regulations and restrictions and in the end independence upon Great Britain."[5]

---

[1] Quoted in P.D.G. Thomas, *British Politics and the Stamp Act Crisis*, p. 294 n. 3. On the circumstances attending the change in ministry and the outlook of the new ministers, see Thomas, as well as John Brooke, *The Chatham Administration, 1766–1768* (London, 1956). On the efforts of colonial agents to secure repeal of the Currency Act and the fate of such attempts during 1767, see Joseph Ernst, *Money and Politics in America, 1750–1775*.
[2] The petition is printed in the *Journals of the House of Commons*, 31:158–60.
[3] *Correspondence of William Pitt, Earl of Chatham*, 3:188–89.
[4] Ibid., pp. 193–94; see Thomas, *Stamp Act Crisis*, p. 301, on the timing of the news.
[5] "Hon. Charles Garth, M. P., the Last Colonial Agent of South Carolina, and Some of His Work," ed. Joseph W. Barnwell, *South Carolina Historical and Genealogical Magazine* 29 (1928): 216–17 (hereafter *SCHGM*).

[II]

As news from America rolled in and the tide of indignation mounted, the cabinet faced a quandary. "Though every body is strongly for enforcing" the Quartering Act, Shelburne wrote to Chatham, "nobody chooses to suggest the mode."[6] The ministry debated a wide range of proposals before finally settling on a variation of a plan that Townshend had initially suggested. This consisted of a statute in which "the governor, Council, and Assembly" of New York were "respectively restrained and prohibited from passing or assenting to any Act of Assembly for any other purpose whatsoever" until provision was made for the army according to the terms of the Quartering Act. This proposal became law in June, but it was never put into effect. The New York assembly proved to be more forthcoming when Governor Moore convened it in May, and though its bill provisioning the troops still contained remnants of the defiance that had marked its conduct the previous session, Shelburne instructed Moore to let the matter drop.

The rationale behind the New York Restraining Act nonetheless deserves attention for the light it sheds on the attitude of the Chatham administration toward American problems. That attitude has usually been seen as harsh and even draconian, and to a certain extent—to judge by the expressions of outrage voiced from all sides of the political spectrum—it certainly was. Expressions of belligerent intent, however, must not be confused with policy. Policy was shaped not merely by the determination to put down the contumacy of New York but to do so in such a way that the other provinces would not come to the aid of the threatened assembly. The belligerence of the British was tempered by fear. It was the combination of these two motives, not merely the former, that shaped the ministry's response to New York.

If, as Shelburne insisted, the issue raised by the action of the New York assembly involved "a far greater question" than that raised by the merits or principles of the Quartering Act, it was indisputable that other assemblies had raised the same question. Other assemblies had not only questioned the constitutional validity of the Quartering and Declaratory acts but had extended their

---

[6] *Chatham*, 3:207. "I presumed to ask the King whether any occurred to his Majesty," Shelburne reported, "but I could not find that any had, except that it should be enforced."

disobedience to other questions as well. The resolutions attending the repeal of the Stamp Act were not put into effect. The rioters were not punished, their victims were not fully compensated. In Massachusetts the general pardon attending the compensation to Hutchinson was a resolution to the Stamp Act riots that the Privy Council's disallowance did nothing to alter.

Yet because of the dangers of provoking a quarrel with all America, the government confined its punitive action to New York. Townshend drew attention to this danger in a speech before the Commons. Although he stressed that the other provinces had for the most part made adequate, though not exact, provision for the troops, he also warned the House to be wary of the colonists uniting in a common cause. Whitehall was determined to deal with only one colony at a time. For this reason Grenville's proposal that a test oath be required of all colonial officials, including assemblymen, was rejected. The British feared, according to William Johnson, that the consequence of applying the test oath "would be a second union of the Colonies against this country, and the same inconveniences that had followed from the Stamp Act."[7]

The appeal of the New York Restraining Act lay in its apparent escape from the "inconveniences" of the previous year. It was agreed by all parties that some response had to be made to American defiance. Appeasement had been tried and found wanting, or so it seemed in the spring of 1767. The room for maneuver was thus narrower than the year before. Yet it was not an easy matter to suggest an alternative to a policy of conciliation, for any suggested alternative still had to answer not only to the consensus that existed in Britain on the need to maintain the sovereignty of Parliament over the colonies, but also to the fears of provoking a conflict with colonies united in their opposition to the mother country. Dealing with New York alone, and making an example of it to the others, seemed to satisfy both imperatives. "The resolution with respect to New York," William Johnson wrote, "is designed as a specimen of their sovereignty, and she is to serve as an example to the other Colonies, who, they flatter themselves, will take no part in the controversy, as they are not immediately attacked. . . . Sensible of the danger of involving all the Colonies in one common contro-

[7] "Letters of William Samuel Johnson to the Governors of Connecticut [1766–1771]," p. 233 (hereafter Trumbull Papers).

versy, the present policy seems to be to attack them singly, as occasion may require, and by degrees reduce them all to that state of subordination and humble obedience which [the British] very injudiciously seem to think necessary to their safety and happiness."[8]

[III]

The ministry's wish to avoid a controversy with "all America" was destined to remain unfulfilled. It was the new program of American taxation, however, not the New York Restraining Act, that led to revived controversy and renewed nonimportation. This resistance came as a profound shock to the ministry that subsequently was required to respond to this defiance, and that would ultimately do so in the only way it knew how—through concession.

The significance of these expectations has seldom been fully appreciated. Because the Townshend Revenue Act ultimately brought forth a crisis in imperial-colonial relations, historians have assumed that the metropolis must have thrown down a challenge; that the intent of the measure was to reaffirm the sovereignty of Parliament, so recently challenged.

Yet, the Townshend Revenue Act sailed through Parliament encountering scarcely a hint, from either the "friends of America" or the colonial agents, that the new program would meet with resistance and nonimportation in the colonies. Indeed, it was from the "friends of America" that several of the new proposals for taxation came. William Dowdeswell, chancellor of the Exchequer under Rockingham, suggested to Townshend in October 1766 that the effective tax on tea be reduced to discourage smuggling from Holland,[9] and both Benjamin Franklin and William Johnson appear to have solicited alterations in the southern European trade. Franklin, in a pro-American tract published in the *London Chronicle* in April 1767, explicitly conceded the legitimacy of taxation on external trade for the purposes of revenue and cast no doubt on its expediency, positions he had earlier maintained in his examination

---

[8] Ibid., p. 232.
[9] See Robert J. Chaffin, "The Townshend Acts of 1767," *William and Mary Quarterly*, 3d ser. 27 (1970):94.

before the Commons.[10] The Chatham administration, in its contemplated alteration of the duties on the tea and southern European
trades, appeared to be doing no more than the Rockingham administration had done the previous year: reducing duties that were
ostensibly burdensome to the Americans but that would succeed
in raising a revenue, primarily through elimination of high duties
that had promoted smuggling or were otherwise burdensome: In
neither proposed alteration of the tea or wine trades was the administration introducing a new principle, and though the new duties
on British manufactures would later be seen to have been based
on novel and uncommercial principles, these new duties aroused
virtually no comment at the time.[11] Within the space of a year, the

[10] *The Papers of Benjamin Franklin*, 14:114–15. There is little reason to suppose that what
was not seen by Franklin was seen by Shelburne, Grafton, or Burke. Yet all three made
retrospective claims that they had either opposed the new taxes or predicted American
defiance. The untrustworthy character of Grafton's *Autobiography* has been emphasized in
both Chaffin, "Townshend Acts," p. 100, and Thomas, *Stamp Act Crisis*, p. 338. Each
insists that Townshend's pledge of an American revenue in a speech of January 26 before
the Commons could not have been unknown to Grafton, as he later claimed in the *Autobiography*; *Autobiography and Political Correspondence of Augustus Henry, Third Duke
of Grafton*, ed. William R. Anson (London, 1898), pp. 126–27. There are indications that
Grafton was reluctant to use the revenues from the Townshend fund to support the civil
establishment in provinces other than New York, but this does not require one to believe
that Grafton either opposed the principle or foresaw the inexpediency of American port
duties to support the American army. Nor was the principle and expediency of American
port duties the source of Shelburne's disagreement with Townshend that emerged in March.
In the March 30, 1767, memorandum on the western problem (which was not in Shelburne's
hand but which historians agree reflected his views), Shelburne mentioned three sources
of revenue that might provide a "Fund for American Expence": (1) on quitrents, (2) "on
such Aids as may be beneficial to the Colonies, at the same time that they lessen the Burthen
of the Mother Country, but [3] chiefly on Requisitions from the different assemblies." It
is difficult to see the second proposal as anything but a reference to the contemplated
alterations in the tea and southern European trades. Both would raise a greater revenue;
both would do so by eliminating burdens on the colonies—in the case of tea, by removing
the one-shilling-a-pound tax collectable in England, and hence making dutied tea much
cheaper in America; in the case of wine, by eliminating the requirement that ships carrying
commodities from southern Europe touch at a British port before sailing to the colonies;
"Reasons for not diminishing American Expence this year," in *The New Regime, 1765–1767*,
11:536–41. Shelburne's assent to the port duties may also be seen in a letter of Townshend
to Grafton; see note 25. On Burke's position, see the introduction by Elliot R. Barkan to
Edmund Burke on the American Revolution: Selected Speeches and Letters (New York,
1966), p. xii.
[11] Thomas, *Stamp Act Crisis*, p. 358. Townshend expected approximately £20,000 from the
cancelled rebate on china exports and from the export duties he placed on glass, paper,
and lead. From the duties on wine, oil, and fruit from southern Europe he anticipated
£23,420, but the final bill did not include these changes; see Thomas, *Stamp Act Crisis*,
pp. 348–49; and Lewis Namier and John Brooke, *Charles Townshend*, pp. 177–78. From
the changes in the tea tax Townshend expected an extra revenue of £20,000. In "Charles
Townshend and American Taxation in 1767," *English Historical Review* 83 (1968): 49,
Thomas wrote that "the purpose of the Townshend duties . . . was not revenue at all," and
this because "if a tax of 3d. a lb. would produce a revenue of £20,000, a rebate of 9d. a lb.

principles on which the commercial legislation of Townshend had been based went from having no opponents to having no supporters. At the time, however, no one thought of the Townshend duties as drawing a line beyond which the Americans would not be suffered to pass. Townshend believed that he was accommodating himself to a line that the Americans had drawn.

It was thus not only the legitimacy of external taxation that was taken for granted in the spring of 1767. Also taken for granted was the expediency of the program. The growing consensus that sovereignty was indivisible became complete only when it became clear that no minister, including George Grenville, would think of imposing internal taxes like the Stamp Act on America ever again. The consensus that formed in 1767 on the absurdity of the distinction between internal and external taxation became widespread only when it became clear that the new administration intended to adhere to it in practice.[12] A startling instance of the climate in which the tax program was discussed is provided by William Johnson's reaction to the withdrawal of the changes with respect to the southern European trade. These changes were given up, he said, because the government thought it "dangerous to relax the Act of Navigation, the chief security of the supremacy of this country, while the Colonies were disputing and denying that very sovereignty which this act was principally intended to establish." Johnson also noted, however, the rumor that "one gentleman objected to those duties because, with a permission to trade directly to Portugal, they would be agreeable to the Americans, and that they ought not at present to do anything that would please us."[13] The

---

should have meant a fall of some £60,000 in net customs receipts." This view is withdrawn in his *Stamp Act Crisis*, but it has been taken up by Ian R. Christie and Benjamin Woods Labaree, *Empire or Independence, 1760–1776*, pp. 103–4, 294 n. 47. This interpretation, however, neglects to consider that the one shilling duty withdrawn was collected on only a fraction of total colonial imports, and that Townshend's purpose in reducing the duty lay in capturing for East Indian dutied tea a market that had theretofore been served illicitly. The £60,000 "lost" to the Exchequer is a hypothetical sum, arrived at by assuming an annual consumption in America of 1.6 million pounds of tea, on which twelve pence a pound was paid. Thus, the decision to allow a total drawback of the duties paid on import into Britain yields a "loss" of £80,000, compensated by the 3 pence duty imposed in America, but nonetheless making for a net loss of £60,000. On the purposes of the reduction, which did not solely concern the revenue, see chapter 5, section IV.

[12] See, e.g., Ryder Diaries, p. 331; HMC, Stopford-Sackville Manuscripts, 1:122; HMC, Lothian Manuscripts p. 275; and "The Bowdoin and Temple Papers," Massachusetts Historical Society, *Collections*, 6th ser., vol. 9 (Boston, 1897), pp. 83.

[13] Trumbull Papers, p. 236.

view that sees the new program of taxation as being intimately connected with the resurgence of a posture of hostility toward the colonies—save in the bizarre sense indicated by Johnson—must be seriously qualified.[14] There was, in the new program of taxation, no malice aforethought, no intention to renew the struggle with America on the legitimacy of internal taxation, no expectation that it would lead to American opposition and another round of non-importation. Only when it became known that the revenues from the new program could be used to relieve the dependence of royal government on the colonial assemblies did consternation arise over the new program.[15] On the legitimacy and expediency of external taxation itself, however, there was not a word.[16]

[IV]

Townshend informed the Commons of the ministry's intention to lay new taxes on the external commerce of America in the same speech announcing the ministry's response to New York. This accorded with pledges he had made to the Commons as early as January, but there was a novel twist to his argument. He wished to use the revenues to remove the dependence of royal government on annual grants from the assemblies. Townshend's proposal to support royal government in America marked an important change in his public pronouncements. It had been in the context of the problem of imperial defense and the ballooning costs of the army that the subject of American taxation had arisen in the Commons. Until late March, the only indications that the ministry may have been contemplating a fund for the support of civil government

[14] Walpole is the source of this view; see his *Memoirs of the Reign of George III*, 3:28–29. Even the recent revisionist accounts appear to accept it. Cf. Chaffin, "Townshend Acts," p. 90; and Thomas, *Stamp Act Crisis*, p. 357.
[15] Trumbull Papers, p. 239; *SCHGM* 29 (1928): 300.
[16] The same may be said for another measure of the Chatham administration which was destined to provoke renewed controversy—the creation of an American Board of Customs Commissioners. Grafton recalled in his *Autobiography*, p. 127, that "I was not aware of the mistrust and jealousy which this appointment would bring on, nor of the mischief of which it was the source: otherwise it should never have had my assent, and I must here confess my want of foresight in this instance." On the reasons for the creation of the Customs Board, see chapter 5, section V.

were inquiries launched during the previous winter by both the Treasury and Shelburne's department into the annual charges of civil government and the taxes laid to support it. Whatever the explanation for these inquiries,[17] both Shelburne and Townshend seem to have focused their attention primarily on the problem of imperial defense.

That problem had been left hanging with the repeal of the Stamp Act and the modification of the Sugar Act. Neither Townshend nor Shelburne was content with the status quo in the west. Both realized that the foundation of Grenville's western program had been radically undermined by the repeal or reduction of the revenue duties. Townshend was aware that his contemplated port duties would defray only a small portion of the costs—although, compared with the revenues expected from the Stamp Act and the Sugar Act, the sum was not insubstantial. To reduce the burden on Great Britain, he urged an immediate withdrawal of the army from the American interior, a plan of action initially proposed by Barrington and seconded by Grenville in early 1767. Townshend presented his plans at a stormy cabinet meeting on March 12, refusing to

---

[17] The circular Shelburne sent to the governors of the continental colonies asked for "an exact Estimate of the annual Charge of Maintaining & Supporting the Entire Establishment of His Majesty's Colony of——distinguishing the different Funds & the different Services to which those Funds are appropriated. You will be very particular in specifying what Funds are fixed & regular, from those which are annually granted or which expire in a given time." This request, as Thomas, *Stamp Act Crisis*, p. 297, notes, "duplicated the Treasury circular of 30 September," but Shelburne, in addition, asked for "a full & clear account of the manner of imposing Quit Rents, & of levying them as also the mode of granting Lands in Your Colony, specifying the Amount of Arrears of Quit Rents, & the Number of Grants hitherto made, & to whom, how many Acres to each, & at what time the Grants have been made"; (*Documents Relating to the Colonial History of New Jersey*, ed. William A. Whitehead, et al., 36 vols. [Newark, 1880–1941], 9:573–74.)

Chaffin, "Townshend Acts," and Thomas, *Stamp Act Crisis*, pp. 298, 354–55, give conflicting interpretations of these circulars. The assumption made here is that these inquiries presage the Townshend scheme in only a very indirect sense and were not written with the intention of supporting civil government in the older British continental colonies. It is likely that Shelburne did consider using the revenue from quitrents to establish a civil list "in America," but the idea seems restricted to "the new and Conquered Provinces." In a December 11, 1766, letter to Gage, around which most of the dispute revolves, Shelburne wrote that "the forming an American Fund, to support the exigencies of Government in the same manner as is done in Ireland . . . might tend to increase rather than diminish the Powers of Government in so distant a Country"; *New Regime*, p. 457. Since Shelburne was toying with the idea of interior colonies as a partial means of resolving the complicated problem of imperial defense, he likely saw quitrents as a means of financing the costs of the new governments in a manner that would relieve Britain of the burden and at the same time "increase rather than diminish the Powers of Government in so distant a Country." On this view, his circular to the governors may be explained as an attempt to gain information and examples that he would apply to the new western governments.

support a vote on the army extraordinaries and threatening resignation "unless the cabinet previously took the whole state of America into consideration, and enabled him to declare to the House the opinion of administration as to the forts, the Indian trade, the disposition of the troops, in short the whole arrangements, considered with a view to a general reduction of expence, and a duty which he undertook should be laid to defray what remained."[18] Both Shelburne and Grafton found his behavior highly offensive. The former, in particular, opposed these "crude and undigested" proceedings, though Shelburne was not yet ready to offer a plan of his own. He warned that "nothing can weaken Government more than the adoption of measures which require subsequent Reformation," and counseled delay in the face of the conflicting reports and recommendations that were still coming from the scene. It would be better to wait: "the affairs of America cannot suffer much by going on one year more in the Channel they

---

The final plan that Shelburne presented to the cabinet in September 1767 is consistent with this view. "Besides the Inconveniences arising from the present System," he said, "the Expence attending the Management of Indian Affairs which has been little diminished since the Peace, continues so considerable that either a Reduction or a certain provision for defraying it is become an indispensable object of consideration for Government. The actual Pay of the Superintendants and the charges attending the civil Establishments at the several Posts are not the only Burthens to be placed to this Account. For the Extraordinaries of the Army as well as the keeping up of the Forts form also a part of it; the present Situation of the Army being so much dependent on Indian Affairs that it is impossible to consider one without the other." He noted the objection that establishing new governments would be costly to Britain—it was the mother country that defrayed the costs of civil government in Nova Scotia, Georgia, East Florida, and Quebec—but "upon Examination" he insisted that "it does not appear that such Governments would be attended with much Expence to Great Britain, for the Quit Rents would in a few years, not only defray the Expence but form a Fund for other purposes."

This interpretation leads to the conclusion (contra Thomas) that Shelburne was considering quitrents as the source of an independent fund from which the civil establishments in the new western governments would draw their salaries (and which could be used "for other purposes," such as financing the army); but that (contra Chaffin) he was not thinking, in December 1766, of the plan subsequently adopted, the intention of which was to lessen the dependence of royal officials on the colonial assemblies in the older colonies. The similarity in the two schemes may have made Shelburne's assent to the Townshend plan all the readier. In addition, some governors (particularly Moore and Bernard) in the older provinces used their response to the circular to deplore their dependence or bemoan the insufficiency of their salaries, and this indicates a genuine, if indirect, connection between the two plans. When the circulars were sent, however, the government seems to have had no plan in mind like that which emerged in May 1767.

[18] *Chatham*, 3:231–36. Removing the troops to the seaboard was an economy measure, not one intended to intimidate the older colonies. Barrington appears to have wanted to withdraw the troops from the seacoast colonies altogether.

have hitherto done."[19] Shelburne was apparently the victor in his confrontation with Townshend. No new arrangements for the west were implemented until 1768, when Shelburne was no longer responsible for American affairs, and the American extraordinaries were voted without Townshend carrying out his threat.

It was some time after the March 12 cabinet meeting that signs appeared that the ministry was considering the revenue from the port duties for another purpose as well. The legislation that the cabinet had previously agreed upon for New York may have sparked this change of plan. Although the ministry confidently announced that it would meet with little resistance in that province—on the usual reasoning that the restoration of British authority required only a rhetorical demonstration of determination and little else[20]— the possibility that a stalemate in government might result from the application of the New York Restraining Act remained open. In that event, the governor and other officials in the King's government would surely be denied their salary, which depended on annual appropriations.[21] Governor Moore's reply to Shelburne's circular of the preceding December arrived on March 25 and served as a pointed reminder of his dependence. His tone was melancholy. He complained that "the difficulties which the present Establishment in this Province labours under at this time, are so many, that it would exceed the bounds of a Letter to animadvert on all the particulars," and therefore plaintively waived "every thing relative to the Governor in Chief here, the Annual Appointment of whose Salary by an Act of Assembly will say more for him than he can for himself."[22]

Moore's complaints were nothing new. Since 1737 the governor of New York had depended for his salary on annual appropriations by the assembly, and a succession of gubernatorial appointments

[19] New Regime, pp. 536–41.
[20] SCHGM 29 (1928): 225.
[21] Although no evidence exists showing that this danger was foreseen by the ministry, it would later be foreseen by Governor William Franklin of New Jersey and it is difficult to see how the ministry could have missed it. In 1771, Governor Franklin was intent on continually proroguing the assembly "till they are brought to a proper sense of their duty" in quartering the soldiers, but he hinted that the colonial government might require some support from home: if the assembly "should happen to hold out any long time the officers of government would be deprived of their salaries which, small as they are, they cannot well do without"; Documents of the American Revolution, 1770–1783, Colonial Office Ser., ed. K. G. Davies, 21 vols. to date (Shannon, Ire., 1972–), 3:104.
[22] Moore to Shelburne, February 21, 1767, Documents Relative to the Colonial History of the State of New York, 7:906–9.

had struggled to secure a permanent revenue against the assembly's defiance and the home government's ultimate indifference, all to no avail. It was with an intention to redress this dependence that a young Charles Townshend had drafted instructions to Danvers Osborn, appointed as governor in 1753, to secure permanent grants from the assembly, but the plan had fallen through, a casualty of Osborn's suicide and the exigencies of the coming war.[23] The impact of these somewhat fortuitous influences on the ministry in the spring of 1767 cannot be established with precision. It does seem clear, however, that the cabinet discussed the New York problem apart from the others. In an undated letter to Grafton, Townshend lamented "that the opportunity has not been taken of soliciting his Majesty's assent to the proposition of independent salaries for the civil officers of North America, especially as he had pledged himself to the House for some measure of this sort, and had the assurances of Lord Shelburne in the last cabinet for the whole extent of the establishment, and the Duke of Grafton on Saturday adopted the idea at least as far as New York."[24]

The breach between Townshend and Grafton may not have been as wide as it seems, for the problem that Townshend was addressing existed in acute form in only four provinces—Massachusetts, New York, New Jersey, and New Hampshire. Elsewhere, the traditional policy of the Board of Trade—to secure a permanent fund that would render the officers of the King's government immune to personal pressure from the assembly—had been applied "with considerable success."[25] The sources of these funds were various. In Maryland and Virginia the civil government derived its support from a permanent revenue granted by the assembly on the export of tobacco. The 4.5 percent duty on sugar not only defrayed the

[23] See Leonard W. Labaree, *Royal Government in America*, pp. 337–41, and Oliver M. Dickerson, *American Colonial Government, 1696–1765* (Cleveland, 1912), pp. 181–85, for a history of the salary question in New York. On Townshend's 1753 instructions see Namier and Brooke, *Townshend*, p. 37.

[24] Quoted in Thomas, *Stamp Act Crisis*, pp. 354–55. Thomas suggests May 25 as the probable date of the letter.

[25] Labaree, *Royal Government*, p. 335. Thomas, *Stamp Act Crisis*, contends that the Townshend civil list plan made the forty thousand pounds Townshend expected from his revenue duties "a matter of no fiscal significance whatever. Since most colonial officials were already paid from American sources, Townshend's proposed use of the new revenue changed the mode of payment rather than the incidence of the burden from Britain to the colonies" (pp. 347–48). He later remarks that "the total annual cost of financing the executive and judiciary in the thirteen colonies that were to break with Britain appears to have been little more

costs of civil government in those provinces from which the revenue was derived—Barbados and the Leeward Islands—but was also used to help pay the salaries of the governors of North and South Carolina. In other colonies the King's government depended on either quitrents or grants from the British Exchequer—the latter case applied particularly to provinces on the outskirts of English civilization which were important for defensive purposes or which had been acquired in 1763. This was true of Nova Scotia, Georgia, and East and West Florida. Elsewhere—in the charter colonies of Connecticut and Rhode Island and in the proprietary colonies of

than £40,000, the same as the estimated yield of the Townshend duties. Townshend had done his sums right, if he had tried to balance the two totals" (p. 361).

This view is not persuasive. Thomas rests his case primarily on the reports of Townshend's May 13 speech announcing his plans for civil government. William Johnson, who was excluded from the galleries but who heard of it from friends, wrote that from the port duties "the Governor and Chief Justices in the King's governments should be rendered more independent by giving the first £2,000:0: and the latter £500:0: per annum"; Trumbull Papers, p. 231. Charles Garth reported that Townshend offered "a Plan for improving the System of Government in the Colonies in order that the Authority of the executive Power might carry with it in the several Departments the Weight and Respect essentially necessary to answer the Ends of its Institution, and for that purpose after shewing in what Manner the Civil Officers of the Crown were provided for and the Extent of such provision, he should propose that, out of the Fund arising from the American Duties now, or to be imposed, His Majesty should be enabled to establish Salaries that might be better suited to support the Dignity of the respective Officers, and for which to be no longer dependent upon the pleasure of any Assembly"; SCHGM 29 (1928):228–29.

According to Ryder, Townshend proposed "that the judges and magistrates who are now in many colonies dependent every year for their salary or at least a part of it on the assembly ought to be made independent."; Ryder Diaries p. 344. As Horace Walpole reported the speech, Townshend said that "the salaries of governors and judges in that part of the world must be made independent of their assemblies; but he advised the House to confine their resolutions to the offending provinces"; Memoirs, 3:31. Another contemporary impression of Townshend's purpose was Edward Sedgwick's: he applauded Townshend "for having provided for the expence of the whole Civil Administration in the Colonies, & made the several Officers concern'd in it independent of the People"; HMC, C. Fleetwood Weston Underwood Manuscripts, pt. 1 p. 406. Franklin reported similar rumors home to Pennsylvania in April; Papers of Franklin, 14:109. What do these reports tell us about Townshend's intentions? Three clearly indicate that the Townshend civil list plan was not to be extended to all the colonies, though the reports of Johnson, Ryder, and Walpole on the precise character of the restriction are not entirely consistent with one another. (The views of Ryder and Walpole, however, are more consistent than may appear at first sight, for the "offending" provinces—New York, Massachusetts, and New Jersey—were the same as those in which the governor depended for his salary on the assembly's annual grant. The exception is New Hampshire, where no troops were stationed.) The reports of both Garth and Sedgwick may be given a more expansive reading, but they, too, show clearly enough that the purpose of the scheme was to alleviate the dependence of the King's government on the "pleasure" of the respective assemblies. Even if these reports are dismissed as being too ambiguous, however, there would remain the question of why Townshend sought to disrupt salary arrangements that ensured the independence of the crown's representatives and that corresponded to the traditional objectives of the Board of Trade.

Pennsylvania and Delaware—the King did not appoint the governor and, consequently, it would have made no sense to pay the executive's salary. In these colonies only the establishment of royal government could have secured influence for the King.

The Townshend program for supporting an independent civil list in America, then, was restricted to those provinces where the King's government depended either partially or totally on annual grants from the assemblies. It may have been even more limited than this. The enabling legislation reserved complete discretion to the King's ministers to apply the funds "in such Provinces where it shall be found necessary," and it was only in 1768 that the first salaries were granted from the fund deriving from the Townshend duties. These grants were limited to the attorney general of New York and the chief justice of Massachusetts. Over thirteen thousand pounds arose from the Townshend duties in its first year of operation; the combined cost of these two salaries was two-hundred fifty pounds in 1768 and four hundred pounds in 1769.[26] Not until 1770 were the next grants made, and these were limited to the governors of Massachusetts and New York. If there existed in ministerial circles a plan to pay the salaries of all royal officials who depended on annual appropriations, why did the ministry move so slowly to implement it? It may have waited until 1768 because only then would a fund have been collected from the Townshend Acts, but this would not explain its failure to act in that year.[27] Townshend's unexpected death in September 1767 is another possible answer. If so, however, it would seem to indicate that the rest of the ministry had misgivings about the plan or had never given their approval to it, if indeed such a "plan" existed. It is certain that Grafton, for whatever reasons, had misgivings about

---

[26] Oliver M. Dickerson, "Use Made of the Revenue from the Tax on Tea," *New England Quarterly* 31 (1958): 240.

[27] After the repeal in 1770 of the Townshend duties (save for the tax on tea), the lack of revenue from the tea duty did apparently act as a constraint on the ministry in further expanding the independent civil list. Hillsborough agreed to pay the salaries of the Massachusetts Superior Court judges, but tentatively recommended to Hutchinson that their number be reduced from five to three, "as five may amount to more than the revenue can bear"; Hillsborough to Hutchinson, June 6, 1772, *Documents of the Revolution*, 5:113. In 1773, Dartmouth, who replaced Hillsborough as American secretary the preceding year, told Governor Franklin of New Jersey that the "Deficiency of fund appropriated by Parliament for civil establishment in America has made proper provision for government in New Jersey difficult, but I will continue solicitations"; Dartmouth to Franklin, August 4, 1773, as summarized in *Documents of the American Revolution, 1770–1783*, 4: no. 1384. Revenue, however, was not a restraint on the ministry in 1768.

extending the plan beyond New York. The assumption of most historians is that these misgivings were laid aside by the time Townshend presented the legislation on June 1. An equally plausible explanation is that the discretion that the legislation vested in the ministry was a way of avoiding a final decision. This view also squares more readily with the overall outlook of the Chatham administration, which was as much intent on avoiding trouble with more than one colony at a time as it was on "reaffirming" the sovereignty of Parliament. If the ministry saw the payment of royal officials as a step that might be treated harshly by the colonists, a "wait and see" attitude was all the more appropriate. The most plausible explanation, in sum, is that no final plan existed, that the ministry sought legislation that would enable it to support royal government when trouble arose and when "necessity" demanded some support from home. The Townshend Revenue Act gave Whitehall a weapon of sorts that might be made use of in the future, and it represented one more step toward an objective that imperial officials had sporadically sought throughout the eighteenth century. At the time of Townshend's death in September, however, the great plan still lay unfulfilled.

[V]

The Chatham administration has traditionally been seen as a ministry riven by internal disputes, driven into harsh American measures only by the forceful personality of Charles Townshend, who espoused programs that the rest of the government—particularly Grafton and Shelburne—opposed but were powerless to stop. "Chatham in full health might have curbed him. No one else could do so."[28] The view is an attractive one if only because it seems to provide a plausible explanation for an otherwise inexplicable circumstance—that it was a ministry headed by the great friend of the Americans which succeeded in reviving the dispute over taxation. The view, however, must be seriously qualified. On the critical American questions, what is striking about the 1767 parliamentary session is the degree of consensus that informed British action. There was widespread disagreement over the proper meas-

[28] Christie and Labaree, *Empire or Independence*, p. 100.

ures to be adopted in response to New York's defiance of the Quartering Act. There was little disagreement over both the need to respond to New York and to isolate it from the others. On both these questions Townshend was in full accord with his colleagues. The program of taxation, too, revealed a widespread consensus on both the principle and expediency of imposing "external" taxes on America. Only on the question of using this revenue to support an independent civil list beyond New York did Grafton hesitate to give his support, though even he would later approve the use of the Townshend fund in Massachusetts.

The only real indictment that can be brought against this program is that it aroused the opposition of the colonies; but to adopt this view is only to acknowledge that the metropolis should have ceased to concern itself with the business of ruling the colonies, because all the bright ideas of imperial administrators were sure to run aground on colonial resistance. Still, it was certainly not the intention of the Chatham ministry to renew the controversy with "all America." With the New York Restraining Act, the administration showed that it had absorbed—or thought it had absorbed—the lessons of the preceding year. Two lessons stood out; one was the necessity of avoiding a controversy with "all America"; the other was the importance of reaffirming the sovereignty of Parliament. The Chatham administration faithfully applied both lessons in the legislation restraining the New York assembly. It did not apply them to the Townshend revenue program because no one foresaw that they were applicable. However much the American position distinguishing internal taxation from other powers of Parliament may have been reprobated in the spring of 1767—and there is considerable evidence that it was sternly condemned not only by George Grenville but also by a few embarrassed Chathamites— the fact remains that Townshend drew up his duties in accordance with a line he believed the Americans themselves had drawn. In theory he thought the distinction absurd and said so on several occasions in the Commons, but he also thought it proper to be adopted in practice—proper because it was expedient to do so, because it would raise a revenue "without offence" to the Americans. These sentiments were genuine and were received without opposition. They acquired a frivolous character only in retrospect.

ELEVEN

The Grafton Ministry

Paper War, 1768–69

[I]

The colonial reaction to the Townshend duties ultimately produced a crisis within the empire similar to the Stamp Act crisis of a few years before. On this later occasion, however, the American reaction was slower and less violent. Although the Commissioners of the Customs received an ominous welcome in Boston when they landed in September 1767, the new duties were executed without great difficulty. Indeed, the difference in the initial dimensions of the two crises showed itself most clearly in the revenues which the two sets of taxes succeeded in raising. The Stamp Act had produced virtually nothing in the continental colonies. By contrast, over thirteen thousand pounds was collected under the Townshend duties in 1768. Yet the precipitous decline in collections thereafter indicates that the passage of time merely served to bring an increase in the dimensions of the crisis. Tempers steadily rose, not cooled. And when the second great crisis had run its course, the collapse of British authority in America had reached—if it had not already passed—the point of no return.

John Dickinson's *Letters from a Farmer* were perhaps most instrumental in rousing the Americans from the complacency into which he believed they had fallen. His letters to a Philadelphia newspaper began arriving in late 1767 and were reprinted widely in America, enjoying a success surpassed in the revolutionary decade only by Thomas Paine's *Common Sense*. Dickinson attacked every feature of Parliament's 1767 American legislation. He found in the New York Restraining Act, in the creation of the Customs Board, and in the Townshend Revenue Act profound threats to American liberties. He acknowledged that the 1767 revenue duties were not especially onerous, but he found their danger to lie precisely in the ease with which they might be paid. The question, for Dickinson, was one of right. It was a point from which he urged his fellow colonists never to retreat. He recommended resistance: vigorous remonstrances to the King and Parliament and measures of economic coercion.[1]

Of these two measures of resistance, the first was more readily undertaken than the second. By the end of 1768, all the colonial assemblies, save New Hampshire, had entered resolves protesting the recent legislation. Most of these contained renewed statements of the rights of the American assemblies. It was more difficult to secure American unity on the question of nonimportation. The Boston merchants entered into a nonimportation agreement as early as March 1768, and the New York merchants swiftly concurred in the appeal from Massachusetts. But both towns made their agreement conditional on Philadelphia's acquiescence, and when the merchants of Philadelphia refused to go along, nonimportation was momentarily defeated in America. Even so, those favoring nonimportation were not easily stayed. A new agreement of the Boston merchants, in August 1768, scheduled to remain in effect from January 1769 to January 1770, was not made conditional on the acceptance of other towns, and New York made a similar agreement later in the year. By March of 1769 Philadelphia finally agreed to nonimportation, and the movement spread to the southern colonies shortly thereafter. By August 1769 nearly all the colonies had adopted nonimportation agreements of varying degrees of effectiveness. The uncertainty of the scope and intensity of American resistance had important implications for British policy. That trouble was brewing—indeed, that Massachusetts was the center of resistance and would not bow easily to British authority—seemed indisputable. But how far American reaction would go, and how successful Whitehall might be in dealing separately with Massachusetts, was much more problematic.[2]

The ministry that would respond to American opposition had

---

[1] *Letters from a Farmer in Pennsylvania to the Inhabitants of the British Colonies* in *The Writings of John Dickinson.*

[2] The standard accounts of the nonimportation movements are Arthur M. Schlesinger, *The Colonial Merchants and the American Revolution, 1763–1776*; and Charles M. Andrews, "The Boston Merchants and the Nonimportation Movement," Colonial Society of Massachusetts, *Publications*, vol. 19 Transactions, 1916–17, pp. 159–259. A critique of these older works may be found in Merrill Jensen, *The Founding of a Nation*, pp. 265–313.

undergone important changes by early 1768. Chatham remained ill and incapable of conducting business, though he would resign from office only in October 1768. With the death of Townshend in September 1767, Grafton clearly assumed the leadership of the ministry. Lord North replaced Townshend as chancellor of the Exchequer, an appointment that foreshadowed the more far-reaching changes at the close of the year. In December, Grafton made his peace with the Bedfordites, and several men of that party, though not Bedford himself, entered the new administration. Of the changes that were made perhaps the most significant was the appointment of Lord Hillsborough as secretary of state of the newly created American Department. Although without full cabinet rank, Hillsborough enjoyed the favor of the King and was to exert real, though not complete, influence on American policy. Overall, the changes in administration seemed to herald an American policy considerably tougher than could be expected from the Chatham-ites. In opposition, the Bedfordites had opposed the repeal of the Stamp Act in 1766. The next few years would demonstrate whether their views would be modified by the responsibilities of office.

In one of his first measures, Hillsborough struck down the plan for interior colonies that Shelburne had developed the previous year. The ministry thus remained committed to the policies set out in the Proclamation of 1763, though the ambitious scheme for regulating the fur trade at assigned posts was abandoned and many responsibilities for Indian affairs were returned to the colonies, who were pressed to work out a consistent policy among themselves. Whitehall also finally gave Gage the authority to alter the distribution of the troops, though the changes that were made were, in the event, less than monumental.[3]

[II]

It was the seaboard, however, and not the west, upon which the ministry concentrated its attention during 1768 and 1769. Throughout this period the Grafton ministry groped to evolve a coherent policy toward the American seaboard colonies, an undertaking that would prove difficult and, in the end, insuperable. The ministry

[3] See John Shy, *Toward Lexington*; pp. 267–74.

was driven by contradictory impulses. At bottom its dilemma was no different from that faced by its predecessors, but the passage of time had sharpened the issues and underlined the ill consequences that would attend either firm action or indisguisable retreat. There were many reasons for avoiding renewed conflict with the American colonies. Once it appeared that resistance was not confined to Massachusetts, the disadvantages of engaging in a contest with America appeared overwhelming. It was possible to draw vastly different conclusions from the widely accepted premise that America was of capital importance to the wealth and power of Great Britain. If the importance of the colonies made it seem all the more essential to retain the sovereignty of Parliament over America, their importance also made the British extremely reluctant to draw the sword. There were widespread expectations that the conflict would prove costly and possibly intractable. Camden regretted that the issue between the two sides was "now joined upon the right, which in my apprehension, is the most untoward ground of dispute that could have been started: fatal to Great Britain, if she miscarries; unprofitable if she succeeds. . . . After both sides are half ruined in the context, we shall at last establish a right, which ought never to be exerted."[4] Dowdeswell was no more sanguine. He wrote to Rockingham that "a contest with the colonies, supported as they will be by the enemies of this country, must be destructive to us."[5]

There was, on the other hand, an instinctive resistance to the demands of the Americans. The two leading features of American opposition—the principle of colonial equality and the threat of economic coercion—represented fundamental challenges to the continuance of British rule in the colonies. Neither the principle nor the threat could be admitted without fatally undermining the supremacy of the British Parliament. The practical exemption from parliamentary taxation claimed by the colonists was, for this reason, less significant than the principle on which the Americans urged the exemption be based. Britain's unwillingness to accept the principle stemmed primarily neither from the belief that its acceptance would foreclose exercise of the right of taxation under circumstances that could not be foreseen, nor from the recognition that its acceptance would jeopardize the 1764 and 1766 revenue legislation,

---

[4] Camden to Grafton, October 4, 1768, *Autobiography and Political Correspondence of Augustus Henry, Third Duke of Grafton*, p. 216.
[5] Quoted in John Brooke, *The Chatham Administration, 1766–1768*, p. 372.

though both considerations were not absent from British calculations.[6] Far more critical and alarming was the evidence indicating that the core American position was unlimited. Before he abandoned his misgivings and launched an attack on the ministry's policy, Dowdeswell warned that the American "claim of right being admitted will give them in my opinion a charter against being bound to any laws passed without their consent." This view gained plausibility by what the British saw as the American redefinition of the meaning of internal taxation in response to the Townshend duties. In back of the American claim to equality the British saw an attack on the Acts of Trade and Navigation, whose continued integrity they deemed critical to Britain's security and well-being.[7]

Nor could the ministry concede from fear of colonial nonimportation without fundamentally undermining its imperial position. The argument that the British repeal the Townshend duties for fear of "the combinations not to import or consume British manufactures, and to establish them amongst themselves," was for North the strongest reason for not repealing. It was an argument, North warned, "which might be applied upon every occasion." If Parliament once yielded to such pressure, it "would find that in future, whenever any act of Parliament was made not perfectly agreeable to the Americans, they would constantly go into the same measures to obtain a repeal, and in the end, by the same means, get rid of all acts of Parliament, even that essential one, the Act of Navigation, the basis of the wealth and power of Great Britain."[8]

Neither set of fears—one aroused by the ruinous costs that might attend armed conflict with America, the other by the threat to British rule held out by concessions exacted under duress—was the exclusive possession of any of the principal factions in British political life. For the most part, preponderant opinion subscribed to both and hoped that it would be possible to avoid the realization of either. Grenville seemed most insistent on a hard line, and he repeatedly criticized the administration for its weakness. Yet he

[6] Cf. ibid., p. 370.
[7] Ibid. See also "Letters of William Samuel Johnson to the Governors of Connecticut [1766–1771]," pp. 305, 307 (Hillsborough),and 337 (North) (hereafter Trumbull Papers); and *Sir Henry Cavendish's Debates of the House of Commons during the Thirteenth Parliament of Great Britain*, 1:203 (Grenville).
[8] Quoted in Trumbull Papers, p. 337.

offered few concrete proposals to stem American defiance. The possibility that a harder line would not have resulted in American meekness and that consequently large-scale military action might be necessary to avoid an even more disastrous retreat was never really addressed by Grenville, who once noted that "a military force should be employed in the last extremity, not in the first"— but failed to say precisely of what the last extremity consisted.[9] Dowdeswell and Camden, whose opinions were representative of most of the Rockinghamites and Chathamites, spelled out more clearly than Grenville ever did the dangers of war with America, but even the doves did not support the movement for total repeal until it became clear that Massachusetts would gain the support of the other colonies. A discernible division of opinion existed in 1768 between hardliners and softliners on the American question; yet the hawks were far from seeing the necessity of armed coercion to enforce the supremacy of Parliament, and the doves were still far from accepting the view they subsequently embraced that the American position was limited and could be accommodated without revolutionary changes in the structure of the empire. Thus the twofold consensus—to avoid the armed coercion of America and to maintain the supremacy of Parliament—continued virtually unchallenged. Recognition that these imperatives of policy were ultimately irreconcilable remained in the still distant future.

The most significant feature of the Grafton ministry was that it proved incapable of choosing between these imperatives. From the spring of 1768 to the spring of 1769 it was capable of neither appeasement nor repression. In consequence, it neither retreated nor advanced throughout 1768 and early 1769—or, what amounted to the same thing, its marginal retreats were made in the worst possible humor, while its advances proved weak and unavailing. The ministry, of course, did not see things this way. It identified its refusal to repeal the Townshend duties as firmness, and it saw its unwillingness to take sterner measures as prudence. What these two diverse springs of policy amounted to, in fact, was a paralysis born of irresolution, a policy—if such it can be called—that led ineluctably to self-contradiction and defeat.

[9] *Cavendish Debates*, 1:201. North later drew attention to Grenville's qualification: "The honorable gentleman disapproves of the employment of the military power, and yet he would have things in America quiet"; 1:204.

The conflicting fears preying on the mind of the Grafton ministry are best illuminated by the attitude it adopted toward the Townshend Revenue Act. The moment the duties came under attack in the colonies, the ministry disowned the work of its predecessor. On several occasions both Hillsborough and North told the colonial agents that they wished the revenue act had never been made, that it was based on uncommercial principles, and that, in fact, they intended to repeal the measure and would have done so had it not been for the nature of colonial opposition.[10]

The ministry's line was difficult to credit, if only because it had been the nonconsumption and nonimportation movements, alongside the threat of the development of American manufactures to supplant the dutied goods, that had made the duties uncommercial. In effect, Whitehall asked the colonists to cease exerting the pressure that had made the ministry change its mind about the wisdom of enacting the duties. Once the economic reasons for repeal had vanished with the collapse of the nonconsumption and nonimportation movements, the ministry would repeal! The government was forced into this awkward position by its genuine desire to remove the immediate causes of contention and by its no less pressing need to limit the political and constitutional consequences of a retreat. The ultimate resolution of the crisis arising from the Townshend Revenue Act—the repeal of all the duties save those on tea—followed from this dilemma. It was the inescapable consequence of a policy based on contradictory premises.

Repeal, however, would not come until 1770. In the interim—and especially until May of 1769—the ministry insisted that the costs of conceding in the face of political challenge and economic pressure outweighed the benefits of removing the immediate bone of contention. This calculation was reinforced by the halting development of the American nonimportation movement. But the central question was whether a bare refusal to repeal represented a sufficient response to American defiance. The ministry concluded that it did not. It did not seem possible to remain idle, waiting for American resistance to expire of its own accord—though the min-

[10] Trumbull Papers, pp. 294, 296, 305; The Papers of Benjamin Franklin, 16:11–12; and SCHGM 30 (1929):234. Cf. Knox's suspicions that the ministry had proposed a deal to the agents, in The Grenville Papers; 4:400–401.

istry was not above hoping that it would do so. The government's response came in a series of measures stretching from the spring of 1768 to the spring of 1769.

[III]

Seething discontent in Massachusetts Bay provoked the first action of the administration. By the end of 1767 the incessant protests in the newspapers against the 1767 American legislation had led a Boston town meeting to instruct its representatives in the General Court to press for repeal. Precisely how far the General Court would go remained a matter of uncertainty throughout January. In that month the Massachusetts assembly dispatched a petition to the King and a series of letters to its agent, Dennys de Berdt, and to those who had sponsored its cause during the Stamp Act crisis— Shelburne, Conway, Rockingham, Camden, and Chatham.[11] Governor Bernard was delighted when the assembly struck down by a two-to-one margin the proposed circular letter to its fellow assemblies on the continent, chagrined when in early February it reversed its vote by the same margin. The letter covered ground already made familiar by Dickinson's *Letters from a Farmer* and by the assembly's letters to the "friends of America." In the assembly's "humble opinion," the "Acts made there, imposing duties on the people of this province, with the sole and express purpose of raising a revenue, are infringements of their natural and constitutional rights." The letter recounted the objection that the colonists were not represented in Parliament and dismissed the practicality of their ever being so. It warned of the dangers of a civil establishment no longer checked by the assemblies, protested the "hardships" imposed on the assemblies by the Quartering Act, and questioned the "commission of the gentlemen appointed commissioners of the customs . . . , which authorizes them to make as many appointments as they think fit, and to pay the appointees what sum they please, for whose malconduct they are not accountable; from whence it may happen that officers of the Crown may

[11] These letters are reprinted in *A Collection of Interesting, Authentic Papers Relative to the Dispute between Great Britain and America, 1764–1775*, pp. 167–91.

be multiplied to such a degree as to become dangerous to the liberty of the people.[12]

Hillsborough's response to the actions of the Massachusetts assembly was immediate. He ordered Bernard to demand the revocation of the circular. If the assembly refused, the governor was to dissolve it and order new elections. At the same time, Hillsborough instructed the governors in the rest of America to prevail upon their assemblies to treat the Massachusetts circular with "the contempt it deserves." If the other assemblies answered, they too were to be dissolved.[13]

Hillsborough's response reveals a great deal about the outlook of the ministry in early 1768.[14] The threat of dissolution made sense only if the promoters and the potential respondents of the circular held opinions at odds with those of their constituents. Promoters of these dangerous and seditious views would thus be turned out of the legislature and called to account if they continued in "this flagitious Attempt to disturb the public Peace." The assumption, however, was profoundly at odds with reality.

In June, when Bernard pressed the ministry's demand that the circular letter be revoked, the assembly refused by a vote of ninety-two to seventeen, and new elections turned out most of the seventeen "rescinders."[15] In the rest of the colonies the result was much the same. The assemblies treated the Massachusetts circular as an affair entirely within their own cognizance. When Governor Sharpe laid Hillsborough's request before the Maryland assembly on June 20, it replied that "what we shall do upon this occasion, or whether in consequence of [the Massachusetts circular], we shall do any thing is not our present business to communicate to your excellency."[16] By the end of the year all the assemblies on the

[12] Ibid., pp. 191–93.

[13] Hillsborough's circular, along with that of the Massachusetts assembly, is reprinted in *English Historical Documents, Vol. IX: American Colonial Documents to 1776*, ed. Merrill Jensen (New York, 1955), pp. 714–16.

[14] Thomas Whately later remarked to Grenville that the "letter for rescinding . . . was, I find, approved by all the Administration"; *Grenville Papers*, 4:392. Cf. *The Correspondence of King George the Third from 1760 to December 1783*, 2:597–98.

[15] Thomas Hutchinson, *The History of the Colony and Province of Massachusetts Bay*, ed. Lawrence Shaw Mayo, 3 vols. (Cambridge, Mass., 1936), 3:166.

[16] *Maryland Archives*, William H. Browne et al., eds., 71 vols. to date (Baltimore, 1883–), 61:413. Governor Franklin of New Jersey had no knowledge of the circular from Massachusetts until he saw from the minutes of the House that it had been received. Hillsborough later unfairly rebuked him for his "very blameable Inattention to Duty." In reply, Franklin noted that the speaker of the House had failed to inform him of the letter. "This too, I

continent had been roused to some defiant act, and many governors warned Hillsborough that the threat of dissolution was worse than useless. After the Maryland assembly passed a series of eight inflammatory resolves, Sharpe told Hillsborough that he would "have immediately dissolved the Assembly had not Experience taught me that no Step is so likely to attach the People to their Representatives as a sudden Dissolution & that on a new Election instantly following None are so likely to be left out as those Members who appeared averse to violent Measures."[17] Thus Hillsborough's first attempt to answer swelling opposition in America ended in failure. Its only result was to demonstrate that imperial authority was weak and that it could be defied with impunity.[18]

---

believe, was the Conduct of every other Speaker who receiv'd such a Letter to every other Governor. They look'd upon it as belonging to the Assembly alone to whom it was directed, and that no other Persons whatever in the Province had or ought to have any Concern with it"; *Documents Relating to the Colonial . . . History of . . . New Jersey*, 10:46, 73.

[17] June 22, 1768, *Maryland Archives*, 14:506.

[18] It is sometimes claimed that the Hillsborough circular did more, that it "produced precisely the result [the ministry] sought most fervently to avoid"; Ian R. Christie and Benjamin W. Labaree, *Empire or Independence, 1760–1776*, p. 114. Merrill Jensen insists that the Massachusetts "Circular Letter did produce a 'union' of the colonies, not because of its merits but because it was answered by a circular letter from England presenting a challenge no colonial legislature could ignore"; *Founding of a Nation*, p. 251. Both views misstate the case against the Hillsborough circular, whose chief difficulty was not that it "produced" a unified opposition to Great Britain but that it threatened a weak and long-discredited sanction—itself intelligible only on a profound misreading of colonial political realities—if the colonies did "unite."

Seven colonial assemblies were in session from the time they had received the Massachusetts circular until Hillsborough's order reached the colonies. Four—Virginia (which sent a circular of its own), New Jersey, Connecticut, and Maryland—responded to Massachusetts and sent a variety of protests back home questioning the right of Parliament to impose revenue taxes. See Lawrence Henry Gipson, *The British Empire before the American Revolution*, 11:167–78; *Documents of New Jersey* 10:34–37; "The Pitkin Papers: Correspondence and Documents during William Pitkin's Governorship of the Colony of Connecticut, 1766–1769," ed. Albert C. Bates, Connecticut Historical Society, *Collections*, vol. 19, Hartford, 1921 pp. 127–139; and *Maryland Archives*, 14:506, 510–11, 61:334, 360, 399, 406–9, 413–20. Two assemblies—Rhode Island and New Hampshire—acted with less dispatch. New Hampshire sent the Massachusetts assembly a letter that approved the latter's action, but a petition to the King was not drawn up until the fall and it appears not to have been sent until 1770; Gipson, *British Empire*, 11:169–70. In February, Rhode Island appointed a committee to draw up a petition to the King and a letter "to one of His Majesty's principal secretaries of state," but the committee did not complete its work until September. The speaker of the Rhode Island assembly, however, did inform the speaker of the Massachusetts house during the summer that Rhode Island's delay should not be construed as timidity; *Journals of the House of Representatives of Massachusetts*, 50 vols. to date (Boston, 1919–), app. p. 13. Of these seven assemblies, only Pennsylvania (whose case will be considered shortly) clearly deferred action on the Massachusetts letter for fear of offending the ministry.

It is impossible to know with certainty what those assemblies meeting after the receipt of both the Massachusetts and Hillsborough circulars would have done in the absence of

[IV]

The failure of the ministry's first American initiative had not become apparent before Whitehall embarked on a second and more hazardous course of action during the summer. Again, events in Massachusetts Bay formed the proximate cause of the ministry's action. On June 8, after Whitehall received reports from Governor Bernard and the customs commissioners detailing the March dis-

---

Whitehall's threat, but it is implausible to assume that they would have done nothing—implausible because it requires one to believe that a sanction that had been employed regularly, though with indifferent success, throughout colonial history aroused in the colonists apprehensions equal to their fears concerning the Townshend Acts. Even if the contrary position is taken, however, and it is assumed that the threat of dissolution was usually effective, there is no reason for believing that the absence of the threat would have given the assemblies an incentive for ignoring the Massachusetts circular.

Of those assemblies that delayed action on the circular, New York and Pennsylvania present the most interesting cases, and it is perhaps on their examples that Jensen's thesis primarily rests. In the former case, the Delanceys wished to repeat and amplify their election triumph of the previous February and consequently hoped that a defiant stance by the assembly would leave Governor Moore with no choice but to dissolve the legislature. The Livingstons, on the other hand, wished to avoid new elections. They contrived to answer the Virginia circular but ignore that of Massachusetts in the hopes that Moore would continue the term, but the strategy collapsed in the face of widespread popular opposition.

New York's experience shows that the threat of dissolution was a blunt as well as ineffective instrument, that the Hillsborough circular became caught up in the dynamics of local politics, and that an antiimperial stance was a sure method for acquiring popular favor. This example scarcely shows, however, that the Livingstons would have ignored the Massachusetts circular in the absence of Hillsborough's threat. If anything, it indicates that the threat of dissolution was the chief moderating influence on their conduct. Out of many challenging, though conflicting, interpretations on the dynamics of New York politics, see particularly Roger Champagne, "Family Politics versus Constitutional Principles: The New York Assembly Elections of 1768 and 1769," *William and Mary Quarterly*, 3d ser., 20(1963):57–79.

In Pennsylvania, the Speaker of the House, Joseph Galloway, succeeded in delaying any action on the Massachusetts circular when the assembly received the letter in May. Still full of hope that Franklin would convince the ministry to oust the proprietors and institute royal government, Galloway and his followers continued to practice what James H. Hutson has called the "politics of ingratiation," avoiding any insult to a ministry in whose hands lay the hope of reform; *Pennsylvania Politics, 1746–1770* (Princeton, 1972), pp. 193–94. This stance, however, made the assembly party politically vulnerable to the attacks of John Dickinson and others associated with the Presbyterian party, whose appeal now centered around its stridently antiimperial platform. When Hillsborough's circular arrived in Pennsylvania in July, the Presbyterians raised a storm of protest. Galloway, needless to say, was not happy with the ministry for complicating his position, yet he still felt he was in control of events. He toned down the petitions to King, Lords, and Commons which the Pennsylvania assembly passed in September, resulting in remonstrances sufficiently respectful to gain an audience in the Commons. After the October elections he still felt confident enough to tell Benjamin Franklin that the design "to raise a Spirit of Violence against the late Act of Parliament . . . was crushed in its Beginning by our Friends, so effectually, that, I think, we shall not soon have it renewed"; *Papers of Franklin*, 16:231.

Shortly thereafter Galloway began to lose control of events. Of the critical factors that came into play to discredit his position, however, the Hillsborough circular was among the least important. Nonimportation was the critical issue for the respective parties, and several

turbances in Boston, Hillsborough ordered Gage to send "one Regiment, or such Force as you shall think necessary, to Boston."[19] Six weeks later, on July 30, Hillsborough augmented these forces by ordering two Irish regiments, scheduled to leave for America in 1769, to depart immediately for Boston. The second decision was reached after the ministry received word of the *Liberty* riots and the panicked flight of the custom commissioners to Castle William. Four regiments would thus descend on Boston sometime in the early fall. It appeared to some observers that the ministry had embarked on the road to coercion; war seemed a distinct possibility. William Knox reported to Grenville, "I find the Administration are all, except Lord Shelburne, agreed upon coercive measures." Camden, who had voted against the Declaratory Act, was "wholly and absolutely of that opinion."[20]

This initiative, too, was destined to end in failure. In retrospect, it is difficult to see how it could have ended otherwise. The troops were under strict orders to support and protect, "when properly and legally called upon, the civil Magistrates and Officers in the Discharge of their Duty."[21] Boston, in other words, was not being placed under martial rule. The troops were to support, not supplant, the civil power.[22] The civil power in Massachusetts Bay, however, had passed some time ago from the hands of the governor. He could not legally request the services of the military on his sole

---

events combined to strengthen its appeal. First, the campaign for royal government had apparently faltered, perhaps irrevocably, removing one principle restraint on behavior offensive to the ministry. Second, Parliament's refusal to repeal the Townshend duties during its winter session led many to the conclusion that Pennsylvania ought to resort to more coercive measures, since petitioning had patently failed. Galloway's public position during 1768 never foreclosed this option, though he did continue to oppose it and had argued in the summer of 1768 that nonimportation would severely disrupt Philadelphia's commerce, that it was a vile commercial trick of the Bostonians, and that it ought to be employed only in the last resort. Finally, the Presbyterians began to argue for nonimportation on economic as well as constitutional grounds and were successful in winning the sympathies of Philadelphia's "mechanics" and "artisans"—the White Oaks—who had remained supporters of the assembly party in the October 1768 elections. On these points, see Hutson, *Pennsylvania Politics*, pp. 224–33; Stephen E. Lucas, *Portents of Rebellion: Rhetoric and Revolution in Philadelphia, 1765–76* (Philadelphia, 1976), pp. 32–41; and Benjamin H. Newcomb, *Franklin and Galloway: A Political Partnership* (New Haven, 1972), pp. 191–99.

[19] *The Correspondence of General Thomas Gage with the Secretaries of State and with the War Office and the Treasury, 1763–1775*, 2:68–69.

[20] Knox to Grenville, September 15, 1768, *Grenville Papers*, 4:364.

[21] Hillsborough to Gage, July 30, 1768, *Gage*, 2:73.

[22] Cf. Charles Fairman, *The Law of Martial Rule* (Chicago, 1930), esp. pp. 31–39.

authority; and the men who staffed the institutions—primarily the Massachusetts council and the justices of the peace—whose consent would be required for any military action were violently opposed to the presence of the army in Boston. The legal use of the army thus depended on a requisition from a civilian "authority," which at least partly lay in the hands of the whigs. From 1768 to the outbreak of war, that requisition never came.

Even this obstacle to the legal use of the troops does not fully reveal the de facto legal restrictions on them. The use of troops against a civilian populace was "a point of delicacy" in the English constitution.[23] Even if called upon by competent authority, local courts retained jurisdiction over the propriety of such actions, and the legal system of Massachusetts Bay was firmly in the hands of those opposed to the presence of the troops in Boston. This jurisdiction extended not only to serious crimes but to minor infractions. All were punishable in the courts of Massachusetts Bay. The most celebrated trial of British soldiers occurred in the aftermath of the Boston "Massacre," but this trial had itself been preceded by a long string of punishments for minor infractions, the fundamental purpose of which was to show the illegality of the army's presence in Boston. Those inhabitants loyal to the metropolis did not enjoy effective possession of the police power in Massachusetts Bay. The point is fundamental. The British could not punish those who defied imperial law; they could not protect those who attempted to enforce it.[24]

The attacks on imperial officials in Massachusetts Bay and the inability of metropolitan officials to respond effectively to these attacks demonstrate how the stakes of the conflict in the Bay Colony had, by 1768, outpaced the initial causes of the dispute. In the postwar program of imperial reform Grenville had given little thought to the means by which the metropolis might maintain order in a

---

[23] Sackville to Irwin, September 22, 1768, *HMC*, Stopford-Sackville Manuscripts, 1:128.
[24] See John Philip Reid's unconventional, though frequently superb, account of the "conditions of law" in revolutionary Massachusetts; *In a Defiant Stance, The Conditions of Law in Massachusetts Bay, the Irish Comparison, and the Coming of the American Revolution* (University Park, Pa., 1977),esp. pp. 100–117. "Boston had become an occupied town but the occupiers were not in control. They had been sent to intimidate and it was they who were intimidated. They were expected to police but it was they who would be policed"; p. 117. Hiller B. Zobel, *The Boston Massacre*, (New York, 1970), and Shy, *Toward Lexington*, also give excellent accounts of the situation facing the troops in Boston.

disorderly colony. Insofar as this question had arisen at all, it had done so within the context of the enforcement mechanism of the Acts of Trade and Navigation. The situation that the British confronted in 1768 had moved far beyond this question. In order to protect their officials, the British had to have some hold on the police power, and this they did not have. They had to be able to ensure the "administration of justice," and this they could not do. To retain the Bay Colony within the empire in any meaningful sense required the British to undertake some changes in the Massachusetts charter—changes that would have made the liberty of the colony dependent on the good faith of its rulers in the metropolis. This was the terrible logic of the situation faced by the Grafton ministry, yet it was a dilemma that at no time the ministry summoned up the courage to confront. The action that the ministry did take—the commitment of the troops to Boston in the absence of the constitutional changes that would have permitted their effective use—was a recipe for a disaster much worse than the one it would have confronted had it simply ignored the challenge or had it sent the army with powers sufficient to the task. The half-measure the government did pursue had all the liabilities, and none of the advantages, of either appeasement or repression.

[V]

It was widely anticipated that Parliament would take some measures to punish Massachusetts when it convened in November 1768. "Something very serious," Hutchinson recalled, "was generally expected," and it was devoutly wished for by those in Massachusetts sympathetic to the establishment of imperial order in their province. Hutchinson warned Thomas Whately that "if no measure shall have been taken to secure this dependence, or nothing more than some declaratory acts or resolves, *it is all over with us*. The friends of government will be utterly disheartened, and the friends of anarchy will be afraid of nothing, be it ever so extravagant."[25] The New York Restraining Act had been passed the previous year in response to offenses almost trivial in comparison with those

[25] Hutchinson, *History*, 3:157–58; and Hutchinson to Whately, December 10, 1768, *Copy of Letters Sent to Great Britain, by His Excellency Thomas Hutchinson* . . . (Boston, 1773), p. 16.

committed in Massachusetts Bay during 1768. The actions that the ministry found offensive, indeed, were duly listed by Hillsborough in a series of eight resolves that he presented to the Lords on December 15. The resolutions condemning Parliament's 1767 American legislation, which the Massachusetts House adopted in January and February, were found by Hillsborough to be "illegal, unconstitutional and derogatory of the rights of the crown and parliament of Great Britain." The Massachusetts circular was denounced in language that Hillsborough had already used—and to similar effect—in his circular to the colonial governors. His third resolution stated that the peace of Boston "has at several times been disturbed by riots and tumults of a dangerous nature, in which the officers of his Majesty's revenue there have been obstructed, by acts of violence, in the execution of the laws, and their lives endangered." His fourth condemned the Massachusetts council and the "ordinary civil magistrates for failing to exert their authority for suppressing the said riots and tumults." He next declared that "in these circumstances . . . the preservation of the public peace, and the due execution of the laws, became impracticable, without the aid of a military force to support and protect the civil magistrates, and the officers of his Majesty's revenue." His sixth resolution condemned the resolutions of the Boston town meetings of June 14 and September 12. The seventh and eighth resolutions dealt with the Massachusetts Convention of towns, which had met in September after a call from the Boston town meeting. He found it "subversive of his Majesty's government, and evidently manifesting a design in the inhabitants of the said town of Boston to set up a new and unconstitutional authority, independent of the crown of Great Britain."[26]

This was an imposing set of indictments. Each contained a charge of either illegality, breach of duty, or usurpation. If true, and they merely recapitulated the reports of Governor Bernard and other imperial officials, the indictments seemed to require a sweeping program of parliamentary action. Yet the only remedy the administration proposed was an address to the King, moved by Lord Bedford, that had two principle components. One expressed "sincere satisfaction in the measures" the administration had taken during the previous year and offered "the strongest assurances that

[26] *PH*, 16:476–79.

we will effectually stand by and support" whatever else the ministry proposed to do in the future. The second feature of the address stated the need to bring "to condign punishment the chief authors and instigators of the late disorders," and requested that the King direct Bernard "to take the most effectual methods for procuring the fullest information that can be obtained touching all treasons, or misprision of treason, committed within" Massachusetts Bay. Bernard was to submit this information to the secretary of state, "in order that your Majesty may issue a special commission for inquiring of, hearing, and determining, the said offences within this realm, pursuant to the provisions of the statute of the 35th year of the reign of king Henry the eight, in case your Majesty shall, upon receiving the said information, see sufficient ground for such a proceeding."[27]

Hillsborough, not content with this program, pressed for sterner measures. In February he presented to the cabinet and later laid before the King a series of measures against Massachusetts Bay. The most important of these was his proposal that Parliament "vest the Appointment of the Council of Massachusetts Bay in the Crown" and declare that any questioning of the principles of the Declaratory Act by the Massachusetts assembly "shall be ipso facto an avoidance and forefeiture of the Charter." He recommended that Bernard be conferred "the dignity of a Baronet" and be recalled from Massachusetts "to Report the State of the Province" to the King. Hutchinson would administer the government during Bernard's absence. The American secretary also recommended that the governor be given discretion to hold the General Court where he wished, and that Gage be allowed to remove from Boston the two regiments he had sent from Halifax.[28]

Most of Hillsborough's proposals were rejected by King and cabinet. The King acknowledged that the royal appointment of the Massachusetts council "may from a continuance of their conduct

---

[27] Ibid., pp. 479–80.

[28] *George III*, 2: nos. 701–701a. Hillsborough made a number of other recommendations, the most significant of which were rejected by the King. These included a proposal to remove four New York councilors who had failed to support Moore's dissolution of the assembly; a suggestion that those New York assembly members occupying important posts in the assembly be rendered ineligible to serve in public office if they refused to retract their offending resolutions; a suggested amendment of the Quartering Act; and a recommendation to repeal the Townshend Revenue Act for those colonies—primarily Virginia and the West Indian Islands—"where Provision has already been amply made for that Service" and to promise any other colony full repeal when it made "permanent Provision for its own Establishment."

become necessary; but till then ought to be avoided as the altering Charters is at all times an odious measure."[29] Hillsborough made no better headway with the cabinet. Barrington had written to Bernard as early as January 2 that measures had been proposed "as will tend to preserve the Obedience of the Colonies," but he was now dejected. "[B]y some fatal catastrophe, two or three men [in the cabinet], with less ability, less credit, less authority & less responsibility than the rest, have carry'd their point and produced that flimsey unavailing Address which has past the Lords."[30] The proposal to alter the charter of Massachusetts Bay, on which Governor Bernard had placed his hopes for restoring the vigor of royal government, had met with defeat.

Thus, the only action the ministry could rouse itself to take was an address to the King approving its actions of the previous year and threatening the colonists with punishment for treason. What the ministry threatened with one hand, however, it removed with the other. An administration spokesman, Grey Cooper, admitted that "it was not meant to put the act [of Henry VIII] in execution, but only to shew to America, what government could do if pushed to it."[31] The gesture was meaningless, since it added nothing to the implicit threat that already existed save the message that the threat would not be implemented. On learning of the address, Governor Bernard became disheartened and told Barrington what the latter already knew: it was a futile gesture that would not "restore the Kings Authority in this Province."

A simple Order to me to make Enquiry into the Proceedings, which have incurred the Penalties of Treason or Misprision of Treason, will have no other Consequence than to show the Impotency of Government; unless I am armed with some extraordinary Power to oblige Persons, whom I shall require to undergo an Examination, to submit to it. But I have no such Power at present; otherwise I should have exercised it long ago. And if I was to call before me, even by special Orders from the King, ever so many Persons knowing of the seditious & treasonable Practices of the Faction here, & was to *beg Leave* to ask them a few Questions, I should be answered, as it is said the Secretaries of State were by Wilkes, "You have leave to ask as many Questions as you please, but I *beg leave* to give no Answer to any of them."[32]

---

[29] Ibid., 2:no. 701a.
[30] Barrington to Bernard, January 2, 1769, *The Barrington-Bernard Correspondence and Illustrative Matter, 1760–1770*, ed. Edward Channing and Archibald Cary Coolidge (Cambridge, Mass., 1912), p. 182.
[31] *PH* 16:507.
[32] *Barrington-Bernard Correspondence*, p. 197.

[VI]

There were two principal lines of attack on the ministry's policy. From one side came the charge that the government's policy was too weak; from the other, that it was too strong. Both united, however, in thinking that the middle ground the ministry had chosen had nothing to recommend it. Many speakers commented on the irregularity of the Act of Henry VIII; questioned whether it could be legally applied to America; and doubted the justice of such a proceeding. Yet the most trenchant critique of the ministry's program came from Grenville. He noted that the address to the King was the remedy proposed to stem the evils summarized in the eight resolutions and asked:

Will the assurances we give his Majesty be an adequate remedy for the votes of the Massachuset's Bay assembly? We say, that the magistrates did not exert their authority for suppressing the riots: will our approving the act of the 35th of Henry the Eighth make those magistrates do their duty? Under these circumstances, a military force is called in: now, a military force should be employed in the last extremity, not in the first instance. When you declare that no magistrate will act, of all the measures that it is possible to conceive, this is the strangest mixture. Hood, Gage, Dalrymple—are they to execute the laws, by their own advice, without the assistance of any civil magistrate? There is nothing in the resolutions tending to remedy the complaint respecting the magistrates.[33]

Like Lord Temple, who had stormed from the Commons in December criticizing this attempt at "paper war with the colonies,"[34] Grenville noted that the ministry did "not mean to send for anybody" under the Act of Henry VIII. "This resolution," he roundly declared, "is so much waste paper." He recurred to the nature of the crisis he believed Britain confronted: "The dispute is not about this or that sum of money, but to establish your jurisdiction and power of every kind, within the words of the act of parliament, over the colonies. Are the Americans to be taught this, by virture of an address of the two Houses of Parliament?" He did not understand how it was possible for the Commons to establish the right of Parliament, "knowing that there is no government in America, that there is no civil power." Nor did Grenville have any kinder words for the Hillsborough circular of the previous April: "Am I

[33] *Cavendish Debates*, 1:201.
[34] *PH*, 16:476.

to recede from it or adopt it? Is it alive, or, like a rickety child, has it died already, by fits or convulsions?"[35]

The ministry's defense of its policy was less than enthusiastic, yet it did make the attempt. Little was said, it is true, on behalf of Hillsborough's circular of the previous April. Nor would the ministry say that treason had been committed. The attorney general doubted "whether [the Americans] have been guilty of an overt act of treason; but I am sure they have come within an hair's breadth of it."[36] The address was a "warning" to go no farther. "It is right to give them notice," North held, "that they are to depend, not upon the impunity of an American jury, but the decision of an English one."[37] To the charge of weakness, North replied "that the not repealing of the act is in itself a measure that will operate in America; where they have been expecting a repeal." Most significant was North's defense of the dispatch of troops to Boston. He held that it had been productive of good consequences. "What, Sir, has been the effect? The riots have been quelled, the tumults have subsided, the act of parliament has been carried into execution, and the officers of the Crown have been re-established. One thing was wanted—the knowledge whether the parliament of Great Britain would approve or disapprove of their conduct." Countering Grenville's charge that there was nothing in the address that would remedy the complaint against the magistrates, North asked: "Could we, Sir, imagine, because the magistrates did not act when they were unprotected, that they would not act when they were protected?"[38]

North's defense of the ministry's conduct was mistaken on several critical points. The threat to try American leaders for treason was scarcely received with fear and trembling. It was, Franklin concluded, of the "same Stamp" as the eight resolutions against Massachusetts: "mere *bruta Fulmina*," not to be taken seriously.[39] Nor did the ministry's refusal to repeal lead the colonists to conclude that their efforts had been unavailing. Instead, it led to the intensification of these efforts. The most critical error, however, was North's interpretation of the reasons for the "restoration of order"

---

[35] *Cavendish Debates*, 1:201–2.
[36] Ibid., p. 196. Cf. p. 198 (Hussey).
[37] Ibid., p. 205.
[38] Ibid., p. 204–5.
[39] *Papers of Franklin*, 16:12. To similar effect, see Hutchinson, *History*, 3:160–61.

in Massachusetts Bay. This had little to do with a supposed new-found willingness of the civil magistrates to act. Even those few civil magistrates who may have sympathized with the metropolis were unwilling to risk public odium or legal prosecution in requesting the troops; whereas the majority of the justices of the peace shared the view of their fellow citizens that the presence of the army in Boston was illegal. The arrival of the troops had brought order to Boston because of the initial uncertainty over the army's powers, the fear of what Parliament might do in its winter session, and the need of the Bostonians to discredit the reports of "anarchy" that Bernard had sent home. The first landing of the troops in Boston, as John Shy has noted, was a display that "combined order, uncertainty, and menace."[40] No one could be sure what secret and terrible instructions had been conveyed to the troops and to the man—Bernard—now identified as the great enemy of the province. It was not unreasonable to suppose, as a writer in the *Boston Gazette* conjectured on September 26, that the mission of the army was more draconian than it would later appear to be. The writer found three purposes in the movement of the troops: "1st That the inhabitants of the province were to be disarmed. 2d That the province was to be governed by martial law. 3rd That a number of gentlemen, who have exerted [themselves] in the cause of their country, are to be seized and sent to Great Britain."[41] That Parliament would deliberate on Massachusetts Bay in the coming winter session was also conducive to quiet. This prospect, too, conveyed alarm.[42] From the standpoint of the whigs, any renewed violence in Boston would only further inflame the disposition of a hostile Parliament and provide fresh proof of the lies and misrepresentations of Bernard.

The inaction of the Grafton ministry during the winter parliamentary session in effect removed the fears that had theretofore made the townspeople apprehensive of the troops and prevented clashes between soldiers and citizens. "As soon as it appeared that all danger was over," Hutchinson recalled, "lenity was construed

[40] *Toward Lexington*, p. 304.
[41] Quoted in Gipson, *British Empire*, 11:161.
[42] Hutchinson recalled that with the arrival of the troops, "short quiet succeeded long disturbance. Troops at first carried terror. There had been no experience of them. The restraint they were under without a civil magistrate was not known to that part of the people most disposed to mobs and riots. Such as were better acquainted with it, seemed willing to hear how parliament would receive what was past"; *History*, 3:157.

into timidity."[43] Clashes between soldiers and citizens began to escalate. "It was soon found, that prosecutions of soldiers for a breach of law were as easily carried on as against any other persons; and that all reports against them more easily obtained credit."[44] The soldiers grew contemptuous of a legal system that obstructed their every move; the citizens of Boston grew emboldened in their attempts to force the troops to quit the town. The upshot, though late in coming, was the Boston Massacre of March 5, 1770. A small group of British soldiers, pinned against the wall by a raging mob, momentarily lost their composure. "Not having the fear of God before their eyes, but being moved and seduced by the instigation of the devil and their own wicked hearts," they fired into the crowd, killing five unarmed men. By the next day, all the troops save those soldiers charged with murder had left the town.[45]

North's defense of the ministry's conduct, then, was full of errors. Does this misunderstanding account for the administration's policy during Parliament's winter session? Did the ministry reject charter reform because it believed such an action was unnecessary to achieve the objective on behalf of which it had sent the troops—the res-

[43] Ibid., p. 161.

[44] Ibid., pp. 173–74.

[45] John Hodgson, The Trial of William Wems . . . [and others], Soldiers in His Majesty's 29th Regiment of Foot, for the Murder of Crispus Attucks . . . [and others] . . . (Boston, 1770), p. 3. The decision to send the troops in the first place was attended by instructions to the governor which also reveal the depth of the initial misunderstanding of the situation in Massachusetts. Hillsborough placed the army under civilian control, but he failed utterly to address the weakness of the governor's position in the province. Consequently, his instructions to Bernard contained very little that the governor could make use of and very much that he could very well have done without, such as the hints impugning Bernard's integrity. British policy, Hillsborough grandly announced, was to induce "a Due Obedience to the Law. . . . No Remissness of Duty will be excusable, upon pretense of Terror and Danger in the Execution of Office." The American secretary ordered Bernard to dismiss the magistrates who had been deficient in their duty, an action that Bernard could not take without the council's consent. The secretary told the governor to "conduct a full inquiry into the late riots and tumults; discover the perpetrators of the violence of June 10; consider the possibility of sending the wrongdoers to England for trial in the King's Bench under authority of a statute dating from Henry VIII." (See the summary of these instructions in Zobel, Boston Massacre, pp. 85–86.) Given the constraints under which the governor labored, however, he could do none of these things. As Zobel notes, Hillsborough was "commanding impossibilities." For Bernard's reply, which placed the difficulty where it belonged—on the irresolution of governments at home and particularly the unwillingness of Whitehall to assure the Massachusetts governor of its support—see Bernard to Hillsborough, September 20, 1768, Francis Bernard, Select Letters On the Trade and Government of America . . . (London, 1774) pp. 61–63. As Bernard had written Shelburne earlier in the year, relating the publication with impunity of a libel against him that he thought seditious: "But after all, these Printers are answerable to Great-Britain, an Hundred Times more than they are to this; and while that Debt remains unsatisfied, we ought not to complain that it is not paid here"; Bernard to Shelburne, March 5, 1768, Letters to the Ministry from Governor Bernard, General Gage, and Commodore Hood . . . (Boston, 1769), p. 10.

toration of order—or because it feared the consequences? Was the administration's unwillingness to execute the statute of Henry VIII an indication of its lenity or its timidity? There are no easy answers to these questions. One must remain skeptical, however, that a better appreciation of the effects that its policy would produce in America would have led the Grafton ministry to take a tougher line. The ministry's understanding was deficient, but it was not totally incomplete. It hoped that some civil magistrates would co-operate with the army, but it knew that a great many magistrates were violently opposed to the presence of the troops and were unremovable by the governor save with the consent of the council.[46] It knew that the council had obstructed Bernard's every move during the previous year. More critically, the ministry knew that there was an "impossibility of obtaining justice upon any past transgression" in Boston, which arose "from a very great defect in the constitutional administration of justice. Neither the great nor the little juries are returned by the sheriffs, but by the colonists: the head of the mob was at the head of the grand jury. It was impossible to bring any man to give testimony: so that the jury were of course dismissed."[47] This appreciation of the "impossibility of obtaining justice upon any past transgression" explains the ministry's recourse to the Act of Henry VIII. It scarcely explains the ministry's unwillingness to execute the act.

One must conclude that the government's policy during the winter of 1768/69 stemmed ultimately from the apprehension with which it contemplated the prospect of a general conflict with the colonies. By the winter of 1768/69 it had become clear to most of the ministry that the cancer of disobedience could not be restricted to Massachusetts Bay, and that any drastic program of constitutional reform in Massachusetts would likely widen the conflict. Nothing was more tempting to Whitehall than a strategy that somehow isolated one colony from the rest. This strategy, such as it was, had informed Parliament's action against New York in 1767, and it had also played a prominent role in the Grafton ministry's earlier policy toward America. Yet the evidence coming in from America appeared to demonstrate that the materials that might allow the British to pursue a policy of *divide et impera* were not present in

[46] *George III*, 2:no. 701a.
[47] *Cavendish Debates*, 1:35 (Stanley).

America. The returns from Hillsborough's April circular convinced many, if not Hillsborough himself, that action taken against one colony would rapidly require action against many others. This prospect the Grafton ministry was not yet prepared to face, and there is little reason to suppose that its views in this respect were contrary to those of the political nation as a whole. If American passivity had allowed Whitehall to believe that it could make an example of Massachusetts Bay and show the other colonies the terrible consequences that might follow from disobedience, it is possible that the Grafton ministry might have screwed up its nerve and presented a program of charter reform to Parliament. The alacrity and unity of the American response, however, made this course of action seem perilous. The same considerations prevented the ministry from seizing a number of Massachusetts whigs and sending them to England for prosecution under the Act of Henry VIII. This, too, might serve only to rally the rest of the colonists behind the martyrs. For the Grafton ministry, the halting commitment to a policy of *divide et impera* meant not merely that it would attempt to rule by division but also, and more critically, that it would not attempt to rule if it could not first succeed in dividing. The unity of the American response had ineluctably set the Grafton ministry on the road to retreat. So long as there was the barest possibility war could be avoided without sacrificing the supremacy of Parliament, the British committed themselves to pursuing it. Only in 1775 would they come to understand that the maintenance of parliamentary sovereignty was impossible without war.

This view of British conduct need not be accepted. Of greater significance is that the colonists did accept it as an explanation of the Grafton ministry's conduct. A new theme entered the correspondence of American leaders, who began to view the administration with approximately equal doses of loathing and contempt. The violent language of Parliament's eight resolutions against Massachusetts Bay taught them that irreconcilable differences existed between Britain and America; its inaction taught them that American resistance, and that alone, had prevented these designs against liberty from reaching completion. The mixture was explosive.

It was William Johnson, perhaps the most acute observer of British political life during this period, who rendered the most damning and perceptive explanation of the Grafton ministry's conduct. He believed that a settlement of the dispute was possible, and, like most Americans, never really saw why Britain remained unwilling to accept the colonial pretension to equality. He also thought, however, that the eight resolutions could not "answer any one good purpose whatsoever, even upon their own principles." At the core of the Grafton ministry he found a divided mind: in truth, he thought, "they know not what to do themselves. Too obstinate to retract, too weak and irresolute to advance, they have chosen this insignificant middle measure of resolution,—seeming to do something, yet really doing nothing,—which can produce only contempt." He noted, in a passage of enduring value, that

wisdom and folly will forever be the same, in private and in political conduct. When an individual has taken a wrong step, true wisdom will forever dictate to him to confess it, to retract it, and mend as soon as possible the mischief of his malconduct. If he will not be wise, he may still perhaps obtain the character of firmness and intrepidity, even by persevering boldly in a wrong measure, and fortifying himself in mischief; but if he has neither the wisdom to repent, nor the firmness to persevere, the light he next appears in is that of insignificancy, and he meets contempt and scorn. The latter, I fancy, will be the character of the present Administration. In a word, the language of their political conduct seems to be this; "We own the late act to be very wrong, yet we will not repeal it, because you first pointed out the error to us, and it will gratify you to disannul it. The act, it is true, is injudicious and injurious; you have reason to complain of it, but when you do so, you are seditious, turbulent, and traitorous. We will be sure not to make another such act, nor will we persevere in the principle upon which this is founded; but we will keep this in existence, that we may still have something to quarrel about. We will obtain a Parliamentary authority and the King's order to punish you, but we assure you we will not do it. We mean to frighten you, and we will even point our artillery against you; but we tell you, at the same time, you need not be frightened, we will not hurt a hair of your heads." Is not this more than silly? Yet such seems to be the wisdom of the present set of politicians.[48]

[VII]

By the spring of 1769 the Grafton ministry had been responsible for three initiatives during the past year. Each had represented an

---

[48] Trumbull Papers, pp. 331–32. Cf. David Ramsay, *History of the American Revolution*, 1:86.

attempt to answer or stem American defiance. Each had failed. In May 1769 what the ministry had been unable to accomplish through ministerial command, the threat of military force, and the threat of political prosecution it now attempted to achieve through artifice. The month before, Thomas Pownall had moved that Parliament repeal the Townshend duties, but the administration remained opposed. After Parliament was prorogued on May 9, however, the ministry sent another circular to the governors of America inform-ing them that the present administration would propose no further measures of taxation and that "it is at present their intention to propose in the next session of Parliament: to take off the duties upon glass, paper and colours upon consideration of such duties having been laid contrary to the true principles of commerce." The decision to retain the tax on tea had narrowly passed the cabinet in a five-to-four vote. Those dissenting were all who remained from the initial Chatham ministry—Grafton, Conway, Camden, and Granby. By the following spring none would be left in the cabinet. [49]

The disagreement within the cabinet, however, was a fairly nar-row one. There was little dispute over the need to repeal the "uncommercial duties"—i.e., all those except tea—and over the strategy of refusing to repeal during 1769 and promising to repeal during 1770. The ministry's motives for acting in this manner fol-lowed from its prior conduct. It saw that a retreat would be nec-essary and wished to put a good face on the repeal. The manifest, though unacknowledged, purpose of *promising* to repeal was to retard, if not destroy, the American nonimportation movement. This done, the ministry could with greater plausibility claim the following year that it had not acted under duress. Indeed, having obtained its moral victory, the administration might have proposed the repeal of all the duties. The maneuver represented an attempt to mitigate the ill consequences that would otherwise attend a retreat, a way of preparing the ground for a proclamation of victory even in the act of defeat. Even so, the ministry's hopes proved unavailing. The colonists also wanted a conclusive demonstration that they had won—just as much as, if not more than, the ministry wished to disguise its defeat. The nonimportation movement spread to the southern colonies, and the colonists refused to acknowledge

---

[49] Grafton, *Autobiography*, pp. 229–34; Christie and Labaree, *Empire or Independence*, p. 129.

the principles of the Declaratory Act. The Grafton ministry had thus failed to make the American problem go away. When Parliament met late in 1769, there the dilemma was, intractable as ever, demanding attention from a ministry that would soon be reorganized under the direction of Lord North.

TWELVE

The North Ministry

The Collapse of Imperial Authority, 1770–73

[I]

The outcome of the events marking the late 1760s bear a striking resemblance to the outcome of the Stamp Act crisis. In 1770 a British government could, once again, find no alternative to a policy of concession. In theory, the ministry now led by Lord North might have retained the Townshend duties, even if this had necessitated—as it likely would have necessitated—adoption of a policy of enforcement. It might have conceded without qualification by total repeal of the 1767 Townshend duties. In practice, the choice was much narrower, and this quite apart from North's commitment to the decision for partial repeal made the previous year by the Grafton administration. Total repeal would not only have been an undisguised defeat for the metropolis on the immediate issue in contention, the Townshend duties, it would have been seen as conceding the issue of right as well. Total repeal would have represented an acknowledgment by the metropolis of the colonial claim to equality, an acknowledgment whose consequences could not be limited to the practice of parliamentary taxation. True, the Declaratory Act would still remain, but its assertion of parliamentary supremacy would now be virtually meaningless. For the colonists had not merely challenged the 1767 American legislation on grounds of equity or expediency; as in the case of the Stamp Act, their principal challenge had been on grounds of constitutional right.

Nor was this all. Total repeal would have been seen as conceding the specific purpose for which the Townshend Revenue Act was presumably undertaken and against which the colonists had remonstrated almost as much as they had the duties themselves. The preamble to the 1767 act declared that the duties were to be applied toward "defraying the charges of the administration of justice and the support of the civil government within all or any of the Plantations." To the colonists, this purpose appeared as a large opening wedge leading to the destruction of self-government in America. To the metropolis, an expanded civil list—particularly in Massachusetts and New York—appeared an indispensable, though still modest, step toward restoring control over colonies in which imperial authority had been placed increasingly on the defensive. The preamble to the Townshend Revenue Act asserted, in effect, a right to support the King's government in America. That right need not have been asserted in the manner it was in the 1767 revenue legislation. It need not have been raised at all. Grenville had refused to consider using the revenues accruing from the 1764 Sugar Act for the purpose of supporting an expanded civil list in the colonies. Even so, once this purpose had been asserted, it is difficult to see how a British government could have backed away gracefully from what had always been considered a right of the metropolis.

A reaffirmation of the Declaratory Act would not have been sufficient in responding to these considerations. The developments in the colonies between 1766 and 1770 were all too clearly a broad assault on the claim set forth in the Declaratory Act. To have abandoned the whole of the Townshend duties while taking refuge in this earlier assertion of parliamentary supremacy would have appeared too transparent an acceptance of the shadow for the substance. If concessions were once again to be made, they would have to be made under a different cover than that taken in 1766, even though the new cover would serve substantially the same purpose as the old. A repeal of the Townshend duties could be made politically palatable to a majority in Parliament only if the preamble and *some* duty were retained. In this way, the repeal of the remaining duties might avoid the appearance of an abject surrender of Parliament's supremacy. The Declaratory Act would thus be reenacted, though now in a form adapted to the circumstances of 1770.

The alternative was a policy of enforcement. There is no evidence that in the late winter of 1770, when the North ministry was moving toward a resolution of the crisis created by the Townshend duties, such policy was given serious consideration by Whitehall. If anything, there was even less support within or without Parliament

for enforcement than there was for total repeal. In the preceding
year, it will be recalled, the Grafton ministry had come very close
to deciding upon a course of total repeal. The Chathamites in the
cabinet had pressed hard for this course out of fear that any other
course would eventuate in a ruinous war with America. Those who
opposed total repeal did so, not because they were in fact ready
to resolve the crisis by force, if necessary, but because they considered total repeal to go beyond what was required by the situation. At most, it may be said that the Bedfordites were willing to
accept a modest risk that force might ultimately have to be employed rather than to accept total repeal. This is still very far from
saying, however, that the group to which North belonged was
seriously prepared to undertake a policy of enforcement rather than
accept total repeal. They were not. Nor was the North ministry in
the spring of 1770. The consensus that had been apparent in the
Stamp Act crisis, and that drew the line short of enforcement when
treating with the continental colonies, was no less apparent in the
crisis over the Townshend duties. The North government would
have been almost as hard pressed as earlier administrations to
breach this consensus, even had it wanted to do so.

[II]

It is against this background that the outcome of the crisis arising
over the Townshend duties must be seen. In moving to repeal the
duties, that on tea excepted, North's strategy paralleled the strategy
of Rockingham four years earlier. The act of repeal had to be
justified primarily on grounds of commercial interest. At the same
time, it could not appear to compromise Parliament's supremacy.
In presenting the motion for repeal to the Commons in early March
1770, North was careful to observe these two imperatives. Most
of the Townshend duties, the King's first minister declared, should
never have been passed, founded as they were on "anti-commercial
principles." The repeal of these duties, he reminded the House,
had been pledged by the preceding ministry, a pledge North had
concurred in at the time and considered himself still bound by,
despite the subsequent defiant behavior of the Americans. Indeed,
had it not been for this behavior, North declared, he would have
been prepared to grant the colonists "further indulgence, and ex-

tend the proposal to the removal of the other duties," which, he said, had been his intention to do the previous year. The pledge of the Grafton ministry, however, did not have the effect of improving the Americans' behavior. Instead, they had persisted in their "unwarrantable and illegal" combinations and associations and had remained generally defiant. Such being the case, the colonists could not expect and ought not to be accorded concession on a duty that did not violate commercial principle. The duty on tea, in contrast to the other duties, was not one laid on a manufacture of Great Britain. An object of luxury, it was the most proper commodity for taxation. Moreover, the duty was light, it was well-established, and it was expected to go "a great way towards effecting the purpose for which it was laid; which was to give additional support to our government and judicatures in America." The tea duty would thus serve as a symbol of Britain's right to tax the colonies as well as continue to provide the financial basis for the plan to pay the salaries of colonial officials in those colonies where this was judged necessary.[1]

North acknowledged that his bill would not satisfy the Americans. What they insisted on was complete repeal of the duties in order to establish that Great Britain had no right to tax them for the purpose of a revenue. Even total repeal would not put an end to their claims, he declared, for having once gained their way on the 1767 revenue act they would go on to complain of the 1764 and 1766 acts. Any duty would therefore be seen as having the purpose of a revenue and, for this reason, rejected. Total repeal would not produce harmony, only further claims against the metropolis. Nor should concessions be made out of fear of the continued effects of nonimportation. These effects, North argued, had been exaggerated for the two preceding years, since the Americans had laid in a greater stock at the outset in order to enable them to hold out the longer. He doubted whether the colonists could continue to do so. The nonimportation movement had already shown signs of weakening and North was confident that "various circumstances portend a dissolution of the associations." America could not immediately supply itself with needed commodities save by smuggling or by manufacturing its own goods. North would prevent

[1] *Sir Henry Cavendish's Debates of the House of Commons during the Thirteenth Parliament of Great Britain*, 1:484–89.

recourse to either alternative. In any event, he would never concede on a point of honor or of right. The motion he proposed made this clear, just as it made clear that he was, to the best of his convictions, "a friend to trade, a friend to America."[2]

North's case for repeal of the Townshend duties was perhaps no more disingenuous than the case earlier made by the Rockingham government for repeal of the Stamp Act. Still, it was disingenuous. The Townshend duties, tea excepted, might have been based on "uncommercial principles," but there is little reason to believe those principles would have prompted the British to repeal the duties in the absence of colonial pressures. The emphasis of the Grafton and North ministries on the uncommercial character of the 1767 duties enabled them to maintain the pretense that in repealing the duties London acted with a free hand and of its own accord. In truth, the Grafton ministry had decided upon repeal in 1769 because it could see no way of responding to colonial resistance, expressed primarily through the nonimportation movement, save by means it was unprepared to take. The same must be said of the North government.

Repeal, on the other hand, held out the prospect of resolving the immediate crisis created in the main by the nonimportation movement. It is clear that North attached great importance to breaking nonimportation, though there was a point beyond which he would not, and probably could not, go to achieve this end. As matters turned out, his calculation proved correct. With the repeal of the duties, the nonimportation movement soon collapsed. And if the retention of the duty on tea carried no broader significance in terms of any intention to impose further taxes on the colonies, it did serve as a symbol of the right claimed by the metropolis and a rejection of the principle of equality on which colonial opposition to the measure had been based. Even more, the retention of the tea duty, along with the preamble to the 1767 Townshend Revenue Act, left open the possibility of supporting imperial officials in the colonies by removing their dependence on the assemblies. But these consequences of repeal had still been dearly bought. The North government was later to give the impression that it had scored a victory by breaking the nonimportation movement. It was

[2] Ibid.

a curious view of what constituted victory, considering that the cost had been to concede five-sixths of the issue.

[III]

At the time, the motion for repeal was attacked not only by the opposition but by administration supporters as well. The attack followed predictable lines. To the Rockingham group and the Chathamites, the motion was defective in that it fell short of total repeal. At the other extreme, the hard liners within the ranks of the government contended that even partial repeal should be granted only to those colonies that had not defied the 1767 act. The most notable attack on the administration, however, was made by Grenville. Disdaining both the government's motion for partial repeal and the opposition amendment for total repeal, Grenville concentrated his fire on the inconstancy of policy toward America since the Stamp Act crisis and the lack of a plan for dealing with the colonies. Distinctions had been drawn with respect to Parliament's powers, Grenville observed, which were without basis. Threats had been made against the colonies that could not have been carried out. "In this situation," he declared, "we now find ourselves: having given way, from one step to another, until we know not upon what ground we stand; without any plan being formed; without a government there, or any thing that looks like a government." In this state of things, the government's motion for repeal could not be expected to give "quiet and ease to America." Grenville would not support a step "which goes to destroy the legislative authority of parliament." Still less would he support total repeal of the Townshend duties. Neither position "embraced a principle of reconciliation." That principle could be found only within the greater principle of the supremacy of Parliament. He closed by posing what was to him no more than a rhetorical question: "Is there any plan formed for establishing a government in the colonies, over which such laws as England shall think fit to be insisted upon may be exercised and enforced?"[3]

The charge that the government had no plan for dealing with America, that it had no policy that went beyond mere improvisa-

[3] Ibid., pp. 494–96.

tion, formed a commonplace among the opposition groups. It was not only voiced in debate over repeal of the Townshend duties but pressed even more insistently in the attack on the government's American policy precipitated by news of the Boston Massacre. The incident provoked a broad, if scarcely illuminating, assault in the Commons on the administration's colonial policy. What Grenville had earlier noted with brevity, Edmund Burke was now to demonstrate with his customary lack of brevity. The result, though seen from an entirely different vantage point, came to the same. For the preceding three years, Burke argued, the government had pursued a course that was consistent only in its inconstancy and futility. Among the resolutions Burke moved, one read: "That a principal cause of the Disorders which have lately prevailed in North America hath arisen from the ill-judged and inconsistent Instructions given, from time to time, by persons in Administration to the governors of some of the provinces in North America."[4] Burke offered no plan of his own. But, then, neither had Grenville.[5]

In terms of the immediate crisis, the charge brought against the government was without merit. The North ministry had a plan and, on balance, it proved quite successful. In repealing the Townshend duties, North undermined the basis of support for the nonimportation movement. The ministry accomplished more with respect to the two centers of trouble, New York and Massachusetts. In the case of New York, the ministry removed a longstanding grievance by obtaining parliamentary approval of an act that enabled the New York assembly to meet its obligations by issuing bills of credit that could be redeemed for public debts. In thus modifying the 1764 legislation, the government gave ground on an issue that had provoked constant complaint in the colonies outside of New England. In the case of Massachusetts, London's response to the Boston Massacre was to acquiesce in the removal of British troops from the city to Castle William. By so doing, the government appeared to convey the message that it desired to avoid the risk of further incidents that might lead to confrontation and that, barring open rebellion, a policy of enforcement was ruled out.

This impression of conciliation was not deceptive. The North government was following a conciliatory policy in the spring of

---

[4] Ibid., 2:14–23.
[5] Of course, Burke did not really acknowledge that any plan was necessary. Grenville did.

1770. It was intent on removing, so far as possible, the immediate causes of contention with the colonies. The view occasionally taken by historians that the North ministry marks the beginning of a new policy of firmness is difficult to sustain.[6] Certainly there was nothing novel in the position of the ministry that it would not yield on issues of constitutional principle. Preceding governments had taken the same position, however ineffective they had been in giving practical expression to it.

The view that the North ministry marks the beginning of a new policy of firmness stems in part from North's earlier record on America. North had voted in 1766 against an earlier resolution for repeal of the Stamp Act and had subsequently supported a later motion for repeal that was restricted to those colonies whose assemblies had expunged from their records any resolutions that were derogatory to the honor and dignity of the crown and Parliament.[7] In 1768 he was reported to have declared in Commons debate over the Townshend Revenue Act "that he would never think of repealing it *until he saw America prostrate at his feet.*"[8] During the same year he took a stand on Parliament's right to tax the colonies which appeared indistinguishable from that of Grenville. "You must possess the whole of your authority," he declared to the Commons, "or no part of it."[9]

What conclusions may be drawn from this record? Certainly it shows that North was not a Colonel Barré or a David Hartley and that he was a firm supporter in principle of Parliament's supremacy over the colonies. Does it establish, however, that he was a hard liner? Although committed to Parliament's right to tax the colonies, North nevertheless agreed in the end to each step along the road that led in practice to the virtual relinquishing of this right. No doubt, North took each step in the conviction that he was not giving way on the issue of right—but the same may be said of many others who have not been considered particularly firm on American issues,

[6] See, e.g., Charles R. Ritcheson, *British Politics and the American Revolution* (Norman, Okla., 1954), pp. 141–42.
[7] Ryder Diaries, pp. 280, 315.
[8] The statement was reported by Connecticut agent William Johnson, "Letters of William Samuel Johnson to the Governors of Connecticut [1766–1771]," p. 303 (hereafter Trumbull Papers). Johnson, a reliable and perceptive observer, went on to quote North to this effect: "America must fear you before they will love you." North had supported sending the army to Boston in the autumn of 1768.
[9] *Cavendish Debates*, 1:84. The statement was made in debate over a Pennsylvania petition submitted to the House of Commons.

let alone as hard liners. Even the Rockinghamites, after all, seem to have been sincerely persuaded that their position entailed no surrender of right.

More significant, perhaps, is the absence of evidence that North had ever been willing to draw the consequences of his supposed firmness. It was one thing to declare that America must prostrate itself before it could expect relief from the Townshend duties and quite another to support the enforcement of those duties. North gave no indication either before or after he became prime minister that, if necessary, he would break the nonimportation movement by forcible means. As matters turned out, he never had to face this choice since his strategy of partial repeal proved a success. It proved a success, though, precisely because it was predicated on the prior concession of most of the disputed duties. America in 1770 was anything but prostrate. The Townshend duties were nevertheless repealed. The collapse of the nonimportation movement can scarcely be attributed to the ministry's firmness. It resulted from what many in the colonies saw, with reason, as a victory sufficiently decisive to justify abandonment of the boycott.

Instead of representing a departure from the essentials of British policy toward America which had emerged in the course of the 1760s, North clung to those essentials until the moment when events were to force him to choose. But this moment lay several years ahead. In 1770, North not only represented continuity in England's colonial policy, he seemed almost to exemplify with exactitude this policy and the dilemma that formed its core. For North appeared as the perfect embodiment of the twofold consensus that made up this core and that gave to British policy its otherwise bewildering inconstancy. Few statesmen professed firmer attachment to the maintenance of Parliament's supremacy over the colonies. At the same time, few were more adept in the attempt to reconcile this attachment with the avoidance of a policy that would lead to enforcement.

The immediate crisis apart, then, the opposition's charge that North had no plan for a general and lasting settlement of differences between Great Britain and the American colonies was perfectly true. North conceded as much in defending his motion for repeal of the Townshend duties against Grenville's attack. In reply to Grenville's criticism that the government had articulated no "principle of reconciliation" and that it had set forth no plan "for establishing a government in the colonies, over which such laws as England shall think fit to be insisted upon may be exercised and enforced," North had replied: "I agree that such a plan is wanted. Everyman feels how desirable it is that the authority of this country should be resumed in those parts. The want of a strong government is obvious; but to effect that requires great abilities, great experience, great knowledge. Gentlemen within doors have been calling out for a plan these five years; but neither within doors nor without has any been proposed, that would place America and this country upon a proper footing."[10]

The exchange was instructive in that it illuminated the core of the difficulty confronting this, or any, British government attempting to effect a real settlement of the imperial-colonial dispute. The British no longer exercised effective authority in the colonies. They had not done so even prior to the Stamp Act crisis. In the wake of that crisis, the erosion of imperial authority—or what was left of it—had dramatically increased. The colonial challenge could not be countered effectively by stopgap measures that did not deal with the heart of the dispute. Such measures might ease and even resolve an immediate crisis, while leaving untouched the deeper and enduring crisis engendered by colonial claims to an autonomy that the metropolis remained quite unwilling to acknowledge, seeing as it did in these claims the aspiration to achieve what was tantamount to de facto independence.

On this reading of the dispute, the call for a plan necessarily entailed measures that might well have to be effected by forcible means, and from this prospect almost all parties—including most hard liners—instinctively recoiled. Of course, it could be argued that this reading of the dispute was fundamentally wrong, that the critical issue was taxation, and that if Parliament would but forego the exercise of this right—and desist from other needless acts of annoyance—the conflict could be soon resolved. Such was the position taken by the Rockinghamites. Given their definition of the colonial problem, the solution seemed clear. London had only to restore the status quo that had prevailed prior to 1763; it had to return to the system of requisitions and, in general, abandon its efforts to impose a greater measure of control over the colonies.

What did the call for a plan mean, however, to those who defined

[10] Ibid., pp. 495–96.

the American problem as George Grenville had done? If one identified the root of the problem in terms of the loss of authority over the colonies, how was imperial authority to be reestablished? One searches in vain for a clear answer. Grenville himself does not appear to have articulated one. Yet it is only reasonable to assume that, having defined the problem as he did, he also appreciated the solution dictated by this definition. Britain's loss of authority in the colonies could be regained only by altering the government of the colonies. The autonomy some now enjoyed—above all, Massachusetts Bay—would have to be curtailed if, as Grenville said, "such laws England shall think fit to be insisted upon may be exercised and enforced." The difficulty, of course, lay in the prospect that any serious curtailment of colonial autonomy would have to be imposed by force. In the years following the Stamp Act crisis, however, Grenville seemed no more disposed to advocate this course than were other hard liners.[11]

[IV]

Although North largely shared Grenville's understanding of the problem the metropolis faced in America, there is little evidence to suggest that in 1770 he was prepared to consider a course of

---

[11] Ibid., p. 496. Grenville's criticism of government policy during the years 1767–70 (he died in November 1770), important and often searching though such criticism was, is not easy to assess. His customary point of departure was, not surprisingly, the mistake made in repealing the Stamp Act. "The repeal of the stamp act," he declared on May 9, 1770, in his last parliamentary speech, "was the capital error of the moment"; Cavendish Debates, 2:34. To this recurring theme was joined the insistence upon the inseparability of taxation and sovereignty. In all ages and in all countries, Grenville repeatedly declared, the surrender of the right of taxation meant the surrender of the right of sovereignty. Finally, Grenville seems to have believed to the end that such colonial opposition to taxation by Parliament as had been manifested was largely the result of groundless fears and misapprehensions owing, as he put it in a letter of July 15, 1768, to William Knox, "to those in England who have weakly or wickedly misled the subjects in America, and not to the colonies themselves, who have done no more than any other people would have done, to whom an immunity from taxes had been holden forth, and who had been encouraged as they have been"; HMC, H. V. Knox Manuscripts, in Various Collections, vol. 6, p. 97.

Given this belief, it is possible Grenville further believed that a firm and consistent government policy intent on colonial submission to the laws of Parliament, inclusive of taxation, could be undertaken without recourse to enforcement. The latter belief, however, is not easily squared with his appreciation that metropolitan authority—particularly in Massachusetts—had eroded to a dangerous degree and that any plan worthy of the name would have to seek the restoration of this authority. In turn, this move implied charter reform, a step that any government would, and did, shy from, since it raised the distinct prospect of enforcement. In the exchange of March 5, 1770, between North and Grenville,

action that even the hard line opposition drew back from proposing. North's policy in the spring and summer of that year was, within the limits described above, one of conciliation. The hope that lay behind that policy was modest. The nonimportation movement might be broken, thereby revealing the difficulties the colonies still labored under to concert their actions. The right would be preserved, though henceforth its exercise would be limited severely. Within those limits, a modestly expanded civil list would be sought which in time might strengthen the metropolitan position in the most troublesome colonies.

If these were the essential features of North's policy, they did not significantly depart from the policy of the preceding ministry. Nor can this occasion surprise; during the first year in office the North government was largely led by ministers who had also formed the Grafton administration. Not all of them were content with policy. One who was clearly unhappy, and who had been so for some time, was the secretary for the American Department, Lord Hillsborough. As already noted, in 1769 Hillsborough had pushed for a more lasting solution in the case of Massachusetts Bay, but his proposals had been turned aside. In the summer of 1770 he returned to his plan for reform of the government of Massachusetts, and in Hillsborough's efforts historians have occasionally found evidence that, at the outset of North's administration, the British government was preparing for a showdown with the colonies.[12] For the attempt to change the Charter of Massachusetts would almost

---

quoted in the text, North intimated just this. The "plan" that would place the metropolis and colonies on a "proper footing" would have to restore "strong government" in America. "I will not say that the object is too great to be ever attained," North complained, "but I tell the House, how arduous I consider the attempt." To this, Grenville dryly replied that it was the prime minister's duty to propose a plan, not his. Grenville's rejoinder, though perhaps well taken, was not uncharacteristic of a position that left contemporaries and posterity in the dark as to precisely where he stood. Indeed, William Johnson reports him as saying to the House on April 19, 1769, when the Commons was debating Thomas Pownall's motion for repeal of the Townshend duties, that in place of a policy of drift it would be preferable to take any part that was open and decisive "and put an end to a controversy equally pernicious to us all"; Trumbull Papers, pp. 340–41. Did this mean Grenville was prepared to endorse enforcement? Is this what was intended by his declaration: "If you do not mean to bend the Colonies by your laws in all cases, even of taxation, tell the Americans so fairly, and conciliate their affections. If you will not make them your subjects, make them at least your allies. If you do mean to bend them in all cases whatsoever, be frank: let it be known and understood, and conduct yourselves accordingly. Let us take some ground or other, and maintain it firmly"? The ground Grenville wished to maintain was clear. The firmness with which he was prepared to maintain it was less than so.
[12] See Christie and Labaree, *Empire or Independence*, pp. 146–50.

certainly have been actively resisted by that colony, and in the manner it would resist the changes subsequently made by Parliament in 1774 in response to the Boston Tea Party. Was Hillsborough prepared to undertake a policy of enforcement in Massachusetts and, if necessary, in other colonies as well? More important, was the ministry prepared to follow his lead?

The answers to these questions cannot turn simply on the government's concern with the course of events in Massachusetts. That concern was apparent and found expression in the hearings undertaken during the early summer of 1770 before a committee of the Privy Council on the "state of the disorders, confusion, and mismanagement which have lately prevailed" in Massachusetts Bay. The hearings issued in a report that pointed out the extent to which metropolitan authority had declined, the executive having "only the shadow of power, not being able to act without the Council who will not consent to any proposal for discountenancing the usurpation of the powers of government by the town of Boston." The recommendations of the committee were approved by the Privy Council and became an Order in Council July 6. Two of the recommendations, that the North American squadron should rendezvous in Boston and that the local fort of Castle William should be garrisoned by British regulars, were scarcely measures calculated to arrest, let alone to reverse, the deteriorating situation in the Bay Colony. It was the third recommendation that was significant. "The weakness of the magistracy and the inefficacy of law," it read, "may be most effectually redressed by the interposition of the wisdom and authority of the legislature; wherefore the Committee humbly submit . . . that it may be advisable for your majesty to recommend the consideration of the state of the province of Massachusetts Bay to Parliament."[13]

To Hillsborough, the Order in Council was taken as a green light to reactivate his proposals for charter reform. In the succeeding weeks and months he reexamined, with the assistance of close aides, the various changes that might be made to the Massachusetts charter in order to reinvigorate executive power in the colony.[14]

[13] See *Documents of the American Revolution, 1770–1783*, 2:110–28, 133–34, for the report of the committee and the subsequent Order in Council. The colonial agents were aware of the inquiry in progress; see Trumbull Papers, p. 442.
[14] These efforts are most reliably known through those who participated in them. One early participant was William Knox, subsequently excluded from deliberations by Hillsborough because he disapproved of any alterations save those which dealt with the council; HMC, Knox, 6:257. Another participant, perhaps the most zealous, was Francis Bernard. Bernard

In letters to Hutchinson and Gage, he indicated that changes in policy would soon be forthcoming and that the most important of these changes would deal with the constitution of Massachusetts.[15] In the late fall of 1770 Hillsborough apparently had prepared—or very nearly so—a bill for the modification of the Bay Colony's charter. Although its precise provisions remain a matter of uncertainty, they almost certainly included changes in the method of selecting councillors as well as of jurors. The effect of these alterations alone, had it been possible to effect them, would have been considerable in strengthening the power of the executive (whose salary would be made independent of the assembly). Talk that the ministry would submit such a bill was common.[16] The bill was never submitted to Parliament, however, and by the spring of 1771 the prospects that charter reform might be undertaken were quite clearly moribund. They would not be revived until the final crisis in 1774.

What is the significance of this ultimately abortive plan to bring Massachusetts under closer control of the metropolis? Does it show that the North government was not in fact pursuing a conciliatory course in 1770? Clearly, the record shows that Hillsborough was not pursuing such a policy and that he was instead intent upon a showdown with the most defiant of the colonies. It is not at all apparent, though, that the American secretary was determined upon altering the charter of Massachusetts even if alteration were synonymous with a policy of enforcement. Earlier, Hillsborough had recommended that changes in the government of the Bay Colony be attended by partial withdrawal of the army from Boston. In 1770, plans for altering the chartered constitution of Massachusetts apparently proceeded with little or no consideration given to the methods by which its proposed changes would be made effective. It may be that Hillsborough was prepared to use force, and on a significant scale, in order to render his plan effective. But there is no clear evidence to this effect. On the contrary, such

---

Bailyn has described Bernard's role in *The Ordeal of Thomas Hutchinson* (Cambridge, 1974), pp. 188–93.

[15] See Hillsborough to Gage, August 4, 1770, *The Correspondence of General Thomas Gage with the Secretaries of State, 1763–1775*, 2:112–13. See also Hillsborough to Hutchinson, July 31, 1770, and Hillsborough to Gage, October 3, 1770, *Documents of the Revolution*, 2:157, 200.

[16] *Trumbull Papers*, p. 466; and "The Bowdoin and Temple Papers," pp. 197–98.

evidence as there is points to the conclusion that the secretary had preferred to avoid dealing seriously with the critical issues of enforcement. [17]

If Hillsborough shrank from confronting this issue, there is all the more reason to assume that North would have done so had he given it serious consideration. Barely able to do so even at the time of the passage of the Coercive Acts, there is little reason to think the prime minister was willing to face the prospect of enforcement in the summer and fall of 1770. Undoubtedly North would have been willing and happy to alter the Charter of Massachusetts if the desirable alteration could have been undertaken without serious danger. Whatever the other illusions he entertained, however, it seems altogether unlikely that this was one. It is quite true that the threat of war with Spain in the winter of 1770/71 afforded solid reason for not bringing matters with Massachusetts to a head. Moreover, the growing signs of collapse of the nonimportation movement, when taken together with other indications that tensions with the Bay Colony might be easing, gave additional incentive not to press for a plan of charter reform. Still, the principal incentive for not doing so was apparent from the outset and, in all likelihood, would have been decisive even in the absence of intervening developments. If anything, those developments, while surely significant in themselves, were welcomed as deliverance from a course that neither North nor a majority in the cabinet could have brought themselves to support in 1770 or 1771. [18]

[17] In his correspondence with Gage during this period, Hillsborough does not raise the critical issue of enforcement. There is no suggestion that an effort be made to strengthen the British military position in Boston. Is it credible that Hillsborough believed Massachusetts would simply accept the intended changes or that Gage could deal with the reaction by the forces he had at hand? Perhaps Hillsborough did, for in February 1769, when he first laid proposals for altering the government of Massachusetts before the King, he remarked that "however those disposed to clamour, may endeavour to represent that Measure, I am almost convinced it will be generally approved at Home, & be popular in the Colony"; *The Correspondence of King George the Third from 1760 to December 1783*, 2:82. If this may be taken at face value, it indicates that Hillsborough's will to take stern measures depended on a profound misunderstanding of political sentiment in the colonies, for which in February 1769 he had no excuse. It is impossible to know what Hillsborough would have been prepared to recommend had he possessed a proper understanding. It has been said of the American secretary that "his statesmanship did not stretch beyond repression"; *The Papers of Benjamin Franklin*, 15:xxvii. It is not clear, however, if it even stretched to that. Hillsborough's extravagantly optimistic reading of the effects that council revision would produce in Massachusetts is illuminating. It indicates that a program of stern measures, whatever its character, was politically acceptable only to the extent that it did not raise the specter of widespread conflict with the colonies.

[18] Christie and Labaree, *Empire or Independence*, pp. 146–49, treat the period from the spring of 1770 to early 1771 as one during which Hillsborough was, in their terms, "the moving spirit" behind the government's American policy. Certainly the American secretary

[V]

It was continuity rather than change that marked the American policy of the North ministry. The government that was to take Great Britain to war with the colonies in 1775 began its long tenure in the hope that somehow the deepening controversy with America might be arrested and imperial-colonial relations stabilized by a policy that failed to address the real sources of the controversy. In this, however, there was nothing novel about the North government. What was novel—at least by early 1771—were the changes taking place in domestic politics. With North, a new era of political stability began. For the first time in nearly a decade, a government had a leader who enjoyed the confidence of the King. By the end of its first year in office it also commanded strong support in the House of Commons. The favorable position of the ministry was in

---

was the principal supporter of plans to reform the constitution of Massachusetts. Whether there is "good reason to believe that . . . Hillsborough had gained control of policy" is another matter. More reason is needed than the authors give. In this regard, the hearings of the Privy Council and the subsequent Order in Council must be seen against the background of the circumstances prevailing in the summer and fall of 1770. The North government had no assurance that its repeal of the Townshend duties would lead to the collapse of the nonimportation movement just as it had no assurance that the situation in Boston would not become even less manageable than it was. A measurable worsening of the crisis would *at some point* have forced the government's hand and necessitated taking such measures as would likely entail enforcement. The recommendation of the Privy Council that "it may be advisable to recommend the consideration of . . . Massachusetts Bay to Parliament" may be seen in this light—and in this light, there is no need to find Hillsborough in control of policy. Instead, it seems more reasonable to see North in control of a policy that was, on balance, conciliatory. If that conciliatory policy were to prove abortive, however, then the "Hillsborough option" would probably have to be taken up. The known activity of the American secretary from July to the end of the year does not contradict this construction. There was no reason for North to place obstacles in the way of Hillsborough's endeavors. They could be considered a form of insurance. As far as Hillsborough's letters to Hutchinson and Gage are concerned, they establish only that the American secretary was in single-minded pursuit of his chosen course, and not that he was in command of affairs or enjoyed the support, as he had assured Gage, of "all the King's confidential servants." Nor is it clear that these servants deserted the ship of charter reform primarily because of the threat of war with Spain that arose in the autumn of 1770 over the Falkland Islands and the desire to avoid a showdown with Massachusetts at the same time the metropolis faced a war with Spain. More plausible is the explanation that the government looked to almost any reason to avoid a showdown with the Bay Colony. Bernard Bailyn, *Hutchinson*, pp. 191–93, illuminates this propensity in his account of the exchange between Hutchinson and Bernard in the autumn of 1770. Hutchinson, in response to a request from Hillsborough to reply to specific questions regarding proposed changes in the Massachusetts charter, had responded by striking a markedly cautionary note. Such changes as Hillsborough—and Bernard—wanted, Hutchinson replied, would meet with "violent opposition." In reply, a bitter Bernard reported to Hutchinson that, since the latter's response, "the intention has cooled" and added, in Bailyn's paraphrase, "that there lay at the heart of the English government such a propensity to avoid troublesome business that any excuse to do so 'is laid hold of.'" This was indeed the heart of the matter and would continue to be so for several years to come.

large measure a function of the decline of the opposition in the House. By 1771 many of the commanding figures of an earlier period had passed from the political scene, either through death or retirement. Their passing signaled the disintegration of the factions they had once led. Of the survivors, a number were absorbed by the government, a step that further strengthened its position in Parliament. After two years in office, only the Rockinghamites and the few supporters of Chatham were left to oppose the government in the House, and their differences prevented effective cooperation. The followers of Grenville and Bedford had either been co-opted by North or neutralized.

The changes made in the ministry during 1771 brought to office men whose record in opposition had been to favor a firmer policy toward the colonies. No significant changes in policy, though, attended this altered composition of the government. Indeed, if the North government comprised men known to favor a harder American policy, it also comprised men who were of moderate view. North himself could not be considered a hard liner, and far less could the man he chose to succeed Hillsborough be so described. Lord Dartmouth, who became the secretary for the American Department in August 1772, had been throughout the preceding years a moderate in his views toward America. His appointment was viewed with favor by a number of colonial leaders. Certainly, he appeared in striking contrast to the man who had preceded him (as well as the man who would succeed him). If the North government were controlled by men of extreme views, they had made a remarkable choice of the man who would bear direct responsibility for carrying out these views.

Still, the parameters of policy were changing, slowly yet surely, in these years. The area of maneuver open to Whitehall for making further concessions to the colonies was steadily narrowing. Concessions could not go on indefinitely; after 1770 there was not much left to concede. The time was drawing near when the metropolis either would have to refuse further retreat or would have to acknowledge that it no longer possessed sovereignty over America.

[VI]

Nowhere were these alternatives more sharply drawn than in the storm center of the growing rebellion, Massachusetts. The acknowledged leader of the colonies, Massachusetts Bay had been from the outset of the Anglo-American controversy the province that preoccupied imperial officialdom. It was in Massachusetts that the challenge to British authority had most insistently been pressed, just as it was in Massachusetts that the insufficiency of government measures to meet this challenge had most clearly been exposed. If the rising colonial assertiveness against the metropolis were to be contained, it would have to be contained here. If Great Britain failed to respond effectively in Massachusetts, the contagion would almost surely spread, and what had not yet become as threatening elsewhere would soon become so.

Massachusetts, then, was critical. Yet by the early 1770s, the metropolis no longer exercised effective authority there and had not done so for some time. Particularly in Boston, it could not govern in the most elementary sense of maintaining public order. This debility of government in the face of an opposition determined to flout it had been apparent from the time of the Stamp Act riots. By the late 1760s the weakness of imperial authority in the province had become still more evident and ominous. The introduction of the army in Boston in the fall of 1768 had not slowed, let alone reversed, the steady erosion. If anything, the army's presence there— in view of the constraints placed on its employment—only contributed further to the erosion of authority. "The Occasion which brought the Regiments to Boston," Thomas Gage wrote to his superior in the days following the Boston Massacre, "rendered them obnoxious to the People, and they may have increased the Odium themselves, as the Disorders of that Place have mostly sprung from Disputes with Great Britain." In any event, the commanding general of British forces in America concluded, "It has indeed been proved, that they were of no other use in the Town of Boston, for the people were as Lawless and Licentious after the Troops arrived, as they were before."[19] Gage meant, of course, that Boston remained quite as defiant of imperial authority in 1770 as it had been in 1768. Given that, in his words, "the troops could not act by Military Authority, and no Person in Civil Authority would ask their Aid," their presence could serve only as a further source of disorder. The lawlessness and licentiousness Gage found in Boston was the opposition's response to an authority now seen as entirely alien and, more important, virtually impotent. The ef-

[19] Gage to Hillsborough, April 10, 1770, Gage, 1:249, 251.

fective authority in Boston, and in Massachusetts generally, was that of the opposition. It was the opposition that was now the source of order, whether as represented in the powers of the legislature, the judiciary, or the executive.[20] The apparent paradox arose of a government that was the principal cause of disorder. The paradox was only apparent, however, since what was termed the government remained so largely in name alone.

Evidence of this striking displacement of authority was everywhere at hand. It was dramatically manifested by the completely ineffective efforts of government to put a stop to the intimidation of those who were opposed to, or who were less than enthusiastic supporters of, the nonimportation movement. It was further illustrated by the inability of government to place any real constraints on the various forms of harassment of royal officials. Such harassment did not stop with the hated customs officials. Although at a higher level it normally took forms other than that of physical threat, the result could be equally effective and, since the target was more exalted, of far greater significance. By 1769, it reached to the highest official in the province. In the spring of that year, the soon-to-be agent of the council, William Bollan, produced confidential letters written by, among others, the governor, Francis Bernard, to the American secretary depicting the precarious situation of government in Boston and recommending certain changes to be made in the Charter of Massachusetts. Bernard was almost instantly proclaimed a usurper and would-be destroyer of the colony's constitution, accusations made first by the council and subsequently, in more formal manner, by the General Court. The demand for his dismissal from office was, in the light of these charges, a matter of course.

The episode was important. Although it led neither to Bernard's dismissal nor to his resignation—outcomes that would have signaled clear victory for the radical leaders—it did lead to the next best thing. In August 1769, an exhausted governor requested an

---

[20] The acting governor characterized his position in 1770 in these terms: "He stood absolutely alone. The house of representatives considered him as inimical to the province, for conforming to the king's instructions, and withstanding their attempts to compel him to give up the prerogative of the crown. The council, instead of supporting him against these attempts, had rather joined with the house against him. Every part of the executive powers of government either concurred in sentiment with the council and house in their opposition to parliament, or was so awed by them, as in no degree to contradict them"; Thomas Hutchinson, *The History of the Colony and Province of Massachusetts Bay*, 3:208.

extended leave of absence. In his place, Thomas Hutchinson, the lieutenant governor, would serve until he, too, would be driven from office in circumstances strikingly similar to those that had led to the departure of Bernard. Four years before this more dramatic and better known event, it had already become apparent that no governor could maintain his position in Massachusetts without betraying his masters in London. Equally, it had already become apparent that the masters in London were quite willing to sacrifice their provincial officials rather than to run the risk of open confrontation with the colonial opposition.

The real problem confronting Whitehall at the turn of the decade, then, was no longer how to maintain Parliament's authority in the Bay Colony but how to establish *any* authority in that province. Any lingering doubts on this score should have been disspelled by the consequences of the Boston Massacre. The chief consequence—the withdrawal of the troops from Boston—laid bare the position of imperial authority in Massachusetts. Of the two regiments in the town, one had been particularly hated by the inhabitants. The commanding officer of the force offered to withdraw this regiment immediately and to station it in the fort—Castle William—five miles from Boston. The selectmen of the town, together with the justices of the county, insisted that both regiments be withdrawn. If they were not, the promise was made to Hutchinson that the troops would be driven out by the townspeople, and that the consequences would be chargeable to Hutchinson alone. The acting governor was further made to understand that refusal to accede to the demand of total withdrawal would, if he remained in Boston, jeopardize his physical safety. Hutchinson, though protesting that he had no power to order removal of the troops, decided to express to the commanding officer his "desire" that the troops be entirely withdrawn, a desire that was at once met.[21]

Why had the troops been withdrawn? The answer was clear, and in his report to Lord Hillsborough Hutchinson was not evasive. He had no alternative but to accede to the demands put to him. He had no source of support to which he might turn. The effective

---

[21] The selectmen had been able to elicit the agreement of the commanding officer that all troops would be withdrawn if the governor would only express his "desire" to this effect. Thus, Hutchinson did not have to order the army out, an order the legality of which the governor seriously doubted and probably would not have issued, see Bailyn, *Hutchinson*, pp. 158ff, for an excellent account of the episode.

government, that is, the opposition, was united in its support of the demands. Thus the council had backed the selectmen of the town in every respect. There were no significant elements of the populace to which he might turn for effective support. Finally, and most important, he had been told that against some six hundred British troops the opposition would pit, if necessary, a force of several thousand. Resistance to the demand that the troops be entirely withdrawn was therefore futile, Hutchinson concluded. "[There] was a moral certainty," he wrote to Hillsborough, "that the people of this town would have taken to their arms and that the neighboring towns would have joined them which would have brought on infinite confusion and, if any violence had been begun, much bloodshed, the spirit being full as high as it was at the time of the Revolution and the people four times as numerous, and it was most probable the confusion would have continued until the troops were overpowered."[22]

The Boston Massacre had thus culminated in a sheer test of power. Hutchinson had expressed his "desire" that all the troops be withdrawn from the town because he had not the military power to act otherwise. Did he possess the authority to act otherwise, even if he did not possess the power? Clearly, Hutchinson doubted that he did in the absence of any support from the provincial council or the local magistrates. It was true, he acknowledged to Hillsborough, that once removed to Castle William the troops were too remote to serve the purpose for which they had been designed. But then, he wrote, "I considered they never had been used for that purpose and there was no probability they ever would be, because no civil magistrate could be found under whose directions they might act and they could be considered only as having a tendency to keep the inhabitants in some degree of awe and even this was every day lessening." For what was by 1770 scarcely more than a nominal government, the troops were indeed a source of disorder.

In the years from 1770 to 1773, Hutchinson sought to restore the authority of royal government in the province. Not surprisingly, his efforts were without substantial result. Indeed, it would have required a political miracle for these efforts to have been productive. Arrayed against Hutchinson was an institutional structure over

[22] Hutchinson to Hillsborough, March 12, 1770, *Documents of the Revolution*, 2:59–60.

which the governor had but very limited control. What powers he did possess served, more often than not, only to inflame further the opposition and to give some plausibility to the charge that Hutchinson intended to implement a plan of tyranny for the province. The vetoing of legislation or the dismissal of a defiant assembly could not redress an imbalance that had been decades in the making and that now was far too advanced to be redressed by methods that might have been effective only at a much earlier date. These methods presupposed the existence of a community that was fundamentally stable and not rent by deeply divisive forces. In such circumstances, the instrument of patronage, if liberally employed, might have been effective in co-opting important elements of the political opposition and in inducing the remainder to pursue a course of moderation.

But the province of Massachusetts in the early 1770s did not conform to these circumstances and had not done so for some time. The radical imbalance that favored the forces of opposition could be redressed, if at all, only by radical methods. Hutchinson's efforts to limit the power of the opposition, particularly through use of the modest patronage at his disposal, accordingly had an air of the pathetic. Although these efforts did not hold out a serious threat to the opposition, they could serve as a provocation for the further discrediting of an already largely discredited imperial authority. By the early 1770s the friends of government were already but a distinct minority. Even among this minority there were not many who were still willing openly to ally themselves with the governor. The power of patronage, on which Hutchinson had based so much of his hopes to restore a vanishing authority, was no more than a weak reed in a storm of ever-mounting intensity.

[VII]

The North government was not oblivious of developments in Massachusetts Bay. Even if by no means alive to the full gravity of these developments, the ministry was nevertheless generally aware of the precarious situation in the province. Its policy response has been described as one of cautious waiting, of playing for time.[23]

[23] Thomas Barrow, *Trade and Empire*, p. 248.

To do what? Was the ministry's policy merely one of avoidance, in the hope that in time the problem might go away? If not, what may account for its apparent passivity during these years? Some historians have found the answer in the government's attempt to control the civil list. On this view, the ministry's passivity was only apparent. Far from remaining inactive, the North government was intent on slowly increasing the number of key colonial officials who received their salaries from Whitehall rather that from the provincial assembly. "This deliberate attempt to control the civil list of that colony," P.D.G. Thomas has written, "was a threat to the financial hold of the provincial legislature over the royal executive and judiciary."[24] "Every year," another historian notes, "saw more colonial officials added to the list of those receiving their salaries from the English government."[25] Presumably, the radical leaders in Massachusetts sensed the danger in North's policy and responded accordingly. They did so because they feared that, given time, this policy, eventuating in a large colonial civil list backed by a substantial revenue, might turn the tide against them. They understood all too well that "the issue was control of government, and [that] in revenue lay the key to sovereignty."[26]

The significance often read into North's policy of expanding control over the civil list thus appears to be supported by the manner in which radical leadership responded to these efforts. The belated discovery in the summer of 1772 that Hutchinson's salary was now paid by the crown had provoked a sharp reaction. Later in the same year, the ministry extended the civil list in Massachusetts to include the salaries of the attorney general, the solicitor general, and the five justices of the superior court. It was this last extension that prompted the Boston town meeting to draw up a statement that marked another significant step along the road leading to rebellion and independence. Titled "List of Infringements and Violations of Rights," the sweeping indictment of British rule in America closely foreshadowed the better known Declaration of Rights and Grievances drawn up by the First Continental Congress almost two years later. The immediate effect of the "List of Infringements," with its almost complete disavowal of British authority whether

---

[24] *Lord North*, (New York, 1976), p. 73.
[25] Barrow, *Trade and Empire*, p. 248.
[26] Ibid., p. 257. To the same general effect, see Christie and Labaree, *Empire or Independence*, p. 154.

exercised by Parliament or crown, was to set the stage for a confrontation between Hutchinson and the provincial assembly that left virtually no room for compromise.

Had the ministry's policy impelled the colonial opposition to respond by escalating the conflict to a new and yet more dangerous level in the winter of 1772/73? Or had this policy merely provided a convenient occasion for the radical leadership to do what they wanted to do and sooner or later would have done in any event? Even if the former question is credited with being the more relevant, it is so only because the radical leaders found in almost any policy response by the metropolis, save that of straightforward concession, the portent of mortal danger to colonial liberties. The expansion of the civil list did not and could not hold out a serious threat to those who now enjoyed effective authority in Massachusetts. It did not and could not hold out a serious threat to the prevailing structure of power in the province. This is so even if it assumed that the financial constraints operating on the North ministry could have been overcome, either through the imposition of new duties or the payment of additional salaries from other funds. Such a policy of indefinite expansion of the civil list, however, presupposed changes in the Charter of Massachusetts. It could scarcely serve the government's purpose to expand the civil list to those whose selection the government could not control. North's strategy required the prior implementation of the Hillsborough proposals or some variation on those proposals. Instead, the strategy was seen as an alternative to a course of action that had been rejected earlier precisely because change in the Massachusetts charter had been deemed too dangerous. In the absence of such change, however, and particularly in the selection of the council, it did not matter if an expanded civil list threatened the financial hold of the provincial legislature over the royal executive and judiciary. Those appointed to office would still be controlled by the opposition, despite the fact that they might be paid by the government.

The limits to the policy of expanding the civil list went still deeper. Even had the government been able to alter the Massachusetts charter, it would have been confronted by a populace in which, by the 1770s, only a small minority yet dared openly to align themselves with government. The shrinking of the circle of those courageous enough to accept the favor of royal patronage was demonstrated time and again to Hutchinson. The mounting fear of the radical movement, and the skepticism that government would provide adequate protection to those who wished to remain its loyal supporters, were barriers not to be overcome by a policy of expanding places and pensions. Such policy was relevant to a society that enjoyed political stability and that did not view its government as an alien entity, destitute of legitimacy.

In these circumstances, the ministry's policy of expanding the civil list could not seriously threaten the effective power structure in Massachusetts. At best, the policy of expanding the civil list could serve a defensive function, to hold the line until a more resolute policy was undertaken. More likely, the purpose of the policy was to demonstrate Whitehall's support to those who had thrown in their lot with the maintenance of imperial authority in the colonies, and who otherwise would have no other source of support. However modest the objectives, though, the policy could act only as a provocation to those intent on challenging any and every attempt by the metropolis to reassert its authority. Not surprisingly, the radical leadership appeared almost to welcome the move by the government in late 1772 to add the judges of the superior court to the civil list. Although the measure scarcely could alter the ever-growing imbalance between government and opposition, it was immediately seized upon by the opposition as a dangerous bid to subvert the charter of the colony and to impose a system of despotism on the province.

[VIII]

There is no need to review the previously mentioned manifestos of the Boston town meeting which formed the immediate reaction to the news that the superior court judges had been added to the civil list. Hutchinson's characterization of the statements prepared by the town meeting's committee of correspondence was on the mark. "Such principles in government were avowed as would be sufficient to justify the colonies in revolting, and forming an independent state; and such instances were given of the infringement of their rights by the exercise of parliamentary authority, that, upon like reasons, would justify an exception to the authority in all cases whatever."[27] What alarmed Hutchinson quite as much as the contents of the declarations was the use to which their sponsors intended to put them. Once they had been concurred in by the towns and districts of Massachusetts, the declarations were to be laid before the assembly of the province. Upon approval by the assembly, they were then to be transmitted to the assemblies of the other colonies. Thus, the dispute in Massachusetts over the extension of the civil list to cover the judges of the superior court was to provide the occasion for a declaration, tantamount in all but name, of independence, first by Massachusetts and subsequently by the other American colonies.

Hutchinson's response to the opposition's plan of action was to call the assembly into emergency session in early January 1773. He had no doubt that his action would "bring on an altercation, which they [the radical leadership] would profess themselves desirous of avoiding; and that they would charge him with raising a flame in the province, under pretence of endeavouring to suppress it."[28] His alternative course was to ignore the plainly seditious declarations of the Boston town meeting and to take a passive attitude toward the opposition's plan to obtain endorsement of the documents by the towns of the province, the Massachusetts assembly and, ultimately perhaps, the entire continent. "I have never had more difficulty to determine what was my most prudent step," Hutchinson wrote at the time to John Pownall. "I was loath to bring this point before the Assembly but when I saw that by neglect the several towns without understanding what they were doing would have bound themselves by their resolves and their Representatives would have thought themselves bound to do nothing in the General Court contrary to the resolves of their towns, I found myself under a necessity of stating the case between the kingdom and the colonies, particularly this colony."[29] To "state the case" for the supremacy of Parliament, now that this supremacy had been challenged so directly, was, Hutchinson reported to his superior, only "consistent with my duty to the King."[30] The governor knew that the new American secretary wished to avoid any confrontation with the opposition. Dartmouth had come to office in the preceding

[27] *History*, 3:262–63.
[28] Ibid., p. 266.
[29] January 7, 1773, *Documents of the Revolution*, 6:45.
[30] Hutchinson to Dartmouth, January 7, 1773, ibid., p. 44.

months intent upon dampening the controversy and hopeful that he would succeed in doing so. It was for this reason, among others, that Hutchinson was, despite his alarm, "greatly perplexed with doubts concerning his own conduct upon the occasion. He had avoided engaging in a dispute upon the authority of parliament, having good reason to think that administration in England expected the colonies would return to their former state of submission to this authority, by lenient measures, without discussing points of right." If he nevertheless had felt compelled in the end to act as he did, he later wrote in his *History*, it was for this reason: "By sitting still, and suffering the assembly to be precluded by the votes of their constituents, he had reason to think he would bring upon himself a charge of conniving at proceedings, the unwarrantableness whereof he ought to have exposed, and the progress whereof to have checked, by every means in his power."[31]

Both at the time and subsequently, the outcome of the celebrated exchange between the governor and the Massachusetts assembly—an exchange that extended over two months and that evoked the best efforts on both sides—has been seen to bear out the conclusion that Hutchinson seriously erred in pursuing his chosen course. In "stating the case" once again for the supremacy of Parliament, he succeeded only in highlighting the already profound gap separating the views entertained of the relationship by the two sides. Hutchinson had nothing to add to an argument that had been set out years before—by Grenville, by Mansfield, by Hutchinson himself. Now he could only repeat the case. Even his oft-quoted assertion that he knew "of no line that can be drawn between the supreme authority of Parliament and the total independence of the colonies" was no more than a paraphrase of a statement that had formed the common currency in parliamentary debate over repeal of the Stamp Act. So, too, Hutchinson's conclusion that "it is rather the mere exercise of this authority which is complained of as a grievance than any heavy burdens which have been brought upon the people by means of it," was an echo of the charge Grenville and his supporters had earlier brought against the colonists.[32]

Hutchinson's mistake, it has often been suggested, was not only revealing a position that remained as rigid as ever but affording

[31] *History*, 3:266.
[32] *Documents of the Revolution*, 6:39–44.

the opposition the opportunity to mark out new ground by its response. The governor had expressly invited a response to his argument from the General Court and the council. In elaborately polite terms he received a response, particularly from the house of representatives, that was virtually an unequivocal rejection of Parliament's supremacy. The choice that was open to the metropolis, the House in effect declared, was to accept the claims to equal status with Parliament that the assembly enjoyed or to risk the eventuality of the colonies declaring their independence. The line that Hutchinson maintained could not be drawn had the consequence "either that the colonies are the vassals of the Parliament or that they are totally independent. As it cannot be supposed to have been the intention of the parties in the compact that we should be reduced to a state of vassalage the conclusion is that it was their sense that we were thus independent." Lest Hutchinson miss the import of this, the House added in a final note of defiance, that "if your Excellency expects to have the line of distinction between the supreme authority of Parliament and the total independence of the colonies drawn by us, we would say that it would be a very arduous undertaking and of very great importance to all the other colonies, and therefore could we conceive of such a line we should be unwilling to propose it without their consent in congress."[33]

Clearly, Hutchinson had lost by the exchange. He was bound to lose if only for the reason that whereas he could only go over well-trodden ground, the opposition could—and did—advance its position. It was, of course, this very advance that Hutchinson believed the Whig opposition would hesitate to make, for to do so would clearly reveal the enormity of its position. As late as the beginning of 1773, the governor believed that the opposition would be disavowed by a majority once its position was fully known and that the "people," if not the hard-core opposition, could be won over through the call to reason. In this he was badly mistaken. Invited to draw out the logic of its position, the opposition had readily complied, with the result that what had theretofore been

---

[33] The texts of Hutchinson's speech to the general court (January 6) and the reply of the House of Representatives (January 26) are given in ibid., pp. 39–44, 66–78. Hutchinson reviewed the exchange, which also included a response by the council, in his *History*, 3:267–75. Hutchinson persisted afterward in believing he had won in the exchange, at least to the extent that he had slowed down the opposition's momentum "until matter was found for fresh disturbance."

largely implicit was now made explicit. A de facto position, as it were, was now given something very close to de jure status. The transformation was significant. Whereas the challenge to authority, however effective, might be overlooked or evaded by Whitehall so long as it was confined largely to acts, once acts were complemented by words—that is, once the challenge to authority was given formal expression—evasion was bound to become much more difficult.

Dartmouth formally upheld Hutchinson, as the American secretary had to do, but his displeasure over the governor's behavior was apparent. In a letter of March 3, 1773, to Hutchinson he praised the governor's "intentions" while reserving all judgment on the expediency and effect of the action. In a subsequent letter he instructed Hutchinson to "avoid further discussion on those questions" and to prorogue or dissolve the assembly if it again drew Parliament's authority into question.[34] Hutchinson's sin, in the eyes of Dartmouth, was clear. By his "imprudence," the governor had upset Darmouth's hopes that the controversy might subside and even perhaps disappear in time if only the parties would avoid raising the critical issues that separated them. To Dartmouth, Hutchinson had reopened a wound that might have healed if only it had been neglected or ignored. Now it had been reopened by words, words that revealed what had long been the reality of political life in Massachusetts. There is a striking irony—perhaps unintended—in the advice Benjamin Franklin gave to a disconsolate Dartmouth on how to respond to the declaration of the General Court. "In my opinion," Franklin recalled telling the American secretary, "it would be better and more prudent to take no Notice of it. It is *words* only. Acts of Parliament are still submitted to there. No Force is used to obstruct their execution." By 1773 the reality in Massachusetts had become very nearly the opposite of Franklin's appreciation. The declaration was indeed words only, but words were about all that was left for Hutchinson in his attempts to deal with the opposition. The executive power in the province, as he had repeatedly stressed to his superiors in London, was simply wanting. It had long been apparent that no reliance could be placed on the courts to enforce royal authority. Since the spring of 1770 it had been clear that, short of a rejection

[34] *Documents of the Revolution*, 6:95, 4:295. Cf. Hutchinson, *History*, 3:276–77.

of imperial authority so overt and blatant that the ministry would be forced to take action or to openly capitulate, there would be no army to fall back on should the need arise. The only thing that Hutchinson could do, then, was to talk. This was the remaining method left, however ineffective, for attempting to uphold British authority. Yet when the governor had attempted to use it for this purpose, Dartmouth had expressed his displeasure over Hutchinson's lack of prudence. He was instructed to avoid all such exchanges in the future, since they could serve only to raise issues that ought not be raised.[35]

In less dramatic and less significant manner, the plight of Hutchinson was indicative of the position in which many imperial officials in the colonies found themselves. The metropolis did not effectively defend its own and, to the end, refused to make a serious effort to do so. Not uncommonly, it almost seemed as though London was intent on pursuing a policy of punishing its officials while rewarding

---

[35] Franklin's statement was made in the course of an interview with Dartmouth on May 5, 1773, the account of which was conveyed by Franklin to Thomas Cushing, the speaker of the Massachusetts House; *Papers of Franklin*, 20:199–203. If Franklin's account is accurate, the interview is extraordinary for the light it casts on British policy at the time and, in particular, on Dartmouth's position. Franklin confirms Dartmouth's chagrin—and possibly North's as well—over Hutchinson's "officiousness" and the difficulties he is alleged to have created for London by his "imprudence." Government's intention—certainly Dartmouth's— had been "to let all Contention subside, and by Degrees suffer Matters to return to the old Channel." Now Hutchinson had "widened the breach" by his foolish behavior. Could not the General Court be induced, the American secretary asked, to withdraw its declaration? To Franklin's response that this was impossible, and that "force can do no good," Dartmouth replied, "I do not know . . . that force would be thought of; but perhaps an Act may pass to lay them under some Inconveniences till they rescind that Declaration." What were the inconveniences? Did they encompass charter reform? Dartmouth did not indicate. What is clear from the exchange is Dartmouth's attitude, which appears almost as that of a supplicant before a stern superior. Franklin warned Dartmouth that, should Parliament attempt by almost any conceivable step to enhance its authority, it would instead diminish that authority and "after abundance of Mischief they must finally lose it." Dartmouth's exchange with Franklin was of a piece with the American secretary's letter the following month to Thomas Cushing. Written in his capacity as a private person to the Massachusetts speaker of the House, and in consequence by-passing the governor, Dartmouth, while rejecting the principles endorsed by the colony's assembly as "wild and extravagant," made clear that if his wishes and sentiments carried weight with Parliament the remaining tax on the colonies "should be suspended and lie dormant" until the need to exercise this power would be obvious to all parties; *Facsimiles of Manuscripts in European Archives Relating to America 1773–1783*, ed. B. F. Stevens, 25 vols. vol. 24, no. 2025 (London, 1889–98). In the circumstances, this could mean only that Dartmouth, for his part, was conceding the issue of taxation *in toto*. In return, he asked of Cushing what he had earlier asked of Franklin. Could not the General Court's declaration be rescinded and the supremacy of Parliament be acknowledged? Cushing's response was the same as Franklin's. Bailyn, *Hutchinson*, pp. 212–20, has given a lucid account of these episodes, along with Dartmouth's treatment of Hutchinson.

colonists who hounded and harrassed those expected to enforce imperial authority. The hated customs officers formed the most apparent case in point. After 1770 they were about all that remained in evidence of the policy of imperial reform undertaken in the 1760s. In Boston, their position had been very nearly unendurable since the Stamp Act crisis. Elsewhere, it had markedly deteriorated since the late 1760s. Yet there is scarcely a case on record of a serious attempt on the part of a British government to punish attacks on those whose duty was to enforce the laws of trade.

Given this passivity in the face of attacks on customs officers, the colonists could reasonably expect a similar response to assault upon yet more important instruments of imperial authority. If royal officials could be attacked with impunity, why not his majesty's warships? The *Gaspee* incident in June 1772 was, in this light, no more than a logical escalation. Nor was it without precedent, for a very similar incident had occurred in 1769 in the case of the government sloop *The Liberty*. The attack on the *Gaspee* was more audacious, however, and the response to the burning of the schooner grounded in Narragansett Bay signaled the determination of the radical leadership in the colonies not to permit the movement to lose momentum. The metropolis was presented with the choice either of acting vigorously and with determination or of responding timidly and with yet another effort at conciliation. Either way, the radical leadership calculated it would benefit. A vigorous response would provide an issue for forging a new unity of the diverse factions. A timid response would earn the metropolis further contempt in America. Predictably, the government chose the latter course. Dartmouth particularly was intent upon following a conciliatory line. A royal commission of inquiry was appointed to investigate the incident. Frustrated at every turn by the colonists, the work of the board was without result. Even so, its very existence was viewed by American patriots as an insufferable provocation. The jurisdictional powers given the board, though they were not exercised and though Dartmouth made clear his disagreement with the power to send the accused to England for trial, were everywhere denounced as further evidence of the intent to extinguish liberty in the colonies. In Virginia, indignation over the inquiry led the Burgesses to initiate intercolonial committees of correspondence. A year after the incident the government terminated the inquiry. The commissioners in their report to Dartmouth made a point of placing a large part of the responsibility for events that led to the burning on the shoulders of the *Gaspee's* commanding officer, who had behaved disrespectfully to the governor of Rhode Island and, presumably worse, had "in some instances" acted "from an intemperate if not a reprehensible zeal to aid the revenue service exceed[ing] the bounds of his duty."[36]

Thus did conditions in the Bay Colony reflect the retreat of imperial authority throughout the thirteen colonies. Although Hutchinson would remain in office until May 1774, by the spring of 1773 he was in an even weaker and more isolated position than he had been prior to his exchange with the assembly. By contrast, the exchange had heightened the confidence of the radical leadership. The ministry, whatever the apprehensions aroused over the defiant stance taken by the assembly, had not responded with resolution. Although it had supported the position taken by the governor—it could scarcely have acted otherwise—the support had been unattended by any new measures. Dartmouth's displeasure with Hutchinson for having precipitated an exchange that had led to the formal disavowal of the supremacy of Parliament and that would now require some response by the metropolis, however inadequate, was known to the opposition. Given the ministry's past record of drift and indecision with respect to events in Massachusetts, the opposition had no more reason to anticipate that any marked turn in policy would occur than did Hutchinson. For over three years Whitehall had left Hutchinson to rely as best he could on his own resources. Never more than meager, they were now virtually exhausted. Isolated and hampered at every turn, subject to the constant vituperative attack on his character and motives by the opposition, Hutchinson was now reduced to a pathetic figure. The question was no longer whether he would be discredited entirely but when and how. Ironically, the *coup de grace* came in a manner that bore striking similarity to the fate of his predecessor. Once again, through the publication of opinions confidentially expressed, a Massachusetts governor was revealed by the opposition as intent upon subverting the liberties of the people. Once again,

[36] See *Documents of the Revolution*, 6:160–64, for the text of the report.

the General Court of the colony petitioned the crown for the recall of the governor.[37]

[IX]

What was the response of the North government to developments in Massachusetts during the winter and spring of 1773? Was it at

[37] The circumstances attending the gathering and ultimate publication of the Hutchinson letters, together with an examination of the motives of those who used them, are examined at length in Bailyn, *Hutchinson*, pp. 221–58. In December 1772, Benjamin Franklin, London agent of the Massachusetts House, sent a group of letters to the speaker of the House, Thomas Cushing. The letters dated from 1767 to 1769 and had been written chiefly by Thomas Hutchinson, lieutenant governor, and Andrew Oliver, then secretary of the province, to Thomas Whately, a one-time secretary to the Treasury. How and from whom Franklin came into possession of the letters (Whately having died) remains unclear. Bailyn believes the supplier of the letters to have been Thomas Pownall, though admitting that, despite considerable circumstantial evidence of Pownall's complicity, the matter remains conjectural. In sending the letters, Franklin instructed that they be neither printed nor copied but instead shown to a few leading people in the assembly and then returned. In early June 1773, the letters were read to the assembly, sitting *in camera*, by Samuel Adams, clerk of the House. The substance of the letters expressed the authors' fears of the direction in which the colonies were then heading, and particularly Massachusetts, and the need to take remedial measures to secure their dependence on the metropolis. The letters contained no startling revelations. The views Hutchinson expressed were well known, since he had expressed them publicly on several occasions at the time and in the following years. Once the pledge of secrecy had been violated by their having been read to the House, the letters were soon published. The same month (June 1773) the assembly petitioned the King to remove Hutchinson and Oliver from their respective posts as governor and lieutenant governor of the colony, the petition charging that the two officials had long conspired to destroy the charter of the province and, beyond this, to annihilate the rights and liberties of the American colonies. Given the circumstances attending the episode, and the contents of the letters themselves, the motives of the radical leaders who made inevitable the publication of the letters and then pushed for the petition to the King appear reasonably clear. The letters were employed to widen the breach between the metropolis and the colonies and, more particularly, to render Hutchinson's position untenable. Franklin's motives are another, and more difficult, matter. His professed motives are not in question, for he stated them at the time of sending the letters as well as on a number of subsequent occasions. His central purpose, he repeatedly insisted, had been to promote the reconciliation of the colonies and metropolis, to restore imperial relations to what they had once been in an earlier and happier period. The letters were intended to further this purpose for they would show the colonial leaders who read them that a few mischievous men had given the King and his ministers a totally misleading impression of the colonies and the aspirations of Americans. These men had misrepresented colonial grievances, had depicted these grievances as something that they were not, and had thereby sown the seeds of what had become consequently an ever more dangerous conflict. The letters would thus show upon whose shoulders the blame for the controversy should be placed—not on the ministry and certainly not on the English nation but on the few miscreants—"those caitiffs," as Franklin called them—who had led astray both the ministry and the nation. The ministry, in turn, could then admit, without apparent loss of face, that it had been misled by its own officials, that it would not have proceeded to most of the measures it had taken in the preceding years had it only known the true conditions in the colonies, and thus begin the

long last moving toward a showdown with the opposition in the Bay Colony? Certainly, imperial officials, and perhaps none more so than the American secretary, were shaken by the events of these months. Between the fall of 1772 and the summer of 1773, Dartmouth's concern over the steadily deteriorating situation in Massachusetts had markedly increased. The optimism with which he had once viewed the prospects for composing the controversy had just as markedly decreased. The methods of reason and persuasion in which Dartmouth had placed his faith had not brought the ex-

---

restoration of the old and harmonious relationship, first, by punishing the authors of evil and, second, by the removal of any and all measures that remained to trouble the imperial-colonial relationship. See, in particular, *Tract Relative to the Affair of Hutchinson's Letters*, in *The Writings of Benjamin Franklin*, ed. Albert Henry Smyth, 10 vols. (New York and London, 1905–07), 6:258–89.

If this was the purpose behind Franklin's action, it was not appreciated by any of the intended beneficiaries. In London, the action was condemned by almost all officials. At the hearing before the Privy Council in January 1774 on the petition of the Massachusetts assembly, the solicitor general, Wedderburn, launched a sustained attack on Franklin while defending Hutchinson. Not only had Franklin's actions been dishonorable, Wedderburn declared, but his purposes—contrary to his professions—had been malign. The Privy Council dismissed the petition and upheld the conduct of Hutchinson and Oliver, while the ministry termed Franklin's action a disgrace and deprived him of his position as postmaster general of North America. Franklin professed shock at the outcome. In a letter to Samuel Cooper he wrote that the ministry's rage "is quite incomprehensible! If they had been wise, they might have made a good Use of the Discovery, by Agreeing to lay the Blame of our Differences on those from whom by those Letters it appear's to have arisen; and by a Change of Measures, which would then have appear'd natural, restor'd the Harmony between the two Countries. But—"; *Papers of Franklin*, 21:124.

Whatever one thinks of Franklin's methods, his alleged strategy and purpose made sense only on the assumption that the two sides wanted to compose the conflict, were in substantial agreement on the substantive issues at stake, and were being impeded either through misunderstanding of each other's true position or through the lack of a face-saving device. How a man as perceptive and as politically sophisticated as Franklin could have assumed this is very difficult to understand. Moreover, the assumption does not square with Franklin's earlier appreciation of the conflict. Although often deploring the lengths to which it had gone, and still threatened to go, he gave every indication of appreciating that its origins were rooted in real—not apparent—differences in goals and aspirations. Why should he suddenly have embarked on a strategy of reconciliation that seemed to deny this earlier understanding? Besides, what was the essential meaning of this strategy as judged—and it must be so judged—by the outcome it was intended to promote? Clearly, the meaning was British capitulation on all the issues in contention. Hutchinson was simply the means to reach this capitulation. The ministry would recall and punish one of its most faithful and competent officials and then proceed to concede its entire position. And for his role in enabling government to "accomplish" this, Franklin professed to believe that he should have merited the gratitude of the ministry.

These considerations certainly do not exhaust the mystery of Franklin's action. They are sufficient to suggest, however, that historians have made a heroic effort to avoid considering the very obvious possibility that Franklin acted as he did because he wanted to ingratiate himself with the radical leadership, to prove his devotion to the cause, and to turn back those who, like Arthur Lee, persisted in their suspicions of his commitment.

pected results. Instead, the opposition in Massachusetts appeared more intransigent than ever. In April, Dartmouth wrote to Hutchinson that it was vain to hope that the assembly and council might be persuaded to yield obedience to the laws of Parliament and, this being so, the "state of the colony" would be seriously considered (an apparent allusion to changing the colony's charter). In the meantime, Hutchinson was instructed to avoid further discussion of Parliament's authority. If the assembly insisted upon again placing this authority in question, the governor was to prorogue or dissolve it.[38] In June 1773, Hutchinson was told by his superior that it was the unanimous opinion of the ministry, in which the King concurred, "that the authority of the supreme legislature must be supported, and that the unwarrantable declarations contained in the addresses and messages of the late Council and House of Representatives ought to be communicated to both Houses of Parliament." Because of the lateness of the session and the occupation of Parliament with the affairs of the East India Company, this portentous step was not to be taken until the next session.[39]

These communications of the American secretary have been taken by historians as evidence that the ministry was now determined to respond to the challenge thrown down by Massachusetts by bringing the matter before Parliament.[40] The important question, however, is what the government would have pressed Parliament to do. Clearly, there was nothing to be gained, if the government's intention was to do little more than obtain from Parliament another Declaratory Act or another address to the King. Neither the making of idle threats nor the reaffirmation of parliamentary supremacy would have sufficed in the circumstances of 1773. Only significant

---

[38] Dartmouth to Hutchinson, April 10, 1773, *Documents of the Revolution*, 4:295.

[39] Dartmouth to Hutchinson, June 2, 1773, ibid., p. 321.

[40] There is other evidence given in support of the presumably hardening attitude of the ministry. Thomas, *Lord North*, p. 73, cites Dartmouth's "complete rebuff" of the Massachusetts petitions on the salaries grievance. This was in May. In June, Dartmouth informed Hutchinson that the provincial assembly must make provision for permanent and adequate salaries to the governor and superior court judges before London would consider withdrawing its financial support for those officials. In addition, the passage of the East India tea legislation in the spring of 1773 is seen as indicative of a hardening attitude toward the colonies. (The significance of the tea legislation is considered later in this chapter. As evidence of a tougher ministerial position, it appears ambiguous.) The position on salaries is another matter. Clearly, the ministry was intent on maintaining its position. Even so, this intention was scarcely indicative of a hardening attitude, unless the refusal to surrender a measure that could have no real effect on the opposition's power is nevertheless seen as such.

changes in the Massachusetts charter could respond to the debility of royal government in the Bay Colony, and then only on condition that Whitehall was prepared, if necessary, to enforce such a change.

What the North ministry might have done in the following session of Parliament had the events culminating in the Boston Tea Party not occurred must remain speculative.[41] In light of the government's record in the preceding three years, however, the view that in the late spring of 1773 the government was intent upon serious confrontation with Massachusetts must be received with a measure of skepticism. His communications to Hutchinson notwithstanding, Dartmouth shrank from the consequences of serious confrontation. Although insistent upon maintaining the supremacy of Parliament, he was yet unready to accept the price this insistence entailed. Even when confronted with the challenge of the Boston Tea Party, which occurred on the night of December 16, 1773, and the news of which reached London in January 1774, Dartmouth's immediate response was to push for a course of action that would avoid the involvement of Parliament. For Parliament's involvement not only would lay bare as never before the issue of constitutional right but would also raise the issue of altering the Massachusetts charter. To avoid these prospects, the government—largely at Dartmouth's urging—initially sought to respond to Boston's defiance of imperial authority by executive action, i.e., closing the port of Boston and punishing the principal perpetrators. It was only when the government concluded that these measures could not be undertaken with strict legality that it turned to Parliament and asked for, among other things, changes in the charter of the Bay Colony. At the very least, this was a curious response for a government that had been presumably intent the preceding spring upon altering the charter; the Boston Tea Party not only

[41] In a letter to a friend, dated July 9, 1774, Hutchinson reported a "long conference" he had had with North the day before, in which North indicated that the government had been intent on changing the Massachusetts charter the year before along lines finally followed in 1774. Hutchinson quotes North to the effect "that the behaviour of the Council and House had been such for some time past, as to render it necessary there should be a change, and that it ought to have been done the last Session, upon the Declaration of Independence, both by the Council and House; that the delay had been occasioned by the state of affairs here in England; that, in general, whatever measure had been proposed by the Ministers, had also been opposed: but that all parties united in the necessity of a change, in order to prevent the Colony from entirely throwing of [off] their dependence"; *The Diary and Letters of His Excellency Thomas Hutchinson, Esq.*, ed. Peter O. Hutchinson, 2 vols. (London, 1883), 1:181.

afforded the clear occasion for alteration but, it may well be argued, virtually dictated the step. Yet Dartmouth and North were plainly reluctant to take the step, and their reluctance, it does not seem unreasonable to conclude, was indicative of their determination— or rather the lack thereof—in the preceding year.

These considerations are not contradicted by the ministry's move in April 1773 for legislation to relieve the financial distress of the East India Company. The tea legislation would lead to the Boston Tea Party, that act of defiance that would finally move a British ministry to take coercive measures it had cringed from taking in previous years. Still, it was not from any determination to provoke a showdown that North proposed the amendments in the legislation affecting the tea trade. The legislation, on its face, was innocuous enough. The 1767 agreement between the government and the East India Company obliged the company to remit to the Treasury the revenues, if any, lost from the withdrawal of all customs duties on teas exported to Ireland and America. In 1772, the act expired. On reenactment, only three-fifths of the duties were drawn back on reexport, but the company was no longer obliged to reimburse the Treasury for any loss of revenue. In 1773, the latter arrangement was continued, but, as in 1767, the duties were wholly drawn back on reexport to America and Ireland, thus lowering the price of dutied tea in America from the higher price it had reached only the year before. The three-pence Townshend tea tax, collected in America, was unaffected by these changes. Together with these changes, the company was permitted by the 1773 legislation to market its tea directly in the colonies through its own export agents rather than having it auctioned in London and then resold to American merchants. Thus, the price of tea in America would be substantially lowered and the straitened condition of the East India Company would be eased.

It was the commercial crisis afflicting the East India Company in late 1772 that had forced North's hand. The tea stocks had risen to extraordinary proportions by late 1772. With warehouses bulging, the European market appeared to offer no prospect of relief. If large quantities of English teas were introduced on the continent, it would depress the price and give smugglers an additional incentive to bring the tea back into England, thus compounding the company's difficulties. North saw in the American market a means to relieve the immediate liquidity crisis of the company by ridding the warehouses of unsold and unsalable tea.

Opposition speakers, however, succeeded in revealing that the government had other motives as well. When Dowdeswell suggested that the Townshend tea duty be repealed, but that an export tax of three pence be retained on English tea exported to America, North refused. It is doubtful that this refusal stemmed from North's desire to expand tea revenues so that the administration might further be enabled to support an expanded civil list in the colonies. It was not the tantalizing opportunities, such as they were, held out by an advance, but the difficulties of a retreat that were decisive for the prime minister.

The commercial crisis of the company forced a choice, then, between what would appear to the British as an unmistakable concession of the right of taxation and what would appear to the colonists as a further confirmation of that right and a precedent for other measures of taxation. Given the decision to market the surpluses of East India tea in the colonies—a decision that was unexceptionable—the choice could not be avoided. Did the ministry anticipate the measures of resistance that the Americans would take in response to the tea legislation? North later declared that he had not foreseen, and could not have foreseen, the consequences of the legislation.[42] There is little reason to question his lack of foresight. At the same time, it remains clear that the government knew its measures entailed a high risk of focusing attention once again on the questions of parliamentary supremacy and colonial equality. These questions were raised in the debate in Parliament on the tea legislation. North recognized their force by refusing the

---

[42] On January 23, 1775, in the course of a debate on petitions for reconciliation with America, North defended himself against the charge that he should have foreseen the consequences of the 1773 legislation. His response—that it was impossible for him to have foreseen the response, that the tea tax had been collected quietly before, that something had to be done to relieve the distress of the company, and that he could not foretell the Americans would resist at being able to drink their tea at 9 pence a pound cheaper—was immediately challenged by Governor Johnstone, who pointed out "it was notorious the Company had requested the repeal of the 3d. per pound in America, and felt and knew the absurdity of giving a drawback here, and laying a duty there: a perfect solicism in commerce and politics. That the East India Company offered their consent, that government should retain 6d. in the pound on the exportation, if the 3d. was remitted in America"; PH 18:177–78. It was, however, highly unlikely that the colonists would have reacted tamely had the import duty, collected in America, been withdrawn and an export duty, collected in Great Britain, been reimposed. The objection of the Americans was to the principle and practice of parliamentary taxation, not to the place designated by Parliament for the collection of the revenue.

opposition's suggestion that the Townshend tea duty be repealed. The King's first minister was not pushing for heightened confrontation with the colonies, but he understood that the tea legislation ran the risk of provoking such a confrontation.

The train of events that culminated on December 16, 1773, in the destruction at Boston of 340 chests of East India Company tea need not be recounted here.[43] Opposition to the East India tea was not confined to Boston. In New York and Philadelphia opposition was manifest from the moment that news of the 1773 legislation reached America. In some measure, this opposition stemmed from the methods now provided for merchandising the tea. In greater measure, it followed from the conviction that the government was now intent on forcing the tax issue and that, if submitted to, the tea duty would soon be followed by other duties. Nowhere was this conviction more strongly felt than in the town that for the preceding three years had been accepting duties tea. With the 1773 legislation, however, Boston suddenly made the tea tax an issue of supreme moment in its ever more pervasive conflict with the metropolis.

In doing so, the opposition leadership likely was intent on precipitating the showdown that followed from the Boston Tea Party. This latest dispute was clearly seen by the leadership as an occasion to maintain the momentum of a movement that was always in danger of moderating and, in consequence, of permitting some restoration of metropolitan authority. The 1773 legislation was itself evidence of the unremitting efforts of government to take away what had been won in previous years of struggle. It had, therefore, to be resisted. But resistance to this latest provocation, even when resulting in the destruction of the tea, was not seen to incur inordinate risk—and certainly not the risk that was soon to follow.

In the event, this view proved mistaken. It proved mistaken because by the end of 1773 the conflict had reached a point where almost any incident would give rise to consequences previously considered as disproportionate by one side. Yet it is not difficult to understand why observers could well have thought that, in the light of the recent past, this point had not yet been reached. For the Boston Tea Party was not an unprecedented act of colonial defiance. The resistance to the Stamp Act eight years earlier may

---

[43] An exhaustive treatment is provided by Benjamin Woods Labaree, *The Boston Tea Party*.

lay claim to that honor with more justice than the destruction of East India tea. Clearly, the Boston Tea Party laid bare the issue of sovereignty and did so in highly dramatic manner, but this was not the first time that issue had been laid bare. Efforts to find in the destruction of the tea something qualitatively different from previous acts of colonial resistance to metropolitan authority stem more from British reaction to the Boston Tea Party than from the intrinsic character and significance of the measures that prompted the reaction. By a process of reasoning that seems only plausible, the assumption is made that if the imperial government finally resorted to unprecedented measures in response to the Boston Tea Party, the explanation must lie in the equally unprecedented nature of the acts that provoked the response. If, however, the destruction of the tea represented "an Epocha in History," in John Adams's inflated phrase, it was simply because the North government chose to make this latest American defiance the occasion for taking measures it had long shunned.

In this perspective, the Boston Tea Party stands out in the history of the imperial-colonial conflict as the psychological "last straw" for Great Britain. Although no ineluctable destiny decreed that the North Government act as it did, there is no mystery in explaining why it so acted. The Boston Tea Party not only appeared as the latest in a long series of colonial challenges to British supremacy, it left the imperial government with almost no room for retreat. The face-saving gesture of a Declaratory Act had been resorted to once. To employ it a second time, or even to turn to a functional equivalent of the Declaratory Act, as the North ministry had done in 1770, would signal the abject surrender, plain and simple, of the metropolis. After the Boston Tea Party the tea duty could have been removed only at the price of capitulation to the colonies, an issue now made all the more dangerous since the vital issues between the two sides had gone far beyond the right of Parliament to tax the Americans. By 1773–74, the Americans were plainly challenging the British claim to supremacy over the colonies. Even in an earlier period, the distinction drawn between Parliament's right to tax and the assertion, in other respects, of parliamentary supremacy had been a tenuous one. At the time of the Boston Tea Party, it had been discarded almost entirely. Now, more than ever, to concede the one remaining assertion of a right to tax would be seen as conceding the right of parliamentary supremacy *in toto*.

If the North government could not concede in the face of colonial destruction of the East India tea, neither could it temporize in the manner it and previous governments had so often done. By the beginning of 1774, the course and momentum of the conflict alone had ruled out this course. Particularly in Massachusetts, a failure to act would be treated by the radical leaders as the capitulation of the metropolis. Of course, London had capitulated before, but in doing so, it still had had some room left for maneuver. Now, in the light of claims that had emerged over the preceding three years, it had almost none. Moreover, in the wake of the Boston Tea Party, even had the government wanted to concede or temporize it probably could not have done so and remain in power, for the consensus in and out of Parliament was that now something had to be done and the rebellious colonists brought to book. This was made abundantly clear when North brought before the House the proposed legislation for Massachusetts.

The legislation carried through Parliament by North's government for the punishment of Boston and the restitution of order in Massachusetts consisted of four acts: the Boston Port Act, which closed the port of Boston until compensation had been rendered both to the East India Company for the destroyed tea and to royal officers injured in public disturbances, and until the King determined that peace and order in the Bay Colony had been restored; the Massachusetts Bay Regulating Act, which amended the colony's charter by substituting a nominated, for an elected, council, authorized the governor to appoint and remove all law officers, and forbade the holding of town meetings without royal consent; the Impartial Regulation of Justice Act, which gave the governor power to remove trials to another colony, or to England, if in his judgment impartiality could not be expected from local juries; and the Quartering Act, which broadened previous legislation for the quartering of British troops by providing that if the need arose they could be accommodated with private families and not only, as had formerly been the case, in uninhabited houses and buildings. These four measures, known to the colonists as the Coercive, or "Intolerable," acts, formed the ministry's response to the defiance of Massachusetts.

PART IV

THE FINAL RECKONING

THIRTEEN

The Coercive Acts, 1774

[I]

In the historiography of the American Revolution the Coercive Acts are generally seen as the most striking mistake of a policy that from 1763 to the outbreak of war had been one long series of mistakes. The Massachusetts legislation not only shocked the colonists by its harshness, it backed them into a corner from which further retreat was all but impossible. A conciliatory response by London in the wake of the Boston Tea Party might have prompted some of the colonists to separate themselves from Massachusetts. Whitehall's response had precisely the opposite effect. So extreme an assertion of parliamentary power appeared to threaten all Americans, thereby creating a degree of consensus in the colonies which had not been apparent before 1774. It persuaded many that a line could not satisfactorily be drawn between the authority of Parliament and the rights of the colonists. For the Coercive Acts appeared to vindicate the position that, once admitted in principle, there were no limits to the exercise of Parliament's supremacy over the colonies, and that even to concede a right of Parliament to control colonial trade was to open wide the door to the prospect of arbitrary action. The measures taken by the government in the spring and summer of 1774 provided new and powerful support for the conviction that the North ministry, following faithfully in the footsteps of its predecessors, had every intention of turning this prospect into reality. Thus, the longstanding charge that successive ministers had been intent on suppressing the liberties of Americans was suddenly given a degree of credibility it had not previously enjoyed. The effect was to make believers of many who had theretofore been skeptics.

In this familiar perspective, the Coercive Acts betrayed an excess that could lead only to results the measures were designed to avoid. Taken to restore London's authority in the most rebellious of American colonies, the measures provoked sharply heightened resistance to this authority. Even then, armed rebellion need not have been the outcome had the government not persisted in taking an intransigent position. At no time, however, did it make a serious attempt to compromise the issues in dispute and to put forth conciliatory proposals that might well have appealed to moderate opinion. Instead, London's position only hardened as the final crisis unfolded. The Coercive Acts led to rebellion, then, because their patently oppressive character was matched by the ministry's determination to enforce them. When that determination became apparent to the colonists, it also became apparent that the only alternative to abject submission was war. Once again, though now for the last time, a British government had forced the Americans into a confrontation that might have been avoided altogether or, at the least, postponed indefinitely.[1]

The prevailing interpretation of the Coercive Acts is thus of a piece with the prevailing interpretation of the imperial-colonial conflict. Here, as elsewhere, this interpretation appears seriously flawed. There is, of course, no question but that the measures taken against Massachusetts had a profound impact throughout the colonies. Many were indeed shocked. But their reaction cannot simply be attributed to the substance of the measures, and to the extent it can be so attributed this is scarcely conclusive evidence that the Coercive Acts were draconian. The Massachusetts legislation was undeniably harsh if judged by the previous measures London had taken in response to colonial defiance of metropolitan authority. If judged by what was required to restore a meaningful semblance of this authority in the Bay Colony, the Coercive Acts appear quite moderate. Subsequent events showed that they were plainly inadequate and that their effect on Massachusetts was not unlike the effect of pin pricks on a bull that is already raging. The very different view taken of them by the colonists, and subsequently by historians, necessarily assumes either that the British government had no right to take the actions it did or that, even if

---

[1] In a large literature dealing with the crisis brought on by the Coercive Acts, and particularly with the response of the Continental Congress, two accounts are particularly valuable: David Ammerman, *In the Common Cause: American Response to the Coercive Acts of 1774* (Charlottesville, Va., 1974), and Jack N. Rakove, "The Decision for American Independence: A Reconstruction," *Perspectives in American History* 10 (1976):215–75.

the issue of right is put to one side, the measures were entirely disproportionate to the situation they were designed to redress.

The latter assumption will not bear serious scrutiny. By the late 1760s the revolutionary movement in Massachusetts—and particularly in Boston—had gained a momentum and strength that made it the de facto governing power. The resistance to the introduction of the East India tea in December 1773 was only the latest demonstration. More significant were the almost daily manifestations of its influence and particularly the effectiveness with which it intimidated those who supported the royal government. In early January 1774, Governor Hutchinson lamented to his superior in London, "There is no spirit left in those who used to be friends to government to support them or any others who oppose the prevailing power."[2] One reason for this impotence of government as against the "prevailing power" lay in the constraints on the executive in upholding a rapidly vanishing authority. In bringing before the House of Commons the bill for regulating the government of Massachusetts, Lord North pointed out

that an executive power was wanting in that country, and that it was highly necessary to strengthen the magistracy of it; that the force of the civil power consisted in the *posse comitatus*; and when it is considered . . . that the *posse* are the very people who have committed all these riots, little obedience to the preservation of the peace is to be expected from them. There appears to be a total defect in the constitutional power throughout. If the democratic part shews that contempt of obedience to the laws, how is the governor to execute any authority vested in him? . . . If the governor issued a proclamation, there was hardly found a magistrate to obey it; the governor, of his own authority, can do nothing; he cannot act, or give out any order without seven of the council consenting; the authority of that government is in so forlorn a situation, that no governor can act; and where there is such a want of civil authority, can it be supposed that the military, be they ever so numerous, can be of the least service?[3]

North's statement went to the heart of the imperial dilemma in Massachusetts. Although the first civil magistrate of the province, the governor was almost entirely without effective means of enforcing royal authority. In the face of riots and disturbances, the executive, for reasons North alluded to, had been unable to take

[2] The letter is dated January 28 to the American Secretary, Lord Dartmouth, *Documents of the American Revolution, 1770–1783*, p. 27.
[3] *PH*, 17:1192–93.

effective action. In the extreme case of "actual rebellious insurrection" he could call upon the aid of the military. Even here, let alone on lesser occasions, he acted at his peril, for constitutional practice was very strict in this respect, as was the government in London, and a heavy onus rested on a governor calling for military assistance in the absence of a request from an ordinary civil magistrate or, more importantly in Massachusetts, without the advice and consent of the provincial council to which North referred.[4] The governor apart, who considered himself unable to act, no civil authority had been willing to call on the army at the time of the Boston Tea Party (just as no civil authority had been willing to call on the army in 1765 during the Stámp Act riots, nor during the "occupation" from 1768 to 1770). No justice of the peace had been willing to do so. The same had been true of the Massachusetts council, a body elected by the assembly and, not surprisingly, reflective of assembly sentiment. This unwillingness was not likely to change so long as the executive was dependent upon a council that was the creature of the assembly and that shared with the governor the power to appoint and to remove magistrates. Moreover, even if the governor might by his own authority call out the army to quell riots and disturbances, there remained the prospect that those employed in such contingencies would find themselves subject to prosecution before hostile local courts for acts performed in the line of duty.[5]

These considerations explain why the North government did not and, indeed, could not content itself simply with asking Parliament for authority to close the port of Boston. The charge of excess and disproportionality brought against the North government has frequently centered on its failure to stop with the Boston Port Act. Why, it is asked, did the ministry feel compelled to go beyond this bill and to propose the serious changes it did in the Massachusetts

---

[4] It is indicative of the constraints placed on the colonial governor that even against the background of events occurring in Massachusetts in late 1773, the governor of that province was cautioned by his superior in London that "the aid of the military except in cases of actual rebellious insurrection cannot be brought forward but upon the requisition of the civil magistrate and for his support in cases of absolute necessity when every other effort has failed"; Dartmouth to Hutchinson, January 8, 1774, *Documents of the Revolution*, 8:25.

[5] These circumstances attending the passage of the Coercive Acts as well as the considerations weighed in the actions taken by the North ministry are examined by Jack M. Sosin, "The Massachusetts Acts of 1774: Coercive or Preventive?" *Huntington Library Quarterly* 26 (1962–63):235–52; and by Bernard Donoughue, *British Politics and the American Revolution: The Path to War, 1773–75* (London, 1964), pp. 73–105.

charter? The answer is that closure of the port did not respond to the critical issue confronting the ministry: How was it to govern in Massachusetts Bay? By 1774 that issue could no longer be avoided. As matters then stood, London had the choice either of reasserting its authority or of acknowledging that in this province at least it was no longer sovereign. There was no prospect of an effective reassertion of authority, however, so long as the governor of the province remained within constraints that deprived him of the means to implement the will of the King in Parliament.

The Massachusetts Bay Regulating Act and the Impartial Administration of Justice Act were intended to remove those constraints. Although altering the charter of the Bay Colony in important respects, however, their effective implementation would not have meant the end of representative government in Massachusetts. At best, they would have placed limits on the purposes and ends for which representative government was then employed and, in consequence, checked the growth and momentum of the revolutionary movement. The point was explicitly made at the time by the government in the restrictions it placed on the holding of town meetings, those "irregular assemblies" as North called them. No doubt, in the act of putting down sedition, a British government might have ended representative forms in a colony, but the North government did not do so and had no intention of doing so. The changes the government made were intended to preserve a mixed constitution, not to end representative government or to establish a despotism.

If the Coercive Acts were not disproportionate to the situation they were intended to redress, were they nevertheless arbitrary? An arbitrary authority is generally understood as one that is uncontrolled by law, unlimited in the power it claims, and, in consequence, despotic and tyrannical. The Coercive Acts apart, this scarcely seems an accurate description of the British government in 1774, particularly when one considers the extreme care with which the North government responded to the latest challenge made to its authority. The initial intention had been to deal with this challenge by executive action alone, that is, to proceed against particular individuals in accordance with existing statute and to close the port of Boston. When the government's chief law officers advised that the measures could not be taken with strict legality, however, they were abandoned. Only then was the decision made to ask Parliament to give government additional powers.

The imposition of the Coercive Acts upon Massachusetts does not establish their arbitrary character, unless one assumes that Parliament had no right to enact the legislation and, equally, that the government had no right to attempt to implement it. The colonies—Massachusetts above all—did claim this absence of right in 1774 and the First Continental Congress gave its full support to the claim. At the same time, the colonists had every reason to know that the metropolis still entertained precisely the contrary position—that it had every right to legislate for the colonies, a right encompassing the power to alter colonial charters. If the colonists were nevertheless shocked by the expression given this claim in the form of the Coercive Acts, this was because Great Britain had gradually relinquished in practice the substance of the claim only to attempt to reverse a state of affairs the Americans had come to regard as legitimate. Having permitted the Bay Colony particularly to attain a position indistinguishable in fact from one of independence, London presumably had no right to attempt the restoration of its all but vanished authority. In effect, the events of a decade and more were considered to have already decided the crucial issue of sovereignty, much as they were considered to have already decided the issue of taxation, and the metropolis, had it been acting in good faith, should have accepted the decision. It was the refusal to do so that the colonists regarded, and that historians continue to regard, as arbitrary. This, it would appear, is the deeper meaning of the contention that, in the crisis that followed the Boston Tea Party, the metropolis should have taken the path of conciliation and that the failure to have done so was not only imprudent but arbitrary. Yet is is apparent that, in the circumstances, conciliation could have no other meaning than the acknowledgment by Whitehall that its authority was no longer supreme in the colonies and certainly not in Massachusetts. Once again we are brought back to the argument of the status quo.

These considerations apart, the shock produced by the Coercive Acts may in large measure be traced simply to the fact that a British government had at long last acted. The colonists had become accustomed to imperial passivity in the face of American defiance. By enacting the Massachusetts legislation the ministry and Parliament had, in John Adams's words, thrown off the mask and revealed the face of unbridled power. Did the subsequent shock come, however, from seeing the face or from realizing that the mask had finally been thrown off? It is difficult to see why the face alone should have caused such shock. After all, its features had been regularly described for a decade in scores of pamphlets, hundreds of newspaper articles, and thousands of speeches. The reaction of the colonists was instead due to the expectation that, despite the shrill and insistent warnings of ever-impending moves by would-be tyrants, the face would never fully be revealed, that a British government would not respond in the manner the North ministry did. The expectation was reasonable. For years, colonial defiance of imperial authority had been met with responses that often appeared even to the colonists as little more than face-saving gestures. From colonial resistance to the Stamp Act to the burning of the *Gaspee*, the metropolis had beaten a path of steady retreat before the Americans. In response to acts of colonial violence, it had but once employed violence and then, though in circumstances of extreme provocation, only involuntarily. Against those who had often intimidated government officials, it had not once meted out punishment. Suddenly, it appeared to turn on those who had persistently and openly flouted its authority, a change shocking enough after nine years of giving way in confrontation.

[II]

Did the Coercive Acts back the colonists into a corner from which they could not retreat? The answer depends largely upon the manner in which the corner is defined. If it is defined in terms of the tax issue, the colonists were in no more of a corner in 1774 than they had been before passage of the Massachusetts legislation. The crisis brought on by the Boston Tea Party and the Coercive Acts had not significantly altered the dispute over taxation but had instead focused the imperial-colonial conflict on the issue of Parliament's right to govern the colonies at all. North had made this clear in introducing the Boston Port Act in the Commons. "[At] Boston," he observed, "we were considered as two independent states; but we were no longer to dispute between legislation and taxation, we were now to consider only whether or not we have any authority there; that it is very clear we have none, if we suffer the property of our subjects to be destroyed."[6] The Boston patriots would scarcely have disagreed with this assessment. For some time they too had defined the conflict in terms of Parliament's right to govern the colonies and not only in terms of a right to tax them. By winter 1774, Great Britain had either to make a credible assertion of parliamentary supremacy over the colonies or to abandon even the pretense that it was still sovereign. A credible assertion of parliamentary supremacy necessarily entailed action that challenged the foundation of the colonial position, and most clearly the position now taken by Massachusetts. In this sense, the Coercive Acts undeniably backed the colonies into a corner from which they could not retreat save by conceding the vital issue of sovereignty. This is only to say, however, that when starkly incompatible claims have been made and given active expression, corners are inevitable. The Coercive Acts no more backed the colonies into a corner than the Boston Tea Party backed the metropolis into a corner. There were two corners, not one.

If anything, as between the positions of the two parties in the summer and fall of 1774, it was the metropolis that appeared to be the more closely constrained. Unless given effect, the passage of the Coercive Acts was an empty gesture. Indeed, unless the Massachusetts legislation was given effect, its passage was likely to prove more injurious to Great Britain than would a policy of inaction. Effective implementation, however, ultimately depended upon the determination and capacity of the government to enforce the acts by military means. In the spring and summer of 1774 the North ministry was still very far from having this determination, let alone from having the requisite means for imposing its will. It is true that in devising the Massachusetts legislation and in guiding the legislation through Parliament, the government made much of its newly found resolve. Henceforth, Whitehall now declared, the government would not hesitate in taking resolute action in the face of colonial defiance to its authority. In opening the debate on the Coercive Acts North asserted in the Commons that "if it is necessary, I should not hesitate a moment to enforce a due obedience to the laws of this country."[7]

---

[6] *PH*, 17:1166–67.
[7] *PH*, p. 1172. Significantly, North prefaced the statement with these words: "The good of this Act [the Boston Port Act] is, that four or five frigates will do the business without any military force."

In fact, the resolution was not there and would not emerge until the end of 1774. Even then it would remain very much qualified. At the outset, it was clearly lacking. The avowal of a determination to enforce the Massachusetts legislation, if necessary, was not to be taken literally. "Enforcement" had a special meaning for the ministry, one that did not encompass forcible measures. The colonies were now to be coerced, but the coercion was to be of a nonforcible character. Historians would later speak of the "failure of the policy of coercion." The failure, however, was not of a policy of coercion, *strictu sensu*, since such policy was not attempted in 1774. In this sense, and it is critical, the Massachusetts legislation was no more coercive than earlier legislation had been. Convenience and established usage, not accuracy, dictate here the use of the term *Coercive Acts*.

Thus, the passage of the Massachusetts legislation did not mark the end of illusions. Instead, illusions persisted, only now the illusions of those who championed a firm policy gained ascendancy. A so-called policy of coercion was made to appear almost as a soft option to a policy of conciliation. If the imperial lion would only bare its teeth, no more would be required, for the colonists would assuredly shrink from further confrontation. Early on in the crisis precipitated by the Boston Tea Party, General Gage told the King that if the British would only "take the resolute part," the colonists would "undoubtedly prove very meek."[8] The resolute part, Gage counseled, was the sending of four regiments to Boston. In the view of a man who had less excuse than most for failing to have known better, and who within several months would be pleading from Boston for twenty thousand troops, it was necessary to make only a modest show of force to subdue the Bostonians. George III was only too ready to accept Gage's sanguine estimate of the effects of showing the flag and urged his chief minister to hear Gage out. In subsequently sending Gage back to Boston with four regiments—a force that did not add to, but only relieved, as many regiments in America—the government satisfied itself that it had accepted the implications of a policy of coercion. Gage was to use his newly combined authority as first magistrate of the Bay Colony and commander-in-chief of British forces in America to reduce Massachusetts to a state of obedience to lawful authority. At the same time, he was given to understand his superior's expectation

[8] The King to Lord North, February 4, 1774, *The Correspondence of King George the Third from 1760 to December 1783*, 3:no. 1379.

that the need to use the King's troops would not occur and that it was his duty to make every endeavor to avoid this contingency. The instructions of April 9, 1774, given by Dartmouth to the departing Gage, expressed the "hope" that Gage's combined authority as first magistrate and commander-in-chief would enable him "to meet every opposition and fully to preserve the public peace by employing those troops with effect," should recourse to the use of troops prove necessary. The American secretary went on to admonish Gage: "The King trusts, however, that such necessity will not occur and commands me to say that it will be your duty to use every endeavour to avoid it." Gage was also instructed to proceed against the "ring leaders in those violences," though he was still to use the ordinary courts of justice within the colony. But if it seemed to him that the "prejudices of the people" would probably prevent conviction, however clear the evidence might be, he was to "desist from prosecution, seeing that an ineffectual attempt would only be triumph to the faction and disgraceful to government."[9] When these instructions were given, only the Boston Port Act had been passed. Gage continued to harbor doubt about his authority in using troops, and not without reason, since the powers he had been formally granted had also been attended by a strong cautionary note. On June 3, 1774, subsequent to passage of the other Coercive Acts and with fresh indication that Boston would not quietly submit to the acts, Dartmouth informed Gage, "As some doubt may possibly arise whether His Majesty's governor can act in any case in the capacity of an ordinary civil magistrate I think it fit to acquaint you that the King's chief law servants are clearly of opinion that the governor by his commission is conservator of the peace in all cases whatsoever."[10] But the doubt was not so much over the formal authority now entrusted him to employ his troops as it was over the government's willingness to take a tolerant view of such employment when later assessing the circumstances of a particular case. The effect of the instructions given him could not but serve as a warning that a heavy burden of proof would be required to establish the necessity for using the armed forces to exact obedience. As time went by, and the seriousness of the situation in Massachusetts finally began to dawn on London, the

[9] *The Correspondence of General Thomas Gage with the Secretaries of State, 1763–1775*, 2:158–62.
[10] Ibid., p. 168.

government would progressively lighten this burden. In the end, it would not only remove the constraints altogether but gratuitously charge Gage with timidity in making use of the quite inadequate forces at this disposal. At the outset, however, it was the constraints on Gage's discretion that were plainly emphasized.

If the North ministry had foreseen that the Massachusetts legislation would ultimately lead to war with the colonies, would it nevertheless have set out on the course it did? Although doubt must persist, the likelihood is that it would have done so and for reasons already outlined. There is no doubt, though, that the course taken by the government was made considerably easier by virtue of assumptions commonly entertained at the time. These assumptions—that the Americans would shrink from the prospect of force, that the Coercive Acts would isolate Massachusetts from the other colonies, and that, thus isolated, the resistance to imperial authority in the Bay Colony would soon collapse—represented more than the mere grasping at straws. They were not simply a reflection of imperial hubris. After all, a good deal of experience could be invoked in support of such assumptions. In varying degree they were shared by many Americans—including not a few of the resistance leaders—who also doubted whether the traditional inability of the colonies to unite their efforts in support of common goals, however desirable, could ever be overcome.

That events were to prove these assumptions mistaken cannot be taken to mean that they were unreasonable. What does seem unreasonable is the apparent ease with which the government and its supporters persuaded themselves that the Coercive Acts could effectively be implemented without incurring the serious risk that at some point armed force would have to be employed on a significant scale. The immediate problem confronting London was not the reaction of the other colonies or the degree of support they might afford Massachusetts, but the reaction of Massachusetts. The fate of the Coercive Acts would be determined in that province— above all, in Boston—and there was little in the experience of the preceding decade to indicate that it could readily be brought to submission. The North ministry was not wrong in considering the Massachusetts legislation as the minimum response required to maintain royal authority in that province. Before royal authority could be maintained, however, it had first to be restored. The changes in the Massachusetts charter could not, of themselves, effect such restoration. Only the immediate and effective assertion of British power could do this, if it could be done at all.[11]

The initial optimism with which Whitehall embarked on a path that would eventually lead to war found a parallel in the optimism with which the colonists expected this latest trial of wills to issue in yet another British defeat. Although not shared by all the colonial leaders, the prevailing expectation was that if the colonies stood united and firm in opposing the Coercive Acts, the government would retreat, draw back from enforcement, and ultimately withdraw the legislation. Given the past record of British governments in dealing with the colonies, the course marked out by the Coercive Acts lacked credibility. Since the metropolis had regularly backed down before, it was reasonable to believe that it would do so again. The repeal of the acts might thus be secured by measures that had earlier secured repeal of the Stamp Act—nonimportation and resistance to attempts to implement the hated legislation. From the outset, the essential elements of a viable strategy for countering the Coercive Acts appeared to follow from past experience. It was the confidence the colonists placed in this strategy that in large measure must account for their unyielding position, a position already set out before the First Continental Congress met in September, though further clarified and strengthened by the deliberations at Philadelphia.

[11] It may be that the initial optimism of the North ministry that Massachusetts would submit to the will of the imperial state was little more than a case of whistling in the dark, that the ministry did not really believe this, and that its early optimism was based on hope rather than solid expectation. This is the view taken by P.D.G. Thomas, *Lord North*, pp. 79–80, who also asserts that, were a confrontation to arise, the ministers, including the "moderate Dartmouth" as well as Lord North, were resolved to face it. "That he [Lord North] was determined on resolute action," Thomas notes, "is known to us from the diary of Thomas Hutchinson." But the Hutchinson diary, even if taken at face value, does not bear out the resolution of the ministers to enforce the Coercive Acts through employing such armed force as might prove necessary in the end. If anything, the diary shows the absence of such resolution through the summer of 1774. Dartmouth's bellicosity rose no higher than expressing the "wish" to see John Adams and John Hancock "brought to the punishment they deserved." North's resolution consists in his insistence that the Coercive Acts not be abandoned and that the colonies "can hurt nobody but themselves" in continuing their defiance; *The Diary and Letters of his Excellency Thomas Hutchinson, Esq.*, 1:201–3, 211–12, 245. Like Dartmouth, North wanted to see the Boston leaders of the rebellious colonists punished (including those who had participated in the First Continental Congress). North was not worried about the colonial trade boycott, but it is important to emphasize that his position on the boycott stemmed not, as Thomas maintains, from the prime minister's view of the relative insignificance for the British economy of the American trade, but rather from his conviction that the radicals would not succeed in forcing the colonial merchants to respect the boycott and from his determination to ensure that the colonies could not trade elsewhere if the boycott were enforced.

This confidence did not seem misplaced. One element of the colonial strategy was almost immediately effective and it was of critical importance. The legislation for altering the Massachusetts charter could not be implemented; at least, it could not be implemented by the measures the government was prepared to employ. These measures assumed that imperial authority still existed in some meaningful sense in the Bay Colony and that, in consequence, the implementation of the Coercive Acts was a matter of administration. The resistance to the implementation of the legislation quickly revealed the illusory character of the assumption. Throughout the summer of 1774 the weakness of royal government in Massachusetts was laid bare with dramatic effect. In response to the Boston Port Act, the radical leaders countered with a "Solemn League and Covenant," pledging the signers to a boycott of British goods and threatening with isolation, and worse, those who did not sign. When Gage ordered the arrest of the organizers of the boycott, no civil official proved willing to execute the order.

This initial show of impotence in June was no more than a modest portent of what followed in August upon reception of the legislation for altering the province's charter. Gage set out to implement the legislation only to find that his newly appointed royal councillors were threatened with violence and forced to resign, that courts were not permitted to function in many parts of the province, and that without the support of the army the cooperation of civil officers almost everywhere was not to be expected. By the end of August the Massachusetts countryside had virtually become enemy-held territory into which British forces could venture only at considerable risk. From this territory to the safety of Boston fled those who had dared to accept appointment to office in accordance with the new legislation. As a precautionary measure, Gage himself quit Salem, where he had been directed in the spring to establish both his residence and the seat of the provincial government, and returned to Boston expressing to London his astonishment over the "enfeebled state in which I found every branch of government."[12] Even this description tended on the side of exaggerating the strength of the government's position in Massachusetts.

Nor did Gage have a viable alternative in the army. Although now aware that he could not restore order and implement the Coercive Acts without employing military force, he was also con-

---

[12] Gage to Dartmouth, September 12, 1774, Gage, 1:374.

scious of the inadequacy of the force at his disposal. There was no prospect that this force might reduce the Massachusetts country-side to obedience while at the same time hold Boston secure. Gage was increasingly apprehensive even of his ability to defend Boston against a determined attack, given the growing strength and height-ened preparation of the forces under control of the radical leaders. In Boston there were fewer than three thousand British troops in late summer. Outside Boston there was a militia force whose num-bers were unknown but calculated to be several times greater than the British force. Gage was understandably reluctant to venture outside the town, quite apart from his persisting uncertainty over whether he could expect London's firm support in using the force at his disposal. The uncertainty was fully justified, for the North ministry had not abandoned its policy of nonforcible coercion.

It is in the light of these circumstances that the corner metaphor must be considered. It seems absurd to contend that it was the colonists who had been placed in a corner from which they could not retreat, or, acknowledging there were two corners rather than one, that it was the colonists who held the more constrained and less tenable position. Clearly, the colonists occupied the more advantageous position. They had successfully defeated British at-tempts to implement the Coercive Acts, they were in command of the Massachusetts countryside, and, for the time being at least, they enjoyed a favorable balance of forces. By contrast, the British had utterly failed to put into effect the changes in the Massachusetts charter, were close to losing the last vestige of their authority in the province, and were now ignominiously confined to Boston. Nor are these considerations affected by the argument that the colonists had only acted "defensively," that they had merely resisted gov-ernment efforts to put the new legislation into effect. For it may be argued with at least equal persuasiveness that the government had only acted defensively in its efforts to change the Massachusetts charter, that it had merely resisted colonial efforts the cumulative effect of which was to deny the substance of imperial authority altogether. This denial was, in fact, the objective consequence of colonial resistance and, in the circumstances, the functional equiv-alent of an offensive action. If the resistance succeeded, the gov-ernment must lose everything. The colonists, then, had only ef-fectively to maintain their "defensive" posture in order to win; for the successful maintenance of this posture meant that imperial authority, in Massachusetts at any rate, was no longer to be taken seriously. The government, however, could not remain content with a defensive posture; it had to reestablish a semblance of authority in order to maintain a viable position at all. In this situation, time was evidently working in favor of the colonists.

These considerations also suggest that it was the colonists, not the metropolis, who were in the better position to temporize and even to make concessions. The contrary view proceeds from the assumption that the British were the stronger party by far and, this being so, could better afford to make concessions. This view, however, is difficult to sustain. In 1774, the colonists were in by far the stronger position. Of course, any plan of reconciliation, if it were to prove at all feasible, had to finesse the sovereignty issue, something neither side was prepared to do by 1774. Even here, though, an asymmetry favored the colonists and permitted them, had they wanted to do so, to draw back from the precipice. For the concession of parliamentary sovereignty clearly did not carry with it the concession of those separate, and ostensibly lesser, claims the colonists had pressed since the middle 1760s. In colonial eyes the sovereignty of Parliament, though acknowledged in 1766, did not imply a right of taxation or, for that matter, a right to legislate generally in matters of internal polity. From the colonial perspective, there had been no indivisibility between admission of the principle of parliamentary sovereignty and admission of these other powers. On the other hand, the denial of parliamentary sovereignty did imply, as a matter of inherent right, the denial of British legislative authority *in toto* over the colonies. Britain could make this concession only by conceding everything. Metropolitan rigidity on the issue of principle was born of necessity, since without that principle there was virtually nothing of solidity on which to stand.

[III]

Although the Coercive Acts did not push the colonists into a corner from which they could not retreat, there is no gainsaying the contention that the legislation did impel them to achieve an increased degree of consensus. The scope and nature of this consensus, it is true, have not infrequently been exaggerated. In 1774, and even in 1775, the commitment to the common cause still required only modest sacrifice from most colonies. Where this commitment appeared to entail the substantial sacrifice only of some—as in the case of nonexportation—it was attended by marked controversy, thus foreshadowing the problems that would later emerge in the course of the war when willingness to sacrifice on behalf of the common cause was subjected to very serious strain. In 1774 the agonies of a prolonged war were still distant, though, and the optimism that attended the acceptance of the strategy for countering the Coercive Acts was indicative of the belief that these agonies might be avoided altogether. These considerations notwithstanding, the colonial consensus that suddenly emerged in the last great crisis with the metropolis prior to the outbreak of war remains impressive.

If London's expectation that Massachusetts could be isolated proved badly misplaced, does it follow that the government would have been well-advised to have pursued a conciliatory policy toward the Bay Colony in the wake of the Boston Tea Party? It would appear to only if previous conciliatory responses can be shown to have created divisions among the colonies and to have moderated their demands. There is little evidence, and no evidence at all in the case of Massachusetts, that such were the earlier effects of a conciliatory policy. Instead, the record shows that for the Bay Colony there was no apparent way to divert the drive for a status tantamount in all but name to independence. That drive might have been slowed—though how much must remain quite speculative—but it could not be stopped. And it could be slowed only by a policy of avoiding confrontation which itself had the invariable effect of further eroding imperial authority. Given these realities, London's choice in 1774 was not one of confronting Massachusetts or of conciliating that province in the expectation that this would substantially moderate the colony's position. Confrontation might and, in the event, did lead to the other colonies making the cause of Massachusetts their cause as well; but conciliation might just as plausibly have led the other colonies to make of Massachusetts an example to be emulated. They had done so on more than one occasion in the past.

The consensus that the metropolis presumably might have avoided had it taken a different course was not merely expressed in the immediately felt need to succor Massachusetts Bay. At a still more significant level it found expression in the rejection in principle of parliamentary supremacy over the colonies. The line that a majority of colonial leaders had been unwilling openly to cross before 1774 was now crossed by virtually all. Thus, when the First Continental Congress met in September at Philadelphia, the vital issue of parliamentary sovereignty that lay at the heart of the imperial-colonial conflict did not, as such, form a matter of serious debate among the delegates. On this issue, the "radical" Samuel Adams and the "conservative" Joseph Galloway shared common ground. In right, Galloway declared, the colonies—and now the Congress—might deny the validity of any act passed by Parliament without regard to time. That Galloway was strongly opposed to the full exercise of this right is far less important than that even the man remembered as the archconservative of the Continental Congress denied that Parliament had any inherent right to legislate for the colonies.[13]

Given this consensus on the limiting issue of the conflict, it is not surprising that on most other major substantive issues a like consensus obtained. Indeed, there is some question whether what are commonly seen as the two serious debates that did occur in the formulation of the statement of the rights and grievances of the colonies may properly be considered as debates on issues of principle. The differences that arose at Philadelphia over whether to limit grievances to acts of Parliament passed since 1763 scarcely appear as such. Dictated for the most part by expediential and tactical considerations, this limitation in time was designed to appeal to the friends of America in Great Britain and, more generally, to demonstrate a conciliatory intent toward those delegates who

[13] In John Adams's notes of debates, September 8, 1774, Galloway is recorded thus: "It is of the essence of the English Constitution that no laws shall be binding, but such as are made by the consent of the proprietors in England. How then, did it stand with our ancestors when they came over here? They could not be bound by any laws made by the British Parliament, excepting those made before. . . . I have ever thought we might reduce our rights to one—an exemption from all laws made by British Parliament since the emigration of our ancestors. It follows, therefore, that all the acts of Parliament made since, are violations of our rights. . . . I am well aware that my arguments tend to an independency of the Colonies, and militate against the maxims that there must be some absolute power to draw together all the wills and strength of the empire" *Letters of Members of the Continental Congress*, ed. Edmund C. Burnett, 8 vols. (Washington, D.C., 1921–36), 1:22. In later presenting his plan of union, Galloway did not qualify his rejection of parliamentary supremacy. The American Congress he proposed, though designated an "inferior branch" of the British legislature, was to enjoy a status of equality with Parliament. The colonies could not be bound by any law of Parliament without first giving their consent. This applied to trade regulation as well as to taxation. In matters of internal polity, each colony was to enjoy complete autonomy. Rejected by the Continental Congress, the plan would nevertheless have given the colonists the substance of what they had long insisted upon—equivalence. It is probably only because Galloway would ultimately oppose the Revolution that his role in 1774 is remembered as that of a conservative. The rejection of parliamentary supremacy was not the mark of a conservative, even in 1774, yet Galloway rejected it. His plan of union was not a device for formalizing the old imperial-colonial relationship, but for establishing a new relationship.

would immediately see in the attempt to go beyond 1763 an attack on the entire system for regulating colonial trade and commerce. Since the matter of parliamentary regulation of colonial trade had already led to the airing of differences that had, for the time being, been left unresolved, the "grievous acts and measures" to which "Americans cannot submit" were restricted to those taken since 1763. But the future did not foreclose the review of a more distant past. The year the Seven Years' War ended formed only a provisional statute of limitations. The statement of grievances did not foreclose the possibility that pre-1763 acts might be challenged at some future time, but promised only that "for the present" the Congress would pass over "many infringements and violations" of colonial rights "from an ardent desire, that harmony and mutual intercourse of affection and interest may be restored."[14]

Much more significant was the division among the delegates over whether Parliament could continue to regulate American trade and, if so, what the basis of this regulation should be. In challenging only the validity of parliamentary legislation enacted after 1763, the Congress left unchallenged—at any rate, for the present—the basic laws governing the system of trade and navigation. These laws could scarcely express an inherent right of Parliament to regulate colonial trade if, as the delegates agreed, Parliament had no inherent right to legislate for the colonies. To be sure, the colonies acting through the Congress might concede to Parliament a "right" to regulate their trade, though only their trade. What was conceded might, if misused, be taken away. They could scarcely acknowledge, however, that Parliament had an inherent right to regulate colonial trade without otherwise seeming to contradict their central position respecting parliamentary supremacy. Even if the admission of an inherent right here and the denial of it elsewhere satisfied the requirements of political logic, it might nevertheless raise serious doubt about the general viability of the colonial rejection of parliamentary supremacy. At least, so the opponents of acknowledging an inherent right of Parliament to regulate colonial trade argued, and their view prevailed.

It is, the statement of rights and grievances reads, "from the necessity of the case, and a regard to the mutual interests of both

---

[14] *Journals of the Continental Congress*, 1:71–73. In the list of grievances, the most notable omission is the Declaratory Act of 1766. This can be seen only as dictated by a desire to placate the friends of America in Parliament, particularly the Rockinghamites.

countries," that the representatives of the colonies, "cheerfully consent to the operation of such acts of the British parliament, as are *bona fide*, restrained to the regulation of our external commerce, for the purpose of securing the commercial advantages of the whole empire to the mother country, and the commercial benefits of its respective members." The carefully qualified formulation is an open invitation to demand such later changes in the trade laws as the colonies might deem necessary or desirable. There is little doubt that, had it been accepted by the metropolis, it would have been subsequently employed to challenge the system of enumeration as well as the constraints placed on manufactures in the colonies.[15]

Even if the debate over parliamentary regulation of American trade is taken as a division on an issue of principle, doubt must still persist over the significance to attach to the division. It does so if for no other reason than the unanimity with which the Congress rejected as unconstitutional the means by which Great Britain had increasingly sought to enforce the old colonial system since 1763. In both the statement of rights and grievances and in the provisions establishing the Continental Association, the delegates made of these means, as the colonists had done for many years, an issue of principle on which they were unyielding. In the provisions of the association, the Congress committed the colonies to observe the embargo on trade until such time as the metropolis should cease to "extend the powers of the admiralty courts beyond their ancient limits, deprive the American subject of trial by jury, authorize the judge's certificate to indemnify the prosecutor from damages, that he might otherwise be liable to from a trial by his peers, require oppressive security from a claimant of ships or goods seized, before he shall be allowed to defend his property."[16] With the repeal of the acts designed to enforce the trade laws, the observance of these laws would be left to the self-interest of the colonists. In effect, then, the dispute over Britain's right to regulate trade could only have had a limited significance, if the effectiveness of this right— even had it been unequivocally acknowledged—nevertheless depended on the assessment the colonists made of their interest in observing the trade laws.

---

[15] The above quotes are from Resolution 4 of the statement of rights and grievances, in ibid., pp. 68–69.
[16] Ibid., pp. 79–80.

However one views the above debates, they remain as the exceptions to the remarkable agreement among delegates to the First Continental Congress on issues of principle. In adopting without division the Suffolk Resolves, the Congress not only promised the support of the other colonies to Massachusetts in resisting the Coercive Acts but committed itself to as uncompromising and militant a position as that expressed in the resolves. So, too, in approving—again without division—the Continental Association, the members entered into a "non-importation, non-consumption, and non-exportation agreement" directed against the metropolis until such time as not only the Coercive Acts were rescinded, but the "ruinous system of colony administration, adopted by the British ministry about the year 1763" was repealed. In support of this complete embargo on trade, the Congress established local committees to enforce the provisions of the association. These committees, which were to prove remarkably effective, gave a structure to the resistance which proved indispensable. Later, they would become equally invaluable in providing the governing infrastructure for waging armed rebellion. More than any other act taken by the Congress, the association was a measure the British could not but view as a signal that the breaking point was at hand. Once made, the commitment to pursue the stringent measures provided for until the metropolis satisfied colonial grievances was one that could be backed away from only at considerable cost. At the same time, the satisfaction of those grievances was impossible to give without conceding in all but name the issue of parliamentary supremacy. Yet, as already noted, the Congress voted approval of the association without division.[17]

This impressive consensus over major issues of principle has long presented something of a problem for historians. On the one hand, the Continental Congress is generally seen as predominantly composed of moderate representatives who sought reconciliation with the metropolis. On the other hand, the moderates are found to have accepted positions and policies virtually indistinguishable from those supported by the radicals prior to and during the Congress. It is quite true that many historians, despite this acknowledged

---

[17] The Suffolk Resolves were endorsed by the Congress on September 18, 1774, and the Continental Association was approved October 20, 1774. For the texts of both, see ibid., pp. 32–43, 75–81.

triumph of the radicals, go on to characterize the overall position taken by the First Continental Congress as on balance conciliatory and to insist that the moderates genuinely believed and had reason for believing that they had left the door open for reconciliation. If this general characterization of the Congress itself creates problems, it does not affect the recognition that moderates did embrace radical positions and policies.[18]

How is one to account for this sudden and surprising conversion—if conversion it was—of moderates? It cannot be adequately explained in terms of the domination of the Congress, particularly in the early stages of its work, by the radical group centered in the Massachusetts and Virginia delegations. Although better organized and possessed of a more developed sense of direction and maneuver, the Adams-Lee group cannot be credited with having seduced and outmaneuvered a substantially larger number of moderates into accepting positions the moderates had not wanted to accept.[19] The broad consensus among the delegates on issues of principle was apparent almost from the very start of the deliberations at Philadelphia. The moderates did not have to be seduced into accepting radical positions. Differences, and on more than one occasion very important differences, over tactics were another matter. Controversy, at times bitter, persisted over the responsiveness

---

[18] John C. Miller, *Origins of the American Revolution* (Boston, 1943), pp. 379ff., presents a Congress that, though initially moderate, ends with the triumph of the radicals. So, too, Ian R. Christie and Benjamin Woods Labaree, *Empire or Independence, 1760–1776*, pp. 208ff., write of a Congress made up of "predominantly moderate men", who, with few exceptions, sought reconciliation. Christie and Labaree conclude that it is "surprising then that in the end they should adopt policies based so closely on radical positions." Why the Congress moved toward "more radical measures and positions" is not explained. Even Ammerman, *Common Cause*, and Rakove, "Decision for Independence," though stressing the consensual character of the Congress on major issues of principle, tend to credit the moderate belief that the work of the Congress did not preclude reconciliation.

[19] H. James Henderson, *Party Politics in the Continental Congress*, (New York, 1974), pp. 32–45, writes that "the record of the first Congress clearly indicates that the radicals achieved a genuine triumph as a result of their superior preparation and organization" (36). But the "triumph" was made possible, as Henderson notes, because "the moderates at once disapproved of radical tactics and supported radical grievances" (23). Even this admission, which substantially narrows the alleged division, does not cover the whole ground. Was the Continental Association, for example, expressive merely of principles (or grievances) rather than of tactics as well? Clearly, it expressed both. Yet the Congress immediately gave it broad support. Indeed, the arguments over the terms and intention of the association were, Henderson writes, largely within radical ranks (43). One reason that Henderson finds a greater triumph of the radicals than in fact occurred is because he misreads the so-called conservative position. Thus, "Conservatives viewed the claim to exclusive legislative power in all cases of taxation and internal policy as an extreme denial of parliamentary authority" (41). But conservatives at Philadelphia endorsed this denial from the outset.

that might be expected from the mother country in dealing with colonial demands. Above all, the prospects for avoiding war with the metropolis elicited divergent responses and gave rise to what was perhaps the most significant division among the delegates. These qualifications, however, which must be considered on their own terms, do not detract from the point at issue. The broad acceptance of radical positions at Philadelphia was not the result of radical guile and intrigue.[20]

There is no need to explain the conversion of the moderates at Philadelphia. There is no need to do so because the dramatic shift to radical positions did not in fact occur. With respect to the great issues that made up the core of the imperial-colonial conflict, the so-called moderates were already radicals—in most cases they had been so for some time. The Coercive Acts did not effect the change. These acts, and the enormity they represented in colonial eyes, merely completed the process of radicalization for many by crystallizing a position that had been years in the making. Suddenly, in the summer of 1774, it was "revealed" to many where they really stood and had indeed long been standing. What James Wilson had experienced several years before when writing his famous pamphlet on the authority of the British Parliament was now experienced by others, though in more mundane fashion, in consequence of the Coercive Acts. Wilson had probably completed his pamphlet in early 1770, though he had then "judged unseasonable" its publication. Now, in August 1774, he wrote in the "advertisement":

---

[20] A persuasive refutation of the view that an initially divided Congress was conquered by a minority of radicals is given by Ammerman, Common Cause, pp. 89–101. Is it fair to say that moderates differed from radicals, not in the substantive position taken on major issues, but in the estimates made of the adversary's "reasonableness"? Certainly, the moderates were distinguished by their expectation in the fall of 1774 that the metropolis would ultimately respond to colonial demands and that it would do so in the form of substantial concessions. It is excessive to say that radicals did not share this expectation. After all, most of them also believed that the mother country would eventually back down before the united stand of the colonies, and particularly before the pressures engendered by the trade boycott. It does seem to be the case, however, that radicals entertained less faith in the outcome of the measures affecting trade than did the moderates. This, in part at least, explains their support for measures of military preparation, measures most moderates opposed at the time. Given the essential agreement on matters of principle, one is tempted to speak of these differences as no more than tactical. But even if they are so categorized, they remain very important. In general, it does not seem far from the mark to conclude that radicals were considerably more prepared to draw the logical consequences that followed from the colonial position than were moderates. (This is the position taken both by Rakove, "Decision for Independence," p. 272, and by Ammerman, Common Cause, p. 96.) We must emphasize the words more prepared, though, since very few were indeed prepared to draw fully these consequences.

Many will, perhaps, be surprised to see the legislative authority of the British parliament over the colonies denied *in every instance*. Those the writer informs, that, when he began this piece, he would probably have been surprised at such an opinion himself; for that it was the *result*, and not the *occasion*, of his disquisitions. He entered upon them with a view and expectation of being able to trace some constitutional line between those cases in which we ought, and those in which we ought not, to acknowledge the power of parliament over us. In the prosecution of his inquiries, he became fully convinced that such a line does not exist; and that there can be no medium between acknowledging and denying that power in all cases.[21]

[IV]

In reaching the destination of total rejection of parliamentary authority, how far had the colonists traveled? Had the distance been considerable between the position marked out in the first great crisis of imperial-colonial relations and the last? In part, the answer evidently depends upon how the distance is measured. If the standard of measurement chosen is the practical rather than the theoretical, that is, *what* Parliament could or could not do rather than *why* it could or could not do, the answer seems reasonably clear. Between the positions advanced in the Stamp Act crisis and the late summer of 1774, the distance is quite short.

It is true that the starting point itself is marked by some uncertainty. What, for example, was precisely intended by the "all due Subordination" the Stamp Act Congress professed to "that August Body the Parliament of Great Britain"? This earlier Congress was not altogether clear, if only for the reason that it was concerned with what Parliament could not do to those who enjoyed the rights of Englishmen yet "are not, and from their local circumstances cannot be," represented in Parliament. Certainly, the Parliament could not tax. Could it, however, legislate in matters otherwise affecting the internal polity? The Stamp Act Congress did not afford an explicit answer (though some of the provincial assemblies did). But the most reasonable inference to be drawn from its declaration is that Parliament might not do so.

---

[21] *Considerations on the Nature and Extent of the Legislative Authority of the British Parliament*, in *The Works of James Wilson*, ed. Robert G. McCloskey, 2 vols. (Cambridge, 1967), 2:721.

This uncertainty was soon clarified. By 1768 little doubt could arise over the subordination the colonies considered they owed to Parliament. In the distinction drawn between matters internal and matters external, the scope of parliamentary authority over the colonies extended no further than the regulation of those matters, by definition external, essential to maintain the common interests of the empire, that is, the power to regulate colonial trade and commerce. This is the distinction drawn and the conclusion reached by John Dickinson in his *Letters from a Farmer*, a statement that may be taken as a representative and authoritative exposition of the colonial position at the time. Yet Dickinson's position could be elaborated. In declaring that the colonists were as much dependent on Great Britain "as one free people could be on another," he laid the ground for the denial, in principle, of Parliament's legislative authority over the colonies.[22]

From the late 1760s, then, it was virtually taken for granted that Parliament had no right to lay any revenue tax, whether internal or external, on the colonies or to legislate in other matters of internal polity. What was left of the sovereign power of the imperial legislature, to which the colonies owed "all due Subordination"? Although a right to regulate the trade and commerce of the colonies was still conceded, it was attended by uncertainty and controversy. In consequence, only the difficulties marking this right were clear, not the solutions.

One difficulty arose from colonial insistence that Parliament could not use its power of regulating trade as a subterfuge for enacting what were, in effect, revenue measures. Since an act for the regulation of trade might also be one that was designed to raise revenue, the determination of when Parliament had supposedly abused its power might prove no easy matter. Nor was a solution readily apparent by inquiry into the intention of the legislature; instead, the intention of Parliament might have to be inferred, if at all, from the nature of the act.[23]

---

[22] *Letters From a Farmer in Pennsylvania to the Inhabitants of the British Colonies*; in *The Writings of John Dickinson*, 1:312–13.

[23] Carl L. Becker remarked of this: "To derive the nature of an act from the intention of its framers, and the intention of its framers from the nature of the act, was no doubt what logicians would call reasoning in a circle"; *The Declaration of Independence: A Study in the History of Political Ideas* (New York, 1942), p. 95. The colonists resolved this dilemma, as Becker noted in paraphrase of Dickinson, by insisting that they had "the same right that all states have, of judging when their privileges are invaded."

This difficulty apart, an act regulating trade might still constitute in American eyes an abuse of parliamentary power if it interfered in matters of internal polity. As the decade-long controversy in American ports revealed, there was in fact no apparent way the metropolis could effectively insure observance of the trade laws save by measures—sanctioned by Parliament—the Americans rejected as beyond Parliament's power to enact.

Given this progressive restriction the colonies placed on Parliament's legislative authority, only marginal significance can be read into the continued profession of "a due subordination" that the colonies would explicitly reject only in 1774. Thomas Hutchinson was later to characterize the admission in theory and denial in practice in these terms: "[At] first, indeed, the supreme authority seemed to be admitted, the case of taxes only excepted; but the exceptions gradually extended from one case to another, until it included all cases whatsoever. A profession of 'subordination,' however, still remained; it was a word without a precise meaning to it."[24] Even at the outset of the crisis in 1765, it had almost no meaning at all.

Thus, what remained to be done by the First Continental Congress was not to effect a change now demanded by those the Coercive Acts had presumably radicalized but to register and give formal expression to a change that had already largely occurred. James Wilson's pamphlet was but one of a number of efforts to formulate a position that would, with little change, find acceptance by the Congress. The famous Resolution 4 of the Declaration of Rights broke no new ground in denying Parliament's authority in all cases of taxation and internal polity but only in denying as a matter of right Parliament's authority to regulate colonial trade. Even here, however, the ground that was broken was not that of practice, for the limitations placed on parliamentary regulation of trade were substantially the same limitations that had been claimed throughout the decade. Only an "inherent right" had been denied, though now explicitly so. The denial was no more than the logical consequence of the position that a constitutional line could not be drawn between cases in which the power of Parliament over the colonies ought, and those in which it ought not, to be acknowledged. By the time of the First Continental Congress, moderates, no less than radicals,

[24] *The History of the Colony and Province of Massachusetts Bay*, 3:256.

had in principle erased that line. The compromise that Resolution 4 is commonly held to represent was a compromise among the delegates, not one with the metropolis. Even as among the delegates, it was a compromise without much meaning.

The shortness of the distance between the practical positions marked out by the colonists at the outset of the crisis with Great Britain and at the end, together with the steadiness and consistency of movement, may be explained by the unvarying purpose that informed American actions. This purpose was to suffer as little interference by the metropolis as possible while still remaining within the protective framework of the empire. Unarticulated at the beginning of the crisis, it would find expression at the end in the claim to equivalent status of the colonial assemblies with the imperial legislature, the tie between them being their common relationship to the King. "The connexion and harmony between Great Britain and us," Wilson concluded his essay, "which it is her interest and ours mutually to cultivate, and on which her prosperity, as well as ours, so materially depends, will be better preserved by the operation of the legal prerogatives of the crown, than by the exertion of an unlimited authority of parliament."[25] A marked consistency of action was dictated by an equal consistency of purpose. The colonists' appetite did not grow with the eating; it was there from the start.

Do the arguments that served to justify purpose show a similar consistency, or do they betray such mutations as to support the view that the Americans used them according to the exigencies of circumstances and interest? There is no question but that the arguments of the colonists did undergo change in the course of the long dispute that eventuated in war. At issue is the scope of the change and the degree to which it responded to the needs imposed by the conflict. Consistency of purpose is of course no guarantee of consistency in justifying purpose. Quite the contrary may be true. To a number of historians it was true in the case of the Americans. Step by step, Carl L. Becker concluded in his review of the process by which the Americans moved toward independence, "the colonists modified their theory to suit their needs." In Becker's view this was unavoidable, given the colonists' very con-

[25] *Wilson*, p. 745.

sistency of purpose: "for the underlying purpose which conditioned their action was always the determination to be free. They felt that they had been free in fact, and that they ought therefore to be free in law."[26]

The modifications in theory are undoubtedly there. Still, what stands out in reviewing the justification given for resisting the claims of Parliament is the consistency with which the colonial argument was developed. Again, it is instructive to compare the Stamp Act Congress and its successor in 1774. The significance of the earlier Congress did not lie in its profession of "all due subordination" to Parliament but the qualifications it made to this subordination. The significance of the First Continental Congress did not lie in the consent it gave to the exercise of certain acts by Parliament but its denial that any subordination was owed to the imperial legislature.

Was a very large step, or a series of large steps, required in theory to move from the first to the second position? Or was the justification of 1774 already implicit in the arguments of 1766? The answer is not apparent in the view that the colonists had progressed from a reliance in 1766 on the rights of Englishmen to a reliance in 1774 on the rights of man. It is not apparent if only because the rights of Englishmen were considered to encompass the rights of man. In this respect, the 1774 Declaration of Rights, though it appealed to "the immutable laws of nature," did not build upon a substantially larger foundation than had the Declaration of the Stamp Act Congress. Whatever the significance one gives the appeal to certain fundamental rights considered as inalienable, and thus beyond the power of any lawgiver to alter or destroy, this appeal formed an integral part of the colonial position from the outset.[27]

---

[26] *Declaration of Independence*, p. 135. Becker's view has drawn severe criticism by later historians. Gordon Wood complains that, for Becker, "the political theory of the Americans takes on an unreal and even fatuous quality"; "Rhetoric and Reality in the American Revolution," p. 8. But Becker did not suggest this. What he did clearly argue was that purpose—the desire to be free—influenced justification. The point seems incontestable. At the same time, Becker's analysis of theory, focused as it was on change, underestimated the essential continuity of colonial arguments.

[27] The most famous proponent of this appeal was that stormy petrel James Otis, whose impact on early American radicalism was considerable. Otis did not question the supremacy of Parliament over the colonies. There was in his thought no distinction between the realm and the dominions. In his 1764 pamphlet, *The Rights of the British Colonies Asserted and*

In denying Parliament's right to tax them, on the grounds that they were not represented at Westminster and could not be so represented, the colonists had not denied the supremacy of Parliament. Taxation was a special form of legislation which presumably required that it be distinguished from other forms. The case was otherwise, however, when legislation dealt with matters of internal polity which did not touch on taxation. Yet by 1768, and in some cases even earlier, the Americans were challenging the right of Parliament to legislate over any matters of internal polity. In 1766 Franklin had anticipated not only this broader claim to exemption from parliamentary authority but the still broader claim to total exemption, just as he had anticipated the grounds on which this progressive denial would be made. Responding to a question put to him in a committee of the House of Commons—whether the Americans' denial of Parliament's right to impose on them an internal tax might not be taken to imply a complete denial of Parliament's authority—he observed: "Many arguments have been lately used here to show them that there is no difference, and that if you have no right to tax them internally, you have none to tax them externally, or make any other law to bind them. At present they do not reason so, but in time they may be convinced by these arguments." "These arguments" were essentially one argument, and Franklin, with his customary lucidity, had in his testimony already alluded to it. The colonies, he declared, "are not supposed to be within the realm; they have assemblies of their own, which are their parliaments."[28]

Here was the essential distinction between the realm and the dominions, between the area within Parliament's reach and those areas that lay beyond its reach because they were not represented. By the 1760s that distinction had long become anathema to the British political nation, which accepted as a sacred tenet of the constitution that the realm and the dominions were one, and over which absolute authority belonged to the King-in-Parliament. The Americans had never seriously contested this interpretation of the

---

Proved, he was at pains to affirm that the empire is one state, with Parliament its sovereign. But if Parliament is sovereign and its power absolute, still that power cannot be arbitrary. It cannot be tyrannical without violating that law which is not within Parliament's power to violate. "[If] every prince since *Nimrod* had been a tyrant, it would not prove a *right* to tyrannize. There can be no prescription old enough to supersede the law of nature and the grant of God Almighty, who has given to all men a natural right to be *free*, and they have it ordinarily in their power to make themselves so if they please"; *Pamphlets of the American Revolution, 1750–1776*, p. 426.

[28] "Examination," in *The Papers of Benjamin Franklin*, 13:153, 156.

British constitution before the 1760s, but neither had they experienced the possible consequences that might be drawn from it. When they did experience these consequences in the form of an exercise of the power of taxation, they denied the interpretation, though at first, and explicitly, only in rejecting Parliament's authority to tax them.

Nonetheless, the basis of an ever-expanding claim of exemption, a claim that would find fulfillment in the complete rejection of Parliament's authority, was laid in this initial denial. Once the claim was made, where were its boundaries to be drawn and on what grounds? The view that they could be limited to Parliament's power to levy a tax, and this because taxation was a special kind of legislation, carried no greater logic and persuasiveness than did the view that there were no boundaries at all, that the legislative power and representation were inseparable. Moreover, once the latter view was applied beyond the sphere of imperial taxation, as was almost immediately the case, the persuasiveness of the argument that a line might be drawn between acknowledging and denying Parliament's power over the colonies was further undermined. An argument might still be made on practical grounds for conceding parliamentary regulation over certain matters—"from the necessity of the case, and a regard to the mutual interests of both countries," as Resolution 4 of the Declaration of Rights puts it—but it could be made only with considerable difficulty on grounds of principle.[29]

The distance, then, between the initial great challenge to Parliament's authority and the final challenge seems to be not appreciably greater in theory than in practice. Neither in their substantive claims to exemption from this authority nor in the principles they invoked in support of these claims did the colonists make sudden and dramatic shifts. They did not make them if only for the reason that after the Stamp Act crisis there was no need to make them. There was only the need to consolidate, while making

---

[29] The point was made succinctly by James Wilson: "Allegiance to the king and obedience to the parliament are. founded on very different principles. The former is founded on protection: the latter, on representation. . . . The American colonies are not bound by the acts of the British parliament, because they are not represented by it." The colonies, Wilson went on to argue, had first denied the right of Parliament to impose taxes on them. A denial of parliamentary supremacy and colonial dependence in instances of taxation "is, in effect, a denial of it in all other instances. For, if dependence is an obligation to conform to the will or law of the superior state, any exceptions to that obligation must destroy the dependence"; *Wilson*, 2:736, 738, 741.

modest additions to, a position that would lead inexorably to the complete rejection of Parliament's authority. The line that many found not to exist in 1774 had only to be lightly brushed over given the developments of the better part of a decade.[30]

[V]

In denying that any subordination was owed to Parliament, the First Continental Congress did not deny the allegiance that was owed to the King. The conflict between Parliament and colonies was not to be interpreted, the Congress insisted, as a conflict between King and colonies. In its petition addressed to George III, the Congress declared: "We wish not a diminution of the prerogative, nor do we solicit the grant of any new right in our favour. Your royal authority over us and our connexion with Great Britain, we shall always carefully and zealously endeavour to support and maintain."[31] The colonies were not bound by, or dependent on, Parliament because they were not represented in it. They were bound by, and dependent on, the King because they enjoyed his protection. The First Continental Congress declared

---

[30] The view taken here does not ignore the position taken by Charles McIlwain in his classic essay, *The American Revolution*, that prior to 1768 the Americans had based their position on the whig doctrine that "the British Empire was one commonwealth, and Parliament was its master" (158), whereas after that date, and particularly by 1774, America's constitutional position "was not Whig at all: it was a position in some respects not merely non-Whig, but anti-Whig; for the doctrine of a parliament both omnipotent and imperial, against which they were really fighting, was more a Whig than a Tory principle" (159). In the contemporaneous classic of Becker, *Declaration of Independence*, p. 97, substantially the same point is made. In quoting Dickinson's 1768 statement that the colonies were "as much dependent on Great Britain as one free people could be on another," Becker noted that "the assumption on which it rests was to be the foundation upon which the colonists built up their theory from this time on. That assumption was that the Americans were one 'people,' the English another, and each a 'free' people." Even if this view of the American position is substantially accurate, there would remain the question of the significance to attach to it, even in theory, if the acknowledgment of Parliament's supremacy was not found to preclude the making of important exceptions to its supreme authority. Whatever the logical objections to admitting that the empire "was one commonwealth, and Parliament was its master" while insisting that there were nevertheless important limits to Parliament's power over the colonies, the point remains that this was precisely the position of the colonies in 1765–66. The Stamp Act Congress, to repeat, speaks of "all due Subordination" to Parliament and not of all subordination. If "all due Subordination" excluded taxation and, quite possibly, other legislation affecting matters of internal polity, then clearly this profession of subordination could be emptied of almost all content, as Hutchinson was to observe. Parliament's omnipotence would then become a principle with hardly any substance—the grin without the Cheshire cat.

[31] *Journals of the Continental Congress*, 1:119.

its independence only from Parliament, not from the King. The latter they would declare their independence from only after the King had proclaimed the colonies in a state of rebellion (August 23, 1775). Even with George III's proclamation, the formal dissolution of colonial government as exercised by the crown did not occur until the following year. At the time of the First Continental Congress, however, there was no disposition to challenge the authority of the King out of Parliament. Allegiance to the same prince, James Wilson declared, "produces a union of hearts [and] a union of measures through the whole British dominions."

What did the Americans intend when they said they wished "not a diminution of the prerogative"? There is no reason to believe that their intention was to acquiesce in the exercise of such powers by the crown as they had denied to Parliament and that what the King might not do in Parliament he might nevertheless do out of Parliament. In the list drawn up at Philadelphia of acts of Parliament considered as "infringements and violations of the rights of the colonists"—a list that comprised almost the entirety of post–1763 legislation for the colonies—there is no measure that would have been accepted simply because its origin lay in prerogative. Surely the colonists would have rejected with equal finality the attempt to effect through prerogative those changes Parliament made in the Massachusetts charter. Nor would it have mattered to them that, once Parliament's authority to legislate for the colonies was denied, they faced, in Charles McIlwain's words, "the alternative of a royal prerogative with no limits to its power except the self-limitation imposed by the promises made by Kings to the colonists in their Charters, a limitation which had proved to be of very doubtful value." McIlwain thought this acceptance of prerogative the "weak spot in the American position," and that in accepting it the colonists "undeniably incurred enormous risk of future oppression through a prerogative unchecked by Parliament."[32] Fortunately, the quick movement to American independence meant that the risk never had to be faced.

The colonists had continued to accept royal prerogative, while rejecting the authority of Parliament, not simply because their immediate struggle was with Parliament. In concentrating upon Parliament, they had not only followed the counsel "sufficient unto

[32] *American Revolution*, pp. 194–95.

the day is the evil thereof." They had accepted royal prerogative because they knew that a century of British constitutional development could not easily be reversed, if it could be reversed at all. The King out of Parliament could not take those measures that would endanger what Americans now considered to be their settled liberties without provoking a first-class constitutional crisis. The hesitancy of government to proceed by way of prerogative in dealing with the colonies had been demonstrated on a number of occasions. In responding to the crisis set off by the Boston Tea Party, the North ministry had backed off from proceeding by way of executive authority, in large part owing to the doubts it entertained over the legality of such procedure and the fear that the actions it then contemplated taking through royal decree—the closing of the port of Boston and punishing those who had been the ring leaders in the recent violence—would evoke the cry of abuse of prerogative. The colonial leaders were not oblivious to all this. They knew that if they were not constrained by action of Parliament they would not be effectively constrained at all.

[VI]

If the work of the men who gathered at Philadelphia further intensified the crisis with the metropolis, it was not because they pressed novel claims but because the claims they did press and the manner in which they pressed them left the imperial state with no alternative but to harden still further its position. The view persists that although the Congress was firm in defense of American claims and insistent that Great Britain bear the burden of initiating negotiations, it did not take an intransigent position. Moderates could believe, this argument runs, "that the program of the First Congress constituted a feasible basis for reconciliation."[33] Nor is this view affected by the fact that the Congress neither made any substantial concessions to metropolitan claims nor, for that matter, provided the least intimation that it might be prepared to make concessions. For the marked asymmetry in the bargaining positions of the parties presumably ruled out this strategy, even had the Congress been disposed to follow it. Holding much the weaker

[33] Rakove, "Decision for Independence," p. 234.

position, the colonies could not afford to make concessions. The metropolis instead ·enjoyed this advantage, though it refused to employ it either to serious attempts toward reconciliation, or, should this have proven impossible, to exploitation of the persisting differences separating radicals and moderates.[34]

In what ways, however, was the conciliatory disposition of the Congress manifested? Clearly, it will not do to point to the constraints the Congress imposed upon Massachusetts as evidence of this disposition. In advising the people of that province to maintain a "defensive" posture toward the government, the Congress assumed that such posture would prove successful in defeating government efforts to implement the Coercive Acts. The course of "peaceable" resistance Massachusetts was urged to follow—a course that was deemed quite compatible with measures of harassment, intimidation, and the assault of government officials and supporters—reflected the dictates of prudence. It was calculated to achieve the ends desired at the least risk. These prudential considerations, however, afford no evidence of a conciliatory disposition. They merely show that so long as a strategy entailing a substantially lower risk appeared successful, there was every reason for holding to it. While satisfying the illusions of many would-be moderates that the door to reconciliation was thus left open, the strategy confronted the British with the alternatives either to concede that they could not govern or to attempt to govern by armed force. If the latter alternative was chosen, the onus for initiating war would fall on London. But by far the prevailing expectation was that in the end the government would shrink from drawing the sword and once again adopt a policy of conciliation.

If the constraints placed on Massachusetts cannot be taken as evidence of a conciliatory disposition, does the substantive position taken by the Congress support the view that the door was left open to compromise? On the fundamental issue of sovereignty, the question seems no more than rhetorical given the unanimity and insistence with which the delegates rejected the claim of parliamentary supremacy. The significance of this rejection was not substantially mitigated by the modest concessions made in the list of grievances

[34] Ibid., p. 272. "If the difference of opinion and attitude among the delegates were relatively narrow, they were nevertheless real, and they could have been easily exploited by a British government willing to adopt even a moderately conciliatory approach toward the demands of the First Congress."

and for the most part evidently dictated by expediential considerations. The imperial state was called upon to repeal the Coercive
Acts and to acknowledge as invalid almost the whole of the post–
1763 measures affecting the colonies. By doing so, it had to concede, and in unmistakable terms, the claim of parliamentary supremacy. In return, the colonies through their Congress were willing to "pass over for the present" a number of unspecified measures
taken prior to 1763 alleged to have violated colonial rights and to
permit Great Britain to continue to regulate their trade, not as a
matter of inherent right but as a concession subject to restrictions
at once indeterminate in character and subject to interpretation as
occasion necessitated by the colonies. In the petition the Congress
addressed to the King, the proposed terms of settlement are rounded
out by the assurance that the colonies would "defray the charge of
the administration of justice, the support of civil government, and
the defense protection and security of the colonies" as their several
legislatures shall judge "just and suitable to their respective circumstances."[35] In a word, the assemblies would remain free to
assess and to act upon their responsibilities as they saw fit. The
status of equivalence could, after all, demand no less.

There was no conciliatory position here, not even the suggestion
of such position. There was no indication of willingness to compromise the issues that formed the core of the imperial-colonial
conflict. Perhaps those issues simply were not susceptible of compromise. Certainly, it is very difficult to see how that issue of issues,
the problem of sovereignty, could have been directly compromised. At best, it might have been finessed, given a willingness
to do so on both sides. What is relevant here is that the effort was
not made by the Congress. The point must not be obscured by the
undoubted desire of the delegates to avoid war and to remain within
the empire. The test of a conciliatory policy cannot be found in
the desire to avoid war but in the price the colonists were willing
to pay to realize that desire. The Congress betrayed throughout a
singular unwillingness to pay any but the most nominal of prices.

Perhaps this intransigence would have been equally apparent
even had the delegates believed that they were dealing from weakness and could not afford a serious effort at compromise. But they
did not so view their position, and the fact that they did not is

[35] *Journals of the Continental Congress*, 1:119.

critical. Once again the metropolis was expected to give way before the resolution of the colonies, this time more united than ever before and possessed of a means of pressure—the Continental Association—that could not but give the British serious pause. At the time, moreover, this conviction of relative strength and advantage did not seem misplaced. In the autumn of 1774 the Americans did hold a position of advantage. They had successfully defied the efforts of the imperial state to impose its will by means short of armed force. They had demonstrated that in Massachusetts metropolitan authority was no more than a thin pretense, thereby raising the distinct prospect that the same might be true in other colonies as well. They had already shown that an aroused, and increasingly armed, populace could be effectively dealt with, if at all, only by measures the British were still unprepared to take.

The colonists did not enter upon the final crisis with the metropolis in the manner of men who felt their backs to the wall. Instead, they responded to the Coercive Acts with a remarkable degree of self-assurance. The First Continental Congress accurately reflected that assurance in the unyielding position it marked out, a position that, once taken, would not be altered. The Second Continental Congress, which met in May 1775, would witness the feeble and abortive attempts of a minority to reopen some of the positions the preceding Congress had adopted. The attempts issued instead in nothing more than another petition to the King, which was duly rejected in the manner of the first petition. The 1775 Congress thus confirmed the policy of the 1774 Congress. It proved no more disposed to reconciliation than was its predecessor, and its significance was in shaping a strategy of armed resistance.

There was only one apparently serious division in the First Continental Congress, and the practical significance even of that division must be questioned. Once parliamentary supremacy over the colonies was rejected in principle, as it was at the outset and without debate, there remained to be drawn the consequences of this rejection. It is no more than a partial truth to say that the moderates at Philadelphia may be characterized by a reluctance to draw these consequences. In most respects, they did draw them— and not only in terms of principle but also in terms of practice. In the unanimous support given to the Suffolk Resolves, the moderates no less than the radicals committed themselves to modes of resisting the imperial state which, once given, could not readily be withdrawn. In the equally unanimous approval of the Continental Association, the moderates no less than the radicals committed themselves to a course of action Great Britain could no more allow to succeed than to suffer indefinitely the successful defiance of Massachusetts. Under these circumstances, acceptance by Great Britain of the principles urged by the "moderates" at Philadelphia would have represented an act indistinguishable from outright capitulation. And this was an outcome that no government in Britain could as yet bring itself to face.

FOURTEEN

The Decision for War, 1775

[I]

It is remarkable, one writer has declared, "that of the men most responsible for British policy in 1774 none should have comprehended clearly the nature of the crisis that confronted the empire."[1] These are not the words of a neo-whig historian but of the distinguished imperial historian, Lawrence Henry Gipson. In this judgment, at least, Gipson is as one with those who otherwise are very far from sharing his admiring view of the First British Empire and his explanation of the dispute that eventuated in its breakup: the failure of the North ministry, in the prevailing view, was at bottom a failure of understanding. In this, the ministry not only followed in the footsteps of its predecessors but managed to go considerably beyond them.

What was it, however, that the North government had so egregiously failed to understand? Certainly, the government did not misunderstand the central issue at stake between the metropolis and the colonies. North had articulated that issue with clarity at the outset of the crisis precipitated by the Boston Tea Party. The dispute, he declared in the winter of 1774, could no longer be defined in terms of Parliament's right simply to tax the colonies but to govern them at all. The American secretary expressed a similar view. "It is not the mere Claim of Exemption from the Authority of Parliament in a particular Case that has brought on the present Crisis," Lord Dartmouth wrote to General Gage in early June 1774, "it is actual Disobedience and open Resistance that have compelled coercive Measures."[2]

The position subsequently marked out by the First Continental Congress vindicated the accuracy of the assessment that the issue

[1] *The British Empire before the American Revolution*, 12:259.
[2] *The Correspondence of General Thomas Gage with the Secretaries of State, 1763–1775*, 2:165.

of sovereignty formed the core of the crisis confronting the empire. This being so, it was not the government, but the opposition in Parliament, that misunderstood the real nature of the crisis. For it was the opposition that persisted in the belief that the Americans were contending for little more than the right to tax themselves. This was the meaning of the argument, brought against the government, that it was "contending for a point of honour" and "struggling to obtain a most ridiculous superiority."[3] The point of honor was the submission by the colonies to a power of Parliament that experience had shown could not effectively be exercised, or, at any rate, could not effectively be exercised save at a cost that was prohibitive. If the colonists would not in fact submit to taxation by Parliament, the attempt to make them concede the principle was indeed a struggle to obtain a most ridiculous superiority, particularly so long as they were not otherwise challenging the sovereign power of Parliament over America. If anywhere, it is here—with the opposition's insistence that the colonies were not otherwise denying Parliament's sovereign power—that may be found the signal misunderstanding of the crisis in the imperial-colonial relationship.

It is quite true that the men most responsible for British policy in 1774 did not comprehend the full dimensions of the crisis they faced. Had they done so, they would have appreciated that the security and well-being of the metropolis would not suffer a crippling—and, to many, even a mortal—blow with the loss of the American colonies. In this sense, the North ministry may fairly be charged with a failure of understanding. In the same sense, however, almost the entire British political nation may also be so charged. A very few seers apart, all shared the assumption that the North American colonies formed the basis of British strength and prosperity and that the loss of America—which was equated with the destruction of parliamentary sovereignty over it—would reduce Great Britain to the status of an impoverished, third-rate nation. The debate between government and opposition was not over this assumption. Accepted as an article of faith by virtually every significant political group in the country, the debate simply took for granted what war and defeat would show to be false.

This is not the failure of understanding with which the North

---

[3] *PH*, 17:100 (Dowdeswell).

government is commonly charged, and, to the extent it is, there is surely nothing remarkable about it. Quite the contrary, what would have been remarkable is precisely that kind of comprehension and insight not to be expected of governments in any age. Even had the ministry possessed these qualities, it could not have translated them into policy. No government could have made the response required to meet the American demands—which, at the very least, meant the repeal of the Coercive Acts—and remained in power. Subsequent events would show that even a policy of limited concessions, though treated with scorn by the Americans, evoked considerable dissatisfaction among supporters of government.

[II]

Once a very imposing and, indeed, altogether unrealistic standard of judgment is put aside, the charge that the government misunderstood the nature of the crisis is placed in clearer perspective. Although the responsible ministers appreciated the principal issue at stake with the colonies clearly enough, they did not act consistently with this appreciation. Was their failure to do so one of understanding or, rather, was it a failure of will? After hostilities had begun, the government understandably preferred the former explanation. It had presumably failed to take more vigorous measures at an earlier stage of the crisis because it had not been aware of the strength and determination of the resistance movement in the colonies. In October 1775, Lord North acknowledged to the Commons that "he had been deceived in events . . . that he had adapted his measures last session to the then state of affairs, not imagining that all America would have armed in the cause. Administration had proceeded upon the information they had received."[4] Dartmouth took substantially the same line as North: he had been deceived by the reports he had received from the colonial governors.

This retrospective defense of a policy that failed to bear the promised results was more than special pleading. The government had been misinformed by many reports from its officials about

[4] *PH*, 18:78–91.

conditions in the colonies. In the case of New York, a province on which Whitehall had based so much of its hopes for splitting the colonies, a superannuated lieutenant governor exuded a misplaced optimism throughout the fall and winter of 1774/75. As late as April 1775, scarcely more than a month before New York would unmistakably show the face of rebellion, Lieutenant Governor Cadwallader Colden advised Dartmouth that "a great part of the people" were against appointing delegates to a second Continental Congress and that the "moderation, loyalty and affection" of the provincial assembly testified to a permanent reconciliation.[5] In Virginia, Governor Dunmore, though confronted since late 1774 with an alternative government backed by substantial and growing armed force, was still assuring London in May 1775 that with a handful of the King's troops he could reestablish royal authority.[6] The deposed governor of North Carolina, outbidding all in his dreams of restoring imperial government, promised his superiors as late as June that if General Gage would only give him support with arms and ammunition he would be able to raise an army "to exceed thirty thousand, and with which I could effectually restore order here and in South Carolina and hold Virginia in such awe as to prevent that province sending any succour to the northward; added to which, such a head made here against rebellion would draw over to it such multitudes of well-affected subjects of His Majesty from other colonies, who only want countenance to induce them to take an open part in favour of government, as would put it in my power to reduce to order and obedience every colony to the southward of Pennsylvania."[7]

These reports, and yet others in a similar vein, surely cannot be dismissed when assessing the government's understanding of the situation in the colonies. At the same time, they must be seen against the very different information also coming to London, in-

[5] Cadwallader Colden to earl of Dartmouth, *Documents of the American Revolution, 1770–1783*, 9:91. Colden's letters were not always suffused with optimism. On December 7, 1774, he wrote to Dartmouth that "however considerable the numbers may be who disapprove of violent riotous measures, yet the spirit of mobbing is so much abroad it is in the power of a few people at any time to raise a mob and that the gentlemen and men of property will not turn out to suppress them. I fear, my Lord, there is too much truth in this representation. It is a dreadful situation. If we are not rescued from it by the wisdom and firmness of Parliament, the colonies must soon fall into distraction and every calamity annexed to a total annihilation of government" *Documents of the Revolution*, 8:238.
[6] Ibid., 9:110–11.
[7] Joseph Martin to Dartmouth, ibid., p. 213.

formation that proved only too accurate. From Boston, beginning in early September 1774 and continuing through to the outbreak of hostilities the following spring, came a steady stream of the most ominous reports on developments in Massachusetts and, eventually, in New England. Their principal source was General Gage. Dartmouth was to complain, both at the time and in retrospect, that Gage's reports were incomplete and misleading. The charge was unfair and gratuitous. Apart from an occasional lapse,[8] Gage's correspondence with the American secretary reflected a remarkably realistic—if pessimistic—assessment of conditions in the storm center of the rebellion.

The import of the commander-in-chief's letters to Dartmouth in the fall of 1774 was that Massachusetts—and New England as a whole—was in a state of rebellion, that the groups supporting the rebellion could not be palmed off as a Boston rabble but had to be taken quite seriously, that the Coercive Acts could be enforced and imperial authority reestablished only by first making a conquest of the New England provinces, that to act prematurely and without adequate forces would be very imprudent and might well result in a decision adverse to the metropolis, that Gage's forces (approximately three thousand) were altogether inadequate to the task, and that in the absence of the forces needed, which were estimated at twenty thousand, a temporary suspension of the Coercive Acts appeared advisable (the latter recommendation being conveyed indirectly to Dartmouth through Thomas Hutchinson).[9] Gage was to suffer the fate of most bearers of bad tidings. Whitehall did not want to hear that in New England it was confronted with war. It was unwilling even to consider seriously the request for an army of twenty thousand. And the advice to suspend the Coercive Acts while building up the British army deeply offended its imperial pride. Gage's fall into disfavor was immediate and irreparable.[10]

---

[8] Inexplicably, after a series of pessimistic, though accurate, reports, Gage sent several mildly optimistic letters to Dartmouth in January and February 1775. The basis for this small ray of optimism was quite insubstantial, including the hopeful signs Gage thought he detected in New York and Pennsylvania—signs which scarcely relieved him of his plight in New England; letters of January 18 and 27, and February 17, *Gage*, 1:390–92.

[9] Ibid., pp. 369–72 (September 2), 372–75 (September 12), 376–77 (September 25), 380–81 (October 30), 381–83 (October 30), and 386–88 (December 15). All letters are from Gage to Dartmouth. On the letter to Hutchinson on suspending the Coercive Acts, see John R. Alden, *General Gage in America* (Baton Rouge, 1948), p. 220.

[10] *The Correspondence of King George the Third from 1760 to December 1783*, 3: no. 1508; *The Diary and Letters of His Excellency Thomas Hutchinson, Esq.*, 1:297.

Yet his estimate not only proved sound, it was substantially corroborated by other officials, as well as by a number of private observers, in the northern colonies.

The government had not been deceived about developments in New England. Was it deceived by the results of the First Continental Congress? Reports on the proceedings at Philadelphia had begun to reach London by early November. By middle December, the ministry was in full possession of the work of the Congress. The demands of the Americans were not obscure. They were not couched in ambiguous terms. The Coercive Acts had provoked a full and explicit articulation of a position that had been long in the making. The complete rejection of Parliament's authority over the colonies, together with the claim of equality between the colonial assemblies and Westminster, was the culmination of a movement that since 1766 had shown few signs of abating. Moreover, the now open challenge to the metropolis had not come from a Congress that could be seen as representing no more than a minority of the colonies. Although its claim to represent all the colonies might still be questioned—and particularly in the case of New York—there was little reason to doubt that the Congress represented politically effective opinion in most of the colonies. Equally, there was little reason to believe in the wake of the Congress that Massachusetts might somehow be isolated from the rest of the provinces.

The argument that the government had been misinformed about the true state of the colonies becomes even more tenuous when one considers the entire course of events from early 1774 to the summer of 1775. After all, the incident that triggered the final crisis was not an isolated event. Although the Boston Tea Party had been the most dramatic act of resistance to British authority, the rejection of East India tea had occurred elsewhere, at Philadelphia and New York. In no place did the tea get past the customs house. This successful defiance of imperial authority pointed to the evident debility of colonial government throughout the provinces. In Massachusetts, Gage reported in the late summer, it no longer existed. By the close of 1774 the same could be said of the other New England states, with the possible exception of New Hampshire. In early January 1775, the American Department informed the colonial governors that they were to use their "utmost endeavours" to prevent appointment of delegates to the next Continental Congress, scheduled to meet in May. But the governors, as most of them were to acknowledge, were helpless to prevent such appointment, whether by provincial assemblies or by popular meetings. Even the irrepressibly optimistic Colden had to report that although the assembly of the province had rejected a motion to appoint delegates to Congress, the appointments would be made by the people and that it was not within his power to prevent this. By the spring of 1775, there were only two colonies north of Virginia that even retained the semblance of royal government, and in the wake of Lexington they, too, were swept away. Only in the southern colonies did British administration hang on, though pathetically so, for a few remaining months.[11]

It is against this general background that the government's subsequent argument of having been misled must be considered. Was the ministry deceived by others or did it deceive itself? Did the North government's failure to act consistently with its appreciation of the principal issue at stake stem from a real misunderstanding of the situation in America or from an unwillingness to face up to the logical implications of a situation it understood well enough? The latter explanation appears much the more persuasive. Despite a great deal of evidence in its possession, and from which only one conclusion could be safely drawn, the ministry continued to cling to its optimistic assessment of conditions in the colonies almost until the summer of 1775. Its alleged misunderstanding, even if in part unconscious, can be attributed only to its lack of will.[12]

[11] See Dartmouth to Governors, circular letter, January 4, and Colden to Dartmouth, April 5, 9:91–93, and pp. 14–17 of Davies's introduction to the decline of royal government in the southern colonies and for references to relevant reports of colonial governors, in *Documents of the Revolution*.

[12] It was presumably the reports of the governors which prompted Dartmouth to the confessions in the Lords (March 14, 1776) that he "was willing to suppose, that the disorders in that country were local, and had chiefly pervaded the hearts of an inconsiderable number of men, who were only formidable because they possessed the power of factious delusion and imposition. I all along expected, that the body of the people . . . would soon perceive the danger in which they were precipitating themselves, and return to their duty"; *PH*, 18:1254. B. D. Bargar, *Lord Dartmouth and the American Revolution* (Columbia, 1965), pp. 158–59, 174, is at pains to emphasize that the American secretary acted on incomplete and misleading information. But Dartmouth had much less excuse for the ignorance he later professed than he cared to admit, and his complaints that Gage's reports left him in the dark were particularly baseless. If Dartmouth was so misinformed as he was later to claim, and that Bargar attempts to support, the ignorance was largely of his own choosing. His persistence in considering the movement in Massachusetts as no more than "merely the Acts of a tumultuous Rabble, without any Appearance of general Concert" had little excuse in the light of the reports he received from Gage; *Gage*, 2: 179. Davies, in *Documents of the Revolution*, 9:8, is right in pointing out that this revealed "an aristocratic incomprehension of the capacity of the colonists to produce leaders when they needed them." It also revealed, however, Dartmouth's unwillingness to confront the prospect of war, a prospect Gage had squarely raised, and urged, and which Dartmouth, in the above quoted letter, rejected almost with an air of resentment.

[III]

This lack of will was apparent from the outset of the final crisis. It must account for a substantial part of the optimism with which the government embarked on its policy of coercing Massachusetts. The assumptions that underlay policy and that proved so misplaced were reflections of more than ignorance and pride. They were also the work of men who badly wanted to believe them to be true, and who did so because they could not bring themselves to confront the prospects either of war with America or of capitulation to its demands. Throughout the spring and summer of 1774 the government found no great difficulty living in its dream world. Although by late summer that world was already beginning visibly to crumble, the news from America—given the usual five weeks to two months delay—allowed optimism to persist. Even so, by early fall, this optimism had received its first hard blows with reports of colonial resistance. By late October and early November, the news from Boston and Philadelphia appeared to give the lie to the assumption that Massachusetts could effectively be intimidated by a policy that stopped short of employing force, just as it placed in grave doubt the assumption that the Bay Colony might be isolated from the other provinces.

Confronted with a breakdown of policy, what did the government do? Its earlier optimism now badly shaken, yet its unwillingness to confront alternatives that seemed equally unpalatable almost as strong as before, the North ministry vacillated. Its indecision accurately reflected the state of mind of responsible officials. A harder rhetoric alternated with a disposition to seek a way out through conciliatory measures. Although America had to "submit," there was a renewed effort to find a formula for exacting submission the colonies might find acceptable precisely because the act of submission would be somehow disguised. The record does not reveal any member of the cabinet committed to tough talk *and* tough measures. This is true of the King as well. The view that George wanted to move to war with the colonies in the fall of 1774 is not borne out by the King's expressed views to his chief ministers. Clearly, the King was more militant than his ministers at this point. Even so, his militancy did not go beyond the measures already being taken in the colonies, measures that had proved plainly inadequate to the ends the North ministry sought.[13]

In adopting a policy of coercion the government had still not faced up to the prospect of war. The Massachusetts legislation had signaled an end to the earlier policy of conciliation. Henceforth, the metropolis would no longer give way before colonial defiance of its authority. But what it would do if defiance nevertheless persisted and, in response to the new policy, even radically escalated had never been determined. If anything, this contingency had been all but precluded by the government; the new policy had been seen as an alternative both to further concessions and to war. At worst, it might require the metropolis to take police action. A police action, however, was still not to be confused with war. In the British drift to armed hostilities with America there was not one rubicon that was crossed but two, and the second was by far the more difficult. Whitehall would only cross the second in the summer of 1775, well over a year after it had crossed the first.

In the meantime, London temporized, unable to choose either war or peace. In the circumstances of the late fall of 1774 peace had become indistinguishable from capitulation to the demands of the First Continental Congress and thus indistinguishable from the de facto independence of America. The only viable alternative, though, was to abandon the hope that the growing rebellion might be contained by a police action and move quickly to war. In essence, this meant that the British would have had to decide upon measures at the end of 1774 that they only decided upon in the course of the following year and then mainly after hostilities had begun. If Gage's reports of the Massachusetts militia were to be credited, and the government had no reasons for not doing so, Boston would have to be strengthened immediately with at least an additional five to seven thousand troops. This in turn would require placing the army on a war footing since there was no assurance that Gage could take offensive measures in the countryside even with a force of ten thousand (a force that would be no better than half of what he had earlier estimated he needed). In response to the American challenge of the Continental Association, let alone to the prospect of the colonies receiving war supplies from Europe, Britain would have to institute a blockade of the colonies, or, at the very least,

---

[13] Cf. King to Lord North, September 11, 1774, *George III*, 3: no. 1508.

attempt to shut off the vital trade in gunpowder. Finally, the persisting hope that Massachusetts—or New England—could be isolated would have to be abandoned and the resistance in the colonies formally recognized for what it was, a rebellion.

When these possible measures are laid alongside the actual measures the government was prepared to take in December/January of 1774/75, the distance that still separated Whitehall from the second rubicon is apparent. Whereas before late fall 1774, London had scarcely given serious thought to the implications of a substantial police action, by the end of the year it was at least prepared to do that. But a police action was still not a war, and the distinction was pointedly drawn by Dartmouth in the important instructions sent to Gage in late January 1775.[14]

Historians have regularly found in these instructions evidence that the British government had decided to initiate war with the colonies. Instead, the instructions indicate that the government had decided to press for more vigorous action by its commander-in-chief, though action that still belonged to a category of measures which stopped well short of full-scale war. Dartmouth did not fail to make this clear to Gage. In reply to the latter's view of the preceding fall that nothing less was required than a conquest of New England, a task estimated to require no less than twenty thousand men, the American secretary roundly declared he was "unwilling to believe that matters are as yet come to that issue." The overall tone of the instructions was to reprimand Gage for what his superiors in London had come to regard as undue passivity. He was told that he might shortly expect reinforcements, though the additional forces would still give him no more than a total of some five thousand. Even so, Dartmouth harbored little doubt that with a force of this magnitude, Gage no longer had any excuse for not taking more aggressive measures. He was instructed that a "first and essential step . . . towards reestablishing government would be to arrest and imprison the principal actors and abettors in the Provincial Congress." Moreover, while keeping possession of Boston, he was also "to give protection to Salem and the friends of government at that place." Since Massachusetts had been judged by the realm's principal law officers to be in a state of rebellion,[15]

[14] *Gage*, 2:179–83.
[15] *Documents of the Revolution*, 8:239–40.

Gage was also informed that he might exercise his power of martial law.[16] Whether he did so or not, however, had to depend upon circumstances on the spot, which only Gage could judge. Throughout this firmest of instructions yet sent to the British commander-in-chief, he was reminded that the expedience and propriety of the measures he would take depended upon his discretionary judgment. In the wake of Concord and Lexington, Dartmouth, blaming Gage for the consequences that the outbreak of hostilities immediately brought, would recall the several cautionary admonitions that attended the instructions.

The instructions tell a great deal about the government's position, Gage's dilemma as commander-in-chief, and the American secretary. Dartmouth's instructions were written after almost three months of relative silence on the part of the ministry. From early November, the few dispatches Gage received from London were mostly of a routine nature. By this time he had clearly fallen from grace. He would have been unceremoniously replaced by late December had it not been for the King's unwillingness to dishonor him in this manner. Gage's supposed sin was his timidity in dealing with the rebels. That he should have been so accused by those who had been models of timidity throughout 1774 was more than ironic. His real sin was that he had told the government unwelcome truths and had offered even more unwelcome advice. For this, he had to go, though the task of finding a replacement proved difficult. Amherst wisely refused the command when offered by the King. Instead, three major generals were sent to assist, and eventually to relieve, Gage—William Howe, Henry Clinton, and John Burgoyne. Howe, the next in line for supreme command, would demonstrate a startling incompetence both in Boston and later in the New York campaign. Clinton would show that he was a brilliant second, but only so long as he remained second. Burgoyne would resolutely lead a British force of seven thousand to defeat at Saratoga, confident almost to the end.

Gage was clearly not a general of considerable talents. Even so, he deserved a kinder fate. Because he served a government that was unwilling to concede the issue to the Americans, yet that also shrank from taking forcible measures until it had no alternative,

---

[16] Gage exercised this power only after Lexington. Gage to Dartmouth, June 12, 1775, *Gage*, 1:405.

the dilemma of the commander-in-chief was complete. When the government finally did order that he go over to the offensive, it typically did so in such manner as to relieve itself of responsibility if the measures it urged on Gage were to turn out badly. This is the meaning of Dartmouth's repeated cautionary admonitions, juxtaposed as they were with the exhortations that Gage bestir himself. The January 27 instructions do no credit to Dartmouth, who began them by accusing Gage of having failed to furnish the facts that the commander-in-chief had been faithfully sending his superior since late summer.

It has been suggested that Dartmouth did not instruct Gage to begin a war, that he reiterated the discretionary nature of the instructions, that Gage interpreted Dartmouth's letter as a call to action, and that Dartmouth was shocked by the reports of bloodshed consequent upon Lexington and Concord.[17] Dartmouth's shock is readily explained. Although intent on the due submission of the colonies, he could not accept responsibility for presiding over the means by which the end would have to be secured. This inability explains his repeated complaints against Gage and, in particular, his inexcusable attempt to place the blame for Concord and Lexington on Gage.[18] It is certainly the case that Gage interpreted Dartmouth's instructions as a call to action, for that is what they plainly were. It is equally the case that the commander-in-chief was not instructed to begin a war. But Gage did not so interpret the instructions. The April 19 move to Concord, undertaken to capture a reported stockpile of rebel arms, was not viewed by Gage as the opening of armed hostilities. He had taken similar moves since September of the preceding year and in October had received direct instructions from Dartmouth to seize rebel arms and ammunition where and when possible.[19] The instructions of January 27 had specifically urged Gage to arrest the rebel leaders in Massachusetts. They did not in any way preclude the action taken by the commander-in-chief.

The most that may be said of these instructions is that they reflected a greater willingness than before to accept the risks of war. This said, however, it must be added that in the circumstances of late 1774 and early 1775 an unwillingness to accept such risks

[17] Bargar, *Dartmouth*, pp. 164–66.
[18] Dartmouth to Gov. Franklin, July 5, 1775, *Documents of the Revolution*, 11:38–39.
[19] *Gage*, 2:176.

was tantamount to capitulation. So long as capitulation to American demands was ruled out, the North government had no choice but to accept risks that escalated as the intensity of the American response escalated. The government, it must be stressed, did not enjoy the tactical initiative by early 1775 and had not enjoyed it for some time. The instructions may be seen as an attempt of sorts to recover this initiative. The attempt was bound to prove abortive, however, since Britain could regain this advantage only by accepting the alternative of war, something the ministry was as yet unprepared to do.[20]

[IV]

The instructions to Gage followed on and responded to the cabinet's deliberations of mid-January. From these deliberations there emerged an altered plan for dealing with America. In response to the continued and ever-growing defiance of New England the government would send reinforcements to its military and naval commands in the colonies. Additionally, it was decided to introduce a bill in Parliament for blockading the trade of the northern provinces with foreign nations. Finally, in place of a proposal by Dartmouth to send commissioners to America with the mission to negotiate a lasting solution of the crisis, the cabinet accepted a proposal by Lord North to the general effect that the metropolis would forego exercise of the right of taxation over the colonies on condition that the Americans pay for their provincial administrations and contribute to the common defense. Such was North's Olive Branch to the colonies. In the course of the following two months, the ministry worked to obtain Parliament's approval of the new measures. The act to restrain the trade of New England was soon followed

---

[20] The follow-up to the instructions of January 27 is Dartmouth's letter to Gage of April 15; *Gage*, 2:190–96. Gage was urged to seize rebel places of strength and destroy them, to seize and destroy all rebel arms and ammunition he could find, and to arrest and imprison all persons who had committed acts of treason and rebellion. Dartmouth referred to Gage's curiously optimistic letter of January 18 in order to point out to his commander-in-chief that since he had now been given a "respectable force" he should be able to accomplish the assigned objectives. Gage was reminded that he had the power to pardon those who had committed treasonable acts, though he was not to do so in the case of leaders of the rebellion. The general tenor of the April 15 instructions is indicative of a government that had taken yet another step towards war but that still clung to the hope of a successful police action.

by a bill extending the provisions of nonintercourse to the other colonies, exception being made of New York, Georgia, and North Carolina, from which the government still entertained high hopes of support. At the end of March, and with the sanction of Parliament, the government also approved—at long last—a proclamation declaring Massachusetts to be in a state of rebellion.

These were the final measures taken by the metropolis prior to the outbreak of hostilities. Although their contents were not fully known in the colonies before Lexington and Concord, they are important if only because they do represent the last peacetime effort of government to deal with the American crisis. Taken overall, the measures reflected the North ministry's continued unwillingness to accept the alternative of war with America. The hope that Massachusetts might be brought to due submission without the use of military force had faded. In its place the new hope emerged that if the metropolis would show fresh determination to enforce its will, the situation might yet be saved. Since it was the northern colonies that were in a state of rebellion, it was against these colonies that firm measures had to be taken. But these measures were not equated with war, even in New England. The additional forces Gage was to be given were to insure that prompt and effective action might be taken to restore government authority. The arrest of the rebel leaders, the seizure of their arms, and, the assertion of royal authority in the countryside were, when taken together with the closing off of northern trade, the means for reducing New England to submission. To be sure, these measures carried the distinct risk of war. Still, they were not the "conquest" of New England Gage earlier counseled. The government, one may say, had taken a substantial step toward war, though in the hope that by doing so war might be avoided. If Gage would only exert himself in New England, and if the middle colonies would come to appreciate the determination of the metropolis, the northern colonies might yet prove manageable. The isolation of New England (rather than, as before, Massachusetts) remained a central consideration in British policy, to be sought after not only by the government's new show of determination but by its offer to compromise the issue that had bedeviled the imperial-colonial relationship since the mid-1760s.

Historians have been almost uniformly harsh in their judgments of this final effort of the North ministry. Perhaps the mildest criticism has been that "the government followed neither the logic of repression nor the logic of conciliation and thus lost the chance to be successful with either."[21] There is much to be said for this view so long as it is acknowledged that the logic of repression meant war and the logic of conciliation meant capitulation. There is less to be said for the far more common judgment that finds in the measures taken by the North ministry the work of a government intent upon war. The ministry was no more intent upon war than were the colonies, and perhaps even less so, but it was intent upon reestablishing at least a measure of its authority in the northern colonies. To permit the status quo of late 1774 and early 1775 to go unchallenged was tantamount to admission of defeat in New England. Negotiations might prove possible once the metropolis had shown by its actions that it was able and determined seriously to contest the forces of rebellion. This it could scarcely do without increasing its military forces to a point where they would no longer be constrained to hold a defensive position. The reinforcements sent out in the early months of 1775 responded to this logic, though the response might have been more impressive. So too, the act restraining colonial trade, though initially confined to the northern provinces, responded to the American refusal to trade with Great Britain and, as North pointed out in Commons, to let New England feel the "inconveniences which they must be exposed to while they denied the authority of parliament."[22]

These measures were not only repressive, they took the government, whatever its intentions, several steps closer to war. What alternative to them, however, would have brought the government no greater danger of war, yet no greater danger of sacrificing its essential position? The opposition to government in Parliament argued that the answer was to pursue a course of conciliation alone, since only conciliatory measures—genuinely conciliatory measures—could avoid the prospect of war. The opposition could take this view, while nevertheless insistent upon retaining British sovereignty, only by virtue of its assumption that the issue of taxation formed the core of the dispute and that the colonists were not

---

[21] John Derry, *English Politics and the American Revolution* (London, 1976), p. 115.
[22] *PH*, 18:395. The act for restraining New England's trade and commerce was to be effective only until the end of 1775 or to the end of the next session of Parliament. The governors of the provinces affected might except particular persons from its operations provided assurance was given of their good behavior.

otherwise seriously challenging the sovereignty of the metropolis. Once that assumption was discarded, however, as it had to be discarded by the government, the futility of pursuing a policy of conciliation alone was apparent. The holding out of conciliatory proposals might induce the colonies—or, at least, some of them— to negotiate if attended by distasteful alternatives. Without such alternative there was little, if any, reason to expect a positive response to offers of compromise, whatever their character. In submitting to the Commons his propositions for conciliating the differences with America, North rejected the arguments that the government attend any conciliatory moves by suspending its "operations of force" in these words: "The putting ourselves off our guard, is certainly not the way to tread on safe grounds or with effect. The ground on which we stand at present, is in all human probability such as will enable us to enforce, what we have a right to demand; and is therefore the most likely to claim attention, and to produce that effect by peace, which we are otherwise in a situation to procure by force of arms."[23]

The repressive measures that attended North's Olive Branch do not warrant the conclusion that the proposal was insincere. Does its substance indicate as much? Many have concluded that it does; even more, that the contents of North's proposal afford perhaps the clearest indication of the government's determination to go to war. For this presumably conciliatory offer was, in effect, a prescription for America's surrender to British demands. It ignored the entire meaning of the conflict and the fears and aspirations that had brought the colonists to the brink of revolt. As such, it betrayed either a shallow Machiavellism in its effort to split the colonies or an utter obtuseness to all that had moved the Americans from resistance to rebellion. The standard work on the abortive attempts at reconciliation between 1774 and 1778 concludes thus: "Words fail completely to describe the utter inadequacy of North's offer. It was not even a halfway measure for peace; it was a stupid gesture."[24]

---

[23] *PH*, p. 321.

[24] Weldon A. Brown, *Empire or Independence: A Study in the Failure of Reconciliation, 1774–1783* (Port Washington, N.Y., 1966), p. 45. "It was a continuation of the movement for centralization which began after 1763; another attempt to obtain a revenue from America; another attempt to take political and judicial power from colonial hands and transfer it to London; an additional assertion of the right of Parliament to regulate colonial commerce and to expect a revenue from America; and a reaffirmation of the determination of Great Britain to keep an army in the colonies."

This judgment of historians follows the earlier judgment of the colonists and of the opposition in Great Britain. To Edmund Burke, North's Olive Branch was "insidious," "a ransom by auction." Charles Fox declared that it carried "two faces"—one of negotiation and conciliation, the other of intransigence. Colonel Barré found it based on the "abominable maxim which has predominated in every measure of our late minister, *divide et impera*." David Hartley, contrasting the proposal with the system of free requisitions, characterized it as saying: "Give me what I ask, leaving likewise the quantity to my discretion, or I will take it by force."[25] These views of the friends of America in Parliament were also the views of American leaders. "We are of opinion," the Second Continental Congress declared in replying to North's proposal,

that the proposition contained in this resolution is unreasonable and insidious: unreasonable, because, if we declare we accede to it, we declare, without reservation, we will purchase the favor of Parliament, not knowing at the same time at what price they will please to estimate their favor; it is insidious, because, individual colonies, having bid and bidden again, till they find the avidity of the seller too great for all their powers to satisfy; are then to return into opposition, divided from their sister colonies whom the minister will have previously detached by a grant of easier terms, or by an artful procrastination of a definitive answer."[26]

Any assessment of North's conciliatory propositions and of the criticism made of them at the time and later must begin by noting that the proposals were far from precise. The text read:

That when the governor, council, and assembly, or general court, of any of his Majesty's provinces or colonies in America, shall propose to make provision, according to the condition, circumstances, and situation, of such province or colony, for contributing their proportion to the common defense (such proportion to be raised under the authority of the general court, or general assembly, of such province or colony, and disposable by parliament) and shall engage to make provision also for the support of the civil government, and the administration of justice, in such province or colony, it will be proper, if such proposal shall be approved by his Majesty and the two Houses of Parliament, and for so long as such provision shall be made accordingly, to forbear, in respect of such province or colony, to levy any duty, tax, or assessment, or to impose any further duty, tax or assessment, except only such duties as it may be expedient to continue to levy or to impose for the regulation of commerce; the nett

[25] *PH*, 18:329, 333, 336, 351.
[26] *Journals of the Continental Congress, 1774–1789*, 2:227.

produce of the duties last mentioned to be carried to the account of such province or colony respectively.[27]

In offering his proposition, North declared that it "marks the ground on which negotiation may take place. It is explicit, and defines the terms, and specifies the persons from whom the proposals must come, and to whom they must be made. It points out the end and purpose for which the contributions are to be given, and the persons from whom the grant of them is to originate."[28] This was excessive, for the proposal was, at a number of points, ambiguous. Nor did North evince much interest in clarifying its ambiguities when pressed to do so in the Commons. The proposal spoke of each colony "engaging" to make provision for the support of civil government and the administration of justice. By contrast, it spoke of each colony "proposing" to make provision for contributing its proportion to the common defense. Presumably, the former provision was not subject to negotiation, whereas the latter was. Indeed, North referred to negotiations on several occasions in the course of the Commons debate. Was negotiation merely a euphemism for imposition, as opponents insisted? Moreover, what was the significance of the engagement to support civil government? Was this a disguised concession by government, in that it signaled a willingness to abandon attempts at creating a civil list? Or was it instead indicative of a resolution, even at this late date, to press after a practice violently opposed by the colonists? Finally, and most importantly, in proposing to make provision for common defense, was the government leaving open the possibility that such provision might be limited to periods of war? And if not, would it have been satisfied in periods of peace with little more than token contributions? Was this, too, a disguised concession in that the government was asking for little more than the acknowledgment in principle of a duty, and a willingness, to contribute to the common defense?[29]

If these questions must remain unanswered, they are nevertheless worth raising unless it is simply assumed that the North pro-

[27] PH, 18: 320.
[28] Ibid.
[29] Although in debate North insisted upon "reserving to Parliament, a right of rejecting or increasing these voluntary aids at pleasure," he also acknowledged that "he did not nor could, at present, pretend to specify the exact sum they ought to raise, as it would probably fluctuate by bearing a certain proportion to the sums raised in Great Britain"; PH, 18: 352.

posal was insincere and even deceitful. This assumption is no more persuasive, however, than the argument that the proposal was the product of sheer obtuseness. The charge of insincerity stems from the fact that the conciliatory proposition was addressed to the separate colonies rather than to the collectivity of colonies, that it conspicuously ignored the Continental Congress, and that it made clear that it could properly be responded to only by each provincial assembly. Thus, the conclusion was and is drawn that a principal intent of the proposal was to split the colonies. No doubt, the government would have been happy with this result. It had never abandoned the hope of isolating the hard core of the rebellion. Even so, this scarcely establishes that the proposal was not made in good faith. In point of fact, it was only the provincial assemblies that could propose to make the provisions called for by the government. Besides, had there been any real interest in North's Olive Branch, there was nothing to prevent its serious consideration in the Continental Congress. Since the Congress took upon itself the authority of rejecting the proposition in the name of the colonies, it might just as well have assumed the authority to respond positively on their behalf. In any event, the North government could hardly have been expected to address its conciliatory proposition to the Congress, and this even if it had appreciated—as it very probably did—that a positive response by the separate colonies would necessitate first a positive response by the body that was now seen by most Americans to represent them in their dispute with the metropolis. By addressing the Congress, the government would in effect have recognized the principal organ of rebellion in the colonies. Before having any assurance that such action would facilitate reconciliation, it would have endowed with legitimacy a body that not only refused to direct any communications to Parliament but had earlier petitioned the King to dismiss "those designing and dangerous men" who formed the ministry.[30]

The charge of obtuseness, or stupidity, is evidently based on the inadequacy of the North proposal in terms of what the Americans

[30] *Journals of Continental Congress*, 1:118. North responded to the charge that his proposal was based on the maxim *divide et impera* by stating: "If propositions that the conscientious and the prudent will accept, will at the same time recover them from under the influence and fascination of the wicked, I avow the using that principle which will thus divide the good from the bad, and give support to the friends of peace and good government"; *PH*, 18: 334.

were demanding. Certainly, it was inadequate when judged by these demands—but then so might any proposal be labeled that fell short of meeting colonial requirements for reconciliation. If this is the measure of obtuseness, wisdom and insight presumably would have dictated capitulation to the Americans, for that is what responding to their demands would have meant. "The American revolution might have been averted, at this point," concludes the historian who judges North's offer as stupid because utterly inadequate, "if the British government had repealed the 'Intolerable Acts,' specifically renounced all intention to tax America in the future, and, in short, restored pre-1763 conditions, as Congress had requested in 1774."[31] There is no reason to doubt this conclusion. Had the British government done what the Congress requested in 1774, there would have been little, if anything, left to rebel against. Parliament's claim to supremacy over the colonies, the issue around which the imperial-colonial dispute centered, would effectively have been relinquished.

Although the North proposal was altogether inadequate when judged by American demands, it did hold out the prospect of modest concessions to the colonies. The promise to abandon the taxation of any colony that agreed to pay the cost of its government as well as its share of the common defense did signal the prospective withdrawal from a previous position. Nor does it detract from this concession that, in making it, government did not, as North wrote at the time to the King, give up any right.[32] In a formal sense, this was true enough. In a practical sense, the promise to forego the exercise of the right was equivalent to giving it up. Of course, the

---

[31] Brown, *Empire or Independence*, p. 58.

[32] In a letter to the King (February 19), North expressed the hope "for great utility (if not in America, at least on this side of the water,) to arise to the publick from this motion; he is confident it gives up no right, and that it contains precisely the plan which ought to be adopted by Great Britain; even if all America were subdued. He has reason to think it would give general satisfaction here, and that it will greatly facilitate the passing the Bill now in the House for restraining the Trade of New England, and the other which must, he fears, be soon brought into the House for subjecting Virginia, Maryland, and other provinces to the same restrictions"; *George III*, 3:177. The King replied that he "very highly" approved of the resolution, "as it plainly defines the line to be held in America, and as it puts an end to Congresses, it certainly will have a good effect in this Country and I should hope in at least some of the Colonies." North's letter, it is well to recall, was written to a King who was committed to the right of taxation and who had insisted, as late as September 1774, "there must always be one tax to keep up the right, and as such I approve of the Tea Duty"; King to North, September 11, 1774, p. 131. Even if North had thought that his proposal did give up the right, for all practical purposes, could he have been expected to admit this to the King?

promise itself was contingent upon the prior approval by Parliament of the proposal made by each colony—thus the cry made alike by the colonists and the opposition in Parliament that the North plan would destroy the very nature of requisitions by making them compulsory. Instead of taxing to obtain a revenue, North was accused of seeking a revenue by the threat of taxation. The Olive Branch, on this view, was no less coercive than the arrangements it promised to displace.

If North was offering no more than his adversaries contended, then he was indeed a fool, since only a fool would have failed to see that the offer was vulnerable to precisely the attack made on it. At the same time, the attack was difficult to avoid since the proposal made to the colonies was not one of returning to the old system of free requisitions but of establishing a system that required the agreement of the metropolis and each colony. The essence of North's conciliatory proposition was its call to negotiate. The element of power—hence, of coercion—would not be absent from the negotiations. Given the nature of the dispute, and the lengths to which it had gone by 1775, this could not be expected. The colonies would indeed have had to negotiate, if they were to have negotiated at all, against the background of the threat, the ever-growing threat, of force. If this circumstance is held to have vitiated the proposal, however, then a negotiated settlement of the crisis was either impossible or superfluous. It was impossible so long as the imperial state pursued a policy of coercion, since the colonies could not be expected to negotiate under threat; it was superfluous once that policy was abandoned, since there would be very little left to negotiate over.

Within the limits that now defined his room for political maneuver, North had offered not only to negotiate an issue heretofore regarded as nonnegotiable but to hold out to the other side the reasonable expectation that the outcome would not be onerous. He had probably gone as far as he could have gone, given the constraints placed on him by supporters of the administration. As it was, the introduction of the conciliatory proposition threatened to provoke a rebellion of sorts within the government's ranks. Nor did the proposal mollify the opposition or embarrass it in the least. Although North's proposition held out the possibility of an arrangement that might have developed into the functional equivalent of free requisitions, the fact remained that on its face it was not an

offer of free requisitions. The government had made no formal
concession of right. Still more important, however, was the ministry's unwillingness to hold out at this juncture any concession
that went beyond the issue of taxation. North made this unwillingness clear when introducing his conciliatory proposition. "[If]
the dispute in which the Americans have engaged goes to the whole
of our authority," he declared, "we can enter into no negociation,
we can meet no compromise. If it be only as to the suspension of
our right, or as to the mode of laying and raising taxes for a contribution towards the common defence, I think it would be just,
it would be wise to meet any fair proposition, which may come in
an authentic way from any province or colony."[33]

The Americans had made clear in the course of the preceding
year, however, that the dispute went far beyond the issue of taxation, that it did indeed go to the whole of the government's authority in the colonies. Even if it had not, the Olive Branch fell
far short of what the colonists were demanding. The Report on
Lord North's Motion, submitted to and approved by the Second
Continental Congress, defined the colonies' "sole and exclusive
privilege of giving and granting their own money" to mean "a right
of deliberating whether they will make any gift, for what purposes
it shall be made, and what shall be its amount."[34] The government's
proposition, the report went on to declare, "seems to have been
held up to the world, to deceive it into a belief that there was
nothing in dispute between us but the *mode* of levying taxes; and
that the parliament having now been so good as to give up this,
the colonies are unreasonable if not perfectly satisfied: Whereas,
in truth, our adversaries still claim a right of demanding *ad libitum*,
and of taxing us themselves to the full amount of their demand, if
we do not comply with it."[35] There was still more important ground
on which to stand, however, "and which they keep out of sight, as
if no such point was now in contest between us." The point was
the claim to supremacy, the claim of right "to alter our charters
and established laws, and leave us without any security for our
lives or liberties."[36] Ultimately, this was the principal justification
for rejecting the proposition. It did not go to the heart of the

33 *PH*, 18:320.
34 *Journals of Continental Congress*, 2:225.
35 Ibid., p. 232.
36 Ibid.

dispute. It did not deal with, let alone relinquish, the claim of Parliament's sovereignty over the colonies. The proposal was "altogether unsatisfactory," not simply because it failed to renounce the "pretended right" to taxation, but because it did not propose to repeal the Coercive Acts and the entirety of the objectionable measures taken by the metropolis since 1763.

In this unqualified rejection of North's conciliatory proposition, the Second Continental Congress kept faithfully to the path marked out by its predecessor. The colonists did not offer the metropolis, as some have suggested, a choice between commerce and taxation, that is, a choice between the right to regulate colonial commerce and the right to exact a revenue from the colonies.[37] The imperial state was told that it had no rights of taxation in any circumstance. Submission to this claimed right, the Congress reiterated, "leaves us without anything we can call property." Even more, submission to the claimed right would mean, the Congress argued, a contribution to the empire double of the proportion to which the metropolis was entitled, and this because of the generous advantages it already received from the monopoly of colonial trade. Should Great Britain nevertheless conclude that these advantages were inadequate and that the colonial contribution to imperial defense fell short of what might be regarded as the Americans' due proportion, the metropolis might remove the restrictions on trade. In that event, the Congress declared, "we will cheerfully contribute such Proportion when constitutionally required."[38] But when was such proportion constitutionally required and, still more significant, who would make this determination? The Congress afforded no answer to the first question. What it did make quite clear was the right of the colonies to determine the proportion required of them. The choice offered Great Britain, then, was one between

[37] Brown, *Empire or Independence*, p. 4. "In 1774, the colonists informed Britain that they would forego their objections to British taxation and guarantee a fixed annual sum if Britain would surrender her rigid control of colonial trade and commerce and allow the colonies to trade with all parts of the empire and the world as their interests might dictate." No such offer was made by the First Continental Congress, nor was one made by the 1775 Congress.

[38] Address to the Inhabitants of Great Britain, July 8, 1775, *Journals of Continental Congress*, 2:168. The passage reads: "It is alledged that we contribute nothing to the common Defence. To this we answer, that the Advantages which *Great Britain* receives from the monopoly of our trade, far exceed our Proportion of the Expence necessary for that Purpose. But should these Advantages be inadequate thereto, let the Restrictions on our Trade be removed, and we will cheerfully contribute such Proportion when constitutionally required."

the continued regulation of colonial trade, though without the effective means of doing so, and the abandonment of regulation in the hope—it could be no more—that the colonists would make their contribution to imperial defense when called upon to do so.

In the spring of 1775 the parties remained as far apart as they had been since the preceding summer. With the outbreak of hostilities, first at Lexington and Concord in April, and then at Bunker Hill in June, the already almost negligible prospects of a negotiated solution diminished even further. Henceforth, negotiations could be pursued only within the context of a growing war, for the news of these initial clashes put an end to the government's policy of neither war nor peace. The North ministry would persist throughout the following year in its abortive efforts at reconciliation. Even so, the vacillation that had marked British policy was abandoned in mid-June. The assumption—rather, the illusion—that the metropolis was involved in a police action had become plainly untenable. Reluctantly, the reality of war was accepted.

FIFTEEN

The Debate over America

[I]

C ould the dispute between Great Britain and the colonies have been compromised after the fall of 1774? Was a peaceful solution of the conflict possible, that is, a solution that would have preserved the essential claims of the contending parties? Writing in 1775, one articulate critic of received truths had the following to say about the need to pursue measures of reconciliation:

This is certainly very good Advice, where it can be followed. But the Misfortune is, that in the Present Case, any Scheme for a *Compromise* is absolutely impracticable. And the reason is, because in all compromising Schemes, it is believed, and taken for granted by both Parties, that what they give up for the Sake of Peace, doth not invalidate their Right and Title to that, which they chuse to retain. But this is by no means the present Case: For the Claim of Right on either Side must be universal, or there must be no Claim at all: and neither Party have it in their Power to recede a Tittle from their Pretensions without subverting the very Foundation of their Claim to all the rest.[1]

It was because the dispute centered on the issue of sovereignty, the "*ne plus ultra* of ruling Power," that Josiah Tucker found "compromising Schemes . . . idle and visionary Things." In such disputes, "there is no common principle to rest upon, no common Medium to apply to," and this because "the nature of the claim is absolutely such, that it must be admitted whole and entire; or be wholly denied and rejected."[2] No scheme for compromising the imperial-colonial dispute was viable unless the issue of sovereignty was first settled. In the absence of such settlement, the parties

[1] Josiah Tucker, *The Respective Pleas and Arguments of the Mother Country and of the Colonies, Distinctly Set Forth* . . . (Gloucester, 1775), Tract 5, pp. 10–11.
[2] Ibid., pp. 38, 48.

were destined to quarrel perpetually, to go to war, or to separate peaceably.

Although Tucker's view of the nature of the dispute was not far removed from the government's, the same cannot be said of his proposed solution. This was "to separate entirely from the colonie; by declaring them to be a free and independent people, over whor.1 we lay no claim."[3] No British government could seriously entertain this solution in 1775, and the North government had no disposition to do so even if it had enjoyed the necessary freedom. Tucker could advocate separation because he was persuaded that while war with America would prove a disaster for the metropolis, British interests, far from suffering, could only benefit from casting off the colonies. The government was of an altogether different persuasion. If it was far from confident of its ability to put down the growing rebellion without making a considerable effort, it was convinced that, all other alternatives failing, British interests required such an effort. This was in large measure the reason the North government came so reluctantly to the conclusion that the dispute could not be compromised. Given the ministry's perception of the interests that would be sacrificed through loss of the colonies, the intractability of the dispute meant war.

[II]

Between a Josiah Tucker and the government, then, there was agreement on the issue that made up the core of the conflict, and disagreement on the "interest" or interests that would be placed in jeopardy by conceding the issue. This distinction between the issue and the interests behind the issue, between sovereignty and the interests sovereignty presumably secured, was partially obscured at the time and, indeed, has remained partially obscured. Although the government was from the outset of the final crisis clear in its insistence that the central issue was, to use North's words, "whether or not we have any authority"—first in Boston, later in New England, finally in America—it was less than articulate, let alone explicit, about the interests for which authority was

---

[3] Josiah Tucker, *The True Interest of Great Britain Set Forth in Regard to the Colonies* (Gloucester, 1774), Tract 4, p. 195.

indispensable. There are exceptions to this rather curious record of silence, but they are quite few.[4]

This relative absence, in the printed versions of the parliamentary debates, of clear articulation of the interests at stake in the conflict has given rise to the persisting view that the government was contending simply for the "submission" of the colonies and that its grand object was, as a leading member of the opposition in the Lords pointed out during debate over the bill to restrain the trade of New England, neither more nor less than "the establishment of supreme dominion, *voluntas pro imperio*."[5] Intended then and now as a criticism of government policy,[6] the criticism slights the consideration that even if sovereignty is not simply seen as a value in itself, it must still be seen as a condition, an indispensable condition, of value. The government had not made sovereignty per se its grand object, while remaining unclear about, or oblivious to or even disdainful of, other objects. The insistence upon the effective assertion of sovereignty, and the submission of the colonies, stemmed from the simple conviction that without this assertion all other interests—tangible and intangible—would of necessity be sacrificed. The conviction may have been misplaced—indeed, it was partially misplaced—but that is a very different matter from arguing that the government was obsessed with establishing its supremacy for little apparent reason other than establishing its supremacy.

---

[4] This is at least the case if one is to judge from the written record of the *Parliamentary History* and the *Parliamentary Register*. Published by those sympathetic to the opposition account of the American problem, both works seldom acknowledge in the speeches of those who led for the government—North in the Commons, Mansfield in the Lords—the ministry's view of the interest behind the issue of sovereignty. Why this is so remains unclear. Others in favor of the government's American policy are reported to speak clearly of the interest behind the issue; *PH*, 18:166 (Townshend), 732 (Acland). Such a view also appears frequently in pamphlets written at the government's behest. See, e.g., Samuel Johnson, *Taxation No Tyranny*, pp. 8–9; and William Knox, *The Interest of the Merchants and Manufactures of Great Britain in the Present Contest with the Colonies Stated and Considered*, pp. 43–49. Cf. *Annual Register* (1775), p. 48.

[5] *PH*, 18:438–39 (Camden).

[6] Even by otherwise sympathetic critics. Richard W. Van Alstyne, in his examination of the parliamentary debate, writes of the government's position: "Practically speaking, all that the Americans need do was to pay lip service to the principle, and all would be forgiven. It seems clear that the ministry did not even intend to hold out on its demand that the colonies share in the cost of imperial defense. 'Submission' was all that was expected. Therein, of course, was the fallacy of the government's approach. It thought it was facing an insurrection; actually it was confronted with a revolution"; "Parliamentary Supremacy versus Independence: Notes and Documents," *Huntington Library Quarterly* 26 (1962–64): 209.

Altogether different is the point that metropolitan insistence on colonial submission was grounded to a marked degree on intangible considerations. This was undeniably the case. The defiance of the colonies was seen by Britain's rulers as a challenge to the nation's dignity and reputation; that defiance cut deeply into imperial pride and sense of grandeur. Even so apparently cool and detached an observer as Tucker himself did not escape the pervasive influence of these passions. Imagining the prospect of being governed by "Vice-Roys sent over from the Court Residencies either at Philadelphia, or New York, or at some other *American* imperial city," he confessed that "the *English* would rather submit to a *French* yoke, than to an *American*; as being the lesser Indignity of the two." The establishment of supreme dominion, *voluntas pro imperio*, cannot be equated only with physical security and material well-being. It must be seen partly in terms of passions that transcended these interests and, perhaps, even on occasion betrayed them, as Tucker argued.[7]

There is surely nothing that is unusual in this. On the contrary, what would be unusual—indeed, unique—is the absence of those passions that must partly account for the insistence on colonial "submission" to the supreme authority of Parliament. At the same time, it is apparent that other, more tangible, interests must also account for the insistence on submission. Of these interests, it is very likely the case that the one spoken of always, taxation, was considered of no more than peripheral significance by 1774 (if not even earlier), whereas the one spoken of but seldom, at least in the printed version of parliamentary debate, was deemed of crucial importance. Whatever aspirations may have been entertained at the beginning of the 1760s over the revenues that might be raised in the American provinces, by 1774 these aspirations had receded greatly. The significance of the trade to the colonies, however, continued to increase. Tucker might argue that separation would not mean the loss of the American trade, since experience had shown that the colonists would trade with their bitterest enemies, provided only it was in their interest to do so. He might contend that with few exceptions interest would so dictate, since it was in Great Britain that the Americans could get the best price for most

---

[7] Tucker, *The True Interest*, Tract 4, pp. 193–94. Cf. Eden to Wederburn, in Van Alstyne, "Parliamentary Supremacy," p. 203; *PH*, 18:1071 (Lyttelton).

of their staple exports just as it was in Great Britain that the Americans could purchase at a cheaper price than elsewhere most of their imports. He might, finally, demonstrate as groundless the widespread fear that an America free from British control would fall under the influence or control of the French, since France was manifestly in no position to acquire the colonies against the opposition of both America and Great Britain.[8]

Tucker's voice, however, was heretical. At the time, very few were ready to listen to his curious message. That the "prodigious increase of trade" the nation had enjoyed was not due to the colonial system and the growth of the American colonies, but was primarily the result of improvements in communications, agriculture, and labor-saving machines, together with reforms in domestic trade practices and taxation, flew in the face of conventional wisdom, as did the view that acquisition of territory and control of colonial trade entailed expenditures that could seldom, if ever, be compensated for by the exclusive commercial advantages thereby accruing to the metropolis. The rulers of Great Britain instead clung to the belief, held as an article of faith, that with the loss of the colonies Britain would sink for want of trade, a prey to its Bourbon enemies who, even if they did not succeed in dominating the colonies, would inevitably profit from the decline of British power. Even those who thought it possible that the preservation of British commerce with America did not require the maintenance of parliamentary sovereignty were skeptical of hazarding the fortunes of the state merely on what "some speculative men had said." In defense of the policy of the government, Adam Ferguson noted that a few had said "that it would be no such fatal stroke to Britain as it generally imagined, were America to be abandoned altogether." He declared that "he had not opinion enough of his own foresight to say with certainty what the consequence would be, but so much benefit had he reaped from these speculations as to hope that the prosperity of Great Britain would not be desperate even were such an event to happen. But who would be bold enough to advise such a measure? and who could, with certainty, answer for the effects of it? If no person would, what remained, but they

[8] Cf. *The Diary and Letters of His Excellency Thomas Hutchinson, Esq.*, 1:262–64; Tucker, *The True Interest*, Tract 4, pp. 195–212.

should exert every nerve to reduce their rebellious subjects to obedience?"[9]

[III]

The opposition to government in Parliament did not disagree with the government's assessment of the interests at stake in the dispute with America. Particularly on the crucial importance of retaining a monopoly of the American trade it was as one with the ministry. Even with respect to the intangible interests at stake there was a marked similarity of outlook. Neither a Chatham nor a Burke was insensitive to those considerations of pride and grandeur which moved their opponents. It was not here that the critical differences were to be found but in the disparate understanding of government and opposition on the issue that defined the imperial-colonial conflict. Whereas the government and its supporters found this issue in the supremacy of Parliament—or rather, the colonial rejection of parliamentary supremacy—the opposition found the issue in colonial resistance to discrete measures taken by the metropolis since 1763 and, above all, to measures of taxation. The colonial challenge was thus deemed to be of limited compass, in the sense that the colonies had not challenged sovereignty as such, and it was by virtue of their understanding that the whig opponents of the North ministry were able to insist well after the dispute had erupted in war that a compromise was still quite possible.

Throughout the almost continuous dispute on American policy that raged in the Commons and Lords from the beginning of 1774 to the spring of 1775, it is this difference in understanding that overshadows all other points at controversy. The debate had many faces and the arguments put forth in its course were often arcane and labyrinthine. Yet when the complexities of the bitter controversy are examined and placed in perspective, it is apparent that the essential position of the opposition rested on the proposition that the government had either misrepresented or misunderstood the position of the Americans. Because of this, the government had also misrepresented or misunderstood the issue at stake with the colonies.

[9] *PH*, 18:739.

The great whig opponents of the North ministry—Chatham, Burke, Shelburne, Fox, Hartley, Camden—have remained for historians figures worthy of attention and respect. It is not difficult to appreciate why this should be so. To most historians of the period, it is the leaders of the opposition who pointed to the road not taken, the road that might have led to a peaceful resolution of the dispute. Even where a more sophisticated and detached historiography has expressed doubt about the viability of the solutions put forward by a Chatham or a Burke, this judgment has nevertheless regularly been attended by praise for the vision and imagination of opposition leaders. These traits are seen in striking contrast with the sterility and poverty of thought found to characterize Whitehall's almost every move.[10]

This affinity of historians for the political opposition in Parliament rests, of course, upon far more than simply the latter's insistence that the dispute might have been settled without war. Of much greater importance is the manner in which the opposition as a whole viewed the conflict with America by 1774–75. In its diagnosis of the origins and course of the quarrel the opposition articulated a position that, in its essential elements, was very close to the position of the colonists. If subsequent generations of historians have refined this position, they have not altered its critical features in any significant respect. The exigencies of political debate, leading as they normally do to marked exaggeration and even to caricature, ought not to obscure the basic similarity of view between the Americans and their friends in Parliament and the similarity of both to past and current historiography. A whig opposition, in substantial agreement with the colonists, has been followed by a predominantly whig history.

The opposition view of the conflict reached full expression only

[10] Bernard Donoughue, *British Politics and the American Revolution*, p. 287, concludes his study by declaring that the government "lacked vision, magnanimity, and the statesmanship which these two qualities make possible. Donoughue, however, does not appear to believe a peaceful solution was possible." He is quite skeptical about the prospects of having satisfied the Americans with any proposal that fell short of what they were demanding. Nor does he believe that the chief opposition spokesmen proposed viable solutions. Yet Burke and others get reasonably high marks for efforts that reflected "vision and imagination." In a similar vein, John Derry, *English Politics and the American Revolution*, pp. 137–51, finds Burke's proposals lacking in realism but characterized by vision, insight, and magnanimity. For Ian R. Christie and Benjamin Woods Labaree, *Empire or Independence, 1760–1776*, p. 233, Burke's conciliatory proposals of March 22, 1775, "were a triumph of creative political imagination," and appeared in striking contrast to the poverty of governmental thought and action.

in 1774. Until this time there had been considerable doubt over whether the individuals associated with the two great opposition groups—the Rockinghamites and the Chathamites—would support or oppose a policy of coercion. At the outset of the crisis brought on by the Boston Tea Party, Chatham strongly condemned the behavior of the colonists and supported the Boston Port Act. So, too, did a number of the Rockinghamites. This early division and confusion of the opposition, however, soon receded with the government's introduction of the later measures that made up the Massachusetts legislation. By the time of the debates over the Coercive Acts, the opposition view of the conflict had been fully articulated and thereafter would go almost unquestioned. Its greatest purveyor was Edmund Burke, though its essential features were sketched by many others as well. Its starting point was an assessment of the historic relationship between metropolis and colonies.

If Burke cannot fairly be charged with idealizing this relationship, he certainly made no serious effort to acknowledge its difficulties. On the contrary, what Burke saw when he looked back beyond 1763 was a dutiful America, always willing to contribute its share to imperial defense. In the Seven Years' War, Burke recalled in his March 22, 1775, speech on conciliation, "the colonies not only gave, but gave to satiety. This nation has formally acknowledged two things: first, that the colonies had gone beyond their abilities, parliament having thought it necessary to reimburse them; secondly, that they had acted legally and laudably in their grants of money, and their maintenance of troops, since the compensation is expressly given as reward and encouragement."[11] This was, to say the least, a partial interpretation of the colonial contribution and the significance of Parliament's subsequent reimbursement. By 1775, however, it represented the opposition's memory—including Chatham's—of the colonial role in the Great War for the Empire. David Hartley gave perhaps the most fulsome endorsement of it in his propositions for reconciliation. The Americans, Hartley declared, "bore, even in our judgment, more than their full proportion." Nor were these efforts unusual. The colonists had presumably always acted thus. In return, what had the mother country done for them? "I believe precisely nothing at all," Hartley

[11] PH, 18:521.

replied, "but just keeping watch and ward over their trade, that they should receive nothing but from ourselves, and at our own price."[12]

In the latter judgment, Hartley went beyond the limits that defined the whig interpretation of the pre–1763 Anglo-American relationship. Whatever the other liberties that might be taken in reconstructing this relationship, with but rare exception condemnation of the old colonial system was not one. Hartley might point to the disadvantages that, in his view, the system held out for the colonists. In doing so, however, he spoke for himself. Neither a Chatham, nor a Burke, nor a Shelburne would have supported such a view. They acknowledged that some of the restrictions placed on colonial trade were onerous, but they insisted that in the happier times which preceded 1763 the system had worked to the mutual advantage of both parties. Burke too believed, like George Grenville, in virtual representation and in the sovereignty and justice of Parliament. Yet that mutuality, Burke discovered in 1774, had been abruptly broken with the Grenville reforms of 1764. Through a "singular degree of anxiety" over the illicit commerce in America, the bonds of the Act of Navigation

were straitened so much, that America was on the point of having no trade, either contraband or legitimate. They found, under the construction and execution then used, the Act no longer tying, but actually strangling them. All this coming with new enumerations of commodities; with regulations which in a manner put a stop to the mutual coasting intercourse of the colonies; with the appointment of courts of admiralty under various improper circumstances; with a sudden extinction of the paper currencies; with a compulsory provision for the quartering of soldiers; the people of America thought themselves proceeded against as delinquents.[13]

Whereas any one of these acts might have been accepted by the colonists, and some even thought reasonable, "the multitude struck them with terror." But the worst was yet to come. With the attempt of the Grenville ministry to tax the colonies without their consent, the growing apprehensions of the Americans over a threat to their liberties were confirmed and, in consequence, provoked acts of resistance. The taxation of the colonists by Parliament was unfortunate not only because it weakened the confidence of the colonies in the mother country but also because it was unnecessary. Had

[12] Ibid., pp. 555–57. This is a recurrent theme in Hartley's speeches. Cf. pp. 351, 562, 1047.
[13] Ibid., 17:1241.

the colonies only been permitted to make free grants, Burke was certain that the metropolis would have received many times what it had otherwise sought in vain.[14] It was thus an empire needlessly torn asunder by the preceding administration that the Rockingham ministry confronted on assuming power in late 1765.

[IV]

The opposition's view respecting the origins of the dispute was complemented by its account of the course the dispute had taken in the years from the Stamp Act to the Coercive Acts. The history of these years was depicted as one in which British governments had forced the quarrel at almost every possible turn. Moreover, they were years in which the saliency that the Stamp Act had given to the problem of taxation was suddenly reinforced. From 1767 onward, taxation would remain to bedevil the imperial-colonial relationship and to overshadow all else, despite the apparent desire of the colonies to reaffirm their loyalty and obedience to the metropolis.

The significance given to the Townshend Revenue Act by Burke is readily explicable. For by his reckoning the Rockingham administration had succeeded in returning the colonies to the state of blessedness that Grenville had disrupted. Not only did the Rockinghamites abandon or modify the vexatious restrictions on commerce that Grenville had introduced; they also "preserved the authority of Great Britain" and "preserved the equity of Great Britain. They made the Declaratory Act; they repealed the Stamp Act." Burke recalled the demonstrations of gratitude throughout America with the repeal of the Stamp Act. So sudden a calm after so violent a storm, he declared, was without parallel in history.[15] Unfortunately, Burke pointed out, the course set by the Rockingham ministry had not been adhered to by its successor. Although headed by a great man, the government of Lord Chatham—"an administration so checkered and speckled . . . a piece of joinery so crossly indented and whimsically dovetailed . . . a cabinet so variously inlaid . . . a piece of diversified mosaic . . . a tessellated

[14] Ibid., p. 1268.
[15] Ibid., pp. 1255–56.

pavement without cement"[16]—gave way to the fatal scheme of its chancellor of the Exchequer, Charles Townshend. With the passage of the Townshend duties, the peace and good will brought by the repeal of the Stamp Act had again been broken, never to return. But instead of attempting to restore good relations between the mother country and the colonies—instead of following the example of the Rockingham administration—the North administration had, by the refusal to repeal the tea tax, inflamed the colonies and yet had not otherwise served any useful object of government. "If you murder, rob," Burke advised, "if you kill, take possession; and do not appear in the character of madmen as well as assassins, violent, vindictive, bloody, and tyrannical, without an object."[17]

Thus did Burke arrive at his claim that the three-pence duty on tea was responsible for bringing the two sides to the brink of war. He remained unshaken before the remarkable candor and clarity with which the Continental Congress had outlined the fundamental position of the American colonies. He resolutely refused to take this position at face value. Only one thing, he said, might make "an honest man the advocate of ministerial measures, namely, that the Americans attack the sovereignty of this country." The idea, however, was preposterous: "the Americans do not attack the sovereignty itself, but a certain exercise and use of that sovereignty."[18] "I do not know," he declared in his speech on conciliation, "that the colonies have, in any general way, or in any cool hour, gone much beyond the demand of immunity in relation to taxes. It is not fair to judge of the tempers and dispositions of any men, or any set of men, when they are composed and at rest, from their conduct or their expressions, in a state of disturbance and irritation."[19]

Even more remarkable than Burke's characterization of American demands was the retrospective view of the conflict taken by the Chathamites. In 1774 and 1775, they believed that the metropolis had forced the conflict at every turn. British policy toward

[16] Ibid., p. 1257.
[17] Ibid., p. 1264.
[18] Ibid., 18:262. To similar effect, see pp. 165, 203 (Chatham), 648 (Fox), 262 (Grafton), 1265 (Richmond).
[19] Ibid., p. 526. The passage is a classic example of what Tucker called Burke's habit of expressing himself "with such Guards and Salvoes, that while you present one Sense to your Readers, you reserve another for yourself in Case of Attack"; *A Letter to Edmund Burke*, p. 46.

the colonies "for many years past," Barre declared, had consisted of "a series of irritating and offensive measures, without policy, principle or moderation. . . . It has seemed to be your study to irritate and inflame them."[20] In the aftermath of the Stamp Act crisis, Chatham declared in 1774, "the Americans had almost forgot, in their excess of gratitude for the repeal of the Stamp Act, any interest but that of the mother country; there seemed an emulation among the different provinces, who should be most dutiful and forward in their expressions of loyalty to their real benefactor."[21] Yet Chatham's memory was deficient. He had by this time forgotten—or had chosen to forget—how the colonies "excess of gratitude" and "expressions of loyalty" were on more than one occasion manifested and his own intense anger over those manifestations. In fact, Chatham had been blinded by rage over American insubordination in the spring of 1767. Only his subsequent illness prevented him from playing a role in the punishment of the colonies that all groups in Parliament, in 1767, thought necessary. Shelburne had contemplated making the denial of parliamentary supremacy an act of high treason punishable in England. The anger and frustration experienced by Shelburne and Chatham during their years in office belied the claims they subsequently made in 1774 and 1775. The Chathamites had not forced a quarrel with the colonies; but they, like others—like the North administration—could not ignore the challenges that the colonists had thrown down. That was one part of the story of the eight-year period from the Stamp Act crisis to the imposition of the Coercive Acts. The other was the ultimate retreat of each ministry before such challenge.

[V]

The interesting question raised by these reconstructions of a recent past is why successive governments had acted so contrary to evident interest. Even the Bute and Grenville ministries had no reasonable cause for having acted as they did, once one accepts the opposition's account of colonial behavior during the Seven Years' War and colonial attitudes on the morrow of victory. Subsequent ministries,

---

[20] *PH*, 17:1203.
[21] Ibid., p. 1354.

and particularly North's, clearly did not have what little excuse might be offered on Grenville's behalf. Yet the North government had repeated the errors of preceding governments and added a substantial number of its own. It had raised the tax issue in a manner the colonists could hardly have been expected to tolerate and for a projected revenue that, even had it been realized, was entirely disproportionate to the dangers incurred. Having provoked a reaction that might easily have been foreseen, the government compounded its predicament by a series of coercive measures the colonies had no alternative but to resist. The effectiveness of the resistance, instead of serving to bring the government back to its senses and to the pursuit of a conciliatory policy, had only prompted it to take even more provocative measures. Thus, step by step, the government had followed a path that could lead only to war with the colonies, a war that either could not be won or, even if ending in a military victory, might well result in the ruin of the mother country. Why?

One answer was the utter incompetence of government, and the North government above all. The high road of opposition argumentation, Burke followed it in his famous speeches and, with an occasional lapse,[22] so did Chatham. They, and others, often did so with considerable effect, moreover, for the record of the North ministry was clearly open to the charge that its American policy was marked by inconsistency and sheer inadvertence. In his speech on American taxation, Burke made the most of this record and, on the whole, it was a telling indictment. The incompetence of the North government, however, was not a theme voiced only by the opposition. Supporters of the ministry's policy often made a similar complaint, though for quite different reasons. In truth, the charge was not without merit coming from either side. The record of the North government was one not only of compromise, but of compromise that had been neither well conceived nor consistently pursued.

There was another explanation. A ruinous policy that surpassed the bounds even of the credibly incompetent pointed to the sinister motives of those in power. "What secret influence has compelled them," Shelburne once asked in debate, "to heap errors on errors, grievance upon grievance, till they have shaken the constitution

22 Cf. ibid., p. 1355.

to its foundation, and brought the whole empire into danger and confusion?" It was, he replied, "an uniform lurking spirit of despotism . . . that produced the Stamp Act in 1765; that fettered the repeal of that Act in 1766; that revived the principles of it in 1767; that has accumulated oppression upon oppression since, till at length it has openly established by the Quebec Bill, popery and arbitrary power over half America."[23] Shelburne's directness was unusual. Normally, the opposition was content simply to intimate a design of despotism in the ministry's American measures, a design to be initially implemented in the colonies though to be ultimately consummated in Great Britain. Thus, in their protest of October 26, 1775, against rejecting an amendment to the address of thanks, the Rockingham supporters in the House of Lords, after excoriating the government for having begun "a cruel civil war, so little supported by justice, and so very fatal in its necessary consequences," declared: "Nor can we impute the misconduct of ministers to mere inability, nor to their ignorance of the state of America, upon which they attempt to justify themselves." What, then, might explain the actions of those "who have deceived parliament, disgraced the nation, lost the colonies, and involved us in a civil war against our clearest interests; and, upon the most unjustifiable grounds, wantonly spilling the blood of thousands of our fellow subjects?"[24] The question, insistently raised in the course of the long debate, apparently did not even require an explicit answer.

The explanation reflected the marked decline in the opposition's political fortunes, a decline that among the Rockinghams encouraged delusions of persecution at the hands of a royal prerogative now working its will through Parliament. At the same time, this decline freed the whigs from the constraints that prospective power might have imposed. The explanation also reflected the opposition's view of the interests at stake in the dispute with America and of the means by which those interests might be preserved. Committed quite as much as the government to the view that retention of America was crucial to Great Britain and that it could be retained only under the fold of a supreme Parliament, the opposition had no choice when opposing government policy but to maintain that the colonies were not challenging parliamentary supremacy. How-

[23] Ibid., 18:725. Cf. pp. 192–93 (Fox).
[24] Ibid., p. 729.

ever tenuous the argument by 1774–75 that the dispute was still a limited one, it was indispensable. Without this argument, the entire structure of the whig position would have immediately collapsed of its own weight. Utter incompetence, then, must have brought the nation to the brink of an unnecessary and ruinous war with America. Where incompetence seemed insufficient to account for the enormity of American policy, this policy had to be found in a design to turn back the clock, to defeat whiggism on both sides of the Atlantic, and to consolidate the power of "as contemptible collection of servile courtiers, renegado whigs, and fawning, bigotted Tories, as ever strove to support the measures of any administration."[25]

[VI]

Given the opposition's understanding of the crisis, it also followed that the means for effecting a satisfactory resolution were, in principle, apparent. If the real dispute with the colonies was indeed of a limited nature; if the issue of taxation defined the essential core of the controversy; if the other American complaints were either of secondary significance or the consequence—as Burke insisted—of the disturbance and irritation resulting from the attempts at taxation; and if the colonists were not posing a serious challenge to the vital interest in the laws which bound their trade and commerce—the way out of the crisis threatening the empire with a disastrous civil war was at hand and had only to be grasped.

"Place us in the same situation that we were at the close of the last war," the First Continental Congress had urged the people of Great Britain, "and our former harmony will be restored." The colonial cry for a return to 1763 formed the opposition's cry as well. It was the critical prescription given for resolving the crisis, and though the precise meaning attached to it might vary from one proponent to the next, the call for a return to the "ancient constitution" that had presumably determined the imperial-colonial relationship prior to 1763 was both pervasive and insistent. Chatham gave expression to it in his Provisional Act of February 1, 1775, for settling the troubles in America. So did Burke in his speech of

25 Ibid., p. 248 (Irnham).

March 22 on conciliation. As the debate dragged on in 1775 the prescription became routine and ritual in opposition speeches.[26]

As a practical matter, the most pressing demand of the opposition had to be the repeal of the Massachusetts legislation. It was the Coercive Acts that had brought the dispute to the point of war, and it was only through the repeal of this legislation that the immediate danger might be removed. Since the Massachusetts legislation was seen as the result of the tax issue, its repeal—though a matter of first priority—was but a corollary of the abandonment of any further efforts at taxation.

In thus urging the repeal of the Coercive Acts, the opposition dismissed the view that the conflict had taken on a life of its own and that it had brought about change that could not be undone. That it had taken on a life of its own was emphasized by Lord Mansfield, who was at pains to dissociate himself from the measures taken by past ministries and, occasionally, by the North government as well. Speaking in defense of the government's policy, he declared that the Stamp Act had been an error, that he had not defended the wisdom of enacting the Declaratory Act, that he regretted the Townshend duties, and that he thought the restoration of the act relative to the trial of persons for offenses committed outside the realm had been a mistake. All this, however, in Mansfield's view, was now beside the point. America was challenging the supremacy of Great Britain. The true bone of contention was sovereignty: "They positively deny the right," he noted, "not the mode of exercising it"—a formulation that reversed the well-known statement of Burke. The government had staked its claim to authority over the colonies on its ability to put the Massachusetts legislation into effect. The colonies had taken up the challenge by denying in word and in deed the validity not only of the Coercive Acts but of Parliament's right to pass any laws governing the colonies. The Coercive Acts had thus come to represent the final test of parliamentary supremacy. If the colonies succeeded in denying the right asserted in the Massachusetts legislation, the vital issue would be decided. The measures proposed by the opposition, particularly those respecting taxation, had to follow the restoration of order in Massachusetts Bay; they could not precede it. If they did, if the Massachusetts acts were undone, the Amer-

---

[26] Ibid., p. 710 (Grafton), 769–70 (Fox), 790 (Adair).

icans "would stand in relation to Great Britain as Hanover now stands; or, more properly speaking, as Scotland stood towards England, previous to the treaty of Union."[27]

The opposition would have none of this. In reply to Mansfield, Shelburne, accurately reflecting the views of the entire opposition, responded that the government would not compromise the vital issue by repeal of the Massachusetts legislation; that, on the contrary, the Coercive Acts, if persisted in, would compromise the vital issue; that the Americans were only contesting for the fundamental right of granting their own money; and that if the claim of taxation "was fairly relinquished . . . the supremacy of the British Parliament would be acknowledged and acquiesced in by America, and peace between both countries be once more happily restored."[28] The repeal of the Stamp Act had brought both peace and subordination; so, too, would the repeal of the Coercive Acts and other objectionable legislation. The policy of coercion, in sum, could not only be abandoned without fatal effect; its retention prevented addressing the true causes of the controversy.

We are thus brought back once again to the opposition's understanding of the imperial-colonial conflict, an understanding that informs the various proposals put forth for a settlement. These proposals differed in their respective specifications for resolving the dispute. The differences were far less important, however, than the essential similarity of the proposals. Each addressed the question, How is it possible to resolve the controversy while preserving British authority? Each answered the question by conceding everything that, in the view of the sponsor, had occasioned the dispute. All agreed that what must not be jeopardized, let alone given up, was the one interest vital to Great Britain: the regulation of colonial trade and commerce. But this interest, it was maintained by all, either had not been seriously challenged by the colonies or, to the extent it had, such challenge was the result of American unhappiness and anxiety over measures that had threatened the right to dispose of property and the security of provincial charters.

In varying degree, the plans of conciliation put forth by the opposition, particularly those moved by Chatham, Hartley, and Burke, reflected the abovementioned characteristics. The plans of

[27] Ibid., pp. 957–58.
[28] Ibid., p. 958.

both Chatham and Hartley provided for the renunciation of Parliament's power to levy taxes on the Americans. Each proposal also provided for a system of free grants or contributions to imperial defense by the provincial assemblies. The old system, whereby the colonies provided supplies to the metropolis on request of the crown, would therefore be reaffirmed, now, if need be, through an act of Parliament. Yet neither of these plans addressed the defects and uncertainties that characterized the past operation of the system. In particular, neither made provision for the eventuality of colonial failure or refusal to respond to requests for aid and supplies by the metropolis. The absence of such provision was consistent with the claim that the colonies had provided their share, and more, in the past for imperial defense. For if the colonies had given their all in the Great War for the Empire, why should there be doubt that they would continue to do so in the future? One answer, of course, might be that Great Britain and America no longer shared a common interest with respect to security and defense. Underlying the proposals of the opposition, however, was the presumption that metropolis and colonies did continue to share such common interest.

In contrast to Chatham and Hartley, Burke did address the primary defect of the requisition system. In his speech on American taxation he declared that, should a colony fail to make its contribution in a war involving the imperial state, Parliament might resort to taxation against the delinquent party. Under such circumstances, he noted, "surely it is proper, that some authority might legally say—'Tax yourselves for the common supply, or parliament will do it for you.' " Burke, however, believed that "this ought to be no ordinary power; nor ever used in the first instance. . . . This is what I meant," he added, "when I have said at various times that I consider the power of taxing in Parliament as an instrument of empire and not as a means of supply."[29]

Burke's proposition, like that of other opposition spokesmen, rested on the assumption that the interests of the metropolis and the colonies were coincident in the past and would remain so in the future. It was here that his position was most vulnerable. The colonial attitude during the Seven Years' War testified to the limited basis on which the presumed commonality of interest in se-

[29] Ibid., 17:1267. Cf. 18:534.

curity and defense had rested. To argue in 1775 that such commonality of interest persisted, and this despite the events of the intervening years, bordered on the absurd. That the interposition of Parliament would be reserved to cases of wartime scarcely improved matters, for it was precisely in war that Great Britain would prove least able to exercise the power in question. Burke's assurance that the colonies would honor their imperial obligations—based as it was on the trust that sprang from ties that, "though light as air, were as strong as links of iron"—was devoid of foundation. It added nothing to the reality that the colonies were to be left quite free to do as they pleased, or, to use the terms of the Hartley plan, that they would enjoy the "inestimable privilege of judging for themselves of the expediency, fixing the amount, and determining the application of the grants."[30]

The abandonment of attempts to insure colonial support for imperial defense was to be attended as well by the abandonment of efforts to maintain a colonial civil list. It is true that in no plan of conciliation is the point made explicit, yet the presumption that the issue of a civil list is no longer to be contended for seems only reasonable. It accords with the general opposition demand for a return to the old relationship and follows from the abandonment of any further efforts to seek a revenue from the colonies. Having once capitulated on the Massachusetts legislation, as well as having repealed most of the other legislation enacted for the colonies since the mid-1760s, the abandonment of a civil list would seem to follow as a matter of course.

There remained the vital interest in preserving imperial regulation of colonial trade. In the plans of conciliation put forth by the opposition, the need to safequard this interest was acknowledged and even emphasized. How were the restraints on trade and navigation to be protected? In Chatham's plan, there is no mechanism left for doing so, save that which was operative prior to 1763. Having proposed either the repeal or suspension of all legislation relating to the colonies passed since 1763, Chatham let the safeguarding of the laws of trade rest upon arrangements that had been in effect prior to this period. Although they might prove quite as inadequate in the future as they had proven in the past, the Chatham proposals afforded no further safeguards. Other proposals, by con-

[30] Ibid., 18:567.

trast, did not go quite so far, Burke would retain the courts of vice-Admiralty with their extended jurisdiction, as "one of the capital securities of the Act of Navigation," though he would provide that these courts be "more commodious to those who sue, or are sued."[31] Shelburne would retain the American board of customs commissioners; "the customs-house laws in America were necessary to the due recognition of trade, and the maintenance of our monopoly."[32]

The meaning of these proposals is difficult to determine. Chatham, in effect, called for capitulation to American demands. The British statesman who had doubled the size of the national debt in a war on behalf of American security was now prepared to abandon any meaningful attempt to control the colonies. The positions of Burke and Shelburne are less easily characterized, for the proposal to maintain and even extend the post-1763 reforms governing the courts of vice-Admiralty certainly did not meet the demands of the Continental Congress, whose opposition to the courts lay not in their inconvenience but in their unconstitutionality. Making the courts more convenient to the litigants would have compounded, not alleviated, the transgression. Still, the point remains that the opposition remained committed, in principle at least, to maintaining the Acts of Trade and Navigation, and there existed the possibility that such a commitment might have to be vindicated through force. The central difficulty presented by opposition thought is how to square this commitment with the assertion, made with equal insistence, that a war with America would prove ruinous to Great Britain whether it ended in victory or defeat for the imperial state.

[VII]

There is no reason to doubt that the opposition was sincere in its commitment to preserve British sovereignty over the colonies, that, no less than the government, it equated this preservation with the integrity of the effective constitution, and that it found the same vital interests protected by continued parliamentary supremacy over America as did the government. This being the case, it had no alternative but to support, as a matter of principle, the

[31] Ibid., p. 525.
[32] Ibid., p. 922.

employment of force if and when sovereignty was placed in question, just as it had no alternative but to support the employment of force if and when necessary in defense of the great objects of empire. Yet it was precisely this commitment, this unavoidable commitment, to force that lay at the center of the opposition's difficulties and created an insoluble dilemma. The problem went deeper than specifying the circumstances in which the opposition would be prepared to make good on its commitment. However ambiguous and evasive this definition might be, there remained the commitment itself. Its acceptance evidently meant that Englishmen might be ruled over without their consent. Its acceptance also meant that force might have to be employed in circumstances holding out the virtual certainty that the cost would prove far in excess of the possible benefits.

The problem created for the opposition, then, was how to reconcile its commitment in principle to force with its conviction that America could not be governed by force. For the Rockinghamites, this was not a moral problem. Their resistance to a policy of coercion rested not on the immorality of ruling over men without their consent but on the inexpediency of doing so. The Rockinghamites, after all, are not to be confused with the true radicals of the day. The minister's followers were very far removed from a Richard Price, who did take an unequivocal stand based on moral principle. But Price's position was rooted in the essential equality of the peoples forming the empire, a political equality that was to be given application at home as well. The Rockinghamites scarcely shared this position. On the contrary, it was as foreign to their outlook as it was to the outlook of the "new tories."[33]

There are passages, it is true, in Burke's great speeches on America that do suggest—but merely so—the illegitimacy of ruling over men without their consent. "To prove that the Americans ought not to be free," he once ruefully noted, "we are obliged to depreciate the value of freedom itself; and we never seem to gain a paltry advantage over them in debate, without attacking some of those principles, or deriding some of those feelings, for which our ancestors have shed their blood."[34] This was undoubtedly the case. It implied that the sovereignty of the British Parliament over the

---

[33] See *Observations on the Nature of Civil Liberty, and the Justice and Policy of the War Against America* (London, 1776), p. 34.
[34] *PH*, 18:499.

American provinces could be asserted and maintained only on principles repugnant to those of the Glorious Revolution. Yet Burke
never drew this conclusion; he merely implied it. His celebrated
refusal to discuss the issue of right stemmed instead from his conviction that a debate with the Americans conducted on grounds of
right would not end—had not ended—to the advantage of the
imperial state. He believed in the legitimacy of parliamentary rule
over the colonies "in all cases whatsoever," but he believed that
an attempt to establish the legitimacy of this power in the principle
of consent could not succeed. He located this legitimacy elsewhere—in settled institutions and practices, in the historic lineaments of the ancient constitution, and thus in his peculiar reading
of the imperial-colonial status quo.

For Burke, then, the error of a policy of coercion lay in its
inexpediency. He rejected force "not as an odious, but as a feeble
instrument." To use it alone could be no more than a temporary
measure, for "a nation is not to be governed which is perpetually
to be conquered." A government does not rule by the forces at its
disposal but by the authority it commands. If Britain were to win
by force of arms, the quiet of the Americans would be "nothing
but the meditation of revenge." Finally, he warned that if conciliation failed, the British could have recourse to arms; "but, force
failing, no further hope of reconciliation is left."[35] Thus, Burke's
position on force was that it was prudent to refrain from exercising
the boundless power of Parliament in any cases where such exercise
would meet with colonial resistance. But for Burke this created no
dilemma. Persuaded that the Americans wanted nothing more than
to remain faithful children of the empire, he believed the task of
policy was simply to permit the real inclinations of the colonies to
find expression.

The opposition considered the practical difficulty of ruling over
men without their consent in the context of a still broader critique
of the hazards that would be incurred by a war with America. By
far the most telling of opposition arguments, the critique is a full
exposition, in the context of the Anglo-American conflict, of the
disutility of force. In war with America, Chatham declared at the
outset of the debate, "it was little matter for whom victory declared,
as ruin and destruction must be the inevitable consequence to both

[35] Ibid., pp. 490–91.

parties."[36] It was by no means clear that the metropolis could win a military victory over the colonies. Certainly, it could not so do without making an immense effort. Quite apart from the resistance the Americans would be able to mount by virtue of their own considerable resources, at some point in the course of such war they must be expected to seek the assistance of Britain's enemies. France would need no encouragement to make the most of such a golden opportunity. At the propitious moment the French, and very likely the Spanish as well, would fall upon Great Britain, then occupied with its American war.[37] The efforts required to meet and to defeat this combination of forces would make the efforts of the previous war pale by comparison, as would the perils thereby incurred in the event of failure. The consequences of failure were chilling: "Reduced to her insular dominions; curtailed in her commerce; the principal source of her wealth and naval power transferred into the hands of her enemies; her blood and treasure exhausted; her revenues lessened; oppressed with an enormous debt, and debilitated with unsuccessful exertions; she will lose her power and consequence in the system of Europe, and be exposed almost a defenceless prey to the first neighbour who shall chuse to invade her."[38]

The ministry shared the opposition's view of the consequences of defeat; indeed, the government's view that these consequences would follow from the loss of America without war formed the compelling motive to spare no expense in retaining the colonies within the empire. Yet the opposition viewed the consequences of victory as being almost equally devastating. The conquest of the colonies would be attended by the exhaustion of Britain's blood and treasure, for the Americans would acknowledge defeat only after having invoked the aid of others and having resisted to the last man. Nor could the cost of victory be compensated for by restoration of the trade and commerce that heretofore had been the foundation of Britain's wealth and power. In victory almost as much as in defeat, the great interest alleged to justify war with America would be compromised, if not destroyed. The "happy consequences" of victory would thus result "in the empty assertion of an unprofitable sovereignty over desolated provinces. . . .

[36] Ibid., p. 203.
[37] Ibid., pp. 962 (Grafton), 491 (Burke).
[38] Ibid., p. 789 (Adair).

[A]cquired by violence and force, it cannot be preserved but by the same means; and our acknowledged revenues, must be still further drained, by the constant expence of fleets and armies, to support our unjust authority." [39] A government á la Prusse, supported by a large occupation force, would be required to hold the colonies. The result would be not only the enslavement of America but eventually the enslavement of Great Britain as well. [40] No victory could prove more pyrrhic.

It might be supposed that the government supported the contrary view; that it countered the black pessimism of the opposition with its own shallow optimism. Such was not the case. Extravagant outbursts that dismissed the martial qualities of the "raw, undisciplined" colonial soldier, such as those occasionally made by Sandwich, [41] reflected his own empty bravado, not the considered view of the government. Neither North in the Commons nor Mansfield in the Lords once allowed himself the consolation, during the long debate of 1775–76, that victory would prove to be easy. Clearly, the North ministry did not go to war with the expectation of defeat. Yet it knew that its chosen path would be difficult and that victory might elude the empire. And it shared more than a little of the apprehension, repeatedly voiced by the opposition, that military victory might be attended by problems that would make very difficult the restoration of a satisfactory relationship with the colonies. Still, the ministry saw no alternative, in the end, to a policy of coercion. As the magnificant armada of the Howe Brothers set sail for New York in the spring of 1776, Mansfield reflected the anxieties of the government, its mind divided to the very end. "This country," he told the Lords, "is now arrived at a very tremendous crisis, just commencing a war of a nature entirely new; a war, that must necessarily be very expensive, and the issue of which no man can foretell." He conceded "that the kingdom will in a great measure be left defenceless; that we can have no certainty that France or Spain will long preserve their present pacific dispositions; that we have been reduced to the necessity of hiring foreign troops, and sending to the parts of other kingdoms for transports." But what, he asked, was the alternative? "America has rebelled; America is in arms; not defensively, but offensively; even if we were willing

[39] Ibid., p. 788 (Adair).
[40] Ibid., p. 755 (Gov. Johnstone).
[41] Ibid., p. 446.

to cease hostilities, they are not. We must therefore act with vigour, and we must at least show ourselves determined to surmount their opposition."[42]

If the opposition's view of the hazards of war with America was more pessimistic than that of the government's, this indicates only that its dilemma was sharper. It does not indicate how the dilemma would have been resolved. The opposition employed its case against coercion to support its case for pursuing a policy of conciliation. If there was no guarantee, however, that conciliation would succeed, the prospect that one day force might have to be employed could not be avoided. Nor would it matter greatly, in the balance of things, that the failure of conciliation would then find the metropolis united over a policy of coercion. The opposition pressed hard upon this consideration, but it carried little persuasiveness. The British political nation was not seriously divided over the government's policy. If anything, preponderant opinion was for showing more determination in bringing the colonies to submission than the North ministry had been willing to show. Besides, a still more united metropolis would not change the hazards incurred by war with America. If the opposition's estimate of these hazards was even approximately correct, there was no alternative to a policy of conciliation. It was not true, as Burke had said, that if conciliation failed, the British might have recourse to arms; but that if force failed, no further hope of conciliation would be left. Instead, the opposition's case on the disutility of force meant that if reconciliation failed, no further hope would be left. Yet the opposition drew precisely the opposite conclusion. After declaring that a war with the colonies would have no victors, Chatham went on to affirm that if he "could once bring himself to be persuaded that the Americans entertained the most distant intentions" of throwing off Parliament's legislative supremacy, he would be "the first and most zealous mover for securing and enforcing that power by every possible exertion.[43]

There was only one way to reconcile the apparent contradiction between the belief in the impossibility of conquering America and the commitment to employ force, if necessary, to preserve Parliament's supremacy over America. It was to insist that if the proper

[42] Ibid., p. 1283.
[43] Ibid., p. 203.

policy—a truly conciliatory policy—were followed, force would never have to be used against the colonies. The opposition had carved out a position that insured against its ever having to face up to the crucial question so long as it remained an opposition. It might, and did, insist as a prerequisite to employing coercive measures that the government make concessions that were impossible to make without the surrender, de facto if not de jure, of parliamentary authority over the colonies. Moreover, it could do so with the assurance that the North government could not possibly make these concessions without committing political suicide. Alternatively, the opposition might, and did, define away the conditions—however ambiguous and lacking in realism—that would, on its own stated grounds, necessitate the use of force. Either method led to the same result. The opposition's understanding of the crisis, and of the means for resolving it, would never have to be put to the test.

Is it idle to ask what the old Whigs might have done had they been in office at the time? Would they have acted consistently with their understanding of the crisis? If they had, would they have moved to the point of conceding, in substance if not in form, the issue of sovereignty? Many years ago, Lewis Namier took the now well known position that, had "Burke and his friends" been in power, the outcome of the quarrel with America would very likely have been the same as it was under the North government. "Their ideas," Namier wrote of the old Whigs, "were no less hierarchical and authoritarian than those of George III and Lord North, and to them, too, trade was the soul of Empire."[44] Namier's position is not really contradicted by Bernard Donoughue's view that the Rockinghamites "had certainly never been coercionists," that they "saw the Americans suffering, like themselves, from the oppressive authority of the royal prerogative as lately exercised," and that they "could, therefore, with genuine conviction take up the cause of the discontented Americans."[45] However genuine their conviction, it stemmed from the condition of political exile in which they had found themselves since the mid-1760s. Their return to power would likely have altered, if not altogether removed, the basis of that conviction. In this event, the Rockinghamites would no longer have found themselves in the same position as the Americans and, to

[44] *England in the Age of the American Revolution*, pp. 39–40.
[45] *British Politics*, p. 133.

this extent at least, would no longer have had the same reasons for identifying with them. In this event as well, the longstanding commitment of the Rockinghamites to maintain British sovereignty intact would have been put to the test in a way it could not possibly be tested so long as they remained in opposition.

The case of Lord Dartmouth, a member of the Rockingham government in 1766, is perhaps indicative of the road the party of his former patron might have taken. The man who held the position of American secretary from 1772 to 1775 had come to office with the reputation of being conciliatory and sympathetic to the colonists. Yet, step by step, Dartmouth had been led to support a policy of coercion which would end in war. More reluctant than any other member of the North cabinet to endorse the use of armed force against America, he nevertheless overcame his deeply felt reservations. His unwillingness to preside over the direction of the war testified to his awareness that he was temperamentally unfit for the task and not to his doubt that the effort must be made to put down the rebellion. On March 14, 1776, several months following his resignation as American secretary, Dartmouth aired his "own particular sentiments" before the House of Lords. Speaking from his own bitter experience and fully supporting the policy of the government, he condemned "that plan of mistaken lenity" of which he himself had once been guilty. Of his past "anxiety" to treat the colonies "with tenderness," he remarked that the Americans "have treated those marks of favour as so many indications of national imbecility; they have abused this lenity in proportion as it has been liberally and affectionately exercised; and have imputed our humanity and forbearance, not to motives of tenderness and maternal affection, but to a timid backwardness and want of ability to assert our rights."[46]

It is quite probable that what happened to Dartmouth would have happened to the Rockingham Whigs or indeed to the Chathamites had either group enjoyed a position of responsibility during the 1770s. To so conclude is not to imply that the opposition was insincere—indeed, their sincerity, or lack thereof, has very little to do with the resolution of the problem posed by Namier. It has much more to do with the view taken of the inevitability of the imperial-colonial conflict. For if the conclusion is drawn that the

[46] *PH*, 18:1255.

controversy was intractable, it must also be supposed that the range
of choice would have been no greater for a Rockingham or Chatham
ministry than it was for the ministry of Lord North, and that the
conciliatory disposition of the opposition groups would have been
tested in a way it had never been tested before. Faced then with
a terrible choice they could not escape—the certain loss of the
colonies without war, the distant hope of retaining the colonies
with war and all its expense—it is very likely that a ministry formed
by Rockingham or Chatham would have been drawn into coercive
action—and ultimately into war—in the same fashion the North
ministry had been drawn.

[VIII]

This conclusion points to the greater consensus within which the
parliamentary debate over America was undertaken and against
which the significance of the debate must be judged. Contemporary
historiography occasionally acknowledges, and even emphasizes,
the limitations this consensus imposed on the possibility of reaching
a settlement of the dispute acceptable to the two sides. Indeed, to
the extent that the war that led to the breakup of the First British
Empire is found inevitable, it is due to the consensus that precluded serious consideration, let alone acceptance, of a settlement
that would have satisfied the colonies while keeping them within
the empire. The Americans demanded the abandonment of parliamentary supremacy and the substitution of loose ties with the
metropolis. They rejected the sovereignty of Parliament but promised continued allegiance to the King and continued acceptance of
royal prerogative. The British could not accept this settlement,
however, given their prevailing constitutional arrangements, which
they had come to regard as sacrosanct. Even if they had been
capable of viewing the world through other than a mercantilist
lens, they were bound to a political structure that would not permit
the settlement demanded by the colonists. In the words of Namier:

Economic considerations impelled British statesmen to take action with
regard to the Empire at a time when, even for constitutional reasons, a
true settlement could not be attained. In 1760 Great Britain had not
reached a stage at which it would have been possible to remodel the
Empire as a federation of self-governing States under a Crown detached

from the actual government of any of its component parts. Royalty, which is now the bond of Empire, was still an active factor in British politics, and to eighteenth-century Englishmen any exercise of its attributes apart from the British Parliament would have seemed a dangerous and unconstitutional reversion to "prerogative." This junction between King and Parliament in Great Britain was by itself bound to carry the supremacy of the British Parliament into the Colonies; and the very fact that George III so thoroughly and loyally stood by the constitutional principles of the time rendered a conflict inevitable.[47]

Namier did not conclude that at the time of the accession of George III a war was inevitable, only a conflict. He saw no way, however, by which this conflict might have been peacefully resolved to the satisfaction of the parties. No "mechanical devices," he wrote, such as representation in the British Parliament or an American union along the lines proposed at the 1754 Albany Congress, bore much promise. He also dismissed the "conscious opinions and professed views" bearing directly on the imperial problem; these opinions and views counted for very little when compared to "the very structure and life of the Empire." Acting under the pressure of circumstances—"which means of mass movements and of the mental climate in their own circles"—statesmen were virtually powerless to deal with the imperial problem in a way that would have led to a true settlement. The "true settlement" Namier had in mind was the settlement the colonists were explicitly demanding in 1774 and had already been moving toward for many years. The rigidity of British political culture precluded its acceptance and thus made inevitable not only a conflict but, in the end, a war.[48]

Does Namier's view have the effect of shifting responsibility for the conflict that resulted in war? Clearly, he relieved individual British statesmen of the responsibility that a neo-whig historiography would assign to them through his emphasis on the "circumstances" that conditioned their actions but that they were powerless to change in any significant degree. In place of the responsibility of individual statesmen there is instead the responsibility of a political order that could not adapt to change. The shoulders of responsibility have broadened, as it were, but they are still unmistakeably British shoulders. This is the conclusion a distinguished

---

[47] *England in the Age of American Revolution*, p. 37.
[48] Ibid., p. 100.

colonial historian has reached in a recent essay that examines the implications of Namier's view. The Namier thesis, Jack P. Greene has written, contains three interdependent hypotheses:

The first is that the devotion of both the King and Parliament to the principle of parliamentary supremacy was *bound* to lead to parliamentary intervention in American affairs in the 1760s. . . . The second hypothesis is that once the Americans had challenged any aspect of Parliament's authority over the colonies the King and Parliament were *bound* to defend that authority and to regard American opposition as "dangerous and unconstitutional." The third hypothesis . . . is that the "terms in which the overwhelming majority of the politically minded public . . . considered" the imperial problem at the time made a "true settlement" of it, that is, a solution along the lines advocated by the Americans, absolutely impossible. If each of these hypotheses is true, only one conclusion can follow: the structure of British politics during the earlier years of the reign of George III made the American Revolution inevitable. The demise of the First British Empire was the necessary result of its own structural failure.[49]

The Namierite view substitutes helpless statesmen for willful and designing statesmen. Bound by ties from which they could not free themselves even had they wanted to, British leaders took their nation into a disastrous war that otherwise might have been avoided. The argument of inevitability advanced by Namier is very far removed from the argument of a Josiah Tucker. In Tucker's view, the essence of the conflict, and the reason for its intractability, was the utterly contradictory character of the claims advanced by each party. What one side claimed the other side had either to deny altogether or to admit and thereby to concede the entirety of its position. Tucker treated the conflict as real, in the sense that the constitutional positions of the parties, being mutually exclusive, could be preserved only by the refusal to compromise, even though he disputed the equation the government drew between the preservation of sovereignty and the retention of British commerce with America. By contrast, in the Namierite view, the constitutional conflict has no integrity of its own. For Namier, what is real are the constraints that prevented the British from resolving the issue of sovereignty without war.

Namier's argument seems a curious one—curious because it identifies structural failure with the inability to adapt to change

[49] "The Plunge of Lemmings," pp. 144–45.

rather than with the inability to resist change dangerous to the interests of the state. Surely, however, both can be indicative of structural failure. It might be argued, and with far greater persuasiveness, that "structural failure" would have existed only had British statesmen lacked the will to preserve, through war if necesssary, the constitutional arrangements in the care of which they had been entrusted, and the continued existence of which they believed (however mistakenly) to be indispensable to the maintenance of Britain's position as a great power. This is at least the case if one assumes that the constitutional settlement imagined by Namier would have represented a surrender of the metropolitan claim to control. Namier, however, appears to have assumed that a "true settlement" of the conflict, though necessitating the abandonment of parliamentary supremacy over the colonies, would nonetheless have preserved a mechanism for effective political control. Yet this view is very difficult to sustain. However important the King may have been in political life at the center of the empire, on the periphery his influence had by this time greatly dimmed. Indeed, the importance of the King's position in British domestic politics—of which Namier himself contributed so much to our understanding—may have obscured the vision of this great historian when he came to consider the lineaments of the imperial problem. In the colonies the King lacked the sources of support that were indispensable to the maintenance of his constitutional role at home. In Great Britain, as David Hume once noted, "the crown has so many offices at its disposal that, when assisted by the honest and disinterested part of the House, it will always command the resolutions of the whole, so far, at least, as to preserve the ancient constitution from danger. We may therefore give to this influence what name we please; we may call it by the invidious appelations of *corruption* and *dependence*; but some degree and some kind of it are inseparable from the very nature of the constitution and necessary to the preservation of our mixed government."[50]

It was the absence of such support to monarchy in the colonies— put differently, the irrelevance of such support to colonial con-

---

[50] "Of the Independence of Parliament," in *David Hume's Political Essays*, ed. Charles W. Hendel (Indianapolis, 1953), p. 70. Cf. Bernard Bailyn, *The Origins of American Politics*; and Adam Smith, *The Wealth of Nations*, pp. 583–84.

ditions, even had it existed—that made the solution advocated by the Americans and endorsed by Namier no solution at all. The very "imbecility" of the colonial governors had sparked much of the reform movement of the early 1760s. A decade later the governors inspired neither fear nor respect. The loss of parliamentary control over the colonies, the British were persuaded, thus meant the loss of any and all effective control. The Americans, Lord Mansfield once declared in articulating this conviction, "would allow the king of Great Britain a nominal sovereignty over them, but nothing else. They would throw off the dependency on the crown of Great Britain, but not on the person of the king, whom they would render a cypher."[51]

It was thus not the fear of a reversion to prerogative that stood in the way of a settlement. The British political nation rejected the American solution of equal legislative bodies under a common sovereign King, not because the King's position was so strong at home, but because that position was so weak in the colonies. Acceptance of the solution to the imperial problem advocated by the Americans and endorsed by Namier would have signaled that the complete unraveling in imperial control had now developed a momentum that was unstoppable. It would have meant that British statesmen had come finally to the realization that the end of empire, and of much else besides, was now at hand.

[51] *PH*, 18:958.

PRIMARY SOURCES

Magazines

Annual Register
Gentleman's Magazine

Contemporary Books and Pamphlets

Adams, John, and Leonard, Daniel. *Novanglus and Massachusettensis; or, Political Essays, Published in the Years 1774 and 1775, on the Principle Points of Controversy between Great Britain and Her Colonies* . . . Boston, 1819.

Bernard, Francis. *Letters to the Ministry from Governor Bernard, General Gage, and Commodore Hood* . . . Boston, 1769.

———. *Select Letters on the Trade and Government of America* . . . London, 1774.

Bolingbroke, Henry St. John, Viscount Lord. *The Works of the Late Right Honorable Henry St. John, Lord Viscount Bolingbroke.* 3 vols. London, 1754.

Brougham, Henry Peter, Lord. *An Inquiry into the Colonial Policy of the European Powers.* 2 vols. Edinburgh, 1803.

Burke, William. *Remarks on the Letter Addressed to Two Great Men.* London, 1760.

[Douglas, John]. *A Letter Addressed to Two Great Men.* London, 1760.

Hume, David. *Essays and Treatises on Several Subjects.* 2 vols. London, 1788.

Hutchinson, Thomas. *The History of the Colony and Province of Massachusetts Bay.* Edited by Lawrence Shaw Mayo. 3 vols. Cambridge, Mass., 1936.

[Hutchinson, Thomas, et al]. *Copy of Letters Sent to Great Britain, by His Excellency Thomas Hutchinson* . . . Boston, 1773.

Johnson, Samuel. *Taxation No Tyranny: An Answer to the Resolutions and Addresses of the American Congress.* London, 1775.

Knox William. *An Appendix to the Present State of the Nation, Containing a Reply to the Observations on that Pamphlet.* London, 1769.

———. *The Controversy Between Great Britain and Her Colonies Reviewed* . . . London, 1769.

————. *Extra Official State Papers Addressed to the Right Hon. Lord Rawdon* . . . 2 vols. London, 1789.

————. *The Interest of the Merchants and Manufacturers of Great Britain in the Present Contest with the Colonies Stated and Considered*. London, 1774.

————. *The Justice and Policy of the Late Act of Parliament for Making more Effectual Provision for the Government of Quebec Asserted and Proved* . . . *London, 1774*.

————. *The Present State of the Nation, Particularly with Respect of its Trade, Finances* . . . London, 1768.

Mauduit, Israel. *Considerations on The Present German War*. 1st ed. London, 1760.

Mitchell, John. *The Contest in America between Britain and France, with Its Consequences and Importance* . . . London, 1757.

Pownall, Thomas. *The Administration of the Colonies*. 2d ed. London, 1765.

Ramsey, David. *The History of the American Revolution*. 2 vols. London, 1793.

Ruffhead, Owen. *The Conduct of the Ministry Impartially Examined* . . . London, 1760.

Sheffield, John Baker Holroyd, Earl of. *Observations on the Commerce of the American States*. London, 1784.

Smith, Adam. *An Inquiry into the Nature and Causes of the Wealth of Nations*. 1776. Reprint. New York, 1937.

Tucker, Josiah. *Four Tracts* . . . Gloucester, 1774.

————. *A Letter to Edmund Burke*. Gloucester, 1775.

————. *The Respective Pleas and Arguments of the Mother Country and of the Colonies, Distinctly Set Forth* . . . Gloucester, 1775.

————. *The True Interest of Great Britain Set Forth in Regard to the Colonies*. Gloucester, 1774.

Whately, Thomas. *Considerations on the Trade and Finances of This Kingdom, Addressed to the Two Houses of Parliament*. London, 1769.

————. *The Regulations Lately Made with Respect to the Colonies Considered*. London, 1765.

Correspondence, Papers, and Memoirs of Individuals

The Diary and Autobiography of John Adams. Edited by Lyman H. Butterfield. 4 vols. Cambridge, Mass., 1961.

The Papers of John Adams. Edited by Robert J. Taylor et al. 4 vols. to date. Cambridge, Mass., 1977–.

The Works of John Adams. Edited by Charles F. Adams. 10 vols. Boston, 1856.

The Writings of Samuel Adams. Edited by Harry A. Cushing. 4 vols. New York, 1904.

Barrington, Shute, ed. *The Political Life of William Wildman Viscount Barrington, Compiled from Original Papers.* London, 1814.

The Barrington-Bernard Correspondence and Illustrative Matter, 1760–1770. Edited by Edward Channing and Archibald Cary Coolidge. Cambridge, Mass., 1912.

Correspondence of John, Fourth Duke of Bedford. Edited by John Russell. 3 vols. London, 1842–46.

"The Bowdoin and Temple Papers." Massachusetts Historical Society. *Collections.* 6th ser., vol. 9. Boston, 1897.

The Correspondence of Edmund Burke. Edited by Thomas W. Copeland et al. 9 vols. Cambridge, 1958–70.

Edmund Burke on the American Revolution: Selected Speeches and Letters. Edited by Elliott Robert Barkan. New York, 1966.

The Works of the Right Honourable Edmund Burke. 16 vols. London, 1826.

Sir Henry Cavendish's Debates of the House of Commons during the Thirteenth Parliament of Great Britain. Edited by John Wright. 2 vols. London, 1841–43.

Correspondence of William Pitt, Earl of Chatham. Edited by W. S. Taylor and J. H. Pringle. 4 vols. London, 1838–40.

"Letters of Dennys De Berdt, 1757–70." Edited by A. Matthews. Colonial Society of Massachusetts. *Publications.* Vol. 13, *Transactions, 1910–1911.* Pp. 203–461.

The Writings of John Dickinson. Edited by Paul L. Ford. 2 vols. Vol. 1: *Political Writings, 1764–1774.* Philadelphia, 1895.

The Political Journal of George Budd Dodington. Edited by J. Carswell and L. A. Dralle. Oxford, 1965.

"The Fitch Papers: Correspondence and Documents during Thomas Fitch's Governorship of the Colony of Connecticut, 1754–1766." Connecticut History Society. *Collections.* Vol. 18. Hartford, 1920.

The Papers of Benjamin Franklin. Edited by Leonard W. Labaree et al. 21 vols. to date. New Haven, 1959–.

The Writings of Benjamin Franklin. Edited by Albert Henry Smyth. 10 vols. New York and London, 1905–7.

Benjamin Franklin's Letters to the Press, 1758–1775. Edited by V. W. Crane. Chapel Hill, 1950.

The Correspondence of General Thomas Cage with the Secretaries of State and with the War Office and the Treasury, 1763–1775. Edited by Clarence E. Carter. 2 vols. New Haven, 1931–33.

"Hon. Charles Garth, M.P., the Last Colonial Agent of South Carolina, and Some of His Work." Edited by J. W. Barnwell. *South Carolina Historical and Genealogical Magazine* 26–33 (1925–32).

[Garth, Charles]. "Stamp Act Papers." *Maryland Historical Magazine* 6 (1911):282–305.

The Correspondence of King George the Third from 1760 to December 1783. Edited by John Fortescue. 6 vols. London, 1927–28.

L. B. Namier. *Additions and Corrections to Sir John Fortescue's Edition of the Correspondence of King George the Third.* Manchester, 1937.

Letters from George III to Lord Bute, 1756–1766. Edited by Romney Sedgwick. London, 1939; cited as Bute Letters.

Autobiography and Political Correspondence of Augustus Henry, Third Duke of Grafton. Edited by William R. Anson. London, 1898.

The Grenville Papers: Being the Correspondence of Richard Grenville, Earl Temple, K.G., and the Right Hon. George Grenville . . . Edited by W. J. Smith. 4 vols. London, 1852–53.

Additional Grenville Papers, 1763–1765. Edited by J. Tomlinson. Manchester, 1962.

The Letters of David Hume. Edited by J.Y.T. Greig. 2 vols. Oxford, 1932.

The Life and Correspondence of Philip Yorke, Earl of Hardwicke. Edited by Philip C. Yorke. 3 vols. Cambridge, 1913.

The Diary and Letters of His Excellency Thomas Hutchinson, Esq. Edited by Peter O. Hutchinson. 2 vols. 1883–86.

The Papers of Thomas Jefferson. Edited by Julian Boyd. 19 vols. to date. Princeton, 1950–.

The Jenkinson Papers, 1760–1766. Edited by Ninetta S. Jucker. London, 1949.

"Letters of William Samuel Johnson to the Governors of Connecticut [1766–1771]." Trumbull Papers. *Massachusetts Historical Society. Collections.* 5th ser., vol. 9. Boston, 1855. Pp. 211–490; cited as Trumbull Papers.

[Knox, William]. "A Project for Imperial Reform: 'Hints Respecting the Settlement for Our American Provinces,' 1763." Edited by Thomas C. Barrow. *William and Mary Quarterly*, 3d ser. 24 (1967): 108–26.

Papers of James Madison. Edited by William T. Hutchinson et al. Vols. 1–10 (Chicago, 1962–77); Vols 11–13 (Charlottesville, 1977–).

The Papers of George Mason. Edited by Robert A. Rutland. 3 vols. Chapel Hill, 1970.

The Papers of Robert Morris, 1781–1784. Edited by E. James Ferguson. 5 vols. to date. Pittsburgh, 1973–.

The Writings of Thomas Paine. Edited by M. D. Conway. 4 vols. New York, 1967.

"Letters of Charles Paxton, 1768–1769." Edited by George G. Wolkins. Massachusetts Historical Society. *Proceedings* 56 (1923).

"The Pitkin Papers: Correspondence and Documents during William Pitkin's Governorship of the Colony of Connecticut, 1766–1769." Edited by Albert C. Bates. Connecticut Historical Society. *Collections*. Vol. 19. Hartford, 1921.

Memoirs of the Marquis of Rockingham and His Contemporaries. Edited by George Thomas, Earl of Albemarle. 2 vols. 1852.

"The Parliamentary Diaries of Nathaniel Ryder, 1764–1767." Edited by P.D.G. Thomas. *Camden Miscellany* 23, pp. 229–351. Camden Fourth Series, vol. 7, London Royal Historical Society, 1969; cited as Ryder Diary.

The Fourth Earl of Sandwich: Diplomatic Correspondence, 1763–1765. Edited by Frank Spencer. Manchester, 1961.

The Private Papers of John, Earl of Sandwich . . ., 1771–1782. Edited by G. R. Barnes and J. H. Owen. Navy Records Society. 4 vols. London, 1932–28.

"Correspondence between William Strahan and David Hall, 1763–1777." *Pennsylvania Magazine of History and Biography* 10 (1886).

Walpole, Horace. *Memoirs of the Reign of King George III*. Edited by Denis Le Marchant. 4 vols. London, 1851.

The Writings of George Washington, 1745–1799. Edited by John C. Fitzpatrick. 39 vols. Washington, D.C., 1931–44.

The Works of James Wilson. Edited by Robert G. McCloskey. 2 vols. Cambridge, Mass., 1967.

Official Documents and Other Printed Sources

Acts of the Privy Council of England: Colonial Series [1613–1783]. Edited by William L. Grant and James Munro. 6 vols. London, 1908–12.

American Archives. Edited by Peter Force. 9 vols. Washington, D.C., 1837–53.

Anglo-French Boundary Disputes in the West, 1749–1763. Edited, with introduction, by Theodore C. Pease. Illinois State Historical Library. *Collections*. Vol. 27. Springfield, Ill., 1936.

Calendar of Home Office Papers of the Reign of George III, 1760–1775. Edited by J. Redington and R. A. Roberts. 4 vols. London, 1878–99.

A Collection of Interesting, Authentic Papers Relative to the Dispute between Great Britain and America, 1764–1775. Edited by John Almon. London, 1777.

Colonial and State Records of North Carolina. Edited by W. L. Saunders et al. 10 vols. Raleigh, N.C., 1886–90.

"Debates on the Declaratory Act and the Repeal of the Stamp Act, 1766." *American Historical Review* 17 (1911/12):536–86.

Documents Relating to the Colonial . . . History of . . . New Jersey. Edited by William A. Whitehead et al. 36 vols. Newark, 1880–1941.

Documents Relating to the Constitutional History of Canada, 1759–1791. Edited by A. Shortt and A. G. Doughty. Ottawa, 1907.

Documents of the American Revolution, 1770–1783. Colonial Office Series. Edited by K. G. Davies. 21 vols. to date. Shannon, Ireland, 1972.

Documents Relating to the Colonial History of the State of New York. Edited by E. B. O'Callaghan. 15 vols. Albany, 1853–87.

English Defenders of American Freedoms, 1774–1778: Six Pamphlets Attacking British Policy. Compiled by Paul H. Smith. Washington, D.C., 1972.

English Historical Documents. Vol. 9, *American Colonial Documents to 1776,* edited by Merrill Jensen. New York and London, 1955.

English Historical Documents. Vol. 10, *1714–1783,* edited by David B. Horn and Mary Ransome. New York, 1957.

Facsimiles of Manuscripts in European Archives Relating to America, 1773–1783. Edited by B. F. Stevens. 25 vols. London, 1889–98.

"Hints Relative to the Division and Government of the Conquered and Newly Acquired Countries in America." Edited by Verner W. Crane. *Mississippi Valley Historical Review* 8 (1921/22):367–73.

Historical Manuscripts Commission (HMC), *Reports.* 162 vols. London, 1860–: Dartmouth Manuscripts, William Legge, Second Earl of Dartmouth, Letters, in the *Eleventh Report* and *Fourteenth Report;* Stopford-Sackville Manuscripts. Viscount George Sackville, Lord Germain, Letters and papers, in the *Ninth Report,* vol. 3; William Knox, Letters, 1757–1808, in H. V. Knox Manuscripts, in *Various Collections,* vol. 6; C. Fleetwood Weston Underwood Manuscripts, Edward Westen, Letters and papers, 1722–70, in the *Tenth Report,* vol. 1; Lothian Manuscripts.

Illinois on the Eve of the Seven Years' War, 1747–1755. Edited by Theodore C. Pease and Ernestine Jenison. Illinois State Historical Library. *Collections.* Vol. 29. Springfield, Ill., 1940.

Journals of the Continental Congress, 1774–1789. Edited by Worthington C. Ford. 34 vols. Washington, D.C., 1904–37.

Journals of the House of Burgesses of Virginia . . . Edited by J. P. Kennedy and H. R. McIlwaine. 13 vols. Richmond, 1905–15.

Journals of the House of Commons.

Journals of the House of Representatives of Massachusetts. 50 vols. to date. Boston, 1919–.

Letters of Members of the Continental Congress. Edited by Edmund C. Burnett. 8 vols. Washington, D.C., 1921–36.

Maryland Archives. Edited by W. H. Browne et al. 71 vols. to date. Baltimore, 1883–.

The New Regime, 1765–1767. Edited by Clarence W. Alvord and C. E. Carter. Illinois State Historical Library. *Collections.* Vol. 11. Springfield, Ill., 1916.

Pamphlets of the American Revolution. Edited by Bernard Bailyn. 1 vol. to date. Cambridge, Mass., 1965–.

The Parliamentary History of England from the Earliest Period to 1803. Edited by William Cobbett and T. C. Hansard. 36 vols. London, 1806–20; cited as *PH.*

Pennsylvania Archives: Selected and Arranged from Original Documents in the Office of the Secretary of the Commonwealth . . . Edited by Samuel Hazard et al. 138 vols. Harrisburg and Philadelphia, 1852–1935.

Proceedings and Debates of the British Parliaments Respecting North America. Edited by Leo Francis Stock. 5 vols. Washington, D.C., 1924–41.

Prologue to Revolution: Sources and Documents on the Stamp Act Crisis, 1764–1766. Edited by Edmund S. Morgan. Chapel Hill, 1959.

Records of the Colony of Rhode Island and Providence Plantations. Edited by John R. Bartlett. 10 vols. Providence, 1856–65.

Royal Instructions to British Colonial Governors, 1670–1776. Edited by Leonard W. Labaree. 2 vols. New York, 1935.

"Stamp Act Papers." *Maryland Historical Magazine* 6 (1911):282–305.

The Statistical History of the United States from Colonial Times to the Present. Edited by Ben Wattenberg. New York, 1976.

The Statutes at Large from Magna Charta to . . . 1761 (continued to 1806). Edited by Danby Pickering. 46 vols. Cambridge, 1762–1807.

Trade and Politics, 1767–1769. Edited by Clarence W. Alvord and C. E. Carter. Illinois State Historical Library. *Collections.* Vol. 16. Springfield, Ill., 1921.

SECONDARY SOURCES

Abarca, Ramon E. "Classical Diplomacy and Bourbon 'Revanche' Strategy, 1763–1770." *Review of Politics* 32 (1970):313–37.

Adams, Randolph G. *Political Ideas of the American Revolution.* 3d ed. New York, 1958.

Alden, John R. *General Gage in America.* Baton Rouge, 1948.

———. *John Stuart and the Southern Colonial Frontier.* Ann Arbor, 1944.

———. *The South in the Revolution, 1763–1789.* Baton Rouge, 1957.

Alvord, Clarence W. *The Mississippi Valley in British Politics: A Study of the Trade, Land Speculation, and Experiments in Imperialism Culminating in the American Revolution.* 2 vols. Cleveland, 1917.

Ammerman, David. *In the Common Cause: American Response to the Coercive Acts of 1774.* Charlottesville, 1974.

Anderson, M. S. "European Diplomatic Relations, 1763–1790." In *The New Cambridge Modern History, Vol. VIII: The American and French Revolution, 1763–1793.* Edited by A. Goodwin. Cambridge, 1965.

———. *Europe in the Eighteenth Century, 1713–1783.* London, 1961.

Andrews, Charles M. "The Boston Merchants and the Nonimportation Movement." Colonial Society of Massachusetts. *Publications,* vol. 19. Transactions. 1916–17. Pp. 159–259.

———. *The Colonial Background of the American Revolution.* New Haven, 1924.

———. *The Colonial Period of American History.* Vol. 4, *England's Commercial and Colonial Policy.* New Haven, 1938.

Bailyn, Bernard. *The Ideological Origins of the American Revolution.* Cambridge, Mass., 1967.

———. *The Ordeal of Thomas Hutchinson.* Cambridge, Mass., 1974.

———. *The Origins of American Politics.* New York, 1967.

Bancroft, George. *History of the United States of America from the Discovery of the Continent.* 6 vols. New York, 1883–85.

Bargar, B. D. *Lord Dartmouth and the American Revolution.* Columbia, 1965.

Barrow, Thomas. "Background to the Grenville Program, 1757–1763." *William and Mary Quarterly,* 3d ser. 22 (1965):93–104.

———. *Trade and Empire: The British Customs Service in Colonial America, 1660–1775.* Cambridge, Mass., 1967.

Basye, A. H. *The Lords Commissioners of Trade and Plantations.* London, 1925.

Becker, Carl L. *The Declaration of Independence: A Study in the History of Political Ideas.* New York, 1942.

Beer, George L. *British Colonial Policy, 1754–1765.* New York, 1907.

Bellot, Leland J. *William Knox: The Life and Thought of an Eighteenth-century Imperialist.* Austin, 1977.

Bemis, Samuel Flagg. *The Diplomacy of the American Revolution.* Bloomington, 1957.

Billington, Ray Allen, ed. *The Reinterpretation of Early American History: Essays in Honor of John Edwin Pomfret.* San Marino, Calif., 1966.

Bjork, Gordon C. "The Weaning of the American Economy: Independence, Market Changes, and Economic Development." *Journal of Economic History* 24 (1964):541–60.

Brewer, John. "The Misfortunes of Lord Bute: A Case Study in Eighteenth-century Political Argument and Public Opinion." *Historical Journal* 16 (1973):3–43.

———. *Party Politics and Popular Ideology at the Accession of George III.* London, 1976.

Brooke, John. *The Chatham Administration, 1766–1768.* London, 1956.

———. *King George III.* London, 1972.

Brown, Peter Douglas. *William Pitt, Earl of Chatham: The Great Commoner.* London, 1978.

Brown, Richard D. "The Massachusetts Convention of Towns, 1768." *William and Mary Quarterly*, 3d ser. 26 (1969).

———. *Revolutionary Politics in Massachusetts: The Boston Committee of Correspondence and the Towns, 1772–1774.* Cambridge, Mass., 1970.

Brown, Weldon A. *Empire or Independence: A Study in the Failure of Reconciliation, 1774–1783.* Port Washington, N.Y., 1966.

Browning, Reed. *The Duke of Newcastle.* New Haven, 1975.

Burt, Alfred Leroy. *The Old Province of Quebec.* Minneapolis and Toronto, 1933.

Butterfield, Herbert. *George III and the Historians.* London, 1957.

———. "The Reconstruction of an Historical Episode: The History of the Enquiry into the Origins of the Seven Years' War" In his *Man on His Past.* Cambridge, 1955.

———. "Review Article: British Foreign Policy, 1762–5." *Historical Journal* 6, no. 1 (1963):131–40.

Chaffin, Robert J. "The Townshend Acts of 1767." *William and Mary Quarterly*, 3d ser. 27 (1970):90–121.

Champagne, Roger. "Family Politics versus Constitutional Principles: The New York Assembly Elections of 1768 and 1769." *William and Mary Quarterly*, 3d ser. 20 (1963):57–79.

Christie, Ian R. "The Earl of Chatham and American Taxation, 1774–75." *The Eighteenth Century* 20 (1979):246–59.

———. *Myth and Reality in Late Eighteenth-century British Politics, and Other Papers.* London, 1970.

———. "William Pitt and American Taxation, 1766: A Problem of Parliamentary Reporting." *Studies in Burke and His Time* 17 (1976):167–79.

———, and Labaree, Benjamin Woods. *Empire or Independence, 1760–1776: A British-American Dialogue on the Coming of the American Revolution.* New York, 1976.

Clark, Dora Mae. "The American Board of Customs, 1767–1783." *American Historical Review* 45 (1940/41).

———. *British Opinion and the American Revolution.* New Haven, 1930.

Coleman, Donald C., ed. *Revisions in Mercantilism*. London, 1969.

Corbett, Julian S. *England in the Seven Years' War: A Study in Combined Strategy*. 2 vols. London, 1907.

Corwin, Edward S. *French Policy and the American Alliance of 1778*. Princeton, 1916.

Davis, Ralph. "English Foreign Trade, 1700–1774." *Economic History Review*, 2d ser. 15 (1962/63): 285–303.

Derry, John. *English Politics and the American Revolution*. London, 1976.

Dickerson, Oliver M. *American Colonial Government, 1696–1765*. Cleveland, 1912.

———. *The Navigation Acts and the American Revolution*. Philadelphia, 1951.

———. "Use Made of the Revenue from the Tax on Tea." *New England Quarterly* 31 (1958): 232–43.

Donoughue, Bernard. *British Politics and the American Revolution: The Path to War, 1773–1775*. London, 1964.

Dorn, Walter L. *Competition for Empire, 1739–1763*. New York, 1940.

———. "Frederick the Great and Lord Bute." *Journal of Modern History* 1 (1929):529–60.

Dull, Jonathan R. *The French Navy and the American Revolution*. Princeton, 1975.

Eccles, W. J. *France in America*. New York, 1972.

Egnal, Marc. "The Economic Development of the Thirteen Continental Colonies, 1720 to 1775." *William and Mary Quarterly*, 3d ser. 32 (1975):191–222.

Eldon, Carl William. *England's Subsidy Policy towards the Continent during the Seven Years' War*. Philadelphia, 1938.

Ericson, Fred J. "British Motives for Expansion in 1763: Territory, Commerce, or Security?" In *Papers of the Michigan Academy of Science, Arts, and Letters*, edited by E. McCartney and W. Steere. Ann Arbor, 1942. 27:581–94.

Ernst, Joseph A. *Money and Politics in America, 1755–1775*. Chapel Hill, 1973.

Fairman, Charles. *The Law of Martial Rule*. Chicago, 1930.

Ferguson, E. James. *The Power of the Purse: A History of American Public Finance, 1776–1790*. Chapel Hill, 1961.

Fieldhouse, David K. "British Imperialism in the Late Eighteenth Century." In *Essays in Imperial Government Presented to Margery Perham*. Edited by K. Robinson and F. Madden. Oxford, 1963.

———. *Economics and Empire, 1830–1914*. Ithaca, 1973.

Fisher, H.E.S. *The Portugal Trade: A Study of Anglo-Portuguese Commerce, 1700–1770*. London, 1971.

Fitzmaurice. *Life of William, Earl of Shelburne*. 2d ed. 2 vols. London, 1912.

Fryer, C. E. "Further Pamphlets for the Canada-Guadeloupe Controversy." *Mississippi Valley Historical Review* 5 (1917):227–30.

Gilbert, Felix. *To the Farewell Address: Ideas of Early American Foreign Policy*. Princeton, 1961.

Gipson, Lawrence Henry "The American Revolution as an Aftermath of the Great War for the Empire, 1754–1763." *Political Science Quarterly* 65 (1950):86–104.

———. *The British Empire before the American Revolution*. 15 vols. New York, 1936–70.

———. *The Coming of the Revolution, 1763–1775*. London, 1954.

Goebel, Dorothy Burne. "The New England Trade and the French West Indies, 1763–1774: A Study in Trade Policies." *William and Mary Quarterly*, 3d ser. 20 (1963):331–72.

Goebel, J. *The Struggle for the Falkland Islands: A Study in Legal and Diplomatic History*. New Haven, 1927.

Graham, Gerald S. "Considerations on the War of American Independence." *Bulletin of the Institute of Historical Research* 22 (1949):22–34.

———. *The Politics of Naval Supremacy: Studies in British Maritime Ascendancy*. London, 1965.

Grant, William L. "Canada versus Guadeloupe, An Episode of the Seven Years' War." *American Historical Review* 17 (1912):735–43.

Greene, Jack P. "Bridge to Revolution: The Wilkes Fund Controversy in South Carolina, 1769–1775." *Journal of Southern History* 29 (1963).

———. "The Plunge of Lemmings: A Consideration of Recent Writings on British Politics and the American Revolution." *South Atlantic Quarterly* 67 (1968).

———. " 'A Posture of Hostility': A Reconsideration of Some Aspects of the Origins of the American Revolution." *Proceedings of the American Antiquarian Society* 87 (1978):27–68.

———. *The Quest for Power: The Lower Houses of Assembly in the Southern Royal Colonies, 1689–1776*. Chapel Hill, 1963.

———. *The Reinterpretation of the American Revolution, 1763–1789*. New York, 1968.

———. "The Seven Years' War and the American Revolution: The Causal Relationship Reconsidered." In *The British Atlantic Empire before the American Revolution*, edited by Peter Marshall and Glyn Williams. London, 1980.

———, ed. *Great Britain and the American Colonies, 1606–1763*. Columbia, S.C., 1970.

———, and Jellison, Richard M. "The Currency Act of 1764 in Imperial-

Colonial Relations, 1764–1776." *William and Mary Quarterly*, 3d ser. 18 (1961).

Guttridge, G. H. *English Whiggism and the American Revolution*. Berkeley, 1942.

Harlow, Vincent T. *The Founding of the Second British Empire: Discovery and Revolution*. 2 vols. London, 1952–64.

Harper, L. A. *The English Navigation Laws*. New York, 1939.

Henderson, H. James. *Party Politics in the Continental Congress*. New York, 1974.

Henretta, James A. *"Salutary Neglect": Colonial Administration under the Duke of Newcastle*. Princeton, 1972.

Higonnet, Patrice Louis-René. "The Origins of the Seven Years' War." *Journal of Modern History* 40 (1968):57–90.

Hoffman, Ross J. S. *The Marquis: A Study of Lord Rockingham, 1730–1782*. New York, 1973.

Horn, David B. "The Diplomatic Revolution." In *The New Cambridge Modern History: Vol. VII: The Old Regime, 1713–1763*, edited by J. O. Lindsay, pp. 440–64. Cambridge, 1957.

—————. *Great Britain and Europe in the Eighteenth Century*. London, 1967.

Hotblack, Kate. "The Peace of Paris, 1763." *Transactions of the Royal Historical Society*, 3d ser. 2 (1908):235–67.

Humphreys, R. A. "Lord Shelburne and the Proclamation of 1763." *English Historical Review* 49 (1934):241–64.

Hutson, James H. "An Investigation of the Inarticulate: Philadelphia's White Oaks." *William and Mary Quarterly*, 3d ser. 28 (1971):3–26.

—————. "The Partition Treaty and the Declaration of American Independence." *Journal of American History* 58 (1971/72):877–96.

—————. *Pennsylvania Politics, 1746–1770*. Princeton, 1972.

Hyam, Ronald. "Imperial Interests and the Peace of Paris (1763)." In *Reappraisals in British Imperial History*, edited by Ronald Hyam and G. Martin. London, 1975.

Jensen, Arthur L. *The Maritime Commerce of Colonial Philadelphia*. Madison, 1963.

Jensen, Merrill. *The Founding of a Nation*. New York, 1968.

Johnson, Allen S. "The Passage of the Sugar Act." *William and Mary Quarterly*, 3d ser. 16 (1959):507–14.

Kammen, Michael G. *A Rope of Sand: The Colonial Agents, British Politics, and the American Revolution*. Ithaca, 1968.

Keith, A. Berriedale. *Constitutional History of the First British Empire*. Oxford, 1930.

Kennedy, Paul M. *The Rise and Fall of British Naval Mastery*. New York, 1976.

Knollenberg, Bernhard. *Origin of the American Revolution, 1759–1766.* Rev. ed. New York, 1965.

Knorr, Klaus. *British Colonial Theories: 1570–1850.* Toronto, 1944.

Koebner, Richard. *Empire.* London, 1961.

Kurtz, Stephen G., and Hutson, James H., ed. *Essays on the American Revolution.* Chapel Hill, 1973.

Labaree, Benjamin Woods. *The Boston Tea Party.* New York, 1964.

Labaree, Leonard W. *Royal Government in America: A Study of the British Colonial System before 1783.* New Haven, 1930.

Langford, Paul. *The First Rockingham Administration, 1765–1766.* Oxford, 1973.

——. *Modern British Foreign Policy: The Eighteenth Century, 1688–1815.* New York, 1976.

Leach, Douglas Edward. *Arms for Empire: A Military History of the British Colonies in North America, 1607–1763.*

Lemisch, Jesse. "Jack Tar in the Streets: Merchant Seamen in the Politics of Revolutionary America." *William and Mary Quarterly,* 3d ser. 25 (1968):371–407.

Lindsay, J. O., ed. *The New Cambridge Modern History, VII: The Old Regime, 1713–1763.* Cambridge, 1957.

Lodge, Richard. *Great Britain and Prussia in the Eighteenth Century.* Oxford, 1923.

Lovejoy, David S. "Rights Imply Equality: The Case against Admiralty Jurisdiction in America, 1764–1776." *William and Mary Quarterly,* 3d ser. 16 (1959):459–84.

Lucas, Stephen E. *Portents of Rebellion: Rhetoric and Revolution in Philadelphia, 1765–76.* Philadelphia, 1976.

Lydon, James G. "Fish and Flour for Gold: Southern Europe and the Colonial American Balance of Payments." *Business History Review* 39 (1965):171–83.

Lynn, Kenneth. "Regressive Historians." *American Scholar,* Autumn 1978, pp. 472–80.

McCormac, Eugene Irving. *Colonial Opposition to Imperial Authority during the French and Indian War.* Berkeley, 1911.

McGill, William J. "The Roots of Policy: Kaunitz in Vienna and Versailles, 1749–1753." *Journal of Modern History* 43 (1971):228–44.

McIlwain, Charles. *The American Revolution: A Constitutional Interpretation.* New York, 1923.

McKelvey, James Lee. *George III and Lord Bute: The Leicester House Years.* Durham, 1973.

MacKesy, Piers. "British Strategy in the War of American Independence." *Yale Review* 52 (1963):539–57.

——. *The War for America, 1775–1783.* Cambridge, Mass., 1964.

McLaughlin, Andrew C. "The Background of American Federalism." *American Political Science Review* 12 (1918):215–40.

Maier, Pauline. *From Resistance to Revolution: Colonial Radicals and the Development of American Opposition to Great Britain, 1765–1776.* New York, 1972.

Marshall, Peter. "The First and Second British Empires: A Question of Demarcation." *History* 49 (1964):13–23.

Martin, Alfred S. "The King's Customs: Philadelphia, 1763–1774." *William and Mary Quarterly*, 3d ser. 5 (1948).

Middleton, Richard. "British Historians and the American Revolution." *Journal of American Studies* 5 (1971):43–58.

Miller, John C. *Origins of the American Revolution.* Boston, 1943.

Morgan, Edmund S. *The Birth of the Republic, 1763–89.* Chicago, 1956.

———. *The Challenge of the American Revolution.* New York, 1976.

———, and Morgan, Helen M. *The Stamp Act Crisis: Prologue to Revolution.* Rev. ed. New York, 1963.

Morris, Richard B., ed. *The Era of the American Revolution.* New York, 1939.

Murrin, John M. "The French and Indian War, the American Revolution, and the Counterfactual Hypothesis: Reflections on Lawrence Henry Gipson and John Shy." *Reviews in American History* 1 (1973):307–18.

Namier, Lewis B. "Charles Garth and His Connections." *English Historical Review* 54 (1939):443–70, 632–52.

———. *Charles Townshend: His Character and Career.* The Leslie Stephen Lecture, Cambridge, 1959.

———. *England in the Age of the American Revolution.* 2d ed. New York, 1961.

———, and Brooke, John, eds. *Charles Townshend.* London, 1964.

———. *The History of Parliament. The House of Commons, 1754–1790.* 3 vols. London, 1964.

Newcomb, Benjamin H. *Franklin and Galloway: A Political Partnership.* New Haven, 1972.

Norris, John. *Shelburne and Reform.* London, 1963.

Olson, Alison Gilbert. *Anglo-American Politics, 1660–1775: The Relationship between Parties in England and Colonial America.* Oxford, 1973.

———. "The British Government and Colonial Union, 1754." *William and Mary Quarterly*, 3d ser. 17 (1960):22–34.

———, and Brown, Richard Maxwell, eds. *Anglo-American Political Relations, 1675–1775.* New Brunswick, N.J., 1970.

Owen, John B. *The Eighteenth Century, 1714–1815.* London, 1974.

Pares, Richard. "American versus Continental Warfare, 1739–1763." *English Historical Review* 51 (1936): 429–65.

———. *King George III and the Politicians.* Oxford, 1953.

———. *War and Trade in the West Indies, 1739–1763.* London, 1936.

Pargellis, Stanley M. *Lord Loudon in North America.* New Haven, 1933.

Pease, Theodore C. "The Mississippi Boundary of 1763: A Reappraisal of Responsibility." *American Historical Review* 40 (1935):278–86.

Peckham, Howard H. *Pontiac and the Indian Uprising.* Princeton, 1947.

Pocock, J.G.A. *The Machiavellian Moment: Florentine Political Thought and the Atlantic Republican Tradition.* Princeton, 1975.

———, ed. *Three British Revolutions: 1641, 1688, 1776.* Princeton, 1980.

Pole, J. R. *Political Representation in England and the Origins of the American Republic.* London, 1966.

Rakove, Jack N. *The Beginnings of National Politics.* New York, 1979.

———. "The Decision for American Independence: A Reconstruction." *Perspectives in American History* 10 (1976):215–75.

Ramsay, J. F. *Anglo-French Relations: A Study of Choiseul's Foreign Policy.* Berkeley, 1939.

Rashed, Zenab Esmat. *The Peace of Paris, 1763.* Liverpool, 1951.

Reid, John Philip. *In a Defiant Stance: The Conditions of Law in Massachusetts Bay, the Irish Comparison, and the Coming of the American Revolution.* University Park, Pa., 1977.

———. *In a Rebellious Spirit: The Argument of Facts, the Liberty Riot, and the Coming of the American Revolution.* University Park, Pa., 1979.

Richmond, Herbert. *Statesmen and Sea Power.* Oxford, 1947.

Ritcheson, Charles R. *British Politics and the American Revolution.* Norman, Okla., 1954.

Roberts, Michael. "Great Britain and the Swedish Revolution of 1772–73." *Historical Journal* 7 (1964):1–46.

———. *Splendid Isolation, 1763–1780.* Reading, Eng., 1970.

Robinson, Ronald, and Gallagher, John. "The Imperialism of Free Trade." *Economic History Review,* 2d ser. 6 (1953):1–15.

———. "The Partition of Africa." In *The New Cambridge Modern History.* Vol. 11, *Material Progress and World-Wide Problems, 1870–98,* edited by F. H. Hinsley. Cambridge, 1962.

Robinson, Ronald, and Gallagher, John, with Alice Denny. *Africa and the Victorians: The Official Mind of Imperialism.* London, 1961.

Robson, Eric. *The American Revolution in its Political and Military Aspects, 1763–1783.* New York, 1966.

Rogers, Alan. *Empire and Liberty: American Resistance to British Authority, 1755–1763.* Berkeley, 1974.

Rogers, H.C.B. *The British Army of the Eighteenth Century*. New York, 1977.

Sachs, William S. and Hoogenboom, Ari. *The Enterprising Colonials: Society on the Eve of the Revolution*. Chicago, 1965.

Savelle, Max. *The Origins of American Diplomacy: The International History of Anglo-America, 1492–1763*. New York, 1967.

Savory, Reginald. *His Britannic Majesty's Army in Germany during the Seven Years' War*. Oxford, 1966.

Schlesinger, Arthur M. *The Colonial Merchants and the American Revolution, 1763–1776*. New York, 1918.

Schweizer, Karl W. "Lord Bute, Newcastle, Prussia, and the Hague Overtures: A Re-examination." *Albion* 9 (1977):72–97.

Scott, H. M. "The Importance of Bourbon Naval Reconstruction to the Strategy of Choiseul after the Seven Years' War." *International History Review* 1 (1979):17–35.

Shepherd, James F. and Walton, Gary M. *Shipping, Maritime Trade, and the Economic Development of Colonial North America*. London, 1972.

Shy, John. *A People Numerous and Armed*. Oxford, 1976.

———. *Toward Lexington: The Role of the British Army in the Coming of the American Revolution*. Princeton, 1965.

Smith, W. Roy. *South Carolina as a Royal Province, 1719–1776*. New York, 1903.

Sorel, Albert. *The Eastern Question in the Eighteenth Century: The Partition of Poland and the Treaty of Kainardji*. Translated by F. C. Bramwell. London, 1898.

———. *Europe and the French Revolution: The Political Traditions of the Old Regime*. Translated and edited by Alfred Cobban and J. W. Hunt. London, 1969.

Sosin, Jack M. *Agents and Merchants: British Colonial Policy and the Origins of the American Revolution, 1763–1775*. Lincoln, Neb., 1965.

———. "Louisbourg and the Peace of Aix-la-Chapelle." *William and Mary Quarterly*, 3d ser. 14 (1957):516–35.

———. "The Massachusetts Acts of 1774: Coercive or Preventive?" *Huntington Library Quarterly* 26 (1962/63):235–52.

———. "A Postscript to the Stamp Act. George Grenville's Revenue Measures: A Drain on Colonial Specie?" *American Historical Review* 63 (1957/58).

———. *Whitehall and the Wilderness: The Middle West in British Colonial Policy, 1760–1775*. Lincoln, Neb., 1961.

Spector, Margaret M. *The American Department of the British Government, 1768–1782*. New York, 1940.

Spencer, Frank. "The Anglo-Prussian Breach of 1762: An Historical Revision." *History* 41 (1956):100–112.

Stourzh, Gerald. *Benjamin Franklin and American Foreign Policy.* Chicago, 1954.

Stout, Neil R. "Manning the Royal Navy in North America, 1763–1775." *American Neptune* 23 (1963):174–85.

———. *The Royal Navy in America, 1760–1775: A Study of Enforcement of British Colonial Policy in the Era of the American Revolution.* Annapolis, 1973.

Sutherland, Lucy S. *The East India Company in Eighteenth-century Politics.* Oxford, 1952.

Tate, Thad W. "The Coming of the Revolution in Virginia: Britain's Challenge to Virginia's Ruling Class, 1763–1776." *William and Mary Quarterly*, 3d ser. 19 (1962):323–43.

Temperly, H.W.V. "The Peace of Paris." In *The Cambridge History of the British Empire. Vol. I: The Old Empire: From the Beginnings to 1783,* Edited by J. H. Rose, A. P. Newton, and E. A. Benians. Cambridge, 1929.

Thomas, P.D.G. *British Politics and the Stamp Act Crisis.* Oxford, 1975.

———. "Charles Townshend and American Taxation in 1767." *English Historical Review* 83 (1968).

———. *Lord North.* New York, 1976.

Thomas, Robert Paul. "A Quantitative Approach to the Study of the Effects of British Imperial Policy upon Colonial Welfare: Some Preliminary Findings." *Journal of Economic History* 25 (1965):615–38.

Tyler, Moses Coit. *The Literary History of the American Revolution, 1763–1783.* 2 vols. New York, 1897.

Ubbelohde, Carl. *The Vice-Admiralty Courts and the American Revolution.* Chapel Hill, 1960.

Van Alstyne, Richard W. "Europe, the Rockingham Whigs, and the War for American Independence: Some Documents." *Huntington Library Quarterly* 25 (1961/62):1–28.

———. "Parliamentary Supremacy versus Independence: Notes and Documents." *Huntington Library Quarterly* 26 (1962–64).

Varga, Nicholas. "The New York Restraining Act: Its Passage and Some Effects, 1766–1768." *New York History* 37 (1956):233–58

Viner, Jacob. "Power versus Plenty as Objectives of Foreign Policy in the Eighteenth Century." *World Politics* 1 (1948):1–29.

Waddington, Richard. *La Guerre de Sept Ans: Histoire diplomatique et militaire.* 5 vols. Paris, 1896–1914.

Walett, Francis G. "The Massachusetts Council, 1766–1774: The Transformation of a Conservative Institution." *William and Mary Quarterly*, 3d ser. 6 (1949):605–27.

Webb, Stephen Saunders. *The Governors-general: The English Army and the Definition of the Empire, 1569–1681*. Chapel Hill, 1979.

Wickwire, Franklin B. *British Subministers and Colonial America, 1763–1783*. Princeton, 1966.

Williams Basil. *Carteret and Newcastle: A Contrast in Contemporaries*. London, 1943.

Wilson, Charles H. *England's Apprenticeship*. New York, 1965.

———. " 'Mercantilism': Some Vicissitudes of an Idea." *Economic History Review*, 2d ser. 10 (1957):181–88.

Wood, Gordon. *The Creation of the American Republic, 1776–1787*. Chapel Hill, 1969.

———. "Rhetoric and Reality in the American Revolution." *William and Mary Quarterly*, 3d ser. 23 (1966):3–15.

Zeller, Gaston. *Les Temps modernes, II: De Louis XIV à 1789*. Paris, 1955.

Zobel, Hiller B. *The Boston Massacre*. New York, 1970.

INDEX

Acadia, 15, 88. *See also* Nova Scotia

Acland, John Dyke, 381 n

Act of Settlement, 31

Acts of Trade and Navigation: misunderstanding of significance of, 47, 110–11, 142, 356–57, 382–83; as form of taxation, 66–67, 101, 113; and British attack on status quo, 66, 198; colonial understanding of conditions for enforcement of, 72, 175, 343; enforcement of, during Seven Years' War, 107, 121–22, 127–29; legitimacy of enforcement of, 107, 132–33, 142–43; as foundation of British wealth and power, 108–14; relationship of, to growth of colonial commerce, 111; shared perception of burdens of, 112–14, 142; revenue vs. prohibitive aims in, and Sugar Act of 1764, 117–27; enforcement of, in Grenville program, 117, 127–33, 194, 263; use of navy in enforcement of, 128–29; nature of colonial offer to observe, 133–44; American demand to retain control of enforcement mechanism of, 137–38, 335–36, 377–78; relationship of, to imperial-colonial conflict, 143; violations of, as precedent limiting powers of Parliament, 144; as assertion of imperial supremacy, 153; reform in machinery for enforcement of, 177–78; severity of reforms of, 200, 387; relaxation of, 240; threatened by concessions to colonies, 254; and First Continental Congress, 335–38; and Second Continental Congress, 377–78; uncertainty attending abandonment of, 383–84; and whig opposition, 387, 395–98. *See also* Commerce, colonial

Adams, John, 204 n, 232 n; on threat from Canadians and Indians, 57; on Boston Tea Party, 315; as deserving of punishment, 329–30 n

Adams, Randolph G., 134 n, 135 n

Adams, Samuel, 308 n

Address to the King (1768), futility of, 264–67

Affection, ties of: and colonial response to Grenville reforms, 141, 178, 199–205; dependence of imperial constitution on, 178

Africa, causes of partition of, 5–6

Aix-la-Chapelle, Treaty of, (1748), terms and significance of, 11–12

Albany Congress (1754), and Indian relations, 89

Albany Plan of Union (1754), 58, 81–82, 407

Alden, John R., 93

Alstyne, Richard W. van, 381 n

Alvord, Clarence W., 27 n

American Board of Customs Commissioners: creation of, 129–30, 234; failure to foresee opposition to, 241 n; reasons for American opposition to, 257–58; flight of, to Castle William, 261; necessity of retaining, 398. *See also* Customs officials

American colonies: security of, as object of British diplomacy, 15, 23–24, 38, 87; dependence of, assumed by British statesmen, 23; importance of, relative to sugar islands, 28–29, 38; importance of, to Great Britain, 32, 53, 84, 111–14, 197, 203–4, 41–42; defensive power of, 47; power of, as affected by Peace of Paris, 56–57; change in security threat to, 57–59; breakdown in security system of, 75–80; alternatives to traditional security system of, 80–87; participation of, in Seven Years' War, 85–86; requirements for defense of, 88; sense of common interest of, 100; self-importance and power of, 111; continuity vs. change in constitutional position of, 134–42, 161–64, 341–48, 377–78; subordination of, to Parliament, 140–41; affection of, to Great Britain, 141, 178, 199–205; peculiar feature of position of, 143; self-understanding of, 151; possible response of metropolis to fears and suspicions of, 164, 209; no sacrifice of interest with acceptance of claims of, 182; pretensions of, with new policy of metropolis, 183–85; charge

American colonies (cont'd.)
brought against metropolis by, 187–88;
responsibility for security of, 194–95;
severity of response to Grenville
reforms by, 199–200; motivation in
behavior of, 202; significance of desire
of, to remain part of empire, 202;
expectations of, identified with moral
order, 203; expectations of imperial-
colonial relationship entertained by,
203–4; political culture of, 205;
reasonable character of response of, to
Grenville reforms, 207; desire for
equality of, 214; strength, audacity, and
sense of direction projected by, 216;
debts of, 226; effect of repeal of Stamp
Act on, 231–32; ingratitude, petulance,
and aggressiveness of, 233; view that
only independence would satisfy, 235;
extent of resistance of, 251; conclusions
drawn from importance of, 253;
instinctive resistance to demands of,
253; two leading features of position of,
253; limited character of position of,
255; explanation of Grafton ministry by,
272–73; repeal of Townshend duties
unsatisfactory for, 279; no plan for
establishing government in, 282, 284–
87; as misled by the wicked, 286 n;
objection of, to tea legislation, 313 n,
314; expectation of, that tyranny would
remain implicit, 324–25; unvarying
purpose of, 344; authority of Parliament
denied to, 349–50; importance vested
in, as failure of understanding, 356
American Constitution (1787), distribution
of powers under, 172–80 passim
American Revolution: consequences of, for
Britain and France, 9; cause of, as
imperial assault on status quo, 45, 65–
66; as struggle for liberty of the
individual and not for independence of
the collective, 187–88
Amherst, Jeffery, 101; relationship of, with
colonial assemblies, 85; and Pontiac's
Rebellion, 92 n
Ammerman, David, 320 n, 339 n, 340 n
Andrews, Charles M., on transformation
from mercantilism to imperialism, 21–
22, 29 n, 67, 189–91
Appeasement: as consequence of fear of
nonimportation, 114; as pattern of

British policy, 229–30; as tried and
found wanting, 237; Grafton ministry
incapable of, 255, 263, 270–73, 325,
390, 405. See also Consensus;
Conciliation
Articles of Confederation (1777):
requisition system under, 99;
subordination of general government to
regional governments under, 174; crisis
of, compared with crisis of imperial
constitution, 177–78
Assemblies, colonial: expansion of powers
of, 59–60, 148–49, 155; refusal of, to
yield on privileges, 60; demand for
return to status quo by, 66; and
Braddock expedition, 84; relationship of,
with British commanders-in-chief, 85;
rights of, 85; reimbursement of, 85,
86 n; resolution of conflicts in favor of,
during Seven Years' War, 86, 160, 177;
response of, to Stamp Act, 100–101;
powers of, as equivalent to House of
Commons, 104, 157, 360; autonomy of,
and Sugar Act, 117; scope of legislative
action of, 149–50; inventiveness,
persistence, and determination of, 153;
power to initiate legislation of, 155–56;
control over finance of, 156–57;
amplitude of legislative competence
inhering in, 163; legislative powers of,
vs. those of Parliament, 174–75;
derivation of authority of, 176; negative
powers of, vs. those of crown, 177;
privileges of, compatible with
parliamentary sovereignty, 179;
Grenville reforms premised on
willingness of colonists to accept limits
to claims of, 181; formal subordination
vs. actual power of, 182; consequences
for, of accepting Grenville reforms, 185;
reaction of, to Hillsborough circular,
258–59, 259–61 n; inefficacy of
dissolutions of, 259, 259–60 n
Atkin, Edmund, 90
Attucks, Crispus, 270 n
Austria, 17; and France, 31, 35; and
Britain, 33–34; and British strategy in
Europe, 51–52
Austrian Netherlands, 11, 19, 35;
importance to Britain of, 32
Austrian Succession, War of, (1740–48),
11, 33, 36, 79; British strategy in, 51

Bailyn, Bernard, 149 n, 288 n, 291 n, 305 n, 410 n; on inflexibility of claim of parliamentary sovereignty, 173; on colonial appeal to federal principles, 175–76; on divisibility of parliamentary sovereignty, 180 n; as "tory" historian, 187 n; on causes of Revolution, 207–9; on publication of Hutchinson letters, 308 n

Balance of power, French threat to, 31, 34

Balance of trade, and legislation affecting West Indies, 120

Bancroft, George, 67, 187

Barbados: taxes on, 121, 246; civil establishment in, 246

Bargar, B. D., 361 n, 366 n

Barré, Isaac, 283, 389–90; on colonial representation in Parliament, 151–52; on North's Olive Branch, 371

Barrington, William Wildman, second viscount, 265

Barrow, Thomas, 106 n, 122 n; on content and volume of American smuggling with Europe, 120 n; on salutary neglect, 159 n; on expansion of civil list by North ministry, 297–98

Becker, Carl L., 343 n, 345, 348 n

Bedford, John Russell, fourth duke of, 20, 232 n; role of, in negotiations leading to Peace of Paris, 21; motion of, to withdraw British troops from Europe, 35 n; and national debt, 39, and use of force against colonies, 230; Address to the King moved by, 264–65

Bedfordites: entrance of, in the administration, 252; willingness of, to resolve American crisis by force, 278; co-optation or neutralization of, by North, 292

Beer, George L., 21 n, 22 n, 28, 88 n, 101–2

Bellisle, 19

Bernard, Francis: and Massachusetts circular, 258; on March 1768 disturbances in Boston, 260; reports of, 264; recall of, 265; on futility of Address to the King, 266; view of, by Massachusetts whigs, 269; weakness of, 270 n; and charter reform, 288 n, 291 n; departure from office of, 294–95

Board of Trade: 1768 report of, 28; and Albany Plan of Union, 81; and proposed taxation of the colonies, 82; and proposed creation of American fund, 83–84, 99; policy of, before Seven Years' War, 160 n; traditional policy of, 245–46

Bolingbroke, Henry St. John, lord viscount, 39 n

Bollan, William, 294

Boscawen, Admiral Edward, 13–14

Boston, 107; vice-Admiralty court at, 131; "List of Infringements and Violations of Rights" by, 298, 300; restrictions placed on town meetings in, 323

Boston Massacre, 262, 269–70; attack on North ministry provoked by news of, 282; withdrawal of army to Castle William after, 295–96

Boston Port Act, 316; failure of ministry to stop with, 322; utility of, 326 n; colonial response to, 331; and prerogative, 350

Boston Tea Party, 287; immediate response of Dartmouth to, 311–12; as psychological last straw, 314–15; as demonstration of strength and momentum of revolutionary movement, 321

Braddock, Major-General Edward: expedition of, 14; Franklin on reason for expedition of, 58; meeting of, with colonial governors, 84; relationship of, with colonial assemblies, 85

"Bread colonies," trade of, 107

British army: stationing of, in North America, 75; contribution of, to victory in Seven Years' War, 85–86; principal functions of, 87–88, 94; cost of, 94 n; redeployment of, in 1768, 95, 252, 260–63; necessity of, for garrison duty, 96–97, 105; as instrument of coercion against colonies, 97–98 n; and requisition system, 98; deployment of, during Stamp Act crisis, 98 n, 219, 221 n; link between stationing of, in North America and American revenue, 122 n; colonial fears of, 198; and American taxation in 1767, 241–44; legal restrictions on employment of, 261–63, 321–22; uselessness of, in Boston, 268–70, 293–94; proposal for partial withdrawal of, from Boston, 289; and enforcement of charter reform, 289–90; withdrawal of, to Castle William, 295–96; political restrictions on employment

British army (cont'd.)
    of, 328; inadequacy of, 332; as required
    to restore King's authority in America,
    359; reinforcement of, 367–68
Brooke, John, 235 n
Brown, Weldon A., 370, 374, 377 n
Bunker Hill, 378
Burgoyne, John, 365
Burke, Edmund: and Bourbon alliance,
    52–53; on conciliation, 69; and
    requisition system, 98, 386–88, 396–97;
    on the colony trade, 111; on colonial
    representation in Parliament, 151; on
    broad constitutional dilemma
    confronting British Empire, 182; on
    purposes and assumptions behind
    "salutary neglect," 193; vision of,
    undermined by circumstances, 194; and
    Townshend Revenue Act, 239 n; on
    inconstancy of colonial policy, 282; on
    North's Olive Branch, 371; and imperial
    pride, 384; historiographical view taken
    of, 385; on imperial-colonial
    relationship, 386–88; and Grenville
    reforms, 387–88; on incompetence of
    North ministry, 391; plan of, for
    resolving conflict, 395–398; on consent
    and force, 399–400
Burke, William, 25 n
Bute, John Stuart, third earl of, 13, 146;
    on Europe, 16, 34–36; role of, in
    negotiations leading to Anglo-Prussian
    breach, 16–18; role of, in resignation of
    Newcastle, 18; historiographical view
    taken of, 22, 43–44, 52; consistency of,
    23; role of, in Canada-Guadeloupe
    controversy, 26; and George III, 34;
    negotiations of, with France (1762), 37–
    41; disagreement of, with Pitt, 46;
    desertion of Frederick by, 48

Camden, Sir Charles Pratt, first earl of,
    257, 381; on right of Parliament, 167–
    69; on dangers of war with America,
    253; and dual consensus, 255; and
    coercive measures, 261; and Townshend
    duties, 275; historiographical view taken
    of, 385
Canada: controversy over Guadeloupe vs.,
    in Seven Years' War, 14–15, 21, 23–30;
    boundary negotiations over, 19; removal
    of French from, as cause of Revolution,

44–45, 53–62; British policy toward
    settlers in, 54; threatened link of, to
    Louisiana, 78; stationing of British army
    in, 87–88; significance of British
    possession of, 94. See also Quebec Act
Cape Breton, 19
Carleton, Guy, 54 n
Carteret, John, second earl of Granville,
    36
Castle William: acquiescence by
    government in withdrawal of troops to,
    282; circumstances of withdrawal of
    army to, 295–96
Catherine II (Russia), 49
Chancery, court of, 169
Charter, colonial: rights conferred by, 161,
    192; right of Parliament to change, 324;
    and Second Continental Congress, 376–
    77
Chatham. See Pitt, William
Chatham administration: American
    legislation of, as response to colonial
    provocation, 234, 249, 390; belligerence
    of, tempered by fear, 236; and New
    York Restraining Act, 236–38; and
    American taxation, 238–41; and western
    policy, 241–44; and colonial civil list,
    244–48; outlook of, 248–49; Burke's
    characterization of, 388–89
Chathamites: and American position on
    taxation, 249; and dual consensus, 255;
    in favor of total repeal of Townshend
    duties, 278; in opposition, 292; and
    coercive policy, 385–86; retrospective
    view of, of conflict 389–90; dilemma of,
    398–406
Chesterfield, Philip Stanhope, fourth earl
    of, 32
Choiseul-Stainville, duc de, 40, 46, 54 n;
    on British policy, 15; negotiations of,
    with Spain, 16; negotiations of, with
    Britain, 19–20
Christie, Ian R., 197 n; and Pitt's view of
    parliamentary taxation, 166–67 n
Christie, Ian R., and Benjamin Woods
    Labaree, 106 n, 287 n, 385 n; on
    rejection of enforcement of Stamp Act,
    218 n, 222 n; on purpose of Townshend
    Revenue Act, 239–40 n; on Chatham
    ministry, 248; on Hillsborough circular
    and colonial union, 259–61 n; on
    Hillsborough's role in North's American
    policy, 290–91 n; on expansion of

colonial civil list, 298 n; on First Continental Congress, 339 n

Civil disturbances, tradition of, and resistance to Stamp Act, 199

Civil establishment: attempts to create permanent revenue for, 156; support of, in Townshend Revenue Act, 234; source of 1767 plan to support, 241–48; and Hillsborough's proposal of repeal of Townshend duties, 265 n; and repeal of Townshend duties, 274–75; tea duty as basis for plan to support, 279; significance of expansion of, in Massachusetts, 297–300; permanent revenue demanded for, as condition of withdrawal of tea tax, 310 n; in North's Olive Branch, 367, 371–72, 374; and whig opposition, 397

Clinton, Henry, 365

Coercion: not attempted with passage of Coercive Acts, 326–27; not identified with war, 363. See also Force; War with America

Coercive Acts: and use of force, 290; terms of, 316; prevailing interpretation of, 319–20; and issue of proportionality, 320–23; right of Parliament to adopt, 320 21, 323 24; reasons for shock produced by, 324–25; colonists backed into corner by, 325–26, 332–33; and nonforcible coercion, 326–30; implementation of, 326–33; use of term dictated by usage, not accuracy, 327; colonial response to, 330–31; colonial consensus not produced by, 334–41; strategy of colonists in opposition to, 351–53; repeal of, as minimum requirement for meeting American demands, 357; and Second Continental Congress, 377; repeal of, urged by parliamentary opposition, 394–95. See also Boston Port Act; Impartial Regulation of Justice Act; Massachusetts Bay Regulating Act; Quartering Act

Colden, Cadwallader, 358

Colonial disunity: as instrument of British rule, 81; dilemma confronted by imperial state as consequence of, 81–82; analysis of, by Townshend, 84; and requisition system, 99–103; and significance of affective ties, 201; New York Restraining Act and attempts by ministry to play upon, 236–38, 249;

expectation of, in response to Coercive Acts, 329; badly misplaced expectation of, 334, 360, 362; assumption of, central consideration in British policy, 364, 368; and North's Olive Branch, 373. See also Colonial unity; Divide et impera

Colonial troops: restrictions on use of, in Seven Years' War, 85; contribution of, to victory in Seven Years' War, 85–86; suitability of, for garrison duty, 97; significance of British contempt for, 98 n, 402

Colonial unity: and power conferred by nonimportation, 111; potential benefits of, shown by repeal of Stamp Act, 231, 330; as restraint on Grafton ministry, 253, 271–72; Hillsborough as creator of, 259–61 n; attempt by Massachusetts to secure, 300; Coercive Acts as creator of, 319, 334–41. See also Colonial disunity

Colonization, new theory of. See Empire

Commerce, colonial: protection of, by British navy, 59, 76; as criterion for allocating burden of imperial defense, 99; predominant pattern of, 107–8; as foundation of British wealth and power, 109–14; relative significance of, 110–11, 330 n, 382–83; growth of, attributed to Acts of Trade and Navigation, 111; growth of, and Currency Act (1764), 114–17; pattern of, and Sugar Act (1764), 117–27; shifting objectives underlying regulation of, 126–27, 136; possible destruction of, by war, 230, 253, 401. See also Acts of Trade and Navigation

Commonwealth, 76, 110

Concert of Europe, 48 n

Conciliation: toward France, 45–46, 55; consequences of, 198–99; during Seven Years' War, 204; cost of, to Americans, 205–7; deeper meaning of, 232; difficulty of finding alternative to, 237; as not producing harmony but discord with metropolis, 279, North's policy of, 282–84, 286–91; limitations of, 292; and Gaspee incident, 306; urged by Franklin, 309 n; meaning of, in Massachusetts 234; vs. coercion, 327–34; expectation that North ministry would adopt policy of, 351–52; and First Continental Congress, 351–54; dissatisfaction evoked by, 357; and

Conciliation (cont'd.)
North's Olive Branch, 368–76. *See also* Appeasement
Concord, 365, 368, 378
Connecticut: civil establishment in, 246–47; and Hillsborough circular, 259 n
Consensus, British: dual or twofold, on maintaining supremacy of Parliament and avoiding use of force against America, 55–56 n, 165, 220, 222 n, 228–31, 236–38, 248–49, 253–55, 270–75, 406; over consequences of American independence, 112; on overall equity of imperial-colonial relationship, 141, 204, 387; on purposes and aspirations of imperial rule, 194; contradictory character of dual, 255; North ministry and dual, 270–74, 284, 362; repeal of Townshend duties and dual, 277–78; Grenville and dual, 286–87 n; Hillsborough and dual, 289–90; as forbidding conciliatory response to Boston Tea Party, 316; on equation of sovereignty with retention of American commerce, 356
Consensus, colonial. *See* Colonial unity
Conspiracy, ministerial, to destroy liberty: and historiography, 187; belief in, and colonial affection, 205; significance of colonial belief in, 207–9; and parliamentary opposition, 390–93
Constitution. *See* American Constitution; Articles of Confederation; Assemblies, colonial; Government by instruction; Governors, colonial; Mixed government; Royal government
Continental Congress (First): and demand for return to status quo, 66–67; Association of, 116, 337–38, 354; solution to imperial problem proposed by, 182, 349–50, 406–10; Statement of Rights and Grievances of, 116, 298, 335–38, 343–44; and strategy of opposition in Massachusetts, 330; differences among delegates to, 335–38; consensus among delegates to, 338–41; significance of, 343–44; conciliatory disposition of, 351–54; on sovereignty, 355–56; reports of, in London, 360; as representative of politically effective opinion, 360
Continental Congress (Second): significance of, in shaping strategy of

armed resistance, 353–54; report of New York opposition to, 358; and North's Olive Branch, 371, 376–78; nature of choice offered Britain by, 377–78
Continental Congress (1776–87): and settlememt of accounts of union, 99 n; collapse of finances of, 103; inflated responsibilities and deflated power of, 178. *See also* Articles of Confederation
Continuity: in colonial position, 134–42, 161–64, 341–48, 377–78; in purposes and aspirations of imperial rule, 192–94 (*see also* Empire, new view of)
Conway, Henry Seymour, 98, 257; on right and policy of parliamentary taxation, 165; and colonial resistance to Stamp Act, 218–19; instructions of, to Gage during Stamp Act crisis, 220–22 n; and Townshend duties, 275
Cooper, Grey, 266
Co-option, strategy of, 150–52
Corbett, Julian S., 32 n, 43 n
Corruption: danger of, 207–8; absence of, 409–10
Country ideology: economic thought in, 39 n; and American resistance, 208–9; and war with America, 230
Courts, colonial: jurisdiction of, over laws of trade, 128, 130–32; jurisdiction of, over army, 261–63; and civil list in Massachusetts, 298–300
Crown Point, 79
Cumberland, William Augustus, duke of, 12; and Stamp Act crisis, 218–20, 222 n
Currency Act (1751), 114
Currency Act (1764), 114–17; modification of, in 1770, 116, 281; modification of, in 1773, 116; colonial efforts to repeal, 233–34
Cushing, Thomas, 305 n, 308 n
Customs officials: enforcement of 1733 Molasses Act by, 121; weakness of, in Seven Years' War, 127–28; Grenville reforms concerning, 129; 1767 reforms concerning, 129–30, 234; harrassment of, 233, 294; failure of metropolis to support, 305–6. *See also* American Board of Customs Commissioners

Dartmouth, William Legge, second earl of: and civil establishment in New

Jersey, 247 n; moderate disposition of, toward colonies, 292, 405; wish of, to avoid any confrontation with America, 301–2; displeasure of, with Hutchinson, 304–5, 307; interview of, with Franklin, 305 n; response of, to *Gaspee* incident, 306–7; concern of, over situation in Massachusetts, 309; and charter reform, 310–12; January 1774 instructions of, to Hutchinson, 322 n; April 1774 instructions of, to Gage, 327–28; resolution of, 329–30 n; claim of, that he had been deceived, 357, 361 n; January 1775 instructions of, to Gage, 364–67; April 1775 instructions of, to Gage, 367 n; proposal of, to send negotiators to America, 367; reflections on mistaken lenity of, 405. *See also* North ministry

Davies, K. D., 361 n

de Berdt, Dennys, 257

Debts, private, owed to British merchants, 114–17

Declaration of Independence (1776), and Stamp Act Crisis, 231

Declaratory Act (1766): as assertion of imperial supremacy, 165; significance of opposition to, by Pitt and Camden, 167; text of, 167 n; and repeal of Stamp Act, 224–25; colonial opposition to, 224, 236, 274; as "waste paper," 232; Chathamites on, 234; effective re-enactment of, in 1770, 276–77; nothing to be gained by mere reaffirmation of, 310, 315; omitted from grievances of First Continental Congress, 336 n; Burke's defense of, 388. *See also* Parliament; Parliamentary sovereignty

Delaware, civil establishment in, 246–47

Denmark, 17–18

Derry, John, 369, 385 n

Dicey, A. V., 180 n

Dickerson, Oliver M., 106 n, 120 n, 129 n, 187 n

Dickinson, John: and prospect of French intervention, 56; demand of, for return to status quo, 66; attack by William Knox on position of, 135 n; on the right "that all free states have," 139; significance of constitutional distinction drawn by, 139–40; on colonial affection, 141; on reasons for repeal of Stamp Act, 232 n; opposition of, to 1767 American legislation, 250–51, 257; in Pennsylvania politics, 260–61 n; on colonists as one free people, 342

Dinwiddie, Robert, 80

Diplomatic Revolution (1756), 11, 31, 53

Disallowance of colonial legislation, 149; power of, incompatible with federal government, 174; power of, for nonlocal, imperial purposes, 177

Dissolution of colonial assemblies, significance of threat of, 259–61 n

Divide et impera: difficulty of pursuing policy of, 271–72; North's Olive Branch and policy of, 368, 371, 373. *See also* Colonial disunity

Domestic (British) politics: importance of considerations relating to, in historiography, 3; importance of, in explaining Peace of 1763, 22, 39–40; and North ministry, 357

Dominica, 19

Donoughue, Bernard, 322 n, 385 n, 404

Dowdeswell, William: and revision of tea duties, 238, 313; on dangers of contest with the colonies, 253; on danger of admitting colonial claim of right, 254; and dual consensus, 255; critique of North ministry by, 356. *See also* Rockinghamites

Dulany, Daniel, on establishing authority of Parliament, 140–41

Dunkirk, fortifications of, in 1762 peace negotiations, 19

Dunmore, John Murray, fourth earl of, 358

East India Company, 123–24, 135 n; commercial crisis of, 312–13

Economic power: significance of, in eighteenth-century war, 109–10. *See also* National debt; Nonimportation

Egremont, Charles Wyndham, second earl of, 40

Elite, colonial: emergence of, 150; possible co-option of, 150–52

Elizabeth (Russia): aims of, in Seven Years' War, 12; significance of death of, 17, 37

Empire: new view of, as cause of Revolution, 3; new view of, as basis for Peace of 1763, 3, 21–30 passim; concept of self-sufficient, 21, 28; Ptolemaic vs. Copernican theories of, 138. *See also* Imperialism.

Enumeration, system of, and British naval power, 110

Equality: status quo and acceptance of colonial claim to, 198–99; essential meaning of, sought by colonists, 201–2, 344; unwillingness of metropolis to concede colonial claim to, 204; failure of metropolis to appreciate intensity of colonial drive for, 214; security impossible without, 214; colonial claim to, 272, 360; colonial claim to, and repeal of Townshend duties, 276, 280

Equity, new ideal of, 195. *See also* Imperial-colonial relationship, (in)equity of

Ernst, Joseph A., 115 n, 235 n

Falkland Islands, 1770 crisis over, 290 n

Federalism, and nature of old imperial constitution, 172–81 passim. *See also* Articles of Confederation

Ferdinand, Prince of Brunswick, 13, 18, 34, 110

Ferguson, Adam, 383–84

Ferguson, E. James, 99 n

Fisheries, 15, 19–20, 22, 39, 107; effect of French removal from, 15, 47

Fleury, Cardinal, 77

"Flags of Truce," illicit trade under cover of, 128

Florida, East and West: acquisition of, 20, 27; stationing of British army in, 88; establishment of provinces of, 90; significance of British possession of, 94; civil establishment in, 246

Force: consensus in Britain against use of, 98 n, 220, 222 n, 237, 253–55, 270–74; use of, proposed by Pitt to secure perfect obedience of colonies, 166; use of, as a moral problem, 181–82, 399; use of, and tyranny, 188; use of, during Stamp Act crisis, 219; Conway's order to employ, during Stamp Act crisis, 220–22 n; effect of use of, on distribution of power at home, 230; disutility of, 230, 253–55, 278, 305 n, 398–404; willingness of Hillsborough to consider use of, 289–90; use of, distinguished from passage of Coercive Acts, 326–29; use of, as alternative to surrender, 351–52; difficulties attending use of, in Massachusetts, 359–60; prospect of, and North's Olive Branch,

375. *See also* British army; Coercion; War with America

Fox, Charles, 371, 385, 389 n

Fox, Henry, 83

France: and threat to American colonies before Seven Years' War, 10, 25, 27, 45, 78–80, 84, 93; and War of Austrian Succession, 11; strategy of, in Seven Years' War, 12–13; and peace negotiations with Britain (1761–62), 15–16, 19–21; and *pacte de famille* with Spain, 16, 44, 46, 52–53; basis of power of, 24, 38, 45–48; relations of, with Indians, 25, 54, 89, 91–92, 95; threat of, to British interests in Europe, 31–32, 35, 43, 48–52; continental diplomacy of, 34; reasons for lenient peace with, 37–41; effects of removal of, from Canada on Anglo-American relationship, 44–45, 53–62; and desire for revenge against England, 46, 48, 78, 197; probability of intervention of, in Anglo-American conflict, 53–57, 230, 253, 401–2; increase in power of, expected as consequence of American independence, 112, 197; commercial policy of, in West Indies, 120–21; and illicit trade during Seven Years' War, 127; in no position to control American colonies, 383

Franklin, Benjamin, 204 n; on imperial-colonial status quo, 2–3; in Canada-Guadeloupe controversy, 25–27; on colonial disunity, 26, 79–80; on Dutch revolt and disutility of force, 56 n; on the objectives of the Seven Years' War, 58; and return to status quo, 66; on unworkability of older security system, 79–80, 194; and Currency Act, 115; on burden of imperial taxation, 200; on legitimacy and expediency of external taxation, 238–39; and Hillsborough circular, 258–59 n; on American policy of Grafton ministry, 268; appreciation of crisis in Massachusetts by, 304–5; motives of, in handling of Hutchinson letters, 308–9 n; on realm and dominions, 346–47

Franklin, William, on salary question in New Jersey, 244 n

Frederick II of Prussia ("the Great"): coalition against, 11; relations of, with Britain, 11–13, 16–18, 21, 110;

desperate position of, 12, 30; reasons for British rupture with, 22–23, 30–37 passim; consequences of British rupture with, 43–44, 48–52, 61–62

Freedom: distinction between individual and collective, 138, 161–62; and imperial constitution, 181–82; colonial claim of, never wholly displacing imperial claim of subordination, 192–93; any policy a mortal threat to, 248, 299

Freedom of action, colonial equation of, with moral order, 204

French Revolution, 110; as consequence of French participation in War of American Independence, 9

Fundamental law, statutory vs., 180 n

Fur trade: importance of, discounted by Hardwicke, 26–27; Grenville program for regulation of, 54, 88–91, 93; as cause of Seven Years' War, 58; regulation of, as departure from status quo, 75; 1768 plan for regulating, 95, 243–44, 252

Gage, Thomas, 90; and Stamp Act crisis, 98 n, 220–22 n; on requisition system, 102 n; and redeployment of army in 1768, 252; and Hillsborough, 289, 291 n; on difficulties facing army in Boston, 293–94; April 1774 instructions to, 327–28; assessment of Massachusetts crisis by, 327, 359–61; weak position of, in Massachusetts, 330–32; fall into disfavor by, 359, 364–65; position of, in Massachusetts in early 1775, 363, 368; January 1775 instructions to, 364–67; move of, to seize rebel arms, 366. See also British army

Galitzin, Count, and Anglo-Prussian breach, 18

Galloway, Joseph: and Hillsborough circular, 260–61 n; as a conservative, 335; plan of union of, 335 n

Garth, Charles, 235, 246 n

Gaspee incident, 305–6, 325

"General good" of empire, and right to regulate trade, 138, 140

George II, 12; view of Pitt, 14

George III, 48; accession to monarchy of, 13; on European war, 16, 33–34; on Pitt and Newcastle, 39–40; on Austria, 52; on seriousness of war with America, 112–13; responsibility of, for Anglo-

American conflict, 192; and Stamp Act crisis, 224 n; relations of, with Hillsborough, 252; Hillsborough's American proposals rejected by, 265–66, 290 n; confidence of, in North, 291; on crisis in Massachusetts, 327; proclamation of colonial rebellion by, 349; and decision for war, 362–63; and North's Olive Branch, 374 n; ideas of, authoritarian and hierarchical, 404

Georgia: maintenance of forces in, 77; civil establishment in, 246; exempted from nonintercourse, 368

Gibraltar, 76, 77 n

Gipson, Lawrence Henry, 106 n; and Great War for the Empire, 45 n; on use of colonials for garrison duty, 97; on vice-Admiralty courts, 132 n; on idea informing British Empire of eighteenth century, 181–82; on failure of understanding among British statesmen, 355

Goree, 14, 19

Government by instruction: rigidity vs. permissiveness of, as cause of progressive debilitation of imperial power, 153–59; causes of breakdown of, and crisis of American Confederation, 178; colonial actions leading to breakdown of, as challenge to status quo, 184. See also Governors, colonial; Requisition system; Royal government

Governors, colonial: responsibility of, exploited by colonists, 60; rights and duties of, 77 n; effect of 1754 Board of Trade plan on powers of, 83; views of, on requisition system, 84; and illicit trade during Seven Years' War, 128; formal powers of, 148–49; decline in position of, 149–50, 155–57, 160; management of provincial elites by, through patronage, 151–52, 157–58, 296–300, 409–10; contribution made by successive British governments to weakness of, 152–53; and government by instruction, 153–54; salaries of, and Townshend program, 157–58, 244–48; limits on powers of, vs. limits on powers of Parliament, 162–63; war of popular parties against, 194; formal powers claimed by, 206; weakness of, demonstrated by Stamp Act crisis, 216–17; inefficacy of dissolutions ordered by, 259; failure of metropolis to

Governors, colonial (cont'd.)
support, 305–6; powers of, as
inadequate basis for imperial control,
410. See also Government by
instruction; Requisition system; Royal
government
Grafton, Augustus Henry Fitzroy, third
duke of, 389 n, 401; and colonial
resistance to Stamp Act, 218–19; and
Townshend Revenue Act, 239 n; and
American Board of Customs
Commissioners, 241; relations of, with
Townshend, 243; and colonial civil list,
245, 247–48; assumes leadership of
ministry, 252; and Townshend duties,
274. See also Grafton ministry
Grafton ministry: make-up of, 251–52;
contradictory impulses driving American
policy of, 252–57; attitude of, toward
Townshend duties, 256, 265 n, 273–74,
276, 280; and Hillsborough circular,
257–61 n; dispatch of army to Boston
by, 260–63; and 1768/69 parliamentary
session, 263–66; parliamentary attack on
American policy of, 267; North's defense
of, 268–71; American policy of, as failure
of will or of understanding, 271–73
Graham, Gerald S., 44
Granby, John Manners, marquess of, 274
Grand Alliance, 11, 36, 48
Greene, Jack P., 68 n, 70–71, 116 n,
149 n; on effects of Canadian cession on
British policy, 55–56 n; on reasons for
and effects of stationing British army in
America, 97–98 n; and redirection of
British colonial policy before Seven
Years' War, 160 n; on workability of
imperial-colonial relationship, 183–84;
on basic substructure of colonial
expectations, 203 n; on Namier's thesis,
408
Grenada, 19
Grenville, George: in 1762 peace
negotiations, 18, 20, 37; attitude of,
toward dependence of American
colonies, 23; failure of, to foresee
opposition to Stamp Act, 55 n, 97–98 n,
217 n, 262; on interposition of
parliamentary power, 103; and Thomas
Whately, 119 n; motivation of, in
reducing molasses duty, 122; on Sugar
Act, 117–18; and right of Parliament to
tax America, 165, 249; views on

parliamentary supremacy compared with
those of Pitt, 172 n; assurances of, not
necessarily binding successors, 185;
responsibility of, for conflict, 192; fall of,
unconnected with American crisis, 218;
support of, for enforcement of Stamp
Act, 218, 220; on Conway's instructions
to employ force against colonies, 221 n;
and dual consensus, 229–30, 254–55,
286–87 n; and consequences of repeal of
Stamp Act, 232 n, 286 n; proposal of, to
require test oath of colonial officials,
237; and willingness to consider internal
taxation after repeal of Stamp Act, 240;
and withdrawal of army from interior,
242; critique of Grafton ministry by,
266–67; and colonial civil list, 277;
critique of North ministry by, 282,
284–85; death of, 286 n; followers of, co-
opted or neutralized by North, 292; and
Hutchinson's defense of parliamentary
supremacy, 302
Grenville reforms: as assault on status quo,
3, 71; role of, in causing Revolution, 45;
weapon for securing success of, 61; as
attempt to preserve status quo, 71; role
and power of provincial assembly as
central issue raised by, 162; federal
arrangements at stake in conflict over,
178; premise of inequality underlying,
180–81; new view of empire and,
189–97; severity of, 199–200; larger
issues attending, 200, 205–7. See also
Acts of Trade and Navigation; Grenville,
George; Imperial defense; Internal
autonomy
Guadeloupe: controversy over Canada vs.,
in Seven Years' War, 14–15, 21–29
passim; return of, to France, 43, 45–48.
See also West Indies (French)

Halifax, establishment of court of vice-
Admiralty at, 131
Halifax, George Montagu-Dunk, second
earl of: on continental connections,
32–33; and proposed taxation of the
colonies, 82–84; and requisition system,
83–84; deprivation of colonial governors
of patronage by, 158; reformist policy of,
before Seven Years' War, 160 n; and
problems of old colonial system, 194;
and dual consensus, 230

Hamilton, Alexander, 177

Hancock, John, 330 n

Hanover, 395; significance of, in Seven Years' War, 12; defense of, before Seven Years' War, 30–32; strategy in protection of, 49; French designs on, 50

Hard liners and soft liners, distinction between, 218–19, 255, 283–87, 292. See also Consensus

Hardwicke, Philip Yorke, first earl of: leaves cabinet, 18; on Canada-Guadeloupe controversy, 26–27; on "continental connections," 31–32; on consequences of Peace of 1763, 44

Harlow, Vincent T., 28 n

Hartley, David, 283, 388; on imperial-colonial relationship, 386–87; plan of, for resolving conflicts, 395–98

Havana, 20, 37

Heckscher, Eli F., 190 n

Henderson, H. James, 339–40 n

Henry VIII, act of: in address to the King, 264; not meant to be executed, 266; application of, to America criticized, 266–67; as "waste paper," 267; threat of, defended by North, 267–68; lenity vs. timidity as explanation of failure of ministry to execute, 270–72

Hesse-Cassel, 30, 35 n

Hillsborough, Wills Hill, first earl of and second viscount, 54 n; and salary question in Massachusetts, 247 n; appointment of, to American department, 252; and western policy, 252; and Townshend duties, 256; circular of, and colonial union, 257–61 n, 267, 271–72, 282; dispatch of army to Boston by, 260–63; eight resolutions of, condemning Massachusetts, 263–64; February 1769 proposals of, 265–66, 290; misunderstanding of situation in Massachusetts by, 270 n, 290 n; and reform of Massachusetts charter, 287–91 n; and dual consensus, 289–90; replacement of, by Dartmouth, 292

Historiography, conventional or whig: central themes of, 2–4; and causes of Peace of 1763, 21–22; and consequences of Peace of 1763, 43–45; and status quo, 65–71, 182–83, 192, 198; and imperial defense, 75–76, 88 n, 91 n, 93–98, 104; and Acts of Trade and Navigation, 106, 127, 132–35, 143; on issue of internal autonomy, 146; on causes of progressive debilitation of imperial power, 153; and virtual representation, 171; and motivation of postwar imperial policy, 187–88; and metropolitan rigidity, 214; and character of British consensus, 220; and Chatham ministry, 248; and North ministry, 287, 290–91 n; and Coercive Acts, 319–20; on conciliatory disposition of First Continental Congress, 351; on British failure of understanding, 355–57; and North's Olive Branch, 368–69; and whig opposition, 384–85; and issue of responsibility, 407

Hodgson, John, 269 n

Holy Roman Empire, 12; constitution of, 32

House of Commons. See Parliament

House of Lords, 263, 392. See also Parliament

Howe, William, 365

Howe Brothers, 402

Hubertusburg, Peace of, (1763), 20

Hume, David, 61, 409–10

Hutchinson, Thomas: on Canadian cession, 44–45; and imperial constitution, 176; and Stamp Act, 216; compensation to, 237; on need to secure dependence of Massachusetts, 263; recommendation that, administer government in Bernard's absence, 265; on lenity construed as timidity, 269; and charter reform, 289, 291 n; impotence of, 294 n, 321; and Boston Massacre, 295–96; departure from office of, 293, 307–8; efforts of, to restore royal government in province, 296–97; salary of, 298; exchange of, with Massachusetts assembly and council, 300–305; and Dartmouth, 300–302, 304–5, 310–11; publication of letters of, 307–9 n; diary of, in assessing resolution of North ministry, 329–30 n; on colonial profession of subordination, 343

Hutson, James H., 260–61 n

Hyam, Ronald, 22, 27 n, 40–41, 43–44, 52 n

Ideological interpretation, of American Revolution, 207–9

Impartial Regulation of Justice Act, 316, 323. See also Coercive Acts

Imperial-colonial conflict: concentration of historians on immediate origins of, 69–71; responsibility for, 69, 191–92, 407–8; fundamental issue in, 144, 196, 209, 267, 325; inevitability of, as a result of new view of empire, 189-90; symbolic issues in, 213–14; pattern of, 213–15; possible compromise of, 379–80; opposition proposals for resolving, 393–98; inevitability of, 405–6

Imperial-colonial relationship: stabilizing elements in, 59–60, 77; "dysfunctions" of, 71; reciprocity of, 77; rights and duties in, 77, 87, 105, 203 n, 204; dissatisfaction of imperial officials with, 159; workability of, 183; (in)equity of, 87, 100–101, 104, 113, 116–17, 141, 154, 161, 171–72, 179, 191, 195, 200, 204 n, 207, 226–27, 387; colonial version of, 192; utilitarian basis of, 202, 203 n; opposition view of, 386–88, 396–97. See also Status quo

Imperial constitution: crisis of, 177; broad dilemma of, 182, 185–86

Imperial defense: and British attack on status quo, 66, 75; nature of security system for, 76–78; breakdown of security system for, 78–80, 194; proposed replacement of security system for, 80–85; during war, 85–87; postwar measures for, 87–97; and taxation, 98–104, 122 n, 195, 207, 241–44

Imperialism: historiography concerning European, 4–6; transformation from mercantilism to, 4, 22–23, 29 n, 67, 106, 127, 189–91; British relations with Europe and the new, 23 n. See also Empire

Impressment, 10, 128

Inconstancy, of British policy: and tyranny, 188; price of, 214–15, 272–73; reflective of attempt by successive government to escape dilemma, 229; and Grafton ministry, 255, 272–73; and North ministry, 281, 391. See also Consensus

Independence, hazards and uncertainties attending, 201

India, 20

Indians: threat from French and, 25; and Grenville program, 27–28, 54, 75, 88–95; American attitude toward, 57, 89, 92; effect of threat from, on imperial-colonial relations, 59–60; threat from, and colonial disunity, 84, 102–3; 1768 plan concerning, 242–44, 252. See also Fur trade; Iroquois

Indian superintendents, 90; powers of, 83

Internal and external objects: distinction between, as federal principle, 175. See also Taxation, distinction between internal and external

Internal autonomy: and British attack on status quo, 66; colonial understanding of, 72; illumination of, by Grenville reforms, 146–47; disparity of view over nature of, 148–49; dependence of, on royal grace and favor, 148–49; colonial representation in Parliament, not a settlement of problem of, 152; momentum given to claims of, by Seven Years' War, 161; as subject to discretion of Parliament, 175; impossible to resolve problems confronting metropolis while honoring colonial claim to, 178, 185–86, 209, 343; as compatible with parliamentary sovereignty, 179; remarkable degree of, 204; loss of, threatened by failure to resist Grenville reforms, 206; colonial claim to, identified with aspiration for de facto independence, 285. See also Assemblies, colonial

Ireland, 127; American independence and loss of, 113; civil list in, 242 n; and tea legislation, 312

Iroquois, 14

Jacobitism, 31

Jellison, Richard M., 116 n

Jenkin's Ear, War of, 77–78. See also Austrian Succession, War of

Jenkinson, Charles, 144 n

Jensen, Merrill, 67 n, 259–61 n

Johnson, Samuel, 114 n, 381 n; and imperial constitution, 176; rigidity of position of, 180 n

Johnson, William, 90, 95, 283 n; on rationale of New York Restraining Act, 237–38; and southern European trade, 238; and purpose of Townshend Revenue Act, 246 n; on Grafton ministry, 272–73

Johnstone, George, criticism of 1773 tea legislation by, 313 n

Kaunitz, Prince, 36. *See also* Austria
Kennebec River, 79
King of Great Britain: rights and duties of, 77; powers of, under Albany Plan, 81; allegiance to, as principal bond of empire, 182, 347–50, 406–10. *See also* Government by instruction; Governors, colonial; Royal government
King's Bench, court of, 169, 270 n
Kloster-Zeven, convention of, 12–13
Knollenberg, Bernhard, 97 n; and Proclamation of 1763, 91 n; and Pontiac's Rebellion, 92; on ignorance and inexperience of British statesmen, 146
Knox, William, 114 n, 201 n, 381 n; view of Peace of 1763, 38, 41 n; 1763 memorandum of, 97 n, 193 n; on distinction between internal and external taxation, 135 n; on parliamentary supremacy, 181 n; on consequences of repeal of Stamp Act, 232 n; on disposition of Grafton ministry, 261; and charter reform in Massachusetts, 288 n

Labaree, Benjamin Woods, 314 n. *See also* Christie, Ian R., and Benjamin Woods Labaree
Labaree, Leonard W., 245; on origin and nature of provincial assembly, 148; on government by instruction, 153–54
Langford, Paul, 30 n, 219 n; on Conway instructions to Gage during Stamp Act crisis, 220–22 n; on case for repeal of Stamp Act, 225; on central problem in repeal of Stamp Act, 228 n
League of Armed Neutrals, 44
Lee, Arthur, 309 n
Leeward Islands: civil establishment in, 246; taxes on, 121, 246
Leonard, Daniel, (Massachusettensis), 57
Lexington, 365, 368, 378
Liberty riots, the, 261, 306
Loudon, Lord, and colonial assemblies, 85
Louisbourg, 11, 14, 79, 85
Louis XIV, 30
Louisiana: considerations behind acquisition of, in 1763, 27; negotiations concerning boundary of, 40–41 n; cession of western, to Spain, 52; and threatened link with Canada, 78

Low Countries. *See* Austrian Netherlands; United Provinces
Loyalists: shrinking number of, in Massachusetts, 299–300; failure of metropolis to support, 305–6; intimidation of, in Massachusetts, 321
Lynn, Kenneth, 187 n
Lyttleton, Sir George, 382 n

McIlwain, Charles, 348 n, 349–50; critique of virtual representation by, 171
McLaughlin, Andrew C., 172–79 passim, 179–81 n
Madison, James, 102 n
Madrid, Treaty of, (1750), 78
Maier, Pauline, 199 n
Manufactures: role of British, in Canada-Guadeloupe controversy, 24–29; dependence of British, on colonial market, 29, 107, 112; bounties on raw materials and British, 110, 226; burden imposed by confinement of colonial market to, 116–17, 141–42 (*see also* Imperial-colonial relationship, (in)equity of); danger of colonial trade in European, 117–19; threat to develop American, dismissed by North, 256, 279–80
Mansfield, William Murray, Lord Chief Justice: justification of parliamentary supremacy by, 167–70, 301; on conflict, 394–95; on necessity of war, 402–3; on settlement proposed by First Continental Congress, 410
Martial law, 261, 365
Martin, Joseph, 358
Martinique, 14, 19, 37 47. *See also* Guadeloupe; West Indies (French)
Maryland, 100; civil establishment in, 246–47; Hillsborough circular and assembly of, 258–59; act restraining trade of, 374 n
Mason, George, 56, 232 n
Massachusetts Bay: 1773 exchange of legislature of, with Hutchinson, 44–45, 173, 300–304; in Albany Plan, 81; and Pontiac's Rebellion, 102; and Sugar Act, 117; revocation of charter of, in 1684, 169; and compensation to victims of Stamp Act riots, 233–34; patronage and civil establishment in, 245, 246 n, 247, 277, 297–300; merchants of, and

Massachusetts Bay (cont'd.)
nonimportation, 251; prospects for
dealing separately with, 251, 271–72 (*see
also* Colonial disunity; Colonial unity;
Divide et impera); circular of, to other
American assemblies, 257–61 n passim;
defects in charter of, 261–63, 286, 300,
310–11; 321–23; reasons for restoration
of order in, 263, 268–70; parliamentary
resolutions condemning, 263–64, 267;
Hillsborough and charter reform in,
265, 287–91 n; conciliatory policy of
North ministry toward, 282; Grenville
and charter reform in, 286; Bernard and
charter reform in, 291 n, 294;
preoccupation of imperial officials with,
293; displacement of imperial authority
in, 293–95, 300; government as principal
source of disorder in, 294–95, 300;
reluctance of North and Dartmouth to
reform charter of, 305 n, 311–12;
petition for recall of Hutchinson by
assembly of, 307–8; imperial dilemma
in, 321; charter reform in, 323–24; right
of metropolis to revoke charter of, 324–
25, 349–50; balance of forces in, in
1774, 329–33; revolutionary movement
in, 361 n; in state of rebellion, 364;
urging of arrest of radical leaders in,
364, 366
Massachusetts Bay Regulating Act: terms
of, 316; intended to preserve mixed
constitution, 323. *See also* Coercive
Acts; Massachusetts
Mauduit, Israel, and continental
connections, 33–34, 36
Mercantile system. *See* Acts of Trade and
Navigation; Imperialism
Merchants: dependence of British, on
colonial market, 112; attitude of British,
toward Currency Act, 115; London
wine, 138; repeal of the Stamp Act and
British, 222–23, 225, 228 n; appeal of
London, 232
Miquelon, 19
Military victory, preoccupation of British
governments with, in Seven Years' War,
60–61, 84–85
Miller, John C., 339 n
Minorca, 14, 19, 76, 77 n
Mississippi River, free navigation of, in
1762 peace negotiations, 19–20
Mississippi Valley. *See* West, the

Mitchell, Andrew, 12, 17
Mitchell, John, 78
Mixed constitution: conditions for, largely
absent in colonies, 151–52, 158, 297–
300, 406–10; preservation of, as purpose
of Massachusetts Bay Regulating Act,
323
Molasses Act (1733), 117, 121–22; colonial
attitude toward, 136–40. *See also* Sugar
Act (1764)
Moore, Sir Henry: and Quartering Act,
236; insufficient salary of, 244; and
Hillsborough circular, 260 n; and
dissolution of New York assembly, 265 n
Morgan, Edmund S., 187 n; on
revolutionary historiography, 22; on
counterfactual history, 68 n; and status
quo, 68, 106, 182; on progress of
American constitutional doctrine, 134–
36; on Britain's fitness to run an empire,
204 n
Morgan, Edmund S., and Helen M.
Morgan, 3; on requisition system, 98 n;
on regulation of trade, 139 n; on Pitt's
view of parliamentary taxation, 166 n
Morris, Robert, 102
Murrin, John M.: on significance of
Canadian cession, 45, 57; and
requisition system, 96–97

Namier, Lewis B., 22 n, 27 n; on Burke
and his friends, 404; on rigidity of
British political culture, 406–10
Napoleon, 32, 48 n, 110
National debt: and colonial trade, 32, 189–
90 n; threat of national bankruptcy as
consequence of rise in, 35; significance
of, for British power, 35, 39, 46, 109;
doubling of, as consequence of Seven
Years' War, 86–87; Grenville reforms
and increase in, 117–18; and war with
America 230
Naval power: and consequences of Peace
of 1763, 44, 45–48, 50–53; protection
conferred by, and decision for
independence, 59, 76–77; and defense
of North America, 88; and Baltic
powers, 110; colonial commerce as
principal foundation of, 110, 112, 141,
189 n, 254
Navy, Royal: cost of, 76–77; and carrying
trade in tea, 124; stationing of, in North

American waters, 128–29; rendezvous of, in Boston, 288; reinforcement of, 367

Necessity, argument of, and individual rights, 138, 188

Newcastle, Thomas Pelham-Holles, duke of, 13–14, 21, 146; role of, in negotiations leading to Anglo-Prussian breach, 17, 36; resignation from cabinet by (1762), 18; attitude in Canada-Guadeloupe controversy, 26–27; and continental diplomacy, 35–36; and George III, 39–40; commitment of, to North America, 61, 84–85

New England: importance of Acadia to, 78; fisheries of, 108; reputation for smuggling of, 131; and Sugar Act, 135; act to restrain trade of, 367–69 n, 374 n. *See also names of individual colonies*

Newfoundland, 36, 107

New Hampshire, 99, 108, 360; civil establishment in, 245, 246 n; and Hillsborough circular, 259 n. *See also* New England

New Jersey, 99; and Quartering Act, 235; salary question in, 244 n, 245, 246 n, 247 n; and Hillsborough circular, 258–59 n

New Orleans, 20

New policy: emergence of, 160 n; as threat to working arrangement between metropolis and colonies, 183; relationship of, to new view of empire, 188–95. *See also* Empire; Imperialism

New York (city), 79, 99, 107; commercial protests of merchants of, 233, 235; merchants of, and nonimportation, 251; as imperial Court Residence, 382

New York (state): threat to, before Seven Years' War, 14, 78–79; relationship between vulnerability of, and rise of assembly in, 60; regular troops in, 77; view of parliamentary right by assembly of, 138–39; and Quartering Act, 234–35; and "the baneful cup of infatuation," 235; salary question in, 244–45, 246 n, 247, 277; Hillsborough circular and political partisanship in, 260 n; proposal to discipline four members of council of, 265 n; conciliated by partial repeal of Currency Act, 282; reports by Colden concerning situation in, 358; exempted from nonintercourse, 368

New York Restraining Act: terms of, 234;

rationale of, 236–38, 271; American opposition to, 250–51

Nonimportation, colonial: logic of, 111–14, 141; dangers of yielding to, 113–14, 227, 253–54, 278–79; and Stamp Act crisis, 222, 225–28; power of, demonstrated by repeal of Stamp Act, 231–32; and Townshend crisis, 251, 256, 275; in Philadelphia, 260–61 n; importance of breaking, 274, 279, 286; effect of repeal of Townshend duties on, 281, 283, 290 n; collapse of, and charter reform, 289, 290 n; North's assessment of, 330 n; adopted by First Continental Congress, 338; colonial expectation that metropolis would back down if faced with, 340 n

North, Lord Frederick, 112; replaces Townshend, 252; on nonimportation, 254, 279–80, 330 n; and use of force in America, 255 n, 402; and Townshend duties, 256; defense of Grafton ministry by, 268–70; ministry reorganized under, 274, 291–92; and partial repeal of Townshend duties, 278–81; as student of Machiavelli, 283 n; and dual consensus, 283–84, 286–87; on difficulties of restoring strong government in America, 286–87 n; not a hard liner, 292; diagnosis of defects of Massachusetts constitution by, 321; hierarchical and authoritarian ideas of, 404. *See also* North ministry

North Carolina, 99; salary of governor in, 246; re-establishment of royal authority promised in, 358; exempted from nonintercourse, 368

Northington, Robert Henley, first earl of, 224 n

North ministry: options of, in resolving crisis over Townshend duties, 276–78; strategy of, in resolving crisis over Townshend duties, 278–81; parliamentary attack on 1770 American policy of, 281–82, 284–86; view that advent of, marks beginning of new policy of firmness, 283–84, 289–91; and charter reform in Massachusetts, 286–91 n; continuity between Grafton ministry and, 287; new era of political stability begun with, 291–92; and expansion of colonial civil list, 297–300; response of, toward developments in

North ministry (cont'd.)
    Massachusetts in early 1773, 304–5,
    306–12; motives of, in 1773 tea
    legislation, 312–14; response of, to
    Boston Tea Party, 315–16; indictment
    of, in passing Coercive Acts, 319–20;
    unwillingness of, to content itself with
    Boston Port Act, 322–23; arbitrary
    character of, 323–24, 350; backed into
    corner, 325–26, 333; absence of
    resolution of, 326, 329–30 n; illusions of,
    327–29; nature of choice confronting,
    334, 351–52; domestic constraints on,
    357; failure of will or of understanding
    as source of policy of, 357–61; January
    1775 instructions of, and decision for
    war, 362–67; view of conflict of,
    distinguished from that of Josiah Tucker,
    380; view of conflict, distinguished from
    that of whig opposition, 384; charge of
    incompetence against, 390–93. See also
    Dartmouth, William Legge, second earl
    of; North, Lord Frederick; Olive
    Branch, North's
Nova Scotia, 107; parliamentary grants for,
    79; civil establishment in, 246. See also
    Acadia

Ohio Valley, 10, 15, 78. See also West,
    the
Old colonial system. See Acts of Trade and
    Navigation
"Old subsidy," adjustment of, in Sugar
    Act, 119
Olive Branch, North's: historiography
    concerning, 368–69; sincerity of, 370,
    372–73; stupidity of, 370, 373–74;
    opposition view of, 371; ambiguity of,
    371–72; American rejection of, 371,
    376–78; and use of force, 375; as call for
    negotiations, 375–76. See also Civil
    establishment; North ministry
Oliver, Andrew, 308 n, 309 n
Olson, Alison Gilbert, 132 n
Osborn, Danvers, 245
Otis, James, 346 n

Paine, Thomas, 58, 202
Panikkar, K. M., 5
Pares, Richard, 30; on Pitt, 22; on Peace

of 1763, 22, 43; on overvaluation of
    colonial trade, 111
Parliament: disjunction between power
    and responsibility (rights and duties) of,
    as consequence of Seven Years' War,
    60–61, 76–81, 86–87, 94–95, 105, 178,
    194; right of, to tax colonies, 76–77,
    103, 107, 126, 133–36, 138–40, 165–72;
    right of, to regulate trade, 77, 107,
    122 n, 133–44, 336–38, 343–44; role of,
    in establishing Albany Plan, 81; power
    of, to be invoked on failure of
    requisitions, 83–84, 103, 396;
    reimbursement of colonial assemblies
    by, 85, 86 n; powers of colonial
    assemblies equivalent to those of, 104,
    149, 157; right of, to regulate colonial
    currency, 116; proposals for colonial
    representation in, 151–52, 179; absence
    until 1760s of overt challenges to
    authority of, 153, 157, 184; intervention
    of, in colonial affairs prompted by
    breakdown of government by
    instruction, 157, 194; authority of,
    founded on representation, 162–63, 168,
    170–72, 176, 181 n; colonial autonomy
    subject to discretion of, 175–76;
    legislative powers of, equal to those of
    assemblies, 176; ability of, to bind
    successors, 180 n; purpose and effect of
    postwar intervention of, in colonial
    affairs, 184–85; resolutions of
    Massachusetts assembly derogatory of
    rights of, 263; right of, to support royal
    government in America, 277;
    interposition of, in Massachusetts called
    for by Privy Council, 288; rights of, and
    First Continental Congress, 334–50,
    passim. See also Parliamentary
    sovereignty
Parliamentary History, 381 n
Parliamentary sovereignty: consensus in
    Britain on retaining, 56 n, 153, 165,
    217, 220, 237, 241, 249, 253, 255, 377;
    compatibility of, with preservation of
    colonial autonomy, 98, 162–63, 179,
    206, 319, 333; inevitability of conflict
    over, in aftermath of Seven Years' War,
    103–4; wisdom of evading question of,
    104, 253, 389, 399–400; equation of,
    with preservation of vital interest,
    114 n, 182, 195–97, 214, 228, 356–57,

380–84, 395, 398–99, 401–2; indivisibility of, 173, 180 n, 195–6, 216, 240, 249, 283, 286 n, 302–3, 341; inconsistency of, with federal principle, 175, 178–79; British definition of, 179, 195–96; British expected to relinquish in practice while continuing to proclaim in theory, 184; possibility of compromising issue of, 195–96, 215–16, 334–35, 352–53; issue of, raised by colonies, 196; as central issue in conflict, 196, 267, 355–56; affirmation of, essential preliminary to repeal of Stamp Act, 223; maintenance of, impossible without war, 272; colonial affirmation of, sought by Dartmouth, 305 n; distinction between issue of, and interests secured by, 380–84; opposition commitment to, difficult to reconcile with view on disutility of force, 388–89, 392, 398–404. See also Declaratory Act

Peace, permanent, 22, 40–41

Peace of Paris (1763): terms of, 1, 9, 18–21; negotiations leading to, 15–16, 18–21; historiographical controversy concerning causes of, 21–23; and Canada-Guadeloupe controversy, 23–30; and continental conflict, 30–37; and desirability of an early peace, 37–41; historiographical controversy concerning consequences of, 43–45; effect of, on Anglo-French relations, 45–48; effect of, on British relations with Europe, 48–52; effect of, on Bourbon alliance, 52–53; effect of, on imperial-colonial relations, 53–62, 82, 88, 194. See also Seven Years' War

Peckham, Howard H., 92 n

Pennsylvania: importance of Ohio Valley to, 78; civil establishment in, 246–47; movement for royal government and Hillsborough circular in, 259–61 n

Peter III (Russia), 17, 37

Petition to the King (1775), 354

Philadelphia, 99, 107, 131; merchants of, and nonimportation, 251, 261 n; as imperial court residence, 382

Pitt, William, first earl of Chatham: in historiography, 13, 43, 61, 146, 385; strategy of, against France, 14, 49–50; as war leader, 14–16, 20; on draconian peace with France, 15–16, 39–40, 43, 46–48; on Canada-Guadeloupe,

controversy, 15, 24, 26, 43, 46–47; resignation of, in 1761, 16; on continental connections, 30, 34–35 n, 52; on international order, 48 n; war policy of, toward colonies, 60–61, 83, 85–86, 105, 160; as bringing on decline of First British Empire, 61, 398; on internal and external taxation, 166–67 n; and use of force against colonies, 166–67, 230, 403; and parliamentary sovereignty, 166, 172 n, 234, 389 n; on virtual representation, 172; and equity of imperial-colonial relationship, 204 n, 387; dependence of Rockinghamites on, 219; on Stamp Act, 223, 232, 390; elevation of, to peerage, 234; formation of administration by, 234; and Chatham ministry, 248; resignation of, in 1768, 252; and imperial pride, 384; on incompetence of North ministry, 391; plan of, for resolving conflict, 395–98. See also Chatham administration; Chathamites

Pitt, William, the younger, 48

Pocock, Admiral, 37

Pocock, J.G.A., 39 n

Poland, partition of, 49, 52

Pole, J.R., 170 n

Political stability, 4; new era of, in England, 291–92; patronage irrelevant in society not enjoying, 296–300

Pontiac's Rebellion: origins and significance of, 91–93; response of colonial assemblies to, 102–3

Portugal: Spanish attack on, 17, 36; and British strategy, 49–50; colonial trade with, 240. See also Wine

Posse comitatus, as rioters, 321

Power: prospect of unlimited, as basis of imperial policy, 179 n, 188, 323–24; vs. plenty as object of empire, 189–90 n. See also Coercion; Economic power; Force; Nonimportation; War with America

Powers, customary view of rising and dominant, toward the status quo, 72

Pownall, John, 300

Pownall, Thomas: on unsettled character of imperial-colonial relationship, 147; and repeal of Townshend duties, 273; as probable supplier of Hutchinson letters, 308 n

Price, Richard, 399

Pride, role of, in refusal to concede claim of sovereignty, 196, 356, 381–82
Privy Council, 149, 234, 237, 288, 291 n, 309 n
Proclamation of 1763, 26–28, 90–91, 93, 252
Property, private: right of Parliament to take, without compensation, 168; significance of security of, in colonial position, 188
Prussia. *See* Frederick II of Prussia
Public credit, stability of, due to colony trade, 189–90 n. *See also* National debt
Public virtue, and requisition system, 102
Puerto Rico, 20

Quartering Act: Gage's requisitions under, 233; enforcement of, 236–38; in New Jersey, 244 n; hardships imposed by, 257; Hillsborough's proposal to revise, 265 n; broadening of, in 1774, 316
Quebec Act, 54, 57, 392

Radicals: as de facto governing power in Massachusetts, 292–97, 321; intentions of, 299; determination of, not to permit movement to lose momentum, 306; motives of, in publication of Hutchinson letters, 308 n; intransigence of, 309–10; motivation of, in Boston Tea Party, 314; and moderates at First Continental Congress, 338–41
Rakove, Jack N., 320 n, 339 n, 340 n, 351 n
Ramsay, David, 146, 231, 273
Realm, distinction between dominion and, 162, 168, 347–48
Reid, John Philip, 262 n
Representation: right of, independent of outside authority, 148, 163–64; disadvantages attending, of colonies in Parliament, 151–52, 179; of colonies in Parliament, as means of co-option of provincial elites, 151, 407; and taxation as inseparable, 163, 167; equation of, with effective authority, 168; requirement of, 169; virtual vs. actual, 170–72; general affirmation that parliamentary sovereignty rested on, 170–72, 176, 181 n
Requisition system: colonial use of, to extract concessions from metropolis, 59–60, 185–86; and status quo, 66; difficulties of, 83–84, 194; contrasted with system of reimbursement, 85–86, 96–97; and constitutional position of colonies during Seven Years' War, 85, 160–61; and Pontiac's Rebellion, 92–93, 102–3, 127; reasons for abandonment of, 98–104; experience of, under Articles of Confederation, 99 n, 100, 102 n, 103, 177–78; and confederal character of old imperial constitution, 175; and North's Olive Branch, 371–72, 374–78; opposition memory of, 386–88; return to, urged by opposition, 395–98
Responsibility: disjunction between power and, 60–61, 76–81, 86–87, 94–95, 105, 178, 194; for Revolution placed on architects of system of government by instruction, 154; depersonalization of issue of, 191–92, 407–8
Rhode Island, 164; civil establishment in, 246–47; and Massachusetts circular, 259 n; disrespectful behavior toward governor of, by commanding officer of *Gaspee*, 306
Rice, 108, 122–23
Richmond, Charles Lennox, third duke of, 389 n
Richmond, Herbert, 44 n
Rigby, Richard, 232 n
Rights, individual vs. collective, 162, 187–88
Rights of Englishmen: colonial demand that enforcement of trade laws respect, 72, 138, 163, 186; as buzzword for violation of trade laws, 142; achievement of, resulting in continual challenge to imperial authority, 157; inalienable character of, 162; and taxation, 162; and rights of man, 170, 345–46
Rigidity: of British colonial policy, 132–33; of government by instruction, 153–59; of British constitutional doctrine, 179–81 n, 301–2; of British political culture, 406–10
Ritcheson, Charles R., 283 n
Robson, Eric, 146
Rockingham, Charles Watson-Wentworth, second marquess of: position of, in ministry, 218; and George III, 224 n
Rockinghamites: on taxation, 166, 283–84, 387, 399–400; and dual consensus, 229,

255, 385–86, 398–406; meaning of plan called for by, 285; in opposition, 292; delusions of persecution of, 392. *See also* Burke, Edmund

Rockingham ministry: and wine trade, 126; modification of Sugar Act by, 136, 235; continuity of, with Grenville ministry on constitutional principle, 165; political restraints on, 217; options of, in Stamp Act crisis, 217–20; strategy and tactics of, in repeal of Stamp Act, 221–27; sincerity of, 227–28; expectations of, in repeal of Stamp Act, 233, 388–89

Rodney, Admiral Sir George Brydges, 37

Royal government: incompatibility of, with federal government, 174–75; effective principle of, 175, 178; as basis of imperial-colonial tie, 344, 349–50, 406–10; collapse of, 360–61. *See also* Government by instruction; Governors, colonial; King of Great Britain; Requisition system

Russia, and Britain, 30, 52. *See also* Catherine II; Elizabeth; Peter III

Rutherford, Captain Walter, 97 n

Saint Domingue, 47

Saint Lucia, 19–20, 40, 41 n

Saint Pierre, 19

Salem, 331, 364

"Salutary neglect": and right to regulate trade, 107; colonial identification of status quo with, 139; and erosion of royal authority in America, 153, 159 n, 192; purposes and assumptions behind policy of, 193–94

Saratoga, 79, 365

Schlesinger, Arthur M., 138

Sedgwick, Edward, 246 n

Seditious libel, 270 n

Senegal, 14, 19

Seven Years' War: origins of, 10–13, 25, 30–32; stake of, in Europe, 11–12; progress of British war aims during, 13–21; influence of, on Europe and diplomacy 48–49; character of British involvement in, 49; British strategy in, 51–52; French strategy before and after, 53–54; colonial revisionism concerning, 57–59; stake of, in North America, 78, 87; pattern of imperial-colonial relations

during, 84–85; cost of, 87; experience of, and British Indian policy, 88–91; enforcement of laws of trade during, 107; British financing of, 110; occupation of French islands during, unpreparedness of British navy before, 128; as forcing ground of imperial-colonial conflict, 159–61, 194, 197. *See also* Peace of 1763

Sharpe, Horatio, 258–59

Shelburne, William Fitzmaurice-Petty, second earl of, 54 n, 257; on American affairs, 234; and New York Restraining Act, 234–35, 236–38, 390; western policy of, 239 n, 241–44, 252; and Townshend Revenue Act, 239 n, 245; and American civil list, 242–43 n, 245, 248; and coercive measures, 261; historiographical view taken of, 385. *See also* Chatham administration; Chathamites

Shirley, William, 79, 85

Shy, John, 97 n, 101 n, 262 n, 269; and decision to station army in America, 88 n; and Pontiac's Rebellion, 92 n; and new view of empire, 190–91, 194

Silesia, 12, 36

Sincerity: of Bute and George III, 39–40; of American colonists, 58–59, 138, 206; of belief on both sides, 208–9; of whig opposition, 398–404

Smith, Adam, 109, 410 n; on national debt, 39 n; on prospect of rupture with the colonies, 41–42, 111–12; on "splendour and glory" of mercantile system, 111; on burdens imposed by confinement of colonial market to British manufacturers, 141–42; on colonial representation in Parliament, 151

Smith, William, 202

Sosin, Jack M., 27 n, 88 n, 122 n, 322 n

South Carolina, 108; and Pitt, 232; salary of governor in, 246

Spain: intervention of, in Seven Years' War, 16; and Portugal, 16–17, 36, 50; and *pacte de famille* with France, 16, 44, 46, 50, 52–53; in 1762 peace negotiations, 20, 40; probability of intervention of, in Anglo-American conflict, 55, 230, 253, 401–2; significance of removal of, from eastern North America, 55 n, 57–58; and Dutch

Spain (cont'd.)
    revolt, 56 n; threat of war with, over
    Falkland Islands, 290, 291 n
Specie, drain of, from colonial economies
    as result of Stamp Act, 100, 224 n, 226,
    226 n
Spotswood, Alexander, 193
Stamp Act: reasons for submission to, 60;
    relationship between imperial defense
    and, 93; metropolitan officials stunned
    by colonial reaction to, 98 n, 199, 217;
    deployment of British army during crisis
    over, 98 n, 219, 221 n; equity of, 100–
    101, 388 (see also Imperial-colonial
    relationship, (in)equity of); inability of
    colonists to comply with, 100, 200, 226–
    27; articulation of character of imperial
    constitution during crisis over, 163–64,
    175–76, 223; effect of, on colonial
    affection for Great Britian, 202; imperial
    policy coherent until reaction to, 214;
    significance of crisis over, in destroying
    metropolitan authority, 215–17, 231–32;
    rejection of policy of enforcement of,
    217–20, 220–22 n; resolutions
    accompanying repeal of, 223–24, 236–
    37; economic effects of, 225–27; revenue
    expected from, 226 n, 250; debate over
    repeal of, move toward repeal of,
    prompted by colonial opposition, 229–
    30; and "lurking spirit" of despotism,
    392
Stamp Act Congress: declaration of, 163,
    348 n; and First Continental Congress,
    342–43, 345–46
Status quo: colonial version of, 2–3, 72–73,
    139, 186; as standard of legitimate
    action, 62, 65, 74; colonial demand for
    return to, 66–67; British assault on, 66,
    75, 106, 146–47; ambiguous character
    of, 72–74, 76, 86, 104–5, 107, 144, 147,
    155; imperial understanding of, 73–74,
    144–45, 184–86; broad vs. narrow (larger
    vs. smaller) versions of, 73, 133, 144,
    186, 200, 205–6, 213; and Currency Act,
    116; change in enforcement of trade
    laws as challenge to, 132–33; importance
    of not disturbing inarticulate and
    undefined nature of, 104, 146–47, 180n,
    183; restoration of, as basis for
    settlement, 182, 186, 192, 209, 308–9 n;
    consisting of two worlds, 183–84;
    departure from, prompted by new view

of empire, 190; implications of
    adherence to, 198–99; ambiguities of,
    found dangerous by colonists, 206, 209,
    and Coercive Acts, 324; return to, urged
    by whig opposition, 393–94. See also
    Imperial-colonial relationship
Stout, Neil R., 110
Stuart, John, 90
Suffolk Resolves, 338, 354
Sugar Act (1764); and British Army, 93,
    122 n; as attack on status quo, 106, 189;
    origins and scope of, 114, 117–27; and
    enforcement of trade laws, 127–33;
    American view of constitutionality of,
    133–42 (see also Taxation, distinction
    between internal and external);
    modification of, by Rockingham (1766),
    136, 219 n, 235, 239; significance of
    sacrificing objectives sought in, 144–45;
    economic effects of, 226–27; revenues
    from, threatened by repeal of
    Townshend duties, 253–54, 279
Sugar trade, in negotiations leading to
    Peace of 1763, 24–25, 27
Suspension, power of, 149
Sweden, 12, 49

Taxation: of American colonies as
    departure from status quo, 75, 198;
    conditions attending Parliament's right
    of, 76–78; in Albany Plan, 81; rejection
    of, in 1754, 82–83; necessity of, 96–104,
    387–88; distinction between internal and
    external, 134–40, 166–67, 169, 175–76,
    238–41, 249, 254; legitimacy of, 161–72
    (see also Parliament; Parliamentary
    sovereignty); right of, distinguished from
    other legislative powers, 163; 1778
    British offer to forego, 181 n; threat of,
    if Grenville program accepted, 185,
    206–7; expediency of 234, 249; practical
    exemption from, less significant than
    principle of exemption, 253–54; policy of
    conciliation and right of, 283; concession
    of right of, by Dartmouth, 305 n; and
    Boston Tea Party, 314; significance of
    issue of, in 1774, 325; and legislative
    intention, 342–43; significance of initial
    denial of right of, 347–48; colonial claim
    of exemption from, not responsible for
    crisis, 355; and North's Olive Branch,
    371–72, 374–78; no choice offered by

colonists between control of commerce and, 377–78; power of, as an instrument of empire, 396

Tea: regulations governing trade in, 123–24, 238–39, 278–80, 312–14; American attitude toward regulation of trade in, 135–37; revenue expected from tax on, 239–40 n; duty on, as symbol of parliamentary right, 279, 313–14, 374 n; widespread resistance to introduction of, 360

Temple, Richard Grenville, second earl of, 267

Theresa, Maria, 36. See also Austria

Thomas, P.D.G.: on Pitt's view of parliamentary taxation, 166 n; on Conway's instructions to employ force against colonies, 222 n; on case for repeal of Stamp Act, 225; on Grafton, 239 n; on purpose of Townshend Revenue Act, 239–40 n, 241 n, 245–46 n, on significance of circulars for information on civil government in America, 242–43 n; on expansion of civil list by North ministry, 298; on hardening attitude of North ministry, 310; on resolution of North ministry, 329–30 n

Thucydides, 106, 213

Tobacco, 108, 115

Tobago, 19

Townshend, Charles, 192, 389; on frailty of 1754 union proposed by Board of Trade, 84; and repeal of Stamp Act, 224 n; and New York Restraining Act, 236–37; and purpose of 1767 program of taxation, 241–48; and western policy, 242–44; 1753 instructions of, to Danvers Osborn, 245; death of, 247–48, 252; sincerity of, 249

Townshend Revenue Act, 56; and regulation of tea trade, 124; colonial attitude toward, 134–40, 250; and legitimacy and expediency of external taxation, 238–41, 249; "uncommercial principles" in, 239–40, 256, 247–80; and western problem, 241–44; and civil establishment, 244–48; repeal of, and colonial civil list, 247 n, 476–77; revenues raised under, 250; refusal to repeal, 255, attitude of Grafton ministry toward, 256, 265 n, 275 Circumstances under which total repeal of, might take place, 256, 274, 278; disingenuous case made for repeal of, 256, 280;

North's justification for repeal of, 278–81; significance of, 388–389

Treason, 264, 266

Tucker, Josiah: on "simple principles of simple peacemaking," 69; on American representation in Parliament, 152 n; on nature of imperial-colonial conflict, 379–80, 382–83, 408; and imperial pride, 382

Tyranny: and British behavior in Stamp Act crisis, 188; alacrity in anticipation of, vs. picture drawn of colonial affection, 205–6; and North ministry, 323–25

Understanding, failure of: and Grenville reforms, 214–15; as basis for American policy of Grafton ministry, 270–71; by Hillsborough, 270–71 n, 290 n; claim of, as basis for settlement of conflict, 308–9 n; by North ministry, 327–29, 355–61; and core of conflict, 384; and whig opposition, 392

United Provinces: neutrality of, during Seven Years' War, 11, 14, and France, 31, 35; importance of, to Britain, 32–33, 35 n, 48–49; and tea trade, 123–24

Utrecht, Peace of, (1713), 77

Veto, power of, 149, 174, 177. See also Governors, colonial; Royal government

Vice-Admiralty courts; reforms in 1760s concerning, 128, 130–32, 177–78; basis of colonial opposition to, 137–38, 162–63; and Stamp Act crisis, 224 n; in opposition proposals for settlement of conflict, 397–98. See also Acts of Trade and Navigation; Courts, colonial

Viner, Jacob, 189–90 n

Virginia: importance of Ohio Valley to, 78; invasion of, by France, 80; in Albany Plan, 81; currency of, 115; 1764 petition to the King, by, 164; civil establishment in, 246–47; and Hillsborough circular, 259 n; and committee of correspondence, 306; reports of Dunmore concerning situation in, 358; act restraining trade of, 374 n

Walpole, Horace, 104, 241
Walpole, Robert, 77, 159 n, 192–94
War of American Independence, 51, 53
War with America: willingness of North
    ministry to confront prospect of, 359,
    361 n, 367–68, 378, 402–3. *See also*
    Consensus; Coercion; Force
Washington, George, 10, 204 n
Webb, Stephen Saunders, 193 n
Wedderburn, Alexander, 309 n
West, the: postwar policy toward, 27–28,
    75, 87–95, 241–44, 252; assumptions
    governing British policy toward, 54;
    growth of French power in, 79–80
West Indian interest, 122, 138, 139 n
West Indies (British): British protection as
    guarantor of dependence of, 60; and
    burden of imperial defense, 99 n; and
    colonial trade, 107–8; and American
    independence, 112; displacement of
    sugar of, from European market, 120;
    commercial policies affecting, 121. *See
    also* Molasses Act; Sugar Act
West Indies (French): as source of power,
    24–25, 27, 39, 47; trade of, with
    continental colonies, 107, 120–21, 129;
    treatment of, in British colonial policy,
    122–23, 136
Westminster, Treaty of (1756), 11
Whately, Thomas, 77 n, on objectives of

Grenville program, 118–19, 123–25,
    128–29, 132, 144; ties of, to Grenville,
    119 n; on virtual representation, 171–72;
    appeal of, to federal character of
    empire, 176; on Hillsborough circular,
    258 n; and Hutchinson letters, 263,
    308 n
Wheare, K. C., 173–74, 180 n
Whig interpretation. *See* Historiography
Whigs, old. *See* Rockinghamites
Wilkes, John, 266
Will: matters of secondary importance
    seen as critical tests of, 214; irresolution
    of imperial, 216; Grafton ministry and
    failure of, 271–72; North ministry and
    failure of, 357–62
Wilson, James, 341, 344, 347–48 n
Wine, 117, 125–26, 139, 238–41
Wolfe, Major-General James, 41
Wood, Gordon, 180 n, 345 n
Wright, Esmond, 106 n
Writs of prohibition, 128

York, Charles, 224
Yorke, Joseph, 17
Yorktown, 44

Zobel, Hiller B., 262, 270

The Johns Hopkins University Press

THE FALL OF THE FIRST BRITISH EMPIRE
Origins of the War of American Independence

*This book was composed in Caledonia text and display type
by FotoTypesetters, Inc., from a design by Alan Carter.
It was printed on S. D. Warren's 50-lb. Sebago Eggshell paper
and bound in Holliston Roxite A by the Maple Press Company.*